"Order and Progress"

A Political History
of Brazil

Ronald M. Schneider

QUEENS COLLEGE, CITY UNIVERSITY OF NEW YORK

Westview Press
BOULDER • SAN FRANCISCO • OXFORD

Copyright © 1991 by Westview Press, Inc.

Published in 1991 in the United States of America by Westview Press, Inc., 5500 Central Avenue, Boulder, Colorado 80301, and in the United Kingdom by Westview Press, 36 Lonsdale Road, Summertown, Oxford OX2 7EW

Library of Congress Cataloging-in-Publication Data
Schneider, Ronald M.
  "Order and progress" : A political history of Brazil /
Ronald M. Schneider.
    p. cm.
  Includes index.
  ISBN 0-8133-1077-6 — ISBN 0-8133-1076-8 (pbk.)
  1. Brazil—Politics and government. I. Title.
F2521.S36 1991
981—dc20
                                                                    90-19463
                                                                         CIP

Printed and bound in the United States of America

The paper used in this publication meets the requirements
of the American National Standard for Permanence of Paper
for Printed Library Materials Z39.48-1984.

10   9   8   7   6   5   4   3   2   1

"Ordem e Progresso" ("Order and Progress")
—Brazilian national motto

Contents

Preface

November 15, 1989, marked both the centennial of the Brazilian Republic and the first direct election of a president there in over twenty-nine years. By this point Brazil had been an independent nation for 167 years. Yet to a very significant extent the armed forces, the Catholic Church, and major property owners remained the chief actors in Brazil's national life. Although present on the scene since at least the 1830s, political parties have failed repeatedly to take root and develop permanent followings. Indeed, their inability to become national institutions was dramatically evident in the 1989 campaign, as 82 million voters overwhelmingly preferred two very different quasi-charismatic personalists of a populist-demagogic stripe—as well as an old-line conservative, a young neoliberal, and a labor leader turned socialist congressman—to the candidates of the country's two major political parties. Yet these same two parties had all but scored a clean sweep as recently as 1986 and had retained a pronounced lead in late 1988 municipal balloting.

This study is focused on demonstrating and explaining both the remarkable continuities and the important changes that have occurred in Brazil's political system from the colonial era to the eve of the twenty-first century. In a forthcoming volume encompassing the early 1990s, I will describe and analyze the functioning of the modern Brazilian nation in terms of its society, economy, and foreign relations as well as its intriguing history and often highly original politics. Together these books culminate a program of research that has extended over more than three decades, a period during which Brazil has undergone very substantial change and has survived, if not always surmounted, a series of formidable challenges—many of which still persist and must be confronted in the years immediately ahead.

Many North Americans and Europeans know at least a little about Brazil from the media. In their eyes it is the land of samba, carnival, Pelé, and a series of Formula 1 race car drivers. For them, most of Brazil's population are descendants of African slaves who practice a voodoo-like religion and live in colorful hillside slums. (Actually, the decided majority of Brazilians are of European extraction and live in houses or apartments comparable to U.S. dwellings of the 1950s.) Many North Americans and Europeans, but far from a majority, know that Brazilians don't speak Spanish, but they are likely to be at a loss with respect to just what language they do speak. Most think that coffee is Brazil's chief export, while in reality the primary exports are automobiles and auto parts, followed by soy, with coffee weighing in at under 8 percent of Brazil's average annual exports. People who pride themselves on following world affairs realize that Brazil is a major debtor and are pretty sure that this bears some relation to the military having been in power. Though a fair proportion of these people have the impression that the armed forces got out of office somewhere along the line, most do not know when, why, or how the change occurred.

The road to demonstrating clearly the true character of Brazil passes through the reconstruction of the country's history. Both past and present must be explained if readers are to understand where Brazil may be headed. The dual challenge, often intimidating if not downright overwhelming, has been first to achieve an adequate understanding of Brazil—an enterprise in which I have been involved for well over three decades—and then to make the insights gained from this lengthy process of having become "part Brazilian" intelligible to non-Brazilian readers. More than a quarter of a century ago, Charles Wagley came very close to accomplishing this double feat in his remarkable *An Introduction to Brazil*,[1] falling short only in the realm of politics and those aspects of economic change most closely related to politics. My inspiration to undertake the second of these formidable tasks dates back to the publication of Wagley's work. I decided then that I would someday provide a "global" interpretation of Brazil that put political processes and problems where they belong, center stage, in a country in which only gross political malperformance can prevent the dreams of past generations and the aspirations of the present one from becoming reality during the lifetime of the generation to come.

My debt to many scholars—including Brazilian, North American, and European—will be apparent in the notes at the end of the book. Although I may often differ from these scholars in my analyses, this results in part from the fact that their rich array of interpretations is not only varied but also often contradictory. In addition, virtually all my adult life has revolved around observing and studying Brazil, which has of course led to my own strongly held views on many matters. A third reason stems from my aim of providing a coherent and integrated interpretation of both the character of Brazil and how—as well as why—this character came to be. As a result, this book is very largely an effort to synthesize both what I have read and what I have observed firsthand, a process in which choices must inevitably be made among the findings and viewpoints existing in the extremely voluminous literature relevant to such a far-ranging endeavor. Indeed, there are at least four hundred Brazilian authors alone whose writings I have found helpful, in addition to the works of over one hundred non-Brazilian scholars—yielding a total corpus of well above fifteen hundred books, monographs, and articles that were specifically used (and many more that were consulted along the way).

I have sought to provide as inclusive a synthesis as possible without sacrificing coherence. Thus, although I have given due consideration to all approaches purporting to explain Brazilian reality, I have of necessity rejected some interpretations in the process of opting for others that seemed to be more persuasive and powerful—in the sense that they seemed to correspond more closely to observable reality. Because Brazilian social science scholarship is often politically engaged and ranges all across the ideological spectrum, it is manifestly impossible to reconcile all approaches and viewpoints. My general rule (applied with generous latitude in light of the varying intellectual quality of the works involved) has been to favor sound empirical studies over those that depart from a preconceived ideological premise—no matter how influential or fashionable a particular work of the latter kind may have been.

In this respect the many probing studies by one outstanding scholar have posed a particular dilemma. The highly sophisticated and more than Marxist ideological position that shapes the inquiry and frames the analysis of Florestan Fernandes is largely incompatible with my fundamental belief that class is only one factor in explaining Brazilian society and politics—and not the most useful factor at that. Yet it is impossible not to find a great many valuable insights in the prolific writings of one of the world's greatest living sociologists. Moreover, the very unacceptability (to me) of Fernandes's most pessimistic conclusions has repeatedly forced me to sharpen arguments to the contrary and reexamine the empirical supports of my belief that Brazil is slowly, but definitely, evolving toward a sufficiently just society.

As Robert Packenham has painstakingly documented, Brazilian social science writing from at least the 1960s through the mid-1970s was dominated by Marxist approaches.[2] More recently, in addition to growing social democratic and liberal tendencies, a vigorous and productive intellectual current has emerged that Packenham calls the New Academic social science. Back in 1971, I identified the key figures in this movement as "a relatively small but growing band of young scholars concerned with a balance between conceptualization and substance, escape from the intellectual confinement of ideological straightjackets, and the disciplined quest for empirical knowledge as the guide to systematic understanding."[3] Confined at that time essentially to publishing seminal articles chiefly through the review *Dados*, these individuals have since each produced a number of influential works. In particular, I have repeatedly encountered stimulation from the writings of Bolívar Lamounier, José Murilo de Carvalho, Simon Schwartzman, and Wanderley Guilherme dos Santos (although there are at least fifteen other scholars who have also made notable contributions to this positive trend, as well as half a dozen journalists and essayists of a similar orientation). Indeed, much of the recent outpouring of valuable monographic studies is by younger scholars who have in turn been influenced by their New Academic mentors.

As precursors of the New Academics, Hélio Jaguaribe and Cândido Mendes de Almeida must be given recognition. The former's *Political De-*

velopment: A General Theory and a Latin American Case (1973) was a pioneering effort to find a synthesis between the dominant and rival consensus/pluralist and Marxist/conflict schools. As with Florestan Fernandes, Jaguaribe's writings span the whole period from the early 1950s to the present and defy categorization in a single discipline. Mendes de Almeida is perhaps as important for having founded and nourished the seminal University Research Institute of Rio de Janeiro (IUPERJ)—where many of Brazil's brightest social scientists have found a congenial home base for their studies—as he is for his own writings and past presidency of the International Political Science Association. Again, even where I view developments quite differently, their opinions have consistently provided stimulation for me for a third of a century.

Over this long span of study and observation I have found that my view of contemporary Brazilian national reality generally has been something different from that depicted by foreign observers—albeit some of these observers have shown extraordinary anthropological or sociological insight. My view is also frequently distinct from that portrayed by Brazilians themselves, although their studies on a wide range of subjects are often highly perceptive and thoughtful. Though the literature in the fields of history and economics provides a rich base upon which to build, until quite recently the analyses by even the best Brazilian political scientists and sociologists have generally either lacked a meaningful comparative perspective or, in the few notable cases of exception to this rule, have been pitched at a very high level of abstraction and conceptualization intelligible only to the intellectual elite. Moreover, such studies have understandably been intended primarily for the Brazilian public, rather than to explain Brazil to "outsiders." Most of these writings are also rather heavily engaged politically, a fact that holds true for the country's newspapers and magazines as well.

Thus, though I take all of these works seriously into account—and couldn't possibly have gotten inside of and stayed abreast of Brazil without them— I am alone responsible for the interpretations contained in this study as well as for the judgments concerning the motives and performance of the very large number of individuals involved in the country's public affairs since its independence in 1822. This caveat is particularly true with respect to the many controversial figures of the post–World War II period, whose actions I have personally had the opportunity to observe.

This responsibility I assume without false reticence, as my interest in Brazil goes back forty years, my firsthand study having spanned thirty-three years and involved thirty-eight separate periods of fieldwork and observation ranging from a few weeks to over six months in duration and totalling more than five years in residence in Brazil. As twenty-two of these research trips have been during the past dozen years, I have had ample opportunity to take a very close and sustained look at recent developments. Though there is still much of this subcontinental country I have not yet had a chance to see, my travels have carried me repeatedly from the interior of Rio Grande do Sul, in the extreme south, to the Amazon above Manaus, together with all the state capitals along the coast and inland to the Paraguayan and Bolivian borders. In the process I have had the pleasure of talking to a great number of Brazilians in all walks of life, each of whom has contributed in some way to opening the window—often just a crack, but sometimes more fully—so that I could get a glimpse of Brazilian culture and character. Collectively these Brazilians deserve considerable credit for any real insight into Brazil this book may reflect, but they certainly bear no responsibility for any failure of this work to provide adequate keys for total comprehension of *a realidade Brasileira*. For the onward march of events both causes this reality to be in near-constant flux and furnishes new clues to the unending task of finding out what the Brazilian reality is and has been.

In addition to the gratitude I owe my wife, Maria Nilza Evangelista Pinto, who has labored diligently alongside me since 1982 and has done a great deal to "Brazilianize" me, I am deeply indebted to the Professional Staff Congress/City University of New York (PSC/CUNY) Faculty Research Award Program for the sustained support given me through nine grants between 1978 and 1990. Good colleagues Harry Psomiades, George Priestley, and Ralph della Cava have individually provided valued stimulation. My association with each of them substantially predates our more than two decades together at Queens College. The final version of this study has benefitted enormously from the very perceptive and extensive comments and suggestions made by Frank D. McCann. His careful reading of an even longer and more detailed version enabled me to forgo redundancy in seeking other scholars' detailed comments on the historical chapters. Dr. Lincoln A. Gordon kindly took time from his forthcoming book on Brazil to provide very constructive comments on the final chapter. A significant portion of the material on the most recent period is adapted from my series of reports on the 1989 and 1990 campaigns and elections. These reports were published by the Center for Strategic and International Studies (CSIS), where William Perry served as a useful sounding board and proved a valuable collaborator on several papers. Indeed, our work together in this area goes back to my coverage of the 1982 campaign that was produced through CSIS's Brazil Program, then headed by Perry.

For turning a complex manuscript into a finished book, many of the able professionals at Westview Press deserve my heartfelt appreciation. Barbara Ellington, as senior acquisitions editor, served as my advocate in convincing the editorial board that this was a viable project. Anna Huff, a skilled cosmetic surgeon of the English language, performed an exceptionally diligent and intelligent job of copyediting, and project editor Martha Leggett conscientiously expedited the passage of my work through the production process. Jane McGraw shouldered the burden of constructing an index requiring elaborate cross-referencing.

The timing of this volume has been consciously designed for a fivefold appropriateness. Symbolically, 1989 marked the centennial of the Brazilian republic, while empirically that year signalled the end of a period of nearly three decades without direct election of the nation's chief executive. In the social sphere, despite dramatic change in many respects, more than a century after the abolition of slavery the descendants of these nonvoluntary African immigrants—who composed the backbone of the nation's workforce for roughly three hundred years—are still at the bottom of the social pyramid. Economically, because 1987, 1988, and 1989 were years of quite limited growth—and 1990 one of economic shrinkage—the process of development needs to be started anew. Finally, on the international scene Brazil's hovering between the first and third worlds has reached a point at which a basic definition of where the country's future lies cannot be long postponed—a fact brought dramatically home by the 1990 Mideast crisis.

Hence, Fernando Collor de Mello, the new president chosen at the end of 1989 who took office in March 1990, finds himself heavily constrained, if not wholly confined, by the legacy of the 1980s. Moreover, a significant share of national-level politicians are still products of the political socialization that took place during the regime of populist corporatism (two-thirds corporatism, one-third populism) under Getúlio Vargas between 1930 and 1945; all senior military figures as well as many key civilians began their careers at least during its reprise as corporatist populism (a populist dog with a corporatist tail) in the first half of the 1950s. Thus, I have striven to analyze these and other parts of the past to facilitate an understanding of Brazil as it copes with the challenges of the 1990s and positions itself for the new century ahead.

Ronald M. Schneider
Montes Claros, M.G., Brazil

Notes

1. Charles Wagley, *An Introduction to Brazil* (New York: Columbia University Press, 1963, revised edition 1971).

2. Robert A. Packenham, "The Changing Political Discourse in Brazil, 1964–1985," in Wayne A. Selcher, ed., *Political Liberalization in Brazil: Dynamics, Dilemmas, and Future Prospects* (Boulder, CO: Westview Press, 1986), pp. 134–173.

3. In the Preface to Ronald M. Schneider, "Modernization and the Military in Brazil: Political Instability, Army Interventions and Institutional Crises, 1889–1966," unpublished manuscript, 1971, pp. vi–vii.

"Order and Progress"

A Political History
of Brazil

Political Map of Brazil (courtesy of the Brazilian-American Chamber of Commerce)

1

What Is Brazil?

A century ago Japan was just breaking out of feudalism, in which Russia was still deeply mired, while the United States was positioning itself for the developmental surge that would make it a world power by the early 1900s. During the 1870s and 1880s Germany was transformed from an essentially agrarian country into a budding industrial power; during the 1890s it came first to equal and then to surpass Great Britain. In many ways Brazil has undergone changes analogous to these during the period since the mid-1960s. Focus upon its present problems, which are many and major, often blinds observers to just how far Brazil has already come along the developmental road.

The essence of the problem of analyzing Brazil is the simultaneous need to explain what the country has been, what it now is, and what it is becoming. For all these aspects coexist uneasily today, much as they did in Bismarckian Germany or in the United States from the 1880s to the beginning of World War I. In cold comparative terms Brazil might be considered—on the basis of social indicators and military strength—as a medium-income, newly industrialized country, a general classification that includes, for example, Mexico and Argentina along with such Eastern Hemisphere nations as South Korea, South Africa, and Yugoslavia. As a member of this group, Brazil might be seen as not particularly special to the United States or the rest of the world if it were not at the same time by far the largest and most populous of such countries and the one moving most rapidly upward within the ranks of the newly industrialized countries (NICs)—particularly in terms of a diversified mining and heavy industry base.

Halfway Along the Road

From another and much more relevant perspective Brazil can appropriately be viewed as an emerging industrial power. It is already the noncommunist world's eighth largest economy (after Canada, but before Spain), as well as fifth in area and sixth in population of all countries. It is this perspective that is valid for those looking ahead to assess the world situation a few years down the road.[1] A mere generation ago Brazil was truly an under-

1

developed country, and within another generation it will be a completely industrialized nation. Right now it is at midstream, with the full array of tensions and problems involved in sustained rapid change and ongoing modernization.

The transition from underdeveloped nation to candidate member of the urbanized-industrialized world is likely to progress even more rapidly during the 1990s than it has during the past generation—dramatic as the changes of the past period have been. For at the time of the post-Vargas "redemocratization" in 1946, Brazil was a country of fewer than 48 million inhabitants that was only 36 percent urban and had very limited industry. By 1990 it had become a nation with a population over 150 million that was 75 percent urban and had aerospace, computer, petrochemical, and armaments industries moving into the high-tech era. As well, Brazil had the newly developed capability to enrich uranium, making it only the eighth country to enter this very exclusive club.

Myths and Misconceptions

Very few people in the rest of the world are at all abreast of the extent of the continuing processes of change in Brazil. For example, there is a mistaken belief that most of the population still dwell in rural areas; in fact, almost 71 million Brazilians live in cities of over 200,000. Though Brazil has always been a big country in a territorial sense, it has now also become large in terms of its population. The state of São Paulo alone has slightly more inhabitants than all of either Argentina or Colombia, and Brazil's second most populous state (Minas Gerais) has the population of Venezuela in an area the size of France. Even its fifth and sixth most populous states each have as many inhabitants as all of either Ecuador or Bolivia. Each year Brazil's population grows by a number equal to the total population of Uruguay.

Misunderstanding about Brazil abounds in the United States and Europe. Most people can at least identify the country with coffee, in which it is indeed first in exports, but few of them would guess that Brazil's coffee export is massively overshadowed by manufactures and accounts for less than a twelfth of the country's total exports. It likely comes as no surprise that Brazil may have the world's largest iron ore reserves or that it is first in hydroelectric potential and second in worldwide exports of soy and cocoa. But few people are aware of Brazil's enormous production of sugar, which dwarfs that of Cuba. Yet the transformation of much of the sugar crop into alcohol for the more than 4 million vehicles that run exclusively on this fuel helps underscore Brazil's unique determination and ability to find original solutions to its developmental bottlenecks. Similarly, not only are Brazilian engines and transmissions found in many U.S. cars, but also in the late 1980s one of the hottest selling cars in the U.S. market was the Volkswagen Fox—built exclusively in São Paulo and long available in Brazil.

The Real Brazil

The salient fact is that Brazil has made dramatic progress in the short span of the last decade alone on a wide range of economic fronts. For example, between 1976 and 1988 it rose from fifteenth to seventh in steel production (passing the United Kingdom in 1980 and France in 1986); moved up two spots in gross domestic product (GDP)—to eighth after having been forty-ninth as recently as 1956; jumped from fourteenth to fifth in gold production; went from being unranked to fifth in aluminum production (with at least 12 percent of the globe's bauxite reserves); and climbed from unranked to eighth in tin reserves and third in tin production. During the same brief period Brazil became an important producer of copper (instead of an importer), developed the world's fifth largest uranium reserves, and came from nowhere to become the sixth biggest market for computers— with a sustained high annual growth in demand that is largely met by local production. Brazilian-made planes fly the skies of over thirty countries, and millions of tons of Brazilian-built ships ply the world's sea lanes conducting the country's foreign trade of well over $50 billion a year.

Of importance is the fact that Brazil's situation with respect to grains and minerals is much more analogous to that of the United States approximately eighty years ago than it is to the emergence as world powers of such countries as West Germany, Japan, or the Soviet Union.[2] Agriculture contributes 9 percent of GDP and employs nearly 30 percent of the economically active population. Recent harvests include highs of over 40 million sacks of coffee, 32 million tons of sugar (much of it converted to alcohol), 27 million tons of corn, 22 million tons of soybeans, 12 million tons of rice, and 7 million tons of wheat. These grains have consolidated the country's position as the world's fourth largest agricultural exporter. But Brazil is also the world's second-ranking meat exporter, drawing on cattle herds surpassing 140 million head. Iron ore may still be well in the lead as far as mining production and export, but in addition to the impressive figures already cited, Brazil is a major factor in manganese production and has very appreciable reserves of lead, nickel, chromium, tungsten, and zinc. Its livestock herds greatly surpass those of beef-famous Argentina, and it has quickly moved up to eighth place in cellulose production even though its forest reserves have only begun to be tapped. Certainly Brazil is not just—or even chiefly—the land of samba, soccer, beaches, and urban slums.

In many ways Brazil has essentially been building momentum for even greater future breakthroughs. Even a cursory glance at some of the sectoral development programs presently underway provides a good indication of where Brazil is headed. Investments of some $23 billion are projected to double steel production to 50 million tons per year by 2000. In the energy field, with the giant Itaipu and Tucuruí hydroelectric complexes still coming on line, installed generating capacity (51,000 megawatts at the end of 1986) is to be increased by nearly 50 percent, to 74,400 megawatts by 1995, through investment of $61.5 billion. The petrochemical industry is to receive $4.7 billion between 1987 and 1991, with paper and cellulose getting almost

$8 billion by 1995. The automotive industry should be capable of producing nearly 1.4 million vehicles annually by 1992, resulting from investment of $4.6 billion during the 1987–1991 period (with a proportional expansion of the auto parts industry). Automotive exports could reach 400,000 units a year, and the number of vehicles on Brazilian roads will probably rise from the present level of roughly 15 million to around 17 million.

Though skepticism concerning development goals is generally healthy in most countries, past performance indicates that in the Brazilian case these goals will be substantially met. Brazil has already broken through the "treadmill" syndrome of a small GDP combined with a high rate of population growth. In real terms its GDP grew 156 times over between 1870 and 1987, moving from 5 percent to about 93 percent of Great Britain's GDP and from two-thirds that of Mexico to two and a half times it.[3] Although throughout the twentieth century Brazil's GDP has averaged an extraordinary 6.5 percent annual increase, until the end of the 1960s the economy was so small that absolute growth had been limited. The 1968–1974 "economic miracle" more than doubled GDP, and even the lower average annual growth rate through 1980 saw GDP rise by an additional 50 percent—more than equalling the absolute growth of the preceding period. Following the brief recession of 1981–1983, the over 24 percent accumulated economic growth of 1984–1986 meant some $60 billion added to GDP—a sum equal to GDP growth for the entire period from 1946 to 1967. Meanwhile the annual rate of population growth declined from over 3 percent in the 1950s to 2.4 percent during the 1970s and fell below 2 percent by the mid-1980s.

Whither Brazil?

As a result of these trends, real per capita GDP is currently five times higher than in 1940, having doubled between 1940 and 1962 and again by 1976. The next doubling of GDP (predicted to occur shortly after the turn of the century) will be from a base of $383 billion to $760 billion, with annual increments averaging nearly $30 billion. The following doubling, which could come as early as 2014, will take Brazil past the $1.5 trillion level. In per capita terms this would yield an increase from the present level of slightly over $2,600 to nearly $4,500 by the dawn of the new century. This would enable Brazil to break out of the middle of the pack in per capita income while possibly moving up at least two places in the absolute country ranking.

In a somewhat backhanded sense, Brazil is also important because of its massive foreign debt of over $110 billion, a good portion of which is held by U.S. banks. Yet much of this indebtedness resulted from fairly sound decisions concerning borrowing to finance infrastructural development and to cover the sharp rise in oil prices after 1974—decisions that do not seem so bad when one considers the harsh alternatives of abandoning development projects and/or decreasing the domestic living standards and the then prevailing low interest rates. More relevant is the fact that Brazil did manage during this time to reduce greatly its dependence upon imported oil. By raising domestic output to well over 600,000 barrels per day and by substituting alcohol for gasoline, Brazil reduced its annual net petroleum expenditures of nearly $10 billion in the early 1980s to under $4 billion by 1985.

Difficult as the debt situation has been, it should not blind observers to Brazil's major accomplishment of producing massive trade surpluses every year since 1984 while achieving satisfactory rates of economic growth for much of this time and managing the transition from twenty-one years of military rule to competitive civilian politics. Indeed, the 1988 surplus of $19.2 billion was third in the world—behind Japan and the Federal Republic of Germany—and the surplus for 1989 reached $16.1 billion despite a sharp increase in imports.

Brazil's developmental experience, however, not only has often departed from textbook models, but also has actually required a fair bit of rethinking and even reworking of the axioms of Anglo-American developmental economics. In addition it has cast grave doubt upon the relevance of Marxist and neo-Marxist formulations. With each crisis comes a chorus of "we told you so" from both extremes of economic thought, while each recovery and surge of unexpected vitality elicits a collective shaking of heads frequently accompanied by a scramble to explain why the recovery is "artificial," "illusory," or "flawed." Yet from any long-term perspective Brazil's economic performance has been impressive, if not all that it might have been or even "should have been" from the vantage point of 20/20 hindsight.[4]

Anyone who has followed Brazil closely over a prolonged period cannot help but be impressed with the pace and extent of change. Yet in terms of social development or quality of life indicators Brazil is still well back, with at least sixty countries ranking ahead of it in worldwide comparisons. Thus, although it has come a long way and has been moving rapidly ahead in recent years, Brazil's "profound but incomplete transition" of economy and society still has a long way to go.[5] But although today's life expectancy in Brazil (in the low to mid-sixties) is far from satisfactory, it is certainly a great improvement over the average life expectancy of only forty-six years as recently as 1940. Basically one can look at the situation in two ways. The first, very common in the writings of the political left, stresses a growing gap between the urban, modernizing, developing part of the country and the backward, traditional, archaic sector. From this perspective stem gloomy predictions and grim implications for the future. The other approach views the disparities as a simple lag rather than a widening chasm. From this perspective, São Paulo today is what much of the rest of the country will be in another generation.

A third of a century of watching Brazil grow and change—albeit not always as quickly as I would wish—leads me to a qualified espousal of the second, more optimistic outlook. But this catching up by the "other Brazil" is not inevitable. It will occur only if the groups holding political power face up to fundamental, pressing problems and deal effectively with them. Palliatives and expedient stopgaps will only buy time at the cost of reducing options. Judgments on how likely one or the other of these future scenarios is to happen must be grounded in a close analysis of Brazil's past experience and how it may be changing at present.

A Country of Cities

A key point to bear in mind is that Brazil is a very urban country, with more than 82 million persons—some 57 percent of its population—residing in cities of 100,000 or more. Three of every eight Brazilians, over 54 million persons, live in the fifteen metropolitan regions of over 1 million inhabitants each. Of these, more than 29 million live in greater São Paulo and metropolitan Rio de Janeiro, while 25 million more dwell in the country's thirteen cities of between 1 and 3.4 million population each. An additional 28.7 million inhabit urban centers in the 100,000–750,000 range. This last group breaks down into 10.6 million in twenty-five major cities of 300,000–750,000; 6.1 million in another twenty-four medium cities of 200,000–299,000; and nearly 12 million in eighty-nine smaller cities with populations between 100,000 and 199,000.

The Federal District is almost 100 percent urban, with more than 93 percent of Rio de Janeiro state's population concentrated in cities of over 100,000. For São Paulo this proportion is above 81 percent (25.9 million of 32 million). Even in sprawling Minas Gerais, noted as an agricultural state, 42.6 percent of the population (6.6 million in a total of 15.5 million) reside in such significant urban centers. Moreover, Minas Gerais has forty-two other cities in the 50,000–99,000 range, eight of which were likely to graduate from this category by the end of 1990. In São Paulo there are thirty-three of these smaller cities and eleven in Rio de Janeiro—containing the lion's share of the population outside the larger urban centers. Even if we discount the developed heartland (São Paulo, Rio de Janeiro, Minas Gerais, etc.), a large proportion of Brazilians in the outlying regions are city dwellers. In Amazonas the figure is nearly 60 percent, with over 54 percent in Rio Grande do Sul and almost 50 percent in Pernambuco—just to take one state each from the northwest, the extreme south, and the northeast. Most foreigners' image of Bahia is that of Salvador (its capital) and a vast rural hinterland, but in reality, in addition to that great city, there are nine regional centers in Bahia ranging from 100,000 to 415,000 inhabitants.

For the six most populous states of Brazil, the proportion of those dwelling in cities of over 100,000 is nearly 65 percent (58.7 million of 90.4 million). Among other things, this means that the national electorate is highly urban, because those six states contain almost 65 percent of the nation's voters (led by São Paulo with 22.3 percent and Minas Gerais at 11.4 percent). But the rest of Brazil is also far from rural: Urban residents make up 42.4 percent of the population (over 23.7 million among 55.8 million persons) of the other eighteen states.[6] Moreover, a very sizeable slice of the remainder live in reasonably good-sized towns. Thus, given the continuing heavy streams of migration from the countryside to the cities and towns, the rural areas are of decreasing importance.

Critical Dimensions and Recurring Problems

The Legacy of Monarchy

The most important differences between Brazil and the Spanish-American countries do not come directly from the fact that the former was a Portuguese colony, although significant aspects of Brazilian society and culture, and to a lesser extent economy and politics, have been heavily influenced by Portuguese traditions and practices. The differences stem rather from the fact that "belonging" to Portugal and sharing its royal family enabled Brazil to escape the double rupture that led to the fragmentation and political instability of Hispanic America during the nineteenth century. For in the Brazilian experience, and only in this case, independence from the mother country and the quest for a new basis of legitimate political authority did not occur simultaneously; instead they were separated by sixty-seven years of national independence under the rule of the very same monarchs who would have governed Brazil had it remained linked to Portugal.

Thus by the time Brazil did finally break with monarchy near the end of the century and embark upon the republican road—which had proven so perilous and fraught with traumatic episodes for the other countries of the region—many of the most serious challenges to national integrity had been overcome. Not only had the vast territory been held together, but some significant gains had been made in the process of securing borders across which there were now nine separate Hispanic American countries plus surviving British, French, and Dutch colonies—on the South American continent alone. Moreover, national political institutions and processes had been consolidated during the monarchy, with the establishment of the armed forces and the alternation of parties in power being the most significant accomplishments. These matters, along with other important aspects of Brazil's pre-republican experience, are explored in Chapter 2.

Certainly nothing had been lost in terms of political development by this late adoption of a presidential republic; in Mexico, republican experience had led by this time only to the Díaz dictatorship (aside from the loss of half of its original territory to the United States). This repressive regime would end through bloody conflict in 1910. In Argentina the double break with Spain and monarchy had ushered in the dictatorship of Rosas (through 1852) and the political separation of Buenos Aires from the interior of the country, which was finally ended in 1861 by the military victory of Buenos Aires over the provinces. Even the long parliamentary experience of the Chilean republic had deteriorated by the end of the 1880s into a civil war between forces supporting a president bent on augmenting his power (executive role expansion) and those backing the primacy of the congress. The conflict ended tragically in 1891, with President José Manuel Balmaceda's defeat and subsequent suicide.

Yet the Brazilian monarchy accomplished more than the avoidance of the extremes of dictatorship or instability: It enabled Brazil to hold together when Simon Bolívar's Grand Colombia and Central America could not (subsequently giving rise to a total of ten present-day countries). Furthermore, the Brazilian monarchy also handled the transition from a society and economy anchored on slavery to ones based essentially upon free European immigrant labor, without massive civil war. The monarchy could not, however, erase either the legacy of African enslavement or the lingering vestiges of separatist movements. Just as important, the empire left behind just a single truly national institution—the armed forces—along with the skeleton of another—the Catholic Church—and the foundations for a strong property-owning stratum. Indeed, in the absence of institutionalized political parties with strong societal roots, the military is still the major national politically relevant organization in Brazil, making it essential to understand how this came to be.

Employing his constitutional "moderating power" (*poder moderador*) throughout his long reign (1840–1889), Pedro II periodically dissolved the parliament, thus providing for a peaceful alternation in power of two factions of the political elite, who in most other Latin American countries had to resort to force to gain access to governmental office. Moreover, with considerable authority resting in the hands of the emperor, partisan political competition was not the all-or-nothing proposition it was elsewhere on the continent; the stakes of the political game were that much lower.

The Military in Politics

When opposition to the monarchy began to take root among urban groups during the third quarter of the nineteenth century, Brazil's preeminent military hero, Luís Alves de Lima e Silva, ennobled as the duke of Caxias (after pacifying Maranhão in 1840, São Paulo in 1842, and Rio Grande do Sul by 1845), lent his full support to the system and remained personally loyal to Pedro. But forces for change were deeply at work, particularly since the Paraguayan War of 1865–1870 (also known as the Triple Alliance War), and a new military generation was emerging from the academy imbued with positivism[7] and favoring a republic as the vehicle for lifting Brazil from economic and social backwardness.

Although these *doutores* had significant disagreements with those officers who had risen the hard way (the *tarimbeiros*), both would come to support military role expansion and political intervention, albeit for different reasons. The former, seeing the soldier as a particular breed of citizen, acted in support of political reforms—a distinguishing characteristic of the "ruler" military.[8] The *tarimbeiros*, on the other hand, joined in overthrowing the monarchy in quest of strengthening the armed forces in terms of equipment and professionalization, without concern for reshaping the society, from which they felt quite separate.[9] Though they did not see themselves, as did their more intellectual rival current, as the "priesthood of national purification," their concentration on obtaining a greater degree of governmental support for the military institution also led to active political involvement.

Moreover, as Alexandre Barros argues, by late in the empire the army—due to recruitment differences that brought changes in the social class and geographic origins of cadets, thereby generally decreasing the Rio de Janeiro bias and coming closer to a middle-class outlook—had become the defender of national interests against the local and sectional interests reflected by the navy and national guard as well as against the state and provincial interests of the militia.[10] Up to this point a Europeanized elite had constructed the Brazilian state, but this elite lost its homogeneity during the years after the Paraguayan War.[11] The resulting vacuum not only drew the military further into politics, but also, as no new cohesive elite emerged, the power vacuum continued into the early years of the republic.

Thus, though the civilian republican movement was gradually gaining adherents during the 1880s, it would be the army, not the Republican Party, that eventually overturned the monarchy in 1889 and assumed the function of the moderating power. Indeed, the military would continue to exercise that power even after it yielded control of the presidency to civilians following six years of essentially military rule. More significant, an actively interventionist current in the Brazilian armed forces has continued to be very important, although only occasionally dominant, down to the present.[12] As shown by Campos Coelho, this situation has been fostered by the repeated propensity of civilian elements to seek military intervention on their behalf.[13]

In the recurrent struggle between legalism and political activism within the Brazilian military, the latter was generally substantially stronger than depicted by most contemporary historians. During the four decades of the Old Republic (1889–1930), very few periods were not marked by military revolts, employment of the military against the regime's opponents, or heavy armed forces tutelage of the government. While a series of São Paulo civilians did govern the country with reasonable security after the initial years of military domination, two of these three presidents faced political-military crises that posed a real threat to their very survival. Prudente de Morais was plagued by Jacobin military opposition allied to extremist Republicans. This was compounded by dissatisfaction over his handling of the Canudos insurgency (see Chapter 3, "The São Paulo Dynasty, 1894–1906"), and in November 1897 he was saved from assassination only through his war minister's willingness to sacrifice his own life.

Following Campos Salles's quite peaceful term, Rodrigues Alves survived with some difficulty the November 1904 revolt of the military school. The first Minas Gerais president, Afonso Pena, died in office of a "moral traumatism" soon after being thwarted in his preferences regarding the presidential succession and being forced to accept the candidacy of his war minister. Nilo Peçanha's brief year in office was little more than a chance to preside over Marshal Hermes da Fonseca's election. Though Hermes faced no military plotting, he was barely settled in office when the Naval Revolt of 1910 broke out as sailors rebelled over discipline. Moreover, protracted and often violent conflicts with entrenched elites in the northeast and social protest insurgencies in the south marked his regime. The latter carried over into the term of Wenceslau Bráz, who otherwise enjoyed stability, although the nation's political kingmaker, Senator Pinheiro Machado, was murdered during Bráz's term.

These episodes of military involvement in political affairs were far from casual, much less accidental. Though most of the military had been directly affected by the civil war in the mid-1890s, this was not the only influence on them. The "professionalizers" would be affected by assignment to Germany and the subsequent arrival of a French training mission. But the Acre affair of 1903–1904 (when Bolivian and Peruvian pretensions had to be met with a show of force in the remote interior of the continent) further convinced the officer corps of the pressing need for a European-type army, not only to protect the Amazon—still internationally important at that time for its production of rubber—from imperial powers but also to counterbalance Argentina's modernization of its armed forces.

The middle-class idea that compulsory military service would, by "militarizing" the civilians, impart their particular vision and virtues upon society failed to pan out. In part this failure was due to the fact that even with substantial expansion of the army—to a peak of 52,000 during the Paraguayan War—the large majority of citizens never experienced military service. Over the 1890 to 1930 period, the army grew by 220 percent to the population's 162 percent, but this still meant in absolute terms that more men came *not* to serve in the armed forces than before.[14] And although the army would expand from 30,000 in 1920 to 50,000 by 1930 and 93,000 a decade later, when World War II dominated the international scene, this expansion barely stayed ahead of population growth.[15]

Hence, it is not surprising that military involvement in politics enjoyed a vigorous resurgence during the 1920s, as repeated military uprisings culminated in the successful 1930 Revolution. Indeed, Brazil's experience became unique as a single military generation exercised a heavy influence over national affairs for a full half century. The *tenentes* (lieutenants), a group of young officers who spearheaded the unrest of the 1920s and furnished a major share of the military component of the subsequent revolution, went on to become in large part the generals of the 1960s and to heavily influence the most protracted period of direct military rule in the nation's life. Yet in some ways this phenomenon was fundamentally similar to that of the young officers who followed Hermes da Fonseca, the leader who had helped put an end to monarchical rule in the late 1880s and shaped events down through the 1921–1922 campaign of the Military Club against the government.

In at least an indirect manner this "Florianist" military generation (perceived as followers of the precepts of former president Floriano Peixoto) spawned the *tenentist* one, and together they exercised a very potent and pervasive influence over nearly the first three-quarters of a century of Brazil's life as a republic. Even though the Hermes faction originally felt that professionalism required that the military stay out of politics and public office, Hermes himself became president (and was ready to return to the presidency in 1922). Furthermore, the continuity stems from the fact that, if events before 1910 were just faint memories to the senior officers of the early 1960s, the same was not true with respect to the Hermes da Fonseca presidency (1910–1914) and the ensuing events, particularly the development of *tenentismo* during the 1920s. With few exceptions, the generals of the post–World War II period were at least already enrolled in the military preparatory school (Colégio Militar), if not studying at the academy (Escola Militar) by the time of the Hermes presidency.

This interpretation—both with respect to the interventionist outcome of otherwise competing concepts of the soldier's role and to the heavy impact of past events upon future actions—is supported by the best Brazilian research on the subject. José Murilo de Carvalho maintains that the "corporative" soldiers during the period from World War I to the early 1930s, as typified by Bertholdo Klinger, though hostile to the *tenentes*, did form a movement in 1930 to oust President Washington Luís. That their chief purpose was to head off the rise to power of the *tenentes* and Getúlio Vargas does not vitiate the import of their actions.[16]

Thus, even these corporative soldiers came to accept—and ultimately to support—military intervention, but only if it was institutional and hierarchical, not the handiwork of some faction with a goal of reshaping society. This corporative view combined with General Pedro Aurélio de Góes Monteiro's concept of "politics *of* the army, not politics *in* the army" would lead to what Carvalho has termed "the interventionism of the generals, or of the general staff, the intervention of the organization as a whole."[17]

As time went on, the increasing division of the officer corps along generational lines would place them on both sides of an accelerating conflict between the established order and the forces of change. Though a constitutionalist current remained strong and was often dominant, historical precedent nourished a continuing belief within military ranks that the armed forces were motivated by national rather than institutional interests or personal ambitions. This view was accepted as well by much of the public and, having served as the gravediggers of the Old Republic—as their predecessors had been its midwives—the officer corps played a central role in the 1937 "Estado Novo" coup, Vargas's ouster in 1945, and the escalating series of crises during the 1954–1964 period that culminated in the establishment of a durable authoritarian military regime. If most of the military had trouble with the concept of the armed forces as the country's ruler, they apparently accepted some version of its mission as final arbiter—at least in times of crisis.

Indeed, Barros has convincingly argued that the military system of training provided a more effective socialization of the officer corps under the republic than did the comparatively ineffective civilian educational system. This socialization increased the military's capabilities to take power relative to the civilians' declining ability to retain it.[18] Moreover, the Brazilian armed forces have generally demonstrated significant independence from regional elites and social classes.[19] This functional autonomy has been accompanied by a set of common values not only rooted in the effective military socialization process, but also reinforced by historical experiences.[20]

The military figures involved in these events had been participants, not just observers, throughout the recurring crises from 1922 on. Hence they felt a sense of responsibility for the outcome of these episodes and second-guessed themselves concerning sins of omission; a valid comprehension of their perceptions in this regard is at least as essential for understanding the sharp regime change of 1964 as is an analysis of developments within the political system itself. Moreover, when the political system underwent fundamental change, so did the military institution insofar as it functioned as a component of the political system. Along with the economic and social processes that underlay political change, the impact of each crisis upon those who would become key actors in subsequent events is examined in Chapters 3 through 8.

The Failure of Parties and Flawed Democracy

Another major theme of Brazilian history has been the effort to institutionalize some viable form of representative government. This has generally involved an excessive faith in the transforming power of constitutions combined with a failure to develop adequate political parties of a truly national scope. As a result there has repeatedly been a substantial gap between the formal framework of government and the prevailing practices rooted in a political culture relatively resistant to change. In part for this reason, the armed forces have been able to retain the role of "moderating power" or ultimate arbiter sanctified in the 1891 constitution and embodied in an essentially similar form in subsequent constitutions.

This overreliance on constitutional engineering to the neglect of more meaningful and empirical institution building is clear in the haphazard process that ensued upon Vargas's removal from office in late 1945. In the midst of the diffuse democratic euphoria that accompanied the Allied victory in World War II, Brazilian democrats thought a liberal constitution that curbed executive powers and spelled out individual rights would be sufficient to allow democracy to flourish at last. No real attention was paid to the question of building a rational party system as distinct from developing an environment of freedom in which all types of political parties could emerge and compete. Hence extreme fragmentation resulted, with the so-called national parties lacking any significant strength in the most important state of all, São Paulo. Instead, in the economic and demographic heartland of Brazil, personalist, regional, and ideological splinter parties proliferated. This in turn contributed to the breakdown of the formally democratic but weakly institutionalized political system in the early 1960s.

The political strength of the armed forces in Brazil is both partially a consequence of the weakness of political parties and a factor perpetuating that weakness. For there has been a pronounced trend for dominant elements within the Brazilian military establishment to oppose the idea of strong political parties. Ironically, this has been an unnecessary preoccupation on their part. The prospects for really strong political parties have never been promising in Brazil, from the days of the manipulated two-party system of the empire through the essentially single and decentralized party of the Old Republic, on past the nonparty system of Vargas's New State and the weak, fragmented multiplicity of parties under the elite-dominated yet populist politics of the 1946–1964 period. This situation failed to change during the prolonged era of military rule, and even as the 1990s open Brazilian parties have no significantly greater substance than they did in these earlier periods. Nor have they earned the loyalty of most of the electorate. Indeed, it is a sad commentary upon Brazilian parties that they were most important during the Juscelino Kubitschek years (1956–1960), a time when almost all analysts put strengthening and rationalizing the party system near the head of the list of the country's political development needs.

Closely related to the parties problem is Brazil's failure to develop real democracy even during periods of formal constitutional representative government. Key to this failure is the fact that cooptation (participation manipulated and controlled from above) has generally prevailed over mobilized participation spurred by social and economic changes. Rooted in the faster and greater growth and differentiation of the governmental structure compared to social modernization or economic development, this situation has led, in the view of one astute Brazilian scholar, to a "simultaneous process of contradictory development."[21] The two poles of this process are São Paulo as the most dynamic economic sector and Rio de Janeiro as the center of a coalition of states jointly controlling political power.

Mobilization of the populace has been a strikingly ineffective force in Brazilian political life. Attributing this ineffectiveness to a political culture stressing conciliation, class harmony, respect for hierarchy, paternalism, clientelism, co-optation, and strong vertical ties (which vitiate class factors), one perceptive U.S. historian concludes that "the failure of virtually all movements of social protest in Brazil since the colonial period attests to the resilience and effectiveness of the political order."[22] Even today, in the labor field most Brazilian efforts at a general strike would be considered embarrassingly weak in almost any other comparable country. Yet overemphasis upon the role of the opposition, particularly regarding actions to mobilize mass support, continues rampant in the bulk of writings on Brazilian politics, including those by foreign scholars. The modern-day counterpart of the long-time overemphasis on the role of civilian forces in the demise of the empire, this misplaced focus obscures the continued decisive role of the military in the transition process.

For exaggeration of the importance of mobilizational efforts creates an artificial need to explain how the armed forces could "again" be so influential as was obviously the case during the late 1980s within the José Sarney government. In the sense that their opinion carries more weight with the political decision makers, including Congress, than does the voice of organized public opinion campaigns and "mass" demonstrations, the military has never been the lesser force. Moreover, as will be amply shown in the following chapters, even when the military has remained at the margin of the process, *conciliação* (the brokered adjustment of interests among astute elements of the governing elites) has as a rule determined the course of affairs in Brazil. Resort to *conciliação* may, however, at times be spurred to action by movements, campaigns, and demonstrations—but rarely if ever have these been the decisive factor. Indeed, the failures of the Brazilian left to become an influential force in the political system have been so consistently repeated that a good share of the explanation must lie within the radical movements themselves; otherwise, the Brazilian conservative forces would have to be extraordinarily strong, skillful, and effective to have retained their dominance.

In part as a result of these considerations, but also contributing to them, is the fact that Brazil has yet to do anything serious in the field of agrarian reform. Indeed, the democratically adopted 1988 constitution provides even stronger obstacles to large-scale expropriation of land for this purpose than did the conservative legislation of the military regime. These obstacles are largely the result of a very effective pressure campaign mobilized by the landowners upon the recent constituent assembly, while organizations professing to speak for the landless millions proved incapable of affecting the final outcome of these proceedings.

Throughout Brazil's life as a nation, immediate political concerns, generally those of the elites and middle class, have taken priority over rational economic planning and responsible fiscal and financial policies. Contrary to much of the conventional wisdom, foreign debt and inflation are not relatively new problems, but rather recurring and even chronic ones—at least through the hundred-year span of the republic. Moreover, throughout at least the past century the "art of not choosing between conflicting objectives" has been highly developed; it has been accompanied in the more recent period by a "proliferation of disguised mechanisms for transferring resources."[23] Much of this resort to disguised mechanisms has stemmed from a lack of clarity in anticipating the consequences of economic policy upon social groups and has been facilitated by the state acting as the distributor of benefits to the holders of political power. For even the Brazilian elites have consistently demonstrated little faith in the market as allocator of power and resources. In this respect liberalism, albeit receiving a good deal of lip service, has not been reflected in the realms of policy and action. (Thus, the forceful moves in this direction by the Collor government mark a major innovation.) On a more positive side, another recurring theme of Brazilian national experience is the repeated ability to recover quite rapidly from adverse economic impacts such as the world economic crisis of 1929 or the 1974 global energy crisis.

One Brazil—or Several?

The final basic themes of Brazil's national experience have to do with regional variations and the racial factor. Brazil's vast size and lack of internal transportation and communications would have created a problem of regionalism in any case. The Portuguese crown's initial decision to make the possession into a large number of separate colonies directly linked to the mother country accentuated this tendency, as did the subsequent experiences of various parts of the country under French, Dutch, or Spanish rule for varying lengths of time. After independence a chain reaction of separatist revolts had to be suppressed by force—although not on the scale of this century's Katangas, Biafras, and Eritreas, which have respectively soaked the soil of Zaire, Nigeria, and Ethiopia with blood. Hence until fairly recently Brazil was in many respects a confederation of regions loosely united by a common language and a widely shared religion. A good deal of national integration has taken place since 1930, particularly in the span of the past generation, both as a result of greatly improved transport and communications and because of very extensive internal migration. Yet regionalism is still a very important factor in national life, and the forms it has taken and its significant manifestations at different junctures are woven into the chronological narrative of Chapters 2 through 8.

But one crucial aspect of the current situation needs to be borne in mind from the start: The economic dominance of São Paulo, a phenomenon essentially of the last hundred years, is one of the factors most strongly retarding and distorting Brazil's political development. The problem has two sides: São Paulo's internal imperialism and the natural reaction in the form of a conspiracy by the lesser states to prevent São Paulo from again exercising the political dominance it enjoyed for a thirty-five-year period that ended in 1930.

The economic preeminence of São Paulo—it exceeds half the national total in many key categories—is often reflected in attitudes toward less developed regions of the country ranging from patronizing through patently superior on to outright arrogance (as reflected in the well-known metaphor of São Paulo as the mighty train engine pulling more than a score of empty boxcars). Not a few São Paulo businessmen appear to believe in a peculiar law of economic gravity whereby all money should flow down from the north, northeast, and west into the center-south and particularly into São Paulo. Proposals to expend significant sums on improving the economic infrastructure of the country are acceptable to these Paulistas, as residents of São Paulo are called, only if they conform to this "self-evident" rule of nature. If, on the other hand, such a proposal appears to bypass São Paulo, it is by definition unnecessary, wasteful, ill-conceived, and even "corrupt"— no matter how much it would benefit those living in other parts of the country.

If it were not for the crying need for infrastructural development in the poorer regions, this self-righteously and often piously proclaimed attitude that "what's good for São Paulo is good for Brazil" might even be amusing. But reflected in such actions as the 1986 knee-jerk rejection of a northeasterner for finance minister (a post God apparently intends for Paulistas only) or the coordinated vituperative attack on the construction of a north-south railroad leading up from Brasília, it is both pernicious and exploitative. Fortunately not all São Paulo entrepreneurs hold such self-serving views.

The other side of this coin is the determination of the smaller states to see that the grotesque underrepresentation of São Paulo in the federal Congress is maintained—an underrepresentation that becomes more pronounced as the Paulista population continues its rapid growth. On a basis of "one man, one vote," São Paulo with 22.5 percent of the country's population should have more than half again the number of seats it has in the lower house of the national Congress. Yet no system short of that practiced between 1964 and 1989—that is, abolition of direct presidential elections—can deny São Paulo, with nearly 19 million voters, enormous weight in choosing the country's chief executive.

In a deeper sense, regional variations go beyond quality of life to the existence of life itself: Though the national average life expectancy is by now well over sixty years, it is still only forty-five years in much of the northeast and fifty-five in the north, contrasting sharply with over sixty-seven in the south and above sixty-four in the southeast and center-west regions. Literacy follows a similar pattern, with over 40 percent illiteracy in the northeast a glaring contrast from the 15 percent rate in the south and southeast. These differences rest upon the bedrock of the extreme imbalance of economic development: Ninety-one percent of all industry is found in the southeast and south, with only 6 percent in the northeast, 1.5 percent in the north, and a scant 1 percent in the center-west.

To Be Black in Brazil

Ethnic composition in general and race relations in particular are also distinctive features of Brazil. Once again performance in this field can be viewed as either striking, in light of the staggering dimensions of the problem, or inadequate, from the perspective of what remains to be done. For if, over a hundred years after abolition of slavery, Brazil is far from the image of racial democracy it has often sought to project, it is also a great distance from the kind and degree of institutionalized racial segregation that was only beginning to be dismantled in the United States a century after the Emancipation Proclamation.

Racially Brazil is a very diverse country, with descendants of African slaves making up over two-fifths of the population, a proportion exceeded only by those whose forebears were European immigrants—Italians even more than Portuguese, but also Germans, Poles, and Spanish in large numbers. There are also noticeable communities of Asian Brazilians, especially those of Japanese extraction, of whom there are well over a million; individuals of Middle Eastern origins, particularly Lebanese, are readily apparent in the larger cities. Indeed, almost the rarest element in the Brazilian ethnic potpourri are the original inhabitants, for identifiable Indians are down to under 200,000, and other descendants of the pre-conquest indigenous population, although very noticeable in some regions, often merge into the ranks of predominantly Afro-Brazilian mixes, rather than the quasi-Indian mestizos found in Spanish America.[24]

The racial/ethnic variations found in Brazil are far from random, although historical differences have been blurred by the heavy flows of internal migration during the post–World War II period. The nature of the pre-independence colony is still discernible in many Brazilian states, particularly those that were centers of population and economic activity in the colonial period. Thus the recent flood of northeasterners to the cities of the center-south does not mask either the largely European immigrant base of São Paulo society nor the Afro-Brazilian foundation of the population in many of the northeastern states.

Blacks in Brazil are much worse off in almost every way than whites, so much so that the reasons for this situation must be a continuing concern throughout this book. Although the heritage of slavery is certainly still a factor, it is simplistic and grossly inadequate to consider slavery as the principal explanation for lower classes, not just in the cities but also in the rural sector, that are preponderantly made up of Afro-Brazilians. This striking correlation of dark color with the lowest rungs of the socioeconomic ladder is manifest in all organizations. In Congress blacks are but six of 559, and the paucity of black or mulatto generals and admirals is matched by their absence from the diplomatic service. The Catholic Church is equally unrepresentative, with only five black bishops out of some 370 and a mere 200 dark-skinned priests in over 14,000. Certainly the educational system contributes to these disparities, but there is much more at work in maintaining the low social mobility of blacks and mulattoes and their exclusion from society's most vital institutions.

The passivity that characterizes the Brazilian underprivileged masses is not only a clear but also a truly striking aspect of Brazilian reality. Even if the historical roots of this docility can be understood, the reasons for its persistence are quite perplexing. Part of the explanation lies in the fact that blacks and mulattoes, given their very large numbers and "majority" status in many regions, typically do not perceive of themselves as a minority. To a considerable degree they accept the myth that their plight is a result of the country's underdevelopment. Yet they are also held back by serious reservations as to whether there is a viable alternative to acquiescing in the hand fate has dealt them. Then, too, the relative ease of survival in tropical and semitropical Brazil—where the vast majority of them live—is another incentive to accommodation.

Brazilian Types and Brazilian Ways

The essence of *Brasilianidade*, the nature of being Brazilian, is an elusive concept, in large part because of the multiple non-Brazilian influences upon Brazilian society and culture. More likely than not cordial, adaptable, and conciliatory (albeit more with respect to form than to substance), the true Brazilian is apt to manifest other traits depending upon the socialization process to which he or she has been subjected. The socialization process, in turn, varies considerably with social origins, for the family is the prime agent of socialization for the still very large numbers not heavily affected by the educational system—as they don't go to school—or by organized religion—as religious education outside of the formal educational system is weak and limited. Yet the influence of television is beginning to be felt, with a fundamentally "homogenizing" effect that spreads a more national culture to the detriment of once very distinct regional variations.

Regional types, although increasingly blurred by internal migration and the effects of the mass media, are still important in Brazil. Indeed, given the lesser impact of formal education and the virtual absence of continuing foreign immigration in Brazil as compared to the United States, Brazilian regional types are probably more distinctive than the analogous U.S. variations (e.g., New Yorker, New Englander, southerner, hillbilly, Texan, midwesterner, Californian). Thus, the prototype Paulista is the country's most pragmatic, materialistic, and hardworking strain—distinguished by a strong sense of superiority—while the Carioca (Rio de Janeiro resident) is by contrast pleasure-seeking, more easygoing, and at least a bit devious (if not a real *malandro*, which is sort of a cross between a conman and an inoffensive scoundrel) behind a facade of openness. Hence both the origin and at least partial continuing relevance of the old saw "earn it in São Paulo and spend it in Rio." Yet there are millions of internal immigrants in both these highly urban states whose socialization took place in other regions and who do not demonstrate the same behavior characteristics as do the lifelong residents of São Paulo and Rio de Janeiro. Moreover, the stereotype fits much better the Paulistanos (residents of São Paulo city) than the inhabitants of the interior of the premier state, while persons residing outside of Rio de Janeiro city are often termed Fluminenses to distinguish them from the true Carioca. (Confusingly, supporters of one of the city's leading soccer teams are also "Fluminenses.")

To the typical Mineiro, as residents of Minas Gerais are called, Paulistas are pushy and often obnoxiously domineering, while Cariocas are seen as apt to be lazy and unreliable, even shiftless—better partners for partying than for business. The Mineiro, in turn, tends to be thoughtful, taciturn, and highly conciliatory, but also is inclined to be rather moody. Inhabitants of Minas Gerais also enjoy a reputation for being wily and sagacious, with this last characteristic in the eyes of the Paulistas and Cariocas often being carried to the point of frustrating inscrutability. As a result of internal migration, several million Mineiros are to be found in other parts of the country.

Bahianos (persons from Bahia) reflect most closely the Afro-Portuguese synthesis relatively free from other ethnic roots, being considered particularly sensuous and perhaps preoccupied with food. In sharp contrast Gaúchos (from Rio Grande do Sul in the extreme south) often seem to be displaced Europeans, demonstrating traits and customs generally identified with Mediterranean peoples, particularly the Italians. Especially to the Mineiro they appear to be loud, direct to the point of rudeness, and unreasonably intransigent—at times veritable "Argentines." The Gaúchos would much prefer to interpret what others view as boisterous and even belligerent as energetic, active, and productive. Between Rio Grande do Sul and São Paulo, the residents of Santa Catarina vary from quite Gaúcho-like to even greater retention of European traits, particularly Germanic, in the north. Similarly, the population of Paraná lacks a distinctive type as those in the upper part of the state think and behave little differently from their neighboring Paulistas, and in some parts Polish cultural residue is still quite pronounced. Other colorful regional types abound, many of them immortalized in Brazilian literature, but their numbers are much smaller and they are much less frequently encountered by most individuals working in or visiting Brazil.

To a very high degree, a person in Brazil is important less for himself than for his relationships and ties. As forcefully portrayed by Roberto DaMatta, individuals without links to persons or institutions of prestige in Brazilian society are treated as inferiors.[25] Faced with a situation in which a North American might expect the law to be applied in a fairly straightforward manner, most Brazilians not near the very bottom of the social pyramid will immediately resort to the classic "Do you know with whom you are speaking?" This is an effort to invoke the individual's status or connection as justification for his or her contention that the law or rule technically violated was intended for the masses, not for a special person such as he or she should be perceived as being. Indeed, for most Brazilians the law may well be appropriate for others, but theirs is almost always an exceptional case to be resolved on a personal basis, not by application of universalistic standards. This projects onto the political scene in the famous dictum, "For my friends everything; for my enemies the law."

Parentela is a fundamental characteristic of Brazilian life, and an understanding of it contributes greatly to comprehending why certain things happen and how many things get done. Essentially this phenomenon is rooted in the importance of the extended family to Brazilians. As vividly and perceptively described by Charles Wagley, this type of kinship group, which at times approaches a clan in extension and inclusiveness, has traditionally been the "most important single institution in Brazil."[26] Including relatives on both the father's and mother's side plus the full array of one's in-laws, the *parentela* has on its fringes an assortment of informally adopted individuals and even family retainers (in the rural areas there are a variety of servants and foremen who are in a very limited sense considered "almost" family). Its range is further extended by the importance still given to godparents as *comadres* and *copadres* of their *afilhados*. Historically, and even today in the more traditional areas of Brazil, *parentelas* are a critical political factor, one far more profound than the North American or European concept of nepotism.[27]

Even for those sectors of modern urban society for whom *parentela* is less important because of the physical distance from the bulk of their kinfolk, family is of great significance. As DaMatta, the leading student of such matters, has so emphatically shown, the domain of the home is important for Brazilians at all social levels. Home is where the individual generally finds the love, harmony, tolerance, decency, generosity, and hospitality so often lacking in the outside world.[28] Within the home everyone is unique and irreplaceable; its security and guarantee of rights and position independent of effort and accomplishment contrasts sharply with the perils and frustrations inherent in those aspects of life outside its purview. In the dog-eat-dog domain of the street, individuals are unable to control their lives and they encounter the harsh realities that stem from the impersonal, competitive, and individualistic nature of the public sphere. Though this may appeal to the wealthy, powerful, and successful, it is not congenial to the vast majority who have none of these attributes and for whom work is not a challenge, but rather a burdensome chore.

Yet these two vital spheres of life interact with a third, that of the transcendental or supernatural, which calls into play sentiments of universal love, altruism, and collectivism.[29] This third sphere holds particular appeal for the poor and unsuccessful, because at its core is the idea that things are evened out in the other world after death. *Umbanda* (a mix of African practices with spiritualism and elements of Christianity), along with the maverick to near-heretical "popular" Catholicism, provides some of the dispossessed with a taste of equality on earth, as within these religions the individual has a chance to be separated from his or her workday temporal status. Individuals who are nobodies in the material world can be important and even play leadership roles within *umbanda* and messianistic movements.

DaMatta stresses that the key to Brazilian society resides in the interaction of the spheres that is represented by Carnival, Holy Week, and the commemoration of national independence on September 7. Study of culture and society through these national rituals leads to essentially the same conclusions as those arrived at through examination of the prism of daily life. The lines of power within these "complementary if dissociated" value spheres are, in DaMatta's analysis, integrated by the search for the perfect leader/good master/messianic figure.[30] During periods when the complementarity of these domains is not seriously questioned, integration is provided through personal relationships and patronage. When this complementarity is challenged, however, there is a marked proclivity in Brazil to call in the providential man, a near-messiah who provides integration in an absolutist manner—this tendency explains the recurring phenomena of populism and authoritarianism. Indeed, at least a partial acceptance of this interpretation is an essential element for understanding the predominantly nonideological and largely nonclass base of Brazilian electoral politics, characteristics vividly driven home in the 1989 elections.

The brokering, clientelistic nature of the Brazilian political-governmental system reflects to a significant degree the pervasive role of the so-called *panelinha*, an informal group of a relatively closed nature bound together by common interests as well as by personal ties. Its very essence lies in the inclusion of members in a variety of complementary positions in the sociopolitical-economic structure, and in its most negative manifestations it may give rise to a kind of amoral (if not immoral) cronyism. One of the most important of the several types of personal links that maintain connections between various interests, organizations, and agencies, *panelinhas* are perhaps the most difficult to identify and trace out because there is no formal record of their existence—unlike kin relationships or "old school ties."[31]

The famous Brazilian *jeitinho*, often mixing a good deal of ingenuity with a dash—or more—of bending the rules, is founded in the deeply felt need to reconcile a personal problem or inconvenience with the bothersome impersonality of the law and rules. Thus in the face of a bureaucratic response that something can't be done, or at least not at that time or in the way the solicitant desires, some factor is invoked to persuade the functionary that this is a special case to be resolved within the flexible spirit of the law rather than its inflexible letter. Certainly this effort may consist of *pistolão* (resorting to influence and connections), but in the typical *jeito/jeitinho* it is more likely an appeal to some common tie that enables the two parties to relate more closely as equals. A common friend, preference for the same soccer team or samba school, or origins in the same state are the kinds of catalysts often invoked.[32] Taken together with the interacting spheres of existence and values, *parentela, panelinha,* and *jeitinho* serve as means for reconciling the modern and the traditional—certainly a continuing need for citizens of changing but not yet transformed Brazil.

The Past Still Shapes the Future

This inquiry has been influenced by a determination to explain Brazilian developments as fully as possible as well as by a desire to portray the Brazilian experience in a manner facilitating comparison. More than three decades of close study and observation of the Brazilian scene has convinced me that most of the military as well as many, if not all, of the civilian politicians and leading figures in the Catholic Church are strongly influenced by their comprehension and perception of relevant antecedent experience. Of course, the real environment within which they operate is at least as important in determining the outcome of events, and I have sought to make its evolution intelligible throughout this study.

Because I am concerned with lessons of the past that have current relevance, special attention is given to those junctures most analogous to what Brazil has recently experienced or is going through at present, particularly regarding efforts to consolidate transitions to representative civilian government. Such transitionary periods include: (1) that in the 1820s immediately following independence; (2) the apogee of the long rule of Pedro II in the 1850s and 1860s; (3) the early years of the republic; (4) the aftermath of the 1930 Revolution; (5) the years immediately following the ouster of Vargas at the end of World War II; (6) the Kubitschek administration in the late 1950s; and (7) the period since 1984. Indeed, nothing is more critical to understanding today's developments and what may lie ahead than a full comprehension of the roots of failure of previous attempts to establish a representative and participant political system under which respect for basic human rights could develop.

Woven into the chronological story will be not only these repeated democratizing efforts, but also a portrayal of how Brazil changed economically and socially between each of them. Similarly, each retrocession to authoritarian rule will be analyzed in terms of its impact upon the ongoing national developmental process rather than viewed merely as an isolated event. Much of what may at first seem incidental detail regarding the episodes of the post-1930 period in particular, but also for earlier times, is intended to explain relationships and behavior in subsequent crises. Thus, while a junior military officer, a state-level politician, or a parish priest may not have played a very important part in a past crisis, his participation in that episode or even his perception of it may often be crucial in determining his actions in a subsequent critical situation in which he occupies a key position.

This factor takes on even greater relevance given the very long careers of many key actors on the Brazilian historical stage. One example is General Augusto Tasso Fragoso, who played a pivotal part in the 1930 crisis: Born at the time of the Paraguayan War, he was a cadet during the political decline of the empire, played an active part in the establishment of the republic as a junior officer, and, after serving as a colonel during the government of Marshal Hermes da Fonseca, became army chief of staff between the first and second *tenente* revolts in the early 1920s. Still in this post at the time of the São Paulo revolt of 1932, Fragoso was minister of the Superior Military Tribunal at the time of the Communist uprising in 1935 and the 1937 seizure of absolute power by Vargas. Hence his active service stretched from the late stages of the monarchy to the midpoint of the Vargas era. Another example is Marshal Oswaldo Cordeiro de Farias, whose career spanned from the 1920s through the 1970s; such half-century careers are duplicated not only by most key military figures, but by many civilian politicians as well.[33] The late Tancredo Neves was on the political scene from the 1930s to 1985, and present-day opposition leader Leonel Brizola began his active electoral career just after World War II. Moreover, Brazil's archbishops and cardinals frequently also reach or exceed a half century of clerical activity.

In light of the importance of formative events upon leading figures, key actors will be introduced into the story at the point when national events first had a crucial impact upon them. By the same token, political organizations of less than lasting direct importance may be discussed if they were either an important breeding ground for new leadership and ideas or a salient example of a recurring phenomenon. This will be seen with increasing frequency as Chapters 4 through 8 carry the story from the late 1920s down to 1984.

Events since 1985, the subject of Chapters 9 and 10, are treated in greater detail than the earlier period for the compelling reason that the recent past and the present provide the foundation from which future developments will arise. When dealing with the more remote past, certain events and developments that appeared important at the time can be treated lightly, mentioned in passing, or even omitted because their consequences proved to be less profound than expected. Similarly, many prominent personalities meriting attention in a study limited to a particular period may be passed over because they did not come to have as much impact on the course of events as once seemed likely.

Of course, when looking ahead to the 1990s, such after-the-fact selectivity is not possible. José Sarney turned out to be the only nationally important figure to emerge from the 1965 crop of governors, but this was neither obvious, predictable, nor even logical at that time—because under normal circumstances no one from a small, poor, peripheral state makes it to the presidency in Brazil (or in the United States for that matter). In the same manner São Paulo Governor Orestes Quércia is the sole representative of the 1974 senatorial harvest to have developed into a major national figure, but at that time he was viewed as well back of a half dozen more senior individuals in his party within his own state and was not even considered likely to become governor of São Paulo, much less a presidential contender. This view was buttressed by the fact that the military and its party still firmly dominated the country, and Quércia was from the opposition party.

Fernando Collor de Mello of the small northeastern state of Alagoas appeared at the time to be one of the least likely members of the gubernatorial-senatorial class of 1986 who would have a major impact on national life. Yet by early 1989 he had already emerged as the front runner in the presidential sweepstakes, subsequently being carried into the presidency on a tidal wave of over 35 million votes and undertaking what may become the most thorough effort at modernizing economic and political life since Vargas jerked the country fully into the twentieth century sixty years earlier. Moreover, others of this cohort are affecting the course of events during this critical juncture at which transition from authoritarian military rule either will or will not be transformed into consolidation of democracy and responsiveness to social needs. Because some of these actors may well eventually emerge to play crucial roles and even become future chief executives, all must at least be presented, if not fully analyzed. Thus, the last chapter will of necessity be more detailed and open-ended. For the future, though it is already crouching in the present, is at least partially hidden behind a series of opaque to translucent screens.

2

Monarchical Brazil: Colony and Empire

The Brazil described in the preceding chapter has resulted from a long and complex historical process. Though many of the most dramatic changes have taken place during the past generation, in most cases these changes resulted chiefly from acceleration of developmental trends long underway. Much as with the British or U.S. experience—as contrasted with that of France or Germany—Brazil's development as a nation has been essentially evolutionary, with few sharp breaks or drastic discontinuities. Indeed, in no instance has there been a real rupture in the sense of the groups previously exercising power being dispossessed rather than just having to share control over national affairs with emergent elements. And such emergent elements typically have been on the political scene for quite some time before causing what can best be described as changes of regime, rather than of the basic system. The old elites have never been plowed under, or even permanently swept aside, as the outcome of even the most important of these substitutions of one political regime for another. Old regimes have at most been displaced, never replaced.

The judgment of one current Brazilian historian regarding the end of the monarchy could well apply to all the subsequent political watersheds as well: "Predictably the new regime they created did not represent a real rupture with the past."[1] Such apparently "revolutionary" events in the political realm as independence (1822), the shift from monarchy to a republic (1889), the overthrow of the oligarchical republic in 1930, the seizure of power by the military in 1964, and the return to civilian rule in 1985 were not in any instance immediately accompanied by sharp social transformations or even dramatic economic innovations. Rather they were partially the result of substantial changes in these realms of national life that had built up over time, and each landmark change of the political regime in turn contributed to a further round of socioeconomic developments that gradually created pressures for yet another major readjustment in the political system.[2]

Because very substantial elements of the old order were always retained after each of these crisis periods, even in the political realm, due attention

24

must be paid to the past in order to understand the present. Indeed, as Nathaniel Leff has pointed out, Brazilian experience has repeatedly demonstrated economic expansion and structural change accompanied by only minimal alteration in the "fundamental relations of power."[3] Yet this does not mean cumulative political change has not been significant, nor does it negate Emília Viotti da Costa's conclusion that "in modern societies, even more than in the past, politics is at the center of human life."[4] It does dictate a need to analyze each major regime change of Brazil's past experience, not only for its own sake, but also to see the present in perspective and to discern the future crouching within the present. This task is made even more urgent by the fact that the transition in the end of the 1980s contained some striking similarities to each of the antecedent ruptures.

Given the lasting impact the colonial order has had upon Brazilian society and economy, which is even more dramatic than that in the political sphere, it is necessary to trace these patterns from their beginnings instead of just starting with Brazil's independence. This will be done very selectively and with a rather broad brush for the period up to the eve of independence. Then, because the continuance of the monarchy provided Brazil with a unique nineteenth-century developmental experience, bypassing the *caudillo* era in the Spanish American countries, treatment will become more detailed on those few trends and events that most strongly influenced the character of republican Brazil. Particular attention will be devoted both to those events that have current parallels and to those features that have proven especially persistent, for in the view of a well-known Brazilian historian writing in the early 1960s, "Traveling through Brazil today we are often surprised by aspects that we thought existed only in history books, and if we ponder them as a whole, we see that they are manifestations of things deeply rooted in the past and not simple anachronistic survivals."[5]

Discovery and Settlement

The discovery of Brazil actually came quite late in Portugal's impressive list of maritime explorations. These explorations had gotten underway following the expulsion of the Moors and the coming to power of the Aviz dynasty in 1385. During the fifteenth century Portuguese sailors made dramatic strides in discovering routes to South Asia. By the death of Prince Henry the Navigator in 1460, these intrepid seafarers had ventured well down the Atlantic coast of Africa and incorporated the Cape Verde Islands into the rapidly expanding Portuguese Empire. In 1488 Bartolomeu Dias turned the Cape of Good Hope and entered the Indian Ocean, and merely ten years later Vasco da Gama reached India by this eastward route. Yet, in vivid contrast with later times, Portugal during this period was at or very near the center of the "world system," leading Europe out of the economic crisis that had prevailed since the beginning of the fourteenth century. Possessing a relatively strong state machinery and "undistracted by internal conflict," Portugal took advantage of its favorable geographic location to become a leader in colonizing the globe.[6]

The First Colonies

With Columbus having accidentally "discovered" North America in 1492, it was only natural that the Portuguese, involved in a spirited competition with Spain that was much like the space race of the 1950s–1980s between the United States and the USSR, would seek to do what the great Genoan had set out to accomplish. Hence in March 1500 Pedro Álvares Cabral set out with a rather large fleet of thirteen vessels in an endeavor to reach Asia. On April 22, either having been blown westward on the equatorial current or wanting to test reports of a western landmass, the Portuguese flotilla sighted land, subsequently claiming it for Portugal's monarch and leaving a handful of lawbreakers behind before sailing on to India on May 2. The original name given to the new land by Cabral was Vera Cruz (quickly changed to Santa Cruz), but it would soon be known throughout Europe as Brazil from the red dyewood of that name, which merchants avidly sought along its extensive coast.

Establishment and consolidation of its New World colonies would prove a formidable task for little Portugal, whose limited human resources were already stretched almost to the breaking point across a variety of African and Asian colonies of greater immediate value and strategic concern. Indeed, Portugal's population at this point was under 1 million, a constraint that would all but determine a pattern of scattered and lightly held settlements in the vast South American territories. Columbus's initial voyage had led to the Treaty of Tordesillas in 1494, by which Portugal recognized Spain's right to all discoveries beyond a line 370 leagues west of the Cape Verde Islands in return for Spain's acknowledgment of Portugal's claims to everything found east of that meridian. But this cozy division of the New World hardly went unchallenged by Great Britain or France, and the Netherlands would subsequently contest the Luso-Iberian monopoly of South America. (It is generally accepted that several Spanish ships may have made a landfall along the coast of what is now Brazil in the late 1490s, but they made no territorial claims, knowing that this area lay within the agreed-upon-Portuguese sphere of influence.)

The initial decades of the sixteenth century saw exploration and colonization go forward at a very deliberate pace. Although trade in dyewood and Indian slaves was lively and many small posts called factories were established up and down the coast between Pernambuco and São Paulo, the first expedition with the aim of permanent settlement was that of Martim Afonso de Souza, which left Lisbon in 1531. São Vicente, near present-day Santos, was founded the next year as the first European town in Brazil. During the ensuing years a system of fifteen captaincies (*capitanias*) was installed, each running inland from the coast to the ill-defined and non-demarcated Tordesillas line. Lacking capital for the extensive colonization necessary to secure the vast New World territories from other expansion-minded empires, the Portuguese crown hoped to achieve this colonization through a semifeudal "donatary" system. This system established large territorial grants to settlers who were to act more as trustees for the country than as private landholders.[7] Yet with the subsidiary granting of *seismarias*, often consisting of from forty to more than one hundred square miles, to enterprising colonists, the foundations were established for a land tenure system based upon large private holdings that has persisted down to the present.

This effort to colonize Brazil essentially through private enterprise with state incentives did not work, as most of the original grantees either went broke or were unable to muster sufficient resources to establish viable permanent settlements, much less provide for the effective defense of such settlements. Because the French had actively cultivated the Tupinambás Indians and used them to attack the Portuguese traders and their generally Tupiniquim allies, defense was a very important consideration to Lisbon. Thus, a combination of the scale of the undertaking and the aggressive interference of other European powers forced the crown to take a more direct role. To this end the crown bought back Bahia from the *donatário* and made it the seat of Governor General Tomé de Souza, who arrived there in 1549 with a full complement of administrative officials, as well as six Jesuit priests under the leadership of Manoel de Nóbrega.[8]

With administration of justice in the hands of an *ouvidor-geral* and finances overseen by a *provedor-mor*, the governor general tried to provide centralization of authority. He and his successors encountered difficulty in coordinating, much less governing the most distant colonies from Bahia. Sugar-rich Pernambuco, headed by original donee Duarte Coelho, sought successfully to maintain its autonomy—which in some respects lasted for another century.

In the middle of the sixteenth century Brazil was still very much a stepchild to the Portuguese, who were generally disappointed that it appeared to lack not only the spices, silks, and jewels found in the Far East but also the silver and gold discovered by the Spaniards in both Mexico and their South American domains (especially at Potosí in what is today Bolivia). Portuguese immigration to the rather precarious colonies in Brazil had been minimal, with the total population (excluding 2.5 -3.5 million unconquered Indians) not exceeding 15,000.[9] Moreover, the great distances between the chief centers—Pernambuco, Bahia, and São Vicente—contributed to a lack of any common identity.

Brazil Begins to Take Shape

With the institution of the governor general came also reinforcement of the Church's position, with a bishop in Bahia as early as 1552 (this post was elevated to that of archbishop in 1646), as well as the first rudimentary elements of a military establishment—precisely the two institutions that would be the first to take on a national scope and that, in the face of sharply defined and long-lasting regionalism, would play key political roles in Brazil's national life down to the present. For in the absence of any significant permanent army, all large landowners were obliged to maintain private military forces from among their retainers and dependents. These evolved over time into organized militia units under the control of the most powerful regional figures, who usually held the rank of colonel (originally *capitão-mor*). These colonels not only were responsible for maintaining law and order in the hinterlands, but, given the lack of regular officials in the rural areas, often also performed other governmental tasks. This was the beginning of the phenomenon of *coronelismo*, a system of rural political bosses and their machine politics that wasn't just a landmark of the monarchy and pre-1930 republic, but also persists in remote interior areas even today.

Consolidation of the Portuguese presence in Brazil progressed slowly in the second half of the seventeenth century. Following the initial steps taken by Tomé de Souza, the second governor general (Duarte da Costa, 1553–1557) accomplished little before being replaced by the experienced and able Mem de Sá, who governed until 1572 and repelled the first serious threat to Portugal's tenuous hold on the coastal areas. In late 1555 Admiral Nicolas Durand de Villegaignon had established "Antarctic France" in Guanabara Bay, and he was soon joined by Protestant groups seeking religious toleration not then available in the mother country. Shortly after taking over as governor general in Brazil, Mem de Sá descended from Bahia and in 1560 destroyed the French fortifications, but he was forced to mount a second offensive against remaining French forces in 1564. Realizing that this was far too attractive a harbor to leave unoccupied, Portugal established the town of São Sebastião de Rio de Janeiro shortly thereafter.

When it was perceived in 1575 that hostile Tamoios Indians up the coast from the new settlement posed a threat, a sizeable expedition crushed the Indian settlement (near present-day Cabo Frio), enslaving an estimated 4,000 after killing half that number along with two Frenchmen and an Englishman found among them. Despite laws intended to protect them, Indians had been enslaved in Brazil from the beginning, but with the increase in European settlement after the hereditary captaincies were created in the mid-1530s, enslavement stepped up sharply. The laws contained exceptions for hostile tribes and those captured in "just wars," and the colonists quickly took advantage of these loopholes to make Indian slaves the backbone of the labor force. In fact, Indian slaves quickly came to constitute the bulk of the workforce, as the total Indian population of Brazil at the time of "discovery" was probably at least 2.5 million. Moreover, as European women were very few in number, Indian females were widely used by the Portuguese as sexual partners, a practice that soon gave rise to a sizeable number of *mamelucos* or *caboclos:* mixed-bloods with European fathers and native mothers.[10]

Yet Indians were considered far from ideal as field hands and could quite easily escape into the vast interior. Hence what was needed was a new source of labor not easily able to survive without the protection and security of the *engenhos* and *fazendas* (plantations and large ranches). This led to the importation of African slaves, which was already fairly common in Portugal, first via Lisbon, then—after 1538—directly from Africa. Perhaps as many as 50,000 of these involuntary immigrants were brought in by 1600 and another 100,000 during the first quarter of the seventeenth century. African slaves totaled 250,000 by 1650 and exceeded 600,000 by the end of the century.[11] Thus the three major components of future Brazilian society were already present and mixing through widespread miscegenation early in the colonial period.

From Colonies to Colony

By the beginning of the seventeenth century sugar was firmly established as Brazil's chief export and was so profitable that it attracted heavy attention from the British and Dutch as well as renewed interest on the part of the French. Each of these empires perceived opportunities to seize control of inviting portions of the Portuguese domains. Owing to the demise of the Portuguese royal family and the consequent unification of the thrones of Spain and Portugal, Brazil was in the middle of a prolonged period of Hapsburg rule that lasted from 1580 to 1640.[12] As the first part of this period coincided with the peak of Spanish-English rivalry, the defeat of the Spanish Armada off England's coast occurring in 1588, the period of Hapsburg rule had marked reflections in Brazil.

Repeated English raids in Brazil culminated in the 1595 attack upon Recife by James Lancaster, while at the same time Portugal, reinforced by Spain's greater military might, moved to expel the French from Maranhão, where the latter had established a fort named after their king. The French were removed by late 1615, but in light of a subsequent Spanish-French rapprochement the name São Luís was soon restored. The victorious Portuguese went on in early 1616 to found Santa Maria de Belém at the mouth of the Amazon, thus effectively confining the French to the small enclave that is still today French Guiana. In 1620 Belém became the seat of a Maranhão and Grão Pará colony that reached down to the edge of Pernambuco and was administered separately from Salvador-based Brazil.

The Dutch Interlude and Penetration of the Interior

The Portuguese were not long to enjoy their victory with respect to this final French threat. In 1624 the Dutch captured Bahia, though they were pushed out the following year by a powerful Portuguese-Spanish expedition. In 1630, however, the Dutch successfully seized all of Pernambuco, and in 1641, by which time the Portuguese no longer enjoyed union with Spain, the Dutch extended their sway southward through Sergipe and northward to Maranhão, thus holding what was then the richest part of Portugal's New World empire. Under Count Johan Maurits de Nassau-Siegen a great deal of material progress was made, especially in the area around Recife. Following this soldier-statesman's return to the Netherlands in 1644, the Portuguese counteroffensive picked up momentum, culminating in a pair of victories at Guarapes in April 1648 and the following February.[13] Finally, in January 1654 the beleaguered Dutch surrendered Recife, then a city of around 8,000 inhabitants, ending the last serious foreign threat to the territorial integrity of Brazil.

By this time the duke of Bragança had effectively claimed the Portuguese throne (in 1640), and the colonial authorities in the growing city of São Salvador da Bahia dos Todos os Santos adhered at once to independent Portugal, while those in Rio de Janeiro hesitated before following suit. Partially in recognition of the colonies' increasing importance, Brazil was elevated to the status of a principality in 1646. Meanwhile the Portuguese had begun to move inland beyond the intimidating escarpment. Francisco de Souza, seventh governor general, had used his long tenure (1591–1602) to encourage exploration of the interior and the search for mineral wealth. Based increasingly from the city of São Paulo, which had been founded by the Jesuits in 1554 on the plateau inland from São Vicente, expeditions called *bandeiras* carried the flag into the interior, bringing back large numbers of Indian slaves.[14]

After 1628 these expeditions had concentrated upon the relatively easy pickings of the Jesuit *reducciones*, cooperatives where substantial numbers of Indians had been brought together and converted into farmers. Subsequently the *bandeirantes* (participants in the *bandeiras*) turned much of their attention to the quest for mineral riches, spurred on to endure great hardships by the limited finds of alluvial gold and silver that had cropped up in São Paulo. These expeditions led in the late 1690s to major discoveries of gold in the region directly north of São Paulo and northwest of Rio de Janeiro, an area that was soon known as "General Mines" (Minas Gerais). Conflict between Paulistas, who thought this wealth should be theirs alone, and the wide variety of "tenderfoots" who quickly flowed into this heretofore frontier grazing area erupted into the War of the Emboabas (1707–1709).[15] As a result, in 1711 a captaincy of São Paulo and Minas was created separate from the jurisdiction of Rio de Janeiro, with Minas Gerais becoming emancipated in 1720.

These troubled times also saw the city of Rio de Janeiro, with its 12,000 inhabitants, fend off a French attack in 1710 but be captured by the 5,800-man expedition of René Dugay-Trauin the following year. Aware of the impracticality of remaining in Rio, the French levied a heavy ransom upon the city's residents and departed. Up in Pernambuco at the same time, Brazilian-born elements carried on a violent conflict with Portuguese merchants in the so-called War of the Mascates (the derisive term *mascates*, meaning "peddler," applied by the former to the latter), which was in great part actually a struggle between debtors and creditors.[16]

Only a short time earlier, in 1694, had the Pernambuco planters managed to destroy the large community of escaped slaves who had for several decades reconstituted an African kingdom at Palmares. The move was based upon the planters' conviction that the African community's continued survival would encourage insubordination among the rapidly growing and increasingly valuable slave population.[17] Runaway slaves had formed a number of communities called *quilombos* during the period of Dutch inroads, and their survival would encourage further flights, so the planter elites insisted upon their destruction. Yet some persisted into the nineteenth century. In addition, the emancipation of the Indians in 1755 made African slaves even more vital to the colonial economy.

The Last Colonial Century

The eighteenth century proved crucial for the basic definition of Brazil's borders with the surrounding Spanish domains. A Portuguese settlement had been established in 1680 at Colônia de Sacramento across the La Plata estuary from Buenos Aires, and towns were founded in Goiás (1724) and at Cuiabá in Mato Grosso (1716). Though the settlement in Goiás was lost to the Spanish in battle, it was regained through the Treaty of Madrid in 1750, which was based essentially on the principle of occupation (*uti possidetis*). The Treaty of Madrid was nullified by the Treaty of El Prado in 1761, which was in turn superseded in 1777 by the Treaty of San Ildefonso. Although the Treaty of San Ildefonso awarded Colônia and the old Jesuit *missiones* to Spain, it confirmed the limits of Portuguese expansion all the way up through the Amazon region. (In addition to Spain getting the territory on the west and north side of the Uruguay River, the population on the other side of the river was to move to the Spanish territory. Their refusal to do so resulted in the so-called Guaraní War.) So that it would be nearer the riches of the mining area and the conflicts with the Spanish in the south, Brazil's capital was moved from Salvador to Rio de Janeiro in 1763.[18] The former was by that time a city of some 50,000—a figure the new capital would reach by 1800.

From the middle of the seventeenth century on, Brazil faced increased competition from the British, French, and Dutch, all of whom began to efficiently produce vast quantities of sugar on their Caribbean possessions. With sugar revenues cut drastically, Brazil's economic salvation lay in its becoming the world's leading source of gold and, after 1729, of diamonds as well. Yet Brazil was cast into what has been described as a "double dependency" by Portugal's acceptance of a marginal position in the British-dominated mercantilist system through the 1703 Treaty of Methuen.[19]

In this treaty Portugal bound itself and its colonies to purchase British manufactures in return for England buying Portuguese wines and agricultural products. As might be expected, Portugal ran chronic trade deficits, which were covered by transfer of gold from Brazil through Lisbon to London. But with gold production dropping sharply after 1760 and sugar in the doldrums, the Brazilian economy stagnated (except for some limited and intermittent gains with respect to cotton and tobacco).

The Arrival of the Portuguese Court

During the period from the Treaty of Madrid to the Treaty of San Ildefonso (1750–1777), Portugal was ruled in the name of the weak King José I by Sebastião José de Carvalho e Mello, the marquês de Pombal. Besides expelling the Jesuits from Brazil in 1759, this towering figure of Portuguese politics re-merged Maranhão–Grão Pará with Brazil, placing the overall capital in Rio de Janeiro, and generally attempted to set Portugal's administrative and economic houses in order.[20] The Brazil of this period had changed substantially since the beginning of the eighteenth century, chiefly as a result of having been supplier of some four-fifths of the world's gold. Not only had many thousands of colonists abandoned their agricultural pursuits and rushed to Minas Gerais in quest of wealth for themselves or their masters, but this El Dorado also served as a magnet for immigration from Portugal as well as drawing adventurers from other European countries. Vila Rica de Ouro Preto became the boomtown not only of Brazil, but also of all South America, achieving a mid-century population of some 30,000.

Although mulattoes had already become a significant social element on the coast, African-European miscegenation in Minas Gerais during the first half of the 1700s turned mulattoes into an element more numerous than the Indian-European *mamelucos*. Moreover, the 33,000 African slaves in Minas Gerais in 1717 trebled to almost 100,000 by the mid-1730s, and in 1786 slaves constituted at least 175,000 to 200,000 of the province's 363,000 inhabitants.[21] Yet on the negative side, gold production had fallen sharply by the mid-1770s, helping put the country into a long recession.

Precursors of Independence

Events that would have a powerful effect upon the course of Brazilian affairs were happening elsewhere in the world during the latter part of the eighteenth century. First came the establishment of an independent and republican United States, with the French Revolution following soon after in 1789. Some Brazilians, already chafing over restraints on trade other than that with Portugal, were further alienated by a 1785 decree prohibiting all manufacturing in Brazil. Subversive talk was rife in all the major urban centers, and in 1789 a highly unsuccessful conspiracy, known as the Inconfidência Mineira and celebrated even today as the harbinger of independence, was broken up. Its leader, Joaquim José da Silva Xavier, better known as "Tiradentes" (Toothpuller), was executed three years later as a warning to other discontents.[22]

By this time hundreds of Brazilians had received degrees from Coimbra University in Portugal and returned home. Most of them viewed Portugal as too limited a country both intellectually and economically, preferring French Enlightenment philosophy combined with some interest in Adam Smith and nascent British liberalism. These disenchanted intellectuals catalyzed a nativist movement in the colony; these influences blended with a growing pride in Brazil, an increased awareness of the U.S. and French republican experiences, and economic dissatisfaction. Hence the Inconfidência Mineira was followed by chain-reaction conspiracies in Rio de Janeiro (1794), Bahia (1798), and Pernambuco (1801). Although all were quickly repressed, they reflected a potentially dangerous degree of alienation, which would be augmented in the years just ahead by the Spanish American wars of independence.[23]

First, however, Napoleon's invasion of Portugal would give rise to important changes for Brazil, ones that would quite directly lead to Brazilian independence. For in November 1807, the royal family, accompanied by much of the civil and military bureaucracies, set sail for Rio de Janeiro under British naval escort. During a brief stopover at Salvador, the prince regent (the future King João VI) opened Brazil's ports to trade with Britain and other countries—more a quid pro quo for British support than a sop to the colonists. Manufacturing was soon permitted, faculties (postsecondary schools) were opened, and naval and military academies were established. More important in the long run was the creation of a new army composed of a mixture of Portuguese troops already stationed in Brazil and local recruits. Finally in 1815 Brazil was elevated to the status of a kingdom, theoretically coequal with Portugal.[24] All these measures served to defuse further a situation in which revolutionary leanings had already been weakened, both by efforts at co-opting Brazilian elites and by the latter's fright over the violence of the French Revolution and the ensuing slave rebellion that virtually eliminated Europeans from Haiti. But the presence of the thousands of Portuguese who accompanied the monarch in this quasi-exile also brought friction with the residents of Rio de Janeiro, some of whom had their homes summarily requisitioned and others who faced more direct economic competition from the displaced but better connected Portuguese elite.

By the end of the Napoleonic Wars, Brazil had a population exceeding 4 million, and Rio de Janeiro had blossomed to a city of over 110,000—a New World giant and large even by European standards of the time. Essentially the colony was fast outgrowing its mother country.[25] The Portuguese Liberals convoked a legislature in which they enjoyed a safe majority of 130 seats to 50 for representatives of Brazil (Brazil was allotted 75 seats, but one-third of those selected to fill those seats never reached Lisbon). Not surprisingly, when this body took measures to reestablish most of Portugal's previous domination, separatist sentiment rose in Brazil. Already there had been a major rebellion in Pernambuco in 1817—in reaction to centralization of power in Rio de Janeiro—that led Portugal to transfer seven regiments to the New World to reinforce 5,000 troops sent in 1815. Landowners who had opposed only those colonial institutions that restricted Brazilian landlords and merchants increasingly leaned toward independence. Thus when the king was required to return to Lisbon in April 1821, he advised his twenty-two-year-old son, Pedro, staying behind as prince regent, to place himself at the head of the movement for independence should it appear to be getting out of control—in this way the Bragança monarchy would be preserved in Brazil.

Independence and the First Emperor, 1822–1831

Young Pedro soon had cause to heed his father's advice. In the midst of clashes between Brazilian-born elements and Portuguese troops, he responded positively to the request of the Rio de Janeiro Municipal Council that he reject an order of the Portuguese Côrtes to return to Lisbon. This famous *fico* (which means "I'm staying") of January 9, 1822, was followed by appointment of a Cabinet in which native Brazilian José Bonifácio de Andrada e Silva was the leading figure. The "Patriarch of Independence" would remain Pedro's chief advisor until mid-1823, by which time independence was an accomplished and irreversible fact.[26] Together they planned for election of a national convention, with the vote indirect and limited, of course, to propertied males. (This was still the rule almost everywhere, including democratic Britain.) Further efforts by Lisbon to tighten Portugal's hold over Brazil resulted in Pedro's dramatic cry, "Independence or death!" on September 7, 1822—the date commemorated as Brazil's Independence Day. Within ninety days of this declaration Pedro was formally crowned (on his twenty-fourth birthday) as the "Constitutional Emperor and Perpetual Defender of Brazil."

Most important, the commencement of national life under the rule of the same individual who had been governing in the name of the mother country allowed Brazil to avoid the vacuum of legitimate authority that plagued most of its neighbors, whose path to independence typically combined rupture with Spain and adoption of a radically different and untried political regime—a republic. Moreover, compared with the protracted wars and large-scale civil strife through which its neighbors had won their independence, Brazil's emancipation was relatively quick, albeit not peaceful. Brazil's emergence was marked by repeated skirmishes and prolonged confrontations with provincial authorities and Portuguese troops loyal to João VI and the Lisbon government; as a result, the newly independent country was obliged to employ European mercenaries as a counterweight to the peninsular units.[27]

Consolidating Brazil

The emperor himself had initially convinced the nearly 5,000-man Auxiliary Division, dug in across the bay from the capital, to depart peacefully in February 1822 (shortly before reinforcements from the mother country arrived). After the reinforcements arrived, General Pedro Labatut (French) and Admiral Lord Thomas Cochrane (British), veterans of the Spanish American struggles for independence, led an expedition to expel Portuguese troops from Bahia and the northern provinces. The clashes were particularly sharp near the old colonial capital of Salvador, where pro-independence forces had been carrying on a quasi-guerrilla struggle since February 1822. For the final stages of the assault against 13,000 entrenched Portuguese troops in June 1823, Brigadier General Francisco de Lima e Silva replaced Labatut in command. It was in this campaign that the general's son, Luís— the future duke of Caxias—experienced his first real taste of battle, which launched a career that was to make him the dominant military figure in Brazil's life as a nation.[28] Admiral Cochrane's armada continued up the coast to Maranhão, where in July 1823 it put an end to armed resistance by Portuguese loyalists. These expeditions involved 12,000 and 18,000 men respectively, each more than the armies of either Simon Bolívar or José de San Martín in the Spanish American independence campaigns.[29] While these conflicts continued in the north, efforts to establish a viable governmental structure were underway in the capital. Elections had hurriedly been held, and Brazil's first constituent assembly began to function on May 3, 1823. But on November 11, after six months of executive-legislative conflict—parallel to the situation that would later occur at the beginning of the republic and nearly be repeated in 1988—Pedro used the army, which was itself displeased with the assembly's proceedings, to close down the legislature.[30] Following this *golpe de estado* (a particular type of coup from above), the promised constitution was drawn up by a hand-picked commission of experts at the monarch's request, submitted for approval indirectly (in this case, it was submitted to the municipal councils), and promulgated by imperial decree on March 25, 1824.

The new document was highly centralized and strongly favored the executive in its allocation of powers; elements of it would later be incorporated in modernized form in the 1967 constitution. Under the 1824 constitution the emperor could both convene and dissolve the General Assembly as well as appoint the presidents of the provinces. Senate members were chosen by the emperor from lists submitted by the provinces and served for life, and the lower house was indirectly elected by a severely limited suffrage. As the country's population was only around 4.5 million, including almost a million slaves and at least 800,000 Indians, this system was quite appropriate, if not particularly advanced, for the times.

Reaction to the closing of the assembly and the establishment of a centralized regime was widespread and violent. Liberal rebels in Pernambuco in July 1824 invited five other provinces of the north to join in a federative republic to be called the Confederation of the Equator. A joint operation by the navy, still under Lord Cochrane, and troops commanded by General Francisco de Lima e Silva repressed this separatist movement, whose leaders were executed as a warning to other dissidents. In Pará, revolts had already occurred in March–April and August 1823, January 1824, and again in December of that year. Maranhão had been in a constant state of unrest since independence; Admiral Cochrane returned there in the latter part of 1824 and established order with a fairly heavy hand.[31] Yet what was of lasting importance was that in the end Brazil's territorial integrity was preserved.

While the problem of recognition of Brazil's independence by Portugal dragged on and Pedro subsequently became involved in Portugal's succession question (following João VI's death in 1826), discontent with the "foreign tyrant" gained headway. The tensions between native-born Brazilian and Portuguese elements combined with the republican-tinged regionalist uprisings were problems enough for the new nation, but the emperor compounded his difficulties by engaging in an expensive and unsuccessful military venture that led to war with the United Provinces of the Rio de La Plata (modern Argentina).

As already indicated, throughout the eighteenth century Spain and Portugal contested for the "Banda Oriental," the territory on the upper side of the Rio de la Plata estuary (modern Uruguay). In 1816 João VI took advantage of the Spanish American independence struggles to occupy this disputed territory, and in 1821 he annexed it to the Brazilian portion of his dual kingdom as the Cisplatine Province. In 1825 the smoldering controversy over the area broke into open fighting, and Pedro was forced to hire large numbers of Irish and German mercenaries to bring his army up to combat strength.[32] The cost of the war pushed the military's share of the budget to over 50 percent and drained away manpower from São Paulo, setting back development of that future key province. By October 1828 Brazil and Argentina had fought to a dubious draw, with the result being the establishment of Uruguay as a neutral buffer state. As much of this territory had been governed by Brazil before the conflict, public opinion generally viewed the war as a fiasco, if not a disaster.

Pedro's Departure

By the end of the decade the stiff-necked, impulsive, and short-tempered emperor found himself in an untenable position. A mutiny by German and Irish mercenaries in June 1828 led Pedro to agree to the dissolution of all foreign units in the army, which deprived him of the very troops that had been assigned to defend the imperial palace. The army leadership was leaning toward the Liberals and the ouster of French King Charles X by the July Revolution of 1830 had had a sharp impact upon elite opinion; consequently, the legislative-executive conflict of 1823 was replayed with the military this time leaning in the opposite direction.[33] The emperor, who had dissolved the parliament in 1829, found the new body no less an infringement upon his neo-absolutist inclinations and his preoccupation with events in Portugal. Under extreme pressure Pedro appointed a Cabinet of Brazilian-born moderate politicians in March 1831. But on April 5 he shifted abruptly, without so much as consulting the legislators, to a Cabinet composed of personal cronies—mostly nobles and senators. This move was viewed as highly suspect by Liberals and nationalists, who were determined to reduce residual Portuguese influence and perceived Pedro's move as a possible prelude to a pro-monarchy coup.

The urban populace, including a significant number of troops, took to the streets, demanding a reversal of this imperial decision, which, however unwise it was politically, was within Pedro's constitutional prerogatives. Brigadier General Francisco de Lima e Silva personally intervened with the emperor as spokesman for the military institution. The proud monarch's response was to abdicate before dawn on April 7 in favor of his five-year-old, Brazilian-born son, expressing his absolutist position in crystal-clear terms.[34] Although it was a victory for the Brazilians over the Portuguese elements at the national level, the abdication left scars and generated divisions throughout the different regions of the country that would not be healed for many years.

The Regency: A Republic in Monarchy's Clothing

In the tripartite regency that emerged, General Lima e Silva functioned as the president and swing man between civilian politicians of differing temperaments and orientations. This role was accepted by the parliament, who pragmatically realized that the regency would require support from the military to withstand efforts to restore Pedro. (The general's brother, José Joaquim, moved up to head the army.) Nonetheless, with the hand of the legislators greatly reinforced vis-à-vis the executive by the recent course of events, Lima e Silva was not in a position to block the establishment of a national guard as a counterweight to the army, which was still suspected of harboring sympathy for the former emperor (who was soon to be king of Portugal). Indeed, at the same time the size of the army was substantially reduced, and its presence in the capital area was all but eliminated.[35] Diogo Antônio Feijó, who as minister of justice would supervise the newly created guard, thus saw his position vastly strengthened, while the army lost control over what had been its reserves. These changes were expected to provide the regime with reasonable security against both the ambitions of military commanders and the insubordination of troops, but the guard soon became a major political factor in its own right. The guard remained under the justice minister's supervision until shortly before its abolition at the time of World War I.

Travail and Instability

The regency period was marked by separatist and republican revolts as well as by frequent troop mutinies and a few uprisings with greater social content. Following an abortive mutiny in the capital, in September 1831 trouble flared up once again in Pernambuco (the so-called Setembrisada) and Maranhão (the Setembrada). In April 1832 there was a mixed resto-rationist-republican uprising in Rio de Janeiro, followed in July by an ill-fated attempt on the part of the Liberals, with the complicity of Feijó himself, to turn the legislature into a national constituent assembly, thus overturning the 1824 constitution. Many other states also experienced unrest, much as in the aftermath of Pedro I's 1823 *golpe*. Pernambuco witnessed yet another uprising, the Abrilada, in April 1832; Colonel Pinto Madeira led a revolt in Ceará in 1831; and Piauí underwent a similar insurgency the following year. In Bahia anti-Portuguese disturbances in 1831 were followed by federalist insurrections in 1832 and 1833. Minas Gerais was the scene of military seditions in March 1833, while the following year Mato Grosso experienced strife in the form of the Rusga, which claimed 100 to 200 lives.[36]

The Additional Act of August 1834 modified the governmental system in the direction of limited but significant decentralization, including giving real powers to the provincial legislative assemblies. The following April, Feijó, the Liberal spokesman, was elected single regent by a slim margin of 2,826 to 2,251, assuming office in October from a most reluctant Lima e Silva. When Pedro's untimely death back in Portugal removed the Liberals' fear of any restoration coup, their unity disappeared. Instead of bringing increased stability to the situation, this election of a single regent and establishment of a Liberal government ushered in a new wave of threats to the territorial integrity of the Brazilian Empire, threats that arose in part from dissatisfaction with the continuing economic downturn.

The so-called Cabanagem erupted in the northernmost provinces at the beginning of 1835 as an outgrowth of popular discontent over the fact that independence had not brought with it any significant redistribution of political and economic power. Turning into protracted banditry-insurgency in the vast interior spaces of the Amazon (with repeated threats to the cities of Belém and Manaus), this movement lasted until 1840 and claimed perhaps 30,000 to 40,000 lives. Bahia was the scene of the bloody Revolt of the Malês in 1835, an uprising of Moslem slaves and freedmen, and in November 1837 the Sabinada broke out in Bahia, leaving nearly 1,100 rebels dead before it was repressed the following March.[37] Autonomists more than separatists, the followers of Dr. Francisco Sabino Alves da Rocha Vieira proclaimed their republic only for the duration of Pedro's minority (the period before he would "come of age" to be emperor), which was due under the Additional Act to end late in 1843.

A major new revolt also exploded in Maranhão. In December 1838 old personal feuds and a general sense of malaise led to a popular uprising directed chiefly against the Portuguese elite who still dominated the provincial society. Pacification of the Balaiada was making little progress until February 1840, when Colonel Luís Alves de Lima e Silva was sent to Maranhão with full powers as provincial president and military commander of an 8,000-man force. With the revolt partially undercut by the sudden end of the regency—which came with the resignation of Regent Pedro de Araújo Lima, who in 1837 had succeeded Feijó—the future duke of Caxias reestablished order in 1841 following the surrender of some 2,000–3,000 rebels.[38]

Finding a Way Out

In the midst of these regional disorders, important developments had taken place in the capital's political arena. Faced with a resurgence of Conservative strength, Feijó resigned as regent in September 1837. Pedro de Araújo Lima—the future marquês de Olinda—won the narrowly based direct election in April of the following year, receiving 4,308 of the 9,492 votes cast nationwide (strict property/income requirements for voting eligibility were still in effect). Back in power these regressive, although not totally reactionary, elements curbed provincial autonomy through the Interpretive Law of 1839. Stung deeply, the Liberals engineered a parliamentary *golpe*, bringing Pedro II to the throne in July 1840—at the ripe age of fourteen.[39]

Pedro II: The First Decade

Though the country had managed to hold together under the regency, it would be consolidated during the early years of Pedro II's long reign.

Luís de Lima e Silva's role in maintaining internal security for the empire had only begun with the success in Maranhão, which earned him promotion to brigadier general and the first of his progressively more elevated titles of nobility. In May 1842 a revolt was launched in São Paulo with the backing of former regent Feijó. The Liberal leader had become increasingly discontented with the dominance of national affairs by Conservatives from the northeast with whom Pedro replaced the Liberal ministry in 1841. The Sorocabana Revolution—to a certain extent a forerunner of the 1924, 1926, and 1932 Paulista revolts—was directed against the strengthening of centralized monarchical authority under Pedro II. By now a baron, Caxias (Lima e Silva) crushed this threat in late June. He then turned to the revolt that had broken out belatedly in Minas Gerais, quashing it in short order.

The most serious threat to the consolidation of Pedro II's empire—and a harbinger of developments to come during the republican era—was the War of the Farrapos, or Farroupilha Revolution. The conflict had ignited in Rio Grande do Sul in mid-1835 and was still going strong when Pedro came to power. Rebelling Liberals, derisively called Ragamuffins, upset over the Conservatives' partisan exploitation of the provincial administration and the economic policies of the monarchy, had seized Porto Alegre in September 1835 and a year later announced the formation of a Riograndense Republic. After successfully invading neighboring Santa Catarina, they proclaimed a more ambitious Piratine Republic.

Because this was the one case in which many large landowners did not back the central government, the insurrection had greater staying power than most others. (One of the leaders at this stage was the Italian Giuseppe Garibaldi, who married a Brazilian, gained military experience that he would soon put to good use back home in another insurrection, and took back with him the combination of red, green, and white that became the Italian tricolor flag.) Once the other regional revolts had been put down, however, Caxias was appointed to preside over Rio Grande do Sul and serve as its military commander. The task of pacifying the Gaúchos, who numbered among their ranks many veterans of the Cisplatine War, proved a greater challenge to Brazil's dominant military figure than had the insurrections in either Maranhão or São Paulo–Minas Gerais, and the job was not completed until March 1845.[40]

A final regional revolt occurred in Recife. Throughout a five-year period of Liberal Cabinets (1844–1848), localized uprisings there had been directed against the entrenched Conservative oligarchy of the Rêgo Barros and Cavalcanti families. In 1848, Europe's year of revolutions and the return of Conservatives to power in Brazil, the Praieira revolt broke out in Pernambuco, where a new generation gloried in family tales of the 1817 and 1824 uprisings. Autonomist, federalist, and, implicitly at least, republican, this movement was suppressed by 1850—ushering in a period of nearly four decades of internal peace and order.[41] Thus by mid-century the causes of some thirty years of instability were sharply curbed, if not ended. The chief factor—centralism versus decentralization—was resolved in favor of the former by military force, and a Brazilian national state was built "from the top down with little or no popular mobilization."[42]

Stability Achieved

Despite the disorder discussed above, important consolidation had taken place, especially with respect to the political elite, military institutions, and structuring of the manipulated parliamentary system under the monarch's scepter. These elements would be the main pillars of the stability Brazil enjoyed for almost forty years and would provide the underpinnings of the empire at its apogee during the 1850s and 1860s. Hence their peculiar nature must be understood before the true character of the longest "civic" interlude in Brazil's often Praetorian life as a nation can be appreciated.[43]

During the colonial period there had been little differentiation between the civil administration and the military. During the course of the eighteenth century, although a few Portuguese regiments remained in Bahia, Rio de Janeiro, and Recife, militia units and a system of reserve units (theoretically comprising all free males between the ages of eighteen and sixty) replaced the informal paramilitary forces of the landowners. Commissions in these forces served to reinforce the political and social dominance of the colonial elite in the interior, much as national guard commissions would later underlie the *coronelismo* form of oligarchical rule in rural areas under the empire and during the first decades of the Old Republic.[44] Then, during the years the Portuguese royal court resided in Rio de Janeiro (1808–1821), the Portuguese became predominant within the centralized bureaucratic stratum, at least in the capital and the major regional centers.[45] Still, outside the key cities the Brazilian-born members of the municipal councils (*senados da câmara*) and the largest landowner of the area, in his capacity as *capitão-mor* (militia colonel), were generally the dominant figures.

Elevation of Brazil to the status of a coequal kingdom in 1815 accentuated the resentment of ambitious and economically successful Brazilian elements, who quite naturally perceived undue favoritism to those Portuguese who had accompanied the king in his transatlantic exile. At the same time the creation of the Brazilian kingdom drew members of the upper classes away from their income-earning agricultural holdings into the expensive, if not extravagant, royal court. This competition between two elite factions, the predominantly Brazilian landowners and the courtier bureaucrats, persisted even after João VI and many of the latter departed with the coming of independence. The balance shifted further in favor of the Brazilians with the abdication of Pedro I, and during the regency and early years of the reign of Pedro II, the Brazilian elite came to occupy an increasing proportion of key positions in the central government. Military men were, however, frequently appointed as provincial presidents, particularly in the peripheral areas—in large part owing to the salience there of the problem of internal order.

With domestic stability achieved by 1850, accompanied by the proliferation and expansion of law schools during that decade, many sons of the provincial elite turned to governmental careers as a springboard to more rapid advancement than was now possible in an increasingly professionalized army. This emergence of the *bacharel* (law school graduate) as an intermediary between the local *coroneis* and the growing imperial bureaucracy further reduced the military's role in the political processes. In addition, that role was even more deeply undercut by changes that took place concurrently in the national guard.

Originally established because of Liberal distrust of an army still largely staffed with Portuguese officers, the guard grew quickly to 200,000 men by the mid-1830s, dwarfing the regular army and playing a major role in the repression of regional revolts. Replacing the *ordenanças* and militia units previously discussed, the national guard soon became the chief arm for maintaining law and order outside the major urban centers. In the process it served as a vehicle for the "militarization of civil society."[46] By 1850 all guard officers were appointed by the central government—though in many cases they had previously been elected—and in the absence of regular administrative and judicial authorities in many areas of the interior, guard officers also performed police functions. Moreover, during the 1840s the predominantly black and mulatto ranks in many areas had often elected mulatto officers; by 1850 this channel of social mobility was choked off. These trends would continue until the guard suffered heavy losses in the bloody 1865–1870 war with Paraguay—following which the guard lost its status as a police force to the expanded professional army and the gradual and incomplete penetration of interior towns by the administrative bureaucracy.

After mid-century the top ranks of the guard were "aristocratized" through the institution of life tenure for guard officers, who were most frequently appointed and promoted as a reward for political services, as well as through requiring commissioned officers to pay a fee for their commission.[47] Then, too, whereas through 1848 only two national guard officers had been granted titles of nobility, this number rose to nineteen between 1849 and 1870 and reached near avalanche proportions just prior to the end of the empire.

The Monarchy at Its Prime

By 1850, then, the elements were in place that would allow Brazil to enjoy over a third of a century of political stability and internal order, accompanied by modest economic development and limited, yet far from insignificant, social progress. Although in the 1830s and 1840s Brazil was not in much better shape than Argentina, Mexico, Colombia, or most of the other Spanish American nations, it would forge well ahead on many fronts during the 1850s and 1860s. Even during the 1830s and 1840s, Pedro II was certainly much preferable to dictators Juan Manuel de Rosas in Argentina and López de Santa Ana in Mexico, and Brazil held together while Bolívar's Grand Colombia split into pieces.[48] At its heyday in the third quarter of the nineteenth century, the Brazilian monarchy would compare very favorably with Mexico's disastrous war with the United States and subsequent French intervention and civil war or with Argentina's long struggle to reincorporate Buenos Aires so as to become a unified nation. Although by the 1870s critics were comparing perceived Brazilian stagnation with the developmental surge of Porfirio Díaz's Mexico or the progress of republican Argentina, Brazil's relative slippage vis-à-vis the other major Latin American countries would not be indisputable until the mid-1880s.

The Socioeconomic Context

Brazil's economy and society had undergone important, if not dramatic, changes since the end of the colonial era. Population had risen to around 7.5 million from just over 5.3 million in 1830, and Rio de Janeiro had grown to a city of some 250,000—110,000 of these were slaves and fewer than that number were white. The provinces of Minas Gerais, Bahia, and Rio de Janeiro had each reached 1 million population, with Pernambuco fast closing in on that mark and São Paulo nearing 500,000. In addition to the descendants of the more than 2.2 million African slaves brought in before 1800, another 1.7 million Africans had been imported by the beginning of the 1850s, when British pressure finally brought an end to the slave trade. By then the more than 2.5 million living slaves made up roughly one-third of the country's population. Although a law of mid-1831 had formally outlawed the slave trade, the law was only "for the English to see" (*para ingles ver*), and from an average of under 20,000 a year in the early 1840s, the flow of slaves actually increased until the very end, running at an average of over 50,000 a year during the late 1840s.

Moreover, between 1821 and 1850 the vast majority of slaves—84 percent— came to southern ports. This stood in marked contrast to the fact that only two-fifths of the 1.15 million slaves at the time of independence were in that part of the country. Nevertheless, even at the beginning of the 1820s, at least 70 percent of Brazil's population was free, and by 1872 this figure would exceed 85 percent (8.6 million free out of a total population of 10.1 million), leaving just over 1.5 million slaves.[49] Though the greatest stream of immigration was still ahead, European immigrants were already the key component of the population in Rio Grande do Sul and Santa Catarina.

Economic growth had averaged 1.6 percent annually between 1822 and 1849, but this included a period of higher growth until 1835, followed by a slowdown that would last through the early 1860s.[50] Industrialization remained in low gear. The treaty with Great Britain, which had been the price for British recognition of Brazilian independence, had limited import duties to 15 percent ad valorem, rendering impossible any real degree of tariff protection. When the treaty expired in 1840, import taxes were nearly doubled, remaining at about 26 or 27 percent during the 1850s and 1860s. Though duty-free importation of machinery was instituted in 1846, this amounted to a policy of protecting newly established industries but fell well short of a policy of industrialization, as aptly put by a Brazilian scholar.[51]

Although its great expansion was still ahead, coffee already provided half of the country's exports—twice that accounted for by sugar, which coffee had first surpassed during the 1830s. Centered in the Paraíba River Valley of northwestern São Paulo and southern Rio de Janeiro, the coffee industry would soon be moving to the interior of São Paulo; the consequent fundamental shift in the center of economic power was reflected first in the emergence of the coffee nobility as a social force, but eventually had profound political ramifications.[52]

In the 1820s coffee contributed less than one-fifth of Brazil's exports, but by the 1880s this figure would rise to over three-fifths. With coffee production steadily rising and cotton staging a modest recovery, the years from 1862 to 1878 were a sustained period of prosperity. Though in the 1830s Brazil supplied 30 percent of the world's coffee, this rose during the next decade to 40 percent and then to 50 percent from the 1850s through the 1870s. As a consequence, by mid-century per capita income levels in the southeast had passed those of the plantation-based northeast, and this trend would continue far into the future. The prime years of the empire also saw the beginnings of railroad construction, which was badly needed to tie coastal ports to interior agricultural production areas in the center-south, where rivers were not suitable for transportation.

Patrimonial Politics

During the monarchy's heyday, Brazil's stability was bolstered by a fairly homogenous political "class" oriented to national unity and stable civilian government. Clearly the large landowners and export producers enjoyed considerable political power. As well, the middle sector–related political/bureaucratic elements (*patronato*) that occupied the upper echelons of the highly centralized state administration had a significant degree of autonomy. Though the *patronato* likely were, as Raymundo Faoro points out, detached from society and indifferent to the suffering and misery of the masses—who were the object of precious little tender concern anywhere in the world in the middle of the past century—they were probably less so than their counterparts in almost any Spanish American nation.[53] Perhaps the most balanced assessment of this elite's role and contribution is the thoughtful conclusion of José Murilo de Carvalho:

> The capacity to process conflicts among dominant groups within constitutional norms accepted by all constitutes the fulcrum of stability of the imperial system. It signifies, on the one hand, a basic extent of conservatism to the degree that the price of legitimacy is the guarantee of the fundamental interests of the large landowners and the reduction of the scope of legitimate political participation in Brazil. On the other hand, it permitted a dynamic process of political coalitions capable of implementing reforms that would have been nonviable in a situation of full domination by the rural landowners.[54]

The elite's ability to co-opt emerging urban elements rested upon perfection of another institution rooted in the colonial era: the *cartorial*[55] state. In this system, public employment is used to provide positions in response to the clientelistic political needs of the elite, rather than bearing any relationship to the requirements of effective public service. The number, type, and regional location of these public positions depends on who is to be co-opted, not on the need for and delivery of services. Because public appointments are exchanged for electoral support, the result is a pyramid of positions through which dossiers are circulated, documents stamped, and the bureaucracy nourished through self-benefitting practices. Such an administratively dysfunctional means of providing for the emerging middle class involves a bargain in which the dominant elite may indirectly subsidize the middle sectors. However, the elite is amply repaid, because in this arrangement "the state served to foster and protect the existing regime while providing the necessary sinecures to insure the political support which the ruling class would otherwise have lacked, and which it needed in order to preserve its economic and political control of the country."[56] Though this best describes the system as it functioned later, its foundations were laid during the empire and subsequent changes were largely a matter of degree and scope rather than substance.

Yet even though this was the picture at the center, a highly decentralized but politically potent power was also exercised by the provincial landed class, whom Fernando Uricoechea compares to the Russian Boyars or Prussian Junkers.[57] This parallel power had been strengthened by the Additional Act of 1834, which transferred significant powers from the central government to the municipalities, but then was partially undercut by the revocation of this authority through recentralization of power in 1841. Yet these local notables remained influential largely through the fact that they continued to overlap substantially with at least one of the major legs of the military establishment: the national guard, whose political role has already been described. Then, too, given the very great distances and the poor communications involved (factors that had undergone only minimal change since colonial days), the Brazilian state—even at the apogee of the monarchy—had to recognize the existence of powerful local interests. These local interests could constrain the policy choices of the national government, but could not force it to follow their preferred course of action.[58]

The mutual awareness that the state and the landowners needed each other in nearly equal measure gave rise to a tacit pact resulting in a pattern of exchanges and reciprocities: The state granted authority and status in exchange for the landowners' cooperation and services. Nearly two generations later, this arrangement would have its functional equivalent in the so-called "politics of the governors," which was practiced by a series of civilian presidents. In the 1850s and 1860s, however, this quid pro quo lay masked behind the stability afforded by an alliance of the monarch and the military.

Parliamentary Government

The regency had given Brazil an opportunity to evolve toward a parliamentary constitutional monarchy, as the chief executives were elected and

Pedro I's absolutism was discredited. Pedro II's acceptance of the parliament as a legitimate participant in governing and his relatively subtle exercise of the "moderating power" took the edge off legislative-executive friction, and the creation after 1847 of a premier (in the form of a president of the Council of Ministers) worked in the same direction. Yet in the final analysis the emperor remained the balance wheel of the system.[59]

Intended to legitimize the emperor's role in "maintaining the independence, harmony and equilibrium of the other political powers," the moderating power included authority to select life-term senators from among the lists of three candidates nominated by the electors of the provinces, dissolve the Chamber of Deputies (the lower house of the legislature), name and dismiss ministers, and suspend judges. Elections were indirect, with a progressively more stringent scale of income requirements for first-stage voters (who had a say only in local elections), provincial electors, and those eligible to be elected. The last feature was in keeping with the times when it was adopted in 1824, but it would not be so another half century later, when the more advanced countries of the world began to broaden the franchise. Although the number of first-stage voters had reached nearly 1.1 million by 1872, the law eliminating the indirect process also toughened provisions for verifying income, reducing the electorate to 117,000 in 1886.[60] Laudatory as was expansion of electoral participation, however, it had become apparent by the 1880s that reform of this one feature disturbed the workings of the system's essentially inflexible elements beyond the point at which the emperor's practice of alternating politically ossifying parties in office could bring the system back into balance.

In the realm of political organization, the Conservative Party had been formed in 1836 as a fusion of the Moderados and a fraction of the Partido Restaurador, which had lost its reason for being with the death of Pedro I. The Conservatives came to power in 1837 and then were briefly pushed out by the Golpe da Maioridade in 1840 (in which it was decided to crown the fourteen-year-old Pedro as emperor rather than wait until he was no longer a minor), but they returned to office the following year and were in power as the 1850s opened. Backed up by the national guard and often manipulated by the emperor, the Conservative Party, along with the Liberal Party—increasingly its mirror image—constituted the linchpin of the system. In this system, controlled elections for the national legislature were a means of ratifying, and to some extent legitimizing, a ministry that in fact had already been chosen and installed in office by the emperor in his exercise of the moderating power.

Pedro II often acted after consultation with the Council of State, which had been reestablished in 1841 and functioned as a sort of privy council.[61] Eleven times during his long reign, Pedro II alternated the parties in power, dissolving the lower house and gaining support for his new Cabinet through elections whose outcome was never really in doubt. Including reshuffles during the tenure of one party or the other, this resulted in thirty-six Cabinets over forty-nine years. This system of pseudo-democracy—at least by present-day standards—based upon manipulation of regularly held elections was firmly implanted during the empire and would continue throughout the Old Republic and the Vargas era, yielding only gradually to more meaningful electoral participation during the period between 1946 and 1964, after which came a reversal of this democratizing trend.

Considerable confusion reigns even among the students of Brazil's parties concerning the social groupings upon which the Conservatives and Liberals drew for their members. In the view of some, including Hélio Jaguaribe and João Camilo de Oliveira Torres, the Conservatives were recruited chiefly from among the landowning class, who were strongly opposed to change in the field of labor relations, particularly regarding slavery. In this analysis the Liberals represented essentially the urban middle class and the law school–graduate element of the provincial elites. Faoro has maintained, however, that the backbone of the Conservative Party was the central administration's bureaucratic stratum, which sought to maintain its dominance against the threat from regional and economic interests wishing to alter the pattern of governmental expenditures. In his analysis many agricultural producers favored the Liberal proposals for decentralization, which would give them a greater voice in policy making.

On the basis of the evidence available it would appear that the Conservative Party contained both substantial rural elements—especially in the decaying areas of the northeast, but also including Rio de Janeiro coffee planters—along with Portuguese-born merchants and a major proportion of the government bureaucrats. The Liberals, on the other hand, drew upon the urban middle class, Brazilian-born merchants, the professional stratum of the provincial elites in the developing regions, and agriculturists producing for the internal market. If these observations are correct, this pattern would roughly parallel that manifested in the 1946–1964 period, with the Conservatives analogous to the Social Democratic Party (Partido Social Democrático, or PSD) and the Liberals having as their remote successors the National Democratic Union (União Democrática Nacional, or UDN). Indeed, as Roderick Barman portrays them near mid-century, the Liberals sound much like the Party of the Brazilian Democratic Movement (Partido do Movimento Democrático Brasileiro, or PMDB) in the late 1980s—a disparate coalition of opposition groups that was so lacking agreement on policy issues as to border on "ideological schizophrenia" and that was extremely factionalized when in power.[62]

The Liberal Party, which during the regency championed provincial autonomy and a more responsible form of parliamentary government with limits upon the moderating power, lost most of its programmatic coherence with its approximation to the emperor in anticipation of his majority in 1840. The differences between the parties subsequently came to be chiefly in terms of personalities and power considerations, a fact that made possible the coalition ministry in the mid-1850s and the following pacific alternation of the parties in office, virtually at the emperor's pleasure.

While contributing to a prolonged period of internal peace and stability, this system had negative implications for further political development, due to the central fact that the parties had lost any capacity to serve as major vehicles for modernization and change. The relative disassociation of economic and political power found at the heyday of the monarchy diminished after industrialization got underway. Yet during the political decay of the empire in the 1880s, the limited political influence of the new economic interests became a salient factor, as did the inability of the Liberals to agree on the abolition effort.[63]

Although the second monarchy left behind a long list of respected, if not revered, politicians and statesmen, their accomplishments were within the rather narrow confines of the system sketched above. The emperor was clearly the central figure, but up until the beginning of the monarchy's decline he enjoyed the collaboration—in the political realm as well as the military one—of the individual who had already done so much to hold the country together: Caxias. For the policy of "conciliation"—implemented in the form of a coalition between the Liberals and Conservatives in 1853— was an adaptation at the national level, engineered by the marquis of Paraná (Honório Hermeto Carneiro Leão), of the policy Caxias had put into effect in pacifying Rio Grande do Sul.

Having already been awarded the title of marquis in recognition of his services in the south, General Luís Alves de Lima e Silva was named war minister in June 1855. He succeeded to the premiership upon Paraná's death in September 1856 and continued to hold this high office for the early stages of Conservative rule, which followed the end of conciliation in 1857. He would become war minister and president of the Council of Ministers again in March 1861, retaining these dual posts until the Liberals came to office in May 1862.[64] Throughout the period until his death in 1880 this combination military leader and Conservative statesman would function also as the chief guarantor of the army's loyalty to the emperor. In this sense he was irreplaceable, and he was sorely missed when the times of difficulty came in the 1880s. For the monarchical system even in its glory days was not as strong or as popular as the monarch was personally, being clearly underinstitutionalized, particularly with respect to parties (a condition that still exists in 1990).

Transformations in the Brazilian Military

Because the armed forces were such a key bulwark of Pedro II's regime and would also be the crucial element in ending the empire and establishing a republic, it is at least as important to comprehend the changes the military underwent during the period from the 1820s through the 1860s as it is to understand the evolution of the political system within which that institution functioned. As with the administrative bureaucracy and the national guard, the changes were essentially gradual, but cumulatively significant. The senior officers of 1820–1850 were largely individuals who had selected a military career before independence. Their recruitment and career patterns contrasted sharply with those of the men who would command the armed forces after

1880, and the 1850–1880 officers were a mixed and transitional group in these regards.

Present at the Beginning

The officers of João VI, both those stationed in Brazil and those who came with him in the 1808 transfer of the court from Lisbon, were sons of civil and military functionaries and small landholders. Many of these officers, who were considered *fidalgos* (grandees) or even lower nobility in the late colonial period, merited this distinction on the strength of their military position rather than any independent economic base.[65] Yet most of them never rose above captain, because the aristocrats, with their advantages of wealth, connections, and education, were quickly advanced past the career officers. Indeed, until the middle of the century the relatively few socially privileged officers could rise rapidly; professionalization during the full flowering of the empire made promotions more competitive and limited opportunity for meteoric rises.

Military career patterns changed in the early years of the empire and again, very sharply, in the 1860s and 1870s. John Schulz has shown that the generals of 1855, who had entered the army between 1800 and 1830, had on the average reached the rank of major by age twenty-seven, while the generals of 1895 (whose military careers began between 1840 and 1870) averaged thirty-nine years of age when first promoted to major. Moreover, 1850 was the dividing line in the social transformation of the army. By this time the officers of Portuguese birth had been eliminated by attrition, and expansion of military education for general staff, engineering, and artillery officers had been expanded and deepened. Thus, by 1857 all officers in these branches had university-level degrees from military institutions; in contrast only thirty-one of 354 infantry officers and twenty of 119 in the cavalry were so educated.

This change in the nature of recruitment and career patterns underscores the uniqueness of Caxias and his family. With a number of brothers having chosen a military career during the late eighteenth century, the Lima e Silvas enjoyed a very strategic and influential position during the first quarter century after independence, one never to be duplicated (although the Mena Baretto family produced an exceptional number of generals over several generations and the da Fonsecas were very important from the 1870s through the early 1920s).

When, as ranking general from the crises of 1823–1824, General Francisco de Lima e Silva had acted as the swing man during the April 1831 crisis, he was seconded by Brigadier General José Joaquim de Lima e Silva. When the former was no longer regent in the mid-1830s, General Manuel da Fonseca de Lima e Silva became war minister and later president of São Paulo, while General João Manuel de Lima e Silva also held critical command positions during this period. In such a situation the rapid rise of the former regent's son should not be surprising. When called upon to show his skills as a "pacifier," Luís Alves de Lima e Silva (born 1803) was already a colonel. Indeed, in April 1832 he had led the troops loyal to the regime in putting down a coup attempt in Rio de Janeiro. Though his military abilities are beyond doubt, his early and repeated opportunities to demonstrate them were far from unrelated to the domination of the command structure by his father and uncles.

Such a situation could not recur after 1850. Although the duke of Caxias was of great importance until 1880, it should be remembered that he had opted for a military career before independence and was already a general when Pedro II came to the throne. After mid-century most of his family, in spite of its glorious military tradition, would seek alternative careers in a changing Brazil—for they were already well placed within the elite. Indeed, by the middle of the century recruitment into the officer corps, which remained at about 1,400, had taken on some politically significant characteristics. Most cadets during this period were sons of military officers, including regular and national guard officers. Thus, 56 percent of those who became generals between 1831 and 1864 were sons of senior officers who on the whole were linked to the Conservative Party. However, for those who reached the rank of general between 1889 and 1894—that is, those who had entered the army during the middle period of the empire—this proportion was only one in five. Before 1850 nearly all generals were from the elite stratum of Brazilian society; by the early years of the republic this would be true of no more than one-half.[66]

Prior to 1850 military men frequently occupied the provincial presidencies—as would again be the case in similar troubled periods such as the years after 1910 and in the 1930s; after mid-century, law school graduates came to predominate in both elected and appointed office. Pedro I had, for example, named a dozen military men to the Senate, but the Senate had only two military members during the regency, four in the 1840s, and two in the 1850s. Subsequently there were only two more in the remaining twenty-nine years of the empire. Figures for the Chamber of Deputies bear out this downward trend: From an average of ten military deputies during Pedro I's reign, there was a decline to a norm of six in the early stages of Pedro II's government and then just one or two in the declining years of the monarchy.[67]

The army itself experienced a series of reorganizations and reductions in strength during the first thirty years of the empire. In 1825 it was cut back from an unwieldy conglomerate of units totalling nearly 30,000 men, and at the end of the Cisplatine War in 1829 it stood at an authorized strength of 23,000. Reduced by the expulsion of foreign troops, it was further cut to a ceiling of just over 14,000 by action of the regency government in 1831, when the national guard was created. By 1837 the Liberal government had reduced this ceiling to only 6,000, but the ceiling was raised again to about 12,000 after the Conservative Pedro de Araújo Lima succeeded Feijó as regent in 1838.[68] A further reorganization in 1839 set the army's size at roughly 14,000, but in the face of regional revolts it actually stayed at between 16,000 and 17,000 toward the end of the decade. The army's numbers peaked at over 23,000 in 1845, during the final push to end the Rio Grande do Sul rebellion. For the next two decades its size fluctuated from around 16,000 to 20,000 men, generally remaining below these authorized strengths.

Another indicator of the armed forces' position in the system, military expenditures, had been highest—as a proportion of total central government expenditures—during the 1823–1824 period of reaction to Pedro I's closing of the constituent assembly, during the final stages of the Cisplatine War (1828–1829), and during the peak of autonomist revolts (1839–1843).[69] For the remainder of the 1840s the armed forces' share of the budget remained relatively steady at about 42 percent, falling during the 1850–1864 period to between 35 and 38 percent.

Professionalization and Reform

The system of military education was repeatedly overhauled and upgraded during the middle third of the century. The Academia Real Militar of 1810 became under the regency the Escola Militar da Corte (EMC). In 1855 the Escola Militar e de Aplicação was established at Praia Vermelha to handle the strictly military specialties, because the EMC was still the country's only engineering school and attracted many students who did not plan on a military career; indeed, the EMC was renamed the Escola Central in 1858 and in 1874 became the civilian Escola Politécnica. In 1858 military academies were opened in Rio de Janeiro and Porto Alegre for relatively poor would-be officers. Then in 1860 the Praia Vermelha institution became the Escola Militar and was essentially the military academy from that time on.[70]

Legislation of September 1850 gave a major advantage in promotions to degree holders over other officers, who subsequently found advancement confined chiefly to the infantry and cavalry branches—for whom a special school existed in Rio Grande do Sul from 1853 to 1911. After 1845 some education had been necessary to gain entrance to the academy, and prior to 1858 such education could be obtained only in secondary schools, which had quite restricted access and were far from inexpensive, or through private tutoring. With the opening of the army's own preparatory schools, an economic barrier to a military career was removed. A partial depoliticization of promotions through the establishment of age and educational criteria could also be viewed as a democratizing measure.

Yet this attention by the government to partial military reform did not fully satisfy the new military generation. From mid-1854 to mid-1855 a group of young officers published a paper in which they called for reforms in the economic and social as well as political spheres. Abolition of slavery, protective tariffs, subsidies for industrialization, railroad construction, improvement of communications, and government-subsidized immigration were among their proposals, and all were compatible with what many Liberal politicians were advocating at the time. Though the officers' actions had little impact at the time, they were a harbinger of what might come with the next generation in the 1880s.

The Paraguayan War and Its Aftermath

As already noted, the Liberals had returned to power in 1862. But before they could more than modestly and hesitantly attack the country's developmental needs, they had to turn their efforts instead to a major international war, one that would strain the nation's resources to the limit and would indirectly allow the Conservatives to regain control of the central government in time to garner the credit for the war's eventual successful outcome. The Paraguayan War of 1865–1870 would also mark a significant watershed in the development of the Brazilian military as an institution.[71]

Uruguay's independence had brought little stability to the River Plate region, and Brazil had become involved in military action with Uruguay against Argentine strongman Rosas in 1850–1851. During the early 1860s Brazil intervened militarily in Uruguay to aid the Colorado Party (Conservatives) in its struggle with the Blancos (Liberals), who turned to Paraguayan dictator Francisco Solano López for help. Small but highly militarized, Paraguay at the end of 1864 sent forces across Argentinian and Brazilian soil to reach Uruguay.

A Difficult Challenge

With a population in excess of 9 million (the 1872 census would show over 10 million Brazilians) and at least the beginnings of an industrial plant, the empire's material advantages over its warlike neighbor were significant. Yet at the outbreak of hostilities Paraguay had 64,000 men under arms and Brazil had only 18,000. It would take considerable time for the monarchical regime to mobilize its manpower resources and bring them to bear on a distant and inaccessible front. Indeed, the length of its supply lines plagued Brazil throughout the conflict and underscored the sad state of the Brazilian transportation system. The ineffectiveness and even corruption of the Brazilian bureaucracy—which was not too dissimilar from the U.S. situation during the early stages of the Civil War—led to considerable resentment toward the civilian political elite on the part of the military.

Because the Liberals were in power and a personal enemy headed the War Ministry, Caxias first turned down an invitation to command the Brazilian Army. But when the allies' forces of over 65,000 troops—including some 57,000 Brazilians plus small contingents of Argentines and Uruguayans—stalled in front of the fortifications at Humaitá, Caxias took command in the field. At the same time, however, his relations with the government went from bad to worse. In a development that would establish a dangerous precedent for the future, in response to the hero's "either him or me" ultimatum in February 1868 the emperor found the ministry of Zacarias de Góes e Vasconcelos to be expendable.[72] Thus, with the Conservatives back in power and an election duly held to manufacture a majority for them, Caxias could concentrate upon winning the war. Humaitá was taken in August and the Paraguayan capital fell at the beginning of 1869. With only a mopping-up operation remaining, Caxias left command of a reduced force of 25,000 Brazilians and 5,000 Argentines to Prince Gastón de Orléans, Conde d'Eu—the emperor's son-in-law.

The War's Consequences

During the more than five years the conflict lasted, Brazil mobilized nearly 200,000 men, sent a total of 139,000 to the war zone, and suffered at least 30,000 casualties. The burdensome financial cost fed inflation and forced the Brazilian government to increase its foreign debt substantially. Moreover, the national guard was very largely absorbed into the army, which in the eyes of some analysts significantly increased the politicization of that key institution.[73] Clearly Brazilian officers came into contact with their far more politically oriented Argentine counterparts. Even more serious in its political implications was the swelling of the officer corps from roughly 1,500 to nearly 10,000, which would later create a major demobilization problem. Then, too, the war created a pantheon of military heroes, many of whom would become major political figures as senior officers by the 1880s. (Frank McCann has intelligently speculated that the occupation of Paraguay to the end of the 1870s may well have had a major impact upon the military's political sense.)

The seeds of the post-1880 decay of the monarchical system may well have been sown during the Paraguayan War, but they were sufficiently irrigated in the superficially calm 1870s to ensure the probability of their subsequent germination. The need to increase revenues to pay for the war had led to an increased level of tariffs, which had a protective effect and thus fostered a significant spurt of industrialization, but there was a built-in lag factor before this would affect society sufficiently to have a heavy impact on politics.[74] In many ways the political system never fully recovered from the dislocations and strains caused, or at least intensified, by the Paraguayan War. Upset at having been ousted abruptly from power in mid-1868 by the emperor (who, as we have seen, had a major assist from Caxias), the Liberals initiated a decade in opposition by issuing a manifesto in 1869 calling for electoral reform, elimination of the moderating power, the disbanding of the national guard, and even the abolition of slavery.

Moreover, time had taken its toll of the system's pillars, and Pedro II faced the 1870s without the most skillful of his Conservative advisors. The sage marquis of Olinda (Pedro de Araújo Lima, the former regent) died in 1870, and in the same year the viscount of Itaboraí (Joaquim José Rodrigues Tôrres) left office—he also was dead within two years. The new generation of Conservative politicians were loyal to the monarchy, but unlike their predecessors they had not lived through the "chaos, anarchy, and threatened disintegration" that had marked the 1830s.[75] Their emphasis upon regeneration of the political system, particularly as it affected the electoral process, was alien—almost incomprehensible—to the older members of the political elite. In 1870 disenchanted Liberals formed the Republican Party, and their ranks would gradually grow as the Liberals endured their longest period ever out of office.[76]

Furthermore, the attack upon slavery had gained impetus through the war, leading to the Rio Branco law (law of free birth) in September 1871. This legislation declared that from that point on all children born to slave mothers would be free—either at age eight, if the owner opted for compensation from the government, or else at twenty-one. In addition, slaveowners were required to allow any bondsman who could come up with the market price to purchase his or her freedom. Since the end of the slave trade in mid-century, sugar planters from the northeast had gradually been selling their slaves to the coffee *fazendeiros* of Rio de Janeiro and São Paulo, so that by 1888 some three-quarters of all remaining slaves were found in this emergent region. By 1884 slaves had declined in number to 1.24 million, and a law then freed all over sixty years of age—albeit not very many reached this ripe age. By 1887, at only 723,000 (plus 500,000 of their children), slaves would constitute just 5 percent of Brazil's population and would be less than one-third as numerous as they had been at the time the slave trade ended.[77]

This significant social trend accompanied and interacted with economic changes, and both were at the center of political debate. Under Pedro II, the government came to intervene fairly actively in the nation's economic life, subsidizing a wide variety of activities such as coastal steamboats, railroad construction, modernization of the sugar industry, and European immigration. Yet only after 1870 did economic development receive as much as 20 percent of the central government's expenditures, a proportion that would reach 33 percent by 1889. Budgetary priority under the monarchy went essentially to the military and civil bureaucracies, which were needed for the crucial task of averting secession—through mid-century—and maintaining stability.

All through the empire, taxes on foreign trade continued to be the major source of government revenue, averaging nearly 75 percent of revenue from 1836 through 1865 and some 70 percent from then through 1885. Failure of agricultural production, despite generally favorable terms of trade, to generate sufficient income was the major restraint on faster growth generally and on industrialization in particular. The small size of the domestic market for manufactured goods, caused chiefly by lack of rising productivity in the agricultural sector, was aggravated by high internal transportation costs stemming from the large distances involved.[78]

Hence it would seem that the governments of the monarchical regime performed reasonably in the economic sphere, as concentration on holding the vast, sprawling nation together and maintaining order were rational priorities for its limited resources. Economic growth, in the doldrums during the early 1850s, picked up after mid-decade, slumped from 1859 through 1862, and then recovered sharply through 1867. Following a further downturn in 1876–1877, the 1870s closed with significant growth during 1878 and 1879.[79] The worldwide banking crisis of 1875 was felt in Brazil through the dramatic collapse of the impressive but overextended entrepreneurial empire of Irineu Evangelista de Souza, Viscount Mauá. Yet by the end of the empire manufacturing establishments had risen from a mere fifty at mid-century to 636, albeit chiefly in the textile field, with the number of industrial workers nearing 55,000.[80] Meanwhile, the land law of 1850, which had primarily benefitted the coffee producers and allowed continuation of *latifundia*, or large landholdings (by providing that only one-tenth of such holdings had to be cultivated within four years to revalidate existing claims), remained the basis of the land tenure system.[81]

Failure of the government to do more to foster economic development appears to have stemmed mainly from its limited financial resources rather than reflecting any philosophical position or ideological restrictions on the state's proper role in the economy. Indeed, foreign borrowing was utilized quite frequently to cover the nearly chronic budget deficits—which occurred in all but eleven years of the 1822–1889 period. A modest effort was also made toward market diversification as Western Europe remained—as it would again be in the 1970s and 1980s—Brazil's principal market, but the United States would gradually replace Great Britain as the largest single market for Brazilian goods. Thus Europe dropped moderately from 74 percent of Brazil's exports in 1840 to 59 percent in 1860 and down to 54 percent by 1880, while sales to the United States over the same time span rose from 23 percent to 29 percent at the intermediate point, reaching 44 percent in 1880.[82]

Military Discontent

Although the abolitionists and Republicans presented the somewhat geriatric monarchy with a more divisive and difficult political agenda, even in the midst of a reasonable economic context, a similar situation of discontent prevailed within the armed forces. A sense of professional frustration accentuated dissatisfaction with the established order. Slowness of promotions, particularly acute between captain and major, compounded by inadequate pay, fed "a burgeoning movement for army reform during the post–Paraguayan War years which assumed a position of utmost importance for army officers interested in the welfare of their corporation, as well as their own careers."[83]

These individuals were well aware of the "Republican Manifesto" issued in 1870, when dissident Liberals had helped to found a new Republican Party to challenge the two ossifying parties of the old elites, but for the moment they were concerned with matters of more immediate and direct import. This same situation would prevail on a number of occasions in the twentieth century, usually leading to increased political involvement as the military's expression of material concerns did not receive what the officers considered a satisfactory response from the government of the day.

Demonstrating a new sense of corporate unity, importance, suspicion of civilians, and perhaps even a broader world view—all in large part a legacy of the Paraguayan War—army intellectuals in the capital area under the leadership of Lieutenant Colonel Floriano Peixoto had organized a Military Institute in 1871 as a forum for debates on matters of interest to the armed forces. Drawn chiefly from the most professionally competent stratum of the general staff, artillery, and engineer corps, this small group would provide a disproportionate share of the army's leadership—and even that of the government—a quarter of a century later. At this juncture, however, having at least partially made their point to the war minister, they discreetly disbanded. But nearly a dozen of this group would soon make themselves heard again—and again.

A series of reform measures passed in 1873–1874 temporarily satisfied much of the officer corps, but only whetted the appetites of some of the more radical figures. Military and civil engineering courses were divorced, "regimental" schools were reformed to upgrade the education of noncommissioned officers, and the national guard was reduced to a "force of officers without soldiers, of ostentatiously uniformed political chiefs" through the establishment of provincial police forces.[84] More important, after a bitter parliamentary struggle a bill was passed providing the basis for replacing the old system of forced recruitment—the so-called manhunt—by a semblance of a conscription system. Yet this cherished goal of military reformers was largely gutted by the implementing legislation of 1875, remaining essentially a dead letter.[85] Hence, rather than closing the breach between the army reformers and the political establishment, this legislation embittered relations, particularly with the Liberals.

On balance, then, those army officers who wished to vigorously reform their service felt misunderstood, and their efforts toward modernization met with indifference, if not active opposition. The civilian elite, lulled into a sense of complacency by the fact that the military had not engaged in political adventures during the Caxias era, perceived no risk in taking the armed forces for granted. Thus the horizon was already clouded when economic depression was aggravated by a coffee crisis after 1880.

Political Decay of the Empire, 1880–1888

Paradoxically, the decline of the monarchical regime was ushered in by what appeared to many observers to be its most important political reform. On January 9, 1881, the government headed by José Antônio Saraiva passed a landmark law making parliamentary elections direct by a single class of electors that included for the first time non-Catholics, freedmen, and naturalized citizens. Although electors still had to meet the restrictive property and literacy requirements, which maintained a situation in which less than 1 percent of the population was effectively enfranchised, this was clearly a step forward.[86] The significance of the measure was quickly demonstrated when the October elections—in which some 96,400 actually voted—dealt the first electoral reverse to the party in power in the nation's history, as the emperor maintained an unaccustomed posture of impartiality. Yet the establishment would adapt rapidly to this modification of the rules of the electoral game, and clientelism at least partially replaced coercion in maintaining the essence of the old electoral politics—manageability. Indeed, the elections of August 1889, just months before the empire's demise, would be manipulated much as had occurred before this reform.[87]

The "New" Military

More of a threat to the system than was the "new" politics, for which the electoral law at least opened the door a crack, was the "new" military. Marshal Manuel Luíz Osório, the marquis of Herval and the Liberals' leading military figure, had passed away in 1879, followed within a year by Caxias—who during 1875–1878 had occupied the war ministry and the presidency of the Council of Ministers for the third time in his distinguished career with the Conservative Party. These two prestigious old-school figures had helped keep discontent within the armed forces from getting out of hand, but their eventual heirs in the military leadership role, Floriano Peixoto and Deodoro da Fonseca, would ride this wave to power instead of seeking to stem it.

The Paraguayan War had opened the way for change in the social origins of the officer corps, and the effects of this development were to be felt during the 1880s.[88] Reforms in the military education system made it attractive to those who could not afford the private preparatory schools that were the main avenue to the law and medical faculties. Often this new breed of cadets were very "nonmilitary" in their outlook, being more concerned with building a society that offered better opportunities for the lower middle class. As they became junior officers, they could not hope to overturn the monarchy by themselves, nor did they have to, because a significant group of the middle-grade officers—the advocates of army reform in the early 1870s—were coming to lean more heavily in this direction.

Indeed, a classic case of a three-generation split existed within the officer corps during the 1880s. The senior stratum was "old soldiers" who were likely to have experienced the provincial revolts of the late regency period, the Argentine campaign of 1851–1852, and the Paraguayan War.[89] The far more numerous middle-grade officers were more likely to be better educated and were combat veterans of the Paraguayan War, while the junior officers lacked battle experience but possessed more education. Those of the older generation who had been successful in their careers and thus were still on active duty were much in the mold of Caxias and Osório, accepting and supporting the system they had helped nourish—and under which they had risen to high social status—as well as the emperor they had known since boyhood.

The mid-career officers were more representative of the officer corps as a whole, not just that element who had made it to the top, including many individuals whose careers were at a standstill and not likely to go forward—at least under the existing system. In many ways this group's cutting edge was the reformers of the early 1870s, with Lieutenant Colonel Benjamin Constant Botelho de Magalhães as the outstanding intellectual figure. The mentor of the junior officers, he was an engineer who had been stationed almost exclusively in Rio de Janeiro as a mathematics professor at the military academy. Although Constant did not become politically active on behalf of his positivist views until after military agitation was peaking in 1886–1887, he quickly became a key figure, chiefly because of his great prestige among the lieutenants and captains who had recently been his students. (Moreover, his brother was an ardent Republican.)

The junior officer generation had witnessed the empire only after its shortcomings had become clearly evident, were with notable exceptions predominantly of middle-sector origins, and as a group were certainly more broadly educated than their seniors. These factors disposed them to be least attached to the monarchical system, and they were the most frustrated by the very limited opportunities for advancement in a peacetime army overloaded with "heroes" of the great war. Not only was their economic situation precarious, but also the military as an institution was experiencing a deteriorating material situation. Indeed, during the 1870–1880 period the military budget was the same as it had been in 1857—substantially less in real terms with inflation taken into account and down two-thirds as a proportion of total central government expenditures. By 1886–1888 military expenditures had dropped even further, and a pay-raise bill of 1887 merely restated the increase that had been promised in 1873 legislation but never implemented.

Failure to put into effect the 1874–1875 recruitment laws further radicalized those officers deeply concerned with the modernization of the army. An estimated 90 percent of the enlisted ranks were still being filled by impressment, officially for six-year terms, but often stretching much longer. Press gangs usually took the unemployed, who were chiefly blacks and mulattoes, a situation that made the officers feel like uniformed overseers. Although the relatively few literates could soon rise to be noncommissioned officers, and in some cases even reach the academy, the bulk of the soldiers represented what the country's elites and the "respectable" middle class considered to be the "worst" segments of Brazilian society. In fact, military support for the government's policy of subsidized European immigration was based in large part on the belief that these new arrivals would make good soldiers once an effective means of conscripting them could be devised.

Breakdown of the Military/Monarchy Marriage

There was, then, a growing difference between the political elite and the military, a divergence that contributed to acceptance by the majority of a coup engineered by a relatively small radicalized faction drawn chiefly from the postwar generation. In this respect the "fall of the Empire was more a phenomenon of political decay, a loss of loyalty to the system, than a consequence of a political action oriented toward its change."[90] And, as will be shown in the pages ahead, "The military intellectuals and their colleagues who adopted the ideals of military professionalism had to resort to politics to gain their ends. The decision to 'take' power developed only as a last resort."[91]

What appeared in the short run to be smart politics actually served to aggravate this potentially serious situation. Both imperial parties cultivated leading military figures, offering them government offices and political advancement in return for their endorsement and support. Moreover, both establishment parties when out of power frequently sought to turn army resentment against the incumbent Cabinet to force it from office. While the Conservatives and Liberals played this game with the senior generals, the small, but growing, Republican Party began to work on the younger officers.

Indeed, as their superiors were elevated to titles of nobility, perhaps even becoming provincial presidents or lifetime senators, while they languished year after year as poorly paid captains and majors, a substantial number of field-grade officers began to wonder whether they might not fare better under a different system. In any case, making politics a major factor for advancement in terms of both assignments and promotions was a sure way to politicize the armed forces. As has proven to be the case repeatedly down to the present, the essentially non-programmatic political parties were concerned with the immediate tactical situation and short-run gains, giving little or no thought to the long-term ramifications of their actions.

The government failed to realize in time that military leaders could provide a quite different type of opposition than had the churchmen in the 1870s during the so-called Religious Question, when the state clashed with the upper clergy over prerogatives. The military officers, along with their very high sense of institutional pride and honor, possessed power capabilities of a very different nature from those of the Catholic hierarchy—which in reality had been quite divided during the Religious Question crisis.[92] The officers could also, as the course of events amply demonstrated, subordinate partisan inclinations and personal rivalries to a prickly sense of corporate pride and strong institutional interests, particularly as successive civilian governments, both Liberal and Conservative, provided issues that united rather than divided the military.

Although during the entire span of the empire civilians occupied the War Ministry with roughly as great a frequency as military men, in 1875 Caxias had kept that portfolio in the Cabinet he headed, and in the succeeding Liberal ministry Marshal Osório (the marquis of Herval) took over that post.[93] Following Osório's death, the viscount of Pelotas (Marshal José Antônio Correia da Câmara) occupied that ministry. Thus, when Carlos Afonso de Assis Figueiredo became war minister in mid-1882, he did so with the distinct handicap of breaking a tradition, albeit one of fairly recent origin, by which prestigious army figures were in charge of military affairs. He encountered an army reform movement much stronger and determined than had been the case a decade earlier. For in reality, the "military question" that was to undermine the empire had its roots in the army's dissatisfaction over the relatively low priority given to its interests by a government that essentially took it for granted and was becoming increasingly concerned with developmental needs.

The first in a series of increasingly serious incidents that were to leave the officer corps substantially alienated from the regime and its governing political elite occurred early in 1883. Ironically it was sparked by the promotion of Floriano Peixoto—who would eventually be the swing man in the 1889 coup—to brigadier general. The war minister's inept handling of a minor protest episode, seen by him as teaching a lesson to the military concerning the firmness and resolve of civilian authority in the face of indiscipline, helped prejudice the army against the Assis Figueiredos, thus creating a problem for future prime minister Afonso Celso (Carlos Afonso's brother).

The next war minister left office quickly as the result of the daylight assassination of a polemical journalist by a group of cavalry officers almost on the steps of the police station. (The most senior of the four officers finally indicted, but not convicted, was Captain Moreira César, who subsequently became infamous for his brutal repressions in Santa Catarina in the wake of the 1893 rebellion and finally perished as a colonel at the head of a military expedition against "insurgents" at Canudos.) The very next year, Lieutenant Colonel Antônio de Sena Madureira, who publicly advocated abolition of slavery, became for the second time the center of the controversy between the miltary and the government over the limits of officers' rights to speak out on political issues.

Finding a Leader

It was at this juncture that fate brought into the picture the confirmed monarchist who a scant five years later was to overthrow the empire. Born in 1827, Manoel Deodoro da Fonseca entered the army during the later stages of the Farroupilha Revolution and first experienced combat during the Praieira Rebellion (1848). The Paraguayan War afforded this ambitious officer, along with his five military brothers, an opportunity to distinguish himself. A colonel by the conflict's end, he was advanced to brigadier general in 1874 at age forty-seven.[94] Promoted to field marshal (the equivalent of major general) in 1884 and named quartermaster general the next year, in 1886 Deodoro was assigned to command all military forces in Rio Grande do Sul. Intent upon attracting him to the Conservative Party, the government also named him first vice-president of that province.

Thus by the time the military question flared up in full force, Deodoro was the acting chief executive of the most turbulent of Brazil's major states. When the ranking hero of that region, the viscount of Pelotas, opened the issue in May with a speech deploring the miserable state into which the army had been allowed to deteriorate under the alleged mismanagement of a series of civilian ministers, the temptation for Deodoro to become embroiled in the controversy was to prove overwhelming. (This would be far from the last time that an apparently nonpolitical general with a long career marked by professionalism and adherence to constituted authority would become highly politicized at a very advanced stage of his career, Marshal Henrique Lott in the mid-1950s and Humberto Castelo Branco a decade later being the most recent salient examples.)

The first war minister in the administration of the baron of Cotegipe (João Maurício Wanderley) resigned in disgrace and was replaced by an individual who as navy minister had senselessly offended naval officers by a fiasco that led to the resignation and premature retirement of the admiral baron of Jaceguaí, Artur Silveira da Mota. Damaging as that episode had been, in his new post Alfredo Chaves soon stumbled into a situation that much more seriously aggravated the military crisis when he ruled that officers could not even respond to criticism through the press without formally receiving prior permission from the war minister. This gag rule for the military was in such striking contrast to the parliamentary immunity enjoyed by most politicians that the viscount of Pelotas immediately leapt to the defense of the soldiers' rights to respond to attacks upon their personal honor.

Sena Madureira deliberately poured oil on the waters with an article in an outspokenly republican journal and was predictably censured by Chaves, who thus found himself at odds with Deodoro's interpretation of the applicable regulations. Thus Prime Minister Cotegipe's dreams of making Deodoro the Conservative Party's new Caxias turned to ashes, as Deodoro aligned himself on this issue with the opposition's leading military figure, Viscount Pelotas. In the aftermath of this imbroglio, aging Adjutant General Manuel Antônio da Fonseca Costa, marquis of Gávea—whose position was very roughly equivalent to that of chief of staff in the twentieth century—resigned after nearly a decade and a half in that key post. (The adjutant general dealt much more with administration and less with planning and operations than does the modern counterpart.)

In view of Deodoro's open defiance, the prime minister relieved him of his command—natural under the circumstances, but it would prove as fatal as the Spanish Republic's decision in the 1930s to send General Francisco Franco to the Canary Islands (whence Franco promptly launched the Spanish Civil War). As the Republicans sympathized with Deodoro over the "illegitimate" nature of the punishment, Deodoro chaired a protest meeting of some 200 officers and was consequently dismissed as quartermaster general, just as one of his brothers had recently been relieved from command of the military academy. As a sign of his willingness to compromise, Cotegipe replaced his war minister, but the opposition was not in a conciliatory mood. In Senate debate on May 18, 1887, Pelotas pointedly reminded the prime minister that Pedro I had been forced to abdicate by a revolt. But as neither Pelotas nor Deodoro had lost his respect for the ailing emperor, an ingenious parliamentary solution was worked out that did not cause the government to fall immediately—a process that would be repeated on several occasions in the twentieth century.

Exhilarated by their success and determined to be ready for future problems, Deodoro and his followers moved quickly to establish the Military Club (Clube Militar).[95] Though the armed forces were not yet prepared to move against the emperor, republican sentiment was spreading rapidly within the ranks of the junior and mid-grade officers—including a majority of those who had attended the academy since the mid-1870s. Although a fairly sharp cleavage on political issues existed between the positivist-oriented disciples of Benjamin Constant and the Paraguayan War generation, common corporate interests brought them progressively closer together during the protracted controversy over the military question, and the Military Club was to provide a continuing forum for exchange of views with their senior colleagues outside the rigid hierarchy of the command structure.

Moreover, the War College, created in March 1889 as an extension of the academy for advanced and specialized training, from the beginning had a faculty loaded with military reformers and would contribute heavily to the coup's leadership. The college was located in São Cristovão right next to the First Cavalry and Second Artillery barracks, a move designed to separate the officer-students from the younger cadets at Praia Vermelha. But the students "subverted" the line troops, rather than being contained by them, and these three units would lead the marching order of the revolutionary column on November 15, 1889.

Establishment of the Republic

Considerable emphasis has conventionally been placed upon abolition as a major contributing cause to the downfall of the empire.[96] Certainly the economic effects of abolition and their political ramifications had some impact, but a more important aspect of the question has generally been overlooked or downplayed. For it was the political involvement of many of the younger generation of the military in the abolitionist campaigns that brought them into contact with civilian political forces who more often than not were also partisans of republicanism. At a time when a direct effort to recruit military supporters for elimination of the monarchy was still so premature as to run the danger of proving counterproductive, the slavery issue provided a common cause upon which an alliance of change-oriented civilian and military elements could be built—within a general framework of modernization and reform.

The Plotting Thickens

Realizing its continued political weakness and the necessity of army support to the achievement of its ultimate purposes, the republican movement strove assiduously to create links of sympathy on any possible ground with military figures. If this required temporarily downplaying their major goal in favor of concentrating on questions of greater immediate interest to the military, such tactics were adopted in the realization that only with the cooperation of the officer corps could the monarchy be ended. Hence, as well as abolition, the Republicans emphasized federalism, which had considerable appeal to many in the military and did not require open opposition to the constituted authorities of the empire. However, the embracement of federalism did carry these officers down the road in the direction of such open opposition.[97] In keeping with this strategy, in July 1887 the abolitionists and Republicans enthusiastically supported the candidacy of Deodoro for senator from Rio de Janeiro, a candidacy originated within the Military Club.[98] Although he was decisively defeated, the marshal's bid aroused strong support from military elements previously linked to the establishment parties. Deodoro, as Military Club president, followed up with pronouncements on all policy issues, including the burning question of abolition. Although the government strove to raise the Argentine menace and to satisfy the military through budget increases, Joaquim Nabuco, recently elected to the parliament, dramatically refocused attention upon the slavery issue. Thus in late October, Deodoro transmitted to Princess Isabel, who was then acting as regent while Pedro II was recuperating from a variety of age-related ailments in Europe, the Military Club's refusal to have the army continue the demeaning task of hunting down runaway slaves.

The pro-slavery Conservative Cabinet of Baron Cotegipe, which had survived the 1887 military crisis with its dignity and moral authority gravely impaired, finally fell over a minor run-in with the military in March 1888. The new Conservative Cabinet came up with the gimmick of making Severiano da Fonseca interim adjutant general—with his tenure dependent upon the political restraint shown by his brother Deodoro—but this ended with the former's death in March 1889.

With the abolition of slavery on May 13, 1888, the monarchy gained a modicum of renewed popular support, but at the price of alienating some of the provincial landowners who were still important in the Conservative Party. That this reaction was not greater resulted from the fact that most of the landowners' slaves had already been freed, or soon would be under an 1884 law freeing those over sixty. Indeed, as of 1888 there were only 650,000 slaves in the whole country, over half in Minas Gerais and Rio de Janeiro and another quarter in the northeast. One of the great ironies of abolition when it finally came was that to a large extent employed slaves became unemployed freedmen.

To curb the growing political role of the Military Club, Deodoro was abruptly assigned to Mato Grosso under the flimsy pretext that the rupture of relations between Bolivia and Paraguay posed a military threat there. As this post was generally occupied by a colonel, often jointly with the presidency of the province, Deodoro felt affronted at his subordination, no matter how nominal, to a provincial chief executive lacking national prestige. The impassioned denunciations of Deodoro's "deportation" to the boondocks by Ruy Barbosa and other republican orators fed the marshal's sense of injustice. The situation eased somewhat in June as the Conservative Cabinet was replaced by a Liberal one under Afonso Celso Assis Figueiredo, the viscount of Ouro Preto. For the first time in seven years, the War Ministry was entrusted to a military man, Marshal Rufino Eneias Galvão (viscount of Maracajú), a cousin and close friend of Deodoro. The navy minister was Paraguayan War hero José da Costa Azevedo, baron of Ladário; the choice for adjutant general was Floriano Peixoto, who, on disability leave in out-of-the-way Alagoas from 1885 to January 1889, had avoided involvement in the military question.[99] But Ladário was soon embroiled in a dispute with prestigious Captain Custódio José de Melo, and Deodoro continued to take offense at any colonel being appointed to govern a province in which he was serving as military commander.

To counter Viscount Ouro Preto's campaign to win military support by conferring titles and honors on many military (as well as civilian) supporters—more than 180 such titles were awarded during the last two years of the monarchy, including 44 to national guard officers—rumors of alleged government plans to build the national guard up again as a counterweight to the army were circulated by the Conservatives as a means of sowing seeds of discontent.[100] By the time Deodoro returned to the capital in September, without government permission, an election had given Ouro Preto an overwhelming 130 to 9 majority in the Chamber of Deputies. In the process, however, the blatant manipulation involved—analogous to the Mexican elections of the 1960s and 1970s, if not that of 1988—further discredited the political structures of the empire. Republican leaders, their party having been credited with less than one-seventh of the vote, realized their need for a prestigious military figure at the head of their movement, while republican sympathizers within the army sought to use the illness of the war minister to launch a new military crisis. Renewed activity of the Military Club featured Deodoro's nephews, Clodoaldo and thirty-four-year-old Hermes Rodrigues da Fonseca (the latter would become president in 1910).

From Conspiracy to Coup

Acting war minister Cândido de Oliveira, a civilian heartily detested by the officer corps, led the government into the trap prepared by the republican firebrands, dismissing the highly respected Lieutenant Colonel João Nepomuceno de Medeiros Mallet from command of the Forteleza Military School for protesting a blatantly political appointment. While the republican press prepared public opinion with a concentrated attack upon the monarchy, the young militant officers of the Military Club signed blood pacts pledging to carry the struggle to the ultimate limit. Then, while all those connected to the imperial court attended a lavish ball honoring visiting Chilean naval officers, on the night of November 9, 1889, the Military Club empowered its vice-president, Benjamin Constant, to resolve the political crisis in a manner "equally honorable for the Army and the nation."[101]

Although such key admirals as Saldanha da Gama and Custódio de Melo were out of the country, fleet commander Eduardo Wandenkolk joined the plot. Deodoro's last scruples were overcome when he was named to head the revolutionary government, and he brought Floriano Peixoto into the picture. Unbeknownst to the government, the composition of the post-coup Cabinet had already been agreed upon. Yet much as João Goulart's military aides would reassure him on the eve of his ouster in 1964, so the war minister informed Ouro Preto that the situation was secure.

Although the original date for the uprising was to be November 20, just before the parliament chosen in the fraud-ridden August elections would meet, hints of precautionary moves by the regime caused the coup to be moved up five days. Responding to false stories that Deodoro's arrest had been ordered, army units were mobilized at midnight on the 14th to "protect" the marshal. The prime minister and most of the Cabinet soon found that army headquarters was the wrong place to go for safety, as Peixoto's 2,000 troops there joined the 600-man rebel column headed by Deodoro and Benjamin Constant.[102] Only on the afternoon of November 15 did Afonso Celso realize that his resignation that morning had spelled the end not just of the Cabinet, but also of the empire. This news was not broken to Pedro II until the following day, when he was told that after eighty-one years in Brazil the Bragança family would have to leave the country within twenty-four hours.

For the first time in the nation's history, a dictatorship was in control, legitimized only by its monopoly of force and significant, but far from overwhelming, popular support for a republic. And for the first time the armed forces were to learn that being in power is a mixed blessing, bringing with it frustrations and vexing problems, not the least of which is maintaining unity.

The ouster of Pedro II and proclamation of the First Republic shared at least one basic feature with the coup that would overthrow the Goulart government nearly seventy-five years later: Its success was more rapid and complete than even its architects had expected. In each case the government had badly overestimated its military strength, seriously misjudged the probable actions of key military figures, and relied on a popularity with the people that would not be reflected in the realm of actions to defend the regime.

For the future course of Brazil's political development the crucial factor was that the Republicans had turned to the armed forces as the one institution that could put an end to the monarchy without this resulting in a drastic change in the distribution of power among contending social groups. Rather than a rupture of political processes, they wanted an alteration in the framework of government so it would accommodate the economic and social changes that had already occurred—indeed, changes that had in large part given rise to their particular movement. It was the fact that São Paulo had only four senators (compared to ten for Minas Gerais, seven for Bahia, and six for Pernambuco), not the sad state of education, public health, or workers' standards of living, that represented the kind of abuses the emerging elite considered outrageous.

The Lessons of 1889

Though it was clearly of some relevance, the economic situation does not appear to have been an especially significant factor in the demise of the monarchy. Although 1884 was the only year of impressive economic growth and the country experienced a recession from 1885 through 1888, prosperity had returned by 1889.[103] Coffee was in a relative slump between 1880 and 1886, with its price hitting bottom in 1882–1883, but had rebounded by the time of the regime's crisis. Providing two-thirds of the country's total exports—almost 5.6 million 132-pound sacks in 1889, compared to but 190,000 at the time of independence—the ascendant coffee producers and their mercantile associates wished a greater role in making national policy than the monarchy seemed able to provide. To them, Ouro Preto's reforms were considerably too little and substantially too late, particularly as the reforms didn't include federalism—perhaps the coffee producers' prime objective.[104] Thus, already serving in the last parliament of the empire were three Republican Party deputies elected from São Paulo in 1884, two of whom would go in a short time from spokesmen for a marginalized minority to become the nation's first civilian presidents: Prudente José de Morais Barros (1894–1898) and Manuel Ferraz de Campos Salles (1898–1902).

Even in present-day comparative perspective, the inflexibility of the Brazilian imperial regime during its last years should not be considered surprising. For as Samuel Huntington has generalized concerning the fate of centralized traditional monarchies: "Such political systems ordinarily have a high degree of legitimacy and effectiveness so long as political participation is limited. Their political institutions, however, remain rigid and fragile in the face of social change. They are unable to adapt to the emergence of middle-class groups into politics."[105] In basic outline, not only did the course of events in Brazil during the 1880s follow this general scenario, but developments after 1889 would also conform to the model Huntington put forth:

> The pattern of politics in the displacement of the traditional or oligarchical rule by military coup d'etat resembles in a more restrained and limited fashion the familiar Crane Brinton model of revolution. In the construction of the coalition of military and civilian elements to carry out the coup, it is usually necessary to stress those objectives which have the broadest appeal and to place at the head of the coup a moderate, conciliatory military leader who is able to acquire the confidence of all the groups participating in the coup and also has more ties than other members of those groups with the old regime.[106]

Contrary to the expectations of many of those who had worked hard to bring it about, the replacement of the monarchy by a republic would prove to be only a political regime change and would not usher in any sharp break in economic policy or new departures in the social realm. Indeed, 1888 rather than 1889 has come to be considered the structural turning point in Brazil's economic development, not for the abolition of slavery— which had largely been discounted in advance—but because of several provisions buried in the ensuing package of reforms. Hence, although these reforms failed to save the monarchy, for by this time its fate rested far more in the hands of military conspirators than with the São Paulo counter-elites, late imperial economic innovations provided much of the foundation for the new regime's policies. Moreover, immigration, already well underway— especially in São Paulo—and not any new program of the republican order would furnish the engine for social change. In fact, immigration had run at the rate of roughly 10,000 a year through the 1850s and 1860s, rising to a total of 194,000 for the 1870s and exploding to 454,000 total for the 1880s.[107]

The demise of the empire and birth of the Old Republic, aside from marking no sharp break in the economic and social spheres, did not even lead in the short run to a drastic change in the distribution of political power. Headed by a conservative militarist who had never believed in republicanism but was attracted to the prospect of ruling Brazil—even if this meant abandoning his initial preferences for a monarchy—the new government involved no rupture of basic political processes. Instead, after a short period of turmoil and strife, the old local and regional elites would reassert their control over all but the most urban and industrializing parts of the country. Thus, just as independence had kept Brazil under the Portuguese royal family, establishment of a republic maintained a representative of the old order in a very kinglike presidency. But first the nation would go through the heady experiences of thinking that a real revolution had taken place and of adopting a new framework of government to replace the centralized monarchical system at the national level.

3

The First Republic

The outlines of several significant features of present-day Brazil can already be discerned in the monarchical period, especially toward its end. The military had emerged to assume an arbiter role in the nation's political life, and the racial composition of the country was rapidly changing as European immigrants were flowing in even faster than had African slaves in earlier periods and Indians had declined to under 1.5 million by 1750, dropping to 800,000 by 1819, and numbering only a half million by 1867. Moreover, the economic heart of the country had shifted southward into São Paulo—whose 1890 population of just under 1.4 million would more than triple to 4.6 million by 1920, largely as a result of immigration. These similarities to present-day Brazil would become much more pronounced during the first decades of republican experience, and other features of modern Brazil would then arrive on the scene, including urbanization and industrialization. At the end of the empire only 11 percent of Brazilians lived in cities of over 10,000 population and industry accounted for only 10 percent of GDP.

As early as the transition to a republic and consolidation of the new regime—1889–1894 and 1895–1902, respectively—there are striking parallels to both the recent military governments and the post-1984 period. These parallels are most salient with respect to the quest for a suitable governmental framework and the establishment of competitive civilian political life, as much at the center of the political stage in the 1890s as in the 1980s and early 1990s. The most apparent differences between these two transitions have to do with sequence: The drafting of a new constitution came first in the earlier case and was followed by getting the military out of power, whereas agreement on a constitution and a form of political administration came after the military had relinquished power in the more recent experience.

The transition from monarchy to republic was initiated under military auspices, to be followed a few years later by transfer of power to civilians. The ensuing regime's demise came in 1930 at the hands of an alliance of military and civilian elements, with the preparatory moves coming from the former, and a new constitution was drawn up several years later. The present-day case again saw the transition initiated in great part by military elements from within the regime itself and, as in the 1930s, power was already in civilian hands before the task of working out a new constitution was undertaken.

In any event it is clear that the present process cannot be understood without a comprehension of not just the more recent 1930 and 1946 transitions, but also that of the 1890s, which so heavily shaped both of the subsequent transitions. Furthermore, as there are also important direct parallels between the actions of the first military presidents and those of the generals who came to power after 1964, a close examination of the initial stages of the Old Republic not only is in order, but is indispensable for an understanding of the present situation—and of what the future may hold. Indeed, with substitution of more current issues for those of slavery and monarchy, what Thomas Skidmore says of the political progressives of the late 1880s applies to their counterparts in the 1920s and 1930s, the mid-1940s, and the 1980s: "The lack of political support for the reformers' prime targets—slavery, the crown, the established Church—misled liberals into thinking that their victory over these enemies would bring the fundamental transformation which liberalism assumed to be the prerequisite for national progress."[1]

Transition Under Military Tutelage

The provisional government that found itself very suddenly in office on November 15, 1889, was not at all agreed upon what kind of a republic should be installed—as is often the case with alliances formed essentially to oust a regime. Historical Republicans, Jacobin younger army officers, and traditional notables seeking to salvage what they could from the sinking of the empire all vied for office and influence. Ideologically, the provisional government was marked by "great confusion" stemming from "poorly absorbed ideas or ideas absorbed in a partial and selective manner."[2] Not only did it contain some elements familiar from Brazil's 1822–1824 experience, but also this scene would be repeated in 1930, partially again in 1964, and in many respects in the mid-1980s. Moreover, the years after 1889 were also similar to the early 1830s regarding both a preoccupation with restorationist plots and the central governing role being filled by military figures.

Socioeconomic Conditions

The Brazil of 1889, if not drastically different from when the empire had entered into decay a decade earlier, had changed substantially since the onset of the Paraguayan War in 1865. Certainly the country had undergone a significant socioeconomic transformation since the heyday of the monarchy in the 1850s. Though Brazil was still essentially a rural and agrarian country, urbanization was beginning to gain momentum, albeit at least as much from immigration as from industrialization. Population had risen to over 14.3 million from 11.75 million in 1880, with over two-fifths of the population still living in the economically declining northeast region.[3] The country as a whole had grown by 2.5 percent annually between 1872 and 1890, but cities of over 50,000 had grown by 3.7 percent. Rio de Janeiro, which had reached 275,000 inhabitants by 1872, now had nearly doubled to 523,000; Salvador had risen from 129,000 to 174,000 in the same period, thus preserving its status as the country's second city. Although São Paulo had only increased from 31,000 to 65,000 over these years, it was about to begin its explosive growth, reaching 240,000 by the turn of the century and 580,000 by 1920. For the whole 1872–1900 period, São Paulo grew at 8.3 percent annually and Rio de Janeiro at 3.7 percent. During the 1890s the growth rate for all cities over 50,000—a category including Recife, Belém, and Porto Alegre—would be a high 6.8 percent yearly, compared to but 2.2 percent for the nation.[4]

Immigration was beginning to change the face of Brazilian society. The flow from Europe jumped from 55,000 in 1887 to over 132,000 in 1888 before dropping in 1889 and 1890 (to 65,000 and 107,000), but more than recovering with a record 215,000 in 1891. Yet this very immigration had— and would continue to have—a chilling effect upon the lot of the rural masses. For as immigrants filled the workforce needs of the developing coffee areas, the former slave population remained fixed just about where they were before emancipation. Moreover, the abundance of labor would help to keep wages down.[5] Although only 14 percent of school-age children were enrolled in classes, this was an improvement over the disgracefully low figure of 10 percent in 1878 and the almost pathetic situation of the early 1850s, when there were 61,700 primary school students in all Brazil and only 3,700 enrolled at the secondary level.[6] The literacy rates reflected this lack of educational opportunity, being 19 percent for males and just a little over 10 percent for females. Thus, the extension of suffrage to all literate males by the republican regime would not lead to anything like mass political participation.

The industrial "genesis" of Brazil occurred during the 1886–1894 period, which bridged the demise of the monarchy and the inception of the republican regime. Textile factories, flour mills, breweries, and light metallurgical works all increased substantially in number during the 1880s and accelerated after 1886 on the crest of expanded exports, which allowed for capital accumulation by the agro-exporting sector and its mercantile allies. Indeed, imports of industrial machinery in 1888–1889 had already risen 37 percent over the rate for the preceding four years, but grew another 30 percent in 1890 and exploded by 70 percent the following year.[7] Railroads, which had totalled just under 300 miles in 1864, reached 780 miles by a decade later and blossomed to 3,800 miles by the middle of the 1880s. By 1894 the rail network would nearly double to 6,900 miles, exceeding 9,950 miles by the turn of the century.[8] British capital played a major part in railroad expansion, through loans in the earlier period and subsequently by means of direct investments; by 1890 there were twenty-five British-connected railroad companies in Brazil.[9]

Even before 1888 the Brazilian government had modestly helped finance the agricultural loans needed to replace those that had been partially secured by slaves as collateral. But more important was the law enacted at the end of 1888 permitting banks to issue paper money. Though the issuance of paper money led to a spurt in inflation and rampant stock market speculation—largely due to euphoria based on the overly optimistic assumption that the establishment of the republic would automatically usher in an era of near-limitless growth—it also resulted in significant permanent development. (The parallel here is striking, in the first place with respect to the unrealistic euphoria that accompanied the 1985–1986 transition from military rule, and in the second place regarding the economic boom of the 1986 Cruzado Plan and the survival of many of the thousands of new enterprises launched in the middle of the somewhat longer period of irresponsible financial speculation that continued through the end of the decade.)

Although philosophically in favor of free trade, Ruy Barbosa, as the republic's first finance minister, implemented a moderate degree of protectionism, considering this politically crucial for consolidation of the new regime. At the same time, the tight-money policies of the late imperial years gave way to rapid implementation of the 1888 law, with banks emitting so much currency that the money supply almost doubled in 1890 and expanded again by just over 50 percent the next year.[10] However, Ruy Barbosa only lasted until January 1891 in this post, and his successor served but four months before giving way to Baron Henrique Pereira de Lucena in July, who lasted only to November.

Indeed, administrative discontinuity in this economic sphere was extreme, if not bordering on truly ridiculous, during the transition stage at the inception of the Old Republic, with nine finance ministers during the first seven years—a phenomenon that was virtually repeated during the period after 1984. Each of these individuals had distinct, occasionally quite personal, ideas concerning what should be done and especially how to go about doing it. Many times the government abandoned its basic goal of a balanced budget accompanied by monetary and exchange stability, most often in response to extraordinary military expenditures, regional natural disasters, or a drop in revenues from deterioration of the international market for Brazil's exports.[11]

Political Patterns

Shadows, if not reflections, of these economic and social changes could be discerned in the political realm. Although some planters had supported the Republican Party because the empire no longer offered an effective vehicle for protecting their interests, from November 1889 to 1894 control of the government was more in the hands of predominantly urban-oriented individuals, chiefly military officers, who took some steps inimical to the planters' interests.[12] The nation's center of gravity had moved away from the northeast (including Bahia) to the center-south, with Minas Gerais (still the country's most populous state at 3.12 million in 1890) occupying a pivotal position as link between the ex-heartland and the soon-to-be dominant region.[13] Yet for all these major changes, the most important factor shaping the course of national life would remain the military. In the view of Fernando H. Cardoso (who would subsequently come to be an important figure in the post-1984 transition to civilian rule), "at the level of real political organization the dismantling of the imperial institutions left a vacuum that, in the short run, could only be filled, as it was, by the great bureaucratic structure that came unglued from the Imperial State: the armed forces."[14]

In most ways the era inaugurated by the overthrow of the monarchy was more complex than the period that preceded it. In the view of Brazil's outstanding Marxist historian, the ouster of the emperor opened the way for a mixed bag of urban middle-class elements who came to take a leading role in political life behind a military vanguard: "power was assumed by a heterogeneous group of men, who by their formation and economic, social, and cultural relations found themselves umbilically tied to the urban middle classes, among which the military constituted, if not the numerically most important sector, at least the strongest and most homogeneous, and who, in addition, possessed weapons."[15]

The self-constituted "provisional government," without any elaborate appeal to principles of revolutionary legitimacy, not only abolished the monarchy but also dissolved the Chamber of Deputies and eliminated the life tenure of senators. Decree No. 1 of November 15, 1889, referred to the republican government as having been "proclaimed by the People, the Army, and the National Fleet." Manoel Deodoro da Fonseca assumed the title of "chief of the provisional government," with Benjamin Constant as war minister, historical Republican Quintino Bocaiúva of Rio de Janeiro occupying the Ministry of Foreign Relations, Ruy Barbosa of Bahia as the finance minister, and São Paulo's forty-eight-year-old Campos Salles holding down the Justice Ministry. As was to be the case again after the Revolution of 1930, military men were appointed to govern a majority of the states (with the notable exceptions of São Paulo under Prudente de Morais and Minas Gerais under an ex-monarchist, along with Rio de Janeiro, Bahia, and five minor states). Needless to say, many imposed governors were not well received. Also similar to the Vargas revolution and the 1964 coup, a special military-judicial commission was set up to deal with advocates of "false and subversive notions" (i.e., monarchists), and 1890 opened with a wave of promotions and forced retirements within the armed forces.[16]

As the military had brought about the foundation of the republic, they continued to dominate the provisional government.[17] Although Ruy Barbosa was named by Deodoro as the first vice-chief, Floriano Peixoto wielded greater real power from his post as adjutant general of the army. One of Deodoro's nephews became secretary general of the provisional government, Deodoro was proclaimed the *generalissimo*, plans were announced for doubling the size of the army, and civilian ministers were made honorary brigadier generals.

At least four major groups had collaborated in the Republican revolution and were represented in the provisional government: the historic Republicans, particularly strong in São Paulo; the young civilian revolutionaries; the positivist-oriented junior officers who followed Benjamin Constant; and the senior military who had joined or accepted the movement because of Deodoro's lead. Not surprisingly, differences over policy as well as personal rivalries soon emerged within the provisional regime—a situation very similar to those that developed after 1930 and in the wake of the 1964 regime change. War Minister Constant was a teacher at heart, and his secretary, Lieutenant Lauro Sodré, was considered by many observers as the major decision maker in the War Ministry. To resolve this problem, Constant was soon shunted aside into a newly created Ministry of Public Instruction and Communications, and fifty-one-year-old Marshal Floriano Peixoto assumed the post of war minister at the end of April 1890. Less than four months later Floriano Peixoto (who would soon come to be known as Floriano) replaced Ruy Barbosa as first vice-chief, the latter's position having been undercut by negative repercussions of his stringent financial reform measures.

With the government exercising a good deal of influence over the choice of candidates, more than one-fourth of the constituent assembly elected on September 15, 1890, was composed of military figures. Moreover, when the assembly met in November the administration presented the body with a complete draft constitution—one that had been drawn up and revised within a closed circle, very much as would be the case in 1966–1967 under the Castelo Branco government.[18] Just after the assembly had completed the task of organization and elected Prudente de Morais as its presiding officer, an assault by army officers on a monarchist newspaper provided the government's critics with an issue upon which to attack the quite "imperial" Deodoro.[19]

Benjamin Constant, who had been at odds with the chief executive, resigned in January and died shortly thereafter at only fifty-four years of age. Not only did the rest of the Cabinet resign on January 21, but several of them went so far as to mobilize opposition within the constituent assembly to Deodoro's bid for the presidency. In this they were supported by Admiral Custódio de Melo, the politically ambitious president of the Military Club, and by Floriano, who agreed to be a candidate against Deodoro. When Floriano's election appeared impossible, these groups shifted their support to Prudente de Morais. The replacement Cabinet installed by Deodoro under Baron Lucena contained very few traces of the historical republicans, leading future president Campos Salles and others to join the opposition. (There are interesting similarities between this situation and the changes in Cabinet composition that took place under Sarney during 1988–1989.)

The new constitution was promulgated on February 24, 1891, and the following day—amidst rumors that the army would revolt if a civilian was elected—Deodoro was chosen president by a vote of 129 to 97, with an overwhelming majority of the 55 military members casting their ballots for the marshal over the São Paulo civilian. Floriano, however, was elected vice-president by a larger majority (153–57). As constitutional president, Deodoro was in a substantially weaker position than he had enjoyed as chief of the provisional government. His prestige within the military establishment had been impaired, and he would have difficulty in dealing with a hostile Congress that was now his constitutional equal and was invested with most of the legislative powers he had been accustomed to exercising. In fact, Deodoro was soon embroiled in a controversy with the Congress similar to those that were later to feature the political crises of the 1946–1964 representative regime.[20]

Deodoro's Fall

Unable any longer to stand what he considered to be unjustified congressional obstruction and criticism, the thin-skinned president followed the advice of his conservative justice minister, Baron Lucena, and dissolved the legislature on November 3, 1891. Although Deodoro calculated correctly that the civilian politicians could not react effectively to his arbitrary move, particularly under the state of siege he imposed, he underestimated his opponents within the military establishment. A revolt broke out in Rio Grande do Sul that forced Júlio de Castilhos, the nineteenth chief executive in that turbulent state in two years, from power.

Aware of a plot against him on the part of naval officers encouraged by Floriano, on November 23 Deodoro ordered the arrest of leading conspirators, but Admiral Custódio de Melo succeeded in reaching the battleship *Riachuelo* and inciting most of the fleet to revolt. Though Navy Chief of Staff Luís Felipe Saldanha da Gama—soon to become involved in even more serious revolutionary activities himself—wished to resist the coup attempt, Deodoro recognized the weakness of his position and resigned rather than precipitate a violent clash. Ill and plagued by some guilt over the precedent he had set by closing Congress, Deodoro preferred to leave public life entirely during the short nine months that preceded his death. A man for whom democracy had at best a "confused meaning," Deodoro was fated to be "combatted on one side by the monarchists, on another by the paulista republicans, on a third front by the historic republicans suspicious of his apparently monarchist attitudes, and on all sides by the press, his power resting only upon some isolated civil elements and small military groups."[21]

"Consolidation" and Civil War

Those who overthrew Deodoro would fare little better at governing the infant republic and would narrowly avoid institutionalizing recourse to force and violence as a means for deciding the control of political power. Rivalry between the army and the navy was to perturb public order for much of the next decade until the admirals who had participated in the ouster of Deodoro were no longer on the scene. Meanwhile, in the absence of institutionalized channels for resolving intra- as well as inter-elite differences, the military would remain arbiter. In response, civilians would learn to overcome their differences sufficiently to engineer the departure from office of the "priests of the state"—as they called the more Jacobin military.

The Florianist Regime

Floriano Peixoto, although he came from a fairly similar background to that of Deodoro, was a very different type of individual. Devious where his predecessor was direct, impassive instead of emotional, distrustful rather than open, and cautiously calculating in contrast to Deodoro's impulsiveness, Floriano managed to arouse extremes of feeling.[22] Though Deodoro had, despite his personal power proclivities, "established" the republic, Floriano was faced with the task of consolidating the new regime. Caught between substantial monarchical sentiment in the navy and continued support on the part of some officers for the deposed president, and impelled as well by his own authoritarian tendencies, Floriano was far from a democratic executive.

He immediately fomented a series of military interventions (*derrubadas*) in the political life of the states to oust all provincial presidents who had supported Deodoro on November 3, thus contributing to the local and regional political strife that was to characterize many of these states for at least another generation. Indeed, the use of federal military forces to influence local power struggles would be more the rule than the exception throughout the Old Republic (1889–1930).

With the War and Navy Ministries in the hands of the two major anti-Deodoro plotters, General José Simeão de Oliveira and Admiral Custódio de Melo, Floriano was able to prevail in his struggle with civilian elements in Congress who argued the need for a direct presidential election. In the face of the constitutional requirement in this respect, Floriano pointed to the exception made for the "initial presidential period," which would not expire until 1894, and maintained the legal fiction of being the "vice-president in exercise of the presidency" rather than acknowledging that he was Brazil's second president. Thus, when in April 1892 a group of thirteen generals and admirals issued a manifesto calling for an immediate election, Floriano responded by forcing them all into involuntary retirement. This was quickly followed by the exiling of a number of Deodoro's supporters to the Amazon region.

The first in a series of military uprisings against Floriano's regime had erupted as early as December 1891, when a group of nearly seventy sailors mutinied against continuing bad conditions and harsh discipline (a foretaste of the 1910 "Revolt of the Lash"). Imprisoned at a fort in Rio de Janeiro harbor, they seized control of it the following month.[23] Demanding the return of Deodoro to power, they held out for nearly forty-eight hours against four battleships and two cruisers.

This was only the prelude to Floriano's difficulties with the navy. Custódio de Melo considered himself, as the "father" of the November 23 coup, to have virtually coequal authority with Floriano, and he manifested a tendency to interfere in government affairs far beyond the normal scope of navy minister or president of the Military Club. Moreover, the situation in Rio Grande do Sul was to afford de Melo an opportunity to make a bid to replace Floriano. Clearly the ambitious admiral's taste for power was much greater than Floriano could accommodate without running the risk of becoming a secondary figure in his own government.

Júlio de Castilhos, the twenty-nine-year-old Gaúcho Republican positivist who had been ousted from office by a coalition headed by long-time Liberal Senator Gaspar da Silveira Martins, returned to power in Rio Grande do Sul through a coup in July 1892. The newly founded Federalist Party, which embraced Castilho's political enemies (known locally as the "Maragatos"), was strongly in favor of a parliamentary form of government, which placed the group in potential conflict with Floriano. Hence the strongman preferred to forgive Castilhos and his "Chimangos" for their earlier support of Deodoro rather than see Silveira Martins, an old monarchist with separatist inclinations, triumph in that key state.

When hostilities broke out in February 1893, some army units aided the insurgent Federalists, while a larger number cooperated with the Republicans' state forces and party militia.[24] Floriano made his position clear when he sent his war minister to Porto Alegre to help direct the military campaign against the Federalists. After 4,500 Republicans trounced 6,000 Federalists at Alegrete on May 3, the latter were reduced to hit-and-run guerrilla raids.

The Navy in Revolt

Yet Floriano could take little pleasure from this success, as his opponents in the navy chose this juncture to mount a major threat to his government and even to the republican regime. Custódio de Melo, sympathetic to the Gaúcho Federalists, broke openly with Floriano in late April, and the most respected admiral, Saldanha da Gama, refused to accept the proffered ministry. The new president of the Military Club, Admiral Eduardo Wandenkolk, rose in arms against the "Iron Marshal." Another invasion from Uruguay by the Federalist exiles was followed on September 6 by a major revolt of the fleet.

De Melo was disappointed in his belief that the threat of the heavy guns of the battleships would force Floriano to quit—as Deodoro had less than two years before. As the politically more astute Saldanha da Gama had rightly observed, the current dictator was a much tougher individual than his older and seriously ill predecessor had been. Deprived of possible military support by his emphasis upon the government's alleged favoritism for the army, Custódio failed to develop a viable strategy once the European and U.S. naval contingents in Rio de Janeiro harbor forbade bombardment of the city (justified under the international rules of the day by the right of these countries to protect their nationals). Admiral Saldanha da Gama, a legalist by inclination, had hoped to keep the cadets of the naval academy— in whom he saw the best hope for the nation's future—from becoming involved in the political struggle. Eventually, however, his strongly developed sense of loyalty to the navy and his fellow officers overcame his reluctance, and he joined the revolt.[25]

With Custódio having taken some ships to Santa Catarina in December, Saldanha commanded the resistance in Rio de Janeiro until the arrival in

March 1894 of a new legalist squadron of ships hurriedly purchased in Europe made him throw in the towel. Meanwhile Custódio had joined forces with the Federalists to capture Paraná, but with Saldanha's capitulation freeing large contingents of government troops for action in the south, the rebels had to abandon plans for an invasion of São Paulo and retreat back into Rio Grande do Sul. Custódio's flagship was lost in action in mid-April, and three days later Colonel Moreira César's troops captured the provisional government in Santa Catarina and summarily executed a large number of distinguished monarchical figures. When Custódio's ships shortly thereafter sought asylum in Buenos Aires, the fate of the revolt was sealed—although resistance on the land continued until mid-1895. Of lasting importance was the fact that the navy was finished as a major political factor.

What Kind of Military? The Quest for a Viable Role

The ideas and attitudes that were to both motivate action and divide opinion among the military for the next seven decades can be found articulated within the officer corps of the army during this turbulent five years of military rule that initiated the republic. While only a submerged minority favored strict legalism and complete abstention from political involvement, many others came to realize the need for internal restraints, if not external limits, upon the armed forces' participation in governmental affairs. As was to be the case down at least to 1964, the majority of the officer corps combined some notion of the military having a special responsibility for safeguarding the nation's basic institutions with a general orientation toward respect for legitimately constituted authority—unless that authority did something to forfeit this respect. In ambiguous situations or in crises in which these principles seemed to be in conflict, the position assumed by their hierarchical superior and the particular way in which the issue was posed would heavily influence the decisions of these officers.

Most officers felt comfortable with one variation or another of the idea that the armed forces, by the act of having established the Federal Republic, had thus assumed the role of moderating power, which previously had been the emperor's. A national institution that viewed itself as standing above the partisan struggle, the military would be prepared to intervene in times of crisis or breakdown of representative processes essential for the "salvation of the Republic."[26]

Tension and misunderstanding between the *farda* and the *casaca* (the uniformed officers and the frock-coated politicians) went back even beyond the "military question" of the 1880s. Just as many civilians felt that the military were unsuited and unprepared to run the country, a significant current within the armed forces doubted the civilians' ability to do so in a patriotic and disinterested manner. Under Benjamin Constant's teaching in the military academy, a whole subgeneration had been exposed to the idea that they should not blindly obey the government. They were not, of course, all equally receptive to these doctrines, as they came from rather diverse social backgrounds—sons of military families continuing in their

fathers' profession, middle- and lower middle-class youth for whom the
chance for an education mattered more than the prospect of a military
career, and even a few mulattoes seeking social acceptance and upward
mobility, along with some representatives of the upper bourgeoisie and
landowning families.

One attitude common among the officer corps was that the military
establishment was too small and its budget too niggardly. Even when they
won substantial pay raises and the troop level was doubled, the army officers
felt that these advances only made up for neglect under the empire, while
many civilians viewed the same measures as an unnecessary burden on
government finances. Moreover, occupation by officers of a wide range of
posts previously held by civilians gave rise to no small amount of resentment.
(Much the same situation would come to prevail after 1964.)

As the 1890s wore on, the constitutionalist reaction to twenty years of
military involvement in politics and a half-decade of military rule spread
to some elements of the armed forces. These elements came to feel that,
in this process of deep politicization of the military, professionalism had
suffered, unity had been sacrificed, and the ability to act as the moderating
power had been compromised. Thus, as would again be the case by the
late 1970s, such elements began to consider the advisability of disengaging
from the direct control of government. As the end of Floriano's term
approached, within the Military Club itself strong sentiment was expressed
in favor of focus upon purely military questions to the complete exclusion
of politics in order that the armed forces might "reacquire its solidarity."[27]

Transition to Civilian Rule

Although the naval revolt and protracted civil war could not directly
dislodge Floriano, they did guarantee that he would leave office at the end
of his term rather than find a means for continuing in power. For while
the chief executive was preoccupied with the survival of his government
through suppressing the strife that had cost the nation perhaps 10,000 lives,
the São Paulo civilian elites were able to establish a basis for the election
to the presidency of one of their spokesmen. To do this they had first to
prove invaluable to Floriano—both by furnishing state troops to keep the
rebels bottled up in the south and by leading the government's support in
Congress.

The Ruling Elites

Yet the new political order inaugurated by the civilian elites would turn
out to be almost as distant from a true parliamentary democracy as was
the military interregnum. In the end much of the patriarchal society was
preserved, and local and regional oligarchies not only survived, but actually
found their hand strengthened—at least at home—against the new political
forces that had begun to challenge their domination during the twilight
years of the empire. A major share of the responsibility for these retrograde

developments would lie with the very São Paulo elites who would establish civilian control of the government in 1894. But the survival of *coronelismo* would be rooted in the fact that the foundation of the republic, as with independence two-thirds of a century earlier, did not change the basic facts of life in the traditional rural areas, especially in the northeast and north. There, even as the old water- or animal-powered *engenho* (traditional sugar plantation) began to give way to the larger-scale steam-run *usina* (mechanized sugar mill), the societal props of the old political system remained firm. The rural patriarchal society had produced an authoritarian paternalism that provided a continuing basis for patrimonial politics.[28]

Co-optation of the middle sectors was the urban counterpart of the maintenance of rural political machines. Largely the product of the substantial urbanization that preceded significant industrialization, the Brazilian middle class during the nineteenth century exceeded the country's limited needs for technical and administrative personnel. Though a minority of its members found a career in the armed forces, most bargained with the ruling stratum of plantation owners and export-import merchants for bureaucratic positions in exchange for the former providing political support to the latter. This style of clientelistic politics existed at all levels as "pacts of mutual interest" were formed in the municipalities and then progressed to the provincial capitals and the federal bureaucracy.

Although it had roots in the empire, this system did not fully flourish until the establishment of a republic had demonstrated the reality of the threat to the dominant elite. With the *cartorial* state functioning as both the product of clientelistic politics and the vehicle for the perpetuation of those politics, the oligarchy was able to stage a strong and rapid political comeback within a few years after the elimination of the monarchy to which it had appeared to be wed.[29]

At the beginning of the republic, the São Paulo elites had been most concerned over influencing economic policy. Closest to their hearts—and to their wallets—was the issue of exchange rates and money supply. Devaluation served to protect the income of the coffee producers, as their sales were overwhelmingly for export. At the same time, however, devaluation caused inflation and fed government budget deficits, for depreciation of the exchange rates made imports more expensive and reduced federal government revenues, which as late as 1897 still depended for over 73 percent of their total on taxes on imports.

Moreover, a drop in tax receipts generally led to renewed foreign borrowing with a consequent rise in the cost of servicing the increased foreign debt, which already required nearly all the hard-to-come-by trade surplus. In 1888 Brazil had contracted a loan of nearly £6.3 million, followed by one of just over £19.8 million the following year. (Thus, the problem of foreign debt and of generating an excess of exports over imports to cover interest and repayment of that debt, so salient in the 1980s, is a matter with which Brazil has had to grapple repeatedly over the span of a full century.)

In his short stint as the republic's first finance minister, Ruy Barbosa had reversed the generally tight money policies of the last eleven years of the monarchy as well as raised tariffs to aid nascent industries. Hence money in circulation expanded nearly 125 percent from 1889 to 1891, with a wide variety of banks issuing paper currency as well as extending agricultural credit. This heavy inflationary pressure was combined with a flood of new stock offerings as a vast array of enterprises organized under the new and more liberal corporation law sought to raise capital. This wild speculative burst, labeled "financial madness" by a leading Brazilian scholar—and known in Brazil as the Encilhamento—ended in late 1891 with a stock market crash and a spectacular wave of bankruptcies.[30]

As most of the new companies had sought—and received—credit, subsidies, concessions, and favors from the government, the subsequent failure of those companies reflected poorly on the new and inexperienced public officials. The crisis of overextended firms was complicated by a nearly 50 percent drop in the exchange rate with the British pound between 1890 and 1892, which caught those who had ordered imported equipment on the wrong foot. Thus, the hangover came just as Floriano replaced Deodoro, and the constitution of 1891 was promulgated in a climate of traumatic economic crisis (which far surpassed that reigning at the launching of the 1988 constitution).

As early as January 1891 Ruy Barbosa's successor in the Finance Ministry attempted to adopt more orthodox fiscal and monetary policies, but these proved unable to stem the inflationary tide. Indeed, prices doubled between 1889 and 1894, with salaries lagging far behind. (As is by now apparent, inflation is another problem with a long history of perturbing the Brazilian economy and providing serious headaches for national policy makers.) With coffee and rubber prices up, the third finance minister of 1891, Baron Henrique Pereira de Lucena, proposed to raise the exchange rate, but he fell from office with Deodoro's ouster.

The São Paulo coffee producers, who had been increasingly in opposition, now participated fully in Floriano's government. With their support, the Bank of Brazil and the Bank of the Republic of Brazil were established at the end of 1892, with the latter authorized to provide financial aid to troubled industries. Moreover, Congress frequently extended tariff exemptions on the imports of selected companies. Having managed to keep control of their provincial government even during the days immediately after the overthrow of the empire, the São Paulo elites had so far elected the presiding officer of the constituent assembly, but had failed to get him in as president. Still, they had benefitted from Deodoro's ouster.

Civilian and Constitutional—Not Democratic

Concerned with maintaining financial stability, obtaining foreign credits, and sustaining European immigration, the São Paulo elites supported Floriano as the best military hope for peace and internal tranquility. With Prudente de Morais as head of the Senate, Bernardino José de Campos presiding over the Chamber, and Rodrigues Alves initially serving as finance minister, the Paulista coffee growers and businessmen were well placed within the government. Yet they did their best to take advantage of Floriano's difficulties, in order to gain his approval of their preferred policies. Beyond this, their goal was a civilian government headed by one of their experienced statesmen-administrators with the armed forces back in the barracks.[31]

Leaving as little as possible to chance, first Prudente de Morais and then Bernardino de Campos as head of São Paulo's provincial government had built up the permanent state police from fewer than 500 to a disciplined and well-armed force of over 3,000 men.[32] (The São Paulo "Força Pública" would prove to be a potent factor in the crises of the 1920s and 1930s, and it would retain some influence as a power factor as late as the 1964 regime change.)

Backed by the Minas Gerais government of Afonso Pena, São Paulo's Francisco Glicério organized a catchall, progovernment Federal Republican Party (PRF), ostensibly to provide the administration with a congressional majority, but also with an eye to use the new party as a vehicle to implement civilian dominance in national politics.[33] The prospects of the PRF in this regard were strengthened by the fact that many civilians from other states were beginning to question the armed forces' assumption of the right to interfere in all spheres of political life and to infringe civil liberties in the name of national security or military honor. Authoritarian overreaction to the monarchist threat served to increase opposition to the very real prospect of continued military rule once the danger to the republican regime and the territorial integrity of the country had been brought under control. (The monarchist threat was used by the government during the 1890s very much as the Communist issue would be used in the 1960s.)

Under these increasingly favorable circumstances, the civilian supporters of the government successfully pressed Floriano in spite of the continuing civil war to hold presidential elections—which he had postponed from the preceding October—on March 1, 1894. With the rebels on the offensive in the south and Saldanha's fleet still in control of Rio de Janeiro's harbor, the government could ill afford to alienate the two largest and richest provinces. Although Floriano tried to launch both military and civilian candidates to head off election of Prudente de Morais, he reluctantly accepted the victory of the PRF nominee, who received nearly 277,000 votes compared to only 38,000 for Afonso Augusto Moreira Pena (who would get his chance to be president a dozen years later). How limited participation still was is reflected by the mere 7,857 votes cast in Rio de Janeiro (this figure rose to just over 13,000 in the 1896 congressional balloting).

Divisions within the armed forces and Floriano's own poor health—which would lead to his death within eight months—appear to have influenced the president's decision to heed the will of the electorate more than did any reverence for constitutional procedures.[34] Indeed, Floriano had earlier pointedly vetoed a provision of the election law that would have made him ineligible for a full term as his own successor.

The São Paulo Dynasty, 1894–1906

Beginning with the inauguration of Prudente José de Morais Barros (known as Prudente de Morais), representatives of the São Paulo elites occupied the presidency for twelve consecutive years. Yet, although it was not apparent to the contemporary observer—whose attention was generally drawn to the political debates in Congress and the articulate expression of views by representatives of civilian interest groups as carried in the generally free, if conservatively oriented, press—the armed forces continued to exert important influence on national political life even after relinquishing direct control of government. Moreover, the oligarchical-clientelistic basis of politics in the rural areas, where the great mass of the population still lived, remained much as it had long been.

As for the military, because its predominant orientation was essentially centrist—neither clearly in support of those opposing all change nor in favor of the still weak radical forces in Brazilian society—it tended to blend in with the political currents of the day. Not faced with a government viewed by a large proportion of officers as hostile to their interpretation of basic national interests or to the well-being of their institution, the armed forces did not appear to be as aggressively interventionist as in many Hispanic American countries at the time. But much of their image as largely above politics or as reasonably disinterested watchdogs of national welfare was a result of the fact that there was no real competition in Brazil between national parties. The dominant coalition of state elite groupings, headed by São Paulo and Minas Gerais with Rio Grande do Sul, Rio de Janeiro, and Bahia playing supporting roles, would generally select the next president with little dissent. When the most powerful state machines fell in line behind a choice that was generally heavily influenced by both the incumbent president and important financial interests, the lesser provinces were left with little alternative but to adhere.

But on those few occasions when a real contest seemed possible, the military took an active part in either opening up or closing down the options. In 1894 and 1898 a group of military figures who had enjoyed substantial influence in the administration of Marshal Floriano opposed the idea of civilian rule and put forth a symbolic candidate from their own ranks. In 1904 they attempted a revolt and in 1910 would impose their views on the government, making Marshal Hermes da Fonseca the official candidate and evening up the number of civilian and military presidents at three each. Throughout this period military figures were actively involved in the political life of the provinces, albeit more often behind the scenes than in the spotlight. Hence it is a mistake to see 1894 as a major watershed, rather than as one more change that failed to result in a fundamental transformation.

Prudente and the Crushing of Popular Movements

Under the circumstances, the government of Prudente de Morais enjoyed considerable success in dealing with the military.[35] Cautious, persistent, tenacious, and, above all, experienced, the new chief executive was aided by the cessation of hostilities in mid-1895. Yet Júlio de Castilhos soon assumed an opposition stance, and Vice-President Manuel Vitorino (of Bahia) imprudently dismissed Prudente's Cabinet while temporarily filling the presidential post from late 1896 to March 1897. Both events were, however, political rather than military crises, as Prudente made the most of divisions within the armed forces to neutralize any potential threat by the army.

Yet to many of Floriano's supporters this taciturn representative of the regional São Paulo aristocracy seemed to represent reactionary interests, while others in the military establishment were concerned by his efforts to reduce its size and cost—both were serious problems because Floriano had irresponsibly promoted in excess of 1,500 officers shortly before leaving office. The relative freedom granted to monarchist groups, contrasted to their stern repression under the military presidents, made Prudente suspect in the eyes of exalted Republicans and militant military Jacobins.

The tragic affair of Canudos soon provided these elements with an opportunity to place renewed pressure upon Prudente and to exploit the weaknesses of his position. Only in an atmosphere of extreme political passions could the existence of a small colony of lower-class religious fanatics in the backlands of Bahia be seen as a monarchist plot and a threat to the existence of the republic. Yet cynical manipulation of this situation to create a politico-military crisis was also a necessary factor.[36]

Antônio Conselheiro, a primitive mystic, and his followers had founded a community in an inaccessible spot buried far in the interior of Bahia. When a police detachment sent to break up this "lawless" gathering of the forgotten and alienated was bloodily repulsed, provincial president Luíz Viana sent in a 100-man punitive expedition of state troops mixed with a small army detachment. Alarmed and disoriented by the destruction of this column in November 1896, Viana appealed to his predecessor, Manuel Vitorino, who as vice-president was temporarily in control of the government while Prudente was convalescing from an operation. A federal-state force of nearly 550 men under Major Febrônio de Britto was dispatched in January 1897, only to be decimated by the determined insurgents even before the force reached the rebel encampment. With this rough equivalent of Custer's last stand, a relatively minor local problem had escalated into a critical national issue.

Because the residents of Canudos were primitive Catholics who felt the republic was both atheistic—for its institution of civil marriage—and Masonic (devout Catholics at this time still viewed Masons as subversive), the belief soon spread widely in the capital that this was a monarchical conspiracy supported with arms and money from abroad. Bahian officials and embarrassed army spokesmen found this possibility to be a convenient way to explain their inability to defeat the mob they had so grossly underestimated. So amidst great public uproar a new expedition was entrusted to Colonel Antônio Moreira César, who just a few years earlier had carried out the bloody repression of the navy-federalist provisional government in Santa

Catarina. The country was dumbfounded when, in mid-March 1897, this force of 1,300 trained troops accompanied by artillery was all but wiped out and its commander killed.

Abruptly returning to the presidency, Prudente found himself in a perilous political situation. Rioting Jacobins in Rio de Janeiro murdered the owner of pro-monarchist newspapers, and the viscount of Ouro Preto and his son narrowly escaped a similar fate. Then on May 26 the military academy mutinied, providing the president with an opportunity to take vigorous action to restore public order. Yet the cost was high, involving a complete break with the strongest leader in Congress, Glicério, and a never-to-be-healed split within the PRF. Indeed, by this point Prudente had aligned himself with political forces who had supported Deodoro rather than with the original Florianistas.

Aware that the various military factions, whose differences and rivalries had allowed him to govern, might unite now that the army's very reputation was on the line at Canudos, the president appointed Marshal Machado Bittencourt as war minister and sent him into the field to support a new expedition under General Artur Oscar de Andrada Guimarães. Many Florianist officers were hoping for a dramatically rapid victory that would return Andrada Guimarães to Rio de Janeiro as the savior of the republic from the monarchist peril, but this experienced officer was not going to become the victim of rashness as his predecessors had. Realizing that Canudos now had all the arms and equipment taken from the previous expeditions, he moved methodically to lay siege to the fortified shantytown, which had grown to a city of some 25,000 inhabitants. His original force of more than 4,000 troops was substantially reinforced until it totalled 10,000 men under five generals. On October 5, after a siege of over three months, Canudos was completely demolished and its defenders annihilated. Thus, with a total loss of some 5,000 on the government side and at least 15,000 humble hillbillies, the affair was ended.[37]

Owing to a further tragic turn of events, what started out as a grave threat to the civilian government ended up reinforcing the president. At a review of the victorious troops, a soldier shouting "Viva Floriano" attempted to kill Prudente, but the war minister took the fatal knife blow instead. Bolstered by public sympathy, Prudente closed down the Military Club, while sobered and chastened army officers reevaluated the dangers of getting the institution embroiled in partisan politics. Discredited by investigations that implicated them in the assassination conspiracy, Vitorino and Glicério posed no further problem. Thus, the election of fifty-seven-year-old São Paulo chief executive Manuel Ferraz de Campos Salles as Brazil's second successive civilian president took place in an atmosphere of comparative calm aided by the candidate's conciliatory statements. The opposition standard-bearer, again 1889 military activist Lauro Sodré, was never really in the race as Florianism reached its ebb. Yet Prudente did not completely have his way, for he would have preferred Bernardino de Campos.

Campos Salles and "Politics of the Governors"

The first direct presidential election in Brazil had taken place under a state of siege and without any balloting in the three southernmost states, where civil war was still raging. In an atmosphere of relative internal peace four years later, Campos Salles received just over 420,000 votes to fewer than 39,000 for his opponent—giving him nearly 91 percent of the votes cast.[38] Because under the constitution all literate males over twenty-one were eligible to vote, this increase in the number of votes cast (compared with the 329,000 votes counted four years earlier) was much less dramatic than most of the middle-class and military advocates of republicanism had expected.

Described as "moderate, opportunist, and vigilant against the excesses of the multitude," the new president was a successful large-scale agriculturalist. Though Campos Salles was often considered the restorer of Brazil's shattered finances and credit, Francisco de Assis Barbosa views him instead as the "consolidator of Brazil's foreign debt."[39] Reversing the policy of his predecessors, Campos Salles ceased to be preoccupied with maintaining his supporters in power at the provincial level, preferring instead to accept whoever won the power struggle in each state as long as their representatives in Congress lent him their support. Thus under the so-called politics of the governors, electoral fraud and coercion by state political machines were tolerated, and victories won by opponents of these machines were not recognized by the Chamber of Deputies group empowered to review election results.

In line with allowing a great deal of de facto local autonomy in exchange for political support—which involved also patronage and services in return for legislative votes—the governors usually extended a similar relationship to local elites as the president did to them. This strengthened the municipal level as a basic political unit, but in such a way as to reinforce the hold of the regional oligarchies and local clientelistic machines. For state power needed votes, and private economic power, with its patron-client leverage, was in the best position to supply this.

Hence in the context of insufficient political institutionalization and the persistence of a traditional sociopolitical order in the rural areas that made up most of the country, the introduction of formal democracy through the extension of the franchise worked not so much for change as to bolster the entrenched elites.[40] There was in fact a reestablishment of the duality between centralized power over national matters in the hands of the federal executive and local autonomy, often bordering on license, in "lesser" matters—which often had life-or-death import to the bulk of the population.

Under these circumstances, the military elements who had been set back by the virtual counter-revolution implicit in the Paulista consolidation of power concentrated on attempts to hold their eroding positions at the provincial level. They met with greatest success on the periphery of the country, where they could still use army influence over federal machinery to enhance their power in what traditionally had been local rivalries. Undercut by the political tactics of Campos Salles, particularly as those tactics were employed by a successor they viewed less favorably, the military "modernizers" would subsequently begin to concentrate on regaining control of the central government.

Ingenious as it appeared at the time, Campos Salles's effort to enable the president to stay above the disputes of shifting factions that had little programmatic content only bought temporary equilibrium at the expense of future crises. Because it virtually eliminated any possibility of peaceful alternation at the state level, it set up tensions that would burst through after 1910. Meanwhile, Campos Salles by 1901 had to deal with the opposition of Vice-President Francisco de Assis Rosa e Silva, former president Prudente de Morais, and PRF head Francisco Glicério. Rooted itself in the absence of any real national political parties, the president's policy had the effect of further weakening the feeble structures of this type that did exist. A chaotic scene of shifting factional alliances predominated, based on the interplay of center-state, interstate, and intrastate maneuvering—a somewhat more rudimentary version of what again prevailed in 1985–1989.

Rodrigues Alves—An Aristocrat Versus the Arbiters

In this environment of domestic peace—despite economic troubles—combined with manipulable political competition, Campos Salles chose for his successor the incumbent president of São Paulo, fifty-four-year-old Francisco de Paula Rodrigues Alves. Having served as finance minister in both the Floriano and Prudente Cabinets (nine months in the first instance and two years in the second), Rodrigues Alves was in many ways admirably prepared for the presidency, but he had to be forced down the throats of historical Republicans. For Rodrigues Alves was an ex-monarchist who had been one of the youngest to be raised to the high position of imperial counselor. His election by over 592,000 to less than 43,000 for Quintino Bocaiúva (a historical and relatively Jacobin Republican from Rio de Janeiro) showed that the system of succession by agreement among the heads of key states was working smoothly. In office Rodrigues Alves personified the shift away from the modest reform and pro-industrialization orientation of Floriano's government toward a "condominium of Conservative oligarchies."[41] Given these circumstances, it is not surprising that Rodrigues Alves would not be as fortunate as his predecessor in avoiding trouble with the military.

At the midpoint of his term Rodrigues Alves was faced with a revolt triggered by a controversy over compulsory smallpox vaccination, but actually involving a reassertion of Florianist views.[42] Proponents of a positivist military dictatorship, headed by senator and lieutenant colonel Lauro Sodré (a chronic presidential aspirant whose support within the army would gain him the Military Club presidency in 1906), sought to escalate popular dissatisfaction into a coup. The November 1904 military academy uprising was put down, and the firmness shown by General Hermes da Fonseca would earn him the post of war minister in the next administration—thus starting him on the road to the presidency. (Among the rebelling cadets were three who would play major roles in events over the next half century: Eurico Gaspar Dutra, Odylio Denys, and Bertholdo Klinger.)

In a move that was to have decisive implications for the future, all cadets were temporarily transferred to Rio Grande do Sul, where they came in close contact with young Gaúcho student politicians who were subsequently to organize the 1930 Revolution. Thus, Getúlio Vargas and João Neves da Fontoura were given an opportunity to forge close ties with Dutra and Pedro Aurélio de Góes Monteiro even before these future heirs to the role of Caxias had gotten a start on their military careers.[43] Significantly, the government proceeded immediately after the 1904 revolt to contract for the construction of a modern fleet including three new battleships, three heavy cruisers, and six speedy destroyers—as the navy's past sins were forgiven by an essentially conservative government inclined to build up the more aristocratic branch of the armed forces. (Only in 1911 would the academy be reopened in a Rio de Janeiro suburb, where it remained until 1944.)

Economy and Society in the New Century

Economically and, to a lesser extent, socially as well, Brazil had moved ahead during these dozen years of at least relative peace and stability. Population at the turn of the century had passed 17 million and, despite the civil war and economic ups and downs, the 1890s saw immigration rise sharply to over 1.2 million, some 690,000 of whom came from Italy, followed by 113,000 Germans. Indeed, in 1900 a full 92 percent of industrial workers in São Paulo were immigrants, 81 percent of them Italians.[44] Of 450,000 immigrants between 1884 and 1890, some 158,000 had come to São Paulo— a figure that grew to 733,000 during the 1891–1900 decade. Factory workers by 1900 totalled 160,000, with life expectancy having risen slightly to 19.4 years. GDP, which had grown only 16 percent from 1889 through 1899— well behind population growth—climbed by 4.2 percent a year during the 1900–1909 period; from 1898 through 1910 coffee accounted for 52.7 percent of exports and rubber rose to 25.7 percent.[45]

Coffee production exploded during the early years of the republic, doubling from 5.55 million sacks in the 1890–1891 harvest to 11.37 million by 1900–1901, with the next crop reaching a grossly excessive (in terms of international demand) 16.27 million sacks. This led to accumulation of carryover stocks of harvested coffee that by 1905 amounted to 11 million sacks—roughly 70 percent of annual world consumption. Indeed, Brazil's share of global coffee production had neared 57 percent in the 1880s, approached 60 percent in the 1890–1898 period, jumped to almost 67 percent for the rest of that decade, and soared to over 75 percent in the 1900–1904 period.

On the policy side, the basic trend of the three Paulista presidents was toward tighter monetary policies and balanced budgets, although the attempt to balance the budget was fairly frequently undercut by military expenditures—such as those incurred for the Canudos campaign—and the burden of debt service. Thus, in the face of a sharp fall in coffee prices at the end of 1896, the Prudente government cancelled the right of banks to issue currency. As coffee prices continued to drop, in part in response to the continuing rise in Brazil's production, devaluation of the exchange rate was stepped up, causing imports to fall and bringing a consequent reduction in government revenues. This deteriorating situation led in June 1898 to the need for a negotiated debt moratorium. All payments on the existing foreign debt were suspended for thirteen years, with the creditors insisting in return upon both elimination of the budget deficit and withdrawal from circulation of currency equal to the funding loan.[46]

Because the 1891 constitution had permitted provinces and even municipalities to contract foreign debt, and they had quickly abused the privilege, the external debt situation had indeed become critical. Much of the money borrowed had gone not for productive investment, but rather to cover government budget deficits—a situation not at all unlike the one that would prevail in the 1970s and 1980s. By 1898 the total owed by Brazil had risen 53 percent since the founding of the republic, and 53 percent of all federal government expenditures went to service the debt. Moreover, government spending had come to be nearly double its revenues, so very substantial emissions of money were made with some regularity.

The Campos Salles years were marked by deflation and recession as the administration strove to put the country's financial house in order. In this light domestic industry was viewed as largely artificial and requiring excessive exchange devaluations and tariff protection. The answer of these advocates of "sound" rather than expansionist policies was to revalue Brazil's currency upward, run up a big trade surplus in 1900—as coffee prices rose once more—and take out a major new loan in 1901 to cover the phasing out of a number of old railroad construction contracts. Yet these policies helped feed a bank panic in September 1900 in which half of the country's lending institutions went under. This resulted in a growing national consensus favoring government intervention in the production of coffee, as the protection of the income of coffee producers through a consistent policy of exchange devaluation was gone. The administration could point with pride to the fact that the cost of living had actually dropped nearly 30 percent between 1898 and 1902—in stark contrast with the 20 percent average annual rise during the Deodoro-Floriano years and a slow but steady upward trend under Prudente.[47]

The Rodrigues Alves years marked the beginning of the economic *reerguimento*, which was characterized by very tight monetary policies whose recessive effects were offset by greatly amplified public works programs stressing rail and port facilities along with sewer and water systems for the capital city—which by now boasted a population exceeding 800,000. In 1905 and 1906 Brazilian money rose in value by nearly 25 percent relative to the British pound, a development that would impact heavily upon Brazil's exports, which were still mostly coffee (at 67.6 percent for the 1889–1897 period) and rubber (some 11.8 percent over the same span).

In this crisis context, the presidents of São Paulo, Minas Gerais, and Rio de Janeiro met in February 1906 at Taubaté, coming up with a scheme to stabilize coffee prices through a pact involving setting of minimum prices, creation of a stabilization fund, and prevention of additional plantings. This package was to be financed by a £15 million loan to be contracted by São Paulo and required federal government participation through both the president's formal blessing and establishment of a Caixa de Conversão to deal with exchange rates.[48]

Although the policies embodied in the Taubaté Agreement conflicted with the president's orthodox financial ideas, he was after all a coffee planter himself, and he dutifully submitted the pact to Congress, where it gained approval at the end of July. By this time, however, Rodrigues Alves was already a lame duck, as a new chief executive had been elected in March— Afonso Augusto Moreira Pena of Minas Gerais—thus ending the twelve-year hold of São Paulo on the federal presidency. The early frontrunner had in fact been Paulista Bernardino de Campos, but his reluctance to support a coffee valorization program centering on a return to regular devaluation of the exchange rate led the politically decisive coffee interests to switch their support to Pena, who was amenable to the policies that would soon be embodied in the Taubaté accord.

Because Minas Gerais had by 1896 replaced Rio de Janeiro as the country's second leading coffee state and as of yet had no significant industry, its representative would protect the interests of "king coffee" more than the rather economically sophisticated Rodrigues Alves had been willing to do. Thus the shift to a president from Minas Gerais did not signify any real change in the distribution of power away from the coffee elite.[49]

Politics Without Parties, 1906–1914

The 1906 succession witnessed the emergence of a new balance wheel in the politics of the governors, one that partially accommodated—but more importantly co-opted and channeled—the interests of states other than São Paulo and Minas Gerais. In August 1905, Rio Grande do Sul Senator José Gomes Pinheiro Machado had masterfully articulated the replacement of Bernardino de Campos as the official candidate by Afonso Pena, defeating in the process both the ambitions of Campos Salles for a return to the presidency and those of Bahia's Ruy Barbosa to achieve an office he felt he merited for his distinguished role in the establishment of the republic (much as in 1988–1989 Ulysses Guimarães was convinced that he deserved to be Brazil's next president).

Pinheiro Machado was clearly the most influential civilian politician of the early twentieth century not to reach the presidency, his real impact on national life from behind the scenes being far greater than that of the celebrated but essentially ineffective role played in front of the footlights by Ruy Barbosa. Pinheiro Machado's kingmaker position stemmed from the fact that he was the permanent head of the Rio Grande do Sul delegation in Congress. He worked in harmony with Antônio Augusto Borges de Medeiros, who had succeeded Castilhos in power in Porto Alegre and was reelected term after term (Rio Grande do Sul being the only province in which reelection of the chief executive was permitted).[50]

In spite of an intense rivalry with former vice-president Rosa e Silva, political boss of Pernambuco, Pinheiro Machado used his great political skills to enlist the quite consistent support of a number of states from the north and northeast in the coalition, called the Bloco, that he orchestrated in Congress. Composed largely of the remainder of Pinheiro's earlier congressional allies plus his more recent conquests, this faction fell under the wily Gaúcho's control. Pinheiro was able to accomplish this both because of his dominant position in the Senate, where he had been the presiding officer since 1903 and where the smaller provinces he led easily had an ample majority, and because of the influence he exercised over "recognition" of disputed election results.

Using the fact that Rodrigues Alves and Leopoldo de Bulhões, Alves's finance minister, were wed to orthodox monetary policies and dead set against the idea of devaluation to aid the coffee interests, Pinheiro waited until Francisco Glicério and other pro-coffee São Paulo politicians turned to him. Although Pena had not been his first choice, Pinheiro was sufficiently astute to perceive that defeat of the president's efforts to put in yet another Paulista would be a substantial step toward achieving two of his goals: opening the presidency to candidates from other states and taking the orchestration of presidential succession out of the hands of the incumbent president. (The latter goal would be attempted and often achieved at later points in Brazil's political life by other spokesmen for Rio Grande do Sul and Rio de Janeiro interests.)

Minas Gerais in the Presidency

As Pena was both an old classmate of Rodrigues Alves and had served as Alves's vice-president after the death of fellow Mineiro Francisco Silvino Brandão before the 1902 inauguration, his presidency did not mark any really significant discontinuity in either politics or policy, except for the greater support for coffee stabilization. Moreover, as Minas Gerais was still first in population, electorate, and congressional seats, elevation of one of its former chief executives to the presidency was not only logical, but perhaps even overdue. Essentially unopposed, with young Rio de Janeiro provincial president Nilo Peçanha as his running mate to offset the fact that he had thrice been a minister under the monarchy, Pena received over 288,000 votes to less than 5,000 for his token opponent—nearly 98 percent of the very low turnout.[51]

As the PRF had never become a real national governing party, being essentially a common front of groupings with varying interests and precious little programmatic outlook—much like the Party of the Brazilian Democratic Movement (PMDB) in the 1980s—it was by this time little more than a rather loose "club of oligarchs." This situation left the military, even with its internal divisions, as the closest approximation to a national political institution.[52] Thus, as had been the case during the empire, dissident state oligarchical groupings could only come to power through a *derrubada* of the entrenched machine by the federal executive exercising the emperor's old moderating power—although the moderating power no longer existed in the 1891 constitution.

Well aware of the realities of the situation, Pena prudently selected as his war minister Marshal Hermes Rodrigues da Fonseca, the legalist hero of the 1904 crisis and, in terms of influence although not role, the period's nearest equivalent to the duke of Caxias. The fact that the presidential succession set off a bloody revolt in Mato Grosso, which lasted from May to November 1906, brought home the need for reestablishing unity and discipline within the army. At the same time that the navy was being rebuilt, Hermes da Fonseca shaped the first real reorganization and reform of the army to take place under the republic, achieving through a law of January 1908 the goal of conscription in place of impressment that the military professionalizers had sought for half a century.[53]

Indeed, Hermes represented the professional strain in the officer corps, which wanted to modernize the army and get it out of politics. Hence he was relatively slow to develop well-defined presidential ambitions, but disunity and intransigence among the civilian elites would create a vacuum Hermes could readily be convinced to fill.

The new president sought to wrest effective control of national politics away from Pinheiro Machado by fostering a new generation of political and governmental leaders who had nothing to do with the Deodoro-Floriano rivalry or the failure of the PRF under Glicério. Minas Gerais President João Pinheiro was Pena's preference for a successor; Davi Campista, the finance minister, along with thirty-five-year-old Carlos Peixoto, who presided over the Chamber, headed the so-called kindergarten cadre of the Pena government. But fortune was not to be on the president's side, as João Pinheiro's death in late 1908 left the Minas Republican Party (PRM) deeply divided. Pena's subsequent efforts to unite his fellow Mineiros behind forty-three-year-old Campista failed. Indeed, Campista's policies were seen as favorable to the São Paulo coffee growers and new industrial interests.

From 1889 Bridesmaid to 1910 Bride

To many opposition politicians Hermes seemed a capable administrator, trusting and good-natured, who would be amenable to their influence, if not subject to their management. For important elements of the armed forces, he seemed to combine the best qualities of his uncle Deodoro with the virtues of Floriano and thus to be the ideal vehicle for the military to reassume control of the nation's destinies from a political class composed chiefly of representatives of the state oligarchies.[54] To combat this resurgence of what he saw as Florianism, Ruy Barbosa launched his own "civilist" candidacy. In this venture he received the backing of the governments of São Paulo, Bahia, and Rio de Janeiro. Thus Brazil's first really competitive direct election of a president was in a general sense parallel to the original presidential contest within the constituent assembly between Deodoro and Prudente. Again the military figure would emerge the victor.

The death of Afonso Pena in June 1909—which was widely attributed to his frustration over failure to block Hermes's candidacy—left the task of presiding over the nation during this bitter campaign to Vice-President Nilo Peçanha, whose own background revealed some Florianist inclinations.[55] Though the champion of civilism carried the cities of the south, the combination of state machines and military support was decisive in the interior, where large majorities were recorded as usual for the government candidate. Hence, November 15, 1910, witnessed the inauguration of Brazil's third military chief executive, and Minas Gerais President Wenceslau Bráz Pereira Gomes took office as national vice-president amidst a series of local uprisings.

The official figures registered a win for the government's slate by 404,000 to 223,000—a record low margin of victory (with just over 60 percent of the vote compared to 84 percent in 1894, 91 percent in 1898, 92 percent in 1902, and 98 percent in 1906). Yet these results were doubted by most observers, as the very high proportion of the vote usually received in each province by whomever was the winning candidate there supports other evidence of fraud having been quite common. Perhaps of greatest significance for the future was the fact that for the first time in five presidential elections, the candidate supported by São Paulo failed to win.

Almost as soon as he took office, Hermes was faced with a revolt by the crews of the nation's proud new battleships, who were seeking a ban on use of the lash.[56] Although from the perspective of the present day this mutiny may appear to have comic opera features, it was at the time a deadly serious matter that shook the capital, if not the whole country. Involved were dreadnoughts that were the largest and most modern fighting ships in an era in which naval forces were at their peak of power and prestige. (As Frank McCann points out, the engineers of these ships were civilian Englishmen.) With over a dozen warships remaining loyal to the government, the possibility of a major naval battle was far from remote. At the root of the rebellion was the fact that the navy was still largely comprised of individuals shanghaied off the streets and required to serve a minimum of fifteen years, and the relatively aristocratic officers treated these rank and file the same as the lowest criminal elements who had enlisted to escape jail sentences. Even after the original revolt was ended with an amnesty on November 25, a marine corps uprising required a large-scale infantry attack on the edge of the downtown district of Rio de Janeiro.

Following the precedent of Deodoro and Floriano, rather than the live-and-let-live stance of the intervening civilian presidents, Hermes strove to overthrow those provincial administrations hostile to his ends and policies. Influenced by a new alliance of middle-class military with some originally anti-Hermes "civilianists," during 1911 Hermes supported their efforts to topple the old oligarchies. First he resolved the case of dual governments in Rio de Janeiro in favor of the insurgent group by partisan use of federal troops. A series of political "salvations" were launched, originally to neutralize the power of Pinheiro Machado's embryonic Conservative Republican Party (PRC), a replacement for the long-moribund PRF, and to satisfy the desires of War Minister Emídio Dantas Barreto (who had been a chief articulator of Hermes's candidacy). The targets of these "salvations" were the oligarchical machines of local political chiefs and powerful landholding families, who had staged an effective comeback during the era of the São Paulo presidents and who were now allied with Pinheiro Machado.

As already indicated, under the politics of the governors the federal government certified as winners the candidates put forth by these provincial governments in return for their support and votes in Congress. The fact that many of these state machines were controlled by former members of the monarchical parties and were often corrupt and tyrannical was overlooked or even justified as allowable autonomy within the federal system so long as their representatives in Rio de Janeiro played ball with the president. The result was the conversion of the country into "feuding groups, large and small, concerned much more with their regional interests than with those of the nation as a whole. . . . The small states gravitated into the orbits of the big ones as if imitating the international balance-of-power game."[57]

Moreover, the high degree of political and administrative autonomy they enjoyed gave the governors a nearly complete control of political life in their states. This control was implemented and maintained through clientelistic appointments and nepotism; electoral corruption that bordered on the absurd, rather than being merely abusive; and, in the ultimate resort, pure and simple violence.[58] Such a system consolidated the leadership of the regional chief in the states and of the colonel in the municipalities through well-mounted political machines in such a way that the peasantry was practically "feudalized": It became totally dependent on a clientelistic policy that, under conditions of absolute loyalty and conformity, delegated to it the partial use of the land and some other goods and services.[59]

This situation undercut the emergence of national political parties capable of disciplining legislative politics. Only in São Paulo, Minas Gerais, and Rio Grande do Sul did strong, coherent Republican Parties exist. Neither the PRF nor the PRC could become anything more than a loose and essentially programless coalition of political "ins," who were dedicated more to manipulating the electoral process than to playing a responsible role in national decision making.[60] That this legacy has hampered the evolution of a meaningful party system down to the present is clearly demonstrated by subsequent developments.

The Oligarchs Survive the Onslaught

Urged on by his sons and other young army officers representative of those who wished to "purify" the republic, and with his brother João Severiano Fonseca Hermes installed as majority leader in the Chamber, Hermes undertook to "rescue" several states from their entrenched machines, but only obtained a partial rotation of oligarchical elites.[61] Pernambuco was the first priority, with General Dantas Barreto, who stepped down from the War Ministry in September 1911, as the instrument for toppling Rosa e Silva—who had been dominant there since 1894 and was a powerful boss even under the monarchy.[62] In Bahia a variation of the dual legislatures tactic—in which each of two separate bodies claims to be made up of the "honestly" elected legislators—was used, along with a shelling of Salvador by the army (quite possibly not approved by Hermes), to pave the way for the elevation of J. J. Seabra.

The toughest nut to crack proved to be Ceará, where Antônio Pinto Nogueira Accioly had been dominant since 1877.[63] The first rounds came out close to the Pernambuco scenario of civil insurrection, providing the pretext for military intervention. But when Lieutenant Colonel Franco Rabelo, installed in mid-1912 in place of the old oligarch, tried to remove the charismatic Padre Cícero Romão Batista as mayor of Juazeiro, he ran into insurmountable difficulties. A much more politically sophisticated individual than Canudos's Antônio Conselheiro had been, the equally mystic Padre Cícero had integrated his stronghold of Juazeiro into the political and economic structure of Ceará and was very much in touch with national, if not international, trends.[64]

Here Pinheiro Machado, who had come to exert very great influence over Hermes during the second half of the latter's term and had decided that the PRC needed the oligarchical machines, found an opportunity to strike back at the "saviors" of Ceará. A majority of provincial legislators, meeting at Juazeiro under Padre Cícero's protection, set up a rival government. After defeating Rabelo's police expeditions against them at the gates of Juazeiro on December 20, 1913, and again nearer Crato on January 22, 1914, Padre Cícero's followers swept across the state. To avoid the prospect of Fortaleza being sacked by the backland hordes, Hermes appointed Colonel Fernando Setembrino de Carvalho as "interventor" (the title used in Brazil for someone named by the central government to replace an elected state chief executive).

Though the early wave of salvations had been successful in Amazonas, Alagoas (under General Clodoaldo da Fonseca), Sergipe, and Espírito Santo, the prestige of Rodrigues Alves as president of São Paulo was unassailable, and Minas Gerais was spared as the vice-president's bailiwick. In Rio Grande do Sul the partnership of Borges de Medeiros (strongman there since Júlio de Castilhos's early death in 1903) and Pinheiro Machado—backed by their disciplined party—withstood the central administration's effort to impose War Minister Antônio Adolfo Mena Barreto as chief executive.[65] Instead Borges himself returned through the 1912 elections. Moreover, from this point on, Hermes tended to side with Pinheiro Machado, turning his back on the salvationists. On balance the provincial oligarchies had not been overturned, and efforts to make the PRC into a real national political party were effectively undermined.

Repression in the Backlands

During the latter stages of his administration, Hermes, as had been the case with Floriano, was plagued with military, or at least internal security, problems that prevented his concentration upon the succession question. Then, too, after his December 1913 marriage to a twenty-seven-year-old, he was wrapped up in his personal life. Beyond the Ceará crisis, which was not resolved until the very eve of the elections, a Canudos-type situation with significant political implications developed in the contested area (marked on maps as "Contestado") between the provinces of Paraná and Santa Catarina.[66]

Availing himself of the popularity of a religious mystic known as "Monk" João Maria (the term meaning a saintly religious lay leader, not an individual member of a holy order), who had been active in the area during the time of the Canudos incident, a deserter from the Paraná police appeared in the region in 1912 claiming to be the monk's nephew and heir. In a period rife with corruption, unemployment, and speculation, he soon built up a following among the superstitious poor. A military expedition managed to kill the fanatic leader in October, but also lost its own commander in the battle and left its weapons in the hands of the guerrillas.

The same mistakes were made by the government as earlier at Canudos: When a new prophet appeared to carry on João Maria's work, which allegedly included restoration of the monarchy, an infantry column of some 200 men sent to repress the "rebellion" was repulsed at the end of 1913 with heavy losses. A reinforced expedition of 750 men with cavalry and artillery detachments destroyed one stronghold in February 1914, but a blow against another center was repulsed a few weeks later. Then a 1,500-man government force under General Carlos Frederico de Mesquita, a veteran of the Canudos campaign, was defeated in May and several towns were raided by the rebels.

Finally, Setembrino de Carvalho, fresh from the pacification of Ceará and just promoted to general, destroyed the main insurgent band in March 1915—but only after his first attacks had been thrown back. Not until October was the last resistance crushed. However, a field army of over 7,000 men was required to regain the rebel-controlled area that once reached 28,000 square kilometers and held 20,000 dissidents. In all, government troops had lost over 300 men, with perhaps twenty times that number of rebels killed—almost all of them humble people participating in an essentially spontaneous protest movement by those marginalized by the existing social order and political process.

The Second Minas Presidency

By the time this Contestado campaign met with success, Hermes had already given way to Wenceslau Bráz, whose 532,000 votes were 92 percent of the total in the March 1914 elections. With Pinheiro Machado vetoed by São Paulo, Minas Gerais, Bahia, and Pernambuco, former president Campos Salles's candidacy cancelled by his death, and Ruy Barbosa at seventy unwilling to abandon the militant civilist stance that rendered him unacceptable to the armed forces, the forty-six-year-old vice-president had emerged as the logical unity candidate. Indeed, Pinheiro Machado himself saw the handwriting on the wall and climbed on Bráz's bandwagon. As Hermes had become generally unpopular, in part because of simultaneous coffee and rubber crises, and the military was again divided over the relative advantages and disadvantages of direct involvement in politics, no effort toward a military candidacy was seriously considered. Although it would still be true in the future that "When things are going badly, a tendency to seek to correct the evils through a formula especially satisfying to the military is formed among the civilians themselves," disenchantment with the uniformed solution, as in the case of Hermes, could come quickly.[67]

Hermismo and the Winds of Change

The armed forces that Wenceslau Bráz inherited when he took office shortly after the outbreak of World War I differed significantly from the military institution under Deodoro or Floriano; by the time Bráz left the presidency in 1918 the processes of restructuring and modernizing would have progressed significantly further. As war minister under Afonso Pena, Hermes da Fonseca had begun a policy of sending young officers to Germany for training and observation. Those who went in 1906, 1908, and 1910 had returned by the midpoint of Hermes's term, and in October 1913 they founded *A Defesa Nacional*, a review that generally put forth these "Young Turks' " case for military professionalism and adherence to constituted authority.[68]

The New Military Generation

Zealots for the cause of military modernization, the Young Turks strongly supported Hermes's reorganization of the army in 1908 along with obligatory conscription and provisions for one-year "special volunteers." These measures also democratized the army in the sense of making it more representative of the Brazilian class structure rather than the lower ranks continuing to be almost exclusively black and mulatto. The Young Turks opposed, however, Hermes's "prostitution" of the army through its employment as a tool for the political salvations. Although they were still relatively few in number and low in grade, they benefitted from the sympathy of Marshal José Caetano de Faria, army chief of staff under Hermes, Military Club president from 1908 to 1912, and Bráz's war minister.

Laws of 1915 and 1918 further modernized the organization of the army, with universal military service, provided for in 1908, actually put into effect and the national guard brought under the war minister rather than continuing to be controlled by the justice minister. At the same time a group of middle-class civilians led by poet Olavo Bilac embraced a romanticized view of military service as a school for order, discipline, cohesion, and patriotism. This group created the National Defense League in September 1916.[69] Although the Young Turks' leading figures went into temporary eclipse after the defeat of Germany in 1918, increasing emphasis upon study and training continued, widening the gap between the old-time "garrison" officers and the new "school" officers. Indeed, the "Indigenous Mission" (a reference to its members being Brazilians rather than imported French experts), made up of many of the key Young Turks, dominated the Realengo Military School until 1922.

The political situation also suffered significant modification during the administration of the well-intentioned but mediocre Bráz. On September 8, 1915, Pinheiro Machado was murdered, an act that had its roots in Pinheiro's campaign to elect Hermes to the Senate from Rio Grande do Sul, and his death would lead to the collapse of the PRC. Although Hermes's presidential candidacy had in large part originated within the army, with the politicians climbing aboard the bandwagon once it was already rolling, public opinion held Pinheiro responsible for playing the kingmaker and blamed him for the marshal's actions as president.[70] The possibility of a political comeback by Hermes excited extreme passions and contributed to the violent act of an emotionally unbalanced "regicide." The sense of crisis was heightened by a series of mutinous movements by noncommissioned officers with close ties to radical politician Maurício de Lacerda.

The Fates Conspire for the Northeast

With the World War I still in progress, the nomination and election of Rodrigues Alves for a second stint as president aroused little opposition— after all it had been a dozen years since he had been the last Paulista to hold this office. In keeping with the general pattern of "coffee with milk" politics—that is, an alliance of São Paulo and Minas Gerais—Mineiro chief executive Delfim Moreira da Costa Ribeiro was chosen as Alves's running mate, and the official slate polled over 99 percent of a very small turnout of just under 400,000.[71]

Mortally ill, Rodrigues Alves was never able to take office and died in January 1919. Besides this, the vice-president, sworn in as acting president on November 15, 1918, was also in very poor health. As the incumbent presidents of São Paulo and Minas Gerais were both young and relatively inexperienced, it was generally felt that they should wait for 1922, a thesis vigorously sustained by Rio Grande do Sul. But in turn the two pivotal states vetoed the candidacy of Gaúcho strongman Borges de Medeiros. As Ruy Barbosa was both old and remained *persona non grata* to the military, the compromise choice was Epitácio Lindolfo da Silva Pessôa, who had gained publicity and prestige as head of Brazil's delegation to the Versailles Peace Conference.

At fifty-four Pessôa had already served as a minister of justice, president of the Supreme Court, attorney general, and senator. He would normally have been barred from serious consideration for the presidency for the unforgivable political sin of having come from the small northeastern state of Paraíba.[72] But in this case the usually fatal handicap was overcome, owing to doubts as to how well the electoral machinery that had delivered spectacularly for Rodrigues Alves in 1918 would perform a year later on behalf of yet another São Paulo or Minas Gerais politico with the popular Ruy Barbosa as opposition candidate. So the presidency fell into the lap of a surprised Pessôa, who on April 19 received 71 percent of the fewer than a half million votes cast, and Barbosa—the William Jennings Bryan of Brazil—in his last hurrah was credited with 116,000 votes to the victor's 286,000.

The Society and Economy by 1920

The sole civilian from outside the center-south to occupy the presidency until the equally accidental tenure of José Sarney (1985–1989), Pessôa was called upon to govern a Brazil that had changed significantly since the early 1900s. Brazil's population had passed the mark of 22 million in 1910, reaching 23.7 million by 1913 and 30.6 million by 1920. Rio de Janeiro had become a city of nearly 1.16 million, with São Paulo next at 580,000 and Salvador hitting 283,000. These were followed by Recife at 239,000, Belém at 236,000, and Porto Alegre at 180,000. The economy, which had expanded some 77 percent from 1900 to 1913—allowing for a significant increase in per capita GDP of 35 percent—slowed down to a very modest 2.4 percent annual growth rate between 1914 and 1918.[73]

Yet qualitative change was evident in the economy as the agricultural sector fell from 45 percent to 35 percent of GDP between 1900 and 1913 and industry rose from 10 percent to 14 percent. (By 1929 agriculture would drop to below 37 percent, with industry rising above 20 percent.) Although coffee still accounted for over 47 percent of the nation's exports in the 1914–1918 period, this was down from its nearly 62 percent share during the Hermes years. Rubber, which had provided 20 percent of Brazil's foreign sales during that earlier period, declined to 12 percent during Bráz's term.[74]

Immigration had fallen off during the first decade of the new century, but the ten-year total of 650,000 was still very substantial, and between 1910 and 1919 the flow would rise again to over 820,000, with Spaniards replacing Italians as the most numerous element (above 300,000). Indeed, the second largest annual total of immigrants in Brazil's history—over 190,000—came in 1913. Between 1901 and 1920 some 857,000 immigrants arrived in São Paulo, and, as the total of arrivals to the country between 1884 and 1920 had approximated 3 million, by 1920 the nation had the largest proportion of foreign born in its history.[75] Life expectancy by 1920 was up to thirty-two years, and the labor force had reached 9.15 million with nearly 70 percent—6.38 million—in agriculture and 1.5 million in the service sector; 275,000 of the 1.26 million in industry were factory workers. The enrollment of school-age children had increased to 29 percent, compared to 20 percent in 1907, and literacy rates by 1920 reached 29 percent for males and 20 percent for females.

Perhaps the most important structural change during the second decade of the twentieth century was the substantial increase in industrialization. Until 1914, and to a lesser extent until the mid-1920s, industrial growth was still limited by the performance of the export sector, but after 1900 the incipient industrial sector was at least partially self-sustaining. The capacity of the Brazilian economy to withstand adverse external shocks and even use them as a stimulus to growth and diversification was demonstrated by World War I. Cut off from some sources of imports, subjected to an abrupt interruption of foreign investment, and deprived of many of its traditional markets, Brazil still grew economically. Having shown zero growth for 1914–1915, the GDP rate of expansion was 4.4 percent, 5.6 percent, and 1.9 percent for 1916, 1917, and 1918 before it climbed to 5.9 percent in 1919 and an impressive 10.1 percent in 1920.

On the industrial side, the coming of the war found Brazil with excess capacity in productive facilities, which had been installed during 1908–1913, and suffering from the 1913–1914 recession. Industry had expanded at an annual average of 9.1 percent over a six-year period before declining by 8.7 percent in 1914 and even with low rates of investment still grew at 4.4 percent a year from 1915 through 1917, followed by a negative 1 percent growth rate in 1918. Indeed, by 1920 4,145 factories in Brazil employed some 84,000 workers. These industrial growth rates masked the fact that wartime growth was limited to those industries processing domestic raw materials, while industries requiring imported inputs or machinery suffered.[76]

The war did clearly focus the attention of both elites and the government on the need for diversifying industrial production to keep from being caught short in any future international crisis. Consequently, during the 1920s the government would provide incentives on a selective basis and extend subsidies to certain priority industries such as cement, steel, paper, cellulose, chemicals, rubber products, and machinery. The government did not, however, yet support industrial development in general.[77] Since 1906 the Taubaté pact had protected the coffee sector, but at the cost of disorganizing the market as a guide to investments. The resulting expansion of coffee production in excess of any possible demand was certainly not a rational allocation of resources.

Moreover, although by mid-1913 São Paulo had paid off the £15 million loan contracted in 1908, a continuing demand for support for coffee came in the form of massive currency emissions in 1915 and 1917—which returned a nice profit when coffee prices rose again in 1919. Meantime, however, this subsidy to the coffee producers further fed the high inflation of the wartime years, and a more than 27 percent fall in coffee revenues in 1920 would lead to even greater reliance upon keeping prices up through loans and expansion of the money supply.

A Contested Succession

In a break with twenty years of tradition, Pessôa had appointed civilians to the War and Navy Ministries, a move that sat very poorly with the armed forces. Indeed, communications between João Pandía Calógeras and the army were never good, and in 1922 this would have near disastrous consequences. Raúl Soares fared little better with the prickly naval officers.

Political passions ran high throughout Pessôa's truncated tenure in office, and his intervention in Bahia on behalf of J. J. Seabra, in which 6,000 troops were employed, aroused vehement opposition.[78] Moreover, although the nomination of Minas Gerais chief executive Artur da Silva Bernardes for the 1922–1926 term—and tacitly that of São Paulo's Washington Luís Pereira de Sousa for the 1926 election—was agreed upon by the nation's political leaders in early 1921, Rio Grande do Sul under Borges de Medeiros did not conform. Thus the 1921–1922 campaign was in certain basic respects a preview of the 1929–1930 battle that would result in the Old Republic's demise.[79]

When the president put forth a compromise nominee to resolve the conflict between two vice-presidential aspirants, Rio Grande do Sul joined with Rio de Janeiro, Bahia, and Pernambuco in the "Republican Reaction" to nominate former president Nilo Peçanha, with Bahia's Seabra as his running mate. Hermes da Fonseca, returning from six years in Europe to find that his absence had indeed made him fonder in the hearts of many Brazilians, threw his support to this opposition slate, which already enjoyed the backing of young reformists and even that of the venerable Ruy Barbosa. Large numbers of the officer corps followed Hermes's lead and with inflamed spirits came to consider Bernardes an enemy of the national good.[80] *Hermismo* was back on the political scene with an explosive potential.

In October 1921, when an influential Rio de Janeiro newspaper printed letters—allegedly written by Bernardes—highly insulting not only to Hermes but also to the armed forces as an institution, indignation in the army came to the point of boiling over.[81] A commission appointed by the Military Club to look into the matter reported back on December 28 that it found the letters to be genuine. Even the admission in May 1922 that the letters were forgeries did not defuse the resolve of a significant proportion of the younger officers to never accept Bernardes as legitimate president.[82]

In the March 1922 balloting, which pitted the two largest states against the next four most populous, the government candidate as always emerged the victor. But with intellectual sectors sensitized by the centennial of independence, the Republican Reaction refused to accept the announced results as valid, and Hermes—presiding over the Military Club—called for a Tribunal of Honor instead of Congress to verify the electoral results. As many of Hermes's partisans had hoped, a worried Pessôa went so far as to suggest that Bernardes withdraw in favor of some unnamed unity figure, but the stubborn Mineiro was determined to take office—and was proclaimed president-elect on June 7 with the lowest margin yet, only 56 percent of the vote, or 467,000 to 318,000.[83] By that time Hermes had been reelected head of the Military Club, which was functioning almost as a shadow government.

Further conflict was not long in coming. The death of the Pernambuco chief executive set off a crisis there in which accusations of favoritism by the federal government to one contending faction prompted Hermes to dash off an abrasive telegram in which he accused Colonel Jaime Pessoa, a relative of the former president, of making the army in Pernambuco the "hangman of the Pernambucan people."[84] Any doubt that the telegram was intended as a gauntlet flung in the face of the government was removed by the closing injunction not to forget that administrations are transitory, but the army is a permanent institution—a pointed call to disregard presidential orders.

The government's response to Hermes's act of gross undiscipline was immediate and vigorous, but also probably exactly what the surviving midwife of the republic wished to provoke. If his arrest was proper, it was probably not prudent, and the manner in which it was carried out was another example of a civilian government trying to reassert its authority in the face of a military challenge by using heavy-handed methods offensive to the armed forces' sense of corporative solidarity. (Deodoro a third of a century earlier had only let Hermes, who was a captain, convince him to move against the monarchy because of the former's personal and professional grievances.) War Minister Pandía Calógeras's relations with the officer corps had often been strained, and in his determination to show who was in control before leaving office he treated Hermes in a manner considered gratuitously insulting by the more "exalted" sectors of the armed forces.[85] Although the final blow would not come until 1930, Pandía Calógeras may well have helped seal the regime's doom. Certainly it was highly undiplomatic to rely upon a law covering anarchists, confidence men, and exploiters of vice to close down the Military Club.

Tenentismo and the Road Toward Revolution

The predictable reaction of Hermes's supporters was to organize a revolt designed to overturn the no-longer-popular government and bring the armed forces to power, at least temporarily. Articulated on quite short notice by a group of romantic young officers, the rebellion had little hope of success unless every part of the plan worked perfectly, which was too much to expect. Consequently it would go down in history as a gallant gesture by a small band of fearless patriots, and thus provide a symbol for further revolts. In addition, it created some leaders for subsequent movements. Its successes were in becoming the new generation's rallying cry and in turning Bernardes into a hated symbol of corrupt politics.

The failure of its senior leader, Marshal Hermes da Fonseca, to make it something more would be the epitaph for Florianism. But out of the heroic behavior of Antônio de Siqueira Campos and Eduardo Gomes, a more potent force—*tenentismo*—was born as a modern movement freed from the shackles of seeking to emulate the successes of an earlier era. Indeed, with Hermes's death on September 9, 1923, as well as that of Nilo Peçanha in March 1924, the break with the past tradition of military movements would become complete. Originally a military movement, *tenentismo* would come to have substantial political ramifications before being absorbed in the new synthesis of the military dialectic in the mid-1930s. And though Siqueira Campos was to perish in 1930, Gomes would twice be a major presidential candidate during the post–World War II period, as would Juarez do Nascimento Fernandes Távora, one of the new leaders the movement developed after 1922. As late as 1967 one of the fringe *tenentes*, Arthur da Costa e Silva, would become president.

The First Angry Shots

In the perspective of 1922, however, the young military rebels looked like anything but the wave of the future. The Pessôa government had vigorously repressed labor unrest during its early years in office and in 1921 had arrested anarchist leaders under a new internal security law. Thus the 1922 revolt would have to succeed as a purely military affair devoid of any effective civilian support.[86] Moreover, the navy had recently been purged of sailors and marines suspected of harboring revolutionary sentiments, and spokesmen for the soon-to-be inaugurated Bernardes were mollifying the officer corps by revealing plans for increases in the army's size and pay with consequent improvements in career and advancement opportunities. Not surprisingly, then, the July 5 revolt involved only a small part of the troops in the Rio de Janeiro area, with its reflex in Mato Grosso being largely a family matter.

Fort Copacabana, commanded by Captain Euclides Hermes da Fonseca, a son of the marshal, rebelled in the early morning hours of July 5. At the same time an effort to mobilize an uprising at the powerful Vila Militar, base of the First Infantry Division, failed completely, thus virtually sealing the failure of the revolt. At the nearby Realengo Military Academy the movement was more successful, and an armed column numbering 600 men, the overwhelming majority of them cadets, departed for the Vila. There they expected to pick up major reinforcements for the march on the presidential palace that was designed to restore Hermes to the presidency. (The marshal's tactical plan was essentially a somewhat more elaborate copy of the 1889 coup, in which the revolutionary column had simply formed up at São Cristovão and proceeded in parade fashion to army headquarters.) When they were received by legalist gunfire instead of adherents, the cadets fell back into a defensive position in the hills, where they held off attacks by government troops until past noon. Then, realizing that the revolt had failed, they returned in an orderly manner to their barracks.[87] (Subsequently 608 were expelled, leaving a massive gap in junior officer ranks that would last for years.) Hermes himself was captured after he attempted to rendezvous with the nonexistent column from the Vila Militar.

Thus the rebels at Fort Copacabana soon found themselves in isolated resistance against the full forces of the government headed by General Setembrino de Carvalho–the conqueror of the Contestado—who was elevated to chief of staff during the crisis. (Captain Eurico Dutra, a future president, led one detachment against the rebels, as did Captain Euclydes Figueiredo, whose son would be Brazil's most recent military chief executive.) Under heavy fire from land, sea, and air, a group of the most militant young officers decided to embark on a suicidal sally against the ground forces besieging them. After bidding farewell to their followers (some 250 enlisted men and a score of other officers), a small band of eighteen men, which was soon reduced to but ten, set out on a running gun battle on the beachfront avenue that ended an hour later with five dead, but the seriously wounded Siqueira Campos and Gomes survived to become national heros.

Fortunately for the future of the country, the score of young officers who led the military academy uprising emerged unscathed to play major roles in future events. Odylio Denys, Juarez Távora, Canrobert Pereira da Costa, Ciro do Espírito Santo Cardoso, Stênio Caio de Albuquerque Lima, Newton Cavalcante, Olympio Falconiére da Cunha, and Edmundo Macedo Soares were exactly the cadre who, along with Luís Carlos Prestes (ill in 1922) and legalist Euclydes Figueiredo, had been carrying the lessons of the 1919 French Military Mission to the academy. Among the cadets following them in raising the banner of reform were such future key figures as Nélson de Melo and Ney Galvão.

Another group who were unable to get their units to rise up but who would gain fame in later episodes of *tenentismo* included Oswaldo Cordeiro de Farias, João Alberto Lins de Barros, Felinto Müller, and Justino Alves Bastos—whose father was removed as army chief of staff during the incident. In Mato Grosso the revolt was led by General Clodoaldo da Fonseca, the other of Deodoro's nephews still on the scene. Ably assisted by Captain Joaquim Távora, Clodoaldo was marching against São Paulo when word of the movement's collapse in the capital arrived. Like the revolt's agent in São Paulo, Isidoro Dias Lopes, Távora and other *tenentes* would almost immediately begin to plan another insurrection—in part at least because they were denied the amnesty that had invariably been granted in earlier cases of politically motivated insubordination.[88]

Continued Conflict

Inaugurated on November 15, 1922, Bernardes was to enjoy little respite from politico-military crises during his four years in office. With General Setembrino de Carvalho as war minister and Admiral Alexandrino de Alencar in charge of the navy, Bernardes sought to retain the relatively strong military position he inherited as a result of his predecessor's repression of the Hermes da Fonseca conspiracy. He also, however, fell heir to thorny situations in Rio de Janeiro and Rio Grande do Sul as to which faction deserved to be in power. Through the less than astute handling of these problems he would make new enemies and once again arouse strong negative passions. As had been the situation both when Hermes came to power in 1910 and also in 1914, a duality of authorities existed in Rio de Janeiro Province. Raúl Fernandes, the candidate of former president Nilo Peçanha, was the leader in the July 22 balloting, but the pro-Bernardes faction refused to recognize the election of this opposition figure. With the state of siege that had been declared at the time of the recent revolt still in effect, Bernardes intervened, paving the way for new elections in which his candidate would be proclaimed the winner (a scenario he would repeat in Bahia in 1924). The situation in Rio Grande do Sul was much more complex and intractable. Borges de Medeiros, his position essentially analogous to that of Júlio de Castilhos at the time of the Federalist revolt three decades earlier, was running for reelection. After initially supporting Hermes in the July crisis, the Gaúcho strongman subsequently condemned the resort to force by the opposition military faction—but only after the revolt's failure was evident.[89] As reelection required at least three-quarters of the vote, Borges's foes hoped to deny him a fifth term. To this end they formed the Liberating Alliance, a coalition of the Federalists with all other anti-Borges elements behind the candidacy of dissident Republican Joaquim Francisco de Assis Brasil. Whatever was the real outcome of the November 25 voting, a special commission of the provincial legislature headed by the rapidly rising young Getúlio Dornelles Vargas announced Borges's reelection by a margin of 106,360 to 32,216.

Because the Libertadores (or "Maragatos," as they were commonly known) would not accept this suspiciously partisan decision, a bloody civil war broke out—one in which old scores remaining from earlier armed struggles were settled by acts of violence that often crossed the line into barbarism. The Republicans ("Chimangos") generally held the upper hand during the ten months of fighting but were unable to inflict a crushing defeat upon their rivals, who hung on hoping for federal intervention. Finally a cessation of hostilities was achieved through the patient, yet firm, mediation of the war minister, who had been a Gaúcho legislator back in the days of Deodoro and enjoyed the added prestige of having recently been once more chosen to preside over the Military Club.[90]

The Pact of Pedras Altas of December 14, 1923, provided for an eventual end to Borges's stranglehold on the governorship through a ban on immediate reelection in the future, as well as postponing congressional elections in Rio Grande do Sul until May 1924 and instituting an amnesty for the insurgents. The elections were to be supervised by the war minister through army officers in each *município* to check against fraud or coercion. (The war minister's chief aide in these difficult negotiations was Major Euclydes Figueiredo, who in 1932, with the backing of both Borges and Assis Brasil, would lead São Paulo forces against a government headed by Vargas!)

The Prestes Column

Long before the civil strife ended in Rio Grande do Sul, plans for a new revolt against the increasingly repressive Bernardes government were going forward. A wave of arrests of suspected military plotters had occurred in April 1923, but this was offset by the number of veterans of the 1922 conspiracy who had been released or had escaped from custody.[91] With prison having been for many a "school for revolutionaries," organization of the new uprising proceeded with greater skill and coherence. The leader of this rebellion, which unlike that of 1922 had São Paulo rather than the capital as its focus, was General Isidoro Dias Lopes, a retired veteran of the 1893 revolt, with Captain Joaquim Távora as his chief of staff.

Captain Newton Estillac Leal, subsequently to be Vargas's most controversial war minister, aided from within the office of the military region commander, while Major Miguel Costa of the São Paulo Força Pública assured the adherence of a substantial proportion of this well-trained and well-equipped state militia. Júlio de Mesquita, J. J. Seabra—who was nearly powerless following Bernardes's successful maneuvering to end Seabra's political control of Bahia—and Maurício de Lacerda (a strikingly effective political orator whose son would become one of the country's leading political figures after 1950) were among the most active civilian participants in the conspiracy.

Launched on the second anniversary of the 1922 revolt, it met with initial success, controlling São Paulo city for eighteen days.[92] Yet by July 27, with Joaquim Távora killed, Eduardo Gomes taken prisoner, and government planes beginning aerial warfare against São Paulo, a strategic withdrawal to the interior was in order.[93] Hoped-for uprisings in other major states failed to take place, but Sergipe was in rebel hands for almost three weeks and Amazonas for five months.[94] More of a real threat to the government was the naval insurrection, which, although its leaders had been arrested in advance, managed on November 4 to seize the battleship *São Paulo*.[95]

Juarez Távora, Siqueira Campos, João Alberto Lins de Barros, and Luís Carlos Prestes had by this time managed to get fighting started in the chronic powder keg of Rio Grande do Sul—where they were allied with the Libertadores.[96] After two months they began a march northward to join with the São Paulo rebels, who themselves had marched over 600 miles to near Iguaçu Falls, a feat achieved in April 1925. Now under the command of Miguel Costa and following a sharp defeat at Catanduvas, a force of some 1,500 men transited Paraguayan territory to attack Mato Grosso. The legendary saga of what was to be called the Prestes Column had begun.[97]

With Prestes as chief of staff, Juarez Távora as his deputy, and Siqueira Campos, João Alberto, Oswaldo Cordeiro de Farias, and Djalma Soares Dutra as battalion commanders, the rebels undertook a more than 15,000-mile campaign—crossing the interior into the northeast and then slogging their way back in a large loop through Bahia. They fought over fifty battles and skirmishes—while averaging more than twenty-one miles a day—before going into exile in Bolivia in February 1927; they caught the country's imagination and succeeded in outlasting the chief target of their hatred, President Bernardes. In fact, a new front had been opened in Rio Grande do Sul on November 14, 1926, the final day of Bernardes's term. A *tenente*-led exile invasion from Uruguay six weeks later was, however, repulsed by provincial government forces. Significant for the future was the fact that the regular army left most of the task of combatting the insurgents to militia or even to the private armies of the interior colonels.[98]

Yet the most important fact was that this would be the last time Gaúcho Republicans fought against the revolutionaries, for in 1930 they would be working closely together behind Vargas to put an end to the Old Republic. But in late 1926 the future strongman of Brazil was just settling into a new job as finance minister in the administration of Washington Luís Pereira de Sousa, Bernardes's chosen successor. Moreover, the military chief of the 1930 Revolution would be Pedro Aurélio de Góes Monteiro, who spent 1925 and 1926 tenaciously combatting the Prestes Column. But times were changing; though the *tenente* revolts of 1922 and 1924 may have been harbingers of these changes, the "long march" of the Prestes Column was the catalyst. A new civilian-military coalition was emerging—one that within a short time would be capable of pushing aside the decaying structures of the past four decades much as the military Jacobins, Deodoro, and the Republican Party had done away with the empire.

As has repeatedly been the case in Brazil, the last-minute—even almost after the fact—adherence of elements hitherto supporting the existing regime would assure that the post-"revolution" synthesis actually preserved much of the content and many of the practices of the old order. Indeed, not only would this be the case in the 1930s, as it had been after 1889, but also it would clearly be so in the years after 1945, in the post-1964 period, and again after 1984.

4

The Vargas Era

By the late 1920s the Brazilian political system was clearly in a state of debilitating disarray and heading for outright decay, just as had been the case with the monarchy in the mid-1880s. This deterioration was a function of the lack of flexibility and capacity to modernize shown by the political structures and processes on the one hand and of the accelerating pace of economic change and resultant societal tensions on the other. Yet the crisis would be relatively slow in unfolding, as it appeared to many participants and observers that the regime had weathered the worst of the political storms with the disbanding of the Prestes Column. Indeed, this time it would require a serious economic crisis—and the grave errors in political judgment this crisis engendered on the part of the administration—to bring about a major regime change. The failure of the "salvations" of the Hermes period had once more underscored the resilience of the oligarchical structures and demonstrated that the middle class could not hope to break through to power without the military serving as its cutting edge. This crucial military role would in very large part be the essence of the 1930 Revolution.

When the demise of the Old Republic did finally occur, it would be seen at the time by important groups as a true system change. However, as in the case of the establishment of the original republic four decades earlier, the 1930 Revolution would instead result in a synthesis characterized more by survival of much of the old order than by emergence of elements of the new order envisaged by the more Jacobin actors. In fact, many changes that the militant elements wished to bring about in the late 1920s would be very long in coming—some not even reaching fruition during Vargas's lifetime. For, as June Hahner concludes her insightful study, as of the 1920s: "Like members of the elite, urban laborers tended to see society as divided into rich and poor rather than working class versus capitalists. . . . When they found themselves in a position to organize—and few did—most turned to reformist labor organizations and politicians' vague promises rather than to militant associations."[1] As for those in control of the system, "Quarrels within this strong, unified elite, with its regional alliances cemented by control of a rural-based elite, never degenerated into bloody fights which might have encouraged some politicians to seek worker support to counterbalance rivals."[2]

The urban middle classes—including the military as well as the liberal professions and public employees—took a leading part in the 1930 Revolution, but lacked the independence to formulate a political program for Brazilian society as a whole or even to establish their autonomy from the dissident oligarchies, who also participated in the movement or quickly aligned with the new regime. Realizing that electoral democracy under the existing socioeconomic system would lead to a return to power by the landowning–export merchant class (whose rural dependents greatly exceeded the urban middle-class vote), these emerging middle-class elements submerged their liberal ideas and accepted a regime without parties or elections, but one in which they could play a major role in a rapidly expanding bureaucracy. (In a different context, the same elements would adopt a similar stance after 1964.)

In 1930, as in 1889, then, the army was the vehicle for dissident elites and the middle class in overturning the old governmental institutions, but when the military returned to the barracks, the civilian middle sectors could not hold on to political power in a still essentially patrimonial society. Yet they could reap individual benefits from the clientelistic-*cartorial* system by agreeing once again to be co-opted.[3] Hence, instead of a pluralist democracy, the populist authoritarian regime of Getúlio Vargas emerged and built up the urban working class as a potential power factor under a corporative institutional structure. The middle class took political control of the *cartorial* state, but did not come to control the political system as a whole. "The apparatus of government continued to service the class that controlled the economy, while it looked after the needs of the middle class, which asked no more than guaranteed State-employment."[4] During this period, however, an industrial bourgeoisie developed as a potentially significant political factor, and Vargas began to turn toward the strategy of an industrialist–working class political base for his increasingly developmentalist and nationalist policies.

The Vargas era not only brought an enhanced role for the middle class; it was also a period during which the state would employ, with substantial success, the "powerful Brazilian institution of patronage" to co-opt effectively much of organized labor into a "system of State tutelage and control."[5] Indeed, this heavy government influence over unions would persist at least through the 1960s. Perhaps most critical to the failure of the 1930 Revolution to develop into a real rupture with the past was the fact that the *tenentes*, the cutting edge of the movement for political reform at this juncture, had no consensus view of any more appropriate role for the working class. Then, too, they were only a minority of the officer corps, perhaps little more than 600 militant individuals in a body that numbered almost 3,500 in 1920 and nearly 5,300 by the end of that decade.[6] Moreover, although the civilian middle class would become politically significant by the end of this period, for all their espousal of political democracy they were not strongly inclined toward social reforms. As a current Brazilian historian aptly describes the 1930s:

> Numerically inexpressive, socially dependent upon the dominant classes (being in large part composed of impoverished branches of the oligarchical families), identified with traditional attitudes and values, the middle class doesn't seem to have managed to surpass the plane of electoral definitions or of liberal demands which are at the same time true ideological points of reference for the dominant elite.[7]

This being the case, the armed forces were to remain the key factor in events of the Vargas period, for, "The occurrence of divisions in the dominant civilian apex stimulated the participation of the military group in the condition of guardian of institutional order. Whenever it found itself involved, or involved itself, in the political debate, the military sector expressed—many times formally—the function of arbiter that the body politic destined for them."[8]

Given these conditions, the following events occurred in succession during the Vargas years: (1) a rapid decomposition of the alliance of the disparate elements that finally overthrew the old regime in 1930; (2) a civil war of brief duration but great intensity; (3) an effort to institutionalize the new regime through a fairly liberal constitution (with many parallels to the situation that would prevail during 1987–1988); (4) an aborted Communist-led revolution (in 1935); (5) establishment of a centralized authoritarian corporativist state (1937); (6) substantial economic diversification and development; and (7) a process of political opening and movement for "re-democratization" in 1944–1945 that was strikingly analogous on many important dimensions to events as they would subsequently unfold during the early 1980s.

Moreover, during the fifteen years of Vargas's prolonged rule, the hegemony of the traditional agricultural elites would be definitively broken, with new urban-industrial elements coming to exert a significant influence on national policy and the middle class beginning to take on real political muscle. Then, too, under stop-and-go government sponsorship, the urban working class would at last emerge from the wings and assume a position on the political stage—albeit not yet any closer to the focus of action than upstage left.

Indeed, Vargas would return to power in 1951, and his political heirs would govern the country for all but brief interludes down to the critical watershed of 1964. During this time, both the increased autonomy of the state (from society) and the assumption of the moderating power role by the armed forces—two fundamental developments that had earlier roots but were greatly solidified during the 1930–1945 period—would come to fruition. Thus, an understanding of the Vargas period in all of its dimensions is as critical to comprehending Brazil today as are the Mexican Revolution and the Perón era in Argentina for appreciating the present situation in those countries. Like these watershed events, the changes during the Vargas era would have much earlier and greater impact at the national government level than at the regional, and they would affect the local level last and least. Vargas's stay in power would accelerate economic development, create a structured albeit co-opted labor movement, strengthen the central government immensely, and greatly expand the scope of the government's activities—in the process raising and broadening aspirations for political participation.[9]

The Breakdown of the Old Republic

At first appearance at least, the presidential succession of 1926 was one of the smoothest the republic had yet experienced, and most sectors of society manifested relief that the troubled Bernardes administration had come to an end. As had been expected even years in advance, the official candidate was São Paulo chief executive Washington Luís, with his Minas Gerais counterpart Fernando de Mello Viana as his running mate. As Hermes da Fonseca, Nilo Peçanha, Ruy Barbosa, and even Raúl Soares had all died, there was no real prospect of an opposition candidate.[10] Indeed, the official results were 688,000 for the government candidate to 1,116 for the opposition.

The Old Republic's Last Gasp

With the country thoroughly tired of rebellions and strife, the new president began his term under highly auspicious circumstances. But by the second half of 1927 the Communist Party had again been proscribed and restrictions were placed on both press freedom and rights of assembly.[11] In this worsening environment, political groupings of "dissident oligarchies" began to take shape, with large coffee planters, São Paulo professionals, and the newer generation of the traditional middle class forming the Democratic Party (PD) in February 1926 to challenge the long-entrenched Paulista Republican Party (PRP). At the same time Antônio Carlos Ribeiro de Andrada achieved the presidency of Minas Gerais on a platform espousing reformist policies.[12] In Rio Grande do Sul the elements that had formed the Liberationist Alliance in 1922–1923 formally constituted the Liberator Party (PL) in March 1928. Tory reformism, or at least defensive modernization, appeared finally to be getting underway. But the situation was slipping past the point at which this modernization might be enough.

By 1928 the republican regime, in its nearly four decades of existence, had reached a point of deterioration and the oligarchic system a degree of political decay that were comparable to the case with the empire by the mid-1880s. Institutions and processes that might well have been suitable for the first years of republican government had failed to evolve beyond the amalgam with traditional practices that had been carried over from the monarchy. This amalgam became entrenched through the federal government's willingness to let state power structures alone as long as they cooperated in Congress and created no undue difficulty over presidential successions. The electoral process was highly fraudulent, national parties simply did not exist, and protests against the inequities of the established order were increasingly met with repression rather than compromise and evolutionary reform. Frequently arbitrary, executive authority often lacked the compensatory merits of strength and effectiveness. The political representatives of the often patriarchal and essentially patrimonial regime could not point with pride to outstanding accomplishments to justify their continuing stewardship of the nation. When they sought to do so, they were only convincing to themselves, while they appeared hypocritical and self-seeking to an increasing proportion of the politically relevant public.

So long as elections might lead to change, there was no strong popular base for revolution, but the people were aware of the fact that never in the history of the republic had the government's candidate lost. Indeed, only on two widely separated occasions had the electorate even been given a shadow of a real choice rather than just the opportunity to ratify the decision of the most powerful state machines. For all intents and purposes the selection of São Paulo's chief executive for the 1926–1930 term had taken place in 1919, when the election of Epitácio Pessôa had been understood within the political class as a temporary "emergency" interruption of the pattern of São Paulo–Minas Gerais alternation. Thus, the presidential succession of 1930 was to be the last chance for the old system to demonstrate significant capacity to adapt. But the course of events from late 1928 on demonstrated that Brazil's political crisis was dual, one both of men and of institutions.

Currents Within the Military

The original core of the revolutionary movement that eventually triumphed in October 1930 was composed of the *tenentes*, who had gained conspiratorial experience as well a significant degree of popular renown during the four years of their armed struggle against the Bernardes government. Though only the Prestes Column veterans kept conspiring from 1927 to 1929, in 1928 and 1929 they successfully exploited the growing dissatisfaction with the regime's policies to recruit additional adherents within the officer corps, especially at the Realengo Military School.[13] The successful revolution would become possible only after the *tenentes* formed an alliance with a broad coalition of political forces possessing significant power bases in key states, but their proselytizing and infiltration of military units throughout the country was essential to the achievement of this purpose. Indeed, without assurance of widespread military adhesions, the rather cautious political leaders, especially the coldly calculating Vargas, would not have risked a revolutionary venture.

Tenentismo as a movement paralleled in many respects the positivistic republicanism of the young officers in the last decade of the empire. On the intellectual side, *tenentismo*'s origins can be found in the Realengo Military Academy, which reopened in 1911–1912. There during the World War I years such future leaders as Eduardo Gomes, Luís Carlos Prestes, Antônio de Siqueira Campos, Oswaldo Cordeiro de Farias, and Stênio Caio de Albuquerque Lima—to name but one group among several—studied and lamented together over a "Brazil laden with problems, beneath the weight of the crisis and in the hands of inept as well as unscrupulous politicians serving as instruments of oligarchies."[14]

The official goal of the academy was to develop competent professional soldiers, well disciplined and essentially obedient to constituted authority. This legalist orientation took with many cadets, but in light of the lower middle-class origin of a large proportion of the cadets and young officers, the fact that the example of their superiors often mixed in politics, the siren call of renewed Florianism (in the broadest sense of the term) through the person of Hermes, and the magnitude of national problems contrasted with the evident selfish interest of the boss-dominated political system, it is not surprising that a significant minority questioned the military's institutional role as a support of the established order.[15] According to Estevão Leitão de Carvalho, the most articulate exponent of the legalist viewpoint among that generation, there existed one current with its "diffusion of a firm concept of discipline, based on obedience, which ennobles the soldier," and a rival grouping "revolted against the march of events of public life which they judged were irreparably prejudicing the interests of the nation and compromising its future."[16]

At that time, as would also be the case in the future, the militant advocates of both the legalist and reformist theses were greatly outnumbered by those for whom the two sides of the nation's motto, "Order and Progress," had equal importance. Because the 1891 constitution enjoined the armed forces to be "essentially obedient, within the law" as well as obligating them to "support the constitutional institutions," it virtually consecrated ambivalence in ambiguous circumstances. Moreover, the increased emphasis upon study and training endorsed so vigorously by the champions of professionalism and embodied in the 1920 regulations, along with the arrival the preceding year of the French training mission, made the young officers more aware of national problems. Growing numbers came to believe that "the Army, and only the Army, was the organized force which could be placed at the service of democratic ideals and popular demands, against the interests of the bosses and oligarchies."[17] Though these officers did not propose a military government as a solution to the nation's problems, they strongly believed in the army's role as ultimate arbiter, with the *tenente* faction at least prepared to act when their hierarchical superiors failed to exercise the moderating power.[18]

The spread of this sentiment among the military coincided with the mounting alienation of urban progressive groups—due not only to the increasingly obvious fact that the political establishment was unresponsive to the middle sectors' desire for a significant say in policy making, but also to the establishment's indisposition to yield to demands for any type of reforms, including any in the electoral realm. Dissention within the political elite over presidential succession combined with the impact of the world economic crisis would both make the regime vulnerable and provide additional impetus to the formation of a revolutionary coalition capable of overthrowing the established order. But this time, in contrast to the termination of the monarchy, a nationwide mobilization and substantial fighting would be required to topple the old regime.

Formation of a "Revolutionary Coalition"

As the 1920s drew to a close, Brazil's population had passed 35 million, with Rio de Janeiro having grown to a city of some 1.5 million, São Paulo nearing 900,000, and Recife approaching 400,000. The economy had expanded at a good pace during the 1920–1923 period—averaging 6.9 percent annual growth in GDP—but Bernardes's hopes of a nonrecessionary adjustment through foreign borrowing had proved to be wishful thinking, and an orthodox monetary shock (consisting of credit restrictions and "tight" money policies designed to diminish inflation by reducing consumption) was belatedly adopted at the end of 1924. After stagnating in 1924–1925, economic expansion recovered to an average of over 11 percent a year for 1927 and 1928. But this recovery had a very fragile basis, for the relative prosperity was highly mortgaged to coffee, which, after providing under 60 percent of export earnings from 1919 through 1923, was responsible for over 72 percent from 1924 through 1929.[19] A high (for the era) 12 percent inflation rate in 1928 preceded a nearly imperceptible 1.2 percent GDP growth for 1929. Between September and December coffee prices fell by one-third, and—with funds to support coffee prices exhausted in November 1929—by the second half of 1930 they would be down an additional 70 percent under the burden of a massive 30-million-sack harvest. Thus, Brazil found itself in a classic J-curve situation, that of a sharp downturn after a sustained rise, with 1929 being a disastrous economic year and 1930 promising to be even worse—and it was, with a negative 2.1 percent real change in GDP magnified as a minus 16.4 percent in terms of prices of the day. Moreover, although the economic policy of the federal government had not always highly favored the corporate interests of São Paulo and coffee producers, the inability of the provincial government to handle the price support problem Bernardes had tossed back into its lap raised a presumption that, following a 1930 electoral victory, a Paulista president would divert national government resources to this end.

The revolutionary movement that took form during 1930 was a quite heterogeneous amalgam of groups desiring sweeping political changes, if not a new social order, with elements violently opposed to the incumbent administration and the president's hand-picked successor but devoid of any wish for more than moderate political and administrative reforms. In both its civilian and military components, the revolutionary coalition was essentially, indeed almost exclusively, bourgeois in nature. The Communists, considering the coalition to be narrowly concerned with regional rivalries within the existing system, refused to participate or even endorse the October 1930 revolt—a fact that would have significant implications for the post-takeover political struggles.

Presidential succession was the issue around which the fragmented opposition forces coalesced into a single movement cohesive insofar as its immediate objective—attainment of power—was concerned. Though Minas Gerais chief executive Antônio Carlos Ribeiro de Andrada would normally have been the leading presidential contender, he had several strikes against him. As a representative of the manufacturing interests around Juiz da Fora (the region nearest Rio de Janeiro) and a very militant Catholic, Ribeiro de Andrada did not have the united support of the state elites behind him. More important, he was a specialist on financial affairs who had served as minister of finance under Wenceslau Bráz; his prescriptions for the economic crisis were at variance with those of President Washington Luís, who strongly desired continuation of his administration's policies.[20]

Hence by 1929 it was already apparent that the president's choice was São Paulo chief executive Júlio Prestes de Albuquerque. If he could not win the coveted presidency for himself, the proud Antônio Carlos was determined to thwart the imposition of the much younger Paulista politician along with this clumsy breaking of a basic understanding upon which the stability of the regime had rested. In this venture Ribeiro de Andrada would require the full cooperation of Rio Grande do Sul, which, as Brazil's third most populous province, had long awaited an opportunity for one of its favorite sons to become president—especially since the 1914 veto of Pinheiro Machado.

With the departure of Borges de Medeiros from the provincial palace in Porto Alegre in January 1928—as required by the Pact of Pedras Altas— the state came under the administration of Getúlio Dornelles Vargas, a forty-four-year-old politician from the interior who had already served as finance minister under Washington Luís.[21] Born in 1883 as the son of a substantial rancher who had risen to the status of a general in the irregular state forces during the federalist revolt and succeeding incidents of civil strife, Vargas had a brief army career, which was to stand him in good stead with the military leaders of the 1930 Revolution and facilitate his dealings with the armed forces during his first fifteen-year stint as the nation's chief executive. This career began with his enlistment at age fifteen in order to be eligible for admission to the Rio Pardo Preparatory and Tactics School, from which he was expelled with a score of other teenagers following a student protest.

Returned to the ranks as Sergeant Vargas, he saw brief service during a 1902 border dispute with Bolivia before entering law school in Porto Alegre. Immediately recognized as possessing unusual leadership talents, he was successful as a student politician and was integrated into the Borges de Medeiros machine. He was elected to the state legislature in 1909 and rose to be its majority leader within a decade. Although brevetted as a lieutenant colonel of militia forces during the 1923 revolt, Vargas spent most of his time as leader of the Rio Grande do Sul congressional delegation. Though he had been named finance minister in 1926, he was called home to be elected to govern the Gaúcho state in November 1927.

Washington Luís's preference for Júlio Prestes was becoming apparent by early 1929, but so was the existence of a determined opposition, still oriented toward electoral channels but already developing capabilities to resort to force. Luís Carlos Prestes had replaced General Isidoro as military leader of the exiled revolutionary forces in 1927, and the São Paulo–based Democratic Party had subsequently reached a tentative working arrangement both with Luís Carlos Prestes and with Assis Brasil's Liberator Party in Rio

Grande do Sul.[22] These conspirators realized that only the defection of Minas Gerais and Rio Grande do Sul from the administration's coalition would open the prospects of electoral victory in 1930.

The conciliatory policies followed by Vargas made possible cooperation between the "Libertadores" and the Republicans in the quest to capture the presidency for their state. The organization of the Liberal Alliance (AL) went forward at the same time, as some of Vargas's advisors saw it as a means of pressuring President Washington Luís into abandoning Prestes and making Vargas the official candidate.[23] By mid-1929 Minas Gerais and Rio Grande do Sul had agreed on a shrewd political ploy. Announcement of a pact to nominate a Gaúcho would be used to try to make Washington Luís reconsider and support Antônio Carlos, in which case Rio Grande do Sul would get the vice-presidency as a consolation prize. If the president failed to see the error of his ways, other states would be recruited behind the Gaúcho candidacy.[24]

A Critical Election

The course of events leading up to the 1930 Revolution was marked by miscalculations on both sides as to the intentions and determination of the other. Washington Luís was certain that Vargas would fall into line and that Antônio Carlos lacked the resolve to go to the mat. For their part, Vargas, Antônio Carlos, and many other political leaders assumed that the president would eventually agree to a compromise unity candidate rather than risk an irreparable split with two of the country's leading states.[25] To minimize confrontation, Vargas made only one campaign appearance outside his own state, and for nearly five months after the March 1, 1930, balloting it seemed that there would be no resort to arms.

Although Minas Gerais and Rio Grande do Sul together gave Vargas nearly 600,000 votes, he was credited with only 200,000 votes in all the rest of the country—including 31,000 in little Paraíba, the home state of running mate João Pessoa (nephew of the former president). In a belt of the most backward states in the north and northeast, the official count gave Vargas only 77,000 to over 480,000 for the government candidate, who also received a suspiciously large majority in São Paulo on his way to an announced national total of nearly 1.1 million. (Of course the 299,000 to 1,000 margin for Vargas in his home state reflected some "preventive" and "countervailing" manipulation of the vote count.) In any case, the country knew that no opposition candidate had ever before run nearly this strongly.

Though convinced that the usual coercion and fraud had contributed decisively to their defeat, the national leaders of the Liberal Alliance seemed very doubtful of their ability to overturn the official results. Vargas himself expressed confidence that needed reforms could be brought about "within the existing order."[26] A series of blatantly partisan political moves spurred indignant protests from the Alliance spokesmen, but only a few on the civilian side—including Oswaldo Aranha and João Neves da Fontoura— were determined not to give up without a fight. Indeed, despite contingency planning over a period of more than a year, the civilians and military who would soon mobilize the most extensive revolutionary movement in Brazil's history—and very possibly in that of all Latin America—were still wary and distrustful of each other.[27]

The Revolution of 1930

The turning point as far as catalyzing the decision to raise the banner of revolt came with the assassination of João Pessoa on July 26, while he was on a visit to Recife. Although his murder was motivated by personal considerations with some ties to local political disputes, opposition spokesmen seized the opportunity to accuse the president of being responsible for this atrocity—Maurício de Lacerda gave a stirring funeral oration in which he likened the corpse to the "cadaver of the nation."[28] Armed with this highly emotional issue, Vargas and Antônio Carlos could finally abandon the cautious attitude imposed by the former's need for federal financial aid and the perilous military position of the latter.[29]

The Preparatory Phase

The most serious problem remaining was the quest for an able and prestigious military chief, a role Prestes had been expected to take. But once he had become a convert to the Communist cause, this popular hero's attitudes and ideology were no longer compatible with the aims of the Liberal Alliance.[30] When Prestes made clear to the other *tenente* leaders— especially Juarez Távora, Siqueira Campos, Miguel Costa, and João Alberto— that he intended to oppose any revolution that included among its backers such "reactionary" figures as former president Bernardes (now a major ally of Antônio Carlos), they ruled him out.[31]

Prestes's logical replacement, Siqueira Campos, perished in an air accident immediately thereafter. As he had been the chief organizer of the revolutionary movement in São Paulo and the popular hero counted upon to overcome the Paulista inclination toward favorite sons Washington Luís and Júlio Prestes, Siquiera's loss was a double blow to the conspiracy. Because Joaquim Távora, the most effective organizer of the 1924 revolt in São Paulo, had died during that struggle, the disappearance from the scene of the only other man who had demonstrated a capacity to dynamize Paulista discontent was a severe enough setback; the fact that he was the only nationally symbolic figure with enough charisma to offset Prestes's defection made the loss almost crushing.[32] When Prestes took advantage of the situation on May 30 to denounce the Liberal Alliance as irrelevant to the real demands and aspirations of the people, the heart had almost gone out of the conspirators.[33] Plans that had tentatively been made to launch a third July 5 uprising—in commemoration of those of 1922 and 1924—had to be abandoned.

The situation was reversed by the public furor over the murder of João Pessoa, the news of a successful revolution in Argentina, and a sense of malaise stemming from the continued economic deterioration. At this juncture forty-year-old Lieutenant Colonel Pedro Aurélio de Góes Monteiro, who in April had tentatively been named as military chief for the forces in Rio Grande do Sul, was confirmed as the Liberal Alliance's chief of staff. A northeasterner—from Alagoas, the state that had produced Deodoro and Floriano and that had long been noted for the frontier violence of its political life—Góes Monteiro had attended military school in Porto Alegre from 1906 to 1909, during which time he had been in close contact with the leaders of the law students there, including Vargas and João Neves da Fontoura. As a junior officer this future heir to a good part of Caxias's role had spent all but two years of his early career in Rio Grande do Sul, both marrying a local girl and becoming a friend of Oswaldo Aranha.[34] A student at the command and general staff school during the 1922 and 1924 revolts, Góes Monteiro subsequently gained considerable combat experience on the legalist side against the Prestes Column.

Efforts were made to recruit General Augusto Tasso Fragoso, who had recently quit as army chief of staff over budgetary restrictions, as well as General João de Deus Mena Barreto, known to be at odds with War Minister Nestor Sezefredo Passos. Although they did not join the conspiracy, these key generals in the capital, along with others who had demonstrated sympathy with the objectives of the Liberal Alliance, were kept informed by Vargas. Though not prepared to commit themselves to a revolutionary venture, they did undertake to maintain order in the Rio de Janeiro area during any interim that might occur between the fall of the government and the arrival of Vargas in the capital.[35]

Yet even in August the military outlook remained poor outside of Rio Grande do Sul. In Rio de Janeiro province, Cristovão Barcellos—who as army chief of staff in 1945 would take the lead in removing Vargas—found few willing to cast their lot with a risky venture, and only in Paraíba were the Liberal Alliance forces fully in control of the situation. There Juarez Távora and Secretary of Security José Américo de Almeida were prepared to launch a second front, but the main effort would have to be in the extreme south and complemented by a hoped-for Minas Gerais uprising. The first military goal was to consolidate control of these bastions before driving on São Paulo and the capital.[36]

The Fighting Stage

Launched on the afternoon of October 3, the revolt quickly swept aside or drew into its wake the powerful 14,000-man federal force in Rio Grande do Sul, dispersed as that force was into twenty-one separate garrisons. Within three days the rebel column was sweeping north through Santa Catarina to Paraná and by the end of the first week was preparing for a showdown with the legalist forces massed at Itararé in southern São Paulo. Meanwhile in the northeast the revolution was scoring a series of rapid successes. Fortaleza and Natal were soon in rebel hands, and fighting in Recife was over in two days.

A rapid march southward by Juarez Távora supported the attack on Salvador that had been undertaken by the troops of *tenente* officers Juracy Magalhães and Agildo Barata, who were already near success when federal resistance collapsed nationwide on October 24. Detachments from Minas Gerais had reached the coast in Espírito Santo, cutting land communications between Rio de Janeiro and the old capital. One legalist regiment put up fierce resistance in Belo Horizonte, but was subdued after five days of heavy rebel attacks. By October 23 rebel forces were on the verge of breaking through from Minas Gerais into Rio de Janeiro province. Overall, then, the military operations of the rebellion were a nearly unqualified success.

At this point the three senior generals in Rio de Janeiro managed to force the resignation of Washington Luís. Tasso Fragoso, perhaps the most respected officer in the army, in conjunction with generals Francisco de Andrade Neves and Alfredo Malan d'Angrogne, argued that the civil war, which threatened to turn into a protracted bloody struggle, could best be ended with the government's replacement by a junta of senior military figures. With a number of ranking officers in the area unhappy about the war minister's arbitrary personnel policies and the government's alleged neglect of the armed forces, the officers in the capital region were somewhat less than lukewarm in their desire to fight their fellows in defense of a quite discredited regime. Under these conditions, the idea of a bloodless military solution that would offer a good chance of maintaining the unity and institutional integrity of the armed forces had considerable appeal. Thus, when he was approached by associates of Tasso Fragoso, Colonel Bertholdo Klinger—Leitão de Carvalho's chief ally in the World War I campaign for apolitical professionalism—saw an opportunity to implement his concept of revolution from above for the purpose of restoring order.[37]

Working with the approval of his superior, General Mena Barreto, inspector of the first group of military regions, Colonel Klinger articulated a "Pacifying Movement." Hence, when the October 22 suggestion to the president that he resign by generals Tasso Fragoso, Mena Barreto, and Andrade Neves brought no result, a broad base of support existed for an ultimatum. Virtually a prisoner in the presidential palace and pressed by his good friend Cardinal Sebastião Leme, Washington Luís agreed to leave the country. On October 24, with thousands of rebel troops poised to launch an offensive against the federal and São Paulo forces, a "pacifying junta" took power in Rio de Janeiro. As was to be the case again in 1964, the potentially decisive and almost certainly costly battle did not actually take place.

Tasso Fragoso—who as a cadet had participated in the ouster of the monarchy—Mena Barreto, and Admiral Isaías de Noronha appointed a provisional government with Afrânio de Mello Franco holding the Justice and Foreign Ministries and Colonel Klinger as chief of police.[38] Although a number of supporters of the newly christened governing junta were reluctant to see Vargas come to power and some of the most extreme revolutionaries had badly wanted to conquer São Paulo and Rio de Janeiro by military force, a peaceful transfer of power took place.[39] Mena Barreto and Klinger were mollified by Vargas's use of the title "chief of the provisional government" rather than "elected president." But it was the issue of how to treat São Paulo that would give rise to continued difficulties culminating in a civil war in 1932.

The Provisional Government and the 1932 Revolt

On November 3, exactly one month after the outbreak of the revolution, Vargas took power, promising a vast program of "national reconstruction."[40] An amalgam of the Liberal Alliance program combined with a laundry list of the specific demands of the several diverse groups that had supported the revolt, Vargas's platform included amnesty for those involved in the insurrections of the 1920s; a purge of corrupt elements; financial austerity; greater priority for education; elimination of protection for the new import-substitution industries, which the agricultural interests viewed as "artificial" industries; diversification of agriculture; establishment of a Labor Ministry; and elections for a constituent assembly.[41]

Problems of Consolidation

Vargas's Cabinet featured Oswaldo Aranha as justice minister, with Foreign Minister Afrânio de Mello Franco and the army and navy ministers confirmed in the posts they had occupied under the junta. São Paulo's José Maria Whitaker was entrusted with the Finance Ministry, with José Américo de Almeida—the leading civilian revolutionary in the northeast—holding the transportation portfolio. The appointment of Assis Brasil as agriculture minister helped clear up the leadership situation in Rio Grande do Sul. Lindolfo Collor became Brazil's first labor minister and Francisco Campos took over the new Ministry of Education and Public Health. (The former's grandson would make good use of his grandfather's distinction as first labor minister in his successful 1989 bid for the presidency.)

Through a series of moves going well beyond those adopted in 1889 by Deodoro's provisional regime—and exceeding in several respects the limits the 1964 Revolution would set upon its arbitrary powers—the provisional government established itself as a dictatorship with vast discretionary authority. Most observers envisioned the arrangement as a temporary expedient to deal with the serious economic crisis and the pending creation of a viable institutional framework. Yet Góes Monteiro and other leaders of the military faction corresponding most closely to the "hardline" position after the 1964 system change expressed the view that at least a decade should pass before the country returned to a competitive political system.[42]

All representative bodies at the federal, state, and local levels were dissolved. Interventors to be appointed by Vargas and removable at his will would have near total power in the states, including authority to name prefects for each municipality as their agents. There was to be no judicial review of interventors' acts. Through steps very similar to those that would be adopted by the victors in 1964, the revolutionary regime undertook to investigate and punish corruption as well as to maintain careful control over the labor movement. Large numbers of politicians associated with the ousted government were arrested, with many being stripped of their political rights.

Although the former war minister and three other generals who had remained loyal to Washington Luís were forcibly retired, Isidoro Dias Lopes and Luís Carlos Prestes were recalled to active service. One of the rising mid-grade officers very nearly purged was Lieutenant Colonel Eurico Gaspar Dutra, who would eventually become Brazil's dominant military figure. Viewed by the *tenentes* with hostility because of his strong legalist stance during the 1920s, Dutra was defended by Klinger. Ironically, Dutra would become one of Vargas's staunchest military supporters, while Klinger would soon head the military side of a revolt against the dictator.[43] The authority of War Minister José Fernandes Leite de Castro was seriously infringed by the continued functioning of the General Staff of the Revolutionary Forces under Góes Monteiro, and influence and prestige within the military depended at least as much upon revolutionary credentials as on formal rank. The brigadier generals who had supported the October 24 coup gained a star in January 1931, and Góes Monteiro became a full colonel. He, Klinger, and eight other colonels became brigadier generals in May.

Yet in the eyes of a large proportion of the senior military chiefs, Vargas had been seen simply as a lesser evil than an extensive civil war. This did not provide a particularly firm basis for their continued cooperation, for they had precious little sympathy for Vargas's program. Their relations with the new regime were further strained by tension with the *tenentes*, many of whom the senior officers viewed as undisciplined troublemakers and politically ambitious upstarts. For their part, the "historical revolutionaries" (those whose plotting against the old republic went back to the first half of the 1920s) mistrusted many of the senior officers and mid-grade legalists as opportunists whose loyalty to revolutionary goals was highly suspect. The issue of prolonged rule by the provisional government versus rapid reconstitutionalization further separated the two groups. The *tenentes* and dissident oligarchies had only gotten together as events moved from the electoral arena to armed revolt, and their marriage of necessity was compounded by another of convenience between them and military elements that joined at the last moment.

Though far from homogeneous in their political orientation, as would soon be evidenced in their evolution in several distinct directions (including both communism and fascism), at this point the *tenentes* generally shared several common attitudes that set them apart from the civilian liberal constitutionalists. In the first place, the *tenentes* mistrusted politicians as a class and were more concerned with the substance of rather vaguely articulated social and economic reforms than with democratic forms. Imbued with a sense of mission and confidence in their technical capacities, they were strongly inclined toward experimentation with practices and institutions in order to further the country's modernization. Although many of them professed a general and often ill-defined socialist leaning—sometimes beginning and ending with support for land reform—they also manifested an elitist approach toward reform and "national regeneration" from the top that frequently shaded into an authoritarian nationalism. Then, too, certain elements of corporativist thought had begun to take root in the minds of those *tenentes* who were concerned about a programmatic basis or ideological underpinning for their movement.[44] With the passage of time different factions of *tenentes* would ally with differing civilian elements, diluting the possible impact of *tenentismo*.

In the northern half of the country the *tenentes* were able to consolidate the control they had established during the October fighting. Only in Paraíba and Pernambuco were civilian governments maintained during the early years of the Vargas era. Moreover, besides the ten northern states controlled by *tenentes* under the coordination of "Viceroy" Juarez Távora, Rio de Janeiro state was governed by a series of military figures, the last being Admiral Ernani do Amaral Peixoto—Vargas's son-in-law and subsequently father-in-law of the 1986–1990 governor of Rio de Janeiro.[45] Paraná was administered by military officers until 1932, and São Paulo and Santa Catarina also experienced periods of *tenente* government. Thus, military figures obtained significantly more experience in governing at the state level during the early Vargas years than they had either under Deodoro and Floriano at the beginning of the republic or during the "salvations" of the Hermes period.

Although in reality the Communists and other radical movements were quite weak, not only the old elites but the emerging middle sectors as well manifested symptoms of a near obsession with the proletarian threat. Heralded as a major progressive reform, the creation of a Labor Ministry was largely designed to provide an effective instrument for government control of the union movement in a situation in which the "social question" had clearly become a matter for policy rather than just police action. Although force would still be used against labor when its demands appeared to the regime to be too great or its political action excessively direct, under Vargas manipulative paternalism came to constitute the federal government's preferred strategy for handling matters in this field. Thus, the operation of the new agency as an integrated Ministry of Labor, Commerce, and Industry with stress upon conciliating worker-employer conflicts was part of Vargas's effort to assure entrepreneurs that their interests would be strongly safeguarded and that those of the workers would not be decisively favored.

The Rival Currents

As the common denominator of the Liberal Alliance had much more to do with opposition to the Washington Luís government than with a fundamentally hostile attitude toward the established order, divisions within the revolutionary coalition came to the surface soon after victory. The "dissident oligarchies" as represented by the São Paulo Democrats and the Minas Gerais Republicans wished for little more than narrowly political reforms. For these centrist (moderately conservative to classically liberal) elements, a formal system of representative democracy would work suitably once the power of the rural oligarchical machines could be curbed by eliminating their ability to manipulate election results as well as engage in various forms of fraudulent balloting. Under an adequate system of electoral justice, the "dissident oligarchies" argued, elimination of the rural bosses' "phantom" voters would reduce the controlled electorate of these bosses to a scale where its weight could be balanced by the growing proportion of urban voters. Even less reform-minded were some of the opposition groups in various smaller states who had joined the Liberal Alliance only as a vehicle for achieving power; all that they wished was to receive the same type of favors from the new government as the local machines they replaced had enjoyed under the old regime.

For certain other groups as well, the Liberal Alliance platform was a maximum program, but for more reformist elements it represented but the first steps in a program of national reorganization and restructuring of the social order. Along with their counterparts in other states, both the Republicans and Liberators in Rio Grande do Sul were essentially rural-oriented if not rancher-dominated. Their participation in the 1930 Revolution was motivated by desires to see a representative of their state as president and to enlarge their voice in national decision making.[46] Their ties to the São Paulo Democrats were in some respect as strong as their commitment to Vargas, whom they considered as a representative more than the unrivaled leader of a national revolution. Hence their support was in large part conditional.

The break between Vargas and João Neves da Fontoura, Vargas's vice-governor in Rio Grande do Sul, was all but complete even before Vargas assumed power in Rio de Janeiro; friction with one of Vargas's chosen interventors, Flôres da Cunha, would soon arise; and old Gaúcho *caudilho* Borges de Medeiros soon developed strong reservations concerning the orientation of the dictatorial regime.[47] Thus, it is obvious in retrospect that the coalition of forces that overthrew the Old Republic was so heterogeneous that there was no real chance of welding it into a coherent party or movement. Indeed, Vargas needed all of his very considerable political skill simply to keep defections down to a manageable level.

The "Case of São Paulo," which was to catalyze the disaggregation of the revolutionary forces, erupted almost immediately. At the end of October, Vargas had patched together an interim administration in São Paulo combining the Paulista Democrats and the *tenentes*. João Alberto was given broad powers as the revolution's "civil and military delegate" but the presidency of the state, coveted by the Democratic Party, remained temporarily vacant. General Isidoro Dias Lopes was placed in command of the military region and Miguel Costa was given the highly professional French-trained state militia (Força Pública). But when João Alberto and Miguel Costa launched the Revolutionary Legion on November 12 as a political movement aimed at supplanting or marginalizing the Democratic Party, the power struggle broke into the open. For in the eyes of the *tenentes*, the Paulista Democratic Party (PDP) leaders were inherently little better than the São Paulo Republicans who had been the backbone of the ousted regime.[48] The Democrats responded by accusing João Alberto of protecting subversive elements, but Vargas appointed him interventor in São Paulo on November 24, with Miguel Costa in the newly created post of secretary of public security. Moreover, repentant figures from the Republican Party replaced Democrats in many posts.

The founding of the Revolutionary Legion in São Paulo was not an isolated action, but rather a step to implement the younger revolutionaries' belief that new political forms were necessary to carry out the objectives for which they had fought. Aranha, Juarez Távora, João Alberto, and Góes Monteiro had agreed upon the need for a vehicle to provide continuity for the radical goals of the revolution. The Revolutionary Legion in São Paulo was matched in Minas Gerais by the khaki-shirted October Legion of Gustavo Capanema and Francisco Campos, with the somewhat uncomfortable participation of the new chief executive there, Olegário Maciel. The October Legion sought to erode the political bases of the Republican Party and to provide a more reliable political support for the Vargas regime.

In the federal capital the October 3 Club brought together the *tenentes* and like-minded civilians, with Góes Monteiro, Aranha, and Federal District Mayor Pedro Ernesto Batista originally among its most active leaders. These three, plus Juarez Távora and João Alberto, made up the nucleus of the inner circle of Vargas's advisors at this point. Although they stressed the civic education and political training functions of the Revolutionary Legion, the liberal constitutionalists saw the group as a threat. Hence the São Paulo situation took a turn for the worse with the Democratic Party breaking with the interventor in late March, which was followed a month later by an abortive Força Pública revolt. As a result Góes Monteiro was sent to São Paulo as military commander, but efforts to agree upon a "civilian and Paulista" interventor were thwarted by the rivalry of João Alberto and Miguel Costa.

Although the military situation was partially normalized in April 1931 with the appointment of Tasso Fragoso as army chief of staff, a final confrontation between the *tenentes* and the constitutionalists could only be postponed, not entirely averted.[49] Borges de Medeiros's call in May for rapid reconstitutionalization coincided with the *tenentes'* promulgation of a revolutionary program clearly dependent upon a continuation of extraordinary powers. Subsequently there was a significant decline in *tenente* influence. In late July, João Alberto was replaced by Paulista politician Laudo de Camargo, and in August, Aranha and the *tenentes* failed to replace the Minas Gerais chief executive with Virgílio de Mello Franco.

Aided by Cordeiro de Farias as São Paulo police chief, in November the *tenentes* engineered the substitution of Colonel Manuel Rabelo for Camargo. With Aranha taking Whitaker's place as finance minister, the São Paulo Democrats found themselves being treated as virtual enemies by the federal government. At the same time the Rio Grande do Sul "United Front" of Borges de Medeiros, Interventor Flôres da Cunha, and the Liberator Party's

Raúl Pilla stepped up pressure on Vargas for election of a constituent assembly. This effort was supported at least implicitly by a manifesto signed by generals Mena Barreto, Klinger, and several others at the end of November, which called for a return of the army to its "true functions" and blamed the *tenentes'* quest for political offices and interference in governmental affairs for a breakdown of military unity and a sharp drop in the prestige of the armed forces. Then in mid-January 1932 the Democratic Party formally declared its opposition to the Vargas government and opened negotiations with the Republicans for a "Paulista United Front."[50]

Although the signing of the long-awaited electoral law and the appointment of a new interventor were designed to defuse the explosive situation in São Paulo, these conciliatory moves came too late. The Paulistas, accustomed to controlling the country's destiny, were thoroughly fed up with being treated as a "conquered territory" by an essentially Gaúcho and northeasterner federal government. Moreover, at the same time a mob with at least two score of army officers in the van wrecked the offices of a newspaper that had been highly critical of the *tenentes*.[51] Several high officials resigned in protest, and Vargas's naming of João Alberto as the new Federal District police chief spurred the former's opponents to step up plans for armed resistance. Concurrently the October 3 Club underwent reorganization, but with no consequent softening of its authoritarian line or hostility toward the São Paulo "divisionists," who were accused of using the issue of constitutionalization as a cloak for a drive for power. Though he stood essentially with the *tenentes*, Vargas sought to stave off the coming revolt by announcing in early April that elections for a constituent assembly would be held in May of the following year.[52]

By May 1932 Brazil found itself on the brink of civil war. On May 23 a mob spearheaded by Democratic Party students burned the Revolutionary Legion's headquarters in São Paulo. When War Minister Leite de Castro resigned at the end of June, Vargas bypassed long-time Chief of Staff Tasso Fragoso and named retired Brigadier General Augusto Inácio do Espírito Santo Cardoso to the post. The general was a figure of little prestige, but one of his sons was a close associate of João Alberto and another was an active *tenente*.[53] The progressive radicalization of the October 3 Club vitiated Vargas's hopes to avoid a violent national confrontation, so Aranha, Góes Monteiro, and José Américo de Almeida resigned from the organization they had founded, thus effectively ending its significance. For events had made it obvious that, with personalist and local factors still so salient in Brazilian politics, it was not possible to build a national reformist party.[54]

A Bloody Civil War

General Klinger, who had been recruited by Miguel Costa to be the military leader of the São Paulo insurgents, precipitated the revolt through an insulting letter to the new war minister on July 6. Eager to avenge the "humiliations" they had received at the hands of the *tenentes* and Vargas, the haughty Paulista conspirators had set the date of the uprising for sometime after July 15 to allow for a coordinated Rio Grande do Sul rebellion. Their hopes for success were pinned upon this, plans for First Region commander General João Gomes Ribeiro Filho to lead a revolt in the capital, the expectation that Klinger would bring 5,000 regular troops with him from Mato Grosso, and the chance that forces led by Bernardes would create enough trouble in Minas Gerais to at least tie up the federal garrisons there. The rebels were to be disappointed on every count. The first hitch in these plans came when 1930 legalist and anti-*tenente* Gomes resigned his command in May over being slighted by Leite de Castro and he was replaced in that strategic position by Góes Monteiro.

Despite his earlier sympathy for the movement, at the last moment Flôres da Cunha in Rio Grande do Sul remained loyal to Vargas (whose dropping of Leite de Castro had been aimed at mollifying Flôres da Cunha), thus neutralizing the United Front there—and probably dooming the revolt. The Minas Gerais government sent state militia against São Paulo, and Klinger arrived there alone with the troops of his old command posing a threat to the rebels' undefended rear. Moreover, there was no military uprising in Rio de Janeiro—from where wave after wave of reinforcements left for the front, bolstered by troops sent by the *tenente* interventors in the north and northeast.[55] To compound problems, Klinger arrived late, and meanwhile the initiative had been lost as Colonel Euclydes Figueiredo, the interim commander, adopted a defensive posture.

A pincers soon developed, with Góes Monteiro leading a powerful column down from Rio de Janeiro and General Waldomiro de Lima, a relative of Vargas, deploying a strong legalist army on São Paulo's southern border. When a counterattack from Minas Gerais got underway combined with a naval blockade, the revolt's fate was sealed. Although the São Paulo insurgents put nearly 40,000 armed men into the field, well over half were poorly trained civilian volunteers. By contrast, government forces eventually totalled at least 75,000 men on the three main fronts and were backed up by nearly limitless reserves. At the end of August, General de Lima alone had 18,000 troops, and Góes Monteiro's command had reached 34,000 by the eve of the end of hostilities on September 29, 1932.[56] Indeed, this was the largest armed conflict in South American history, its nearest rival being the peak of the Paraguayan War sixty-five years earlier.

There was not, however, complete harmony on the government side concerning conduct of this campaign. Having advocated compromise rather than the risk of civil war, Tasso Fragoso resigned as army chief of staff in August and was replaced by Andrade Neves. Moreover, Góes Monteiro and Waldomiro de Lima developed a considerable rivalry.[57] The latter faced acts of insubordination in August by units of the Rio Grande do Sul "Brigada Militar," as the Gaúchos belatedly launched an armed revolt. But when Borges de Medeiros was captured on September 20, hope for a second front able to take pressure off São Paulo perished. Indeed, exploratory negotiations concerning a cease-fire had already been initiated by General Klinger as federal troops drove to within 100 miles of the rebel capital and air strikes became more frequent. On October 2 the São Paulo government resigned, ending a valiant twelve-week struggle against overwhelming odds.

Given the extent to which the Paulistas felt victimized by the 1930 Revolution, without which their dominance of the central government would have extended at least until 1934, the rebellion was perhaps all but inevitable. Had the provisional regime been able to find a figure it trusted for interventor who satisfied both the Paulista demand for one of their own and the *tenente* requirement for unquestioned loyalty to revolutionary goals, the course of events might have been quite different. Whereas Siquiera Campos might have muted the conflict between the *tenentes* and the Democratic Party, João Alberto intensified it. Driven to a pact with Republican Party elements in key states in order to broaden the base of their revolt, the Paulista insurgents paid the price of appearing linked to retrograde forces.

For its part, the Vargas government played skillfully upon still-fresh memories of São Paulo domination and Paulista "imperialism" to arouse latent hostility toward the province believed by many Brazilians to harbor separatist proclivities. Lacking the major grievances that motivated them in 1930 and seeing in Vargas's concessions a strong possibility for reconstitutionalization without the risk of resort to force, Rio Grande do Sul and Minas Gerais refrained from joining the revolt, which left São Paulo isolated. Then, too, the Paulista elites failed to enlist the effective support of the working class—fear of whose greater political involvement was one of the causes of the elites' attrition with Vargas. Most important for the future, the Paulistas learned from this bitter and costly experience not to place themselves again in such an exposed position, a rule that would govern their conduct in subsequent crises.

Although the *tenentes* were firm in their support for Vargas and provided a large contingent of the army's future leaders, many of the officers who were active on the constitutionalist side would also play significant roles in future events. Justino Alves Bastos and his brother-in-law Nestor Penha Brasil, who in the early 1960s would each command the powerful Third Army at a critical juncture, were with the revolt, and in Rio Grande do Sul lieutenants and brothers Henrique Geisel and Orlando Geisel sympathized with the constitutionalist cause—a sentiment shared by their younger brother Ernesto (who would be president from 1974–1978). Though in large part the military leadership of the 1932 revolt was comprised of officers linked to the "pacifying junta" and was assisted by some who had remained loyal to Washington Luís, the developments of the next half dozen years would create new lines of division cross-cutting those of 1930–1932, so that the alignments in subsequent crises would be substantially different.[58]

The Constitutional Interlude

Roughly 200 constitutionalists, including seven generals, were exiled to Portugal in the wake of the revolt's collapse, and a sweeping decree deprived several categories of rebels of their political rights for three years, lumping many of the legislators of the Washington Luís period together with all the active participants in the 1932 rebellion.[59] Yet in spite of opposition from the *tenentes*, who felt that reconstitutionalization was still premature, Vargas chose to follow through on the concessions he had made and to honor commitments made to the governments of Minas Gerais and Rio Grande do Sul—which had weighed heavily in their not joining the Paulistas. Though this policy of conciliation did serve to undercut efforts for a new revolt, it also opened the door for a political resurgence of the pre-1930 elites.[60]

Almost as soon as hostilities ended, a special commission under the chairmanship of Foreign Minister Afránio de Mello Franco—and including Góes Monteiro, Aranha, and José Américo de Almeida—began work on drafting a new constitution, finishing its task in May 1933. With a healthy São Paulo crucial to the economic recovery of the country and with that state's delegation slated to be the second largest in the constitutional assembly—which would also elect the next president—Vargas hoped to achieve a rapid normalization. Hence General Waldomiro de Lima as São Paulo interventor avoided repeating the policies of João Alberto and permitted organization of a wide variety of political movements, including several representing groups that had supported the revolt.

Combined with Flôres da Cunha's stronghold over Rio Grande do Sul politics through the Republican Party—with old Borges de Medeiros exiled to Recife—and Olegário Maciel's dominance of the Minas Gerais political situation, this coalition of political forces effectively blocked the *tenentes'* renewed efforts to establish a national party as a vehicle for the radical reformist aims of the 1930 Revolution. Though several of the *tenente* interventors did set up parties of this type in their states, the majority ended up working with or even actively seeking the support of traditional political forces.[61]

Writing a New Constitution

Thus, the May 1933 elections for the new National Constituent Assembly were marked by the participation of a confusingly large number of new parties that existed solely at the state level, most of which really represented old established political interests and leaders. The chief innovation, then, was the participation of women for the first time in the nation's history. *Tenente*-backed Social Democratic Parties in several states met with little success. Indeed, the election's victors included a large proportion of political notables and relatively few representatives of the various *tenente*-backed reformist movements. To redress this conservative balance somewhat, but more to strengthen the government's hand in the new legislative body, forty "class" representatives chosen through a carefully controlled process of indirect elections were subsequently added to the 214 members elected on May 3. Eighteen of these hand-picked delegates came from labor unions, seventeen from employer organizations, three from liberal professions, and two represented government employees. The total number of military men elected was a relatively modest seventeen.[62]

In São Paulo the "Single Slate for the Good of São Paulo," an alliance of the old Republican and Democratic machines behind a variety of new organizations and labels, elected seventeen congressmen.[63] General de Lima's usefulness as interventor was ended by the electoral failure of his "São Paulo Coalition for Defense of the Revolution of October 1930"; caught between the resurgent constitutionalists' demands for a "civilian and Paulista" interventor and the thinly veiled hostility of Góes Monteiro—and subject to increasingly vocal criticism from the *tenentes*—he resigned. But whereas they were successful in thwarting de Lima, the *tenentes* were not able to influence Vargas's choice of the new interventor, and over their vocal opposition the São Paulo government was entrusted in October to Armando de Sales Oliveira, brother-in-law of *O Estado de S. Paulo* publisher Júlio de Mesquita. Vargas had decided to gain the support of his old political enemies even at the cost of alienating some of his earliest allies, so that, unlike Deodoro, he would not be faced with unified Paulista opposition to his presidential bid.

No sooner had the dictator worked out a resolution to his São Paulo political headache than he was faced with a serious political dilemma involving Minas Gerais—and its crucial thirty-seven votes in the presidential contest. Even more than had the São Paulo episode, this new crisis divided Vargas's closest political associates. Maciel's death abruptly raised the succession question in Minas Gerais at a most inconvenient time for the provisional chief executive. Flôres da Cunha and Antônio Carlos, the former harboring his own presidential ambitions and the latter in the strategic position of going to preside over the constitutional convention, backed acting provisional president Gustavo Capanema. For his part, Afrânio de Mello Franco demanded the appointment of his son Virgílio, whose distinguished role in the 1930 Revolution earned him the support of Aranha and many of the *tenentes*.[64]

Consistent with his general proclivity toward compromise and congruent with his strategy of maximizing his political maneuvering space, Vargas instead selected young Minas Gerais congressman-elect Benedicto Valladares. The Mello Francos would not, of course, forget this slight and would within a few years become major leaders of the opposition, contributing significantly to Vargas's ouster in 1945. But as Valladares owed his unexpected elevation entirely to Vargas's goodwill and his wife was a relative of the strongman, Vargas assured himself control of the Minas Gerais government by a loyal satrap rather than having there an independent political leader with national ambitions. Significant for the future was Valladares's choice for his staff chief: Juscelino Kubitschek de Oliveira, a young doctor whose nascent political ambitions would carry him to the presidency two decades later.

While the constituent assembly, which opened on November 15 under the presidency of Antônio Carlos and with Aranha as majority leader, was engaged in approving a new constitution and preparing to elect a president for the 1934–1938 term, Vargas found himself in a strengthened position on the military side as well as in the political realm. Prestigious senior officers had passed away or gone into retirement, the luster of the *tenentes* had been dimmed considerably by the 1933 politicking, and internal differences had reduced the October 3 Club from a broad spectrum of the revolution's authentic spokesmen to the mouthpiece for one faction of *tenentismo*. Officers who had proved themselves loyal to the government in 1932 had been promoted at the end of the revolt and by now occupied key positions in the command structure. Also, the 1931–1932 furor over the reincorporation of the 1922 cadets as first lieutenants had died down with the creation of a "parallel" promotion pool. Symbolic of this changed situation of general legalist dominance was the election of Brigadier General Dutra to preside over the Military Club.[65]

Under these circumstances Góes Monteiro encountered scant opportunities to translate his political ambitions into action, and all other leaders of the 1930 Revolution had been trimmed down to size. In the eyes of an overwhelming majority of Brazil's political leaders there was no real alternative, much less rival or threat, to Vargas in the presidential sweepstakes. But just as in 1891 there had been an abortive attempt to block Deodoro's election by launching the candidacy of Floriano—a military figure from within the regime—so in 1934 elements of the October 3 Club supported the idea of Góes Monteiro as a presidential candidate. Vargas aptly placed them in checkmate by appointing Góes Monteiro to be war minister in January 1934.

The functioning and outcome of the 1933–1934 constituent assembly did not differ substantially from those of its 1890–1891 predecessor. Just as the first republican constitution had been drafted by a special commission named by the provisional chief executive, so the new charter was drawn up.[66] Following the organizational sessions in mid-November, the executive's rather eclectic project and proposed amendments were considered by a special commission, whose membership was more a microcosm of the larger body than a collection of the most distinguished jurists and substantive specialists. The commission's draft went to the floor in March 1934.

Meanwhile, as had been the case four decades earlier, the authority and actions of the provisional chief executive were amply recognized. Most of the *constituentes* intended to campaign for election to the new national legislature as soon as their work in Rio de Janeiro was finished, and they were also subject to considerable psychological pressure from the military to give Vargas most of what he wanted. Hence, although the constitution promulgated on July 16, 1934—pushed through by a "steamroller" of the major states—differed from the government's proposal in some significant respects, these were not considered critical by Vargas, who had never committed himself publicly either to the "Itamaraty" draft or to that which subsequently emerged from the "Commission of 26." Indeed, he was much more concerned with preparing his election to a four-year term than with the details of the framework within which he would have to govern.

On July 17 Vargas was chosen constitutional president by a comfortable margin of 175 votes to 59 for Borges de Medeiros—who had been put forth as a symbol of protest by the opposition, who had no illusions about winning—and 13 votes split among nine other individuals. Within the limits of a sometimes conveniently ambivalent constitution, Vargas was free to continue with his work of gradual modernization of the Brazilian nation.

The contradictions within the constitution reflected the divisions within the body politic, in which slightly renovated rural oligarchic structures and liberal constitutionalist movements representing urban bourgeois aspirations coexisted with disparate emerging middle-class elements who had not yet translated their aspirations into viable programs, ideologies, or movements. In this sense the 1934 constitution was a valid symbol of its times. Much of the core of the 1891 charter and its classical republican institutions were preserved, but grafted onto it were the political reforms so dear to the liberal constitutionalists along with the socioeconomic guarantees demanded by the *tenentes* and their reformist civilian counterparts. Thus, the secret ballot, women's suffrage, and an independent system of electoral courts were combined with a beginning of class representation. Though 250 deputies would be elected territorially, 50 others would represent labor unions and professional syndicates.

Greater centralization was partially offset by new limitations upon presidential authority. On the one hand the powers of the Senate were sharply curbed—to reduce the excessive influence of small traditional states—while on the other hand the basis for representation in the Chamber of Deputies (one deputy per 150,000 population up to a total of twenty deputies, then one deputy per 250,000 inhabitants) was designed to restrict the dominance of São Paulo and Minas Gerais. Broad provisions of the sections on the "economic and social order" established the basis for an active and interventionist national government, but the distribution of revenues was shifted slightly in favor of the states and municipalities. Article 162 declared that the armed forces were "permanent national institutions and within the law, essentially obedient to their hierarchical superiors." Their function was "to defend the Fatherland and guarantee the Constitutional powers." This was little changed from the 1891 charter, which had been repeatedly interpreted as justifying military intervention into politics in exercise of the moderating power. Yet in many ways the document was, reflecting the currents and cleavages of the times, "ambiguous, dissatisfying both sides."[67] Though augmenting the competence of central power, it gave the states great influence in the legislative branch. It was this increased state influence that would lead Vargas to turn to the military as his allies in the struggle to strengthen the national government vis-à-vis the state oligarchies.

Vargas as Constitutional President

The legal transition from dictator to constitutional president meant that Vargas, who had been following an essentially centrist course since coming to office, would need to pay even greater attention to the claims of organized political groups. In line with the new realities, the Cabinet was reconstituted with the exception of the two armed forces ministers. Regional political balance appears to have been the chief consideration in the composition of the new government, although Aranha's going to Washington, D.C., as ambassador removed this major figure from the political scene.

As Vargas was ineligible to succeed himself, maneuvering for 1938 began almost right away, with the 1934 congressional balloting and the subsequent indirect election of governors critical to the ambitions of the several presidential aspirants. (The electorate at this point had reached 1.47 million.) The state elections of October 14 yielded mixed results, with victory perhaps going more frequently to middle-of-the-road elements than to either the pre-1930 oligarchic machines or the strongly reformist movements. In all major states the forces supporting the interventors emerged on top. Thus, Armando de Sales in São Paulo, Valladares in Minas Gerais, Flôres da Cunha in Rio Grande do Sul, Carlos de Lima Cavalcanti in Pernambuco, and Juracy Magalhães in Bahia all gained election to full terms as governors from their new state legislatures. Similarly, Pedro Ernesto was elected mayor of the Federal District. In Rio de Janeiro state the election was delayed by an impasse until late 1935, when Navy Minister Protógenes Guimarães finally defeated General Cristovão Barcellos, who was strongly backed by Flôres da Cunha. (Flôres da Cunha was seeking at that time to build a network of alliances that would facilitate his election to the presidency in 1938.) In most of the minor states candidates friendly to Vargas won election; indeed, after the 1937 coup Vargas would appoint nearly all of them as interventors of their respective states.[68]

Vargas's knack for expanding the powers of the presidency was given a boost by the National Security Law of April 4. The law was aimed against the Communists, but it was to result in a radicalization of the liberal opposition, which saw in it a dangerous step toward arbitrary executive power and a possible return to dictatorship. On May 6 Góes Monteiro resigned (in a move that may have been intended to elicit a vote of confidence from Vargas) and was replaced by General João Gomes. Compromised by his long-term rivalry with Flôres da Cunha—who had emphatically accused him of Bonapartist proclivities and even of plotting to seize power—Góes Monteiro remained without assignment until January 1936. Whether Vargas consciously engineered it that way or not, he had effectively undercut the most powerful and ambitious military figure and divided the army to the point where he could play one faction against another to maximize his own freedom of action. And Góes Monteiro would also remain Vargas's chief instrument for eventually eliminating Rio Grande do Sul strongman Flôres da Cunha from the presidential lists. For by October 1935, Vargas already had this in mind.[69]

The Communist Revolt and Its Aftermath

More serious than the military crisis of the first half of 1935 was the marked radicalization of politics. The emergence of strong ideological political movements on the Left and Right overshadowed the contest between the oligarchical forces and *tenente* reformism which had characterized the politics of the early 1930s. With the leadership of the liberal democrats exiled after the 1932 revolt and their political organizations greatly weakened, a political vacuum existed that was deepened by the inability of the *tenentes* to launch a national political movement during the 1933 campaign. Benefitting from a situation in which the Vargas regime showed no inclination toward building a national party, the Left began to develop the beginnings of a mass base, while in reaction a militant ideological movement emerged on the Right.

In view of the political trends in Europe at the time and Brazil's marked permeability to external influences, such a polarization was to be expected; the absence of any indigenous modern party or unified political movement merely facilitated the process. Indeed, one of the reasons that the *tenentes'* effort in late 1933 to gain middle-class or labor support failed was that many of the leaders of these groups and even some of the *tenentes* themselves were already looking elsewhere—to the coalition of radical forces coalescing around the Communist Party and to the incipient Brazilian fascist movement, each of which possessed both the ideological underpinning and the fresh, potentially charismatic leadership that the *tenentes* lacked.

Red Versus Green

Luís Carlos Prestes and Plínio Salgado were the figures who by 1935 were increasingly capturing the attention of the urban populace. Returning from Russia a full-fledged Communist in April 1935, the "Knight of Hope" (Prestes) had a powerful attraction for elements who felt he had been correct in predicting that the 1930 Revolution and the "placebo" program of the Liberal Alliance would lead to no significant improvement in the lot of the proletariat or rural masses. On the other hand, many of the less radical petty bourgeoisie as well as staunch Catholics and military figures listened attentively to the siren song of a budding native fascism that called for a strong, almost authoritarian, syndicalist state and an "integral" society. The radical and authoritarian strains foreshadowed in *tenentismo* were now transformed into the leitmotifs of ideological political movements.

Integralism, which was to flourish and fade in a span of only six years, had its origin as a political movement during the campaign preceding the constituent assembly elections. Plínio Salgado, a young and prolific writer who had previously authored the original manifesto of Miguel Costa's Revolutionary Legion, set up a Society of Political Studies in São Paulo that attracted the interest of dissatisfied young middle-class intellectuals. These included Olbiano de Melo in Minas Gerais; Lieutenant Severino Sombra (who had organized a Cearense Legion) and Padre Helder Câmara in Fortaleza; a group in Rio de Janeiro led by Augusto Frederico Schmidt, Francisco Clementino de San Thiago Dantas, Lourival Fontes, and Raimundo Padilha—all of whom would play significant political roles in the 1950–1964 period; and such Paulistas as Miguel Reale, José Loureiro Júnior, and Roland Corbisier. Gustavo Barroso, president of the prestigious Brazilian Academy of Letters, was one of the movement's leading theoreticians and leaned more toward nazism, in contrast to Salgado's great admiration for the Italian brand of fascism. Launched in October 1932, Brazilian Integralist Action drew most of its inspiration from the Portuguese regime of Antônio Salazar and from Mussolini's Italy. The Integralist candidate polled only 4,600 votes in São Paulo during the May 1933 balloting for the Constituent Assembly.

Placing heavy emphasis upon the family, nation, and God, the doctrine of the movement called for corporatist representation and municipal autonomy. All the trappings of fascism were utilized, with the Greek letter sigma serving in place of the Nazi swastika and green shirts instead of brown or black. Its stress on hierarchy and discipline, which appealed to traditional forces seeking to articulate defense of the "Christian" order against a presumed Communist threat, and the endorsement of many elements of the Catholic Church won integralism the support of middle-class sectors searching for leadership and a program following the eclipse of liberal constitutionalism and the decline of *tenentismo*.[70]

Although the Integralists were gathering strength during 1934–1935, their political enemies on the Left were preparing even more rapidly to make a bid for power. In March 1935, during the debate over the National Security Law and a divisive controversy over the issue of military pay raises, the National Liberation Alliance (ANL) was launched as a united front of radical leftist forces including the illegal Brazilian Communist Party (PCB). Although the PCB was certainly a moving force of the ANL and came to exercise a more decisive voice with the passage of time, the radical wing of *tenentismo* and alienated liberal democrats were also active in the ANL's formation.[71]

The ANL's president was Captain Herculino Cascardo, a historical revolutionary with a distinguished record of leadership in the *tenente* revolts of the 1920s, and Captain Roberto Sisson, a socialist, served as its secretary general. Radical *tenentes* including João Cabanas and Nemo Canabarro Lucas in São Paulo participated in the work of the ANL there under the direction of Miguel Costa and Communist intellectual Caio Prado Júnior. Agildo Barata, a radical *tenente* who had supported the constitutionalist revolt, returned from exile to join the Communist Party and help coordinate ANL activities in Rio Grande do Sul. At the March 30 ANL convention Luís Carlos Prestes, then in transit from Moscow, was proclaimed honorary president of the movement. The resolution to this effect was introduced by young Carlos Lacerda (son of the old radical politician Maurício de Lacerda), who, as a conservative populist, would become one of Brazil's most powerful political figures during the 1950s and early 1960s.

At the same time that the revolutionary and strongly anti-imperialist program of the ANL was being disseminated throughout the country, the Chamber of Deputies passed the National Security Law, giving the government new legal weapons to use against the ANL—which the Chamber depicted as a front for the subversive PCB. Having such strongly authoritarian overtones as to provoke criticism from the Military Club, in the short run this legislation probably helped the ANL's rapid growth. Through the PCB and, to a lesser extent, anarchist and socialist elements, the ANL enjoyed very substantial influence among the more militant and politicized labor unions, and a wave of strikes was unleashed. This further alarmed the Brazilian bourgeoisie, which saw in the specter of working-class mobilization by radical political forces a threat to their favored position. Clashes between ANL partisans and Integralist elements occurred in various parts of the country, in several instances resulting in fatalities.

At a July 5 ANL rally commemorating the 1922 and 1924 *tenente* uprisings, Prestes surprised many of his supporters with the revolutionary extremism of his speech. Denouncing Vargas for having permitted the expansion of imperialist influences, he called for a popular revolutionary government to combat this, to liquidate the fascist peril, and to destroy feudalism. His ringing cry of "Down with the odious government of Vargas! All power to the National Liberation Alliance!" was a direct defiance of the regime, which responded quickly by closing the ANL for six months and arresting a number of Communists. This incident put an end to the debate within the PCB between supporters of the popular front approach and advocates of violent revolution, with the latter group carrying the day.

From Protest to Revolution

Even before the closing of the ANL, contingency plans for a coup had been prepared, and in August and September preparations were accelerated.[72] The PCB's plans for armed struggle in the name of the National Liberation Alliance were both based upon an unrealistic assessment of the situation, which attributed to the masses a militancy that they lacked, and undercut by the unwillingness of many middle-class radical politicians to undertake such an extreme and risky step. Moreover, the conspiracy was extensively penetrated by the Vargas government aided by British and German intelligence services.

Thus, instead of a mighty explosion, the November 1935 revolt erupted more as a string of firecrackers—a series of local military uprisings easily subdued by the regime. Rio Grande do Norte, where dissatisfaction with the gubernatorial elections was widespread and increasingly harsh discipline upset many soldiers, afforded the best prospects for success. There several units of the Twenty-first Battalion rose up prematurely on the night of November 23 and, with the aid of sympathetic civilians, soon controlled Natal. In Recife the Twenty-ninth Battalion revolted on November 24 and was joined by railroad workers, but within twenty-four hours legalist forces were reasserting control of the situation—at the cost of 1,000 lives. Following the collapse of the Recife revolt, the rebels in Natal also fled, so by the time hostilities began in the capital on the originally scheduled date of November 27, the danger in the northeast was already over. With a state of siege already in effect, the government quickly contained the revolt of the Third Infantry Regiment at Praia Vermelha (at the foot of famed Sugar Loaf Mountain) and that of the Aviation School some fifteen miles beyond the edge of the city. Military region commander Dutra received the surrender of Agildo Barata's forces at noon, following artillery and aerial bombardment, while around daybreak Colonel Eduardo Gomes, the surviving hero of the 1922 revolt, had already put down the mutiny of the First Aviation Regiment.

Brief as was the Communist-led revolt of 1935, it was to leave a legacy of anticommunism on the part of most of the Brazilian officer corps that would still be highly operative well beyond 1964. Indeed, the anniversary commemorations would be favorite occasions for impassioned oratory against the menace of leftist subversion even in the late 1980s. The revolt's immediate effects were to strengthen Vargas's hand substantially and to induce the vast majority of the officer corps to close ranks against the "subversive" Left. It also brought the Church and propertied interests into alliance with the military to combat all radical and progressive forces that could be viewed as allies of the Communists.[73]

The Aftermath

In the weeks preceding the revolt a crisis had occurred within the army as the war minister refused to promote Newton Cavalcante, whose Integralist sympathies were well known, to brigadier general over a number of colonels with greater seniority.[74] The tension between Vargas and Flôres da Cunha had also reached the breaking point through the protracted struggle to see their surrogates triumph in the contest for the governorship of Rio de Janeiro state. Bolstered by the mid-November victory of Admiral Guimarães, Vargas dismissed General Pantaleão Pessôa, a close friend of Flôres, from his influential post as chief military aide.

The Communist revolt pushed these problems onto the back burner and enabled Vargas to convince Congress to make the National Security Law even more stringent. Furthermore, he obtained three amendments to the 1934 constitution. The first allowed the president to equate a "grave internal commotion" having subversive intentions to the "State of War" provided in Article 161, thus greatly increasing his emergency powers. The second authorized him to dismiss military figures—active, reserve, or retired—who took part in a subversive movement, and the third made it possible for him to do the same to civil servants.[75]

Many of the rising ex-*tenentes*, including Gomes and Cordeiro de Farias, did not like the implications of Amendment No. 2, but they were in no position to create an issue over it. Góes Monteiro, on the other hand, felt the situation called for even more drastic action. In a foreshadowing of the events of 1937, he advocated as a possible line of action a coup through which the constitution would be abolished and full powers would be concentrated in the hands of the president.[76] Although the government did not go that far, a special National Security Tribunal was established to try those accused of involvement in the plot. By a vote of 190 to 59 in July 1936, Congress suspended the immunity of suspect legislators. Among the several thousand arrested in the aftermath of the revolt was Federal District Mayor Pedro Ernesto Batista, the former president of the October 3 Club.

Aided by congressional willingness to extend the state of war every ninety days, Vargas went on with his unannounced task of destroying all remaining capabilities of the Brazilian Left and intimidating his more vocal liberal critics. In fact, as subsequent events were to prove, the abortive revolt enabled Vargas to lay the groundwork for his own coup and the establishment in 1937 of a long-term dictatorship. For even in the midst of electoral campaigning in March 1937, Vargas was able to convince the dominant conservative forces in Congress that the Communist threat was still sufficiently real to justify yet another extension of emergency provisions. When they finally refused to extend emergency powers again in July, it would be too late to upset Vargas's carefully laid plans. As the most meticulous study of the period concludes: "Vargas managed with extreme competence the complex regional political game, creating or redefining loyalties, isolating resistances and shaping a new system of subordination to the priority goals of a new power center. To this end he could count on his distilled experience as a politician coming from the Old Republic, something he never ceased to be."[77]

The Estado Novo

The year 1937 was the most momentous for Brazil since 1930, although the profound changes that took place were far from those most Brazilians or foreign observers expected. While the public's attention during the first ten months was focused upon the contest for Vargas's successor, scheduled to be chosen in January 1938, the really crucial developments were largely behind the scenes, where the president skillfully carried to fruition his undermining of political rivals and creation of a favorable situation among the military. Indeed, Vargas had already begun his double game of appearing to accept, if not positively facilitate, the electoral process while at the same time preparing for his own unconstitutional continuance in power.

Background of the Coup

Vargas knew he could manipulate the political parties, including the Integralists and Communists, to achieve his ends, but Flôres da Cunha and his 20,000 "provisional" troops in Rio Grande do Sul constituted a major obstacle to Vargas's continuist ambitions. The Gaúcho governor, though anxious to become president himself, had endorsed the candidacy of Armando de Sales by São Paulo at the end of 1936, in part to force Vargas to show his hand.

Long hostile to Flôres, his rival since 1930 as the second most powerful figure in the country, Góes Monteiro accepted appointment as inspector of southern military regions with the unspoken understanding that his principal task was to devise a plan to eliminate Flôres's military strength.[78] The decision to move against Flôres deeply divided the army high command, but in a manner advantageous to Vargas. João Gomes left the War Ministry in early December of 1936 over his opposition to Góes Monteiro's plans for bringing matters to a head, opening the way for Vargas to appoint Dutra as Gomes's replacement—and Dutra would be a bulwark of support to

Vargas in this post until 1945. Then in mid-1937 Góes Monteiro became army chief of staff, while politically ambitious rival Waldomiro de Lima was arrested.

During the first half of 1937 Vargas was extremely busy anticipating or countering the moves of civilian political elements who threatened to get in his way. Alert to the president's interest in continuing in office, Bahia Governor Juracy Magalhães had attempted to forge an alliance of his state with São Paulo, Rio Grande do Sul, Minas Gerais, and Pernambuco to compel Vargas to abide by the constitution.[79] But Vargas was already weakening Sales's position by wooing the latter's successor as São Paulo governor, articulating a second Paulista candidacy, and reminding politicians that in light of the short time since the 1932 revolt, thought of a Paulista presidency was premature and certain to divide the country.

In reaction to this, on April 1 agreement was reached by Sales, Flôres, and Magalhães to view a threat to one of their states as an aggression against all three.[80] Vargas responded to this provocation by a show of authority, which, among other interventions, involved imposition of a state of siege in Rio Grande do Sul and removal of Antônio Carlos as the presiding officer of Congress. Antônio Carlos's replacement was a young deputy from Minas Gerais, Pedro Aleixo, who had been serving Vargas well as majority leader. (During the postwar period Aleixo would be a key congressional leader of anti-Vargas forces before serving as vice-president in 1967–1969.)

Both the presidential campaign and Vargas's conspiracy to abort it went into high gear in mid-year. The newly formed Constitutionalist Party formally nominated Sales, while Minas Gerais Governor Valladares, backed by all states except São Paulo and Rio Grande do Sul, put forth the candidacy of José Américo de Almeida. Although he never received Vargas's direct endorsement, the latter was considered to be the official candidate and received the support of the São Paulo Republicans as well as that of the anti-Flôres forces in Rio Grande do Sul.

The field of candidates was soon enriched by the addition of Salgado, but the wily Vargas was about to blow the campaign apart. Sales expressed confidence in the ability of liberal constitutionalism to withstand blows from extremists of Left and Right, while José Américo, true to his pro-*tenente* orientation, attacked the oligarchs, denounced the Integralists, and stressed honesty and political morality.[81] His increasingly radical pronouncements struck many of his original backers as dangerously demagogic. With violent conflicts marking many Integralist campaign rallies—sometimes as a result of attacks by left-wing elements possibly encouraged by some of Vargas's henchmen—a significant proportion of the political elite and a growing number of the urban middle class were susceptible to the idea that perhaps the elections should be postponed if a suitable unity candidate could not be found. Indeed, as the most careful study of this period points out, Sales' campaign showed that São Paulo liberalism was "more oligarchical than plutocratic," while the failure of José Américo's populist campaign demonstrated the continued strength of "agrarian and oligarchic bases" elsewhere in the country.[82] The former polarized regionalism; the latter polarized classes.

Vargas moved astutely to exploit the changing mood and engineered a controlled escalation of the crisis. Polarization was fostered by encouragement of Integralism on the one hand and reactivation of the specter of Communist subversion on the other. Inflammatory addresses by Vargas and pro-Integralist General Newton Cavalcante on September 20 set the stage for the bombshell that exploded in the press ten days later—a new Communist plot to seize power by force of arms. The so-called Cohen Plan—replete with vivid detail on the liquidation of anti-Communists, burning of churches, and other violent acts—had a profound impact upon public opinion. Generally accepted at the time as authentic, it induced an atmosphere of near hysteria.[83]

Buffaloed by Dutra and Góes Monteiro, Congress approved a new state of war decree, reinstituting the emergency powers Vargas needed to carry out his continuist designs. On October 14 the Rio Grande do Sul, São Paulo, and Pernambuco state militia were "requisitioned" by the war minister. Three days later Flôres—who had recently avoided impeachment by the margin of a single vote—fled the country when the governor's palace in Porto Alegre was surrounded by federal troops. (Their commander, Lieutenant Colonel Odylio Denys, would become one of the two most influential military leaders in the country between 1950 and 1964.)

A Bloodless Golpe

With Flôres out of the way, Vargas required only three weeks before ending the electoral charade. Sales had been isolated as merely a São Paulo candidate; now Valladares was put in charge of destroying his own creation, the candidacy of José Américo—leaving only Salgado. Here the Integralists' unrealistic assessment of their strength facilitated the task, for, convinced that the days of the old nonideological politics were over, they had viewed the smashing of the Left in 1936 as paving the way for their rise to power. Although their ranks had grown to as many as 200,000 by 1937, including a number of persons in second-echelon positions in the government and many navy officers, they lacked roots in the masses.

In late September Salgado was shown a draft of a new, essentially authoritarian constitution by Francisco Campos, Vargas's original education minister, who hinted that Integralism might become the official ideology of the proposed "Estado Novo."[84] This paved the way for Integralist acceptance of Vargas's imminent coup in return for continued official tolerance and control of the Education Ministry. Seeing no viable alternative in view of the overwhelming military support for Vargas's plans, Salgado reaffirmed Integralist "solidarity with the President of the Republic and the armed forces in their fight against Communism and anarchical democracy."[85]

Not only did Vargas have the support of a majority of northeastern governors for his coup, but on November 5 São Paulo's José Joaquim Cardoso de Melo Neto fell into line. Dutra had smoothly handled mobilization of support by key generals, leaving only the commander of the Fourth Military

Region, Lúcio Esteves, opposed. Góes Monteiro's successor as president of the Military Club, this staunch legalist had been placed in check by a recent transfer to Minas Gerais. Only when Góes Monteiro declared that the armed forces were not moving to establish a military dictatorship and that in case of a change of regime they sought no benefits for themselves did the opposition begin to emerge from their fool's paradise.[86] On November 8 Campos took over as justice minister, and on the morning of the 10th Congress was closed and the new constitution was declared to be in effect. The eight-year run of the "New State" had begun.

As with the original republic nearly a half century earlier, the military's role had again been critical. Although the Estado Novo itself was "a Bonapartist authoritarian formula conducted by a leader apparently acting above classes," the coup installing it was "without any doubt a military *golpe* in civilian dress."[87] Vargas worked with Góes Monteiro and Dutra to reestablish discipline and hierarchy and to consolidate the army's influence as a pillar of central government power. In stages from 1932 until the critical September 27, 1937, meeting during which a group of military commanders decided to go ahead with the coup, it fell principally to Góes Monteiro to:

> define a new strategy which consisted in strengthening the principles of a lost hierarchy, preaching at the same time an elimination of political contests within the army. In other words, it suited the corporation to amplify spaces within the State, assume effective conditions for its functioning and participate in the construction of a national project above regionalisms, without involving itself directly in the lesser questions which divided the political class in the direct struggle for power. Within this proposal, it concerned itself with assuring an arbitral role for the military apex while combatting involvement at a lower level.[88]

The democratic regime installed with the 1934 constitution had really died in November 1935; two years later the armed forces helped Vargas bury it.

The armed forces were largely responsible for permitting Vargas to establish this dictatorial regime, although few officers expected the administration to last past the end of the decade, and the forces drew several lessons for this experience. First and foremost they resolved not to be again maneuvered into permitting a chief executive to maintain himself in power beyond his constitutional term. Thus, "an autonomous and interventionist army capable of acting with its own legitimacy" would keep a very close watch on Vargas in 1954 and a decade later would oust his political heir rather than run the risk of João Goulart imposing a "syndicalist republic" upon the nation.[89] Whereas the early 1930s had been a period of learning as well as disillusionment for the *tenentes* in regard to competitive politics, the years after 1937 taught them that an authoritarian dictatorship under a civilian "indispensable man" also had critical disadvantages for the controlled modernization of the country to which they aspired.

After 1937 the military would find no real turning back from an active involvement in determining the course of political affairs, at least as long as the *tenentes* remained on the scene. Hence their perceptions of the Estado Novo period, during which, for example, future presidents Castelo Branco and Costa e Silva advanced from fairly junior majors to senior colonels, would decisively affect attitudes and actions not only in 1945, but also in all subsequent crises through the 1960s.

The New Order

The early weeks of the Estado Novo were filled with government initiatives reminiscent in gross terms of the first moves of the provisional government seven years earlier. Reaction against the swift and decisive *golpe* had been scattered, taking the form of the resignations of governors Magalhães of Bahia and Lima Cavalcanti of Pernambuco—both of whom had been pointedly left out of the pre-coup consultations. With Governor Guimarães in Rio de Janeiro state fatally ill, Vargas named naval Captain Ernani do Amaral Peixoto, soon to become his son-in-law, as interventor. General Manuel de Cerqueira Daltro Filho had been serving as Rio Grande do Sul interventor since the ouster of Flôres, and all governors who supported the coup were confirmed in power as interventors, with Valladares allowed to keep the title of governor.

Essentially Vargas's action was accepted by most elements of Brazilian society with varying degrees of resignation or enthusiasm as necessary under the emergency conditions.[90] Astutely, Vargas portrayed himself as a servant of the people who, responding to the needs of the country, had reluctantly agreed to forgo his well-earned leisure and, at great personal sacrifice, to bring Brazil a "strong government of peace, justice, and work."[91] In reality, he had been aiming toward this moment ever since reconstitutionalization had been forced upon him by the 1932 revolt. All of his apparent twistings and turnings were undertaken with this final goal in mind.

Tenentes, the senior military, the new civilian elites, the old oligarchical machines, the Integralists, and even the radical leftists dedicated to his overthrow had been used by Vargas in one way or another as he quietly and effectively mobilized discontent against the constitutional system, hence diverting that discontent away from himself, the country's chief executive. Thus, he was able in November 1937 to assume the stance of a unifying symbol in a situation where ideological polarization not only had provided salience to both communism and fascism, but also had divided those who rejected radicalism between the traditional liberal constitutionalism of Sales and the fundamental, often incoherent populism of José Américo. In all politically relevant strata, developments—aided by Vargas's manipulations—had raised broadly held doubts as to the viability of conventional democracy in Brazil.[92]

For, although the military had been critical in the establishment of the Estado Novo, the Church and propertied interests had also facilitated Vargas's plans. As Camargo and her associates have shown:

The Church, politically mobilized, also represented a relevant role in the legitimization of the coup, to the extent in which it supported the government in measures against communism, giving needed backing to its fight in aspects of social life over which it exercised, at the time, extreme influence. . . . What the Church received in return for its decisive collaboration wasn't little: in the first place, aid to religious schools in detriment to lay education, and, in second place, the insertion of important Catholic cadres in official institutions, as well as the attention of important ministries, like Education, to its principal political demands. . . . With respect to the entrepreneurial sectors, this period saw the emergence of new leaders such as Roberto Simonsen and Euvaldo Lodi. . . . These new leaders collaborated with the industrialization policy initiated by the government after 1937 and defended the protectionism indispensable to national economic development, coming to have places on the technical councils involved in redirecting the Brazilian economy.[93]

The 1937 constitution, largely the handiwork of Francisco Campos but shaped to Vargas's general specifications, laid down elaborate provisions for the restructuring of the country's political institutions. These articles concerning representation and legislation, which drew heavily upon the Polish constitution and Italian legislation, never went into effect, as Vargas purposely failed to schedule the national referendum on the constitution after which elections were to have been called.[94] Hence he continued to enjoy complete decree powers augmented by those pertaining to the state of national emergency that remained permanently in effect. Moreover, he retained the power to amend the constitution by presidential decree and did so on several occasions.

In keeping with the Estado Novo's centralizing and authoritarian character, Article 161 defined the armed forces as "permanent national institutions, organized upon the base of hierarchical discipline and faithful obedience to the authority of the President of the Republic." Thus, this article withdrew any legal basis for exercising the moderating power.

Stability and Change Under the Dictatorship

Vargas encountered few serious difficulties during the consolidation of his dictatorial regime. The death of General Daltro Filho at the beginning of 1938 provided him with an opportunity to assuage Gaúcho sensibilities by naming Colonel Cordeiro de Farias as interventor, and this politically astute former *tenente* governed effectively for nearly six years. However, wanting someone loyal to him administering São Paulo, in April Vargas selected energetic young Adhemar de Barros, thus launching this conservative populist on a career that would include two serious bids for the presidency as well as a major role in the 1964 Revolution. Then Vargas lured Aranha back from Washington to be foreign minister in March 1938, using the latter's strong liberal personality to balance the authoritarian Francisco Campos—thus reestablishing Vargas's favorite situation in which he could play off the personal and political rivalry of leadership figures to keep their ambitions in check.[95]

Buttressed by the censorship provisions of the constitution and the December 1937 Press Code, Getúlio, as Vargas was popularly known, enjoyed a secure position of unchallenged control—at least so long as he kept his fences well mended with the military. This was quite easy at first, as the army was kept happy with its own growth and the curbing of state paramilitary forces as well as with such gestures of national unification as the symbolic burning of state flags. Federal armed forces nearly doubled in size between 1927 and 1937 while the strength of the states' Força Pública units grew by less than 36 percent.[96]

The Integralists hoped their leader, Plínio Salgado, would emerge as the Hitler to Vargas's Hindenburg, but Brazil's all-time master politician had other plans, being cut more from the Bismarckian mold. Although nationalism and the beginnings of a paternalistic social policy were to be carried forward under a corporativist, semi-authoritarian state, it would not be the Integralists who gave orientation to the regime and benefitted from its actions. With the "communist threat" laid to rest by Vargas's strong government, many Brazilians who had backed the Integralists when it appeared that Vargas would be forced to step down by the constitutional ban on reelection now preferred the dictator's pragmatic approach to the doctrinaire program of the Brazilian Integralist Action Party. Moreover, there was a nearly unbroken string of bitter disappointments for the Integralists, as Vargas included them in the December 2 decree outlawing all political parties and did not allow their continuation in the guise of cultural associations and physical education clubs. And although General Cavalcante resigned his command of the Vila Militar over the regime's moves against the Integralists, he would subsequently make his peace with the dictator and refuse to be the military leader of the 1938 Integralist revolt.[97]

The Integralists Shoot Their Bolt

The only threat to Vargas's new order of things came in May 1938 when Integralists joined with some liberal constitutionalist conspirators in a poorly executed coup attempt, one that reflected as great a detachment from reality in their assessment of the situation as had the Communist-led revolt of 1935. A premature naval uprising on March 11 led to the arrest of many of the most important non-Integralist leaders including Colonel Euclydes Figueiredo, the non-Integralists' most experienced military figure, and Otávio Mangabeira, the most prestigious civilian.[98] As approved by General João Castro Júnior, plans for the revolt centered on carefully coordinated attacks by small groups composed chiefly of military men upon nearly seventy strategic targets in the capital. The president himself was to be surprised at his residence and taken prisoner on the night of May 10, because on that date one of the conspirators would be in charge of the marine corps detachment on guard duty there.

With almost everything going wrong even before dawn, many of the attackers were hunted down and shot, while others were fortunate enough to find asylum in the Italian Embassy. In the aftermath Vargas amended the constitution to further strengthen his extraordinary powers and established a personal guard made up of loyal roughnecks from his home area in Rio Grande do Sul. The hundreds of arrests that followed helped convince the chief opposition leaders—Sales, Mesquita Filho, Bernardes, and Mangabeira—to accompany the coup's financial backer, Flôres da Cunha, into exile, where they were soon joined by Salgado.

Institutionalization Through the State, Not Parties

Even after this abortive coup, Vargas continued to govern without a political party and made no effort to channel his support into any type of an organized movement. In part he was manifesting his suspicion that parties might prove a vehicle for the rise of political rivals, but to a high degree Vargas viewed parties as merely electoral trappings—the only role they had ever really played in Brazil—and thus irrelevant to his needs and objectives. For as the months turned into years, it became increasingly apparent that elections were far from the president's thoughts.[99]

Indeed, in Vargas's experience parties had tended to cramp his political style. The well-organized and disciplined Republican Party in Rio Grande do Sul had never been under his control; in fact it had been turned against him by Borges de Medeiros in 1932 and subsequently by Flôres. The Democratic Party in São Paulo, more attuned to the new politics of the post-1930 era, had been used to mobilize effective opposition to the Gaúcho *caudilho* and then to launch a revolt against him. Moreover, São Paulo remained a major political vulnerability for the dictator and by virtue of its very size would almost certainly become an extremely influential, if not dominant, factor in any national party. The only ideological parties Vargas had seen in action were extremist, and radicalization was against his political nature. The efforts of the *tenentes* in 1931 and again in 1933–1934 to found a national party embodying the goals of the 1930 Revolution had not met with success.

In sum, Vargas saw no need for a party and preferred the flexibility of a partyless political system. Even the shifting of his basic political technique of manipulative paternalism toward personalistic populism did not, at that point at least, call for any new intermediary structures. In this area Vargas was not innovative, preferring to turn existing forces and institutions to his use if at all possible and destroying those he could not utilize. In addition, he thrived on exploiting personal rivalries among leading figures, often turning yesterday's opponents into today's allies, rather than having to cope with institutionalized power contenders.

Although Vargas did not significantly change his political style or fundamentally modify the institutional structure of the Estado Novo during the seven years following the elimination of the Integralists as a political factor, Brazil itself was changing and he would adapt pragmatically to altered conditions. The processes of industrialization and urbanization, though not achieving the growth rates they would in the postwar period, were modifying the societal foundations of the polity. With the prolonged moratorium on normal political life continuing into the wartime emergency, neither the shifts in the composition of the potential electorate nor changes in their orientation to politics and alliance patterns were readily apparent, but in reaction to external as well as internal stimuli these changes definitely were taking place. By 1945 Brazil would be substantially, if not dramatically, different from the Brazil of 1937, even more so from that of 1930.

National integration continued to progress, in large part as a result of the government's pronounced centralizing tendencies, and the federal executive branch—particularly its bureaucratic structures—developed capabilities far beyond those of an earlier era. One at a time rather than wholesale, an impressive array of administrative agencies were established to deal with matters previously outside the scope of public policy, but with which the centralized, increasingly interventionist state under Vargas was beginning to concern itself. Most readily visible, a wide variety of government corporations and mixed capital enterprises came into being to play an ever more important role in economic development.[100] Also in the spotlight was an array of new organizations designed to tie the urban workers more closely to the government through both the dependent union movement and a rudimentary social welfare system.[101]

Social and Economic Change Under Vargas

To understand the roots and setting of this increasingly complex and differentiated state, it must be borne in mind that social and economic change picked up steam during the Vargas years—chiefly through acceleration of trends already discernible in the late 1920s. By 1940 the country's population had grown to over 41 million—and would reach 52 million by 1950—with São Paulo finally having surpassed Minas Gerais, the former at 3.67 million to the latter's 3.39 million. Urbanization had progressed to the point at which Rio de Janeiro city had a population of about 1.9 million and São Paulo city over 1.3 million (followed by Recife at 550,000 and Salvador with 338,000). The labor force had expanded to over 14.7 million workers—almost 12 million of them male—with agriculture still leading the way employment-wise at over 9.7 million, followed by the service sector with some 3.4 million and industry with more than 1.5 million. Indeed, almost 900,000 of the 1.5 million in industry were employed in nearly 50,000 registered factories. By 1945 industry's share of GDP was up to 28 percent, with agriculture having declined to 28.6 percent.[102]

During the Vargas period there was a very substantial and sustained surge of import substitution industrialization. Prior to this time industrial growth had been heavily dependent upon the export earnings generated chiefly by coffee sales; after 1930 it became more self-sustaining. Though exports dropped from 14 percent to but 8 percent of GDP from 1930 through 1932, industrial production declined only 10 percent and recovered in 1933 to the predepression level, subsequently rising 50 percent by 1937. Indeed, on the strength of an 11.2 percent annual rate of expansion from 1933 through 1939, Brazilian industry's output actually doubled during the 1930s. Although industrial growth would subsequently slow down, mainly because of World War II and the resulting scarcity of capital goods, it still rose at a yearly average of 5.4 percent from 1940 through 1945. Propelled by this industrial growth, GDP rose by nearly 4.3 percent annually during the 1930s and continued to grow over 3.3 percent annually from 1940 through 1945—resulting in an average annual growth for the sixteen-year period of just under 4 percent.[103] This stands in striking contrast with most of Latin America during this period and should be considered one of the major accomplishments of the Vargas era.

The Brazilian economy, then, recovered relatively quickly and well from the initial traumatic impact of the global depression. Although real GDP fell over 5 percent in 1930 and 1931, this loss was largely offset in 1932 alone. Because of the crisis of the export sector, a distinct break developed between this coffee-led factor and industrial growth. Certainly export earnings were still necessary to generate a capacity to import basic industrial inputs and capital goods. But whereas export receipts plus money supply accounted for 80 percent of investment capacity prior to 1914, this proportion had declined to just under 70 percent during the 1914–1929 period before it dropped sharply to only 33 percent from 1930 on.[104] Reduced capacity to import at the beginning of the Vargas era stimulated the already existing consumer goods industry—for a currency depreciation reaching over 100 percent by 1935 sharply increased the relative price of imports. As the Vargas period stretched on, favorable conditions were created for an expansion of the incipient intermediate goods industry and even a beginning of production of capital goods.[105]

Thus, by the time of Vargas's departure from power at the end of 1945, internal economic activity had replaced external demand as the principal determinant of the accumulation of industrial capital. As a natural result of these developments, the hegemony of the traditional "coffee" bourgeoisie came to an end as the obverse side of the rise of the newer urban, industry-related bourgeoisie.[106]

Although debate continues over the impact of government coffee policy upon this quite rapid recovery from the depression, the fact is that the coffee sector's income declined only 25–30 percent compared to a 60 percent drop in the international price of coffee. But in the process over 78 million sacks of coffee were removed from the surplus stocks by burning. At first this was done through a National Coffee Council (CNC) established in May 1931 and made up of representatives of the producing states, but the council was replaced in February 1933 by the National Coffee Department, which was directly subordinate to the finance minister.[107]

In the process of attempting to support the price of coffee through reducing the supply, Brazil's share of world sales slid to 48 percent in 1934–1937 compared to near 70 percent for 1930–1933. Hence the establishment of the Estado Novo was accompanied by a return to a marketing policy designed to press other producing countries toward an international agreement. Pursuant to this agreement, Brazil's exports rose sharply from 12.2 million sacks in 1937 to 17.2 million and 16.5 million during the next two years—just over 57 percent of the global total. At the end of 1940 Brazil convinced the United States to set up a quota system that allocated to the latter 9.3 million sacks per year out of a total of a little over 15.5 million.

Meanwhile diversification was taking place as coffee fell from 48 percent of the total value of Brazil's agricultural production in the late 1920s to under 30 percent for the 1932–1936 period and only a bit over 16 percent between 1939 and 1943. The slack was mainly taken up by cotton and rice, which together rose from 11 percent in 1939 to nearly 28 percent by 1943.[108] Moreover, during the first stages of the Vargas regime banking institutions were finally established to handle the growing need to finance expansion of productive capacity. The Department of Banking Mobilization began to exercise rudimentary central bank functions in 1932, and in 1937 an Agricultural and Industrial Credit Department was created within the Bank of Brazil.

The growth and differentiation of the Brazilian state was reflected in a wide range of areas besides coffee and banking. In contrast to the relative simplicity of the central government during the highly federalistic Old Republic, institutes, autonomous agencies, and consultative councils proliferated, particularly after establishment of the Estado Novo. Policy with respect to production and trade came to be formulated by the Technical Council of Economics and Finances of the Finance Ministry (1937), the National Petroleum Council (1938), the Water and Energy Council (1939), the Executive Commission of the National Steel Plan (1940), and the Fuel and Lubricants Commission (1941). With the establishment of the National Steel Company (1941) and the National Alkali Company (1943), the government moved into the area of actual production.

The institutional footings for planning were established with the Federal Foreign Trade Council, the National Council for Industrial and Business Policy, and the Economic Policy Commission.[109] Particular sectors were served—and co-opted—by the Alcohol and Sugar Institute (1933) and its subsequent counterparts for cocoa, maté, salt, and pinewood. This bureaucracy remained a rather ramshackle and jerry-built structure with considerable overlapping of functions and lack of mechanisms for effective coordination short of the presidency. Yet these agencies served rather well their primary political purpose, that of "transferring the conflict among the different dominant groups to within the State bureaucracy itself through self-representation of interests in these technical organs."[110]

Development of Interest Groups

Essentially, the process of economic and social change underway during the Vargas years did not result in any sudden replacement of the hitherto dominant coffee-led agricultural elite by the urban industrial sector, much less by the middle class. Instead, the end of the first group's near hegemony resulted in a state not exclusively serving the interests of any one socio-economic sector—all of which lacked adequate political vehicles for attempting to gain control of the governmental machinery. There were now a multiplicity of interests seeking to attain their ends in terms of impact upon public policy, but after 1937 there was no longer either a legislative arena or an opportunity to mobilize electoral support and bring it to bear upon the executive. Both interest articulation—the effective expression of political demands—and interest aggregation—the reduction of those demands into a manageable number of policy alternatives—had to take place without political parties as intermediaries between societal sectors and the policy-making apparatus of the Vargas state.

Though Vargas was a very astute political balancer, conciliator, and manipulator, he could only concern himself with the most important matters. Indeed, the Vargas presidency lacked the elaborate staff that has subsequently evolved, and the dictator worked almost directly with his ministers, assisted only by a small group of personal aides. Although the Administrative Public Service Department (DASP) was created in 1938, it was essentially a technical and administrative agency designed to make coordination possible and to increase bureaucratic efficiency, not any kind of a superministry.[111]

In this context there was a pressing need to develop some structures to link state and society. With parties ruled out, the answer was a network tying together the Vargas-appointed interventors, the growing array of governmental agencies, and the sectoral organizations fostered by the basically corporativist design of the Estado Novo. This, as orchestrated by Vargas, who retained ultimate decision-making authority, would provide a means for accommodating emerging interests while at the same time easing the decline of traditional elites by continuing to provide them with the opportunity to influence the decisions most vital to their economic interests. Centralization was made more palatable by furnishing a widening variety of groups with new avenues of quite direct access to policy making and implementation just above the working level. The resulting system of co-optative clientelism enhanced the viability of the Vargas-designed state by channeling the concerns and energies of politically relevant elements into relatively narrow struggles over policy in particular areas—hence away from broader questions of the regime's basic orientation and underlying priorities.

At the state level, the Vargas system worked through having local branches of the DASP in the capitals serving as limited functional equivalents of the nonfunctioning legislatures. Thus, the interventor could act largely as a political coordinator for the president, and Vargas could also use the state DASPs—which reported to him through the justice minister—as a parallel channel of information and a check upon the activities and loyalty of each interventor. The functioning of this mechanism was crucial for the viability of the Estado Novo, because in essence a unitary form of government had been imposed upon a country long used to an exaggerated degree of federalism and effective local autonomy.[112] Yet the interventors still had considerable leeway for accommodating to local realities in keeping with the balance between the emerging urban forces and the established agrarian interests with their clientelistic machines.[113]

The workings of party and electoral representation had led to a predominance of local over national and private over public interest—both before 1930 and in the 1933 and 1934 balloting. Hence the architects of the Estado Novo wished to integrate social groups into the political system "through a mechanism of controlled participation, under the direction of the State, which would thus preserve sufficient freedom of action to function as arbiter of conflicts in the name of the nation's general interests."[114] To this end the regime set out to "institutionalize the confrontation among dominant groups, reinforcing the avenues of access of the victorious power coalition of 1930, excluding at the same time ideologically undesirable forces, and simultaneously reducing the political influence of traditionally dominant sectors."[115] Therefore the state's autonomy was relative, not absolute, and far from monolithic or equidistant from the different social forces. This manipulation of participation with the state as arbiter was foreshadowed in the 1930–1937 period and subsequently given a more defined structure by the Estado Novo.

As the 1930s moved toward their end, the emerging industrial elite's view of the desirability of state intervention in the economy came to coincide with that held by key regime figures—as well as that of some important elements in the armed forces.[116] Hence there was a very gradual shifting of resources and benefits away from the traditional agrarian sector toward emerging urban interests, particularly those involving building the foundations for industrial capitalism.[117] This trend was facilitated to the degree that the industrial entrepreneurs gained experience in forming alliances with other "modernizing" elements and working effectively with the governmental machine. Recognizing the new opportunities it afforded, the Federation of Industries of the State of São Paulo adjusted promptly to the corporative structure of interest representation, while in contrast the declining coffee interests lamented their loss of control over policy and moved toward opposition to the Vargas regime.[118]

Clearly the governmental capabilities of the Brazilian executive grew from 1930, through 1937, and on to 1945—accompanied by the state's increasing penetration of at least the urban, modernizing sectors of society. As the central government came to affect directly the lives of a larger proportion of the population, both more frequently and in a wider variety of ways, the regime built a multiclass base, even if this was not reflected in the sphere of political organization. Hence, although there was very little mobilization, the base for a future move in this direction was laid. Lacking representative institutions, yet without a markedly high component of coercion, the structures of the Estado Novo were fulfilling the functional requisites of a modernizing, albeit still far from modern, political system.

The Critical Role of Leadership

Though Vargas had clearly consolidated his dominance within this Brazilian political-governmental system by mid-1938, maintenance of this favorable position continued to depend to a high degree upon employment of his political skills, not the least of which was discretion. The military still constituted a significant restraint upon his actions, but any substantial conflict was avoided because he did not attempt to move in directions contrary to their perception of national needs and interests. Moreover, for the first time in a generation no consequential civilian opposition to the regime was calling upon the armed forces to exercise their power as a veto group.

Placing a high priority upon internal peace and order after nearly two decades marked by instability and unrest, the armed services accepted a role of guardian of the regime, although not unconditionally. Indeed, in 1937 and 1938 opponents of the Estado Novo coup were elected to preside over the Military Club. Thus, John Wirth could conclude that "As the political arbiter of Vargas's regimes, the Army exercised great influence on policy at every turn of the political wheel."[119] Significant in Vargas's successful relations with the military was his use of economic nationalism and the key role in industrialization policy given to the military after 1937 through the National Security Council—in which they were predominant—and the National Petroleum Council under General Júlio Caetano Horta Barbosa.

It was the coming of World War II, however, that was most important of all in Vargas's maintenance of effective power and authority vis-à-vis the armed forces. Not only did it enable him to channel military energies into the war effort while rallying popular support in the name of national defense, but it also provided an opportunity for sending a large proportion of the more activist officers to the United States for training and, subsequently, to combat in Italy. Furthermore, the armed forces were substantially satisfied with the new equipment they received from the United States and the very favorable position relative to Argentina that Brazil came to enjoy in terms of military strength. All this would be jeopardized by any move against Vargas, who exploited the image of President Franklin Roosevelt's most valued ally in the hemisphere.

Brazil and the War

World War II was to have a profound impact upon the Brazilian armed forces, chiefly those officers of the *tenente* generation. Although pro-Axis sentiment existed on the part of a large proportion of the officer corps, particularly those who had been attracted to Integralism in the mid-1930s, the course of events led to close collaboration with the U.S. military and a quite thoroughgoing reorientation of those officers most deeply involved in this process. Among the key figures who underwent a shift from a position of substantial sympathy for Hitler's Germany to being exponents of hemispheric solidarity and eventually ostensible champions of liberal democracy were both Dutra and Góes Monteiro. The first phase of this transformation accompanied that of Vargas himself; the second carried them to a point at which they joined the movement to oust the dictator from power—in part to negate the danger of being dragged down with him in the face of nearly overwhelming opinion among the armed forces as well as civilian groups that a return to representative government was overdue.

From the early days of the Estado Novo, Foreign Minister Aranha worked assiduously to bring Vargas around to the side of the United States in the intense competition with Germany for Brazil's cooperation. Ability to deliver concrete benefits and fundamental geopolitical realities won out, and in September 1940 agreement was finally reached on an Export-Import Bank loan of $20 million, later raised to $45 million, to build the Volta Redonda Steel Mill of the government's National Steel Company. For with the war raging in Europe and the Allies in control of the Atlantic, there was little chance of receiving further shipments of the $55 million in armaments ordered from Germany under a 1938 contract with Krupp Industries.[120]

Yet the United States was unwilling to furnish war material on the large scale Brazil requested, and the Vargas government could not agree to the stationing of thousands of U.S. troops in the strategic bulge of the northeast. This changed with the U.S. entry into the war, but only over the objections of Dutra and Góes Monteiro and in the face of concessions by the United States on both military hardware and economic assistance. The torpedoing of numerous Brazilian ships beginning in March 1942 led to Brazil's declaration of war against Germany and Italy on August 22.[121] Góes Monteiro presented a plan for military collaboration to Navy Secretary Frank Knox in Rio de Janeiro in September, but the proposal of Leitão de Carvalho, the head of Brazil's military delegation in Washington, went further: a full army corps of three divisions to be trained for combat in the European theater.[122] With Dutra's endorsement this plan was discussed between Vargas and Roosevelt in Natal in February 1943. Bitter over being left out of what was increasingly Dutra's show, Góes Monteiro resigned as chief of staff and at the beginning of 1944 was given a powerless post in Montevideo—leaving him in a poor position to maneuver to be Vargas's successor.[123]

The Brazilian Expeditionary Force (FEB) was to have a profound influence in reshaping the outlook of a major portion of the Brazilian military, and this new outlook would remain generally dominant down past the 1964 Revolution. One reinforced division under General João Batista Mascarenhas de Morais actually arrived in Italy in late 1944 and fought valiantly and effectively at Monte Castello, Castelnuovo, and Montese. Sustaining over 450 combat deaths and with some 2,000 of its over 25,000 combat troops wounded in action, the FEB developed a heroic reputation—one that would give its returning veterans strategic leverage in the political maneuvering that characterized the second half of 1945. In alliance with important civilian groups, one wing of FEB veterans would be instrumental in forcing Vargas from office within a few months of their return home, and in 1964—along with essentially the same political forces—this element would still constitute the backbone of the movement that overthrew Goulart and the remnants of the Vargas system.

The "Reestablishment of Democracy"

By 1943 Vargas himself was aware that the Estado Novo could not carry over into the postwar era without substantial modifications. Students had been agitating for some time, particularly through the National Union of Students (UNE).[124] In the wake of an Allied victory pressures for a return to competitive politics would be well-nigh irresistible. Hence the regime would need a political organization capable of functioning effectively in mobilizing public support for an eventual contest at the polls. Building upon the foundation of amplified social programs for urban workers and the government's close control over their unions—through the power of legal recognition, influence over choice of officers, patronage leverage, and financial dependence—Labor Minister Alexandre Marcondes Filho began to organize a machine that could rapidly be transformed into a party. At the same time, the dictator's public pronouncements took on an increasingly populist tone, with references to change and economic development mixing with nationalist exhortations. Industrialization became the touchstone of a still diffuse program designed to appeal to workers, urban commercial and entrepreneurial interests, government employees, and—of course—the military.

The Political Chess Game

Vargas apparently believed that he would be able to ride out the growing pressures toward ending his arbitrary rule and retain power as he had when faced by demands for constitutionalization in 1932 and again when the question of presidential succession arose in 1937. But, in part because of a shift in the position of the military that was buttressed by external factors and also because of the widespread domestic feeling that fifteen years of unbroken rule was enough for any one man, no matter how exceptional (as even Roosevelt, Hitler, and Mussolini were all gone from the scene), the situation in 1945 moved beyond Vargas's control. Nonetheless, through generally adroit maneuvering the dictator retained a great deal of initiative over the course of affairs until the very end and left office in a way that maximized his possibilities for mounting a political comeback.[125]

The first dramatic sign of opposition to the regime was the founding on January 1, 1943, of the Society of Friends of America with such leaders as Aranha and the Mello Francos. Of even greater impact was the "Mineiro Manifesto" dated for symbolic reasons October 24, 1943, the thirteenth anniversary of the ouster of Washington Luís—Brazil's last popularly elected president.[126] Bearing the signatures of ninety distinguished personalities of Minas Gerais, this eloquent call to the nation's conscience clearly articulated the question that had risen in the minds of many Brazilians in other parts of the country: "If we fight against Fascism at the side of the United Nations so that liberty and democracy may be restored to all peoples, certainly we are not asking too much in demanding for ourselves such rights and guarantees?" (More than a half dozen of the signers would play leading roles twenty-one years later in the ouster of Vargas heir Goulart.)

Vargas's angry reaction took the form of a campaign to depict such agitation for elections as unpatriotic combined with a renewed appeal for national unity to pursue the war effort. Indeed, the regime held that the war emergency period should not count against Vargas's term in office, asserting that he would have fourteen months left to serve after the cessation of hostilities. Moreover, Aranha was harassed into resigning as foreign minister in August 1944. This in turn contributed significantly to the alienation of Góes Monteiro, who quit his post in Montevideo and returned to Brazil— where he entered into consultation with such military advocates of a transition as Juarez Távora, Eduardo Gomes, and Juracy Magalhães. The election of a long-time critic of the Estado Novo to preside over the Military Club served further notice that the officer corps was growing impatient.[127]

At the beginning of 1945 the First Congress of Brazilian Writers called for immediate elections and the sympathetic Jefferson Caffery was replaced as U.S. Ambassador by Adolf Berle. Then on February 22 a Rio de Janeiro newspaper openly, if somewhat belatedly, challenged censorship by printing Carlos Lacerda's sensational interview with José Américo in which the frustrated 1938 presidential candidate expounded a series of cogent arguments against Vargas's continuation, even through direct elections, and set the stage for the launching of Brigadier General Gomes's candidacy.[128] Vargas's hand was forced, and he decreed a constitutional amendment authorizing elections.[129] But instead of buying some relief, this decree was followed by a barrage of attacks by jurists on the de facto nature of the regime— including one by Francisco Campos, the author of the Estado Novo constitution. The question was increasingly not whether Vargas would leave office, but when and under what circumstances.

Vargas countered the opposition's move to establish an electoral vehicle for Gomes's campaign by authorizing Valladares and his justice minister to articulate the candidacy of Dutra in a strategy of "a sword to fight a sword."[130] The introduction of military contenders destroyed the parallel with 1937, as Dutra could not be used and pushed aside as easily as had been the case with José Américo, and Gomes possessed great support in the armed forces and popular prestige that Sales had sorely lacked. Determined that if he could not hold on to power directly, it must pass to his allies and supporters rather than to his critics, Vargas demonstrated his resourcefulness and flexibility by reaching a political accord with Luís Carlos Prestes, the Communist Party leader he had kept in prison for nearly a decade. Freed along with over 500 other political prisoners through an amnesty in April, this popular hero subsequently surprised the nation by rejecting Gomes's candidacy as well as that of Dutra and calling for a third alternative. Moreover, he insisted that the road to "National Union" required Vargas's remaining in the presidency until after elections were held, and in July he reiterated the PCB's "frank, open, and determined" support of the government.[131]

On April 7 representatives of all political currents opposed to Vargas had come together in Rio de Janeiro to found the National Democratic

Union (UDN). Its formal leadership included former president Bernardes and the three former presidential candidates victimized by Vargas (Júlio Prestes, José Américo, and Sales).[132] Also active were the full array of Vargas enemies including such former allies as Borges de Medeiros, Flôres da Cunha, Raúl Pilla, and the Mello Francos.[133] On April 8 the Social Democratic Party (PSD) was launched in Minas Gerais, and the interventors in other states took up the work of organizing the local political establishment into branches of the new party. Then at the end of May Vargas convoked elections for December 2 for president and Congress, with state elections set to follow on May 6, 1946.

Formally nominated by the PSD on July 17, Dutra stepped down as war minister shortly thereafter.[134] In a clear sign that events were beginning to develop a momentum of their own, Vargas found himself compelled to appoint Góes Monteiro to that key post in spite of being aware that this strong figure would be very difficult, if not impossible, to control. Although the campaign was officially underway, great skepticism remained as to Vargas's real intentions.

With the date for the election nearing, Vargas was again acting very much as he had in 1937, roiling the waters where possible and interjecting disquieting initiatives. The president gave no aid to Dutra's sputtering candidacy, informing Góes Monteiro that his predecessor as war minister had forfeited support by consorting with some of Vargas's critics. Knowing full well that Góes considered himself much more qualified to take the country's helm than was Dutra, Vargas tempted the former with the possibility of entering the lists as a compromise candidate, suggesting that Dutra and Gomes would both withdraw.[135] The dictator followed a similar tactic with Cordeiro de Farias, recently returned from Italy, and even with Valladares— who was the PSD's first vice-president behind Vargas as the party's head.

Vargas's chief interest came to focus upon the newly formed Brazilian Labor Party (PTB), through which Marcondes Filho, ably seconded by José Segadas Viana, was organizing the support of the government-controlled unions for Vargas's objectives.[136] With this party at his disposal and many of the interventors still essentially loyal to him, Vargas had in hand at least the minimum political elements needed for a bid to retain power. Although the military *dispositivo* to guarantee his maneuvers was absent, the sharp division of the army's preferences between Gomes and Dutra still afforded exploitable opportunities.

Having Juan Perón's recent successes in Argentina in mind, particularly Perón's exploitation of labor support to solidify his power position within the armed forces, Vargas pushed ahead with moves designed to create a situation in which his permanence in office might be acceptable as an alternative to disorder. In late June he decreed an antitrust law aimed both at attracting support from the Left, agitated over rising inflation and "imperialist" influence, and at giving the government a big stick with which to intimidate its opponents and bring wavering businessmen into line. Thus, an Administrative Commission for Defense of the Economy (CADE), subordinate to the president, was given sweeping powers to punish acts "contrary to the interest of the national economy," with intervention or expropriation authorized in a wide range of cases embracing many relatively common Brazilian business practices.

Forces supporting Vargas portrayed this as a nationalist act to defend the urban masses against continued exploitation, but it was roundly denounced by the opposition. This conflict played into the president's aim of stripping the UDN of any image as a broad and representative coalition behind the "peoples' candidate" and making it appear instead as a champion of essentially bourgeois capitalist interests linked closely to foreign investors. In this regard the anguished wails of U.S. companies over the antitrust law led many nationalistic Brazilians to believe that this measure had indeed been aimed at protecting the Brazilian economy from excessive foreign penetration and possible dominance.

By September Dutra found himself in a dilemma as Vargas's supporters argued for postponing the presidential election so that the president could preside over the nation while the constituent assembly was at work on a new constitution. For their part the opposition articulated the battle cry of "All power to the Judiciary," requesting that Vargas step down at once in favor of the head of the Supreme Court. With Góes Monteiro unambiguously reaffirming that the armed forces would guarantee the elections, Vargas had to wonder if this was meant as much as a warning to him as an assurance to the democratic forces. In late September the "We Want Getúlio" ("Queremos Getúlio") elements were upset by a speech by U.S. Ambassador Berle, which stressed U.S. confidence that the electoral calendar would be respected. Then on October 3—the fifteenth anniversary of the launching of the 1930 Revolution—a mass rally of the "Queremistas" urged Vargas to stay on at least until the new constitution was promulgated.

Vargas's Ouster

A week later the dictator precipitated a confrontation by abruptly moving the state elections up to December 2 and permitting the interventors to be candidates for their own succession. The ploy also had the effect of weakening the UDN by accentuating its rivalries at the state and local levels. Moreover, if it proved impossible to mount the state campaigns on such extremely short notice, the possibility of postponing the elections would be increased.[137]

As has universally been the case in Brazilian political-military crises since the establishment of the republic, the army chief of staff became a pivotal figure during the weeks before Vargas's fall. General Cristovão Barcellos, who had followed an essentially independent and legalist road since his rise to prominence in the 1932 civil war, presided over a meeting of generals that delegated authority to Góes Monteiro to present Vargas with an ultimatum. Their demands involved having the ranking judge in each state take over at once from the interventor and no further changes being made in electoral rules or calendar. It appears that Dutra's military supporters were allying with those of Gomes against any efforts by Vargas to short-circuit these candidacies. The events of mid-October in Argentina, where the army ousted Perón only to see him ride back to power on the strength of mass popular demonstrations, alerted the Brazilian military to the dangers of a marriage of political demagoguery with mob action—as well as the costs of military indecision. Hence the armed forces leadership vetoed the monster rally planned by the pro-Vargas forces for the night of October 26.

Vargas responded by naming his brother Benjamin as Federal District chief of police, a move interpreted by the military as preparatory to some decisive initiative. Not having been consulted with regard to this key personnel change, Góes Monteiro resigned as war minister, assuming instead the pretentious title of "commander-in-chief of the army" and appointing General Cordeiro de Farias as his chief of staff. Together with both of the major presidential candidates, they decided that Vargas must step down— a message relayed to the president by Cordeiro de Farias, once Vargas's close associate. At the suggestion of both Dutra and Gomes, who suspected that Góes Monteiro intended to seize power, Supreme Court head José Linhares was immediately invited to assume the presidency, with the oath of office administered at the War Ministry at 2:30 A.M. on October 30. The next day, just three weeks after it had precipitated the crisis, the decree law moving up the state elections was rescinded. The Estado Novo was at its end.

Although most of the senior officers favored severe measures against Vargas, the moderate views of Góes Monteiro—who successfully maneuvered to stay on as war minister—prevailed, and the former dictator returned to his home in Rio Grande do Sul.[138] The campaign was resumed where it had been interrupted by the Queremista episode, but the bloodless coup would have its reflexes in 1950 and 1954, when Vargas was returned to power and then once more forced out. Again in 1945, as had occurred on repeated occasions since the overthrow of the empire fifty-six years earlier, it was the military who had taken the decisive action, with civilian forces divided and uncertain.

By yielding to the irresistible forces for change, albeit at the last possible moment, Vargas was able to depart from office with honor and dignity and, even more important for his political future, without having opened an irreparable breach with the armed forces—whom he explicitly absolved from any blame in his valedictory message. Thus, Vargas could be quite certain that "history and time" would exonerate him. In fact, the next five years were more a period of drift than of reversal of Vargas's policies, which would be resumed in 1951.

5

The Quest for Development and Democracy, 1946–1960

Studying the long span of the Vargas regime is certainly crucial to understanding Brazil's development as a nation in all respects—economic, social, and political. This is as true of the decade and a half after World War II as for the preceding period. Whereas corporatism had been woven deeply into the fabric of the Brazilian nation between 1930 and 1945, the 1950s would witness the development of populism, nationalism, and developmentalism—all of which would contribute both to the profound crisis of the early 1960s and to the nature of the authoritarian regime that ensued. More than anyone else, Vargas would continue to be the central figure in the events of this period, first in person, then through his legacy of parties, organs, and practices as well as by his political heirs. Indeed, there would be a common line running through the regime crises of 1945, 1954, and 1964: the desire of conservative forces, both civilian and military, to end the hold of the Varguista elements. Moreover, the elimination of direct presidential elections after 1964 was chiefly a result of the frustration of these forces in having seen the electorate return verdicts favorable to Vargas in 1946 and 1950, as well as to his heirs in 1955, and in having to swallow the "accidental" accession to power of his protégé, João Goulart, in 1961 (through the abrupt resignation of President Jânio Quadros).

Thus, although Vargas had been forcibly removed from the helm of government in October 1945, this short, middle-aged man would continue to cast a long shadow over Brazilian politics. First, even the 1946–1950 period would prove to be much more of a pause than a sharp change in course, in large part because of the carryover momentum of the processes of economic and social change stimulated during Vargas's fruitful 1930–1945 stewardship.[1] Indeed, Vargas's ouster in 1945 was largely a reaction by the old landowning and mercantile elite in alliance with the middle class against the processes of change. More than directly hurting their pocketbooks, these changes threatened in the longer run to undermine the viability of continued conservative dominance of politics and use of the state to further the interests of the dominant groups rather than those of an emerging urban working class.[2] The middle class itself was undergoing a transformation at this juncture, with the entrance of a new generation of technical and administratively oriented personnel and a "new intelligentsia" concerned with development problems. These yet insecure elements of the middle class still feared the possibility of losing their recent gains as a consequence of the rise of the working class and extension of expensive social benefits to them.

The governments from the reelection of Vargas in 1950 through the overthrow of Goulart in 1964 would all be based to a significant degree upon a loose coalition of industrialists, with the commercial sectors linked to the internal market, the "technical" elements of the middle class, and the organized sector of the urban working class. But it would be the military—with the support of the more traditional component of the middle class as well as that of conservative interests—who would intervene repeatedly when the process of development threatened to bring with it significant socioeconomic changes. The progressive forces failed to create a new party, resting instead upon the inadequate basis of the Vargas-forged alliance between the Social Democratic Party (PSD), strong in Congress, and the Brazilian Labor Party (PTB), which possessed popular support in urban areas. The middle class, more concerned with its patronage positions than with any radical changes in the system, had failed to fulfill a revolutionary role in the 1930s and in the postwar period permitted consolidation of democratic forms without correlative social policies. Thus, even with the 1945 reestablishment of representative politics, "all the important organizations functioning as mediators between the State and the individual are really entities annexed to the State itself rather than effectively autonomous organizations."[3] In a framework of direct contact between the state and urban masses through the intermediary of populist leaders, personalities took precedence over programs, and even more so over ideologies.

Although not enough to establish a permanent basis for combining fully competitive politics with institutional stability, some significant political change did take place. The transformations were not as obvious as those in 1945–1946, which were highlighted by the emergence of parties and the adoption of a new constitution. Still the early 1950s were to witness a continuance of fundamental adaptations and adjustments in the Brazilian political system, which was changing in response to the increased rate of social mobilization and broadened participation in restored electoral politics. The established parties, suffering from a lack of coherence and inadequate organization as well as from their essentially conservative orientation, were inadequate vehicles for the socialization of the new urban masses entering the electorate. Alongside the still relatively effective clientelistic politics, new types of populist leaders were called forth by the situation, partially filling the vacuum resulting from the elimination of the one ideological party of the Left, the Brazilian Communist Party (PCB).

During the postwar period, the problem of political absorption of the growing urban masses would prove to be a factor in all crises, because the realities of the electoral process and influence of the entrenched interests led to a situation in which the president was generally faced with a Cabinet and Congress much more conservative than were the voters to whom he owed his election. The basically conservative orientation of the major political parties and the heavy, if not predominant, rural influence in the leadership of those parties prevented the urban voter from any close identification with them.

Hence, as would be repeated in the late 1980s, while vociferous nationalists proclaimed the advent of the era of ideological politics and were followed by the relatively highly politicized leadership of unions and "popular" organizations, the masses turned instead to a direct link between their votes and a political leader with a significant degree of charisma.[4] Clientelism continued to serve as the basis for holding much of the middle class to the established political leadership and the existing parties in terms of an exchange of votes for employment or a specific favor. But it could not work for the urban masses as a whole as the electorate expanded far beyond the patronage potential of even the *cartorial* state. From roughly 1 million in 1908 and 2.7 million for the 1934 balloting, the electorate had expanded to over 7.4 million by 1945—and would grow even faster thereafter (to eleven times that figure by 1989).

The peculiarly Brazilian form of populism, combining in different proportions features of urban machine politics with personalism and appeals of emotional affect with effective performance in the material realm, would assume several distinct forms during the 1950s: (1) the labor-oriented nationalism of Vargas; (2) the conservative nationalism of Adhemar de Barros, which blended massive public works expenditures with demagogic campaigning and large-scale exploitation of graft and patronage for electoral ends; (3) the moralistic messianism of Jânio Quadros, the ascetic giant-killer who capitalized on popular desires for an end to the corruption and controversy of Vargism and Adhemarism; and (4) the crusading anti-Communist zeal of Carlos Lacerda and his developing mystique of intransigent oppositionism in a system where opportunism and accommodation predominated.

Although Juscelino Kubitschek—greatest of the post-Vargas leaders— would rely more upon developmentalism and nationalism than populism, the period of his administration (1956–1960) would witness the introduction of two new varieties of populism to fill the vacuum left by Vargas's death. Thus, Leonel Brizola modernized the *trabalhista* (appeal to workers) line by adding a more ideological brand of nationalism and, like his archrival Lacerda, effectively exploiting the new medium of television to transcend the limitations of communication with the masses on the basis of personal appearances. Miguel Arraes, not gifted as a speaker, began to evolve a mystique as spokesman for the "other" Brazil, the forgotten masses of the northeast. Confronted with the residual strength of *coronelism*, he adopted the coloration of a dedicated reformer while utilizing the program and organization of the Communist movement, albeit not all of that movement's ideology.[5]

What these several strains of populism shared was their appeal to the poorly assimilated mass urban population, which was being fed by heavy migration from the countryside and which was plagued by the insecurities of city life as well as by dissatisfaction with its standard of living in the midst of sustained dramatic development. Restless, but largely nonradical, the middle sectors would also give substantial support to populist politicians. Though this tendency was still not evident during the Dutra years, it grew in importance through the crises of the 1950s and was crucial to the "Jânio phenomenon" at the decade's end. Betrayed and disoriented by Quadros's August 1961 resignation, the middle classes would be important to Goulart's early successes before giving substantial support to the movement that overthrew him.

To a very considerable degree the 1964 "revolution" was a reflection, if not a direct continuation, of the political crises and repeated military interventions of 1954–1955, which saw the final elimination of Vargas and a struggle over whether the victors of the 1955 elections should be allowed to take office. What the armed forces did and refrained from doing in 1954–1955 had a profound impact upon their actions in both 1961 and 1964. Indeed, the roles of the main actors in the 1964 crisis are intelligible only against the background of the positions assumed a decade earlier. For the chief actors in the 1964 system change had not only held key command positions in 1961, but also had been generals or senior colonels during the 1954–1955 crisis. In fact, as has already been shown, many had played consequential roles in the 1945 deposition of Vargas, and their memories of the 1937 *golpe*, the 1930 Revolution, and even of the *tenente* revolts of the 1920s were often the memories of participants as well as observers. This continuity of leadership was nearly as pronounced on the civilian side, with the physical absence of Vargas after 1954 more than offset by the pervasive influence of his political legacy and the prominent role of his political heirs.

For even after hounding him to his grave, Vargas's opponents could not engineer anything more than a temporary detour, and a mere year and a half later his political heirs would reclaim control of the nation's destinies and resume headway along the course Vargas had charted from 1930 to 1945 and refined during the early 1950s. Yet like Vargas, they too would run up against the continued obstruction of any progress in rural Brazil by determined political elements both closely linked to the old agrarian interests and entrenched in the governmental machinery. The intransigent Right was greatly aided by the gross overrepresentation of the less developed rural states and the increasingly grotesque underrepresentation of those that were most advanced economically, socially, politically—especially São Paulo. Thus land tenure patterns remained virtually unchanged and the rural working population was excluded from effective political participation and the benefits of a limited welfare state.[6]

Dutra and the Conservative Republic

Brazil's return to constitutional ways began, as had the republic itself and the post-1930 experiments, with the civilian political groups indebted to the military for having ousted the "decadent" regime. Indeed, the striking fact about Brazil in the immediate postwar period is not the armed forces' assumption of responsibility for intervening in politics on behalf of the civilian democratic elements, but the latter's acceptance of this as a proper and legitimate function of the army as a national institution.[7] The selection of military candidates for the 1945 presidential succession involved considerations of fundamental political strategy with respect to public familiarity as national figures, but recognition that the "reestablishment of democracy" required the sponsorship of the armed forces was probably a more decisive factor. Indeed, the liberal constitutionalists had begun to woo the army even earlier—much as the Republicans had done during the 1880s. As titular leader of the democratic opposition, from 1939 on Armando de Sales repeatedly urged the armed forces to intervene. Thus, in the eyes of the liberal constitutionalists, the military's action to end the dictatorship on October 29, 1945, both was justified by the armed forces' institutionalized role as holder of the moderating power and served to justify the continuance of that role.

The 1945–1946 Transition

Although Vargas was at last out of the presidency, the institutional structure he had devised continued untouched. Góes Monteiro did step down as war minister in mid-November owing to serious health problems, but despite the naming of new interventors, the electorally crucial mayors, who were overwhelmingly tied to the PSD, remained in office, and the state elections were returned to their original 1946 date. Reluctantly and impelled by a realization that Gomes would reverse the policies he had established, Vargas finally endorsed Dutra on November 28. This move gravely disappointed the Communists, who had put up Yedo Fiúza, the mayor of Petrópolis, in hopes that this old friend might receive Vargas's backing. Nominated for senator or deputy in a number of different states, Vargas was able to blanket the campaign with his political shadow.

Indeed, Dutra's election depended far more upon the durability of forces entrenched in control of the majority of states plus the urban masses responsive to Vargas's populist appeals than upon anything the candidate said or did. Gomes, on the other hand, relied upon the resurgence of liberal constitutionalist sentiment, the desire of many middle-class elements for a change in the holders of political office, and the votes of the fragmented opposition groups at the state level—who knew that a PSD victory nationally would consolidate the control enjoyed for years by their rivals. With Vargas not so easy to attack effectively in "retirement" down on his ranch, the Gomes campaign had great difficulty in avoiding an essentially negative image—that of being against everything Vargas stood for. The carefully qualified positions of the National Democratic Union (UDN) program were meaningful to the more sophisticated component of the middle sectors, but its restrictions on industrialization, emphasis upon economic liberalism and freeing the productive forces of capitalism from excessive governmental controls, and hammering away on anti-Communist themes evoked little enthusiasm from the working class, which preferred the PTB or the PCB.

With nearly 7.5 million voters registered—nearly three times the number in 1934—and with almost 6.2 million voting, the preferences of the electorate could only be the subject of speculation not of informed prognostication, much less scientific prediction, as the vast majority would be voting for the first time. The three states of São Paulo, Minas Gerais, and Rio Grande do Sul together with the Federal District continued to embrace well over half the nation's eligible voters, with the addition of Rio de Janeiro state, Bahia, Pernambuco, and Ceará raising the proportion to more than three-fourths. As would be the case in all subsequent presidential elections, the contest was decided in these pivotal major states.

When the December 2 election results were finally tabulated, Dutra had defeated Gomes by a margin of better than three to two (3,251,507 to 2,039,341), and the Communist Party nominee trailed far behind with a still respectable 569,818 votes. Well over 60 percent of the victor's margin came from Rio Grande do Sul and São Paulo, with much of the rest run up in Minas Gerais, as the Vargas-founded parties delivered massive pluralities. Vargas, to his substantial satisfaction, found himself senator-elect from both Rio Grande do Sul and São Paulo, where his presence on the PSD and PTB tickets had been crucial to Dutra's success; he was also elected as federal deputy by six different states. PSD candidates received nearly 43 percent of the congressional vote, and the PTB, limited chiefly to urban centers, won over 10 percent—thus the two parties together doubled the UDN's not quite 27 percent.[8] Prestes was elected to the Senate from the Federal District and fourteen fellow Communists gained seats in the 286-member Chamber of Deputies. The established political forces of the Vargas era were resoundingly confirmed in power, and the UDN—which had fully expected victory—was shocked by the result. (This experience would be repeated in 1950 and in 1954–1955 and would push the UDN far down the road of seeking power through a military coup.)

Dutra, a sixty-year-old career officer experienced in the intra-regime politics of the Vargas era, took office on January 31, 1946, as Brazil's first popularly elected chief executive in over fifteen years. Of modest provincial origins, he would keep his earlier authoritarian inclinations well under control as president, appearing generally not to be too far from a Brazilian version of Dwight D. Eisenhower. Often uncertain in a situation that provided few guidelines for the development of an effective presidential leadership style, Dutra could occasionally be resolute when his background and experience were relevant to the problem at hand. Though he could rely upon the support of the armed forces, and thus be free from the necessity of concerning himself with the calculus of survival, he was highly conscious of the fact that his every action set a precedent in the new experiment with democratic government.

Combined with the absence of an appropriate constitutional framework for most of his initial year in office, this self-consciousness contributed to an appearance of indecisiveness and a tendency toward inaction, at times bordering upon drift. Indeed, until the promulgation of the 1946 constitution, Dutra's administration had much the character of a caretaker regime, and after that time the president was very scrupulous about not infringing on the prerogatives of Congress, the courts, or even those of the parties. Thus, Brazil failed to receive strong or imaginative presidential leadership during this crucial period of transition from a relatively closed discretionary regime toward an open, competitive, and representative system.

Meeting with full constituent powers on February 8, the Congress—in which the PSD held 177 seats (151 of 286 deputies along with 26 of 42 in the Senate) and the PTB held 24 (22 in the lower house and 2 in the upper) to the UDN's 87 votes (77 deputies and 10 senators)—chose as its presiding officer Fernando de Mello Viana, senator from Minas Gerais and Brazil's most recent vice-president (1926–1930).[9] As would again be the case during 1987–1988, the old authoritarian constitution remained in effect until promulgation of the new one, and there was no already prepared government-approved draft proposal to consider. A thirty-seven member Grand Commission (composed of nineteen PSD representatives and two from the PTB against ten from the UDN) worked from March 15 to May 27 under the direction of Senator Nereu Ramos to produce a draft, with ensuing floor debate lasting until September 18. The resulting document was designed to curb the executive's powers and to guarantee the preservation of true federalism while providing an institutional framework for continued national integration and development. Following its promulgation, majority leader Ramos was elected to the newly created post of vice-president of the republic. Dutra simultaneously reconstituted his Cabinet with General Canrobert Pereira da Costa, who had substituted for Góes Monteiro, confirmed as war minister and the UDN's Raúl Fernandes—an old Vargas foe—as foreign minister.

Emergence of a Flawed Party System

In the supplemental election of January 1947 the PSD scored a major victory, gaining twelve of the twenty-one Senate seats and six of eighteen new federal deputy posts. Moreover, the party won six governorships, plus six more in coalition with the PTB, along with 364 state legislative posts. The UDN trailed with five senators, four governors plus three others elected in coalition with smaller parties, and 244 state deputies. With eighty-eight state legislators, plus junior partner status in a number of state administrations, the PTB demonstrated some progress toward becoming a national party. The PCB won control of the Federal District municipal council, gained two additional congressional seats, and attained representation in fifteen state legislatures.[10] The elections were also marked by the appearance of a number of new parties. several of which would develop into consequential political forces. Most significant was the victory of Adhemar de Barros for the governorship of São Paulo, which had come to surpass Minas Gerais as Brazil's most populous state. Chosen by Vargas to be his interventor in São Paulo in 1933, Adhemar had been removed by the dictator three years later and subsequently joined in the formation of the UDN. In 1946 he engineered the merger of three small splinter movements into the Social Progressive Party (PSP). Now he had defeated Vargas's chosen gubernatorial candidate, but would within a few years become one of Vargas's most valuable allies.

During Dutra's term parties were still in their infancy and schisms, mergers, and realignments were almost routine occurrences. The nature of the political parties and the party system that emerged in 1945 set significant limits upon what could be attempted, much less accomplished, during Dutra's administration. At the same time Vargas's continuation as the potentially dominant figure for two of the three major parties drastically inhibited the parties' development either along modern programmatic lines or into institutionalized vehicles for political mobilization. With anti-Vargism the unifying factor and the guiding principle of the UDN, while the power-oriented PSD remained closely tied to the former dictator, policy differences would be subordinated to emotional issues of Vargism, and divisions stemming from the Estado Novo days would generally override the class and interest similarities between much of the UDN and the PSD—keeping the latter in increasingly uneasy alliance with the PTB.

The PSD, preeminently the party of the political "ins," supplied the majority in the 1946–1950 Congress, occupied the lion's share of executive positions in Dutra's Cabinet, and controlled the greater proportion of state administrations. Essentially nonideological, it combined the dominant state machines of the post-1930 period, chiefly rurally based, with the businessmen and industrialists who had benefitted under the Estado Novo from Vargas's increasing orientation toward objectives of economic development. A high proportion of the new bureaucratic elite, whose numbers had multiplied through the steady expansion of government activities during the Vargas era, also leaned toward the PSD, whose ranks were swelled by all those who sought advantage from being associated with the administration party in Brazil's patronage-oriented *cartorial* state. Essentially these groups wanted more of what they had been receiving from the Estado Novo, and they pressed Dutra for special favors as well as increased support for programs beneficial to their diverse interests.

Indeed, the PSD was more a loose confederation of regional parties than a unified and coherent national organization. With a few notable exceptions, PSD leaders were significantly more conservative than their rhetoric would generally indicate, and the party's diverse components were substantially satisfied with the status quo so long as opportunities existed for squeezing advantage out of the system. During the late 1940s, its resemblance to the several Republican Parties of the pre-1930 regime was striking in spite of the fundamental changes that had taken place in Brazilian society since that time.[11]

In its early years the UDN was almost as distinctively an alliance of political "outs" as the PSD was a coalition of the holders of power. In fact, in much of the country the two parties were not very different in their social bases or policy objectives. With bi-factionalism by far the predominant pattern on the local level in rural areas, the UDN label was often adopted in 1945 by the political chief of the clan that was not linked to the state interventor's power structure—which at times brought the largest and most reactionary landowners into the UDN.

Similarly, in the cities the UDN was supported heavily by commercial-industrial interests, although many other members of these interests opted for the PSD. The UDN contained especially high proportions of bankers, administrators of large companies, and offspring of prestigious families. Whereas the pro-Vargas Center-conservative party attracted many middle-class voters tied to the expanding government bureaucracy, the UDN recruited heavily from among the professional men and white-collar employees of the private sector. Strong among the intellectuals and students in the larger cities, who at the time of the party's founding were intensely against the dictator on juridical and libertarian grounds, the UDN represented a classically liberal tendency. The so-called bachelors (holders of law degrees) were most prominent in the party's position and activity on the national scene. But as socialist, moderately progressive, and populist segments of the originally broad coalition of anti-dictatorial forces broke away to constitute their own parties, on social and economic issues the UDN came increasingly under the influence of its conservative rural constituents.[12] As a minority party it became accustomed to the role of public critic even though many of its component interests dealt with the government for whatever patronage and favors they could extract. In fact, in many ways the UDN in its early years was much like the Party of the Brazilian Democratic Movement (PMDB) of the mid- and late 1980s.

At the beginning of Dutra's administration the PTB was more significant for its potential than for its existing strength, being an effective electoral force only in the major industrial centers. Yet few politicians could be blind to the fact that with the continued mobilization of urban groups and the development of the working class, the PTB would almost surely continue to grow—and would be the prime beneficiary of any drop in support for the Communists or the loss of that party's legal status. With Vargas at its head, the PTB would be a formidable power contender and hence merited respect well beyond its 1945 and 1947 electoral performances.

For its part, the PCB enjoyed the advantage of being led by a man who was for many Brazilians a legendary hero and living symbol of the struggle against oppression and neglect of the lower classes. Luís Carlos Prestes was as much the PCB's leading electoral asset as Vargas was for the PTB. Moreover, the Communists possessed a discipline and ideological base that was lacking in the ranks of the *trabalhistas*. With the Soviet Union for the moment respectable and a valiant ally of Brazil in the triumph over European fascism, the Communist movement as of 1945–1946 was in a position to emphasize its democratic orientation and its function as a nonviolent alternative to the existing order. By choosing a non-Communist engineer as its 1945 presidential candidate rather than former *tenente* Prestes, the PCB dramatized its opposition to the military tutelage of Brazil's political life and sought to capitalize on what "civilist" sentiment remained in the Brazilian electorate. The party's stress upon alliance with the national bourgeoisie helped blunt attacks upon it as a revolutionary threat.[13]

Governing with little opposition from the UDN, whose "realist" elements even favored alliance with the PSD, Dutra repeatedly called for a pacification of spirits and political tranquility as he strove to establish the basis for long-term stability under a successor who might well be a civilian.[14] In his eyes and those of Justice Minister Carlos Luz, who in 1955 would briefly reach the presidency in the midst of a major military crisis, the chief threat to domestic order came from the Communists. A statement by Prestes that in case of a war involving Brazil and the USSR the PCB would have to side with the latter aggravated the situation, as did Communist gains in the January 1947 balloting. Consequently the administration welcomed the superior electoral tribunal's ruling in May that the party's statutes conflicted with constitutional provisions and that it thus forfeited its legal status.[15]

Follow-up action by Congress at the end of the year and early in 1948 deprived all PCB elected officials of their seats, while a loyalty oath provision of the labor code was invoked to eliminate Communists and their supporters from the unions—many of which were intervened by the government. Moreover, the Brazilian Workers' Confederation (CTB) was closed down, as Brazilian law did not provide for an overall national labor organization.[16] The fact that the Cold War had come to Brazil was made more apparent by the ensuing break in diplomatic relations with the Soviet Union.

Dutra's Dull, Dead-in-the-Water Democracy

In any case the reestablishment of a representative legislative body and the emergence of political parties would have seriously affected the operations of the policy-making mechanisms and administrative machinery inherited from the Estado Novo. But the undermining of executive authority was accentuated during the 1946–1950 period by the fragmented and factionalized nature of the parties, constitutional provisions and structural modifications designed to decentralize power, and the political style of Dutra. A "born again" military man of previously authoritarian leanings, the president was determined to govern entirely within the limits of the recently reinstituted formal democracy. In his single-minded pursuit of this goal he failed to take an adequate role in resolving the difficult adjustments necessary if the representative system of the renewed republic was to demonstrate the effectiveness required for long-run viability.

Thus, though characterized by freedom and stability, the Dutra years were also a period of lost opportunities for a lasting consolidation of the transition from authoritarian rule. Many of the major vices of the Estado Novo were eliminated, but its major virtues were also lost, and a number of the least desirable features of the pre-Vargas system reemerged. Hence despite the high hopes of the constitutionalists, instead of liberal democracy being legitimized in the eyes of the populace by its achievements in the aftermath of the dictatorship, its shortcomings were too often underscored by a policy of drift and accommodation with retrograde forces. Indeed, the return to regular elections and a functioning Congress enabled the old agricultural interests through their controlled voters to regain much of the power they had held before 1937—though not quite as much as they had held before 1930. Thus, a timid agrarian reform proposed in 1947 never got out of committee in spite of the Catholic Church finally having awakened to this pressing social issue.[17]

The "Conservative Republic" turned out to be a period marked by immobility—in part as a result of the relative balance in terms of political influence that existed among the economic elites. The large agriculturalists and associated mercantile interests sought with considerable success to reassert their influence on national policy in the face of the challenges from business, banking groups, and an emerging industrial sector. The former strove to preserve an economic order based on export of agricultural products and unhindered access to imported manufactured goods, while the latter increasingly demanded fiscal policies promoting industrialization and tariff protection for their products. Although the proponents of free trade and minimal governmental controls were dominant during the first part of the Dutra administration, the tide was turning toward the advocates of industry. In the face of rapidly shrinking foreign exchange reserves, a system of import licensing was instituted in June 1947, which, combined with an artificially high official rate for the cruzeiro, led to increased investment for domestic production. An eased credit policy in the late stages of Dutra's term also encouraged industrialization.[18]

Despite the unimaginative nature of the government program, which started out attacking inflation and the government deficit by orthodox contractionist policies, the annual real increase in GDP did average 6 percent, which was slightly more than double the rate of population growth. Although this was very satisfactory by comparative standards, it made little dent in the massive social needs of the Brazilian people, and debate over the proper path to economic development would continue to be a constant feature of national life. The 1949 Abbink Report, as the final document emerging from the work of the Joint Brazil–United States Technical Commission was generally called, stressed orthodox fiscal policies, private enterprise, and the curbing of inflation—much as International Monetary Fund (IMF) and World Bank (whose proper name is the International Bank for Reconstruction and Development, or IBRD) documents would do through the late 1980s. Though the Abbink Report called for state investment in basic infrastructural sectors such as transportation and energy, it essentially downplayed manufacturing and recommended restriction of credit.

With ups and downs in terms of influence on governmental policies, the ensuing debate over this orthodox approach or the pursuit of development with relatively little regard to the problem of inflation would continue for at least a generation. Indeed, economic development was to emerge as the fundamental issue of the new decade, with most of public opinion unable to follow the technical debate but alert to the popularized—and generally oversimplified—interpretations of journalists and political leaders. Although intense sporadic attention would be paid to specific policy controversies and campaigns to mobilize support within the electorate for certain measures, the fundamental schools of thought regarding Brazil's optimum road to development would take form gradually throughout the 1950s before becoming more crystallized in the 1960s. At the same time, the military's doctrine of national security would become more fully elaborated, setting up a confrontation between radical nationalism as it was finally adopted in the early 1960s by the Goulart regime and the armed forces' brand of "security and development," which was premised upon close association with the United States.

The Military Sphere

The essentially conservative character of the Dutra government reflected the dominant orientation of the senior officers during the late 1940s. This outlook was increasingly out of step with the views of many of the younger military generation, who often took on a more nationalist and developmentalist cast. Rather heavily imbued with a legalist tradition, in contrast to the penchant for political activism of those who immediately preceded them—the renowned *tenentes*—these officers who had gone through the military academy in the late 1920s and early 1930s frequently took Captain Henrique Duffles Teixeira Lott as their model nonpolitical career soldier. A few years later this role came to be filled by Major Humberto de Alencar Castelo Branco, tactics instructor at the military academy during the first few years of the Vargas era.[19]

But to more fully understand the differing attitudes of the Brazilian military in the postwar period, social and geographic origins as well as patterns of socialization and subsequent links to societal sectors must be taken into account. The Rio de Janeiro Colégio Militar was free for orphaned sons of officers, and sons of living military men paying half tuition. Thus this chief channel into the academy attracted a fair proportion of the offspring of army officers of modest circumstances as well as some from families with a long military tradition. The other two military preparatory schools were in Porto Alegre and Fortaleza, so a fairly high proportion of those seeking an army career came from Rio Grande do Sul or the northeast. The dominant states, São Paulo and Minas Gerais, furnished relatively few officers. Not surprisingly under these circumstances, a deep division developed. On one side were arrayed those who as a result of participation in the several uprisings of the 1920s had their military careers suspended until after the 1930 Revolution, by which time many of them were too busy with governmental posts and political activity to make up for courses they had missed. Their opponents were the "professionals" who had remained on active duty throughout. The latter not only went through all the various levels of military education, but also subsequently served as instructors in these courses.

Thus, for example, Lott and Castelo Branco, two of the four most influential generals in the period from 1954 to 1967, attended the officers' advancement course (Escola de Aperfeiçoamento de Oficiais, or ESAO) together in 1924, graduating in first and second place, respectively. Lott, several years senior to Castelo, passed directly to the general staff school (Escola de Estado Maior, or EEM), graduating in first place in 1927 and returning to the faculty of the ESAO, then to that of the academy. He remained in this professorial function through 1935 and took it up again after graduating from the French War College in 1939, becoming subdirector of training at the EEM before being named its commandant in 1943. Thus virtually a whole generation of officers was very directly influenced by Lott and would in large part follow his lead when this paladin of professionalism "reluctantly" became deeply involved in politics in the mid-1950s.

Like Lott, Castelo Branco spent most of the crucial period of the late 1920s and early 1930s involved in military education rather than attached to a troop command or even a position with the general staff or War Ministry. After the war, in which he gained prominence as chief of the operations section of the Brazilian Expeditionary Force (FEB) divisional staff, he became director of teaching at the staff and command school (the Escola do Comando e Estado Maior de Exército, or ECEME, successor to the EEM).[20] After the founding of the National War College (Escola Superior da Guerra, or ESG) in 1949, Castelo became associated with that pinnacle of military study, which was first commanded by Juarez Távora.

Thus, during the 1946–1950 period Lott (who reached major general in 1948) and Castelo Branco (still a colonel but recognized by all as a probable future army chief of staff) came to represent the non-*tenente* officers rising to top command posts just behind the senior generals of that period, who were contemporaries of Dutra and Góes Monteiro. Still a neck ahead of Lott and Castelo Branco at this juncture were generals Canrobert Pereira da Costa and Euclides Zenóbio da Costa, the leading rivals for top authority within the army once the two military bulwarks of the Estado Novo had become president and senator. But whereas Dutra and Góes Monteiro had been the dominant military figures for a twenty-year period—1930–1950— the stars of Canrobert and Zenóbio would shine for only five years.

The 1948 Military Club elections had been won by General Salvador César Obino, with staunch legalist Leitão de Carvalho as his running mate. The salient issue around which military politics revolved at this point was that of petroleum policy. Though the Dutra administration was relatively favorable to U.S. participation in the exploration and development of Brazil's apparently inadequate petroleum resources, a strong current in the armed forces opposed foreign involvement in such a strategic area. Leitão de Carvalho joined a number of other retired generals in the foundation of a Center for the Defense of Petroleum and the National Economy (CEDPEN).[21]

As basic legislation in this field was being considered in Congress from 1948 on, the matter remained at the forefront of military concern. The 1950 Military Club elections thus came to center on a question parallel to one of the major issues in the concurrent presidential campaign, that of economic nationalism—a theme upon which Vargas was placing increasing emphasis in his successful quest to mobilize popular support for his return to power as constitutional president.[22] In the realities of Brazilian politics, the attitude of the armed forces was at least as important to Vargas as was the response of the electorate, as the former could effectively veto his candidacy. Hence the victory of the "nationalist" slate in the Military Club balloting in May removed this threat to Vargas's comeback.

Yet in the longer run the defeated "anti-Communists" would come to constitute the backbone of the 1964 movement that ousted Vargas heir Goulart and ushered in a protracted period of their own rule. Having forced Vargas from office in 1945 only to see him elected to the presidency in 1950, then driving him to suicide in 1954 but seeing his political supporters triumph in the 1955 elections, these elements of the armed forces would become disposed toward decisive action to end the Vargist succession. When the defeat of Vargas's heirs at the polls in 1960 was reversed by Goulart's elevation to the presidency the following year, these elements would indeed stop standing by and, in the process, would put an end to Brazil's experiment with a competitive democratic system and open political process.

Vargas Again

As attention turned to the question of presidential succession, the UDN was confident that their defeat in 1945 had occurred because the elections were held in the shadow of the Estado Novo and that the people had since matured sufficiently under the democratic regime to appreciate their party's brand of liberalism. Although much of public opinion appeared disenchanted with the Dutra government, the UDN strategists argued that this would hurt the PSD and redound to their benefit. Moreover, Vargas's oratory during 1949 and early 1950 had been directed chiefly against the government, not the UDN. They were optimistic that Brigadier General Gomes would be the next president and hence rebuffed overtures for a unity candidate with the PSD.[23] In addition their decision to accept the support of Plínio Salgado's Popular Representation Party (PRP) was a serious mistake, for the relatively small number of votes this neofascist grouping could deliver would be more than offset by the loss of centrist support from elements that viewed this move as rank opportunism contradictory to the lofty moral principles of Gomes's campaign.

On April 19, 1950, his sixty-seventh birthday, Vargas accepted a PTB "draft," having already reached a bargain with Adhemar de Barros for PSP support in return for PTB assistance in the São Paulo elections and a vague commitment of sympathy toward Adhemar's future presidential aspirations. Although neither Vargas nor the São Paulo governor was very happy with the choice, PSP dissident João Café Filho, a federal deputy from Rio Grande do Norte, became the coalition's vice-presidential nominee.[24]

Vargas realized that his electoral prospects also required support from at least a major faction of the PSD. Vargas understood the PSD politicians, most of whom had been his collaborators during the Estado Novo and were carefully cultivated by him during the ensuing years, much more thoroughly than did Dutra. Using his influence within the PSD, Vargas assured the selection of a weak candidate who would be unacceptable to important elements of the Social Democratic electorate and would have an appeal limited essentially to the same sectors as that of the UDN standard-bearer. In addition to the support of the party's Rio Grande do Sul branch and that of Rio de Janeiro state, which was led by son-in-law Amaral Peixoto (whose political career would end only with his death in 1989), Vargas could count upon many key figures in the powerful Minas Gerais section.

Thus the PSD nomination went to a relatively obscure Minas Gerais congressman, Cristiano Machado, enabling Vargas to exploit his old and still strong ties to PSD state and local leaders—whose loyalty to a party label only five years old could not outweigh associations with Vargas, which went back as far as twenty years. Moreover, capitalizing upon the continued appeal of his name to their constituents, Vargas made a host of deals with PSD legislative and gubernatorial candidates, promising PTB votes in return for their support in the presidential balloting. One of his chief agents in this work was the young and little-known João Goulart, who was destined to become his protégé and successor as leader of the PTB.[25]

Election and Political Base

Thus, although PSD candidates were victorious throughout most of the country, Machado's presidential candidacy was deeply undercut—Vargas carried seventeen states plus the Federal District. Even in his home state, where the PSD gubernatorial candidate was victorious, Machado lost to both Vargas and Gomes. In São Paulo, the PSP stronghold, Vargas beat Machado by more than six to one and nearly trebled Gomes's vote; in the Federal District he also won by a margin of well over two to one, despite the UDN's predominance in the mass media there. Nationally Vargas received nearly 3,850,000 votes (48.7 percent) to a little more than 2,340,000 (29.7 percent) for Gomes and fewer than 1,700,000 votes (21.5 percent) for the humiliated Machado. (At this point the voting public, 8.25 million in a registered electorate of almost 11.5 million, was just 16 percent of Brazil's nearly 52 million population.) The fact that the PSD's congressional candidates received roughly a million more votes than the party's presidential nominee demonstrates the deep inroads made by Vargas.[26]

The marriage of the predominantly rural-based traditionalist political forces of the PSD and the largely urban, development-oriented groups backing the PTB that Vargas was able to construct would survive, albeit with some mutual infidelity and considerable bickering, until after the 1964 Revolution. The blend of clientelistic and populist politics inaugurated by

Vargas shaped the PTB and profoundly affected the PSD despite repeated efforts to introduce meaningful programmatic or even ideological content into these parties. The proportions of the mix were, however, to vary as the PTB grew in strength relative to the PSD and as developmentalists and reformers, if not true modernizers, increased within the ranks of both parties. Yet in the 1951–1954 period Vargas's style would help keep these parties functioning essentially as electoral vehicles, not as effective participants in the processes of government.

Even after Vargas's victory, important political forces with a very substantial reflection in the military were hostile to his return to power. However, the younger and more nationalist officers had served notice of their increasing influence in the Military Club election of May 1950, in which generals Newton Estillac Leal and Júlio Caetano Horta Barbosa defeated the slate headed by the essentially conservative former *tenente* Cordeiro de Farias— and including many of the future leaders of the 1964 Revolution.[27] Coming to office on January 31, 1951, Vargas sought to build himself a strong military *dispositivo* (power structure of support) that would support his nationalist-populist policies. Estillac Leal was named war minister, Zenóbio da Costa remained in command of the eastern military zone, Álvaro Fiúza de Castro became army chief of staff, and Espírito Santo Cardoso was named as the president's chief military aide.

On the civilian side Vargas had selected a heterogeneous Cabinet made up chiefly of PSD figures of varying prestige and orientation who either had backed his candidacy or represented groups with substantial support in Congress. The PTB and PSP received only a single ministry each, as did a dissident UDN faction. Vargas opted at first toward an eclectic and generally pragmatic policy that fully satisfied neither the economic liberals nor the radical nationalists but that laid down the basic guidelines for the "developmentalist" programs and doctrine that would be followed with greater success by the Kubitschek administration in the second half of the decade.

Accustomed to governing relatively free from restraints, Vargas was not comfortable operating within an institutional structure designed to minimize his freedom of action. Moreover, Dutra's quite narrow interpretation of presidential powers created a situation in which each move by Vargas to provide strong presidential leadership was criticized by the generally hostile media as an indication of his "dictatorial" proclivities. Thus, although matters went reasonably well at first, attritions built up quite quickly, with the opposition strongly suspicious of the motives behind Vargas's every initiative. For his part the president was impatient with the short-sighted obstruction of policies designed for the gradual modernization of the nation and with the attacks upon his essentially evolutionary approach to social welfare for the urban working class. Cognizant of the fact that Brazil's urban and suburban population had grown nearly three times as fast as that of rural areas during the past decade, Vargas was increasingly concerned with industrialization and concomitant problems of guided change rather than with maintenance of the status quo.[28]

Variant Approaches to Development

Although their positions would remain somewhat fluid until the late stages of the Vargas administration and their specific policy packages might not become fully defined until the Kubitschek period, three basic schools of thought on public policy related to development were taking shape during the early 1950s. The first accepted orthodox principles concerning fiscal and monetary policy as espoused by mainstream economists in the developed capitalist countries and embodied in the Abbink Report. For them the market and price mechanisms were sacrosanct and government controls taboo, with balanced budgets and a hospitable environment for foreign investment highly prized. Eugênio Gudin (who was to live to 100 in the late 1980s and publish to the end) and Octávio Gouveia de Bulhões (head of the economics side of the Getúlio Vargas Foundation and post-1964 finance minister who at eighty-four would help inspire the Sarney government's 1989 austerity program) were their leading spokesmen, and they were strongly supported by the conservative press. Highly compatible with the interests of the traditional elite, this "cosmopolitan" or neoliberal position was on the defensive by the early 1950s, but remained vigorous and able to weather the political storms until its dramatic resurgence with the 1964 Revolution. The traditional elements within the armed forces generally held to views fundamentally congruent with this policy option.

The approach of "nationalist developmentalism" or developmental nationalism was still largely inchoate in 1951, but would rapidly take form and be elaborated.[29] Finding their early theoretical justification in the Prebisch Doctrine of the U.N. Economic Commission for Latin America (ECLA) and subsequently in the writings of its Brazilian veterans, led by Celso Furtado, these "structuralists" saw the state as the engine of development and argued that the outdated formula of their conservative rivals would condemn the country to perpetual underdevelopment. Planning and centralized direction were seen as essential, a view congenial to much of the government personnel and many of the groups pushing for a policy of industrialization—as well as to younger elements in the armed forces.

To the Left there existed a numerically much weaker current that held that even the mixed economy with a strong and active public sector advocated by the developmentalists would prove inadequate for the country's needs. In the view of this radical nationalist, anti-imperialist school, a determined attack upon the semi-feudal domestic agrarian structure needed to be mounted at once and accompanied by strict restraints upon exploitative foreign investment.[30] Though lacking significant political support at this time, they would be able to contribute to the polarization of the late stage of the Vargas administration through an articulate political rhetoric that would often pass beyond radical to revolutionary and extend from nationalist to xenophobic. Most important, their small but influential reflection within the armed forces provoked a reaction that by mid-1952 shifted the political disposition of the military rather sharply toward the Right and to a position bordering on open hostility toward the Vargas regime as that administration moved in the direction of economic statism.

As he entered the presidency for this last time, Vargas wished to function as the manipulator of existing political interests as well as mediator between existing and emergent groups. Preferring to let the contending political forces, especially those within the regime, articulate the issues and policy alternatives, Vargas remained the resourceful conciliator. Opportunities to play the great broker of conflicting interests were abundant in 1951–1952. The PSD retained 112 seats in the new 304-man Chamber of Deputies and the PTB held an additional 51, giving the government a congressional majority when this alliance of disparate elements could be held in line. Moreover, Adhemar de Barros's generally friendly PSP had twenty-four seats, whereas the backbone of the opposition, the UDN, could only muster eighty-one deputies. The eight minor parties, led by the conservative Republican Party (PR) but ranging over the political spectrum, divided the remaining thirty-six seats.

With the urban-oriented wing of the PSD basically developmentalist but more than balanced out by the traditional liberal views of the rural-based elements of the party and the PTB being developmentalist with a leftist fringe leaning toward radical nationalism, Vargas found himself obliged to pursue a mixed and often ambivalent policy. As characterized by a close student of the period, in light of the "tumultuous and contradictory relations of the party with the government everything had to be resolved case by case, with individual resolutions, and whatever solution might be found had to be the product of negotiations which eternally began all over again from zero."[31] The UDN's predominant adherence to neoliberal policies, which in the long run cost it substantial middle-class support, and the fact that economic nationalist sentiment extended across a vociferous spectrum of public opinion substantially wider than the Communist movement or even the broader range of Marxist thought meant that most policies adopted by the Vargas administration were subject to attack from both Right and Left.[32]

Reaction to Vargas's policies varied sharply among the major class and interest groupings within the electorate. Chambers of commerce and trade associations generally leaned toward the opposition on the grounds that protectionist measures for industry, exchange controls, and import restrictions were harmful to their interests. The administrative and managerial personnel of the private sector and members of the expanding government bureaucracy had come to make up the backbone of the urban middle class. Whereas the government bureaucrats were generally aware of the need for industrialization and modernization of the economy, the private sector managers in large part did not see a direct relationship between increased opportunities and Brazil's transition from an agricultural exporter toward a diversified economy based on growth of manufacturing. Although their ties to the traditional agrarian elites were fewer and weaker than in the case of the provincial middle class, this group still generally identified its interests with these of the foreign trade–oriented commercial elements. Thus divided, the Brazilian bourgeoisie in the early 1950s was far from ready to assume a leadership role in national economic modernization.[33]

Vargas began his presidency in a mixed but relatively favorable economic situation—but one that would soon deteriorate. His initial plan was to stabilize the economy first, then move quickly on to ambitious development projects—much as had been the case under Campos Salles and as would again be attempted by Collor de Mello in 1990. Having catered during the campaign to a wide variety of regional economic interests, Vargas was faced with the task of making industrialization and, to a somewhat lesser degree, diversification into common denominators for national economic policy. Aided by the demand for Brazilian exports spurred by the Korean War, he was able to win reasonably broad acceptance of a return to a more active economic role for the state, including a significant degree of government planning, with incentives and subsidies much more favorably received than controls—a situation still prevailing in the late 1980s. As most of the agencies necessary for this level of state intervention in an essentially capitalist economy already existed as institutional legacies of the Estado Novo, the executive could move forward without depending upon Congress.

Under the impulse provided by a group of young technicians on the presidential staff, proposals for massive investments in the economic infra-structure, especially transportation and energy, took shape during 1951. In the political arena, however, short-term concern was focused upon signs of economic deterioration and the threat of rising inflation (held in Vargas's first year to the 1950 level of 11 percent). The nub of this problem was stimulation of imports by an overvalued cruzeiro, which also led to increases in remittances of profits and in capital outflow. Hence, as would become essentially chronic, balance of payments problems became a major constraint on economic policy making.[34]

Given the Truman administration's willingness to provide technical as-sistance for basic planning studies and tacit, if not explicit, commitment to long-term loans in support of priority development projects, Vargas initially tended to accept the established rules of the international economic system, turning a deaf ear to the radical nationalists. A Joint Brazil–United States Economic Development Commission began work in mid-1951, and, though its final report was not issued until December 1953, Vargas's administration welcomed the by-products of its deliberations. During late 1951 and 1952 the government followed the five-year plan of Finance Minister Horácio Lafer, which featured establishment of the National Economic Development Bank (BNDE). The development bank served as a training ground for a group of young economists who would play increasing prominent roles in subsequent administrations—most notably Rómulo de Almeida, still active until his death in 1988, and Roberto de Oliveira Campos, post-1964 planning minister and the leading spokesman for free enterprise capitalism in the 1987–1988 constituent assembly.[35]

At the same time, however, Vargas maintained his populist stance by advocating measures of economic nationalism. In contrast to the tendency of the Dutra government to open the petroleum field to foreign investment, at the end of 1951 Vargas submitted a bill to Congress calling for the creation of a mixed capital (government and domestic private) corporation to explore and exploit Brazil's oil resources. Thus, the military's running debate on the oil question came to center around the administration's proposal, making this Vargas policy a divisive issue within the armed forces. The president may well have thought in light of the 1950 Military Club elections and his war minister's favorable attitude that this bill would win him army as well as civilian support. In fact it was to have the opposite effect, leading to a victory within the arena of military politics for the opponents of radical nationalism—whose anti-Communist sentiments were aroused by the leading role assumed by the illegal PCB in the "Oil is Ours" campaign for "national economic emancipation."[36]

The Process of Polarization

Even during this period of quite moderate and democratic behavior by Vargas, important armed forces leaders outside the regime's power scheme launched a strong campaign against the administration's military pillars, particularly Estillac Leal. The victory of the nationalist slate in the 1950 Military Club elections had resulted not only from the popularity of their political views, but also perhaps even more from their championing of a new promotions law and pay raise. Thus, it was not necessarily a mandate for radical political positions.[37] Moreover, the balloting had taken place before the outbreak of the Korean War, an event that rallied the veterans of the FEB quite strongly to the side of the United States and gave a powerful impetus to anti-Communism among the officer corps. Hence in 1951 the alignment within the military, which had been quite favorable for Vargas when petroleum policy was the line of division, shifted markedly over the question of Brazil's stance toward the Korean conflict.

This impingement of international considerations led very directly to a serious deterioration in Vargas's military *dispositivo*, which was built upon the leftist nationalist faction of the army. The Communist Party at this point opened an aggressive anti-U.S. attack, and its sympathizers within the military followed the PCB line of seeking to identify economic nationalism with anti-imperialism. As a result of pressures from the sectarian leftist minority in the Military Club, a very vocal segment of his constituency, Estillac Leal found himself pushed toward radical positions. These positions in turn cost him the support of less exalted nationalist elements and led to an escalation of attacks from pro-UDN officers.

As 1951 progressed, the focus of conflict shifted to the United States–Brazil Military Agreement negotiated by Foreign Minister Neves da Fontoura, and in March 1952, Vargas, under heavy pressure from the Center and Right, dismissed Estillac and signed the pact so fiercely opposed by the leftist-nationalist faction. Góes Monteiro, in the newly created post of chief of the armed forces general staff; Cordeiro de Farias, as commandant of the ESG; and Juarez Távora had effectively flexed their muscles. Whereas Góes Monteiro soon moved up to a seat on the superior military tribunal, new War Minister Espírito Santo Cardoso was only a brigadier general and thus seriously lacking in prestige among the senior officers. Zenóbio da Costa, as well as Gomes and Canrobert da Costa, lent support to a staunchly anti-Communist "Democratic Crusade" slate, which soundly trounced Estillac and the nationalists (8,288 to 4,489) in the May 1952 Military Club balloting. In the aftermath of this severe blow to the Left, a series of military police inquiries (IPMs) dealt harshly with leftist and ultranationalist officers.[38] Gomes continued to exert moral influence over the air force, and strongly anti-Communist admirals kept pressure on Vargas's centrist navy minister.

The increasingly dominant faction within the military advocated cooperation with the United States and was highly sensitive to the freedom of action the Communists seemed to be enjoying.[39] Against this backdrop a polarization of political life affording a foretaste of the event that would end civilian government a decade later took place during the latter half of 1953. This was kicked off by the replacement of the moderate José Segadas Viana as labor minister by Goulart, whose admiration for Argentine strongman Perón was no secret. For although relations with the United States were a factor in this as in all the subsequent crises, in the eyes of the armed forces Argentina was an equally important consideration. Vargas's perception of Argentine developments had influenced his actions in October 1945, and under Dutra Brazil stood as an obstacle to Perón's quest for continental hegemony.

Vargas, by way of sharp contrast, respected the accomplishments of the Argentine dictator in establishing a new type of popular authoritarian regime based upon manipulation of both labor and the military. Moreover, following the defeat of his candidate for governor of São Paulo in January 1947, Vargas had found himself in dire need of financial assistance for his future electoral campaign. Charges of Peronist monetary aid to Vargas were made as early as August 1950 by General Newton Cavalcante—then Dutra's chief military aide—and one of Vargas's first acts following his inauguration was to send his crony Batista Luzardo back to his former post as ambassador in Buenos Aires.[40]

The mid-year resignation of Neves da Fontoura as foreign minister turned in large part upon the regime's unofficial links to Perón, and the army's ability to force the dismissal of Batista Luzardo in August 1953 ushered in a period of increasing military pressure upon Vargas that ended with his death a year later. Not only did the armed forces once again suspect Vargas of harboring continuist objectives, but also this time they felt he did so with the backing of the Argentine regime, which could never hope that any other Brazilian government would be so friendly. Indeed, a major component of the military hostility toward Goulart at this time—as well as in 1955, 1961, and 1964 (when they would resort to naked force to expel him from the presidency)—stemmed from his sympathy toward Perón and his behind-the-scenes dealings with the Argentine regime.[41]

Vargas's thirty-five-year-old neighbor from São Borja was known to favor a labor policy well to the Left of that pursued by his centrist predecessor, who had generally urged restraint on union leaders and utilized the ministry more as a vehicle for keeping radical elements of the working class under control than for building labor up as a political force. Goulart's appointment was not depicted by the media as heralding a populist policy aimed at undermining Adhemar de Barros's presidential bid and strengthening the PTB—as it may well have been intended by Vargas. Rather it was attacked as a prelude to an assault by radical forces upon the Brazilian social order and established democratic institutions. No effort was spared in the press or in Congress to create a climate of suspicion that would thwart Vargas's emerging strategy of a turn to populism and nationalism as the difficulty of continued reconciliation tactics became apparent to the president.[42]

Spearheaded by the biting press and radio attacks of UDN Congressman Carlos Lacerda and his so-called Lantern Club, Vargas's opponents lambasted the government for its alleged reopening of the labor movement to Communist penetration as well as for generalized incompetence and corruption. Lacerda centered his attacks upon large-scale Bank of Brazil loans to Samuel Wainer, a reporter who had become friendly with Vargas during the 1950 campaign, to set up a pro-Vargas daily newspaper, Ultima Hora.[43] A formal congressional investigation kept this "scandal" in the public eye from May through November 1953. In point of fact, Vargas badly needed a paper that would sympathetically explain his progressive policies, and no such venture was feasible without a heavy initial investment, which could not be found from private sources for such a risky undertaking.

Ultima Hora quickly built a strong following among middle- and working-class readers and developed as an essentially pro-PTB organ. Although Vargas was certainly—and naturally—moving to strengthen the PTB's hand in the October 1954 congressional elections and to realign his political base for the 1955 presidential succession, his opponents were seeking to impute a subversive intent to his actions. Goulart, the rancher suddenly turned champion of the urban working class, became the lightning rod attracting their attacks (a role Brizola would play vis-à-vis Goulart a decade later). These attacks intensified sharply after he began to foster organization of rural labor unions.[44]

Vargas's cultivation of labor and appeals to nationalism in the latter half of 1953—like the "independent foreign policy" of Jânio Quadros in 1961—can best be understood as efforts to offset the unfavorable impact upon the working class of a deflationary program of economic stabilization. Aranha was recalled to the Finance Ministry in a mid-1953 shakeup triggered by Vargas's desire to broaden his political base in response to the defeat of his candidate by Jânio Quadros in the São Paulo mayoral election. Back in a job he had held two decades earlier, Aranha inherited a situation that had deteriorated badly as a result of the conflict between his predecessor's efforts to hold the line on credit expansion and the Bank of Brazil's generous loan policy toward São Paulo industrialists. In October Aranha instituted a complex system of multiple exchange rates aimed at discouraging luxury imports, channeling investment toward sectors linked to development, and quasi-subsidizing the continued importation of capital goods needed for industrialization. At the same time, as part of his policy of balancing moves welcome to the Right with measures popular with the Left, Vargas gave considerable attention to the enactment of the law creating Petrobrás, a government-controlled oil company with a monopoly on drilling but no exclusive rights in the refining, distribution, or petrochemical fields.[45]

As would again be the case in the early 1960s, inflation served as the catalyst of social tensions and raised the dilemmas of financial policy that the administration had sought to avoid, forcing it to disappoint the groups it was most seeking to court. Wage restraints and credit restrictions, essential as they might be for economic reasons, seriously undercut Vargas's efforts to build up political support among labor and the new industrialists. The cost of living in 1952 had risen 21 percent—nearly double the inflation of the preceding years—and was threatening to go even higher. The middle class was badly squeezed by the hike in prices, while labor cried for more substantial wage increases rather than kind words or gestures. Thus, wage policy was to prove a critical factor in the collapse of Vargas's conciliatory strategy and the replacement of compromise by confrontation during 1954.

The Dutra administration had firmly controlled the labor movement and failed to raise minimum wages in the face of substantial price increases. In December 1951 Vargas granted an increase that helped workers recover their losses in purchasing power. At the same time unions were allowed to pursue their bargaining with management in a more aggressive manner than had been permitted by the preceding regime. As organized labor sought wage adjustments in the face of mounting inflation, the number of strikes went up significantly in 1952 and 1953 (from 173 in 1951 to 264 the following year, with 800,000 workers involved in 1953).[46]

The United States Turns on Vargas

Vargas's problems were accentuated by the change of administrations in the United States. Under the influence of Treasury Secretary George Humphrey and Secretary of State John Foster Dulles, willingness to use public funds to aid Brazil's development programs was replaced by a policy of insisting that U.S. private investment would do the job if the Brazilian government would only create a sufficiently attractive climate. The Eisenhower administration decided to phase out the Joint Economic Development Commission with no commitment to help finance the projects it had agreed were essential to Brazil's development.

Opposition to the Petrobrás law was openly expressed as private U.S. interests attacked it as Communist-inspired. Vargas's foes were quick to exploit this new difficulty, and the president quite naturally reacted by increasing the nationalistic tenor of his public pronouncements. He had already extended his economic nationalism into the field of profit remittances during 1951 and 1952, when the overvaluation of the cruzeiro had led foreign firms to send their profits home instead of reinvesting them. Now, in December 1953, he struck back at U.S. investors' attacks upon the Petrobrás law by stridently denouncing their "sabotage" of Brazil's developmental efforts. This tactic of attributing Brazil's economic troubles to external forces made sub-stantial political sense in diverting resentment over austerity away from the administration. Yet this stress on nationalism, which struck a responsive chord not only among the urban working class but also with a very large proportion of the middle sectors, did not prove at this time to be the unifying force its intellectual advocates expected. The very vocal role of the radical nationalists in championing the causes that Vargas espoused for populist rather than revolutionary reasons led to the identification of nationalism with basic societal as well as economic changes. At the same time the role of such radical leftists fed apprehension among many middle-class elements.

What was crucial was the fact that by the end of 1953—as would be the case again a decade later—there was a propaganda war going on between the rightist opponents of the government and those on the other side of the spectrum who hoped to turn anti–foreign capital sentiment against the domestic capitalist system. Polemics largely replaced dialogue as radicalizers on both extremes played upon class interests and the tensions and insecurity engendered by the process of modernization. In particular, the conservative propagandists strove to drive a wedge between the urban middle sectors and the working class by depicting the political rise of the latter as a threat to the former and by grossly exaggerating the extent of the Communist menace.

The Coup of August 1954

The new year saw Vargas go farther down the road of diverting attention away from the unsatisfactory domestic situation through resort to an in-creasingly strident nationalism. On the U.S. side a senatorial investigation of "exorbitant" Brazilian coffee prices, which were in fact the normal result of a serious freeze, was an ill-disguised slap at the Vargas regime over its petroleum policy. Moreover, a situation parallel to the one that would lead to the system-shaking crisis of 1964 arose as Aranha's efforts to implement the shaky anti-inflation policy—undercut by São Paulo's massive deficit—came into direct conflict with Goulart's desire to raise the minimum wage sharply in response to labor unrest and leftist agitation.[47]

Then, too, the deficiencies of the party system were also to be a major factor in both the 1954 and 1964 crises and interventions. The UDN was not an adequate vehicle for the middle sectors, particularly those elements favoring industrialization and some degree of nationalism. Given the middle sectors' positive orientation toward moralism as a political value, the PSD held no significant appeal to them, and the PTB's brand of *trabalhismo* stressed class interests distinct from those of the urban middle groups. Adhemar de Barros's type of electoral populism overlaying a cynical ex-ploitation of opportunities for graft and favoritism to economic special interests represented the features of Brazilian politics that the middle class most disliked. Although in São Paulo many of them found a new symbol with the election of Jânio Quadros as mayor in March 1953, it would still be a number of years before the exciting young critic of the clientelistic system could emerge as a national figure. In the strategically critical Rio de Janeiro area the middle class was divided between support for Vargas in his developmentalist policies and adherence to the brand of conservative liberalism represented by the local leadership of the UDN, and Carlos Lacerda emerged as someone with whom many of them could identify, at least with regard to their fears and uncertainties.[48]

Military Divisions

More sharply than in 1945 and very much as would be the case in 1964, the backbone of the anti-Vargas movement was an alliance of the UDN with the strongly anti-Communist wing of the armed forces. The victory of the Democratic Crusade within the Military Club in May 1952 had been in large part a function of many of the middle-of-the-road officers reacting against the club's leftward swing. Though the nationalist fringe clearly represented a limited minority current among the armed forces, the neoliberal faction, with its militantly anti-Communist stance masking in many cases a preference for the status quo, was far from representing majority opinion regarding the proper road to economic development and the sociopolitical modernization of Brazil. The broad centrist spectrum of the military reflected the same ambivalences of the civilian middle class, complicated by varying attitudes on the "constitutional" responsibilities of the armed forces and differential perceptions on the nature of past military interventions in the political life of the nation. Moreover, a continuing value for the military that did not concern the civilian sectors was preservation of the armed forces' unity. For the overwhelming majority of the officers, a fundamental consensus capable of supporting discipline had to be preserved in order that the army could maintain its capacity for resolving any really critical political crisis. Threats to the basic institutional integrity of the armed forces could not be tolerated.

At the beginning of 1954 the military was divided much as it would be a decade later, with attitudes on legalism partially cross-cutting those on nationalism. Events of the ensuing eight months would move the armed forces closer to consensus on the need to exercise the moderating power once again, but without resolving differences on major questions of national policy, particularly in the economic and social realms. Thus, once having performed their "surgical" intervention, the vast bulk of the officer corps would favor leaving these matters to the interim regime headed by the vice-president. As most officers turned against Vargas only after the military had been drawn into the crisis by an incident in which one of their colleagues was killed, they were not highly concerned with presidential succession. But a politicized fringe, generally with ties to the National War College (ESG), was very actively organizing the candidacy of either Cordeiro de Farias or Juarez Távora.

Bringing together many civilian politicians, journalists, and businessmen with officers of all the services, the ESG was the arena for the development of a doctrine of national security that saw Brazil's future as firmly allied with the Western Judeo-Christian world in its confrontation with the communist bloc. Wishing the rapid emergence of a strong Brazilian nation, the exponents of this worldview saw this alliance with the West as best resulting from "the cooperation which can be given to us by foreign initiative, technology, and capital."[49] Among the ESG students in 1954 was Lacerda, who there cemented his close ties with a group of the rising young anti-Communist officers, and he would emerge as the detonator of the fatal crisis.

The military movement that was to result in Vargas's ouster and death made its first overt move in February 1954, issuing the so-called Colonels' Manifesto. In this rather curious document that reflected legalist scruples while bordering on an ultimatum, a group of eighty-two senior field-grade officers strongly expressed their dissatisfaction with neglect of the armed forces' need for modernization of equipment, their concern over labor agitation, and their disapproval of political corruption.[50] These officers were, with few exceptions, too young to have been part of the *tenente* movement, and this gesture was in their eyes the functional equivalent of the patriotic and moralizing actions of those who had come along a few years earlier. This idea had been nurtured, if not implanted, by Juarez Távora, Cordeiro de Farias, and other former *tenentes* who had broken with Vargas. Professing to speak for lower-ranking officers as well, the group lamented the "dangerous atmosphere of intranquility" in which the Communists might exploit the "unmistakable crisis of authority." Most critical at this particular juncture was their opposition to a proposed increase in the minimum wage that would place the lowest-paid worker equal to a junior officer.

Instead of reacting vigorously to enforce military discipline, Vargas dismissed both Goulart and the war minister, replacing the latter with Zenóbio da Costa—who had felt himself entitled to this high post since 1951. Like Góes Monteiro in 1945, he would be as much a constraint upon the president as a guarantor of his authority.

Rather than satisfying Vargas's critics, Goulart's removal was taken as a sign of weakness that called for escalation of the offensive against the president; Vargas responded by turning up the volume of his nationalist pronouncements. A doubling of the minimum wage, decreed on May Day— quite similar in intent and effect to Goulart's decision to pull out the stops on "basic reforms" in March 1964—represented a willingness to alienate important groups in order to solidify his leadership of the workers and gain votes in the scheduled October congressional elections. His bold, even reckless, tactics were in large part a reaction to the April 4 revelation by Neves da Fontoura that Vargas had entered into a pact with Perón to act jointly against U.S. hegemony in the continent. Although efforts at impeachment fell short in early June, in many respects serious damage had been done.[51]

Opposition Becomes Conspiracy

The Military Club elections of May 1954 confirmed the strength of anti-Vargas forces. Despite an alliance between War Minister Zenóbio da Costa and the remnants of the nationalist faction, the victors were Canrobert da Costa—Dutra's war minister—and Juarez Távora. This setback to the Left came by a decisive margin of roughly 7,000 to 4,000, as many centrist officers had moved over to support the anti-Communists. At the same time the moralist campaign against the Vargas regime was stepped up by the UDN, with the almost diabolically effective journalistic crusader Lacerda leading the attack.

When on August 5 an attempt was made on Lacerda's life, it unleashed a process that within three weeks would cost the president his life instead. While Lacerda was merely wounded in the foot, stray shots killed Air Force Major Rubens Florentino Vaz. An IPM set up at the main air force base traced the attempt to individuals closely linked to the presidency, in the process giving the public a good look at some of the unsavory types found there as well as uncovering a wide variety of shady dealings in which Vargas's cronies and advisors were involved.[52]

Although Vargas strove to ride out the storm, almost daily revelations concerning the "sea of mud" on which the presidency seemed to rest eroded his public support. Though Zenóbio da Costa was having some success holding the army in line, the air and navy ministers had lost control of the situation. Formulae to find a "constitutional" road out of the crisis all ran up against Vargas's unwillingness to be disgraced and the opposition's solidifying opinion that any solution short of his departure from office would be a temporary palliative at best. Former president Dutra concurred in this view, and on August 22 most of the leading generals demanded the president's resignation. Vargas insisted that if they came to depose him, they would find only his body, and when they rejected his offer to take a temporary leave, he shot himself neatly in the heart. At seventy-one, he felt "too old to be demoralized" and "no longer with any reason to fear death."[53] At his bedside was found his political testament, a brief document roundly condemning the "international economic and financial groups" that had thwarted his efforts to emancipate the Brazilian nation and brought inescapable pressure upon the Brazilian economy. Offering his life as the "price of their ransom," he told the Brazilian people that he "serenely" left life to "enter history."[54]

Vargas had indeed avoided the final humiliation of a second deposition through his suicide and the shrewdly designed testament. From a tragic failure he was immediately transformed into a patriotic martyr.[55] Instead of mass demonstrations against his regime, the country was swept by a wave of attacks upon his enemies and upon symbols of U.S. imperialism.[56]

The Café Filho Government and the November 1955 Counter-Coup

Although Vargas was dead and most of his close associates had been pushed out of the center of the political arena, the tension between pro- and anti-Vargas forces continued to dominate the political scene. The administration headed by Vice-President Café Filho, composed of a mixture of nearly all non-Vargist political forces including the Dutra wing of the PSD, assumed a "caretaker" role. This was in keeping with the fact that it found the country already in the advanced stages of campaigning for the October 1954 legislative and partial gubernatorial elections, with the presidential balloting only a little over a year away.[57] In terms of key positions and policies, however, it was more a UDN government than one of professed "national unity." Orthodox economic guru Gudin was finance minister (albeit only for the first seven months), with Eduardo Gomes heading the air force and Raúl Fernandes back for another stint as foreign minister. Although Café personally maintained a nonpartisan stance, the forces that had finished off Vargas strove to undercut, if not fully dismantle, the political machine he had left behind and to discredit the Vargas myth by continuing to expose evidence of corruption and governmental mismanagement under the preceding regime.[58]

Vargas's heirs, for their part, sought to capitalize on his martyrdom and depicted the UDN and its allies as power-grasping *golpistas* and tools of imperialism who had hounded the champion of the people into his grave. Though the exalted Lacerda wing of the UDN called for a dictatorial regime, the more conciliatory majority elements of that party were satisfied with seeking to obtain maximum electoral benefits from their control of government positions. The greater part of the military scheme of the Café Filho government was composed of officers who had been active in Vargas's ouster. General Canrobert da Costa headed the armed forces general staff, Álvaro Fiúza de Castro served as army chief of staff, and Juarez Távora became the president's chief military aide—with Lott brought in to be war minister and General Odylio Denys staying on as First Army commander.

A Year of "Relative" Stability

The outcome of the October 3 elections, held only forty days after Vargas's death, was surprisingly normal, with 9.9 million of the 15.1 million registered actually voting. The results demonstrated a relative stand-off between Vargas heirs and foes.[59] In the Federal District Lacerda received an impressive political support of some 160,000 votes for a return to the Chamber of Deputies, but Luthero Vargas also benefitted from a massive popular mandate with over 120,000 votes. Goulart's bid for the Senate in Rio Grande do Sul was, however, unsuccessful. Yet his brother-in-law, Leonel Brizola, polled a record 103,000 votes for Congress by emotionally capitalizing on Vargas's corpse. In many states the PTB and UDN allied as if the blood of Vargas was not between them and in complete disregard of the PSD-PTB coalition in Congress. As usual, the chief concern of politicians was winning, and national issues took a back seat to local questions and alliances of convenience. When the dust settled, the PSD held on to its dominant position with 114 Chamber seats, while the PTB gained slightly to 56 seats and the UDN slipped marginally to 74. Thus Café Filho and his successors would have to govern until February 1959 with a Congress little changed from that elected along with Vargas in 1950.

Brazil was to have no respite from political campaigning, as maneuvering was already well underway for the next year's presidential sweepstakes. Concerned that the campaign would further inflame passions and prolong the unsettled political situation, the military chiefs called for a national unity candidate.[60] To this end Café Filho sought in vain to persuade the PSD to shelve the candidacy of Juscelino Kubitschek, who had begun campaigning even before Vargas's death. Afonso Arinos de Mello Franco (who had advised both his father and his brother back in the 1930s and would be a leading figure in the 1987–1988 constituent assembly) sought to convince fellow UDN leaders that a firm alliance with the PSD was needed to keep the nation's largest party from joining with the PTB and thus returning the Vargas forces to power.[61] But for most UDN politicians a national unity candidate would be a good thing only as long as it was their Juarez Távora, while PSD influentials thought that it would be fine only if the UDN wanted to back Kubitschek.[62] Moreover, Kubitschek decided to call the bluff of a threatened military veto of his candidacy. (Ernesto Geisel was serving at this time as deputy military aide to the president; eighteen years later he would himself become Brazil's chief executive.)

Once the PTB formally allied with the PSD on the basis of Goulart for vice-president, Juarez Távora accepted the nomination of the Christian Democratic Party (PDC)—in order to appear as more than just the UDN's man—with the UDN, as the long leg of the coalition, indicating former Minas Gerais governor Milton Campos for the number two spot—a move designed to draw votes in that key state away from native son Kubitschek. Adhemar de Barros decided to make a determined bid, with PTB dissident Danton Coelho as his running mate. Adhemar had been promised administration support in return for backing Vargas in 1950, but the latter's death negated this deal. Moreover, the rise of Jânio Quadros to the governorship of São Paulo in 1954 threatened the future of Adhemar's base there.

As one more example in Brazil's long recurrent chain of subordinating rational economic policy to political exigencies, José Maria Whitaker replaced Gudin as finance minister in return for Quadros's pledge of electoral support to the government's candidate in the presidential contest.[63] (Thus, Whitaker returned to the post he had first held in 1930, which, as with the Aranha example, was a strong reminder that former finance ministers may very well be recycled in Brazil.)

In the midst of virulent UDN attacks on the bid of Vargas's heirs to recapture control of the government, the May 1 death of Estillac Leal deprived the nationalist-progressive faction of the armed forces of their chief. Opposition to the dominant Democratic Crusade grouping came to center upon the Constitutionalist Military Movement (MMC) of General Zenóbio da Costa—which was no match for the forces headed by the ailing General Canrobert da Costa and presidential hopeful Juarez Távora.[64] With the Brazilian Anti-Communist Movement, presided over by Admiral Carlos Pena Bôto, commander-in-chief of the fleet, denouncing Kubitschek for having accepted support of the illegal PCB, the seriously ill Canrobert da Costa

all but directly called for a coup to keep Goulart out if elected. Adding to
the tension, Lacerda attacked Goulart on the basis of the so-called Brandi
Letter, in which, back in 1953, an Argentine congressman appeared to have
been arranging with the PTB leader details for coordination of labor activities
between the two countries and discussing trade in contraband war material
across the border into Rio Grande do Sul. Very probably spurious, this letter
did tie in well with the April 1954 Neves da Fontoura denunciation of
Vargas's secret pact with Perón and provided Lacerda with an opportunity
to make public documentation linking Goulart to the Argentine strongman.

The elections gave a slim plurality to Kubitschek and Goulart with the
former receiving nearly 3.1 million votes—almost 470,000 more than Juarez
Távora—and Goulart edging Campos by less than half that margin. As
Kubitschek's victory in Minas Gerais by some 430,000 votes nearly equalled
his national plurality, his election resulted almost exclusively from his strength
in his home state. Adhemar de Barros, not Kubitschek or Juarez Távora,
carried São Paulo and the Federal District.[65] "Juscelino" (as Kubitschek was
called in public life) had received only 34 percent of the total presidential
vote cast—a high 9.1 million votes. With this as their pretext, the UDN
and its military allies refused to accept his election as legitimate, arguing
that an absolute majority was required and that votes given to the winning
slate by supporters of the PCB should be nullified. The UDN's small but
extremely loud and visible *golpista* wing spoke repeatedly of the need to
use force to keep "corrupt and subversive" elements from taking office.
They were apparently depending upon General Canrobert da Costa to lead
the coup, but the country's ranking military figure died of cancer.

With Estillac Leal and Canrobert da Costa both dead, Juarez Távora's
luster dimmed by the failure of his electoral campaign, and Zenóbio da
Costa censured by the president, War Minister Lott became the dominant
army figure. But as he had become more powerful, his stance with respect
to the political situation underwent a basic transformation. Whereas in April
he had warned of the disruptive influence of Goulart's candidacy, by October
all of his hostility toward the PTB leader seems to have disappeared—in
part because of his resentment of Juarez Távora's "excessive" influence as
well as in reaction to Lacerda's vituperative attacks upon his legalist position.

Development of a Crisis

Lott reacted vigorously to an inflammatory speech by Colonel Jurandir
da Bizarria Mamede at Canrobert da Costa's funeral on November 2.[66] The
PSD and PTB were denounced for "suicidally insane" intransigence. Effusive
praise for the deceased as a "true military leader" who "in the midst of
confusion and complexity knew how to define clearly and in a straightforward manner, the way of honor and duty" was intended as much as a
rebuke to Lott as a tribute to his predecessor. Indeed, this address was as
articulate a call for the armed forces to exercise the moderating power as
could be made without directly advocating a coup. Lott, who had shortly
before censured and reassigned Zenóbio da Costa and several other MMC

officers for speaking out in favor of inauguration of Kubitschek and Goulart, decided to view Mamede's words as a serious breach of discipline and a threat to his authority.

A potentially manageable episode escalated quickly into a major crisis, in part because even before becoming aware of the exact content of Mamede's speech, the president suffered a mild heart attack leading to his hospitalization.[67] On November 8 the military ministers were informed of Café Filho's intention, on medical advice, to turn the presidential office over temporarily to Carlos Luz—as presiding officer of the Chamber of Deputies Luz was first in the constitutional line of succession. The ties of the new acting chief executive to the coup-minded officers and their UDN allies were clearly close, if not truly intimate, and he was certainly a rival of Kubitschek within Minas Gerais politics.[68] The supporters of the victorious candidates harbored mistrust with respect to the intentions of Café Filho, who had consistently guaranteed that they would be inaugurated if confirmed by the electoral courts. Their suspicions of the new acting president were far greater. Indeed, many of them doubted that Café Filho was really ill, seeing in his hospitalization a move to clear the decks for a coup.

When Luz accepted the ruling of the chief of the armed forces general staff, backed up by the attorney general, that Mamede had not violated military regulations, Lott felt that the loss of face involved was unacceptable. Thus, he could either resign or depose the temporary president. When informed by Luz that his replacement would be Fiúza de Castro, Lott came to suspect that his forced resignation was being engineered as part of a plot to prevent the inauguration of the president-elect and the vice-president-elect. Concerned with what he saw as "pro-Communist" leanings of the Constitutionalist Military Movement (MMC), capital area army commander Denys did not want them to be able to claim credit for insuring Kubitschek's coming to office. So while Lott agonized over whether or not to relinquish the War Ministry, Denys was busy organizing a powerful military scheme to oppose that supporting the "acting, acting" president. Lott agreed to become its titular leader, and well before dawn the capital was in their hands.

Reaction to this smoothly executed military action was minimal. President Luz and his associates, including Lacerda, took refuge on a cruiser commanded by Captain Silvio Heck (who would be navy minister in the late 1960s) and set sail for Santos while Gomes and other loyal air force officers flew to São Paulo. Although Governor Quadros, who had been a major backer of the Juarez Távora candidacy, was in sympathy, resistance fizzled out in the face of opposition by the Second Army and military region commanders— both old *tenentes*. On November 11 the PSD-PTB majority in Congress voted Luz's "impediment" by a count of 185 to 72.[69] Bitterly attacked by the UDN, this move was justified by the majority leader on the grounds that any "constitutional" way out was preferable to a naked military takeover. Senate presiding officer Nereu Ramos accepted the presidency to preserve civil authority, declaring he would turn it back to Café Filho when the latter had sufficiently recovered. But on November 21 Café Filho's impediment was also voted, and troops kept him a virtual prisoner in his apartment until Kubitschek had been inaugurated.

As no proof was ever presented of plans to actually mount a coup to keep Juscelino and Jango (as João Goulart had come to be known) from office—as distinct from a strong desire to do so by Lacerda and some junior officers—the "preventive coup" was to persist as a major bone of contention within the military as well as the broader political arena. Indeed, during his presidential campaign in 1960, Lott would be attacked for having cloaked a naked power grab as the "Movement to Return to Existing Constitutional Norms." The question of which side was truly that of "legality" would remain highly ambiguous in succeeding crises. Thus, while the "August 24" and "November 11" military factions would be numerically far inferior to the centrist majority of the officer corps, in periods of political polarization the latter would tend to inaction, leaving the initiative to the more militant minorities.

The Kubitschek Administration:
Development and Independence

Juscelino Kubitschek, the grandson of a Czech immigrant, earned a unique place in Brazilian history as the only president to enjoy greater popularity and to be more firmly in control of the political-governmental situation at the end of his mandate than at the beginning. Born in 1902, he lost his father at an early age and had to struggle to gain a medical education. At the time of the 1930 Revolution he was an ambitious young Belo Horizonte doctor about to enter into a quite advantageous marriage. After serving as a noncombatant on the government side in the 1932 civil war, he was tabbed by Valladares to be chief of staff for the Minas Gerais interventor. Elected to Congress in 1934, he returned to his medical practice when that body was put out of business by the 1937 Estado Novo *golpe*. Appointed mayor of Belo Horizonte in April 1940, he quickly established a reputation as an energetic and effective administrator. Returned to Congress in the 1945 voting, he was elected by the PSD to the Minas Gerais governorship in 1950.[70]

Kubitschek's successes caught most observers by surprise, as in 1956 or 1957 few of them were inclined to predict that he would even complete his term in office.[71] But he brought to the tasks of reestablishing stability and putting the country squarely on the road to development all the legendary facility for political maneuvering and compromise of an experienced Mineiro politician. This ability was coupled with a solid background of administrative experience as mayor of Brazil's third city and governor of its second state. He also possessed both a penchant for building and a blueprint for the construction of a modern Brazilian nation.

His Program of Goals (Programa de Metas) set ambitious targets to be achieved, promising "Fifty Years' Progress in Five," with emphasis upon transportation, energy, and manufacturing—as well as on construction of a new capital in the sparsely settled interior. From a political point of view, the program offered something to nearly every relevant group, with its long-run effect being to consolidate Brazil's industrialization by building up the requisite infrastructure while implanting heavy industry—especially auto-motive—and fostering a capital goods sector. For, essentially a dynamic and pragmatic centrist, Kubitschek gave economic development marked priority over social welfare measures.[72]

Kubitschek's Political Style: A Model for the Future?

This prototype of the Brazilian "amiable man," whose political centrism and conciliatory style made few enemies, carefully avoided the kind of confrontation that had so recently cost Vargas both this office and his life and that would lead to Goulart's downfall within a few years. In tacit alliance with the landowning forces so powerful within his PSD, he would leave their economic and political interests untouched in exchange for a free hand in promoting industry and taking some steps toward modernization of urban society. (This was in keeping with what Samuel Huntington would subsequently advocate as a combination of "Fabian," or gradualist, strategy and blitzkrieg tactics.) In adopting a policy that Hélio Jaguaribe has aptly termed "strategic postponement," Kubitschek believed that a process of forced-draft industrialization would indirectly bring change to the countryside. The validity of this assumption was only partially borne out, largely because he would never have the second term in the late 1960s upon which he was counting to complete his modernization of the country. Moreover, the relatively painless economic growth of Juscelino's years in office could not be duplicated—owing to the limits reached on import-substitution indus-trialization and the high level of inflation that was the negative side of the Kubitschek legacy. This meant that successor administrations would face hard and politically divisive choices that he had been able to avoid.

A good indication of Kubitschek's essential moderation was the fact that even the rural social service he implemented in mid-1956 had been proposed to Congress by Vargas and enacted into law during the Café Filho gov-ernment.[73] Although Vice-President Goulart and his PTB submitted a rural workers' statute to Congress, it failed passage in even a watered-down version (finally being enacted in March 1963). For his part, Kubitschek skillfully redirected attention away from this issue to the development of the laggard northeast. Setting up a Development Council for the Northeast (CODENO) in February 1959, he got it transformed into the Superintendency for the Economic Development of the Northeast (SUDENE) at the end of that year.[74] But before he could even begin to move ahead with his efforts at national development, Kubitschek had to deal with the immediate political problems hanging over from the 1954–1955 crises—and do this before he could have time to build up public support from the just over one-third of the vote he had received.

The only elements of the intransigently opposed "August 24" faction in the military to translate their dissatisfaction into action against the regime were air force officers linked to Lacerda. On February 11, 1956, Major Haroldo Coimbra Veloso raised the standard of revolt in an inaccessible Amazon region, hoping that the government would overreact or mishandle the task of repression and that this might lead to additional uprisings.[75] This intended parallel to the *tenente* revolts of the 1920s did capture significant public sympathy for the insurgents, hence the new government was obliged by this air-age emulation of the Prestes Column to appear ineffectual, if not impotent, for eighteen days before a contingent of the elite paratroopers captured the rebels.

Kubitschek believed that a magnanimous measure was preferable to creating martyrs, so his reaction was a prompt amnesty. His more serious military problem was the fact that while Lott constituted a strong bulwark against the continued refusal of some UDN elements to accept the new administration as legitimate, this proud army strongman also infringed upon the president's authority and freedom of action. Given Lott's long friendship with General Denys, there was no viable alternative to Lott as war minister, so Kubitschek could never consider replacing him—a situation that naturally led the vain Lott to role expansion.[76]

Born in Minas Gerais in late 1894, Lott was a 1914 academy graduate and one of the relatively few in his age bracket to avoid involvement in both the *tenente* movements and the 1930 Revolution. Widely considered apolitical and concerned only with professional matters, he reached the army's top rank in mid-1955, after he was already war minister. Although a graduate of the French War College, he was more the Prussian type of career soldier.[77] Though he was not widely read nor particularly well informed on many aspects of public affairs, as the man responsible for having guaranteed Kubitschek's inauguration his every pronouncement on policy matters and political questions received heavy media play. His egotism provided the occasion for a serious military crisis in November 1956, but he subsequently succeeded—with the aid of his staunch ally, General Denys—in reestablishing discipline within the army as well as that service's dominance over the more opposition-minded navy and air force.[78]

Kubitschek managed progressively to exert his leadership within the government during the course of 1957. His responsible conduct and development policies did more to dispel lingering military suspicions than did his quite diplomatic dealings with the armed forces. His emphasis upon growth, moderate nationalism, and conciliation held considerable appeal for the centrist majority of the officer corps. As the president demonstrated that he was a Vargas heir only in the most constructive sense of the term and that, instead of any authoritarian or demagogic tendencies, he represented the better side of the PSD establishment, he neutralized military reservations. A modernizer more than reformer, Kubitschek's infectious enthusiasm for Brazil's future disarmed all but the most hardened of his opponents and moved the country closer to a national consensus on many basic issues than had existed since before the 1920s.[79]

Even the construction of a new capital, Brasília, on the interior plateau a thousand miles northwest of Rio de Janeiro, while generating considerable controversy, contributed to the new national psychology and caught the imagination of a large proportion of the military as well as that of the civilian populace. Criticism of his government by the far Left removed much of the lingering distrust on the part of conservative elements stemming from his alliance with Goulart and the PTB as well as his receipt of Communist support in the 1955 campaign. The president's closing of the National Emancipation League (LEN) in mid-1956 as a Communist-dominated organization and his lack of sympathy for politically motivated strikes helped gain further Center-Right support.

The navy and air force, in which *golpista* tendencies were significantly stronger than in the army, were kept divided by a protracted dispute over which force would fly from the obsolescent British aircraft carrier purchased in December 1956 and incorporated into the fleet as the *Minas Gerais* after refitting in the Netherlands. Even if Juscelino did not consciously foster this dispute, his politically wise decision not to reach a definitive resolution of the interservice conflict certainly maintained both the navy and air force on their best behavior with respect to the president's wishes and inhibited collaboration between opposition elements within their respective ranks. At the same time, the army was kept satisfied by the relatively large quantities of military hardware received from the United States under augmented mutual assistance programs resulting from negotiations for permission to construct an missile tracking facility on Fernando de Noronha Island off the bulge of Brazil's northeast.

Moreover, a not inconsequential number of military officers came to occupy important executive positions in state enterprises and mixed corporations.[80] Thus, on the military side Kubitschek had increasing support and freedom of action as his administration reached its midpoint. It is not surprising then that the May 1958 Military Club elections were won by the incumbent "November 11" faction associated with Lott and Denys, as Justino Alves Bastos defeated Castelo Branco—candidate of the Democratic Crusade—by roughly 4,500 to 2,500 votes.[81] In the long run, however, the Democratic Crusade would come out on top, with Castelo Branco becoming Brazil's president in 1964.

The Kubitschek period, although clearly the apex of reasonably functioning and representative politics down to the present, was not without considerable political controversy and an active and often effective opposition. But, in contrast with what was to come as well as with the past, this was kept within the bounds of normal political competition. The UDN finally settled into routine criticism and minor obstructionism; although radical leftist and ultranationalist elements exercised little influence upon administration policies, these same elements were also generally unable to mobilize strong opposition to such policies. Repeatedly Kubitschek assumed a stance just nationalistic enough to take some of the wind from their sails, and the quite high rate of economic growth—around 7 percent each year—allowed for substantial wage concessions to the urban working class without disturbing the highly satisfactory profits of the business and industrial sectors. Indeed, "stabilization" efforts were only aimed at pulling inflation back to liveable levels without even seriously sacrificing development.

A past master in the use of patronage as a means of political persuasion, Kubitschek dealt with all but the most radical extremes of Left and Right as potential allies and collaborators rather than treating them as confirmed opponents. His repeated Cabinet reshuffling was generally more the result of the political convenience of rewarding different groups and individuals than a reflection of serious political difficulties. Thus, from a labor minister named by Goulart and the PTB at the beginning of his administration, Kubitschek progressed to one selected from several names proposed by the PTB, and before the end of his term only afforded that allied party a possible veto of names he had selected from among their ranks.[82] The several concerted nationalist campaigns during 1956, 1957, and 1958 on such issues as export of atomic minerals, opposition to the entrance of American Can Company into Brazil, and against the Hanna mining interests did not seriously inconvenience Kubitschek, who was very adept at balancing the demands of the conservatives and radicals while following an essentially centrist course.[83]

The congressional elections of October 1958 (with concurrent gubernatorial balloting in half the states) came at a time when the financial problems that were to plague the administration for the rest of its term were not yet out of hand. The 326-member Chamber of Deputies chosen to serve for the last two years of Kubitschek's term and the first years of his successor's was little changed from that elected four years earlier. Benefitting from an alliance with the illegal Communist Party, the PTB gained to sixty-six seats (from fifty-six) on the strength of nearly 20 percent of the vote. But the president's PSD easily retained its lead with 116 federal deputies and 32 percent of the national vote, while the UDN won 70 seats with its 20 percent of the ballots cast.[84] The outcome of a number of state races had important implications for the future, particularly the election of Brizola as governor of Rio Grande do Sul and the defeat of Adhemar de Barros by Quadros's candidate in São Paulo. The key northeastern state of Pernambuco saw a UDN-PTB alliance turn the entrenched PSD machine out of office for the first time, thus paving the way for political ferment and a move to the Left four years later. Impressive was the fact that while the electorate had been pared to 13.8 million by a new registration process, almost 12.7 million actually voted.

"Fifty Years' Progress in Five"

With the elections out of the way, a new phase opened, one characterized by marked progress toward fulfillment of Kubitschek's development goals, an ever-increasing rate of inflation—which brought with it international complications and some domestic social tensions—adoption of a more active and positive foreign policy, and the beginnings of maneuvering with regard to succession. At about this same time, the PCB chose to take a more aggressive stance in the "struggle against North American Imperialism" and to push for its own legalization and reestablishment of trade and diplomatic relations with the Soviet Union.[85] In part this revivification of the Communist movement was a reflection of the coming to power of Fidel Castro in Cuba, but the opportunities afforded by the rapidly rising cost of living and the escalating debate over economic and financial policies were probably more fundamental. Within Congress, the supra-party Nationalist Parliamentary Front (FPN), founded in 1957 by a majority of the PTB deputies and the leftist elements of other parties, came to play an increasingly important role in setting the tone for consideration of economic and foreign policy matters.

In this changed environment, the failure of the government's economic stabilization measures to hold inflation in check and the consequent stiffening of the attitudes of U.S. and international financial institutions led to tensions in U.S.-Brazilian relations that provided a foretaste of the disagreements that were to mark the Goulart period. After a generally successful year in 1957, the policies of Finance Minister José Maria Alkmim had not been able to contain inflation during the first half of 1958 as Brazil's balance of payments deficit grew sharply with the continued deterioration of terms of trade. The new team of Lucas Lopes as finance minister and Roberto Campos as head of the National Economic Development Bank (BNDE) designed a program that promised to combine sustained rapid economic growth with financial stability. The increase in the cost of living was to be held to only 5 percent for 1959, while real wages would rise and Kubitschek's sacred Program of Goals would continue at full throttle.[86]

In practice—as was to be the case under successive efforts of at least the next eight administrations—a high rate of investment and economic growth did not prove compatible with price stability no matter what plans might project. The structuralist-monetarist controversy, which had been previewed under Vargas and sidestepped by the Café Filho administration, was joined full force, with the Brazilian government fearing possible stagnation and consequent political difficulties, while the sources of financial assistance, particularly the U.S. government, were stressing the overriding dangers of inflation.

The situation in mid-1959 was aggravated by the failure of the United States to respond positively to Kubitschek's proposal, first formulated in a May 1958 letter following the disaster of Vice-President Richard Nixon's South American trip, for a joint crusade against underdevelopment in the hemisphere. Kubitschek viewed this Operation Pan American as a statesmanlike initiative to meet Latin America's obvious priority problems and to undercut communism by eliminating its breeding ground. The visit of Secretary of State Dulles in August 1958 dramatically underscored the wide gap between Kubitschek's views on the problem and the perspective of the U.S. administration, which pushed hard for vigorous anticommunist actions in the political sphere combined with orthodox economic remedies.

Subsequent delays and misunderstandings over the implementation of Operation Pan American, accompanied by pressure by the United States to abandon "unrealistic" and overly ambitious development goals in favor of an all-out attack on inflation through stringent wage and credit controls, led Kubitschek to opt for a policy of continued development at all costs. The president was unwilling to back away from his commitment to industrialization and was becoming concerned over stepped-up political attacks from the Left—at the same time as producers' groups were vociferously complaining about the adverse impact of tighter credit and reduced subsidies. Hence he was not inclined to take the further steps, particularly those with respect to exchange reform, insisted upon by the U.S. government and the IMF.[87]

With the PTB and the nationalist wing of the PSD already criticizing Lopes and Campos as "handing over" Brazil to the United States, Kubitschek chose to drop them and blame foreign obstructionism for the upsurge in inflation that followed. Thus, U.S. policy, which called for keeping Kubitschek on a "short leash" and providing only enough external assistance to maintain Brazil on a fairly even keel, ran up against a significantly greater determination on Kubitschek's part than had been foreseen. Inside Brazil the consensus on developmental nationalism that had been skillfully built up in the 1956–1958 period began to disintegrate in the face of the impassioned debate and political polemics between the economic liberals' advocacy of orthodox fiscal measures and the radical nationalists' attacks on foreign capital and external influences.

This shift toward a more "Vargas-like" policy was sealed in June 1959 when Kubitschek broke off negotiations with the IMF. From a pragmatic political viewpoint, he had little choice, for following the tough stabilization line insisted upon by the IMF would almost surely have brought him to the end of his term without having fulfilled his promises in the development field. Moreover, this would have left his successor to benefit from the country's sanitized finances at the almost certain sacrifice of Kubitschek's ambitions for winning a second term in 1965. The dramatic strategy he did adopt, in sharp contrast, rallied support around the national goal of development, clouded the issue of whether the rising cost of living was an inevitable side effect of the drive for development or the result of U.S. unwillingness to accord Brazil the special consideration Brazilians felt their country merited, and projected him as a fearless patriot.

Such a forceful assertion of independence clearly suited the new and more nationalistic mood that was one of the by-products of Kubitschek's successful campaign to demonstrate to his compatriots that they were fully capable of determining their own destiny. By taking a course so distinct from those recently followed by the Argentine, Chilean, and Bolivian governments—which in Brazilian eyes had led to economic stagnation through application of orthodox monetarist prescriptions—Kubitschek effectively rallied support from diverse sectors. These included not only the radical Left, but also the armed forces and industrial interests. Brazil was no longer content, he emphasized, to be part of the "international proletariat." The "land of the future" was coming of age and the "poor relative" was not satisfied with being shut off in the kitchen and would insist upon access to the living room.[88]

The dedication of the new capital in April 1960 attracted favorable international interest and afforded Kubitschek an opportunity to bring home to the Brazilian people the positive accomplishments of his administration, centering upon very substantial completion of the greater number of the thirty targets of his Program of Goals. Though the president's prestige and personal popularity remained high and may well even have continued to grow during his last year in office, the campaign for his succession also focused attention upon some of the shortcomings and neglected areas. Had the constitution permitted, he might well have been able to gain reelection, but as it was, the interest of the electorate turned increasingly toward the succession race.

The Brazil Kubitschek prepared to hand over had changed a great deal since the end of World War II and the Estado Novo. Population was up to 70 million, with over 31 million classified as urban dwellers. Life expectancy was nearing fifty-three (compared to under forty-three around 1940), and infant mortality had dropped from 145 per 1,000 live births in the 1940s to around 117. The doubling of industrial production during his term was reflected in the presence of over 2.9 million employees of industry in the labor force of more than 22.7 million—a very significant rise from 2.2 million in 1950 and only 1.6 million a decade earlier. By 1960 industry accounted for 25.2 percent of GDP, compared to only 22.5 percent for agriculture, an inversion of their relationship in 1950.[89] Industrial establishments had reached 111,000 for a rise of almost 30 percent in a decade. Total nonagricultural employment had shot up from 6.7 million in 1950 to over 10.3 million—twice the increase in agricultural employment (up to 12.3 million from 10.4 million).

Income was still very unevenly distributed, with nearly 40 percent going to the highly favored top one-tenth of the population and 36 percent to the next 30 percent, leaving only 25 percent for the bottom three-fifths of the social pyramid. But Kubitschek had done all humanly possible to build a base for economic development on a scale that would assure that in the future there would be something much more adequate to distribute. GDP growth had slowed in 1956 to only 2.9 percent, chiefly as a result of the drift and hesitation during the crisis period of the latter part of 1955.

Over the next five years—the period of Kubitschek's responsibility—the economy expanded in real terms at an annual rate of 8.3 percent, permitting a per capita gain of well over 5 percent a year. (During the Dutra administration the average rate of economic growth—buoyed by favorable international conditions—had been a healthy 6.9 percent yearly, and this annual rate had held fairly steady at 6.8 percent during the Vargas government.) In the process of this expansion, Kubitschek had doubled iron production to 7.5 million tons a year; raised steel-making capacity from 1.15 million to over 2.5 million tons (which would reach 3.5 million by 1964 when the projects he launched were completed); expanded oil production from 5,500 to 82,000 barrels a day; and upped oil refining from 108,000 to 308,000 barrels daily (by 1961). In addition, he had increased installed electrical generating capacity from 3,000 kilowatts to 4,750 kilowatts, with projects under construction that would bring this capacity to 8,500 kilowatts by 1965, and he had built from scratch an automotive industry that produced 321,000 vehicles in 1960.[90]

Thus, the Kubitschek years did, indeed, mark the consolidation of industrialization in Brazil and provide the foundation for the post-1967 economic takeoff. First, however, three years of poor management of the economy in the midst of renewed political instability would lead to an overturning of the political system Kubitschek's adroitness and economic successes had done so much to bolster.

6

Decay, Crises, and "Revolution," 1961–1964

The positive heritage left by Kubitschek was quickly dissipated by his successors, paving the way for perhaps the most dismal decade in Brazil's life as a nation—1963 to 1973. Although it is conventional to take 1964 as the dramatic watershed, with 1985 as the next, the processes that produced the 1964 "revolution"—like those that led to the major regime changes of 1889 and 1930—began their work several years earlier. Similarly, the transition toward democracy that would eventually bear fruit in January 1985 with the return of the presidency to civilian hands actually got underway in 1974. Hence the period running from Quadros's inauguration in early 1961 through the deepest trough of military authoritarianism—yet also the peak of economic growth—can best be understood as a pair of three-act tragedies.

The first of these tragedies consisted of (1) Quadros's erratic and irresponsible mini-administration from January to August 1961; (2) Goulart's accidental and ineffective stewardship between September 1961 and March 1964; and (3) the armed forces' 1964 intervention to put an end to the government's leftward shift. The second would include (1) the installation of long-term military rule, first under an interim junta and then with Castelo Branco as president from April 1964 to March 1967; (2) deterioration under Costa e Silva between March 1967 and September 1969; and (3) institutionalized authoritarianism under Emílio Garrastazú Médici from October 1969 through 1973. This chapter will analyze the process of breakdown and the military's transition from arbiter to ruler, with the heyday of the authoritarian regime and its subsequent decline constituting the heart of the next two chapters.

Underlying the undeniable political decay of the early 1960s was the tension between the modernizing sectors of Brazilian society and those opposed to any fundamental change in the essentially patrimonial order—rooted in clientelism, co-optation, and the *cartorial* state—which had successfully withstood attack even in the immediate aftermath of the 1930 Revolution and the postwar "reestablishment of democracy." The modernizing sectors were largely concentrated in the center-south, with the conservative traditional forces still dominant in the northeast and north—a situation that would only slowly change over the next quarter century. This fundamental cleavage would prove resistant to repeated efforts to bridge it through formulae for accommodation and compromise and would lead to increased political polarization as direct popular election of the president gave the more advanced sectors a major voice in choosing the executive, whereas the continued gross overrepresentation of the most backward states guaranteed at least veto group power for the traditional conservative forces.

In short, economic development of the postwar era had by the early 1960s so transformed urban Brazilian society that the old rules of the control–conciliation-clientelism–co-optation political game no longer applied there. But these changes had not yet reached the hinterlands, where—owing to the grotesque congressional underrepresentation of the most populous states—the locus of political power still resided. At the local and state levels of the northeast, north, and center-west, the patrimonial political structures proved very resistant to the limited reflections there of the ongoing economic and social transformations of the area below the eighteenth parallel. Thus, not only through the 1950s, but also on into the 1960s "the representatives elected by the rural and small city vote, above all in the underdeveloped [part of] Brazil, acted as a bloc in the direction of impeding any substantial modification of the agrarian structure of the country."[1]

Moreover, co-optation, rather than true representation, was rooted in the fact that strong governmental structures had been established before efforts to mobilize social groups. As a result, "the more intimate the participation in the governmental bureaucracy on the part of the leader, the greater his political force, since he would have greater resources to maintain control of his political base."[2] From this stemmed the repeated electoral victories at the state level that enabled these rural-based conservative elites to exert very heavy influence, if not always control, within the decentralized national structures of the UDN and the PSD.

Thus, at the national level patronage politics survived in the face of sustained economic growth and modernizing influences in society that might have been expected to give rise to interest groups, if not ideological politics. With parties rendered incapable of representing group interests, the latter sought to express themselves through their respective "class" organizations, unions, and commercial associations. Inadequately organized in this respect, the middle classes would come to look toward the army as defender of their basic interests, which led to a breakdown of the developmentalist coalition of forces that had functioned effectively during the Kubitschek era. Within this environment Quadros's effort to switch development strategies would founder on the impossibility of playing a Bonapartist role "in the service of a reformist design, but without the control and support of Bonapartist armies."[3]

In this context, political issues, particularly those with deep social and economic roots, not only proved highly divisive during the Quadros presidency, but also became positively indigestible through the Goulart years.

This was a dual tragedy. First, it paved the way for the military's seizure of power and retention of control over government for two decades, with a resultant narrowing and atrophy of political processes. Agrarian interests demonstrated ability to find allies in Congress for their efforts to thwart executive initiatives; when in 1963 and 1964 they found themselves dislodged from the levers of political power and facing the prospect of major changes in the rural sector becoming law, they responded by doing away with the electoral and legislative processes that no longer served their purposes. To accomplish this they needed to convince centrist elements of the desirability of putting an end to "demagogic" politics by force, while their allies within the armed forces did the same vis-à-vis the moderates in that decisive institution. For there was a well-defined military nucleus who had been frustrated by the fact that every time they had pushed Vargas and his populist heirs out of power—1945, 1954, and 1960—the "misguided" electorate quickly opened the door for the return to power of these same populists (1950, 1955, and 1961). Hence they decided that the next time the voters must not be given a chance to repeat this "mistake."

The second facet of the tragedy was that even when fully competitive civilian political life was resumed in 1985 after the long hiatus, many of the same unresolved and polarizing issues would return to the policy arena. This was particularly true—and most significant—with respect to the inability in the early 1960s to reach any agreement on a meaningful program of agrarian reform.[4] The lost opportunity resided largely in the Quadros fiasco, for Goulart would subsequently arrive in office with too many liabilities for him to have any real chance of success.

The Quadros Regime—A Peaceful Revolution Fails

By 1960 the balance in the PSD-PTB alliance had shifted to a point where the latter demanded a greater say in picking the presidential candidate, with his nationalist credentials of key importance. Unfortunately the candidate selected—Lott—lacked both popular appeal and Kubitschek's proven genius for working within the system to get the most out of it. Hence the electorate's hopes came to rest upon Jânio da Silva Quadros, a new and exciting type of populist politician who promised to reform or sweep aside the system rather than manipulate it. This dynamic if erratic former governor of São Paulo came to share the center of the Brazilian political stage with Kubitschek during 1959 and 1960 and then to dominate it in 1961. Viewed by many as a miracle worker, if not a political messiah, the mystical man with the broom as his symbol pledged to sweep out the accumulated corruption and inefficiency of three decades of the Vargas succession while setting Brazil's administrative house in order, maintaining the momentum of development, and remembering the little people whose interests had been largely neglected by Kubitschek's emphasis upon infrastructual growth over social development.[5]

This was a tall order indeed, but paradoxically one that the new confidence engendered by Kubitschek led many Brazilians to believe was attainable—

given leadership and direction by the providential man. The disappointment bordering on betrayal of these hopes was to lend depth to the multiple crises of the 1962–1964 period and contribute to a pernicious radicalization as some elements sought in more doctrinaire programs or ideology the remaking of institutions and practices that the demagogic populist leader so roundly failed to deliver.

The Roots of the "Jânio Phenomenon"

Before being catapulted to national prominence by his upset victory over Adhemar de Barros in the 1954 São Paulo gubernatorial contest, Quadros had risen from the obscurity of a secondary school teacher in only a few years. In sharp contrast to Kubitschek's step-by-step rise through the PSD machine, Quadros relied upon a charismatic appeal and highly unorthodox campaign techniques in which he frequently changed party labels in order to build an image and following that transcended the lines of Brazil's fragmented political organizations.[6] His political debut came in November 1947, when at the age of thirty he barely won election to the São Paulo municipal council with 1,707 votes—mostly obtained from the families of his former students and law clients. During the next two years this young erstwhile Christian Democrat earned a reputation as the most assiduous champion of the little man. Nurturing the image more than the physical man, he often appeared in public unshaven, unkempt, and munching on a sandwich to demonstrate that he was too busy representing the people to take proper care of himself.

By dint of almost constant activity and association with almost any cause or manifesto, Jânio built a following in the poorer working-class sections of the city that enabled him to gain a seat in the state legislature in the 1950 balloting with a highly respectable 17,840 votes. By the time he was only halfway through his first term as a state deputy, Quadros had already set his sights upon the São Paulo mayoralty. Taking on a coalition of the four largest national parties plus four regional ones, he exploited to the hilt his position as underdog, coining the slogan "the poor man's nickel (*tostão*) against the millions of the powerbrokers." The "March 22 Movement" (named for the date of the election), which operated outside the regular party structures, and his innovative populist style provided an eye-opening victory. With nearly 285,000 votes to but 115,000 for the establishment candidate, overnight he became a national figure. On a more basic level, his electoral feat had laid bare the weakness of the ties between the existing parties and the urban electorate.

Merely a year and a half after his election as mayor of Brazil's largest metropolis (a position to which he would again be elected some twenty-five years later), Quadros established himself as a probable future president by defeating the redoubtable Adhemar de Barros for the São Paulo governorship, bringing his dramatic score to three formidable electoral triumphs in the brief span of four years. With the National Workers' Party (PTN), a São Paulo state political vehicle "owned" by Federal Deputy Emílio Carlos, replacing the PDC as Quadros's sponsor on the ballot, the populist had unveiled a campaign style that would take him to a record national vote just six years later. Waving his broom and with "Here comes Jânio" as his catchy slogan, he offset the lack of a political machine in the interior of the state with a hyper-energetic personal appearance marathon that alternately played on his underdog status and his role as a man of destiny who would triumph against all odds on the shoulders of the people so often shortchanged in the past by opportunistic and self-serving politicians.[7] By the paper-thin margin of 18,304 votes out of nearly 2 million cast, the "anti-politician" became the country's most successful political figure.

Although Quadros's assistance was not enough to carry Juarez Távora to victory over Kubitschek in 1955 and as São Paulo governor he lacked the military strength to keep Luz in office in the face of the powerful Lott-Denys military movement during the November 1955 crisis, his prominent role in these events helped make him better known on the national scene. Controversial as much as colorful, he built a reputation as an effective administrator as well as an unbeatable campaigner. Prickly to a fault when his authority was questioned, Quadros possessed a knack for turning hot water into his cup of tea. Blessed with the gift of appearing sincere even when Pinocchio's nose would have been growing at an alarming rate and with a rare ability to gain the support of the people through direct, often emotional appeals stating his side of a given case as that of the angels, Quadros was able to cover even arbitrary actions with the cloak of a moral crusade. He had chosen very able men to occupy key posts in his administrations, and by making respected Finance Secretary Carlos Alberto Alves de Carvalho Pinto his successor in the 1958 elections—when he exploited a loophole in the electoral code to become federal deputy from Paraná on the PTB ticket—Quadros assured himself of entering the 1960 presidential sweepstakes as one of the favorites.

Revolution Through the Ballot—The 1960 Elections

By the beginning of 1959 Quadros had gained the backing of Lacerda, who saw him as the best possibility for defeating the PSD-PTB coalition. Lacerda also felt that Quadros would be relatively favorable to his own presidential candidacy in 1965. While letting Lacerda, José de Magalhães Pinto of Minas Gerais, and his Paulista allies work to gain the UDN nomination for him, Jânio got the PTN nomination in April—assuring himself first place on the ballot—and formed the Popular Movement for Jânio Quadros (PMJQ) to mobilize popular support outside the parties.[8] In mid-October the PDC nominated him, and the UDN convention on November 11 also fell in line, rebuffing the pretensions of party stalwart Juracy Magalhães—an old *tenente*—by a vote of 205 to 83.

But on November 26 the country was shocked by the news that Quadros had withdrawn from the race as a result of an alleged lack of "unity and harmony" among the various political groups participating in his campaign. His statement that he would "rather be a free citizen than a prisoner president" was an ominous harbinger of the destructive action he was to take ten months later. At the time, however, the most serious consequence was a "vest pocket" rebellion by air force elements hostile to Lott and Goulart—the latter was again the PSD-PTB vice-presidential candidate— led by Lieutenant Colonel Haroldo Coimbra Veloso, from the early 1956 prototype revolt, and João Paulo Burnier.[9] Launched at Aragarças in a remote Amazon region on December 2, this revolt provided Quadros with a plausible justification for reentering the presidential race, which he did on December 5. Subsequently, as Lott's campaign lagged badly, Goulart and the PTB machines in a number of major urban centers gave encouragement to the "Jan-Jan" movement (short for Jânio and Jango, Goulart's nickname) in favor of vote splitting.[10] Meanwhile, Denys, who had succeeded to the War Ministry, gathered around himself a group of highly competent, strongly anti-Communist officers including the Geisel brothers—with Orlando (war minister in 1969–1974) as head of his staff and Ernesto (president from 1974 through early 1979) as his intelligence chief.

The October 3 voting carried Quadros into the presidency with nearly 5,640,000 votes to Lott's fewer than 3,850,000 as Adhemar de Barros finished a distant third on the strength of almost 2,200,000 votes. At the same time Goulart achieved reelection, receiving just under 4,550,000 votes compared to 4,240,000 for the UDN's Milton Campos and roughly 2 million for dissident *trabalhista* Fernando Ferrari. In amassing this record plurality of some 1.8 million votes more than the government candidate, Quadros carried all of Brazil's major states—something neither Dutra, Vargas, nor Kubitschek had been able to accomplish. Yet the vote in seven states was nearly even, reflecting the increased degree of honesty in ballot counting that was noticeable in Brazil from 1958 on. Wherever a significant urban electorate existed, Quadros's effective campaigning and time-for-a-change sentiment neutralized the enormous advantages enjoyed by the administration candidate in terms of patronage, money, and the support of entrenched political machines capable of delivering a controlled rural vote. Among the governors elected with Jânio who would play leading roles in the events of the ensuing years were Lacerda in Guanabara (the old Federal District) and Magalhães Pinto in Minas Gerais.

Jânio in Power—High Hopes Dashed

In assessing the balance of strength between foes and supporters of the system, it should be remembered that Kubitschek did not utilize the national government machinery heavily on behalf of Lott, nor did he make a maximum effort to hold all PSD elements firmly behind the party's nominee. Although principle was certainly involved in Kubitschek's maintenance of an Eisenhower-like stance with respect to the election of his successor, he was also quite clearly pleased with the prospect of Quadros's removal as a rival for the presidency in 1965. The satisfaction of São Paulo's strong desire to gain control of the presidency was also to Kubitschek's advantage, as Lott was also from Minas Gerais and, if he had been elected, in the 1965 campaign

Kubitschek would have faced attacks against a Mineiro dynasty.[11] With a need for austerity looming and a near certainty that the rate of economic growth would drop off in the 1961–1965 period, Kubitschek could be confident that his developmentalist platform would have enhanced appeal to the voters in 1965. His opposition, on the other hand, would have to shoulder responsibility for the downturn.

The Cabinet appointed by Quadros was, like most of those to follow in the next three years, neither exceptionally capable nor excessively weak. Normal rules of geographic distribution were followed, and the parties supporting his election received representation roughly proportional to their strength. There were several veterans of the Dutra administration, and Afonso Arinos de Mello Franco, son of the foreign minister of the early 1930s, assumed that post, with José Aparecido de Oliveira—a Minas Gerais congressman who would be Federal District governor and minister of culture in the late 1980s—serving as presidential private secretary. On the military side, Denys was kept on as war minister, Admiral Silvio Heck (who had striven to keep Luz in the presidency in the 1955 crisis) was navy minister, and old *tenente* Cordeiro de Farias served as chief of the armed forces general staff.

Key was Denys, known as the "Army Fox," who had compiled an enviable record of professional achievement and command decisiveness. A *tenente* of 1922, he returned to the active ranks through the 1930 Revolution and as a brigadier general supported Vargas in the October 1945 crisis. A full general in 1954, he did not adhere to the anti-Vargas movement and the next year was the chief organizer of the "preventive counter-coup" that ousted Luz. Allowed by an act of Congress to remain in command of the First Army beyond retirement age, he was the natural choice to succeed Lott as war minister, and Quadros wished him to continue his effective work of healing old wounds within the army.[12]

From his inaugural address on, Quadros emphasized the gravity of financial problems and the deficient condition of the administrative machinery. His stress on accumulated inefficiency and corruption was a gauntlet the PSD and PTB picked up. Knowing that the measures he was proposing would encounter strong opposition from entrenched interests and offend some of his original backers, Quadros realized that he needed to develop new links between his government and the people, whose votes had brought him to power and whose hopes were deposited in him and his administration.[13] He had little idea, however, of how to accomplish this task. His move to establish branches of the presidential office in state capitals aroused a furor in Congress as legislators perceived a major threat to their traditional game of bargaining with mayors and governors for electoral advantage in return for advocating the latter's interests with the federal bureaucracy. The National Service of Assistance to Municipalities was viewed in a similar light. Members of this 1958 vintage Congress, with their eyes on the 1962 legislative elections, were also less than enthusiastic about the new president's policy of regional meetings with governors to discuss state needs and federal assistance—which usurped their role as brokers.[14]

Quadros also disturbed the PSD and PTB by immediately launching a series of special crash investigations into the workings of government agencies believed to have been particularly exploited for patronage or profit by political figures under past administrations. But it was when he moved into the field of pressing economic and financial measures that Jânio encountered a more serious side of the dilemma of arousing the ire of important interests without gaining more employable public support than he had already with a series of "moralization" measures.

Inflation, which had begun to get out of hand during the Kubitschek years, was seen by the new administration as a priority problem, so Octávio Gouveia de Bulhões, head of the Superintendency of Money and Credit (Brazil's rudimentary beginning of a central bank), abolished the system of multiple exchange rates that had been requiring massive emissions of currency to subsidize imported oil, wheat, and newsprint—a move that required a 100 percent devaluation of the cruzeiro.[15] Price control machinery proved inadequate to the task of curbing speculative profits (a condition that would still prevail nearly three decades later), so on April 5 Quadros submitted an antitrust law to Congress, followed on July 7 by a bill disciplining the repatriation of profits. The sensitive subject of agrarian reform was entrusted to a study group headed by Senator Milton Campos, but the resulting bill was stalled by the PSD shortly before Quadros's untimely resignation.[16]

The reaction of economic groups to these reform measures was highly defensive if not wholly negative. Moreover, in late July the president and the opposition congressional majority locked horns over his veto of a bill of the type Quadros held had led to the bloating of the federal bureaucracy during the years of PSD control. When his veto was overridden, the president's manifest disgust with Congress took on new dimensions. Congress, accustomed to the continuous wooing and concern for its interests and sensibilities that had characterized Kubitschek's legislative relations, resented Quadros's techniques of neglect, appealing over its head to the public, and chastising it for obstructionism. Jânio, in contrast, was used to a relatively docile state legislature in which, owing to the fact that no party had more than a fifth of the seats, he had been able to manipulate a shifting coalition for nearly any measure he desired. Yet, despite the fact that the administration had ignored or criticized Congress instead of trying to work with it, the government's legislative record from March to August was far from entirely negative.

"Independent" Foreign Policy

The issue that precipitated the August 1961 crisis was a foreign policy matter that only indirectly involved the Congress. Quadros's emphasis on an "independent" foreign policy arose out of his own desire to see Brazil achieve a more prominent position in international affairs and his reading of the domestic political situation. Knowing that his economic policies would prove highly unpopular with the political Left and organized labor in particular, he set out to offset this and at least partially neutralize the opposition leaning of these groups by following a dramatically nationalist line in foreign affairs that would have considerable appeal to them. Fundamentally, his policy was based on a blending of continued close relations with the United States and a strong assertion of independence when Brazil's national interests appeared to so dictate. As it worked out in the short span of only seven months in office, the third world aspects of Quadros's international policy cost him much of his conservative support without gaining him significant new strength from the Left. Though his independent foreign policy, which was in many respects an accentuation of trends undertaken by Kubitschek after 1959, did not lose Quadros the continued support of the armed forces, it did lead to a complete rupture with Lacerda, who once again proved to be a very dangerous foe.

In his March 15 state of the union message, Quadros had quite clearly defined the basic tenets of his foreign policy.[17] His pursuit of new markets for Brazil's exports and of sources of credit for manufactured imports found widespread support within Brazil, and Afonso Arinos and San Thiago Dantas eloquently defended his foreign policy. But hostile economic interests perceived Quadros's vulnerability on this front and joined Lacerda's criticism.[18] By mid-August the campaign against Quadros's foreign policy was in high gear, with an increasing proportion of the UDN congressional delegation lined up alongside the great bulk of the PSD against the president. Progressive and nationalistic elements of these parties, as represented by Magalhães Pinto and Goiás Governor Mauro Borges Teixeira, still stood by Jânio.[19]

The Resignation Crisis

The crisis that was to bring Brazil perilously close to civil war began on the night of August 18, when Governor Lacerda arrived to confer with the president.[20] Not only was the encounter highly unsatisfactory, but also the next morning, as an enraged Lacerda returned to Rio de Janeiro, a beaming Ernesto "Che" Guevara received Brazil's Order of the Cruzeiro do Sul from Quadros's hands. Following a final encounter with the president at Laranjeiras Palace in Rio de Janeiro, on August 22 Lacerda bitterly criticized Quadros's foreign policy in a televised speech, while for his part Goulart was enjoying a state visit to Communist China (a "coincidence" that both underscored Goulart's alleged procommunist sympathies and would handicap his efforts to lay claim to the presidency when it suddenly became available).

Lacerda as Catalyst

In a dramatic new twist, on August 24 (which happened to be the seventh anniversary of Vargas's demise), Lacerda, while threatening to resign as Guanabara governor, revealed that Justice Minister Oscar Pedroso d'Horta had told him that the president intended to close Congress and implement a series of institutional reforms that would subsequently be legitimized by means of a plebiscite.[21] This denunciation exploded like a bombshell in Brasília, where Quadros was additionally upset by receipt of the war minister's proposed proclamation for Soldiers' Day. Although the proclamation's references to foreign policy appeared on the surface to support the president, he chose to interpret them as a form of military pressure impinging upon his authority. Yet Quadros had been honored earlier that day at a banquet attended by sixty ranking officers, and the army was clearly not preparing to abandon him, much less to take part in his ouster.

Perhaps influenced by the unaccustomed solitude of Brasília and very likely drinking more than was advisable under the circumstances, Quadros insisted in seeing a congressional plot to undermine the presidency. He was determined to avoid the kind of dead end in which Vargas had found himself seven years earlier. Hence he chose to take the initiative, subsequently claiming that to govern Brazil effectively he required powers similar to those possessed at the end of the 1950s by de Gaulle in his successful efforts to transform the decadent French Fourth Republic into the vibrant and dynamic Fifth Republic. These, he knew, Congress would not grant him, so a way had to be found to bypass that obstructionist body. (Little wonder that in popular mythology August has come to be considered the month of troubles and crises.)

But once his plans to bring about the requisite "grand modification of the system of government itself" were exposed by Lacerda's denunciation, Quadros opted for an all-out gamble. Remembering the success of his resignation gambit in November 1959 and aware of how Fidel Castro had used such a ploy to rid himself of an unwanted president and become the untrammelled guide of Cuba's destinies, he decided to employ this technique as a last resort to salvage something from the disaster that threatened to engulf his administration. Aware that the military and most conservative elements—particularly those linked to Lacerda, who were the source of his greatest difficulties—would not accept Goulart as president, Quadros hoped that the dilemma would be resolved in his favor. Jânio with extraordinary powers would be a lesser evil in the eyes of many of these elements, both military and civilian, than would the rise of Goulart and the PTB to power or a breakdown of constitutional order and establishment of a military regime.

Although events did not work out as he wished, his basic assumptions were in large part valid, especially in that the military leaders would neither be willing to take power themselves nor to permit Goulart to do so. His chief—and fatal—miscalculations lay in underestimating the Congress he scorned and in assuming that the armed forces high command could impose its will on the entire military establishment.[22] Quadros has asserted that his line of reasoning was that "either a formula would be encountered as a consequence of which he would emerge as chief executive within a new institutional regime or the armed forces would undertake to establish this new regime without him."[23]

After appearing at the Soldiers' Day ceremonies on the morning of August 25, Quadros informed his military ministers of his intention to resign. Denying any Gaullist or Nasserist ambitions, he dropped the problem squarely in their laps and departed from Brasília for São Paulo. While the military leaders continued to grope for a way out of the impasse in which Jânio had placed them, the president's resignation letter heaped fuel on the fire. Patterned along the lines of Vargas's suicide note, his perplexing missive denounced "corruption, lies and cowardice that subordinate general interests to the appetites and ambitions of groups and individuals, some of them foreign." Yet it praised the armed forces for their "exemplary conduct" and support, thus completely dissociating them from the "terrible forces" of reaction that had defeated him. In Congress, the kind of telegrams from governors urging a rejection of the presidential resignation that he must have counted upon to have effect were brushed aside as irrelevant, and Chamber of Deputies presiding officer Ranieri Mazilli was quickly sworn in as acting president with the military ministers being confirmed in office. Although confusion still reigned concerning Quadros's motives, a large number of legislators suspected a power play on his part and were relieved that the crucial first step to thwart this had been taken.

Avoiding Civil War

Indeed, the focus of interest in Brasília soon turned to the question of whether Goulart would succeed to the office without an armed struggle. The rest of the country remained confused and stunned. Unfortunately for Jânio's plans, the atmosphere of shock and dismay tended to play out in terms of "how could he do such a thing to us" rather than "how could they do such a thing to him." Furthermore, the isolation of Brasília rendered the Congress relatively impervious to the type of popular manifestations that had influenced its actions in the 1954 and 1955 crises, when the mobs were at the very doors of the legislature. Moreover, with the PSD's Mazilli as interim chief executive, Sérgio Magalhães of the PTB, a leader of the Nationalist Parliamentary Front, became the presiding officer of the Chamber. He dedicated his every effort to seeing that his party's leader would not be blocked from coming to power by the UDN idea—acceptable to some PSD elements—of having Congress name Juracy Magalhães as president on the grounds that Goulart's absence from the country forfeited his claim.

Yet even by the 27th and 28th, while Lacerda and associates were plotting a way to keep Goulart from office and the vice-president was slowly returning from China by way of Paris, the situation was changing as a result of developments in Rio Grande do Sul, where Governor Brizola announced his intention to use force to guarantee legality, which he defined as including the right of his brother-in-law, Goulart, to the presidency.[24] Kubitschek pulled back from his tentative acceptance of the UDN proposal and the PSD issued a note giving full support to Goulart. Asked by the military ministers to vote Goulart's impediment, the PSD-PTB majority in Congress refused to do to one of theirs what they had willingly done to Luz and Café Filho less than six years earlier. (With significant implications for the future, the reasons for the military's veto of Goulart were presented by the acting president's chief military aide—General Ernesto Geisel, who would himself be selected to govern the country a dozen years later.)

Most critically, the military's united front was broken by the decision of Third Army commander General José Lopes Machado to cast his lot with Brizola rather than with the interim government.[25] Although this move would prevent Lopes Machado from going much further in his career, the generals serving under him who also opted for "legality" would rise to top positions under Goulart. Jair Dantas Ribeiro would be Goulart's last war minister and Colonel Argemiro de Assis Brasil would serve as Goulart's chief military aide.

In an effort to head off a violent confrontation, a special committee of the Chamber of Deputies, which had been established some weeks earlier to consider a constitutional amendment instituting a parliamentary system, was urgently activated. Will within Congress to resist the pressures of Denys and his associates had been strengthened by signs of increasing military disunity. It was now the turn of the military ministers to give ground, very reluctantly agreeing to accept a parliamentary system, because with Goulart nearing Buenos Aires control of the situation was rapidly slipping out of their hands. Dramatically Kubitschek took to the Senate rostrum to "ask the War Minister not to insist upon opposing the law and the will of the people, placing the armed forces in opposition to the nation."[26] With Afonso Arinos throwing his considerable prestige behind the parliamentary amend- ment on August 30 and confirmation of Goulart's willingness to accept such a curtailment of presidential powers in order to avoid conflict brought back from Montevideo by Tancredo de Almeida Neves, the scales tipped decisively to the side of compromise. On Saturday, September 2, the Chamber passed the "Additional Act" the required two times (by votes of 236 to 59 and 235 to 5); the Senate followed suit with votes of 47 to 5 and 48 to 6. As part of his campaign to regain the presidency in 1965, Kubitschek—who had played a leading role in engineering the compromise—voted symbolically against it.

What had threatened to be the most serious crisis since the 1930 Revolution had ended with a victory for reason and moderation. On September 7, Brazil's Independence Day, a full two weeks after Quadros's rash resignation had precipitated the crisis, João Belchior Marques Goulart took the oath of office. The next day the parliamentary experiment began in earnest as the Chamber approved by a vote of 259 to 22, with 7 abstentions, a Council of Ministers headed by Tancredo Neves—who also held the Justice Ministry, a post he had previously occupied during the last days of Vargas's admin- istration. The disaster of civil war had been avoided without resort to a rupture of legality and implantation of military rule. But this would prove to be only a stay of execution rather than a permanent reprieve.

The Parliamentary Regime and the 1962 Elections

Brief as would be the Goulart government—albeit lasting almost four times as long as that of Quadros—the events that occurred during this period make it crucial to an understanding of present-day Brazil. Whereas the administration's first stage would be a period of impasse, the latter part was to be a tragic case of political mobilization leading to a preemptive counter-revolution instead of to the structural reforms that were its banners and—for many of the participants—its actual goals. During this time a real breakdown of democracy did take place, one involving an abject failure of the Brazilian knack for compromise and conciliation so recently demonstrated during the Quadros resignation crisis.[27] Both the intransigence of the conservative elements and a striking detachment from reality on the part of the extreme Left were important factors in the triumph of polarization following the evaporation of the flimsy and partial consensus achieved in the Kubitschek years. Undoubtably the far Right was extremely short-sighted in its opposition to further change—much as it had been in the late 1880s, at the end of the 1920s, and even in the mid-1950s. For its part the Left would let wishful thinking run amok in 1963 and early 1964 until that wishful thinking turned into suicidal self-delusion that very possibly exceeded that of the National Liberation Alliance (ANL) militants in 1935.

Both extremes clearly must bear a heavy share of responsibility for the sad events of 1964–1973. The failure of the parliamentary regime to function in even a minimally adequate manner—in large part owing to the weakness and lack of discipline fundamental to Brazil's political parties—started matters down the slippery path of decline, once Jânio's intemperance and impatience had put the country on this disastrous road.[28] Although the situation would have been extremely difficult for any chief executive, Goulart's manifold shortcomings helped aggravate the crisis and bring on its unfortunate denouement. As president Goulart proved to be a very poor student of what Vargas had tried to teach him. Indeed, Tancredo Neves as well as Kubitschek had learned the lessons of the astute Vargas much better than had the new chief executive. Yet the dilemmas inherent in the situation of the early 1960s would have severely tested the mettle of even a Vargas or a Kubitschek. As seen by one of Brazil's leading political scientists, "the 1961–1964 period was truly characterized by the transformation of a reasonably operational political system into one incapable of producing decisions with respect to the most pressing questions of the epoch."[29] Ideological radicalization, fragility and instability of political coalitions, fragmentation of power resources, and high turnover in key governmental positions were major elements in this process of decay.

The Parliamentary Experiment

As was natural given the coerced nature of the 1961 compromise, reluctantly accepted as it was by both sides as a lesser evil and certainly not as a positive good, the year following Goulart's inauguration was marked by increasing conflict between Congress and the president. At the center of the dispute were the latter's efforts to prove the new hybrid system unworkable and to engineer a return to presidentialism. Although the Brazilian gift for compromise, as often postponing the showdown as avoiding it, brought the country through several potentially serious crises during 1962, the price was very steep in terms of economic and social problems left unattended and a legacy of deepening mistrust and mutual suspicion. This negative heritage was aggravated by a polarizing legislative election campaign in which the clash between Right and Left was greatly intensified.

During the period from September 1961 to the elections of October 7, 1962, Brazil was governed by a series of Cabinets, the first of which possessed an extremely broad base of support, but which was followed by two abortive efforts to form a government and finally by a pair of Cabinets that could barely survive, much less gain congressional approval for a coherent program. One feature these Cabinets shared was that the prime ministers made no effort to contest with the president for executive powers. Indeed, the prime ministers actually functioned more as allies of Goulart in his struggle with the Congress.[30]

Generally satisfied with their role in bringing about a solution of the 1961 crisis, the main political forces undertook initially to collaborate with the newly installed regime. The PSD, as befit its status as the ranking national party, was represented in the Cabinet not only by the prime minister, but also by São Paulo Federal Deputy Ulysses Guimarães as minister of commerce and industry and three other portfolios. Goulart's PTB occupied the Foreign Ministry through San Thiago Dantas of Minas Gerais as well as the Health Ministry under Pernambuco's Eustácio Souto Maior (whose chief claim to fame is probably as father of three-time Formula One Grand Prix driving champion Nelson Piquet). Each of the rival wings of the UDN had a ministry, with the PDC's André Franco Montoro as minister of labor and social welfare. (That this Cabinet possessed potential is demonstrated by the facts that Neves would go on to be elected president in 1985, Guimarães remained a candidate in the 1989 presidential sweepstakes, and Montoro sought a ministerial appointment in 1990.) As an advocate of conciliation during the recent crisis and the senior active duty officer, João de Segadas Viana became war minister.

Reflecting as it did a coalition of the country's major parties, the first parliamentary Cabinet easily gained approval from the Chamber of Deputies by a 246 to 10 margin, but one of the new system's fatal flaws resided in the fact that Cabinet members did not have to come from Congress and would be subject to the old law—incompatible with any real parliamentary system—that they resign from the Cabinet in order to stand for election to Congress.

As international affairs had precipitated the August 1961 crisis, a foreign policy issue would be the first divisive question facing the new government as Goulart pushed ahead on reestablishment of diplomatic relations with the Soviet Union.[31] This completed in November, Brazil's continuing adherence to an independent foreign policy was underscored by its position at the January 1962 Inter-American Foreign Ministers' meeting at Punta del Este, where the Brazilian delegation resisted all U.S. arguments and refused to support the exclusion of Cuba from the Organization of American States.[32]

Domestically Goulart followed an initially cautious and moderate course that won him grudging acceptance from most centrist and some conservative sectors.

His April visit to Washington, D.C., and conversations with President John Kennedy were generally a success and went far to allay suspicions both as to Goulart's orientation and with respect to his capabilities. Following his return from the United States, however, Goulart was concerned by the deterioration of his position with the working class. He soon became preoccupied with the possibility of being seriously outflanked on the Left by Brizola, who continued to make it clear that he would not have agreed to have his powers emasculated as Goulart readily had. Hence the president adopted a more leftist tack, strongly criticizing Congress for failure to enact basic reforms and proposing that the new legislature to be elected in October be granted constituent assembly powers to deal with agrarian reform and other pressing matters. As subsequent events were to confirm, his primary goal was early repeal of the Additional Act and recovery of full presidential powers.

The Conspiratorial Components

With campaigning already underway, the more militantly anti-Goulart elements of Democratic Parliamentary Action (ADP), an anti-Communist ideological supraparty bloc that had come into being in early 1962 to counter the Nationalist Parliamentary Front, came out in an increasingly aggressive manner against any and all presidential policies.[33] Through links to the Brazilian Institute of Democratic Action (IBAD), an organization headed by Ivan Hasslocker and dedicated to anti-Communist activities, and its network of Popular Democratic Action (ADEP) groups in several states, this U.S.-supported movement sought to offset the influence of the emerging National Liberation Front of Brizola, Recife Mayor Miguel Arraes (in the late 1980s governor of Pernambuco and a presidential candidate), and Peasant Leagues organizer Francisco Julião. So by mid-year the forces making for polarization and radicalization of Brazilian political life again were in many respects outweighing efforts toward continued conciliation.

Still shaken by the stiff military opposition to his becoming president, Goulart scrupulously avoided conflicts or even significant policy differences with the armed forces during his initial year in office. Steering clear of any initiative in which the military establishment might perceive their interests as threatened, he made generally skillful use of selective promotions, intelligent assignment policies, wide expansion of his personal and social contacts with key officers, and even sponsorship of measures designed to improve the military's rather precarious economic situation. As a result the armed forces were really one of his most effective allies in mounting a return to full presidential powers. Yet with the end of the semi-parliamentary system, Goulart was to find it increasingly difficult to avoid friction with the military without losing his support from the nationalist Left.

Indeed, Goulart's lack of really relevant political experience was all too apparent in his relations with the military once he became accustomed to complete presidential powers. Never having been a governor or even a mayor and with only a short passage through the Labor Ministry in 1953–1954, he knew little of the special sensitivities of the military—in diametrical contrast to his mentor, Vargas, and his sometime role model, Perón, a career army officer. He dealt with key military figures in essentially the same way as he did with Brazil's rather undistinguished crop of labor leaders, apparently expecting that senior officers would be grateful to him for their positions of prestige and perquisites as was the case with most union careerists. He failed to understand that in the armed forces general officers felt that they had earned the top posts on the basis of professional performance within the military institution. Clearly a few officers promoted by Goulart over the heads of more highly regarded peers might feel some personal loyalty to him. Yet over all, politicization of promotions generated countervailing dissatisfactions by those prejudiced in the process, which often shaded past resentment into conspiratorial activity.

The biennial Military Club elections held in May 1962 saw the nationalist faction rebuffed in their effort to regain control. As a result of this defeat Goulart's backers were denied use of a prestigious entity through which a good deal of propagandizing and proselytizing might be carried out as in the 1950–1952 period. Instead, as during the 1954 crisis Vargas had faced a Military Club controlled by his enemies, Goulart would feel the weight of the club's increasing hostility during the events leading to his downfall. In this the anti-Goulart officers would have militant and well-organized allies, as the Institute for Social Research and Studies (IPES) was organized by elements of the commercial and industrial classes following the 1961 crisis. Aware of the need for a more active and direct political role than that feasible through their traditional sectoral organizations, a group of Rio de Janeiro and São Paulo entrepreneurs and economists of a strong anti-Communist but essentially modern orientation agreed to establish a political action arm.[34] The São Paulo branch of IPES quickly took an active role in behind-the-scenes politics. The Rio de Janeiro group chose to operate in a less direct manner, in part because of the greater federal government influence and leftist strength there, but also as a result of a more liberal bent of its leaders and the very active role being played there in the political action field by IBAD.

Organized in 1959, IPES did not become a significant factor until the early months of 1962, when it began to collect funds to support anti-Communist candidates and to combat leftist movements. Considering IPES's leaders as a group of "poets" because they shunned direct involvement in electoral battles in favor of propaganda activities and concern for public opinion, IBAD's prime mover, Hasslocker, also played a dominant role in ADEP.[35]

Military plotting against the Goulart regime was also underway by mid-1962. General Olympio Mourão Filho was the first of the senior active duty officers to try to organize a military movement to overthrow the government.[36] In the same manner as Mourão professed to have been spurred to action by Brizola's alleged advocacy of plans for a syndicalist regime to replace Brazil's "outmoded" liberal democratic system, Orlando Geisel and José Pinheiro de Ulhoa Cintra along with other generals claim to have been spurred to action by a comparable conversation between Goulart and Adhemar de Barros. The mentors of these generals among retired officers included Denys and Cordeiro de Farias, both of whom still enjoyed very significant followings among their former juniors.

Polarization and the 1962 Elections

When the Senate shortsightedly—with some of its members fearing electoral competition from ministers—refused to waive the constitutional requirement that congressional candidates not have occupied executive positions in the months preceding the elections, the Tancredo Neves Cabinet abruptly resigned in late June. Goulart, who for his own political ends wished to dramatize the shortcomings of the parliamentary system and to get a prime minister and Cabinet fully compliant with his wishes, chose San Thiago Dantas to form a new Cabinet. The UDN and a majority of the PSD promptly rejected the PTB leader as prime minister—the latter doing so because they felt strongly that this was their prerogative as the strongest party in the Chamber—sending him down to defeat by a 174 to 110 vote.[37] With the country already experiencing a protracted student strike, a major proportion of the labor movement poised to walk off the job, and the metropolitan regions suffering from serious shortages of basic food supplies, the political situation was serious and deteriorating daily as a result of the governmental vacuum.

Whereas it was probably expected that he would be balked by the PSD's stand, Goulart caught the opposition off guard on July 2 by suddenly selecting Senate President Auro de Moura Andrade, a PSD stalwart from São Paulo. Although approved by a 222 to 51 margin, Andrade was repeatedly hampered by the president in his efforts to form a Cabinet and quickly threw in the towel in the face of a July 5 "general" strike accompanied by serious food riots in the proletarian suburbs of Rio de Janeiro that resulted in a score of deaths and hundreds injured. Quick to emphasize that this unrest demonstrated the danger of drift and immobilism under an "unworkable" hybrid system, Goulart promptly moved to take advantage of congressional desires to return to the campaign trail, where their rivals were benefitting from the incumbents' absence. His new nominee on July 8 was someone who would never have been acceptable if put forth earlier, Francisco Brochado da Rocha—a Rio Grande do Sul jurist of no real national projection, who although closely aligned with Brizola was nominally a PSD dissident— thus allowing that party to save face. In reality, Brochado da Rocha's acceptance by the Chamber on July 13 by a vote of 215 to 58 spelled an end to the fiction that the prime minister was representative of Congress. For the rather parochial Goulart now had a fellow Gaúcho of no political consequence as nominal head of government. Indeed, it is very likely that this was his goal in "burning" Minas Gerais and São Paulo candidates before pulling Brochado out of his sleeve.

More narrowly based than its predecessor and largely devoid of significant political figures, most of whom were candidates in the October elections, Brochado's Cabinet did not inspire a great deal of confidence. Most important were the move of General Nélson de Melo to the War Ministry and the naming of Pedro Paulo de Araújo Suzano, one of the very few naval officers with leftist sympathies, to head the Navy Ministry—a development that drove a group of admirals to resign in protest, with most of them soon entering the ranks of the anti-Goulart conspirators and gaining their revenge in 1964. Indeed, within less than two months the new war minister would himself become seriously estranged from the president and begin to align himself with the plotters. For when Congress reconvened in August, Brochado requested an emergency delegation of broad powers—nearly equal to that Quadros had dreamed of the preceding year—and insisted upon constitutional amendments to facilitate meaningful agrarian reform and provide for a prompt plebiscite on return to the presidential system.[38]

As the situation became increasingly tense, the Brazilian genius for compromise came through once again. Though resisting the notion of constituent powers for the incoming Congress, opposition leaders did agree that this body would be committed in advance to a plebiscite on the form of government. But the September "concentrated effort" that brought legislators back to Brasília saw a new and more serious crisis rather than the resolution of differences that had been planned. Coming at the height of a very heated election campaign in which positions were in many cases sharply polarized and grave accusations were being exchanged between politicians of the Left and Right, the spirit of compromise had all but ebbed away. Spurred on by the incendiary Brizola, Brochado chose to make holding of the plebiscite on October 7 a vote of confidence, and heavy pressure was brought to bear on Congress by leftist groups that were orchestrated by Brizola.

Although the public credit for the elaborate solution went to Kubitschek along with his Mineiro confidants Gustavo Capanema in the Chamber and Valladares in the Senate, the accords were really hammered out by three other Minas Gerais conciliators, each from a different party—Tancredo Neves of the PSD, San Thiago Dantas for the PTB, and Afonso Arinos representing the UDN. Stretching the constitution a bit by handling through a law, albeit a very special one, matters that should technically have been the subject of a constitutional amendment, the authors of Complementary Act No. 2 of September 16 provided for a limited temporary delegation of powers and for a referendum on the parliamentary system to be held on January 6, 1963.[39] A "provisional" Cabinet headed by Hermes Lima, labor minister under Brochado, rested on an even narrower parliamentary base than had its short-lived predecessor. The new war minister was General Amaury Kruel, who until then had been Goulart's chief military aide.

In an atmosphere of relief mixed with lingering tension, nearly 15 million Brazilians—of 18.5 million registered—cast their votes on October 7 for a complete Chamber of Deputies that was to hold office until February 1967, two senators from each state (with terms lasting until early 1971), and—in half the states—new governors for the next four years. Climaxing the most extensive, expensive, and bitterly contested campaign in the nation's history, the balloting would have a decisive impact upon the course of events leading to the 1964 Revolution.[40] In the great urban centers the electoral battles polarized sharply around the antithetical themes of "basic reforms" and "Communist menace." Yet with patronage, personalism, and local political disputes determining the outcome in most of the interior, the overall results were very mixed. As the Left and Right each experienced spectacular victories and dismaying defeats in the majority elections, the legislative balloting under Brazil's peculiar form of proportional representation returned most of the incumbents to Congress along with a heterogeneous array of newcomers. All but a few governorships remained in the hands of moderates, a fact that was to have very important ramifications in the 1964 crisis. Yet workers' votes, estimated at no more than 1.2 million in 1945 and perhaps 3 million by 1958, may well have risen to around 3.5 million.[41]

Former president Kubitschek's favored position for the 1965 presidential sweepstakes was strengthened—largely as a result of the reverses suffered by his leading rivals. But Quadros failed in his bid to get a running start on the road back to national political leadership, instead suffering the first electoral defeat in his meteoric career (but he would come back through election as mayor of São Paulo in 1985). The man who nosed him out by a bit more than 100,000 votes was Adhemar de Barros, the conservative populist who had run third in the 1955 and 1960 presidential voting. The two long-time rivals were a study in contrast. With "an arrogant and distant attitude toward the parties and an authoritarian-charismatic position toward the masses," Quadros represented the ultimate in the populist style, unadulterated by vestiges of clientelism.[42] His appeal was relatively greater to the more satisfied sectors of the urban masses than was that of Adhemar, a patronage populist who promised direct benefits rather than moralization of the system. Unlike the ascetic-appearing Quadros, the rotund gladhander of the PSP had the support of his own party—a political machine built up carefully on the basis of patronage over a period of more than fifteen years. Thus by the time of the 1962 São Paulo governorship race, Adhemar's last campaign, there was as much co-optative clientelism to this style as populism per se.

Most important, on the far Left Brizola consolidated his position as a national political figure by polling an all-time record vote for a federal deputy candidate. Although his opponents won handily in his home state of Rio Grande do Sul, where he had just ended a nearly four-year stint as governor, the president's brother-in-law successfully transferred his political base to Guanabara (the state comprising the city of Rio de Janeiro) as 269,000

Carioca (residents of Rio de Janeiro city) voters cast their ballots for him. The close victory of Arraes for governor in Pernambuco also gave the extreme leftists a cause for celebration—although their candidates in the equally important states of Bahia and Ceará were soundly defeated.

The congressional balloting, which was to give rise to significant investigations of corruption and economic abuses by both the IBAD-backed anti-Communists and the many leftists who benefitted from administration favors and assistance, resulted in a Chamber of Deputies in which the PSD, PTB, and UDN possessed relatively equal strength with 119, 104, and 97 seats, respectively—for a total of 320 to only 89 for the other ten parties combined. Party strength in the Senate was quite proportional to these results, so maintenance of a PTB-PSD alliance provided the prospect of a fairly firm congressional base for the administration, if Goulart could walk a line between the insistent demands for reforms coming from the majority component of the PTB and the essential conservatism of the rural-based core of the PSD.

As measured by the elections, the Left was gaining strength, but not as fast as its leaders and spokesmen expected. The nation had spoken decisively neither for nor against change. Radical leaders could and soon would argue that the distortions caused by the influence of economic power in the elections as well as disfranchisement of the illiterates masked the true support of popular demands for drastic change, while the Center-conservative forces would counter that Congress did fully represent the people's will. In any case, with the elections over the prospects for conciliation and moderate reform appeared better than they had for the preceding six months.[43]

Plebiscite and End of the Parliamentary Regime

At least in the short run the elections had helped consolidate Goulart's position, and the president continued assiduously to cultivate his military support. With the faithful Jair Dantas Ribeiro heading the Third Army, Brazil's most powerful battle force, and the strongly leftist-nationalist Osvino Ferreira Alves keeping Lacerda in check as First Army commander, Goulart temporarily enjoyed a high degree of security. Not satisfied with this, he undertook a successful campaign to gain the loyalty of sergeants and warrant officers. Following up on the actions favorable to these echelons that Lott had undertaken during the 1956–1960 period, Goulart proposed raising their pay, making them eligible to stand for election, and facilitating their becoming homeowners. In exchange he asked for their support for a return to the presidential system and his drive for basic reforms.[44]

Little enthusiasm remained for the travesty of a parliamentary system functioning in Brazil. Indeed, even many of Goulart's enemies felt that a return to full presidential powers was preferable to letting him hide behind the excuse of an unworkable system and continue to blame it and Congress for the lack of progress in dealing with the country's pressing problems. Only at the end of November did the Chamber of Deputies finally get around to formally approving the Hermes Lima Cabinet, and it was December 5 before the prime minister presented his program of government.

Unquestionably Goulart had maneuvered through political shoals with considerable skill in pursuit of his primary objective—the plebiscite—but this was all he could show for nearly sixteen months as chief executive. The dissension within the government between radicals and moderates over economic policies, to become acute during 1963, was foreshadowed by an incident in which Labor Minister João Pinheiro Neto denounced the IMF's "economic dictatorship" over Brazil. In the course of his diatribe he accused two eminent conservative members of the government, Roberto Campos and Octávio de Bulhões, of being the IMF's chief agents.

More important, the emphasis upon the agrarian problem that was to characterize the second half of Goulart's presidential tenure was presaged by the enactment, after a long and bitter legislative battle, of the "Rural Workers' Statute." Another four months would pass before the statute received Goulart's signature, because it had originally been sponsored by an archrival from his home state. But its passage marked a realization that the countryside was awakening and that the claims of the rural masses would for the first time receive a sympathetic hearing from the national executive. The name of Peasant Leagues organizer Julião was already well known outside of his northeast stomping grounds, and rural conflict had been experienced in several key states as squatters and land speculators clashed with increasing frequency and much greater intensity than the traditional violence stemming from tensions between landowners and tenants or fieldhands. In Rio Grande do Sul, Brizola as governor had given active sponsorship to an organization of landless rural dwellers, and in São Paulo Governor Carvalho Pinto had undertaken a very moderate program of agrarian reform.[45]

Presidentialism and Polarization, 1963

The early months of 1963 were the highwater mark of the Goulart government and the lowest point for the fortunes of the military conspirators. The January 6 plebiscite favored a return to pure presidentialism by nearly 9.5 million votes to only 2 million opposed. But as subsequent events were to demonstrate, by interpreting the five to one margin as an overwhelming vote of confidence and personal mandate, Goulart badly miscalculated his position. Opposition was to rise rapidly as he began to push for policies injurious to the interests of the established power structure rather than just campaigning for a return to the accepted and traditional governmental system.

Except for the reappearance of several members of Congress, Goulart's first presidential Cabinet differed relatively little from the caretaker ministry that preceded it. The three service ministers were carried over along with four civilians, and there were eight new faces—the most interesting of whom was Celso Furtado as minister without portfolio for economic development planning. For a short time at least, it seemed that Goulart could counterbalance the radical Left with the PSD and implement a consistent program of sound development measures and moderate reforms. Such a three-year plan, essentially building upon the accomplishments of the Kubitschek period, was drawn up by Furtado and Finance Minister San Thiago Dantas.[46]

The Collapse of Conciliation

However, within a matter of weeks Goulart's attempt to combine a general political policy of conciliation with a push for significant economic and social changes was proving nonviable. The development program and financial stabilization plan were criticized by businessmen from one side and labor from the other—as usual the former objecting strenuously to tight credit policies and the latter refusing to accept a wage freeze. The Left acrimoniously attacked the government's proposal for settling the problem of expropriated U.S. power companies—which had been triggered by Brizola during his term as governor—and the Right held firm against meaningful agrarian reform. Concerned about losing ground in their competition with radical elements for control of the unions, moderate labor leaders joined in insisting that the "U.S.-imposed" austerity program be scrapped.[47] Indeed, from this point on organized labor would prove a major force propelling Goulart leftward.

The biennial elections of the million-member National Confederation of Industrial Workers (CNTI) in December 1961 had posed a major test of the president's strength in what had always been his political base, the labor movement. During Quadros's short stay in office, an effort had been made to undercut Goulart, particularly among the industrial sector, but the incumbent anti-Communist leadership subsequently proved no match for Goulart's power and experience in using a combination of controls and patronage to gain election of a slate inclined toward closer cooperation with the president and the PTB.[48] The CNTI and other unions threw their weight around during the mid-1962 Cabinet crisis, making demands for an end to conciliation and a concerted offensive for basic reforms. Cooperating with the Communist-controlled maritime, longshoremen's, and bankworkers' confederations, the CNTI officers helped constitute a General Workers' Command (CGT), which would have an increasingly effective role during 1963 although it could not receive legal recognition under the existing legislation that barred an overall national labor organization.[49]

Always wary of losing the support of his original political base, Goulart wavered during the first part of 1963 with respect to implementing the very policies his Cabinet had just formulated and adopted. Thus the prospects for Brazil finding a path toward consensus and a compromise solution of its manifold problems appeared once more to be slipping away. Indeed, in retrospect the series of crises that led almost directly to the March 1964 overthrow of the existing regime germinated almost a year earlier as the last major effort at conciliation foundered in April and May. The keystone of Goulart's experiment in this direction was the "Furtado Plan," which had been hurriedly announced on the eve of the plebiscite.[50] Formalized as the Plano Trienial, it called for an annual GDP growth rate of 7 percent with inflation reduced from 1962's 52 percent level to 25 percent for 1963 and a target of only 15 percent set for 1964.

Stabilization and development were to be achieved at the same time, along with administrative, banking, tax, and agrarian reforms. Less than an economic plan in the strict sense of the word, this was essentially a statement of policy objectives and was more nearly a mix of Kubitschek and Quadros administration aims than a markedly nationalizing or socializing program. (Furtado would serve after 1985 as the centrist Sarney government's minister of culture.) The plan called for increased foreign investment and was designed in large part with a view to impressing the U.S. government with the seriousness of Goulart's intention to pursue Alliance for Progress goals and meet Brazil's international obligations.

Goulart's lukewarm commitment to this plan, based as it was upon political convenience and lacking any conviction on his part regarding its economic necessity or even desirability, would quickly crumble. The generally favorable external reaction to these policies spurred the radical Left to increasingly strident criticism—to which Goulart was first sensitive, then responsive. Hence instead of moderation, the most dramatic development of the year was to be the growth and increasing assertiveness of the nationalist Left as manifested through a network of political, labor, and student groups. All of these elements enjoyed close ties to Brizola, and in the struggle between the conciliatory and radical advisors to Goulart, they threw their full support to the radicals while denouncing and undermining the efforts of the conciliators. Too elite and intellectual for the task, San Thiago Dantas would prove unable to retool as a populist leader, and neither he nor Furtado, who lacked any real political base, was sufficiently adept at the manipulation of politicians to prevail over the more radical forces.

The Nationalist Parliamentary Front (FPN), reorganized to incorporate newly elected deputies, issued a program in February 1963 calling for an independent foreign policy and structural reforms.[51] With Brizola as one of its vice-presidents, this very vocal group came out strongly for vigorous implementation of the restrictive legislation on remittance of profits, against any compromise in the expropriation controversy, and in adamant opposition to the plans of the Hanna mining company to exploit a disputed concession in Minas Gerais. As these were exactly the matters of greatest particular concern to the U.S. government, Dantas's hopes for successful conclusion of large-scale financial negotiations with the United States depended upon considerable flexibility in these disputes, which had caused new foreign investment to dry up to a mere trickle.[52] Moreover, the Plano Trienial— which linked the growth rates achieved during the Kubitschek years to price stability not attained since the 1940s—was not "doable," and as Goulart gradually abandoned it under political pressures the balance sheet for 1963 was to show an actual decrease in per capita GDP and a cost of living increase of over 80 percent.

Even back in troubled 1961 economic growth had been 7.9 percent, compared to 1963's 2.8 percent, and inflation, albeit on the rise, had been half that of 1963, so the relative economic debacle was apparent to all. With industrial expansion down from 8 percent in 1962 to only 2.8 percent and agricultural growth up an insignificant .1 percent compared to a 6 percent increase the previous year, the government was extremely vulnerable to charges of economic mismanagement. The promise to step up growth while bringing inflation under control required a high level of public investment financed through noninflationary means. But Goulart would not bite the bullet on higher taxes instead of increasing the money supply, nor would he seriously consider significantly altering the firmly rooted pattern of heavy subsidies imbedded in the inefficient government-controlled sector of the transportation system—especially the railroads. Resolute, even heroic, measures in this respect were more the style of a Quadros than of a wavering Goulart—and Quadros had thrown in the towel before following through on his initiatives, essentially worsening the problem for his successor. In light of fundamental political realities, a tight wage policy was as difficult politically for the labor-oriented Goulart as stringent budget cuts and credit restrictions were for the developmental-minded Kubitschek when he chose to scrap the Campos-Lopes Plan in 1959.

Had Goulart decided to really implement the three-year plan, Brazil's capacity to import would have had to be maintained through a refinancing of the foreign debt, as short- and medium-term obligations plus repatriation of profits had equaled nearly half the country's exports in 1962. But given the water already over the dam, these negotiations were bound to be much more difficult than those successfully concluded by the Quadros administration. Moreover, the Goulart effort to blend growth with financial stability also involved basic reforms as a way of neutralizing working-class anguish over the limitations on wage increases inherent in such an undertaking.

The best chance to enact such controversial provisions lay in the formation of a coalition of political interests each of which would support compromise measures for its own differing reasons. Hence land reform was advocated on economic grounds as a necessary modification of an outmoded system of land tenure that blocked increased agricultural production, a view that had some appeal for urban consumers highly concerned with food shortages and high prices. It was also put forward as a way of incorporating into the money economy marginal rural masses that presently lacked any significant purchasing power—a line of reasoning in which industrialists and industrial workers could find some merit. Whereas such developmental arguments for structural reforms struck a responsive chord among centrist elements, justification on the grounds of social justice also appealed to more progressive groups.

Extremists of both the Left and Right, however, were more concerned with the power implications of the government's proposed reforms. The radicals viewed essentially moderate measures as inadequate or designed as palliatives to deaden the revolutionary impulses of the Brazilian people, while the reactionaries saw the same proposals as dangerous wedges that would lead to more drastic changes that would upset the social order and shift political power perilously far to the Left. Hence the acerbic polemic of the 1962 election campaign persisted through the following year. The opposition continued to portray the president as essentially in agreement with Brizola and the other PTB radicals who supported "Communistic" measures, while these radical elements strove mightily to pull Goulart to the Left and to transform his administration into a truly "nationalist and popular" regime.[53] In this context the rather sparse results of Foreign Minister Dantas's March trip to Washington were inadequate for his aim of proving to the president and public opinion that there were greater advantages to continued cooperation with the United States than might be brought by adoption of a go-it-alone course of action analogous to that of Kubitschek in 1959.

Meanwhile, while Goulart still hesitated, price rises were far outrunning the government's predictions—a situation that had been the case in 1961 and would be the prevailing experience under almost all governments down to the present. Thus Goulart decided against holding the line on government pay raises—a key element of the agreement with the United States and the assumptions of the soon-to-arrive IMF mission. At the same time the resolution of the expropriation problem worked out by Dantas and U.S. Ambassador Lincoln Gordon, which involved Brazilian payment of a fair price in return for the proceeds being invested in Brazil by the U.S. parent companies, was attacked by the Left as a "sellout" of national interests. This attack was led by Brizola, who trumpeted that implementation of this agreement would lead to a final rupture between the president and "popular and nationalist" forces.

The Rise of Radicalization

Although party lines had come to have relatively little significance by this time, division of centrist forces as a result of traditional partisan disputes—going back to the Estado Novo, hardened in the series of crises since 1954, and reinforced by the bitterness of the 1962 political battles— hamstrung efforts at conciliation. Competing political ambitions including rival presidential aspirations on the part of key figures further impeded cooperation in support of a program of economic recovery and development accompanied by moderate reforms. In sharp contrast, formidable radicalizing forces existed on both the Left and the Right. Within the UDN, Lacerda— selected as the party's presidential standard-bearer in April—headed the intransigent faction, a group as determined that the ouster of the president was essential as they had been a decade earlier when they began maneuvering to bring about Vargas's downfall. The power struggle within the PTB also turned increasingly in favor of the radical wing, which moved steadily toward complete repudiation of the established order. To maintain PTB support, Goulart sacrificed Dantas and Furtado.

Within the PTB of the early 1960s, Goulart represented a Center position rather than that of champion of the radical wing. His brand of patronage-oriented, quite paternalistic populism was largely devoid of ideological content. Indeed, until he became president, Goulart had made life within the PTB uncomfortable for reformers who wished to give the party a coherent programmatic orientation. A true disciple of Vargas in this respect, he felt uncomfortable without room to maneuver and generally was most at ease in a relatively fluid bargaining situation where he could play competing interests against each other and follow a somewhat zigzag course toward his objectives. Often viewed as a weak personality, which he was by the standards for a major political leader, he was not prone to run risks for causes in which he felt no great stake, much less for abstruse principles. A moderately shrewd political manipulator with no great vision who was inclined to look for the path of least resistance, Goulart was not without ambitions that transcended mere holding of office and exercising of power. He definitely did not want to go down in history as a weak and indecisive man unable to deal effectively with the problems of governing Brazil. He was disposed neither to become a nearly powerless tool of the established groups nor to be upstaged and superseded by a more authentic and popular figure on the Left, brother-in-law or not.

Goulart's indecisiveness was most clearly reflected in his agonizing over what road to follow to make his mark as a worthy successor to Vargas. His irresoluteness was a function of both inadequate training and preparation to deal with technical problems and of a lack of the patience necessary to study complex matters. He remained a rather provincial Gaúcho, never coming to understand fully the thinking and style of Paulistas or Mineiros. Moreover, as a French journalist with years of residence in Brazil perceptively pointed out, Goulart was a man who had "an appetite to live well, the instinct for power, but few ideas and even less education."[54] In the judicious view of Jaguaribe:

> President Goulart, party leader but no statesman, excellent tactician but poor strategist, gifted with keen political intuition but bereft of practical knowhow, showed himself incapable of controlling events and reconciling short-term advantages—which he was always adroit in securing—with the longer-term interests of his Government, which he was prone to sacrifice to the expediency of the moment.[55]

Indeed, Brizola was, potentially at least, a far more formidable populist leader than Goulart, being "aggressively virile where the President was subject to derogatory rumors about his wife's amatory adventures; handsome and strong where Goulart was sensitive about his partially shriveled leg; and decisive where Jango appeared irresolute."[56] A political speaker matched only by Lacerda but with far greater appeal to the urban working class, Brizola tended to alienate other leftist figures, some of whom envied and feared his popularity while others were left apprehensive by his unbridled ambition.

Born in 1922, Leonel de Moura Brizola was four years younger than his brother-in-law but had started in elective politics at the same time, polling 3,839 votes for a state legislature seat in 1947 compared to Goulart's 4,150 for another seat in that year's at-large elections. In winning reelection in 1950 he raised his tally to an impressive 16,691—at the same time as, on the strength of Vargas's sponsorship, Goulart was elected to Congress with nearly 40,000 votes. An engineer, Brizola served as Rio Grande do Sul secretary of public works, with Goulart holding the state's justice portfolio, before he went on to a short but eventful stint as labor minister. Demagogically "exploiting Vargas' corpse" in the eyes of his enemies or picking up the torch in his supporters' view, Brizola was the third most highly voted federal deputy in all Brazil in 1954, with some 103,000 votes, while Goulart in the same year lost a Senate bid. The next year Brizola was elected as mayor of Porto Alegre and in 1958, at age thirty-six, won the governorship. Once inaugurated, he quickly gained national attention by expropriating the U.S.-owned local power company.

His leading role during the 1961 succession crisis elevated Brizola to a position of national leadership among the forces of the radical Left, and in 1962 he was massively voted back into Congress in the former Federal District. By mid-1963 in a very real sense he had the president on a string, because, worried about Brizola capturing the leadership of organized labor, Goulart would move leftward to head this off. Moreover, the conservative opposition held Goulart responsible for his brother-in-law's frequently revolutionary pronouncements, while in reality Goulart had very little influence with, much less control over, firebrand Brizola—who never doubted that he was the better man in every respect.

As of mid-1963, neither the extreme Right nor the radical Left wished to see moderate reforms enacted, an unfortunate situation clearest in the crucial struggle over agrarian reform—the pivotal issue upon which the prospects for political peace through accommodation rested. The crux of the problem was the constitutional provision calling for full and prompt payment in cash for any land expropriated. Vargas had failed to get Congress to modify this a decade earlier, and a two-thirds majority was needed to change the constitution. However, the UDN was firmly opposed, the PSD was willing to consider a compromise protecting the landowners against the effects of inflation, and Brizola's Popular Mobilization Front wanted to make the measure more sweeping.[57] As many PSD congressmen held that agrarian reform would be political suicide for their largely rural-based party—enabling the PTB to overtake them faster than it already was—a variety of bills went down to defeat. Goulart may well have scored points with the Left by declaring that this conservative Congress would never support significant reforms, but this remark also further fed legislative mistrust, for in the Center and Center-Right lawmakers' eyes the president had far from exhausted the possibilities for bargaining and compromise. Hence by the second half of the year Goulart's intentions were often viewed with suspicion mixed with apprehension.[58]

This made the job of Tancredo Neves as majority leader in the Chamber very difficult and thwarted efforts to gain support for the administration's policies from the younger and more progressive Bossa Nova wing of the

UDN. Had this initiative been successful, it would have given José Sarney (who had rejected an offer in 1961 from Quadros to be ambassador to Cuba) a Cabinet post, rendering him *persona non grata* to the military when they took over in 1964, thus all but certainly keeping him from becoming Brazil's first civilian president since Quadros.[59]

Military Stirrings—Ambivalences Accentuated

Even more than the political situation, the military scene deteriorated for Goulart during the latter part of 1963. The congressional impasse of September–November gave new life to the historical conspirators, as the lines between the leftist-nationalist and anti-Communist military groups would increasingly be drawn in such a manner as to involve the centrist-legalist majority of the officer corps through the issue of discipline. Moreover, the pay question, so crucial in the pre-crisis tensions of 1954, was again boiling up within the armed forces. Indeed, in July the Military Club issued an ultimatum to Congress to act at once (which a worried Congress did). With opponents of Goulart's agrarian reform bill charging that his insistence on a constitutional amendment was the entering wedge for a plan to remove the prohibition on his reelection, accusations of coup and counter-coup punctuated the acrimonious debate.

Whereas the mid-June Cabinet reshuffle was intended by Goulart to realign his support preparatory to a leftward shift without abandoning conciliation of centrist groups, it brought radical João Pinheiro Neto to head the infant Agrarian Policy Superintendency (SUPRA) and put politically inexperienced anthropologist Darcy Ribeiro into the sensitive job of presidential chief of staff.[60] (Darcy Ribeiro's political ineptness would be manifest in a disastrous campaign for the governorship of Rio de Janeiro in 1986.) New War Minister Jair Dantas Ribeiro was a strong legalist who had backed Goulart all down the line, but Brizola and his radical leftist associates had wanted their "peoples' general," Osvino Ferreira Alves. At the same time UDN party president Bilac Pinto had escalated the confrontation at mid-year by charging on the floor of the Chamber that the president was planning a coup.[61] As agrarian reform legislation painfully moved at a snail's pace through the legislative process, conservative PSD leaders had increasingly given thought to breaking off their coalition with the leftward drifting PTB— being held in line only by the prospect of Goulart's possible support for Kubitschek's 1965 bid to return to the presidency. For his part, Rio de Janeiro Governor Lacerda accused the federal government of having "declared war" against his state.

Although the month of August passed without a major crisis, the agitation within military ranks that General Amaury Kruel had denounced in May— an act that had led Goulart to replace Kruel as war minister almost immediately—exploded into an open rebellion that dramatized the seriousness of inroads into military discipline.[62] For almost a year the question of the eligibility of noncommissioned officers to run for elective office had been "hanging fire" (a problem for which there has been no real movement toward resolution). When the Supreme Court upheld the electoral tribunal's ruling against such eligibility, a sizeable group of air force and naval noncommissioned officers (noncoms) reacted by seizing control of Brasília on the morning of September 12. When Goulart, who was vacationing in Rio Grande do Sul at this critical juncture, issued an incendiary declaration that "the Constitution of 1946 was designed much more to care for the interests of economic groups and privileged minorities than those of the majority of the Brazilian people," many officers and opposition political figures suspected more than a touch of complicity with the noncom uprising.

The revolt was contained within the Federal District, but only after the country was treated to the spectacle of the presiding officer of the Chamber of Deputies and a Supreme Court justice being held prisoner by the rebels. (Although some 550 participants were subsequently arrested, an amnesty bill endorsed by Goulart was pending at the time of his ouster.) The appearance at rebel headquarters of leaders of the Nationalist Parliamentary Front to manifest their solidarity with the "just demands" of the sergeants was not lost upon the military, contributing to the subsequent entrance of a significant number of dismayed officers into the ranks of the anti-Goulart conspiracy. Symptomatic of this tendency to move toward active plotting were the remarks made the next day by Castelo Branco while he was being sworn in as the new army chief of staff—the critical swing man position in past military interventions—as he criticized "opportunistic reformers" seeking to undermine the army and "agitate the country."[63]

The crisis entered a new stage with a change of venue to São Paulo, when Second Army commander Pery Constant Beviláqua, just four months earlier the leftist-nationalists' candidate to head the Military Club, deeply disturbed by labor support for the sergeants' revolt, condemned radical union leaders as "enemies of democracy."[64] While the loss of one of the president's highest-ranking military supporters was itself a serious blow—much more so than Goulart dreamed at the time—concern over signs of government efforts to undermine discipline now extended from the high command to the junior officers in most immediate contact with the troops. The officers were by now acutely sensitive to any further efforts to build a "sandwich" scheme of military support for the regime—a *dispositivo* combining a relatively small number of senior officers in the top command positions with strong support from the warrant officers and noncoms. As events would soon prove, this "brilliant"—at least in the eyes of its architects— plan cost the government the support of a very large proportion of the legalist-democratic majority sentiment in the officer corps, upon whose constitutionalist scruples the government's security really rested, while few sergeants made any significant contribution to the defense of the president when the final crisis came.

With many officers in São Paulo now listening sympathetically to the plans being articulated there by Cordeiro de Farias and former Second Army commander and former war minister Nélson de Melo, the Goulart regime was more than a little beleaguered as the Brazilian spring moved along in October and November. Clearly some new initiative was in order to regain forward momentum, but the one undertaken was ill-conceived and self-defeating. On October 4, Goulart presented Congress with a request for approval of a thirty-day state of siege throughout the entire country. As the facts gradually became known over the next two weeks, it seemed evident that this was to have been but a first step to facilitate more drastic action. Plans had been made for a detachment of paratroopers to seize Lacerda, after which intervention of Guanabara state would have been decreed, but these plans were aborted by the refusal of two mid-grade officers to carry out the illegal act.[65] The government was further embarrassed by the negative response in Congress, with the fiasco completed by the opposition to the state of siege from labor, students, and nationalist politicians—the very groups upon whom Goulart intended to base his regime. Sheepishly withdrawing the request in the face of a lack of support within his own party, Goulart had to reconsider his idea of having Congress assume constituent powers to alter the constitution in favor of far-reaching socio-economic reforms.

Eventually fatal, however, was the reaction within the armed forces, where Castelo Branco actually censured the war minister for having acted in the name of the army without having consulted its high command.[66] Denounced in public for having unilaterally committed the army to a political venture that could only bring discredit upon it, Dantas Ribeiro never recovered from the loss of prestige suffered as a result of this episode. Thus, although the regime was not yet in immediate jeopardy, it was treading on very thin ice. The Right was encouraged by having seen Goulart once again ineffective and having to retreat abruptly in disarray from an imbroglio of his own making. The forces of the Left, in turn, suspected that his actions had been in compliance with the service ministers' desire for an emergency regime in order to crack down on both radical extremes. To these as well as to the legality-oriented centrist groups, Goulart's October actions smacked too much of the maneuvering preparatory to Vargas's continuist coup of 1937.

Radicalization, Reforms, and Resistance

The state-of-siege fiasco was interpreted by the opposition and a significant proportion of the military as showing to what extremes Goulart would go in his quest for greater power. It also seriously damaged his position by revealing to his enemies the degree to which he was not fully master in his own political house. Indeed, the opposition's distrust was so great that the Senate convoked in advance an extraordinary session to run through the normal mid-December to March recess to prevent the president from exercising any emergency powers during this time. Yet on the other side, the Brizola- and Arraes-led Popular Mobilization Front (FMP) decided to assume a position of "total independence" in the face of Goulart's not having moved far enough to the Left to satisfy their rapidly expanding aspirations. Indeed, Brizola to a very marked degree and Arraes in a less pronounced manner were more concerned with maneuvering to succeed

Goulart through the scheduled 1965 elections than they were with any prospect that getting there would prove to be a major problem.

Goulart himself painted a gloomy picture at the end of November, predicting a "social disaster of catastrophic proportions" and appearing to lean toward the idea of a moratorium on foreign debt.[67] With nearly $2 billion due to be paid before the end of his term and Finance Minister Carvalho Pinto unable to obtain a major rescheduling owing to Brazil's virtual abandonment of the three-year plan, the situation was grave—and it was made worse by Carvalho Pinto's resignation in mid-December. Adding to Goulart's woes, the FMP and associated organizations pushed for Brizola's appointment as finance minister, but Goulart named Bank of Brazil head Ney Galvão to the post instead.[68]

The Radical Left Triumphs Within the Regime

The struggle between the "positive Left" and the "negative Left," to use San Thiago Dantas's distinction, was, in effect, over.[69] Though the progressive wing of the Church and UDN moderates like Magalhães Pinto were still in accord with Dantas's objectives, they, like he, were minority voices within their own organizations—overshadowed if not drowned out by radicalizers and reactionaries.[70] As Jaguaribe saw it:

> It was precisely because the negative Left, under Brizola's irresponsible adventurism, could address to the masses the most revolutionary promises and appeals, that the viable compromise offered by the positive Left was made to look irrelevant, if not disguising a social treason. Correspondingly, the fallacious appeal, by the Right wing conservatives, to unrestricted advantages for the bourgeoisie, could mislead the national entrepreneurs.[71]

Exhilarated by their defeat of the conciliatory policies of Dantas and his moderate allies, the radical reformers and revolutionaries felt increasingly certain that the future was theirs. Just as they credited the triumph of legalism in the 1961 crisis to their efforts rather than to the divisions within the military and the generally legalist attitude of Center elements, these leftist groups felt that they had brought the president around to a more radical stand. What they did not perceive was that their insistence upon socialism and anti-U.S. foreign policy—instead of the social justice measures and independent foreign policy advocated by Dantas and Furtado—would drive the "national bourgeoisie from the progressive camp to that of the reactionary forces."[72]

In the eyes of its often self-proclaimed leaders, the coalition of workers, peasants, students, and nationalist military was making great progress during the opening months of 1964. It was felt that establishment of a truly "nationalist and popular" government should come immediately, with revolutionary changes to follow closely in its wake. The CGT, despite its lack of legal status and heavy dependence upon the government, had a highly inflated opinion of its political strength—although its leaders had yet to organize a truly national movement of any kind or stage a reasonably effective general strike. The organization of rural workers was proceeding rapidly, but the would-be architects of the prospective new "syndicalist" political order overlooked the fact that these were still infant groups with little experienced leadership and lacking even a fraction of the cohesion necessary to play the role the FMP and the CGT envisioned for them. A sober analyst would have seen that the small groups' potential in this respect could only be realized, at the soonest, two or three years hence.[73] In contrast to this immature overoptimism, the Prestes-led Brazilian Communist Party, a cat once scalded by its own lack of realism in 1935 and guilty of adopting an unrealistic, leftist, armed struggle line in 1950, consistently adhered to a cautious position and warned against adventurism based on overestimation of the strength and organizational capacity of "popular forces." Whereas Brizola and his cohorts scorned continued collaboration with the national bourgeoisie, the PCB saw this collaboration as the only viable strategy. The Communists were enjoying very substantial success in identifying themselves with the rising tide of nationalism, in infiltrating the PTB and the Brazilian Socialist Party (PSB), and in gaining control over important elements of organized labor and the student movement as well as building a network of front groups through which they could influence other components of the Left.[74] In the view of the Prestes-led orthodox mainstream current, a nationalist and popular government was good enough for the time being. (This had been foreshadowed when this group backed Kubitschek in 1955 after having strongly opposed Vargas.)

The Communist movement had, however, been undergoing serious internal dissension since the beginning of de-Stalinization and the Soviet-aborted 1956 Hungarian Revolution.[75] Agildo Barata led a significant group of militants out of the PCB in 1957, and important intellectual sympathizers withdrew from active support of party causes. After the Moscow-Peking split in the international communist movement became well defined, Prestes and his allies first downgraded and then expelled the leftist faction led by Maurício Grabois, João Amazonas, and Pedro Pomar—who subsequently formed the Communist Party of Brazil (PCdoB). The PCB decision to back Lott in the 1960 election against pro-Castro Quadros caused further defections.

When Goulart came to power Prestes and his followers supported the president, pressing him toward neutralism and radical reforms and seeking full legalization for the party before the next elections. But whereas the PCB strove to be a restraining force on extreme leftist elements, the PCdoB urged those same elements toward violent revolution. Heading four of the six national labor confederations, in spite of the fact that only 10 percent of the country's 1,600 recognized unions were under its direct control, the PCB played a major part in the Arraes administration in Pernambuco and enjoyed close relations with several of Goulart's key aides. With only 1,500 members, the PCdoB only managed to launch several small ventures in rural violence, but these were widely played up by anti-Communist forces. While the PCB was urging the foundation of a broad popular front, the PCdoB was calling upon university students to go into the countryside to organize the peasants for armed revolution.[76] The PCdoB pursued this course despite the abysmal failure of such an effort during 1961–1962 by the Tiradentes Revolutionary Movement (MRT) and Peasant League elements led by Clodomir Santos de Morais.[77]

For its part, the PCB was deeply concerned about both the extent of Brizola's popular following, which was undercutting the party in some areas, and the possibility that his bravado could result in a rash resort to violence that might bring about a disastrous reaction on the part of conservative military elements. Once a career army officer, Prestes understood military attitudes much better than did either Brizola or the president.[78] In Prestes's view, objective revolutionary conditions did not yet exist and would take some time to be brought into being.[79]

The accelerating political mobilization at the end of the old year and beginning of the new brought far more recruits to the radical movements than the relatively few who enlisted in support of conciliation. Moreover, the Basic Education Movement (MEB), a literacy program with heavy political content, and the student-sponsored Popular Culture Movement might over time offset the control of the mass media and educational system by the established Center-conservative groups—adding large numbers of newly participant citizens to the ranks of those clamoring for structural changes. Given sufficient time, continued organization of rural workers and agitation for agrarian reform would also work against the political dominance of the economic and social elite and the established class of clientelistic politicians. With the active encouragement of the government, these changes could come about sooner, rather than later, but not as quickly as the radical Left required.

This extreme of the political spectrum included not only the dissident Communists, but also the Popular Action (AP) youth elements, who had evolved from their original Catholic base into fervent, albeit often romantic, revolutionaries as they escaped the doctrinal fetters of the Church-oriented Catholic University Youth (JUC).[80] Immature and volatile, these strongly anti-imperialist students had become the dominant element in the Union of Students (UNE) and through this peak organization exerted a heavy influence on the political position of the younger generation.[81]

Succession Rears Its Head

Even as the crisis deepened, the position of major political leaders was still largely determined by their presidential ambitions. Though Adhemar de Barros, whose electoral prospects were not very strong, had already opted for revolution, other major contenders were understandably afraid that a coup would upset the electoral timetable and introduce changes in the rules of the game that could adversely affect their prospects. Kubitschek, the early frontrunner, was trying strenuously to hold together the traditional PSD-PTB alliance by pulling Goulart toward moderation and urging his congressional followers to be more receptive to the president's pleas for basic reforms. Kubitschek's closest competitor, Lacerda, was torn between his virulent opposition to Goulart and his desire not to jeopardize his promising electoral possibilities. Clearly the most direct opposition candidate, his presidential bid gained strength among the Center and even some moderate Left voters as the Goulart regime failed to deal effectively with the nation's urgent problems and the possibility of a radical PTB candidate loomed larger.

Magalhães Pinto, on the other hand, was steadily losing ground to Lacerda within the UDN and sought a base as a potential reconciliation candidate acceptable to those moderate elements of the Left who wished to block the election of the violently anti-PTB Lacerda. (In this Magalhães Pinto also faced the problem of substantial popular support for former finance minister Carvalho Pinto.)[82] Eventually the civilian swing man of the conspiracy, Magalhães Pinto represented the more progressive wing of the UDN and was reasonably open to reforms—as long as such reforms did not seriously infringe on property rights or undermine an essentially capitalist system. His role as an articulator of dialogue and compromise stemmed both from his essential beliefs and character and his political ambitions. As long as he could foresee the possibility of some assistance to his candidacy from the president, he remained on quite amicable terms with Goulart.

On the Left, Pernambuco Governor Arraes was viewed as a presidential contender in light of the ineligibility of both Goulart and Brizola—the latter seen as ineligible because he was the president's brother-in-law. But having few illusions concerning his chances in 1965, Arraes feared both a conservative coup and an effort to remove Brizola's ineligibility. Isolated and exposed, he shared the same suspicion that Goulart intended to stay in office rather than permit a free election of his successor that led other leading politicians to join or condone the conspiracy against the president.[83]

During 1963 the political atmosphere had been further radicalized by renewed accusations and counteraccusations of corruption and improper use of large sums of money to influence the outcome of the 1962 elections. Brizola went so far as to use this to impugn the moral authority, if not the very legitimacy, of Congress, and a congressional investigating committee plowed through this mucky ground.[84] Although Goulart issued a decree in August 1963 dissolving both IBAD and ADEP, the controversy continued as the radical Left attempted to rub some of these organizations' bad odor off on IPES and the Right launched an investigation of alleged "buying" of control of UNE by Brizola.

Very ostensibly engaged in propagandistic campaigns for modernization of Brazilian capitalism and against communism, IPES was behind the scenes playing a very important role in preparing Goulart's downfall. Given the formidable disadvantages for a Brazilian businessman of actively opposing the government, upon whom he was highly dependent for credit and who could create grave problems for him through strict enforcement of many essentially dead-letter regulations, the growth of IPES was an index of the solidification of opposition to Goulart on the part of the urban propertied class. From about eighty members in early 1962, the organization's rolls expanded to some 500 by mid-1963. Particularly in Rio de Janeiro, IPES's staff came chiefly from among the ranks of retired military officers, with General Golbery do Couto e Silva, a noted author on geopolitics who had run the national security· council staff under Quadros, as chief of the strategic "Research Group," the organization's intelligence arm.[85] (Closely linked to Castelo Branco, Golbery would become the government's intelligence director after Goulart's ouster.) Alongside IPES there was a conspiratorial group tied to *O Estado de S. Paulo* and the Civil-Military Patriotic Front of former navy minister Silvio Heck.[86] Yet the plotters badly needed a prestigious senior general on active duty in the Rio de Janeiro area to assume a leadership role, and Castelo Branco admirably filled this bill.

The Road Toward Intervention

A hero of the Italian campaign who enjoyed a reputation for having scrupulously avoided involvement in civilian political affairs, Castelo Branco had developed a large following among those who were by now middle-grade officers during his long tenure with the command and general staff school and among more senior officers through his service as ESG commandant. In seeking to win him over to the anti-Goulart cause, Marshal Adhemar de Queiroz, a close friend since academy days, and others committed to the coup reminded the scholarly Castelo Branco of their joint struggle against leftist elements in the 1950 Military Club elections. Deeply concerned with the government's course, by late 1963 he had agreed to assume military leadership of the conspiracy.[87] His adherence was, however, conditioned upon all plans to move against Goulart being contingent upon the president's violation of the accepted rules of the game. As long as Goulart did not close Congress, show clear indications of attempting to continue in office beyond the expiration of his term, or otherwise act illegally, he would still be considered the legitimate commander-in-chief of Brazil's armed forces. But Castelo Branco's subsequent addresses and circulars as army chief of staff demonstrated an increasing perception that Goulart was treading on very dangerous ground.

By February the conspirators had drafted a document setting forth their main premises. Entitled "LEEX" (from the Portuguese for Loyalty to the Army), it emphasized the movement's objective as preservation of representative democracy.[88] Including a series of questions as to precisely what state of affairs would justify action against the government, the document was a way of ascertaining the conditions under which a coup would find support from officers in the outlying parts of the country. Yet even before the results were in from this sounding, a naval crisis would present an issue that could better serve as a trigger for a successful coup than any of the contingencies conceived by the revolution's strategists. But first Goulart took a series of populist measures at the end of February that at least bordered on demagoguery and indicated that he had stopped listening to Kubitschek and was falling more under the. influence of Brizola. Instances of land seizures increased, allegedly with SUPRA encouragement, and Brizola boasted openly of organizing a peoples' militia in the form of the Groups of Eleven, giving highly inflated claims of 200,000 members—which served more to arouse the opposition than to intimidate it.[89]

This provided grist for the mill of the Right's newly inaugurated political offensive—a campaign denouncing the existence of a government-encouraged "state of revolutionary war." Building on the foundation of Bilac Pinto's Chamber speech of the preceding June, this pressed home accusations that rural unions and port workers were storing arms for a revolution.[90] At the end of February both an address by Brizola and a highly publicized congress of a pro-Castro Latin American regional labor organization were forced out of the Minas Gerais capital by well-orchestrated anti-Communist demonstrations.

Still the government felt that its military power scheme—which rested on a few leftist officers, the legalist orientation of most of the others, the long record of avoidance of involvement in politics on the part of Castelo Branco, and the personal ties between Goulart and Second Army commander Amaury Kruel—was more than adequate to cope with whatever might be planned by what they perceived to be a small nucleus of military conspirators. In fact, however, the plotters were already far more numerous than the government thought, and events of March were to rapidly strengthen their ranks while eroding the regime's support. Indeed, the state military forces of São Paulo and Minas Gerais had already been built up and the former partially reequipped with arms produced by local industry whose leaders were ready to "double the effort of '32 in '64" if necessary.

The Demise of Democracy

By the beginning of March neither of the key Mineiro conciliators had given up hope, but few were heeding their words. Magalhães Pinto, although more than half convinced that a coup would be necessary, called once again for reason and restraint. On the government side, Dantas's dreams of a "broad front for reforms" were dashed by the increasing aggressiveness of his own party's radicals, who rejected the idea of PTB support for Kubitschek in 1965 and threatened to break with Goulart unless he veered sharply to the Left. Indeed, Brizola's Mayrink Veiga radio station and weekly *Panfleto* often flagellated the government as violently as did Lacerda.[91] As for the administration, it was increasingly obsessed with getting rid of this Guanabara governor, while the "producing classes" of the nation as represented by a convention of some 300 businessmen, industrialists, and bankers resolved that, unless the president abandoned his leftward tack and dropped any ideas of continuism, direct action would be justified.[92]

In the interior, land seizures by newly organized peasant groups were matched and often overmatched by armed resistance on the part of landowners. In the classic dilemma of the reformer fighting a two-front war against Left and Right, Goulart—relying upon his staff's advice that his military support was sufficiently strong to overwhelm any foreseeable reaction—decided to go all out for mobilization of mass pressures for basic structural reforms. This decision lit the fuse on the powder keg of accumulated tensions and conflicts that had gotten only partial release in the 1961 crisis. Intended to strengthen the president's hand, it not only cost him his job, but also spelled an end to competitive civilian politics for over two decades.

Friday the Thirteenth and "Basic Reforms"

The self-perceived high point of the Goulart administration came on Friday, March 13, as the president addressed a cheering crowd estimated at above 150,000 gathered in the square opposite the War Ministry in Rio de Janeiro. Surrounded by leftist leaders of mass organizations, Goulart announced an agrarian reform by decree, the nationalization of private oil refineries, and an urban reform law establishing rent controls on vacant apartments. In by far the most effective speech of his career, Goulart lashed out at his enemies for exploiting the people's Christianity by "mystifying them with anti-Communism," condemned the constitution for legalizing an "inhumane" social and economic system, and made an impassioned appeal for mass support for "great structural changes."[93] Yet it was Brizola's denunciation of Congress and open invitation for a popular revolution that aroused the most enthusiastic response from the crowd—and elicited the most negative reaction from the middle class, military, and businessmen watching with dismay on television. His ultimatum to Congress, to enact the whole package of basic reforms demanded by the "popular and nationalist" forces within thirty days or the people would "know what to do," helped the government's opponents depict the rally as a gathering of extremist elements inaugurating a campaign of subversion of the Brazilian way of life.[94] Skillfully the conservative-controlled media concentrated on the red banners and placards demanding immediate legalization of the PCB carried by the Communist claque in the front rows.

It is very possible that in the heat of the moment Goulart went farther than he had intended to on March 13, but his subsequent state of the union address to the new session of Congress contained a number of proposals with far-reaching implications: amendment of the constitution to provide for expropriation of land without immediate cash payment; extension of the franchise to illiterates; delegation of legislative powers to the executive; legalization of the Communist Party; and elimination of tenure for university professors.[95] Most controversial was his proposal for a plebiscite involving the entire adult population—illiterates included—on the question of basic reforms. Moreover, Brizola took over the formal leadership of the PTB and began mobilization for a May 1 plebiscite—giving every appearance of being a presidential candidate.

Although it seemed to many at first that the opposition had been caught off guard, thrown on the defensive, and even intimidated by the momentum of the campaign for basic reforms and a popular-nationalist government, this was far from the case. Congress decided to move ahead with its own program of reforms, beginning with the moderate Christian Democratic agrarian reform bill. Brizola and allied labor leaders went on mapping out increasingly ambitious policy initiatives and the president scheduled a series of mass rallies in key cities—to culminate in São Paulo on May Day with an attendance target of 1 million. But underneath the surface waves they were making, the tide was turning against them.

On March 18 former president Dutra broke his long silence on political matters to issue a call for unity in defense of democracy and the constitution. The "army of quiet men" was beginning to speak out against the "army of loudmouths."[96] Indeed, it was the euphoric and immature Brazilian Left rather than the wily old soldiers who were increasingly detached from reality to the point of living in a fool's paradise. The Brizolistas and exhalted presidential advisors confused ability to mobilize a turnout for their rallies and a series of uncoordinated land seizures accompanied by a flood of revolutionary rhetoric with the capacity to bring into being and into action an "irreversible" popular movement for structural reforms. In the heady emotions of the moment, the government forces lost sight of the need for effective organization and institutionalization of these newly unleashed forces.

Symbolic of the radical Left's growing separation from a realistic view of the situation was the fact that on March 19, just as their congressional spokesmen were demanding replacement of centrist Cabinet members by "representatives of the people," by which they meant Brizola and his associates, a mass demonstration in São Paulo of nearly 500,000 men and women dramatically expressed their feeling that the country had already moved too far to the Left. The "Family March with God for Liberty" sponsored by the Feminine Civic Union under the patronage of Governor Adhemar de Barros marked the commencement of a major counterattack by the regime's opponents.[97]

Designed explicitly as a dramatic answer to the Left's March 13 show of force, the march benefitted from the assistance of businessmen's and land-owners' organizations as well as from that of the state administration. The government tried to play down the demonstration as artificial and manipulated—as if the March 13 crowd had turned up spontaneously in the middle of Rio de Janeiro. But in its contribution to an atmosphere propitious for a successful coup, the family march was much more than a bunch of fanatically Catholic housewives clutching their rosaries and followed by a mob of their domestic servants—as the Brizolistas sought to make it appear. As regime and opposition alike realized, as long as General Kruel and the Second Army remained loyal the regime was probably safe from any threat from the Right. With the São Paulo anti-regime rally taking place in front of their eyes, these officers were undoubtably impressed. Then, too, on the same day Magalhães Pinto pointedly reminded the president that a revolution from above was no more legitimate than a coup, and Kubitschek urged respect for the integrity of Congress.

As the Easter holidays neared, the obviously increasing polarization appeared to the government to be contained within the political arena. The close cooperation coming into being among the governors of five of the country's six most important states—with many of their colleagues from smaller states falling into line—meant little to the administration. Instead and shortsightedly, it was more concerned with both the PSD's precipitation of the succession question by formally launching Kubitschek's candidacy and with Brizola's call for a constituent assembly election under new rules banning "economic interests" to take matters out of the hands of Congress.[98] As Brizola's radical line elicited more enthusiasm from PTB elements than did Goulart's inconsistent and rather haphazard leftism, Dantas's essentially moderate "broad front" program finally announced on March 23 was not in keeping with the polarizing atmosphere.

The most serious development, although out of the public eye, was that Castelo Branco had officially circulated a message to the army officer corps denouncing Brizola's initiative as a step toward dictatorship and refuting the thesis that legality necessarily meant support of a president bent on crossing the permissible limits toward subversion.[99] The military's constitutional task, the chief of staff emphasized, was to guarantee the functioning of the constitutional powers and the application of the law—not to "defend programs of the Government, much less its propaganda." In a clear reminder of the moderating power role, he affirmed that military respect for the president's authority was always conditional upon the president remaining "within the limits of the law."[100]

The Naval Crisis: An Affront to Military Discipline

The presidential staff feverishly prepared new decrees for radical reform measures to be announced at each of the mass rallies during April, upon which Goulart was counting to keep attention focused on the issue of progressive policies rather than on possible continuist designs. But for him as the country's chief executive, April would never come. Instead the crisis that, although catching the conspirators as well as the government by surprise, was to lay Goulart low within a week began on the night of Wednesday, March 25. Disobeying a ban by the navy minister, officers of the Association of Sailors and Marines had attended a political meeting at the Communist-led Bankworkers Union two days earlier.[101] While Goulart went off to spend the holidays on his ranch, the navy minister attempted to bolster eroding discipline by arresting defiant officers of the association, including the organizers of its anniversary commemoration, which brought 2,000 discontented servicemen together at the headquarters of the metalworkers' union. Here they heard an inflammatory address by their leader, José Anselmo dos Santos—denounced then as a Communist militant, later as an *agent provocateur* working for the anti-Goulart conspiracy—excoriating the forces of domestic reaction and imperialism and linking the navy minister to them. Egged on by radical labor leaders and nationalist politicians, the mutineers resolved to hold out until all punishments were revoked and a new minister sympathetic to their movement was appointed.[102] Leftist Admiral Cândido Aragão was replaced as head of the marine corps for refusing to move to repress the mass insubordination, and the CGT threatened a general strike in support of the mutineers.

Returning from his interrupted vacation, Goulart found the situation getting out of control, as Brizola had seized the opportunity to denounce the coup intentions of the military ministers in their "persecution" of the sailors and marines. In the face of a lack of any presidential support for strict enforcement of the law, the navy minister resigned. With almost all senior navy officers hostile to his position and Aragão being too much Brizola's man either for the president's comfort or for the military to swallow, Goulart resorted to a lesser evil of calling seventy-three-year-old anti-imperialist Admiral Paulo Mário da Cunha Rodrigues out of retirement. While Goulart, grossly underestimating the seriousness of the situation, flew off to Brasília for the Easter weekend, the clearly over-the-hill navy minister had important assistance in mishandling the crisis from General Assis Brasil, the president's erratic chief military aide, who accepted a hearsay version of Goulart's wishes and went along with the almost immediate release of the mutineers. The insurgents held a jubilant celebration in the center of the city that sent shock waves through the officer corps of all three services as well as through civilian advocates of order. The sight of reinstated marine corps commandant Aragão and former minister Suzano (just named chief of naval operations) being carried through the streets on the shoulders of unpunished mutineers caused many to decide that legality at this juncture was clearly not on the side of the government.[103]

Although it was not yet apparent, what Goulart and his advisors congratulated themselves upon as the end of the crisis was really the beginning of the end for the regime. On the public side the Naval and Military Clubs gathered in protest and Rio de Janeiro's major newspapers prepared extraordinary Saturday editions (with that of the *Jornal do Brasil* featuring a front-page editorial dramatically titled "Illegality") as well as publishing editions on Easter Sunday—unheard of in Catholic Brazil. Very quietly Marshal Denys left for a meeting in Juiz da Fora, Minas Gerais, with General Mourão Filho and Magalhães Pinto.[104] On Monday, March 30, General Arthur da Costa e Silva recommended to all the officers serving in his department of the War Ministry that they consider acting before army and air force discipline was also be subverted by the "Communists."[105] Planned to pave the way for a "General Union of Military Workers" as a link between the labor movement and the military, the event of the preceding Wednesday had instead united the armed forces against the presumed Peronist-type ambitions of the soon-to-be-former president.

The Sergeants' Rally—The Last Straw

As oblivious to the impending disaster as the emperor had been three-quarters of a century earlier, Goulart devoted Monday to an address he was to make that evening to the Association of Sub-officials and Sergeants of the Military Police at the Rio de Janeiro Automobile Club. Even after there were clear indications that something serious was afoot in Minas

Gerais, instead of mobilizing troops for a possible move in that direction, the administration was wrapped up in arranging transportation to carry even more First Army noncoms away from their units to a rally that would last into the early hours of what would turn out to be the government's last morning. Before only a fraction of the 10,000 or more sergeants he had been told to expect, the president—who had ignored Tancredo Neves's advice to cancel—gave his enemies the further provocation they were seeking in an exalted ninety-minute nationally broadcast speech.[106]

His nightmare began with sunup the next day, as the *Correio da Manhã* headline, which the day before had been "Enough," now read simply "Out!" By afternoon the worst rumors were confirmed: Minas Gerais was in open revolt. Although Jair Dantas Ribeiro returned from his hospital bed to assume direction of the regime's defense, within hours he had suffered a relapse. As for the regime's scheme of military support, it simply evaporated—for in large part it had only existed on paper or in the heads of incompetent aides operating on misfounded assumptions.

Military Action on Five Fronts

Although it lasted less than two full days, the military side of the 1964 Revolution took on a distinctive character in each main region of the country: in the First Army, sharp divisions and open confrontation as the troops from Minas Gerais marched on Rio de Janeiro; in the Second Army, hesitation while Paulista civilians and troop commanders waited for General Kruel to make up his mind to lead them against legalist forces in Rio de Janeiro; in the Third Army, the divisional commanders leading their troops against the commanding general; and in the Fourth Army, coordinated action by all units under the leadership of its commander. On all fronts success came relatively quickly and with a minimum of bloodshed. Respecting the position of their opponents, who were fighting for legality as they saw it, revolutionary forces preferred to outmaneuver and outnegotiate rather than overpower. While military action was decisive, the support of organized civilian groups— particularly the cooperation of state administrations—was of great importance. For within Brazilian society, activity on behalf of the revolution was much greater than were the scattered efforts to mobilize in defense of the regime, a far cry from the enormously more successful "legality movement" of 1961.

The distinction of launching the revolution fell to Minas Gerais, for São Paulo had paid a stiff price for sticking its neck out alone in 1932. Moreover, a revolt in Minas Gerais would sever communications between Rio de Janeiro and Brasília, and a small number of troops there could hold off much larger forces trying to come up the mountainous terrain from the coast.[107] Success was complete, and by late afternoon loyalist troops withdrew from positions along the Minas Gerais–Rio de Janeiro border, allowing the troops of generals Mourão Filho and Luís Carlos Guedes to proceed on a triumphal mechanized march to Brazil's second metropolis, where they arrived by dawn.

There Lacerda had begun to mobilize state forces on the 29th, when he received word from Deputies José Costa Cavalcanti and Armando Falcão—

both subsequently to hold key ministerial posts—that agreement had been reached with Castelo Branco for initiation of hostilities during the course of the coming week.[108] When confirmation of Minas Gerais having jumped the gun came in the early hours of the 31st, Lacerda and his allies moved to tie down as much of the legalist forces as possible, while the military conspirators acted effectively and with dispatch to sap the will and ability to resist of the rest of the First Army. With bastions in the National War College under General Mamede and the command and general staff school headed by General Orlando Geisel (to become war minister in 1969), by afternoon they would also control the War Ministry, where Costa e Silva took over.[109] By that time Goulart had fled to Brasília, where Darcy Ribeiro was trying with little success to organize government workers into resistance units, but, deciding that the situation was too exposed, the president flew on to Porto Alegre at 10:00 P.M.—having remained in the capital a bare seven hours.[110]

Although the revolution appeared to unfold relatively slowly in São Paulo, there was never any cause to doubt its success there. In light of their past friendship, Kruel was unwilling to take a leading role in Goulart's ouster and insisted on giving Goulart a chance to save himself by breaking with the radical Left.[111] When after a series of phone calls Goulart still refused to do so, Kruel gave orders on the evening of the 31st for the Second Army to move against Rio de Janeiro, leaving the 30,000-man state militia to contain isolated pro-regime demonstrations by labor unions. A conflict near the Agulhas Negras Military Academy was avoided when acting War Minister Armando de Morais Ancora realized that the government he was defending had ceased to exist.

While the Second Army then turned its attention southward on the night of April 1, the revolution was already consolidating its victory there. For in sharp contrast to the 1961 crisis, the Rio Grande do Sul state government was in the hands of long-time opponents of Goulart and the Brigada Militar could be counted upon to neutralize many of the legalist units of the Third Army. General Adalberto Pereira dos Santos's Sixth Infantry Division posed a threat to pro-Goulart forces in Porto Alegre, while the Third Infantry, along with the Second and Third Cavalry Divisions, secured the interior for the insurgents before also marching on the state capital.[112] Thus, when Goulart arrived there at dawn on April 2, he found a hopeless situation and quickly departed for his ranch near the Uruguayan border—leaving Brizola the impossible task of trying to mount armed resistance. For even in Paraná the revolt had also triumphed more easily than its architects had expected in their most optimistic moments.

Although this was but frosting on the cake, avoiding the need for a mopping-up campaign, the revolution's success in the northeast also exceeded all but the most optimistic hopes of its leaders—easily beating the 1930 timetable. Fourth Army commander Alves Bastos—having been preceded in that post by Costa e Silva and Castelo Branco—was in full control of the military situation and promptly deposed Governor Arraes, while in the rest of the region it was the governors themselves, several of whom were former career officers, who took leading roles (the only exception being in Sergipe).[113]

Thus, although in retrospect the weaknesses and errors of the Goulart regime stand out—pronounced in lack of a coherent project, debilitating internal divisions, and gross underestimation of their foes—from a technical point of view the uprising was extremely well planned and executed. Indeed, a number of the government's chief shortcomings resulted from intelligent tactical exploitation of potential vulnerabilities by the leadership of the rebel forces. Rapid and virtually bloodless, the movement enjoyed some of its most striking successes exactly where Goulart's defensive scheme was touted to be its strongest. The greatest contrast between the two sides was in the leadership sphere, as the revolution could call upon the army general staff, the ESG, and the command and general staff school, as well as members of the armed forces high command of the Quadros government. In a very general sense, the *tenentes* of the 1920s, with their subsequent experience in the 1930 Revolution and World War II, were much more able when it came down to a military operation than were their opponents. As Castelo Branco, Cordeiro de Farias, Adhemar de Queiroz, Nélson de Melo, Mamede, and Sizeno Sarmento had all been on the ticket defeated by that of Estillac Leal in the bitterly contested 1950 Military Club elections, victory was particularly sweet to them.

Moreover, even though they never needed to be employed, the armed and organized civilian reserves of the rebel forces greatly overmatched the vaunted "mass organizations" and "popular forces" of an immature radical Left equipped with mouths much bigger than their real appetite for a fight.[114] As for Goulart's military advisors, besides grossly underestimating Minas Gerais—for them merely the tail on the First Army dog—they handled politically unreliable officers by giving them school and staff assignments in Rio de Janeiro, arguing that without troop commands they were no threat. But in this way they actually built up a critical mass of alienated officers who came themselves to constitute a formidable strike force reinforced by a large contingent of retired and reserve officers. With Goulart overthrown, it would be the Rio de Janeiro–based leadership of the revolt who would give shape to the new regime, for during the critical first half of April all key political events would be centered there, not in Brasília.

7

The Military as Ruler, 1964–1973

Having once again exercised the moderating power, the armed forces were now going to have to decide what to do next. The first decision would be to establish a semi-constitutional regime to replace the interim junta, but this would be followed by disagreement stretching over the course of the next several years over whether to remain in control of the government or return to a role of tutor, if not go all the way back to being again "just" the arbiter of national political life. Once the die was cast for at least a second consecutive military government, the country would embark upon a much longer period of rule by the armed forces than anyone imagined— with the first decade spent on getting in deeper and deeper as abortive "normalization" efforts led instead to an increasingly authoritarian political system. During this time the military would develop very close ties with the property-owning groups, while these groups in turn would greatly diversify as a result of the marked economic development. For its part, the Church—or at least a major faction of it—would become spokesman for the muzzled masses, a role that would place it in unaccustomed opposition to the government.

The forces that so easily overthrew the Goulart government were united chiefly by their agreement that the radicalization and indiscipline of the preceding three weeks was intolerable. Beyond their shared desire to put an end to "subversion" as they perceived it, the various components of the triumphant March 31st Movement possessed no consensus as to what should come next. "Historical conspirators" within the military who had never accepted Goulart as legitimate stood alongside conservative UDN elements who, now that the Vargas heirs were finally out, wanted the lengthy period of political dominance they had expected to enjoy after the 1960 elections. Each only coexisted uneasily with moderate constitutionalists both in uniform and in business suits, for whom Goulart had been acceptable as long as they could expect a return of Kubitschek to power by 1966. The constitutionalists' relations were at least equally shaky with the numerous legalists who had reluctantly acted only when they were convinced of Goulart-Brizola efforts to subvert military discipline and "unconstitutionally" change the constitution.

Indeed, the situation was parallel to that in late 1930—when the radical *tenentes* were contending for power with the representatives of politically marginalized states, the dissident oligarchy of Minas Gerais, and the last-minute adherents from the senior ranks of the armed forces. Very simply, the "revolution" as it came to power at the beginning of April had too many self-proclaimed owners with incompatible aspirations and contradictory, albeit overlapping, visions of the new order.[1] At one extreme, the historical conspirators advocated a prolonged period of purges under a regime of extraordinary powers, while at the other were found Social Democratic Party (PSD) elements led by former president Kubitschek, who fully expected elections to be held as scheduled in 1965—as had been the case in 1955 after Vargas's downfall in the preceding year.

In between were UDN forces divided between the presidential pretensions of Lacerda and Magalhães Pinto and favoring elections without Kubitschek's participation, on the one hand, and São Paulo groups led by Adhemar de Barros eager to exploit the situation to attain the presidential office, which had eluded them in 1955 and 1960. Within the military there was a general feeling that power could not be allowed to fall back into the hands of the Vargas lineage as it had in 1951, 1956, and 1961. Yet there was little consensus on how this was to be avoided, and only a small minority foresaw anything like the over twenty years of military rule that was to take place.[2]

Castelo Branco and the Arbiter-Ruler Dilemma

Under such circumstances it was almost inevitable that the significant array of forces advocating a brief implementation of an arbiter function by the military in keeping with its past exercise of the moderating power would be able to stave off defeat for some time. In fact, they would carry the day in April 1964 and remain in control of the situation until October 1965 initiated a series of reversals for the champions of early normalization. Only with the 1967 presidential succession was the die decisively cast for a long authoritarian night under a military determined to be the nation's ruler.[3]

The First Months: The Negative Phase

The immediate aftermath of the Goulart government's ouster was a short period of intense purges. In Rio de Janeiro, Costa e Silva—assuming the post of war minister as the senior active-duty officer there—quickly organized a Revolutionary Supreme Command composed of himself, Admiral Augusto Rademaker Grünewald, and Air Force Chief of Staff Francisco de Assis Correia de Melo. At the same time, officers of the less extreme "Sorbonne" group—composed of members of the ESG, the command and general staff school, and the army chief of staff's collaborators—worked effectively behind the scenes to articulate Castelo Branco's candidacy to fill the rest of the Quadros-Goulart term.

Almost all leading politicians accepted the idea of a military man who could be expected to provide a stable interim regime and preside over election of a constitutional successor with relative impartiality. So over Costa e Silva's preference for at least a month's delay in replacing his junta with a legitimized chief executive, Castelo Branco was chosen by the key governors and military leaders, being duly ratified by Congress on April 11 by 361 to 72 abstentions and 5 votes for historical figures Dutra and Juarez Távora.[4]

By this time, however, the Revolutionary Supreme Command had taken decisive action to ensure that the "subversive" and "corrupt" elements linked to the overthrown regime were effectively removed from political life. The author of the 1937 Estado Novo constitution, Francisco Campos, and his onetime assistant, Carlos Medeiros da Silva—Vargas's solicitor general, Kubitschek's attorney general, and a member of the Supreme Court—drafted an Institutional Act adequate to the imperatives of a revolutionary regime. Bearing only the signatures of Costa e Silva, Rademaker, and Correia de Melo, the act made clear the military's view that their rescue of the nation left the armed forces vested with legitimate authority to decree a new institutional order.

Besides greatly strengthening the powers of the president, this overriding of the existing constitution suspended for six months all constitutional and legal rights of job tenure, thus allowing the president and governors to dismiss public employees for "threatening national security, the democratic regime, or public order." Moreover, it authorized the junta to suspend political rights of citizens for ten years and to cancel the mandates of congressmen, state legislators, and members of municipal councils—with the president to enjoy the same powers for a period of sixty days.

The first round of cassations on April 10 caught nearly the entire leadership of the Nationalist Parliamentary Front, as well as former presidents Goulart and Quadros, PCB chief Prestes, and Pernambuco Governor Arraes. Almost the entire General Workers' Command leadership was also included along with most Goulart advisors. Four days later a few additional politicians and a considerable number of writers also became political nonpersons as did two dozen military figures. By this time all leading figures of anti-imperialist congressional investigations—even those of the mid-1950s—had been purged. On April 11 some 122 military officers were retired against their will, with most of them and many from the lower ranks also deprived of their political rights for a decade. Far-reaching as were these purges, at least by Brazilian standards, they affected only a small proportion of the total officer corps—in no way matching the draconian measures taken in Argentina during the months after Perón's ouster in 1955.[5] Still, when Castelo Branco was inaugurated on April 15, Brazilian democracy was already in the process of being severely restricted.

Sensing that the regime's political axe was being sharpened for his neck, on May 25 Kubitschek addressed a message to the Brazilian people declaring that they had already judged him at the polls and seemed eager to have another opportunity to demonstrate their faith in him at the ballot box.

Although Castelo Branco was extremely reluctant to do so, he deprived Kubitschek of his political rights on June 8, acting under heavy pressure from the "hard line" and Costa e Silva—who had remained as war minister and whose presidential ambitions were ill-concealed. Then on June 15, the sixtieth day of Castelo Branco's administration, an additional seventy-one persons lost their political rights in what was thought at the time to be the final wave of cassations under the Institutional Act.

Castelo Branco, born in 1900 in Ceará as the son of an army officer, attended the military school in Porto Alegre as a classmate of Costa e Silva and the Kruel brothers. A graduate of the French War College and of the U.S. Staff and Command School, he commanded the Fourth Army before being named army chief of staff. As president, he quickly assembled a generally centrist-conservative Cabinet with relatively high technical qualifications in which civilians were numerically preponderant. Bulhões was retained as finance minister, with National Democratic Union (UDN) senator and former Minas Gerais governor Milton Campos as justice minister. Juarez Távora returned to the Transportation Ministry, a position he had held more than thirty years before; Roberto Campos was named planning minister; and Bahian UDN Deputy Luíz Viana Filho, a distinguished academic figure, became presidential chief of staff. Viana Filho, who would still be a leading figure in the Senate in 1990, had been a congressman during the 1934–1937 period and again from 1946 until his Cabinet appointment.

The first period of this administration was characterized, on the surface at least, by a continuation of "clean-up" activities, with hundreds of individuals linked to the Goulart regime remaining under arrest—although most of the more important leaders had been able to find asylum in foreign embassies and begin the steady procession into political exile.[6]

With Castelo Branco publicly manifesting considerable reluctance, his originally interim term was extended by nearly fourteen months to March 15, 1967, through amendment of the constitution on July 22. A companion measure extended electoral eligibility to the military.[7] An amendment eliminating the cash payment requirement for land expropriations was also passed, but a proposal to extend the vote to illiterates failed to gain congressional approval. Yet even these reforms stirred up some controversy within the military—where old divisions began quickly to reemerge over the question of direction and dimensions of change. In 1960–1961 the leaders of the November 11 movement—Lott and Denys—had chosen opposite directions, and many of the Vargas period cleavages had been overridden, although not forgotten, in the face of the Goulart administration's assault on the principles of military discipline and hierarchy in early 1964.

Divisions Within the Military

This artificially high degree of cohesion in the armed forces was further bolstered in April by the expulsion of the small but previously influential group of leftist nationalists—a total of just over 2,000 military officers were called before inquiry boards to justify their prior actions and 149 of those involved in the mutinous events of March 25–27 received five-year prison sentences. But the seeds of new divergences were already germinating. At the senior level the original intransigent conspirators of the Mourão Filho, Guedes, et al. stripe deeply resented being deprived of the personal fruits of victory—as none of them received the top positions they felt their roles should have earned. They and others who hoped to compensate for this short shrift through the electoral road would break with Castelo Branco when the president frustrated their political ambitions.

More significant was the emergence of the hardliners, an influential group of younger officers of a generally radical rightist position. This "Linha Dura" faction enjoyed control initially over the large number of military police investigations (IPMs) set up under the junta to investigate alleged subversive activities during the defunct regime. When, against their advice, the president allowed his major discretionary powers under the Institutional Act to lapse on June 15, they became increasingly uneasy over the government's stress on moderation and rationality. They were particularly upset by public attention turning toward rectification of abuses committed by them in the heat and zeal of April and May—when by their standards hundreds if not thousands of "subversives" had not yet been rooted out. In fact, they called over 10,000 persons to testify, indicted almost 6,400 of them, and punished more than 2,100, with forced retirements from government service nearing 4,500— roughly 1,700 civilian and almost 2,800 military.[8]

Moreover, Castelo Branco's appeal to the "nonsubversive" Left to join in support of a program of reforms and the increasing prominence within the government of modernizing technocrats sat crossways in the hardliners' throats. For the "in" group of the Castelo Branco administration was the moderate, or Sorbonne, group, for whom the regrettable necessity of military exercise of the moderating power arose from basic flaws in the country's political structures and not as a result of evil men in public life who had subverted and corrupted the system.

Prior to the 1964 Revolution this generally more reflective and school-oriented group within the army had on several occasions come very close to having political power and even control of the government in their hands. Vargas's victory over Brigadier General Eduardo Gomes in 1950 had been a major disappointment in this regard, although the group's institutional base, the ESG, was still in its infancy at this time. With Juarez Távora as perhaps the most influential figure in the Café Filho interregnum of 1954–1955, the Sorbonnists enjoyed substantial influence. This, however, was a caretaker regime, not one able or disposed to undertake major policy revisions or institutional reordering.

The 1955 elections held out promise of overcoming this obstacle to their updated version of the essential core of the *tenentist* tradition, but instead of electing Juarez Távora, they were forced to swallow the bitter pill of a Kubitschek victory. Subsequently the Quadros period was again one of frustration of high hopes. With Cordeiro de Farias as chief of the armed forces general staff and Golbery and Ernesto Geisel well placed on the presidential staff, the prospects seemed good for expansion of their influence—only to be dashed by the abrupt turn of events in August 1961 and Goulart's rise to power. Under this antithesis of their program (the Goulart administration), the ESG increasingly became a dumping ground for officers the administration preferred not to see in troop commands. With the triumph of the 1964 Revolution and the elevation to the presidency of one of their leaders, the Sorbonne group finally had an opportunity to play a dominant role in policy making.

Through the long association of its ESG-linked core with politicians, businessmen, industrialists, journalists, and bureaucrats who made up a majority of its students—as well as the central role of Golbery in IPES—the Sorbonne group appeared to have manpower adequate to its self-assumed task of thoroughly overhauling the nation's political and administrative institutions. Strongly anti-Communist, they could still distinguish between subversives and nationalist reformers—something the *duristas* (hardliners) rarely did. Although there were certain limits upon and rigidities within their worldview, it was much more sophisticated and cosmopolitan than that of either the military hardliners or the radical leftists of the Goulart regime.

Thus, it was not surprising that the Sorbonne group tended to look down on the historical plotters as lacking in political sense and to oppose the hardliners in preferring to retain as much of the normal order as possible, reforming and renovating the system rather than supplanting it by implanting a permanent military regime. But in the eyes of their rivals, who typically resented the academic accomplishments and perceived air of superiority of the Sorbonnists, the latter were trying to seize control of a movement they had joined at a late stage, were compromising with a corrupt political class, and were preserving discredited institutions.[9]

The Sorbonne elements, though generally convinced of their own abilities and understanding of national problems, had a more realistic view of the level of competence and experience required for complex governmental tasks than did the rest of the officer corps, whose careers had largely been with troop commands. This led them toward the concept of a fused technocracy rather than rule by a military caste. Whereas for their rightist rivals subversion and corruption were still the fundamental problems, for them it was essential to put the punitive phase of the revolution behind and come to grips with the underlying structural problems. During the second half of 1964 the president's technique of resisting hardline pressures as much as possible and, when forced to give ground, countering with reformist moves in other areas became well defined. Thus, in November Castelo Branco yielded to the hardliners' insistence that he remove Goiás Governor Mauro Borges Teixeira, but he followed this by insisting on holding the partial state elections as scheduled for October 1965. Subsequently the government's decision to play a leading role in the Inter-American Peace Force sent to the Dominican Republic in the wake of the civil war there and the ensuing U.S. intervention was well received by the hardliners.

Austerity, Institutional Reforms, and
Accentuated Dissension

Planning Minister Campos's emergency measures announced at the end of April had been glumly accepted as necessary in light of the country's financial chaos and galloping inflation. In his role of ambassador to the United States Campos had been a coauthor of the policies advocated by Dantas and Carvalho Pinto within the Goulart administration, and these were firmer applications of the measures put forth at that time plus a return to some of those Lucas Lopes and he had put into effect in 1958 only to see them scrapped by Kubitschek the following year, yet briefly readopted under Quadros.

When the Program of Government Economic Action (PAEG) was unveiled in mid-August, groans turned to screams of anguish. Feeling essentially free from the considerations of political feasibility that had constrained previous stabilization efforts—with which they had personally been associated from the Dutra administration on—Campos and Bulhões took a strictly technocratic approach to the complex and intractable problems of economic policy. The contrast with the past was less in the plans than in the determination to follow through on their implementation, as their architects were confident that this time they would receive full presidential backing instead of being sacrificed in the face of the inevitable and shrill protests from labor and producers.

Jesuit-educated and, by self-admission, prone to the "un-Brazilian" vice of excessive rationality, Campos was determined that for once a technically sound program would not be diluted and compromised away in the face of interest-group criticism. With like-minded economists, rather than bankers or businessmen, in the other top-echelon economic policy positions—including the Bank of Brazil—a homogeneous and largely harmonious team was in charge of economic policy (a rarity in Brazil to this day). Most important, however, was Castelo Branco's unwavering support for containment of inflation as the government's first priority. Yet this containment was seen consistently as a means to the end of preparing the country for renewed growth. Indeed, in comparison to the early or late 1980s, GDP growth of 3.4 percent in 1964, 2.4 percent for 1965, 6.7 percent in 1966, and 4.2 percent the next year appears quite positive for a period of adjustment and austerity.

The goals of the PAEG were not in themselves highly controversial. The rate of economic growth was to be restored to a level of 7 percent annually, with regional, sectoral, and social imbalances ameliorated. But the emphasis upon disinflation, with virtual price stability targeted for 1966, and the containment of government expenditures were not palatable to important sectors of society who wished to continue receiving the breaks, benefits, and subsidies to which they had become accustomed. Hence not only were individuals of a nationalist and socialist orientation opposed to the administration's plans to rationalize and open up—including internationally—the

Brazilian quasi-capitalist system, but many businessmen also frowned upon the major readjustments implied by this determination.[10]

Certainly, austerity measures like those implemented by the Campos team are never politically popular. Moreover, in a country where economic nationalism had been heavily stressed for the better part of a generation, the repeal of several nationalist provisions of Goulart-period legislation—particularly limitations on profits sent abroad and expropriation of public utilities—gave rise to protests that the Brazilian economy was again being handed over to North American imperialism.

The government's hopes of sharply reducing inflation while returning to a high rate of economic expansion depended heavily upon international financial assistance and a sharp increase in foreign investment, so a series of actions were taken designed to elicit a favorable response from the Johnson administration and business circles in the United States. The latter's skepticism as to the probable brief duration of the Campos policies, based on the Kubitschek and Quadros experiences, contributed to a situation in which Castelo Branco committed himself to complete and continued support for his planning minister. Indeed, the cassation of Kubitschek's political rights and the ensuing extension of Castelo Branco's own presidential mandate were done in part to assuage such doubts.

Well aware that elections in key states were a mere six months away and that the positive results of its economic sanitation measures would be slow in coming, the administration commemorated the revolution's first anniversary by issuing a series of decrees implementing the basic agrarian reform legislation enacted the preceding November. The Brazilian Institute of Agrarian Reform (IBRA) and the National Institute of Agricultural Development (INDA) were more adequately structured, and criteria were established for the survey of landholdings and the classification of appropriate productive uses needed before thought could be given to possible large-scale redistribution of underutilized properties.[11]

Then, in the face of not only warnings from the hardliners, but also cautions by Costa e Silva as well, the president went ahead with balloting in March for a new São Paulo mayor—a major step toward maintaining important participant-representative features of the regime. The results of this first test justified Castelo Branco's confidence, as Brigadier General Faria Lima, once closely associated with Quadros but a firm supporter of the 1964 Revolution, was the winner in a campaign in which local issues appeared to take precedence over national questions.

While those opposed to a reopening of political competition so soon issued dire forecasts, Castelo pushed ahead with direct elections of governors in the eleven states where they had been elected in 1960. (Governors elected in 1962 had terms through 1966.) Magalhães Pinto, who had gone ahead with a one-year extension of his term designed to strengthen his presidential possibilities, broke with Castelo Branco when the president reversed this decision by a docile state legislature. So with strengthened legislation on ineligibility, designed to allay military fears that some yet "unpunished" subversives and *corruptos* might run, the regime headed toward an electoral test of public reaction to its brand of tutelary democracy and institutional renovation.

Although the labor movement, with many of its key unions still under government intervention, was causing no real difficulty, and other dem- onstrations of opposition to the regime were small and sporadic, the government's popularity was not high. Moreover, the broadened and inten- sified debate engendered by the electoral campaigns led not to the regime's desired renewal of political leadership and move toward increased normalcy, but resulted instead in the implantation of a more authoritarian regime armed with emergency powers—a process that would be repeated three years later as again a regime of qualified participation would give way to one of arbitrary authority and hardline hegemony.

The 1965 Elections and the Revolution
Within the Revolution

Although the government realized the dangers involved in permitting balloting at a time when the full brunt of deflationary policies was being felt by the electorate, this was considered a worthwhile risk. With the revolution itself as one of the most important political issues, the regime had a great stake in these gubernatorial races, and it developed a sophisticated strategy to minimize the chances of a major setback. Heretics Lacerda and Magalhães Pinto would be eliminated as presidential contenders through the defeat of their hand-picked choices by individuals who—although nominally from opposition ranks—could be counted upon to collaborate with the federal government and to cause far fewer problems for it than would these politically ambitious governors. For most voters the sharply rising cost of living, scarcity of basic foodstuffs, and shortcomings in public services led to a widespread feeling that the government's economic policies were failing. Hence the opposition candidates won in both Guanabara and Minas Gerais.[12]

As "revolutionary" candidates carried the day in most of the other states, when the dust settled regime strategists could make a reasonable case that, taking all factors into account, things had not gone badly. But public perception was that of a repudiation of the administration in major urban centers. The inner circle and the most politically savvy outsiders knew that the isolation and undermining of Lacerda and Magalhães Pinto—two of the cardinals of the revolution—were the regime's priority goals. The vast majority, however, saw only that UDN candidates in the most important states where voting took place—Minas Gerais and Guanabara—had been trounced by at least nominal opponents of the government elected on the strength of PTB as well as PSD votes. Operationally crucial was the fact that hardline officers, convinced from the beginning that the elections were unwise and unnecessary, viewed the results as too similar to those of 1954, which had served as a precursor to the return of the Vargas crowd behind the Kubitschek-Goulart ticket the following year.

The Second Institutional Act

Thus a military crisis, albeit relatively quiet and largely concealed from the general public, developed as soon as the trend was clear from the early Guanabara returns—for Francisco Negrão de Lima was a Kubitschek man, as was Israel Pinheiro in Minas Gerais, and the former president had dramatically returned from sixteen months of exile on the morning of the elections. Never a good loser, Lacerda feverishly incited his still numerous contacts within hardline ranks to take matters into their own hands. With extreme right-wing elements calling for Castelo Branco's ouster, the war minister worked out the basic outlines of a compromise that included his pledge that the government would move strongly to reinvigorate the revolution and would not hesitate to issue a second institutional act if the situation required such a drastic step. As a result, while Castelo Branco retained the presidency, Costa e Silva consolidated his position as the leading contender to be his successor.

Then as Congress failed to come up with the three-fifths majority needed to pass a series of constitutional amendments significantly strengthening the executive's hand, a second sweeping Institutional Act was indeed decreed on October 27. Under its provisions, presidents would henceforth be chosen by Congress and the existing political parties were dissolved.[13] Certainly the government was correct in its assessment that they could not rely on a wavering and uncertain PSD; the administration's desire to weaken the influence of governors—particularly those elected in 1962—was also understandable. What was regrettable, particularly in the light of further developments, was the Castelo Branco government's failure to really change the nature rather than just the number of political parties. There would not be another opportunity to do this during the ensuing quarter century.

Despite the sacrifice of important features of democratic formalism, the Castelo Branco government was far from finished by the "coup within a coup," which forced it to abandon a strategy of reforming the political infrastructure while permitting the components of that infrastructure to function with some degree of autonomy. Tutelage moved closer to control in the president's dealings with Congress and political groupings, but with regard to pursuit of other fundamental goals—including those in the economic realm—Castelo Branco's remained far from a lame duck administration. Indeed, in the sixteen and a half months remaining of his mandate, Castelo Branco accomplished considerably more in the legislative field than he had prior to the October crisis.[14]

By late November a foundation was laid for a two-party system by providing for provisional registration of parties sponsored by at least 120 members of the lower house and a score of senators. For reasons of conviction or convenience 254 of the former and 43 of the latter joined the government-sponsored National Renovating Alliance (ARENA), giving opposition elements no choice but to also band together in a single organization, the Brazilian Democratic Movement (MDB). The MDB had but 21 senators and 150 deputies, yet these included such a wide range of interests and ideological positions that the opposition party would never achieve a significant degree of unity and coherence (this being exactly the result desired by Castelo Branco's brain trust). All but a handful of the UDN, most of the PSD, and a majority of the minor party legislators joined ARENA; the backbone of the MDB was the old PTB plus PSD elements who could not coexist at the state level with long-time UDN rivals. Rio Grande do Sul Senator Daniel Krieger was entrusted with the task of shaping ARENA into a reliable base of parliamentary and electoral support for the regime.[15]

Costa e Silva formally launched his presidential candidacy in early January amidst rumors that many of Castelo Branco's key advisors were still looking for an alternative candidate. After a substantial reshaping of his Cabinet, sparing the economic side, the president agreed to support his war minister's bid for the ARENA nomination in return for a commitment to continuance of his program, particularly in the economic-financial sphere, and selection of a war minister capable of securing military unity.[16] Then on February 5, Institutional Act No. 3 implanted indirect selection of governors, scheduled congressional elections for November 15, and eliminated election of mayors of capital cities.

Castelo Branco thus yielded significantly to the hardline pressures he had resisted the previous year and established a system—subsequently perfected by a series of complementary acts—under which the government candidates for president and governor could not lose, thus avoiding another crisis of the October 1965 variety. In late May Costa e Silva was formally nominated by ARENA—to the chagrin of many of the president's advisors, both military and civilian. Then on June 5 Adhemar de Barros was removed as governor of São Paulo, a move that signified increased centralization and concentration of power in the hands of the federal executive as well as elimination of a powerful focus of efforts to complicate the presidential succession.

In the face of administration threats to limit severely Congress's role in shaping the new constitution or even to bypass that role entirely, the MDB legislators adopted obstructionist tactics. At this juncture Lacerda returned to the political wars with a masterful (diabolically so in the eyes of the administration) interview in *Visão*. Also in the second half of August, Goulart expressed his support for a "broad front" of opposition elements including both Lacerda and Kubitschek—the two of whom added fuel to the fire by issuing a letter saying that approval of Castelo Branco's proposed constitution would be "an international humiliation."[17]

Neither Authoritarian nor Democratic

Personally selected in most cases by the president without much regard for their electoral appeal, the twelve new governors chosen on September 3 were relatively young and came chiefly from within incumbent administrations.[18] Costa e Silva's election—given the rules newly established for this limited balloting—was never in doubt, and the MDB decided not to run a candidate. On October 3 the former war minister received the vote of 252 ARENA deputies and the party's 40 senators, plus 3 independents. Whereas the congressmen voting for him had received just over 4.6 million votes in 1962, compared to 2.8 million for the abstaining MDB legislators, opposition figures who had been stripped of office represented another 1.5 million 1962 electors. Thus, on his sixty-fourth birthday Marshal Costa e Silva became Brazil's president-elect, but under circumstances closely paralleling those of Floriano's selection nearly three-quarters of a century before.

When Congress showed signs of unacceptable independence, Castelo Branco canceled the mandates of six federal deputies, serving notice that he would not permit individuals whom the regime considered subversive or corrupt to stand for reelection. Then as the Chamber continued to manifest indications of defiance, the president issued a complementary act placing Congress in recess until a week after the November 15 elections.

The existence of some 22.4 million registered voters in a population of 85 million reflected not only population growth, but also the significantly higher literacy rate among those who had turned eighteen since 1962 and the provision in the 1965 electoral code requiring registration for non-employed women. São Paulo (4.9 million), Minas Gerais (3.1 million), Rio Grande do Sul (over 1.9 million), Guanabara and Paraná (1.5 million each), Bahia (1.4 million), and Rio de Janeiro state (more than 1.3 million) together contained nearly two-thirds of the national electorate. When the results were in, the government had strengthened its hand, electing roughly two-thirds of the new Chamber and eighteen of twenty-two senators. ARENA had won 277 seats in the lower house on well over 8.7 million votes, while the MDB's nearly 4.9 million votes were good for 132 seats. Yet in Guanabara, Rio de Janeiro, and Rio Grande do Sul the opposition held decisive edges, and in São Paulo the MDB candidates ran a close second. Even in the states where ARENA won big, the MDB did quite well in the larger cities, with the government's pluralities coming from the traditional rural areas.[19]

Combined with the fact that all governors were now either from ARENA ranks or inclined toward it, the government party appeared almost as hegemonic as its counterpart in Mexico. Yet a close look at the results showed that ARENA was weakest in the modernizing urban centers—where the MDB rolled up impressive margins—and that the large proportion of blank or null protest votes cast by the most militant elements of the opposition actually aided the ARENA candidates by weakening their MDB challengers. At the state level ARENA came away with 731 legislative seats on a total of just over 9 million votes, while the MDB won 345 state assembly posts on the strength of over 5 million votes. Still, in many states this performance by ARENA represented an improvement over the existing situation. Yet the party would not figure highly in the regime's plans, as Congress was to have a very limited role compared to the centralization of decision-making authority in the hands of the executive and the latter's concentration on "technocratic" rather than traditional political considerations.

At a higher and more sophisticated level, at least if the relative states of national development are not taken into account, the real situation came to fundamentally resemble that of the Estado Novo despite the fact that this time the national legislature continued to function—albeit under significant restraints. For the indirectly chosen governors were interventors in almost every respect except in name.

Even before the elections, the regime had been shaping up a new constitution, rebuffing congressional desires for a significant voice in the process. Thus, while Costa e Silva was beginning to organize his new administration—mixing old allies from his April 1964 interim government with elements that had subsequently become alienated from Castelo Branco—the president and his advisors undertook to institutionalize as much of their blueprint for a reformed and renovated political system as the limited time remaining to them would allow. To this end, on the eve of the reopening of Congress Castelo Branco issued a series of nearly forty decree laws. On December 6 a draft constitution freshly reshaped by the pen of Medeiros Silva was unveiled to hot criticism from the MDB and icy glares from the more liberal elements of ARENA itself.[20] Institutional Act No. 4, issued the following day, summoned Congress to meet in special session over the holidays to approve the new constitution. This approval was given after minor revisions by a vote of 223 to 110 in the Chamber and 37 to 17 with 7 abstentions in the Senate, but 107 ARENA deputies expressed grave reservations and their intention to seek fundamental changes once the new administration was in office—after the government's power to cancel their mandates had expired.

The president demonstrated his determination to govern to the end and to clear the ground for his successor by suspending the political rights of an additional ninety individuals during his last weeks in office. In addition to a major administrative reform and a new currency, Castelo Branco also promulgated by executive fiat a tough national security law incorporating important elements of the Sorbonne doctrine into the nation's juridical structure.

Despite significant limitations on political competition, Castelo Branco turned over to his old classmate a Brazil in substantially better shape than had been the case when he took over the helm from Costa e Silva nearly three years before. Indeed, inflation was finally coming under control and the process of accelerating growth—which would be sustained through the next two presidencies—had begun.

Costa e Silva and the Failure of "Humanization"

The inauguration of the fairly amiable but essentially quite ordinary Costa e Silva ushered in a fourth stage in the military's post-1964 exercise of power—the first stage being the junta, the second signified by Castelo Branco as would-be normalizer, and the third characterized by the armed forces as a reluctant builder of the foundation for prolonged military rule.

Costa e Silva's abbreviated term would be the first of three periods during which the presidency would be occupied by someone committed to the idea of the armed forces as the country's proper and semipermanent ruler, for Costa e Silva was clearly the choice of the hardliners.[21] Moreover, his premature departure from power would be followed by a short-lived junta that would bequeath a full term to General Emílio Garrastazú Médici— under whom the regime would be the most authoritarian, although this was partially masked by the "economic miracle." Only after the end of this administration in 1974 would the road start up from authoritarian depths through slow evolution toward more competitive politics with "decompression" under General Ernesto Geisel and "opening" during the subsequent term of General João Baptista de Oliveira Figueiredo.

Though during the military's second decade in power the issue of arbiter or ruler—moderating power or direct holder of the reins of power—would again come to the fore, as of 1967 it appeared to be resolved in favor of the broader and deeper role. Costa e Silva's government would mark the culmination of five and a half years on the slippery downward road to the most institutionalized form of authoritarianism, the "National Security State," which would remain for about an equal period of time before twice as long was required for its dismantling. Thus military rule in its purest and most naked form would be in full flower only from late 1969 through early 1974. But the thirty months of Costa e Silva's government provided that military rule with a solid foundation.

Dominance by the Duros

Ironically, Costa e Silva's outgoing personality and "hail-fellow well-met" style—contrasted to the austere aloofness of Castelo Branco and his quasi-puritanical aides—led many Brazilians to expect him to loosen the reins, a prospect that had been implied by his campaign talk of "humanizing" the revolution. Yet those whose expectations lay in this direction would shortly be bitterly disappointed, for the departure of the Sorbonne generals from office opened the way for the resurgence of the hardliners.

By late 1967 Brazil would experience unrest greater than that at any point of the Castelo Branco government; further deterioration would lead to a crisis situation in the latter half of 1968 that would result in another coup-within-a-coup, issuance of a stringent Institutional Act No. 5, dissolution of Congress, and cassation of many individuals whose actions during the first phases of the revolution had marked them as moderates and liberal constitutionalists. Far from a more humane tutelary democracy—no matter what the new president's personal desires may have been—Brazil under Costa e Silva was to slide right into the type of unrestricted military dictatorship that Castelo Branco had largely been able to avoid.[22]

The personnel of the Costa e Silva government included a fair proportion of individuals who had become critics of Castelo Branco. A line officer accustomed to troop command, in contrast with his predecessor's long experience in school and general staff positions, the president was relatively adept at routine military politics but inadequately prepared for other areas of national policy making. Moreover, his executive staff clearly lacked the intellectual qualities of Castelo Branco's advisors. Brigadier General Jayme Portela as chief military aide had neither the governmental experience nor the leadership qualities of the man he replaced, future President Ernesto Geisel, while General Médici, who took over as head of the National Intelligence Service (SNI) from Golbery do Couto e Silva, its founder, could not rival the intellectual ability or political astuteness of this exceptional figure—a fact that would become clearer during Médici's subsequent tenure as president.

Although Magalhães Pinto brought a long political career to the Foreign Ministry, this was not a position from which he could exercise much influence over domestic policy, and presidential chief of staff Rondon Pacheco was a run-of-the-mill congressman. Thus the way was open for thirty-eight-year-old Antônio Delfim Netto, a Paulista economist, to quickly emerge as the new administration's leading light.[23] Presiding over a reasonably homogeneous economic team featuring Hélio Beltrão as planning minister, Delfim would move ahead while the rest of the government was painfully slow to define policies and programs.

The Frente Ampla, or "broad front" of opposition forces, with Lacerda as its moving force, had offered itself to Costa e Silva as an alternative base of support should he wish to break out of the political straitjacket of ARENA bequeathed to him by Castelo Branco. Rebuffed, Frente Ampla moved quickly to probe the government's intentions and present the regime with the dilemma of having to choose between campaign commitments to normalization and the hardliners' insistence upon revolutionary continuity. To this point many participants in the political game viewed Lacerda's alienation from the government as a falling out with Castelo Branco and the Sorbonne group rather than an irrevocable break with the revolution itself. With Brizola in exile, Lacerda was probably the most controversial figure in Brazilian public life, having in the course of his career assumed positions spanning from one end of the political spectrum to the other.

The brilliant son of an aristocratic radical father, Lacerda was a paternalistically populist intellectual whose political successes had been more oratorical and parliamentary than organizational. Making his mark first as a young Communist journalist when Maurício de Lacerda was at his peak as the tribune of the people, by 1946 he was the country's most widely discussed columnist and the next year was elected to the municipal council of the then Federal District. Swept into the Chamber of Deputies in 1950, he quickly emerged as Vargas's most caustic critic. After polling a record 160,000 votes in 1954—all this within the conservative UDN—he was reelected again in 1958, and in 1960 became the first elected governor of newly created Guanabara state, a position from which he was highly instrumental in both Quadros's rise and fall. Impressed in 1962 with arch-foe Brizola's electoral triumph as a carpetbagger in the former Federal District, Lacerda worked tirelessly for the ouster of the Goulart regime while becoming increasingly determined to broaden his own political base from the urban middle class to embrace the workers and the lower-class social groups politically orphaned by the 1964 purge of leftist politicians.

Far from a centrist in the usual connotation of a tendency toward conciliation, the complex and volatile Lacerda was also neither a reactionary nor a revolutionary. The requirements of being a successful urban populist in a repeatedly changing system help explain his political inconsistencies much more than does "opportunism." Although his tactics and message changed, his objectives remained fundamentally unaltered—to gain popular election to the presidency, which he had seen held by a series of individuals he considered of distinctly inferior abilities. Thus he would have to be against any government whose succession options excluded his candidacy— especially a regime inclined to perpetuate military rule.

The political balance within the revolution was upset abruptly on July 18 with Castelo Branco's death in a mid-air collision just outside Fortaleza— an event that resolved the struggle for the loyalty of ARENA leaders in favor of the president. It also brought disarray to the ranks of the Frente Ampla leadership, who that very day had decided upon a strategy of exploiting the cleavage between Castelistas and the Costa e Silva administration.[24] Shortly thereafter the government barred Lacerda from television, but he continued his devastating attacks upon the government in the press— a fact that influenced the regime's determination to show firmness rather than any flexibility that might be mistaken for weakness. In late September Lacerda managed to create a climate of tension and expectation through a dramatic trip to Uruguay to establish a political alliance with historical archenemy Goulart as a further extension of the opposition front into a "popular union for direct elections."[25]

Although it was really only an alliance at the top—mutual distrust still reigned within this melange of Lacerdistas, Juscelinistas, Janistas, and Janguistas (Goulart supporters)—the government viewed this agreement as a potentially dangerous threat to be neutralized, if not destroyed, at any cost, even though Brizola had denounced the agreement as an unholy alliance. ARENA spokesmen who argued in favor of meeting the challenge through popularization of the government by means of wage concessions, a return to direct elections, and a gradual reduction of military influence were promptly squelched—but some of them would emerge again in 1984 to join with the moderate opposition in support of redemocratization through the election of Tancredo Neves. Indeed, by the final months of 1967 a majority of ARENA congressmen disagreed with basic elements of the administration's programs, so the executive branch found itself faced with a significant end-of-the-session parliamentary revolt much as Castelo Branco had experienced in 1965 and 1966. When Lacerda renewed his attacks in the new year, he was banned from radio.

While the Frente Ampla was consuming a very great proportion of the opposition's energies during 1967, developments of greater lasting significance and with even broader ramifications had been taking place, particularly within the student movement and the Church. To a more pronounced degree than in 1963–1964, these two institutions would be critical elements in a radicalization and polarization of positions that this time would result in the implantation of an openly dictatorial regime. Though friction between the government and student groups had begun immediately after the 1964 seizure of power, this conflict had been brought under control through dissolution of existing student organizations.[26] As president-elect, Costa e Silva had spoken bravely of a meaningful dialogue with students, but instead his government quickly experienced increasing friction with them. Misunderstanding and conflict developed over the government's efforts to modernize the educational system through a series of agreements with the United States, leading to violent clashes in April and May 1967, with the Church drawn into the fray during July and August.

Church-State Tensions

During the second half of the year increasing attention focused upon the escalating frictions between the regime and the Church as well as on dissension within that institution. Under the empire the Church had depended heavily upon the state, a fact demonstrated by Pedro's sharp pulling on the reins during the 1872–1875 Church-state conflict regarding the Religious Question (discussed in Chapter 2). A period of increased vitality ensued after the Church's disestablishment in 1890, despite its inadequate staffing and structure, with important modernizing trends apparent after 1916, but as a bulwark of the Vargas regime it again began to receive substantial public funds. Through the two decades of strong leadership by Dom Sebastião Leme, archbishop and cardinal of Rio de Janeiro (1921–1942), the Church's attentions remained largely focused on the urban middle class. Even after Leme's death, the Church remained an essentially conservative force marked by a strong anti-Communist orientation.[27]

Concerned over the inroads being made by Protestantism and spiritualism in the rapidly growing urban areas and increasingly aware of the social problems vitally affecting the gradually awakening masses, during the 1950s the Church began to undergo significant changes. The most obvious outward manifestations of this trend were Popular Action (AP), the Catholic University Youth (JUC), the Young Catholic Workers (JOC), the Basic Education Movement (MEB), and the Peasant Leagues—all spheres of activity involving considerable interaction and cooperation with Marxist elements.[28]

The turbulent and polarizing events of the early 1960s impacted heavily upon the Church and contributed to its internal divisions. The development of relatively distinct currents of conservatives, defensive modernizers, and reformers was not only a response to societal change within Brazil, but was also related to developments within the international Roman Catholic Church. Pope John XXIII's encyclicals *Mater et Magistra* in 1961 and *Pacem in Terris* two years later, in conjunction with the work of the Second Vatican Council (1962–1965, also known as Vatican II), gave encouragement to the more progressive elements within the Brazilian hierarchy. The conservative modernizers remained in control of the Church's higher echelons, but in the aftermath of the Medellín (1968) meeting of the Latin American Episcopal Conference (CELAM) the reformers came to dominate the National Conference of Brazilian Bishops (CNBB). Indeed, the advocates of "liberation theology" and a radical preferential option for the poor found a highly placed champion in Dom Aloísio Lorscheider, the dominant figure of the CNBB in the 1970s, and in Dom Paulo Evaristo Arns, after 1973 the influental cardinal of São Paulo.

Founded in 1952, the CNBB was heavily influenced by its secretary-general, the progressive Dom Helder Câmara of Recife. In 1964 a conservative slate headed by then Archbishop of São Paulo Dom Agnelo Rossi defeated the reformists, but by the late 1960s a significant proportion of the moderates became alienated from the regime. By and large they came to accept the view that the Church needed to speak out for the powerless under an authoritarian regime that had shut off most channels of opposition and protest. This viewpoint was reflected in the 1968 election of Dom Aloísio Lorscheider as secretary-general of the CNBB.

Accustomed to viewing the Catholic Church as a bulwark of stability, many in the armed forces confused its newly found social conscience with the giving of aid and comfort to subversive agitators.[29] Though the numerically predominant moderate current within the religious hierarchy was not inclined to mount a struggle against the government or even to condemn the regime for injustices that had not been corrected, it was not willing to forgo its right to speak out in the future. Many Catholic leaders felt the tutelary nature of the regime accentuated the Church's role as the interpreter of popular sentiments that were in danger of not being heard in the clamor of polarizing politics. Then, too, churchmen demonstrated a tendency to defend fellow priests when they might be under attack even if they did not entirely approve of these fellow priests' actions.

At the end of its first year in power and the fourth anniversary of the revolution, the Costa e Silva government experienced a serious breakdown of meaningful communication with both the Church and students, which deeply buried the feelings of relief and expressions of hope that had predominated less than a year earlier. Marshal Mario Poppe de Figueiredo had called for the restoration of direct elections in 1970 to be followed by amnesty the following year, and Lacerda claimed that General Portela rather than the president was really running the government. Then a relatively small student protest exploded into rioting as the fatal police shooting of a young student gave the militants the martyr and symbol they had been lacking. As sympathy demonstrations spread to other cities, the government chose to treat the protests as part of a subversive plot, using this "plot" as a pretext to close off the channels of normal political disagreement by banning the Frente Ampla—although the regime resisted hardline demands for a new institutional act. Whereas in March liberalization seemed possible, by April the regime was closing up and hardening in the direction of an Argentine-like authoritarianism. Clashes between students and the security forces escalated in scale and intensity, while the extreme Left began terrorist actions.

Prior to the 1964 Revolution, the Communist movement in Brazil had been divided into the Moscow-oriented PCB, the pro-Chinese PCdoB, and the Revolutionary Workers' Party (Trotskyite)—the POR(T). Moreover, a group of students and journalists grouped around the publication *Política Operária* of the Marxist Revolutionary Movement (ORM) became known as POLOP. During the Castelo Branco period the left-wing Catholics of Popular Action (AP) became further radicalized.[30] By 1968 only the PCB and the orthodox Trotskyites still clung to the peaceful road. In late 1967 yet another significant schism had taken place in the PCB, with a Cuban-influenced faction headed by Carlos Marighella, Mário Alves, and Joaquim Câmara Ferreira being expelled.[31]

Part of these elements founded the National Liberating Action (ALN) and carried out a large number of bank robberies. Others established the Revolutionary Brazilian Communist Party (PCBR), with a few joining the PCdoB instead.[32] The Red Wing (Ala Vermelha) of the PCdoB—with roots going back to 1966 as did those of the Revolutionary Communist Party (PCR)—turned to armed action, as did factions of POLOP that took the names of National Liberation Command (COLINA) and Popular Revolutionary Vanguard (VPR). These subsequently merged in mid-1969 into the Armed Revolutionary Vanguard-Palmares (VAR-Palmares), which army Captain Carlos Lamarca and his small band of followers then joined.[33] Hence, divided as was the extraparliamentary opposition in 1968, they had greatly increased both their inclination and capability to use violent tactics. This tendency would, however, meet with a more than offsetting escalation of repression with tragic human results. Indeed, a first small-scale guerrilla effort, launched in November 1966, had been stamped out by March 1967.[34]

From Confrontation to the Edge of Conflict

The opening of the second half of the 1968 legislative year found Congress in much the kind of insubordinate mood as the preceding August. Amnesty for students and strikers was actively debated while the president called for "understanding and tranquility." Although the amnesty bill was eventually defeated by a vote of 198 to 145, no fewer than thirty-five ARENA legislators rebelled against party discipline and crossed the aisle to vote in favor of this anti-government measure. (Leaders of this ARENA faction would be among the first to be deprived of their mandates following the denouement of the year-end crisis.) Then August 19 brought a triple bombing of political police headquarters in São Paulo, followed shortly by arrest of students there and in Brasília who were supposed members of an alleged terrorist ring—with violent sympathy demonstrations resulting in Rio de Janeiro.

By mid-1968, nearly a year after Castelo Branco's death, the complex pattern of military politics—both on the level of factions and cliques and in terms of doctrinal differences—had undergone significant modification. The distinction between Sorbonne and hardline had become much less clear and very possibly no longer meaningful for officers below those lieutenant colonels who had already attended the Army General Staff and Command School (ECEME). For captains and majors, of whom only about a third could look forward to being selected for that institution, which opened the door to the higher career ranks, popular discontent was a more immediate concern than it was for their superiors, who had been more thoroughly indoctrinated into the mysteries of Brazilian national security doctrine.

The content of the military's internal education system had been instrumental in determining the political orientation of the armed forces since the positivism of the academy in the 1870s gave rise to republicanism within the army. Now it would again prove decisive in the cleavages and misunderstandings that would spell an end to the last chance for Brazil to avoid a long authoritarian night, for a type of neo-Florianism in modern dress was becoming resurgent—much as had been the case in the 1920s with the *tenentes*.[35] The *tenentes*, in part as a result of their indoctrination with Hermes's brand of liberal democratic ideals reinforced by the French Military Mission, four decades later were still attached to the formal trappings of representative processes.

Thus Castelo Branco had striven to maintain as much as possible of the formal institutions of representative government even while centralizing, concentrating, and strengthening executive authority, but he and Costa e Silva represented the end of the generation whose political socialization had followed this course. The active duty generals of 1968 were a mixed transitional group in this regard, while the colonels had gone through the ECEME during the Cold War period—having perhaps been cadets at the time of World War II and junior officers through the turbulent 1950s.[36]

At the level of doctrine, the ESG integrated development and national security as "the two complementary, although distinct sides of the exercise of National Power," but in practice the two were not so easily harmonized.[37] In late August a meeting of the national security council to discuss the "National Strategic Concept" revealed the existence of two rival, almost antagonistic, groups within the Cabinet—Interior Minister General Afonso de Albuquerque Lima was quite clearly at odds with the finance and planning ministers. It was one thing to compile a laundry list of "Permanent National Objectives" but quite another to transform these into prioritized "Essential Elements of Government Policy" that would influence budgetary shares.[38]

By the beginning of September there were abundant signs that Brazil was headed for another political crisis, but events during the ensuing three months were to guarantee that this crisis would involve more serious consequences than even the naysayers foresaw. Though a good part of the responsibility for renewed terrorism during this period must be borne by the leftist revolutionaries, the right-wing extremists were even more instrumental in escalating violence. By mid-1968 it was apparent that the revived Anti-Communist Movement (MAC) and the Communist-Hunting Command (CCC) were seeking to provoke a witch hunt by carrying out acts of terrorism for which the leftist opposition would be blamed.[39] Lack of firm presidential leadership was another major contributing factor to the growing sense of malaise. The president, resting at the old winter palace in Petrópolis, was being criticized as indolent, and the situation described by regime spokesmen as "normalcy" was viewed by less involved observers as more of a vacuum. Moreover, intense maneuvering was already going on with respect to the 1970 gubernatorial and senate races, accompanied by efforts of contending state forces to manipulate the November municipal elections to their advantage.

The question of presidential succession aroused civilist attitudes in some ARENA leaders while feeding ambitions and rivalries within the military. Early in October in a lecture at the ESG, Albuquerque Lima made clear his disagreement with the monetarist orientation of Delfim Netto and Beltrão, manifesting a desire for the military to have a greater say in economic policy and fiscal priorities.[40] Although in launching his candidacy independent of Costa e Silva's will Albuquerque Lima was following a strategy similar to that the president had himself employed, he was not working from nearly as strong a position. Far from being the army's ranking officer and holder of the pivotal service ministry, Albuquerque Lima faced serious competition in bidding for the presidency both from officers senior to him and from several below his rank but closer to the president. Among the latter were General Portela and Transportation Minister Colonel Mário David Andreazza (who left active duty in October 1968).

To add to the mounting tension, Brazil experienced another major student crisis when, on October 12, military and state authorities broke up the thirtieth Union of Students (UNE) congress in a small São Paulo town.[41] In this context of escalating violence, the elections in nearly 1,500 municipalities were all but anticlimactic. ARENA candidates won in most areas, with the balloting serving to underscore the vices and limitations of the system. Much more important was the brewing confrontation between Congress and the military. The crisis of April had demonstrated the dilemma of a military partially but not completely in power, and there were very clear signs of serious unrest among junior and mid-grade officers. In May, Brazilian Democratic Movement (MDB) Chamber Leader Mário Covas had accused the government of complicity in a plot to destroy the opposition. An insecure government was prone to exaggerate the subversive threat of demonstrations—which had been channeled into the streets because other effective means of protest had been foreclosed—and hence met them with excessive repression. A dominant part of the government and thus themselves at the heart of the crisis, the armed forces were not in a position to exercise their historical role of moderating power.

The incident that would result in the implantation of full dictatorship had its roots in the August 30 invasion of the University of Brasília by the army. On September 3 Deputy Márcio Moreira Alves, member of the MDB's radical wing and author of books and articles considered subversive by military authorities, issued an impassioned plea for a "boycott of militarism." Considering this not only to be insulting and unpatriotic, but also part of a concerted conspiracy to discredit the armed forces in the eyes of the public, the military demanded that the young journalist-politician be punished.[42] To this end in late October heavy pressure was placed on the Chamber to strip Moreira Alves of his parliamentary immunity. Miscalculations carried the day as the military felt sure that Congress would yield, but, just as it had during each of the preceding three years, the usually compliant lower house chose to demonstrate its independence near the end of the legislative session.

On December 12, with 372 members present (249 ARENA and 123 MDB), the Chamber voted down action against Moreira Alves by 216 to 141 with 12 abstentions. No fewer than ninety-four government party congressmen balked on a measure considered vital by the executive, convincing the military that Congress could not be allowed to function. Many of the officer corps carried a military concept of discipline over into the sphere of party politics, viewing abandonment of the government on a critical issue as the equivalent of desertion in the face of the enemy.[43] This viewpoint was, of course, completely alien to the amorphous nature of Brazilian parties. But in the minds of hardline officers punitive action was required.

The Fifth Institutional Act and the Defeat of Normalization

The government's reaction was both swift and devastating. As opposition leaders and militant critics of the regime were arrested by the hundreds, Institutional Act No. 5 appeared out of the portfolio of hardline Justice Minister Luíz Antônio da Gama e Silva. Draconian as the act's provisions were, the citizenry were reassured that these measures would be employed only to "directly and immediately confront the problems of restoring internal order and the international prestige of our country."[44] The act granted the president authority to recess legislative bodies, to intervene in the states without limit, to cancel elective mandates and take away political rights, to suspend constitutional guarantees with regard to civil service tenure, to confiscate property acquired by illicit means, and to set aside the protection afforded by habeas corpus—with all such actions beyond review by the courts. Complementary Act No. 38, decreed at the same time, closed Congress indefinitely. With the imposition of censorship even more stringent than that of the Estado Novo, a state burial had been given to both the promised "humanization" of the revolution and to any lingering hopes that the armed forces would soon return to an arbiter role.

From Purges to a Junta

In the administration's eyes, ARENA had failed to provide an effective parliamentary base for the regime, having "deteriorated" from occasional insubordination to desertion by a third of its members in the late 1968 crisis vote. When an interparty bloc let him down in October 1965, Castelo Branco had dissolved the existing parties and created ARENA; now the response to indiscipline would be a thorough purging of Congress before its eventual reopening.

The political heads of the first eleven congressmen rolled on December 30, with Lacerda being turned into a political nonperson as well. Mid-January witnessed a much more extensive purge as two senators had their mandates terminated along with thirty-five federal deputies—including Covas—accompanied by the forced retirements of three members of the Supreme Court (with two others quitting in protest). Institutional Act No. 6 on the last day of the month eliminated these five seats on the court, reducing the tribunal to eleven members as it had been constituted before Castelo Branco had "packed" it under the second Institutional Act. A week later another pair of senators and thirty-three more from the lower house were expelled—bringing the total to 77 of 409 in the Congress, including two-fifths of the MDB's representation and most of its leadership.[45] A number of prospective gubernatorial candidates unacceptable to the regime were included along with the most independent centrists from ARENA ranks. Five state legislatures were also recessed and—as in 1964—a General Investigations Commission (CGI) was set up to supervise the new host of IPMs constituted to root out and prosecute subversion. Eventually almost 1,400 individuals would be punished under "AI-5" (as the fifth Institutional Act became known in the lexicon of Brazilian political life). Then at the end of February Institutional Act No. 7 eliminated all elections scheduled to be held prior to November 1970.

Thus as Brazil entered the third year of Costa e Silva's administration and the sixth year of the 1964 Revolution, only the faintest traces of representative processes remained. On the economic side the situation was less bleak, as 1967's 4.2 percent rise in GDP had been followed by one of 9.8 percent in 1968 and inflation was kept to under 25 percent for two consecutive years.[46] But the collective resignation of ARENA leadership and further stiffening of the national security law underlined the continuing retrogression in the political sphere. Moreover, "fostering of animosity toward the armed forces" by civilians, even in private, was now punishable by the military courts.

Although most politicians—wrongly as events were soon to prove—viewed the developments of the preceding months as temporary measures arising from a crisis in which they had badly underestimated the military's "hypersensitivity," acute observers questioned whether the course of events might not indicate instead that the longed-for "normalcy" could be not only distant, but actually getting further away. The armed forces were clearly in control of the country but were deeply divided over how best to exercise the responsibility they had assumed; political parties were virtually non-functioning; stringent censorship was strongly resented by media accustomed to substantial freedom; universities were crippled by purges of distinguished faculty; and even the Catholic Church was torn between a fear of being identified as "subversive" and repugnance for the regime's repressive measures.[47]

A mass purge next hit the University of São Paulo—South America's finest institution of higher education—and the Foreign Ministry and more federal and a slew of state legislators were dismissed. Yet at the same time Vice-President Pedro Aleixo was entrusted with the task of drawing up consitutional changes to bring the regime into line with a state of law. Whereas Costa e Silva was inclined toward promulgation of a new constitution by the beginning of September, to be followed immediately by reopening of Congress, this would be going too far too fast for much of the military establishment. These same measures, however, were viewed as far too timid and half-hearted by the rivals of the military. In addition, Castelista elements were moving toward alliance with Albuquerque Lima's faction, a development that further undercut the president.[48] The growing extent of military division, owing in part to the relative ineffectiveness of Army Minister Aurélio de Lyra Tavares, was reflected in heavy criticism of the government by four-star General Augusto César Moniz de Aragão, who had presided over the Military Club from 1964 to 1968.[49]

Indications of turbulent political waters ahead were abundant—but the crisis was nearer at hand than anyone imagined. On August 31, 1969, the country awoke to the startling news that, in light of a cardiovascular problem that had incapacitated Costa e Silva, the three service ministers had formed a junta to govern the country temporarily. As this clearly signified that the armed forces had vetoed assumption of the presidential office by the civilian vice-president, it was obvious that for the fourth time since 1964 perceived progress toward political normalcy had been bulldozed into oblivion by military imposition of an even more arbitrary regime than had previously existed. It quickly became evident that the trend toward liberalization would be stopped dead in its tracks, if not reversed.

The dramatic kidnapping by leftist terrorists of U.S. Ambassador C. Burke Elbrick on September 4 created a major headache for the junta, but did not divert it from finding a military replacement for the president and installing the new executive for a full presidential term, rather than merely for the remainder of Costa e Silva's period.[50] Acting essentially as a "College of Cardinals," the ranking generals and admirals distilled the preferences of the flag officers serving under each of them, and a seven-man Armed Forces High Command on October 7 ratified the army's choice of General Médici, with Admiral Rademaker as vice-president. Runner-up Orlando Geisel would become army minister, with third-place finisher Antônio Carlos Muricy being kept on as chief of staff. Although he enjoyed substantial support from colonels and mid-grade officers, Albuquerque Lima was not able to overturn the junta-engineered selection of the former chief of the National Intelligence Service (SNI). Moreover, the extensive set of constitutional amendments— virtually equivalent to a new constitution—decreed ten days later increased centralization of power in the hands of the federal government, augmented the concentration of authority in the executive, and further extended the scope of the national security law and military courts.[51]

Subsequently, after more than ten months of enforced recess and minus the large number of its most determined members who had fallen afoul of the institutional act, Congress was summoned back to Brasília to ratify the military's decision. This it dutifully did by a vote of 293 against 76 abstentions—as the MDB had been reduced to but 66 seats from their post-election high of 127 by the repeated rounds of cassations. In all eighty-eight members of the lower house had been purged and another six resigned, while the Senate lost five members.

The Médici Years:
Growth, Stability, and Repression

A member of the 1927 military academy class and the academy commandant during the better part of the Goulart administration, Médici had left Brasília for command of the Third Army after his early 1969 promotion to the rank of four-star general. In addition to Army Minister Orlando Geisel, the strongmen in Médici's government would be holdover Finance Minister Delfim Netto and Presidential Chief of Staff João Leitão de Abreu (brother-in-law of Lyra Tavares). In a move that would have important consequences a decade later, Brigadier General João Figueiredo became chief military aide and secretary general of the security council—in 1979 he would become the last link in the chain of military presidents. "Project Brazil: Great Power" was to become the leitmotif of Médici's administration, a regime in which record rates of economic growth would coexist with ruthlessly effective repression of all but the most docile opposition.[52]

Consolidation of ARENA Hegemony

Municipal elections on November 30 in ten states saw the government party consolidate its hold over the smaller towns and rural areas, with the MDB deprived of an opportunity to score any major gains by the continued appointment of mayors of the state capitals. Feeling strengthened by the capture-killing of the armed opposition's chief leader, National Liberating Action leader Carlos Marighella, by security forces in São Paulo on November 4, Médici made it clear that in his concept of the "revolutionary state" the president retained extraordinary emergency powers both in his role as leader of the revolutionary movement as well as in his constitutional authority as chief executive.[53]

With economic growth having held at 9.5 percent in 1969—after an astounding jump to 9.8 percent in 1968 compared to only 4.2 percent for 1967—and continuing to accelerate, the regime found it quite easy to keep public attention focused away from politics during 1970. In this respect the World Cup soccer finals in Mexico helped significantly as, led by the incomparable Pelé (Edson Arantes do Nascimento), Brazil won its third title in the past four tries, making up for its poor showing in 1966. Identifying teamwork and collective will as the keys to this momentous victory, Médici astutely called for the application of these virtues to the "struggle for national development."[54]

In the afterglow of the *futebol* triumph, a 4 to 1 rout of Italy in the championship game, on October 3 all but one state legislature duly confirmed the governors hand-picked by Médici to provide—it was hoped by the regime—effective administration of technically sound programs, which were isolated insofar as possible from "distorting" political considerations.[55] Even Guanabara, where ARENA lacked a majority in the legislative assembly, provided no real problem for this most imperial of presidents. There Antônio de Padua Chagas Freitas, an old-line patronage populist who had earlier been a follower of Adhemar de Barros, controlled the MDB and became governor. His administration bespoke much more of Chicago's Mayor Richard Daly than of any of the reformist principles embodied in the party's program. Even more than had been the case with Negrão de Lima in 1966, from day one Chagas Freitas had close cooperation with Brasília in mind as a keystone of his administration.[56]

With the size of the Chamber of Deputies having been reduced, the basis for apportionment shifted to electorate instead of population, and with voters required to make their congressional and state legislative choices from the same party, national elections followed on November 15. Nearly 29 million registered voters, in a population approaching 95 million, gave the government party 220 of 310 lower house seats and victories in 40 of 46 Senate races. Among the fifty-nine ARENA senators (to only seven for the MDB) in the new Congress was José Ribamar Ferreira de Araújo Costa of Maranhão, known in the literary world and in political life as José Sarney, whom the vagaries of fate were to elevate to the presidency in 1985. On the strength of 10.9 million valid votes racked up by ARENA to but 4.8 million for the MDB in the Chamber voting, the balloting was a definite triumph for the regime.

Yet the MDB had won once again in Guanabara and had come fairly close in Rio Grande do Sul as well as running well in São Paulo city—thus demonstrating that the opposition retained a solid base in the most advanced regions of the country. Moreover, this provided an indication that the regime's political support might well have peaked, an interpretation bolstered by the abnormally high proportion of blank and nullified ballots as well as by the relatively low turnout of only 77.5 percent of those eligible to vote. Radical elements' claims to have been responsible for instigating the phenomenon of the "blank vote" in major urban centers were given some credibility by the continuing episodes of kidnapping of foreign diplomats, even though the government had arrested at least 4,000 suspected subversives during November alone.

Crushing Insurgency and Institutionalizing Technocracy

Determined to end armed opposition, the Médici government combined improved intelligence, more systematic use of torture, and more sophisticated counterinsurgency tactics to destroy the violent Left. Revolutionary Brazilian Communist Party (PCBR) leader Mário Alves had been eliminated in January 1970, and Marighella's successor as head of the ALN was captured in October and subsequently killed. Stuart Angel Jones, chief of the 8th of October Revolutionary Movement (MR-8), which had carried out the kidnapping of U.S. Ambassador Elbrick, met a similar fate in May 1971. Lamarca, who had left the reconstituted VPR for the MR-8, was hunted down and shot in the interior of Bahia in September, while the PCdoB's enclave in the southern reaches of the Amazon Basin near Araguaia would be exterminated in late 1973 and early 1974—the vast majority of the sixty-nine guerrillas met their deaths on the spot.[57]

Much of this success was obtained through resort to torture, which was masked behind a veil of censorship that allowed no mention of what was really going on with respect to internal security while trumpeting the regime's accomplishments in the economic sphere and its promises regarding social policy.[58] Not surprisingly, this was the heyday of out-of-control secret repressive organizations within the sprawling security apparatus and of officially condoned "death squads" among the civilian police, especially in São Paulo and Rio de Janeiro. Results were what mattered, and there was little concern in governing circles over the methods by which those results were being obtained. Operation Bandeirantes (OBAN) had in 1969 organized cooperation among intelligence agencies, security forces, and anticommunist businessmen—particularly in São Paulo. The subsequent creation of Internal Defense Operational Commands (CODIs) at the military region level, with Internal Operations Detachments (DOIs) to actually carry out repressive blows against urban subversives, further institutionalized the National Security State.[59] Behind the cloak of censorship, repression was brutally efficient, although it was not nearly on the same scale or marked with as great a disregard for human life as would be the case in Argentina once the military took over again from the Peronists in 1976 or as would be the case in Chile after September 1973.

Long viewed as the only truly national institution in Brazil aside from the armed forces, the Catholic Church became the chief critic of human rights violations and, to an increasing degree, of social injustice as well. Yet substantial elements of the hierarchy sympathized with the technocratic side of the regime, if not necessarily with its military pillars. Indeed, much of the religious hierarchy was preoccupied with their own problems of greatly inadequate manpower combined with the loss of formerly Catholic rural workers to Pentecostal sects of Protestantism and to *umbanda* (see Chapter 1) as these workers migrated to the outskirts of Brazil's cities.[60] Whereas the Church in the impoverished northeast worked to champion the interests of the downtrodden, that in the more developed southeast and south was only slowly responding to the challenge posed by the apparently institutionalized role of torture and repression.

The military-technocratic alliance as it enjoyed its heyday under Médici was based not as much upon a special affinity between the two groups— or even close policy agreement in all areas—as it was upon the foundation rock of mutual advantage. The military required a high rate of economic growth both to satisfy their ambitions to make Brazil into a country that would be taken seriously by the major powers and to gain public acceptance for the stringent restrictions the ruling junta had placed on political freedoms. It was important for the plans of this military-technocratic alliance that the working class trade liberty for jobs and that the middle class swap acquiescence in authoritarianism for a steadily rising standard of living. In attaining this goal the skilled economic technocrats were an indispensable ally, for the armed forces realized the complexity of the Brazilian economy and their own lack of qualifications to manage it effectively.

For the technocrats, the opportunity to implement their well-conceived plans over the span of time necessary to see significant results was irresistible—especially given Brazil's long history of civilian governments sacrificing economic rationality to political expediency. The technocrats held state and municipal expenditures under control while giving birth to a vastly expanded array of state enterprises. Thus it was not a love match, but rather a marriage based upon mutual convenience and buttressed by substantial shared interests.

Nonetheless, the salient fact and major lesson of the Médici period may well have centered on how great a degree of acceptance and even popularity could be engendered by a repressive government through sustained economic growth, with the gains loudly proclaimed and the costs swept under the rug of censorship. Yet the regime's rosy picture of the country's development and progress did not go uncontested. To confront such hymns of praise as Murilo Melo Filho's four popular volumes—*The Brazilian Challenge, The Brazilian Miracle, The Brazilian Model,* and *Brazilian Progress*—there were a series of hostile critical analyses of the shortcomings of this approach to development, though many of them unfortunately were as polemical and unbalanced, if not highly exaggerated, as those of the regime's apologists.[61] The dramatic positive side of the coin was economic growth, which, fueled by heavy industrial investment, steamed ahead at 10.4 percent for 1970, 11.3 percent in 1971, 12.1 percent during 1972, and a startling 14.0 percent for 1973. This "economic miracle" provided the foundation for the national mood of optimism bordering on euphoria generated by the regime's carefully orchestrated campaigns behind such slogans as "Nobody can hold Brazil back any longer" and "Brazil: Love it or leave it."

Critics stressed extremely inequitable income distribution, the failure of this growth to result in any appreciable improvement in the standard of living for the uneducated urban and rural masses, "wasteful" expenditures on showy infrastructural projects such as the TransAmazon highway, and neglect of pressing social problems—especially in the fields of health, housing, and education.[62] While industry grew annually at 12.6 percent from 1968 through 1974, agriculture expanded at only a yearly 5.3 percent. Yet often lost in the debate on income distribution was the fact that inflation—generally the dragon in Brazil's economic garden—averaged well under 20 percent a year during this period, while foreign exchange reserves increased almost tenfold (from under $660 million to over $6.4 billion). Foreign trade flourished, with exports of $2.7 billion and imports of $2.8 billion in 1970 rising to $6.2 billion and $7.0 billion for 1973.

With capital inflows growing equally rapidly, there was little serious alarm over the doubling of foreign debt between 1970 and the end of 1973, as $12.6 billion seemed at the time very manageable. Leftist economists might criticize the key role of expanding the automobile industry, with its positive impact on related industries but its aggravation of Brazil's oil problems—yet most of the politically relevant groups looked forward to acquiring cars, just as they had become used to having televisions during the late 1960s and early 1970s. To them, the hundreds of thousands of new cars on the streets and highways were a highly visible sign that Brazil was beginning to catch up with the developed countries of the West.

In this environment the government scored resounding victories in the November 1972 municipal elections, coming away with 3,349 mayors and 29,331 municipal councilmen to only 436 and 5,936, respectively, for the MDB. Although 746 municipalities, including all state capitals, had been excluded from choosing their chief executives, these impressive election results increased Médici's ability to keep the succession process from slipping out of control as it had for both Castelo Branco and Costa e Silva. Still, he too would not be able to control it fully and install his personal choice in office. For Médici had delegated a great deal of authority in the military field to Orlando Geisel, who as army minister restored military unity much as Denys had done in 1960–1961.[63] Thus, although SNI chief General Carlos Alberto Fontoura was strongly opposed to a return of the Castelistas to power, a position shared by other hardliners, Médici preferred to keep his strong army minister satisfied and accepted the countervailing view of chief military aide Figueiredo, who guaranteed that General Ernesto Geisel had broken with Golbery—the true nemesis of the hardliners. Hence the younger Geisel, an austere Lutheran who was heading Petrobrás (the government petroleum corporation), was announced officially as the government candidate in mid-June of 1973.

Duly ratified by the ARENA convention, Geisel was named to the presidency on January 15, 1974, by an electoral college composed almost exclusively of the incumbent Congress. The vote was 400 to 76 with 23 abstentions over the MDB's "anti-candidate," party president Ulysses Guimarães—an individual who would become a key actor in the events of the ensuing fifteen years.

8

The Road Back

Brazil had taken half a decade to slide into a fully authoritarian regime under armed forces increasingly inclined to the role of long-term rulers of the country, then spent almost an equal period under a repressive government apparently determined to institutionalize military rule into a permanent system. Yet, though it was unperceived at the time, by 1974 the midnight of military rule had already passed, and the next five years would be a reversal of the late 1960s as the champions of the military-as-arbiter role outwitted and outfought the entrenched hardline advocates of indefinite military rule. The new president, in the face of heavy resistance within his "internal constituency"—the armed forces—and with only limited understanding and sporadic cooperation from a distrustful civilian opposition, would steer the country through a phase of "decompression" of the repressively authoritarian regime and set Brazil on the path to political opening (*abertura*).

The first chief executive since 1926 to successfully see his preferred successor installed in office—Médici having been lukewarm about that successor—Geisel would then watch from the sidelines while, after a promising start, Figueiredo faltered in providing leadership once political opening shaded into transition during the early 1980s. Yet by 1984 civilian elements would recover enough initiative to take the ball from Figueiredo's hands and finally reestablish civilian government and fully competitive political processes after a hiatus of over two decades.

This reversal of the authoritarian drift would be possible only because by that time a very definite majority of the officer corps had come to believe that military disengagement from the direct control of government was necessary under the circumstances and, for many of them, probably even desirable. In no way, however, did this willingness to "extricate" from power mean that the officer corps as a whole was prepared to relinquish the role of moderating power. It did imply, however, that for some time the armed forces would probably be very reluctant to exercise the moderating power in a manner involving direct intervention.

Geisel: The End of the Economic Miracle
and the Beginning of Decompression

Back in power after seven years in the political wilderness, the heirs of Castelo Branco would face very serious obstacles in their effort to get Brazil up politically at least to where it had been before the fifth Institutional Act and the Médici administration. But for them this was preliminary to trying to move the country to where Castelo Branco had wished to see it headed before he was forced to accept Costa e Silva as his successor. Their efforts in this direction were generally neither understood nor appreciated, even by those who would eventually benefit most from the obstinate devotion of Castelo Branco's heirs to the only viable road away from the dead end of repression and from the more deeply rooted radicalization this repression would inevitably spawn. Indeed, the civilian opposition generally viewed these efforts as mere cosmetic surgery designed to enhance the military regime's viability and thus delay even longer the armed forces' departure from power. As some elements within the regime were thinking in these terms, such suspicions were understandable, albeit not constructive.

Although coming to power in the midst of a continuing economic boom, Geisel was clearly not going to be able to outperform his predecessor in the realm of growth. This would probably have been true even if the international environment had remained favorable, because marks as high as 12 percent and 13 percent GDP growth have rarely been strung together for a decade or more by any developing country. But the global energy crisis had already begun during the last quarter of 1973, so the boom was due to moderate, if not end. Instead of placing his bets on more of the unbridled pursuit of economic expansion—which he and his advisors did not disparage or belittle—Geisel assumed office with a definite agenda and a tentative, but flexible, timetable for dismantling the repressive apparatus that had burgeoned under Médici and for turning the country out of the cul-de-sac of authoritarianism.[1] Knowing that this would be a long and arduous task—one almost certainly well beyond the scope of a single presidential term—he at least provisionally selected his successor at the very beginning and to this end moved Figueiredo to the post of SNI chief.[2]

The heart of the new government consisted of individuals who had been closely associated with the administration of Castelo Branco. Geisel had himself served Castelo Branco as chief military aide, and his choice for presidential chief of staff (minister-chief of the civil Cabinet) was General Golbery, who had organized the SNI for the first revolutionary president back in 1964 with Figueiredo as one of the SNI staff. Continuity with the Médici government was provided by Planning Minister João Paulo dos Reis Velloso, while the brilliant young (at thirty-nine) economist Mário Henrique Simonsen was brought in to replace Delfim Netto as finance minister. On the military side General Vicente Dale Coutinho, very closely attuned to the president's basic orientation, was chosen to be army minister, but his untimely death very early in the administration led to the naming of Sylvio

Coelho da Frota, who as First Army commander since 1971 had combatted the use of torture and worked to keep the security apparatus under a reasonable degree of control. Yet he was not a Sorbonnist and in many respects was more closely identified with moderately hardline positions. Compounding the loss of Coutinho was a temporarily disabling accident that kept General Dilermando Gomes Monteiro from succeeding Figueiredo as chief of the military Cabinet (the formal title of the chief military aide). Instead this strategic post went to a tough paratroop commander, General Hugo de Andrade Abreu. Both of these second choices would provide major headaches for Geisel during the latter stages of his term.

Aims, Strategy, and Tactics

During the first meeting of his Cabinet, Geisel expressed a goal of "gradual, but sure democratic refinement" that would involve increased participation by "responsible elites" as well as the people in general in the quest for "finished institutionalization of the principles of the Revolution of 1964."[3] The government's exceptional powers would be retained, but not used except as a last resort, until a set of "effective safeguards within the constitutional context" had been devised and were in place. Certainly, no promise of a return to a fully competitive civilian political system was made by the incoming president—not even in the medium term, much less the short run. There was, however, a sober statement of an objective—that of institutionalizing a more representative and participant regime within the framework of a constitutional order—and a clear expression of an intention to work toward that objective. Only through the lenses of wishful thinking, however (which are often worn by opposition politicians), could these words be interpreted as involving a rapid return to democracy.

Indeed, to a very large degree "decompression" (*distensão*), as the Geisel administration's project came to be known, was designed in its initial stages at least to stabilize the regime, not to rush toward what the opposition had in mind as liberalization, much less democratization.[4] In fact, Geisel could not have attempted to do more than this, as he would have to work extremely hard to mobilize support within the armed forces for even the initial steps of diminishing rampant authoritarianism. He was president largely because of his brother's endorsement (for the much more conservative Orlando Geisel could almost certainly have had the job if he had wanted it) and had inherited a situation in which the hardliners were very well dug in within the military establishment. Consolidating and exercising his presidential authority, so that he would become the leader of the military institution as well as the head of government, would have to be his first priority if he was to be able to implement the changes he had in mind for making the regime more viable over the long run through legitimization without loss of control and direction.

Geisel's plans foresaw a political system of safe competition, dominated by a strong ARENA and with the MDB functioning as a loyal opposition, leaving the far Left isolated. New life was to be infused into the two-party system through competitive elections, for a living—but not too lively—parliamentary opposition could be used as a counterweight to hardline elements. But this opposition was not to be allowed to get out of hand; indeed, it would be manipulated by playing on fears of hardline reaction and changing the rules of the electoral game, and it would be disciplined if not fully controlled by the continued existence of AI-5—the atom bomb of Brazilian political life.

At the center of the decision by Geisel, who was urged on by Golbery to begin decompression, was the perception that the effective repression of the violence-oriented opposition during Médici's term had led to a dangerous degree of autonomy on the part of the security apparatus. This autonomy had resulted in a widening gap between essentially centrist to moderately reformist forces in Brazilian society and the military—which was held responsible by such centrists and reformists for abuses of human rights. Moreover, as continuation of such vigorous repression was clearly unnecessary—the guerrilla threat no longer existed—the armed forces themselves were becoming deeply divided over the issue.[5] Yet it would be necessary for Geisel to demonstrate that he would brook no subversive activity, for, if he wished to do away with extralegal repressive capabilities, he would have to convince the bulk of the officer corps that he would use the regime's "revolutionary" powers without hesitation to maintain internal security.

Once again, much as had been the case in 1967 when Costa e Silva took office or even when Médici had pledged to leave Brazil a democracy, many Brazilians clung to overoptimistic and unrealistic expectations regarding the possible rate and extent of liberalization. Thus, Geisel's August speech warning the opposition against attempts to mobilize public opinion as a means of forcing the government's hand on decompression hit the opposition like a bucket of cold water. Meanwhile, centralizing decision-making power in his own hands, Geisel—shunning the limelight and publicity as much as his predecessor had reveled in them—began patient efforts to get the security apparatus back under control. Stress on caution, consistency, and coherence was dictated by a determination to avoid breakdowns and reversals of attempts at political normalization such as had occurred in October 1965, December 1968, and September 1969.

Geisel, Golbery, Figueiredo, and their associates were convinced that the regime's range of choice might soon be unacceptably narrowed if steps were not taken to accommodate the social mobilization and desire for participation unleashed by such side effects of the economic development process as increased urbanization, expanded education, and improved communications. They realized, however, that the pace of such accommodation must be carefully orchestrated so as not to catalyze a backlash within the military establishment that might bring on a repetition of the rejection and subsequent reversal of Castelo Branco's and Costa e Silva's analogous efforts. Hence decompression had to be accompanied by at least an equal rate of progress in increasing professionalization of the armed forces and by consolidation of military sentiment in favor of doing away with the most repressive aspects of the national security state. Then, as headway was made in this respect—for the military remained the government's key constituency—an improved strategy for the co-optation of moderate opposition elements could be implemented. To this end decompression needed to go forward sufficiently to justify self-restraint and cooperation with the government on the part of the MDB's "responsible" elements, but changes could not be allowed to build up their own momentum; the impulse for liberalization had to remain channeled, with the initiative at every stage firmly in the government's hands.[6]

For this strategy to work, major elements of the opposition would have to be willing to accept limited and piecemeal reforms spread out over an extended period of time. More difficult for the opposition to swallow would be the harsh fact that they would be expected to go along with adverse changes in the rules of the political game when the government felt such changes were necessary to assuage military fears that the process was going too fast and threatening the military's continued control over the situation. Such outstanding political scientists as Wanderley Guilherme dos Santos—himself a target of the hardline in the mid-1960s—might argue persuasively for the need for the opposition to be "incrementalist" and to cooperate in this regard so as to minimize "the risks of recompression."[7] But for too many politicians this approach seemed unnecessarily cautious and appeared to leave the initiative indefinitely in the regime's hands.

Yet it was fundamentally to cultivate an understanding of the limitations on the government's freedom to move forward quickly in this field, as well as to convince important sectors of society of the sincerity of his regime's commitment to do what was possible, that Golbery even before taking office began a series of meetings with representatives of the Church, the major press organs, and the bar association. Subsequently, as a sign of its good intentions, the new government prosecuted radical Congressman Francisco "Chico" Pinto for insulting comments he made about Chilean President Augusto Pinochet—who was present for Geisel's inauguration—using the national security law as grounds for its case rather than resorting to AI-5.

Despite repeated setbacks encountered in what he knew from the beginning would be a very difficult struggle, Geisel pushed ahead with determination. At times he was required to behave autocratically to remove obstacles from the road and to resort to authoritarian measures when failure to do so would run a serious risk of losing "uncommitted" military support to the siren songs of the hardline foes of *distensão*. Thus throughout 1975 and 1976 Geisel would repeatedly be forced by these conservative elements to apply his extraordinary powers under AI-5 whenever the regime's authority was sharply challenged by intransigent elements of the opposition. Yet as soon as circumstances allowed it he would doggedly return to his effort toward normalizing the political situation.[8] In the eyes of Geisel, an experienced veteran of Brazil's political wars, the country had taken from 1967 to 1974 to get into its current difficult straits, and the road back would almost certainly be as long.[9]

The 1974 Elections

The first step in the political realm was the careful handpicking of governors, all of whom were duly confirmed by their state legislatures in October. Then Geisel insisted, over hardline reservations, on holding essentially free congressional elections on November 15—just eight months after he had taken office. At 35.8 million in a population nearing 105 million, Brazil's electorate had grown sharply since 1970, with the actual turnout of just under 29 million matching 1970's number of registered voters. Indeed, the electorate was more than double that of 1962 and three times the 1950 total. (Expansion would continue at the same high rate, doubling again by 1986.) The balloting resulted in a surprisingly strong comeback by the MDB, which scored a sixteen to six victory in the Senate races and elected 45 percent of the lower house.

The government was more sobered than shaken by this poor showing of its party's senatorial candidates, as it retained a decisive 204 to 160 edge in the Chamber of Deputies—compared to its previous 220–90 advantage—and had an even more comfortable margin in the upper house, where holdovers gave ARENA forty-six seats to the MDB's twenty. Moreover, the government party continued to control sixteen state legislatures, although the opposition now had majorities in such major states as São Paulo, Rio Grande do Sul, and Rio de Janeiro (now merged with Guanabara).[10] (The fusion of Rio de Janeiro and Guanabara allowed the central government to appoint the first governor, thus keeping control of this crucial urban center in the hands of a loyal subordinate.)

From the government strategists' point of view the opposition gains were healthy to the extent that these gains reflected a return to the normal channels of electoral politics by alienated elements who had abstained or nullified their ballots in 1970. To keep this renewed interest going it was necessary to hold out hope to the MDB that they might eventually win power within the existing system. The inner circle of the administration was disturbed by ARENA complacency and hoped that the changing political scene would create a more propitious environment for shaping ARENA into a more effective party. In addition, these presidential confidants saw the election results as a repudiation of the legacy of Médici's four and a half years, not an adverse verdict on their programs, which were only beginning. Then, too, Geisel was in the unique position of being able of preside over another full set of elections before leaving office—municipal voting in 1976 and the whole array of congressional and state legislative posts, plus the governorships, in 1978. This meant that the 1974 elections were not his only chance to try to achieve electoral results that would create a more viable situation for his successor.[11]

The most important single outcome of the elections, although not clearly so at the time, was the victory of the MDB's Orestes Quércia over former governor Carvalho Pinto in the São Paulo senatorial race. The former mayor of Campinas, Quércia won 70 percent of the vote in the capital—to but 19 percent for the ARENA candidate and 11 percent blank or null. Within the electorate of 8 million only the upper and middle classes voted for the government's candidate, with part of the middle class and the overwhelming proportion of the lower classes preferring the opposition standard-bearer.[12] São Paulo would continue to be the backbone of opposition strength during the ensuing decade, and by 1987 Quércia would be its governor, emerging during 1988 as a serious presidential contender, albeit with his eye more on 1994 than 1989. But even by 1974 Quércia had already had two important and constructive effects upon the MDB. First, while still Campinas mayor, he had helped engineer the gaining of control over the São Paulo MDB by moderates, arguing effectively that the party needed to accept the 1964 Revolution as irreversible and should concentrate upon developing a strategy to come to power within the system's constraints. He also helped establish the party in many smaller municipalities where ARENA had previously had the field to itself.[13]

The Trials and Tribulations of Geisel's Second Year

March 1975 saw both the resumption of the full functioning of Congress and the installation of the new state administrations. Indeed, progress toward decompression peaked with Geisel's March 1 message to the new Congress and with the hopes expressed elsewhere that incoming governors in states where the MDB had a majority in legislative assemblies would be able to work out viable relationships with the opposition legislators.[14] Golbery, chief architect and advocate of decompression—who in the course of his duties would normally see the president at least two or three times a day—was forced by serious eye problems to take extended leave. Uncertainty over whether he would be able to reassume his key functions worked to the advantage of the opponents of his enlightened political policy. Moreover, he never fully regained the influence he had exerted on Geisel prior to this forced absence.

In early May the president invoked the extraordinary powers of AI-5 after years of disuse, a move designed as much to remind the MDB of the need to be prudent as it was to satisfy the military hardliners. Then a group of discontented young hardline officers expressed the view that, in light of the results of the November 1974 elections, the revolution had been defeated and more than a decade of effort by the armed forces was in danger of going down the drain. The army minister responded with an order of the day reiterating his belief that AI-5 and the decree law that had placed severe restrictions on political activities of students were "indispensable to assure the climate of peace, order, security, and stability in which Brazil lives, a climate so different from that of the international arena."

After the Senate voted to drop charges of corruption against one of its members, the president used his exceptional powers again to remove the offending legislator from office, thus underscoring that AI-5 was a deterrent to corruption within the regime as well as a safeguard against subversion by its opponents. At the beginning of August, on the eve of the reopening of Congress after its winter recess, Geisel reaffirmed his determination to continue using extraconstitutional powers if necessary, stressed that decompression was as much economic and social as political, reiterated that the decompression process must be gradual if the reforms were to be long-lasting, and warned that there were no shortcuts to political development. Subsequently the term *development* was increasingly substituted for decompression in the government's policy statements, with the clear implication that this was a long-term process.

By the last quarter of 1975 *distensão* was clearly at a standstill, if not permanently sidetracked. Hardline elements, particularly in São Paulo, were heating up the issue of communism and subversion in answer to the opposition's efforts to focus attention upon the questions of torture and violations of civil liberties. On October 25 the death of young journalist Vladimir Herzog while he was undergoing interrogation at Second Army headquarters brought matters to a head; in spite of the authorities' assertion that the death had been a suicide, public opinion overwhelmingly considered Herzog to be a victim of torture.[15]

In the midst of substantial unrest over this incident and rumors of military-centered conspiracies against him—conspiracies said to be supported by businessmen opposed to the burgeoning economic role of the state—Geisel swept into São Paulo and turned the situation to his decided advantage. Temporarily at least, many wavering officers reacted against the hardliners' excesses and rallied to the president's vigorous leadership initiatives. Yet military outrage over criticism by an MDB senator stemming from the Herzog incident was contained only by means of a retraction hastily engineered by leaders of both parties who were interested in avoiding any repetition of the events that had led to the fifth Institutional Act just seven years earlier. When two young São Paulo MDB state legislators refused to retract charges that constituents had been coerced and possibly tortured, Geisel acquiesced in starting off the new year by stripping them of both their positions and their political rights.

At this juncture the president resisted hardline pressures to use AI-5 against a much larger number of opposition figures. Then, when Manoel Fiel Filho, a worker accused of distributing Communist propaganda, died while in custody of a Second Army security unit, Geisel swiftly relieved General Ednardo D'Avila Mello of his command, replacing D'Avila Mello with close personal friend Dilermando Monteiro, who was at that point the most junior of four-star generals.[16] Thus, prospects for improvement in the political environment of São Paulo brightened from the crisis atmosphere that had been recurrent there since the Médici years. Yet the removal of D'Avila Mello also appears to have marked a definite drifting away from the president on the part of Army Minister Frota, who swore he would not let another ranking general be "demoralized" as D'Avila Mello had been.[17]

Decompression was soon to encounter additional difficulties. With campaigning for the municipal elections—scheduled for November 15—underway, two Rio Grande do Sul MDB congressmen were either carried away with the enthusiasm of a party rally or went too far in consciously testing the limits of the regime's toleration of criticism. Once again there were concerted right-wing pressures for application of AI-5, and only with difficulty did the government devise a formula that would not involve purges on such a scale as to place the elections under a serious cloud. Only the two relatively junior national legislators directly involved and one excessively vociferous defender from among the MDB's leadership ranks lost their seats, while divisions within the opposition were accentuated by disagreement over the appropriate response, with the moderate leadership seeking a graceful way to avoid confrontation with the regime. Meanwhile the March and July 1976 army promotions were a step forward for Geisel in his effort to reshape the high command more in his own image: The five new four-star generals included three who had worked well under Geisel at earlier stages of their careers. The support of these three new generals would be critical when the president and the army minister reached a showdown.

Winning the Succession Battle

At the midpoint of Geisel's term in September–October, decompression appeared to be stalled rather than either abandoned or moving forward. Over a dozen years after the armed forces had seized power, the Brazilian military remained divided over the fundamental nature of the political system they wished to help bring into being. Critics of decompression cited the U.S. defeat in Southeast Asia; events in Portugal, Greece, India, and Italy; the situation in Angola; and the continuing instability in the Middle East to argue that with the world in such a mess and Brazil increasingly required to care for its own defense and security, this was definitely not the time to weaken the regime by introducing the divisiveness of political competition or by permitting congressional restraint of the executive branch. Still smarting over the outcome of the 1974 elections, the hardliners maintained that there was not sufficient time before national and state elections in 1978 to adequately strengthen the government party and that, with the bloom off the economic miracle, all electoral advantages were on the side of the opposition. Moreover, in their view, decompression had unleashed distributive pressures that jeopardized continued development and thus were undermining national security.[18]

Military liberals drew very different conclusions from the domestic and foreign panoramas. They felt that after a long period of authoritarian rule a political boiling point is eventually reached at which a radical turn to the Left—so evident in post-Salazar Portugal, which was very much on their minds—becomes a real possibility. Then, too, they held, the economic pie had grown enough to make some distributive measures desirable—at least to counterbalance the pronounced concentration of income evident since 1960—particularly to the degree that such measures might well broaden the internal market sufficiently to sustain economic growth. Furthermore, the liberal officers pointed out, the political situation was the only negative factor in Brazil's substantially improved international image, and it clouded the country's potential for leadership.

Supporters of ARENA argued it was premature to say that the party could not bring decompression to fruition. Rather than viewing an opposition victory in 1978 as all but inevitable, ARENA President Francelino Pereira and Secretary-General Nélson Marchezan believed that their party had not really begun to exploit effectively those issues that could carry it to victory in the 1976 municipal elections as well as in the state and congressional balloting of 1978. They pointed to Geisel's increasing prestige and popularity, recent potentially rich petroleum discoveries, and a number of nationalist foreign policy initiatives. Many military leaders agreed at least in large part with this optimistic assessment, to which the president and his closest advisors generally subscribed.

The Weight of Leadership

At this point a majority of the officer corps was aligned neither with the hardliners nor with the moderates. Most harbored ambivalent attitudes based upon their perception of the situation as markedly ambiguous. Under such conditions leadership would be a critical element in determining the future course of military politics and hence of national affairs. In this regard turnover in the upper reaches of the military hierarchy was continuing apace, with another wave of retirements and promotions due after the November elections and more to follow in March 1977.

The November local elections saw over 18 million votes cast for ARENA's municipal council candidates compared with nearly 13 million for those of the MDB. Yet the opposition elected either the mayor or a majority of the councilmen in 63 percent of cities over 250,000 population, up sharply from a comparable measure of 32 percent that the opposition had won in 1972.[19] But with the electorate swollen to 41.3 million, ARENA still came away with 83 percent of the mayors (2,457 to 491) and roughly 20,000 of 28,000 municipal legislators. These results were made possible in part by the so-called Falcão law, which denied candidates any significant access to television—use of the medium was viewed by the regime as having been the chief fly in the ointment during the 1974 campaign.[20]

The most important impact of these elections was to confirm the government's belief that it could retain sufficient control of the system at the national and state levels in 1978 with ARENA as its vehicle—albeit only through further tinkering with the electoral rules. Yet Geisel, who had to a considerable degree taken over personal direction of ARENA, had encountered considerable resistance on the part of "old pros" to his desire to mobilize new elements—particularly youth and women. These old pros were motivated by a well-founded fear that in the wake of such broadening of the party's base they might lose their seats to representatives of the new groups.

The year 1977 would prove to be the critical one for the Geisel government and for the continuation of Brazil's progress toward a less restricted democracy. Multiple problems faced Geisel and his lieutenants, involving not only the succession process but also the degree of control over the military institution required to effectively see the succession through. Former Minas Gerais governor and foreign minister Magalhães Pinto had decided that this would be his last chance to attain a goal he had sought since 1960, and Frota was moving toward establishing himself as the candidate of the armed forces. Moreover, the relaunching of *distensão* was complicated by mediocre performance in the economic realm—exactly the factor that had served so effectively to ease opposition during the Médici years.

The Economic Context

The Geisel administration had announced ambitious economic goals shortly after coming to office—to have done anything else would have burst the balloon of public confidence and optimism that had carried over from the sustained boom of the Médici years. This Second National Development Plan: 1975–1979, promulgated in September 1974, called for a shift of emphasis to intermediate and capital goods in order to maintain high growth rates. Yet the plan would be undermined from the beginning by the soaring price of crude oil and the heavy investments required by subsequent efforts to reduce Brazil's dependence upon petroleum imports.[21] During 1974 problems were most evident in the trade field, where imports more than doubled— from $6.2 billion for 1973 to over $12.6 billion—resulting in the preceding year's equilibrium between exports and imports turning into a $4.7 billion trade deficit. This produced a large current account deficit of $7.1 billion and a somewhat more manageable balance of payments shortfall of just under $1 billion (courtesy of a heavy inflow of loans, credits, and import financing). Hence foreign exchange reserves dropped from $6.5 billion to $5.3 billion as foreign debt rose to $17.2 billion. GDP growth, in large part a carryover from the dynamism of the Médici period, was 9 percent, with inflation edging up to nearly 28 percent.

The economic downturn was somewhat more noticeable during 1975. Export earnings were a disappointing $8.7 billion, while imports were contained at $12.2 billion, cutting the trade deficit to $3.5 billion, which, with a net outflow for services of approximately the same magnitude, yielded a current accounts deficit of $6.9 billion. With a net capital inflow almost matching that of the preceding year, the balance of payments deficit came to $1.2 billion—bringing Brazil's foreign exchange reserves down to the $4 billion mark. GDP growth fell to 6.1 percent—but was reported at the time as significantly lower—and inflation leveled off at 29 percent. Although 1976 saw GDP growth improve to 10.1 percent, inflation jumped to 42 percent. The crucial last years of the Geisel government would take place in a deteriorating economic environment as the growth rate fell to 5.4 percent for 1977 and only 4.8 percent in 1978—both well below historical averages. Moreover, inflation remained near 40 percent.[22] A harbinger of problems ahead was the rapid rise of Brazil's foreign debt, which, after climbing by a total of $15 billion over the 1975–1977 span, would jump a whopping $11.5 billion the next year to a total of $43.5 billion. Thus, while Brazil achieved a balance between exports and imports in 1977 and 1978, the time bomb was ticking because debt service was coming to require a large sustained net capital inflow.[23]

Structurally the Brazilian economy of the mid-1970s was substantially changed from the one that had existed prior to the military's seizure of power. Both industry and services had come to overshadow the previously dominant agricultural sector. Whereas in 1947 the latter accounted for almost 28 percent of GDP with industry a bit below 20 percent, by the end of the 1960s the two sectors were roughly even. Yet by 1978 agriculture was down to 14 percent of GDP and industry was up to 33 percent. Within this dynamic industrial sector, metallurgy, manufacturing, and chemicals had caught up with if not overtaken food processing and textiles—the traditional leaders of the sector. Steel production exceeded 9 million tons by 1979, triple that of 1964. The auto industry, started from scratch by Kubitschek in the late 1950s, was producing nearly 1 million vehicles per year. Installed electrical generating capacity had doubled between 1964 and 1971 and again by 1978.

These profound changes were reflected in the workforce. As late as 1950 only a little over 14 percent of the economically active population (EAP)— then numbering just above 17 million—were found in industry, with just under 60 percent in agriculture and 26 percent in the service sector. By 1978 some 20 percent of an EAP swollen to over 40 million were employed in industry, with agriculture down to about 36 percent and services up to some 40 percent. The trend was much more dramatic with respect to new jobs: In the 1960s agriculture only provided one in eight new jobs and a net of zero during the 1970s, while industrial jobs came to grow by well over 500,000 a year and those in the service area by nearly 900,000 annually. School enrollments exploded during this time, from 8.7 million in 1960 to over 20 million by 1978, with the greatest relative growth coming in higher education—where 1960's enrollment of a mere 93,000 had become roughly 1.4 million.

In early 1977 the regime was faced with finding a way to guarantee some form of ARENA victory in the next year's national elections while heading off the unwanted presidential candidacies of Magalhães Pinto and Army Minister Frota—the former unacceptable because they felt it was too soon to end military control of the presidency and the latter because he could not be relied upon to continue decompression. The crux of the electoral dilemma was the fact that the governorship elections were slated to be direct, and this could lead to a situation similar to that in 1965, in which the results would be unsatisfactory to the hardliners and therefore would lead to an explosive military crisis.[24] The most "normal" way to get around the electoral problem would be through a constitutional amendment, so the government sought to negotiate the requisite two-thirds majority with the MDB leadership—composed of Ulysses Guimarães, Tancredo Neves, and Thales Ramalho, all of whom would play key roles in the 1984–1989 transition. But when the opposition flexed its muscles by rejecting an amendment restructuring the judiciary, Geisel acted decisively. (The Chamber vote was 237 to 155 in favor of the restructuring amendment, but a two-thirds majority was needed for passage.)

The April "Package"

Placing Congress in temporary recess on April 2, the president subsequently decreed a package of changes that not only made the gubernatorial elections once again indirect, but also added representatives of municipalities to the state legislatures in the electoral colleges to make ARENA victories more certain. Moreover, Amendment No. 7 (April 13) put into effect the judicial reform, while Amendment No. 8 (April 14) provided that one senator from each state would be chosen indirectly (these were the so-called bionic senators, in reference to the then popular *Six Million Dollar Man* television program); that a simple congressional majority would be sufficient to amend the constitution in the future; that representation in the Chamber would be based on registered voters, not total population; and that state legislatures and municipal councils would have some representation in the electoral college that would choose the next president—although Congress would still be predominant in the electoral body. It also extended the Falcão law to cover the 1978 campaign and provided a six-year term for Geisel's successor.[25] Thus the government could be assured of retaining control of the Senate after 1978 and of having a reinforced majority in the body that would elect the next president.

Although the opposition protested vigorously—for censorship had been significantly relaxed during the first three years of Geisel's government—they had no real option but to increase their efforts to do well in the 1978 elections despite these new handicaps. Indeed, privately, albeit certainly not for public consumption, several of the MDB's more cosmopolitan leaders agreed that these *causimos* were little more severe than those that were employed under the French Fourth Republic (1946–1958) to greatly disadvantage the Communists and Gaullists. Though this realization did not keep them from continuing denunciations of the "April Package" as arbitrary and authoritarian, it did help restrain their protests within limits the regime found acceptable. Criticism of specific policies and measures was permissible, but fundamental contestation of the 1964 Revolution that implied the desirability of a return to the status quo prior to the revolution was not. Moreover, the reopening of Congress within two weeks contrasted favorably in the eyes of the opposition with the much greater length of previous executive-imposed legislative recesses.

To the extent that the decisive modification of the electoral rules reaffirmed Geisel's determination to keep decompression within the confines he had dictated and to control its pace firmly, this electoral modification contributed to the consolidation of military support necessary for dealing with the succession question. In fact, Geisel's decisive action removed one of the hardline's most telling arguments: that the president's policies would lead to an MDB victory in 1978. As 1977 wore on, Frota increasingly became the spokesman for military hardliners and archconservative civilian elements, who by September had created a bloc of some seventy to eighty ARENA legislators favoring the army minister's candidacy. While the president maintained publicly that the succession question should wait for the new year, in large part to avoid dividing the military, he allowed several members of his inner circle to launch Figueiredo's candidacy. The need to go slowly in this regard was dictated by Chief Military Aide Abreu's firm opposition to a bid by an officer slightly inferior to him in seniority as well as by the broader problem of the SNI head not yet having achieved four-star rank. As this matter of "the pope should come from among the cardinals" had proved insurmountable for Albuquerque Lima in 1969, it was a weighty consideration, but one that time could resolve through an expedient promotion. First, however, the president had to dispose of the Frota problem.

Outfoxing Frota

Geisel had no intention of allowing his army minister's understandable ambitions to jeopardize his long-term project. The president was painfully aware of how both his mentor, Castelo Branco, and his nemesis, Costa e Silva, had lost control over the succession process and, as a result, were stymied in their quests to accomplish the normalization needed if the country was to find a viable middle ground between repressive rule and irresponsible populism. Moreover, no one could be more aware than Geisel of how avoiding trouble by acquiescing to a choice desired by his army minister had forced Médici to sit by and watch as many of his favorite policies were abandoned or reversed by a successor—Geisel—with not only different priorities, but a distinctly variant view of what the future should bring. Proud and determined, Geisel was not going to let what he viewed as an unfortunate complication stemming from Dale Coutinho's unforeseeable death stand in the way of what he was sincerely convinced was best for the country.

The active involvement of General Jayme Portela, a leading architect of the Castelistas' humiliating defeat in 1966–1967, in Frota's corner only added to Geisel's resolve. The president's concern was how to get rid of Frota in a manner that would not leave deep or lasting scars on the military unity he had been working hard to achieve—unity that he knew Figueiredo would require to carry on his work effectively.[26] Thus, Geisel's strategy was to attempt to disassociate Frota's dismissal from the question of presidential succession. Indeed, this disassociation was essential if Geisel was to retain the support of the military Cabinet head and not push Abreu over to Frota's side.[27]

Frota—who was heavily outgunned in the realm of political savvy by Geisel, Golbery, et al.—was astutely maneuvered into overplaying his hand and was consequently dismissed on October 12 without a major military crisis. Geisel managed to convince most senior officers that Frota had been seriously out of line and that there were no ideological implications to the army minister's removal. In this the president was aided by the fact that a frustrated Frota reacted with a series of wild and irresponsible accusations, most of which were plausible only to the extreme Right. Moreover, a hardliner was appointed as the new army minister while other hardliners were advanced in the November promotions.[28] Free at last of the threat of being forced to accept Frota as his successor or even of being placed in an untenable position by having a majority of the army high command aligned against decompression, Geisel was still faced with important elements who feared that renewed liberalization and reforms of the political system could threaten the primacy of the military within the regime.

Essentially, however, affairs would go Geisel's way during 1978. At the beginning of January, Figueiredo's selection to be the next chief executive was made public. Although this choice precipitated General Abreu's resignation and his subsequent alignment with opposition forces, Figueiredo's promotion to four-star rank was pushed through at the end of March, and he was formally nominated by ARENA at its convention in early April.[29] The naming of Minas Gerais Governor Aureliano Chaves da Mendonça as Figueiredo's running mate effectively put the last nail in the coffin of Magalhães Pinto's candidacy. There still remained, however, the question of what the MDB would choose to do, as their active participation was an important element in the regime's quest for legitimization. What was needed was for the opposition to select a candidate who they could convince themselves had a chance of winning, but who really would pose no threat, and who—in the remote possibility that the government's plans went awry and the opposition candidate was elected—would prove acceptable to the armed forces. After considerable vacillation the MDB, thinking that they were outsmarting and crossing Geisel and his essentially military brain trust, obliged the administration by taking the bait.[30]

Outmaneuvering the MDB

The candidacy of General Euler Bentes Monteiro had as its godfather Severo Fagundes Gomes, a São Paulo businessman tapped by Geisel to be his minister of industry and commerce. Taking a leading role in articulating the views of Paulista industrialists, Gomes soon entered into repeated policy disagreements with Simonsen and Reis Velloso, who were much closer to the inner circle than he was and had the president's ear on economic matters. Although the media stressed Gomes's more nationalist policy stand, particularly his opposition to letting foreign companies explore for oil, as the cause for his departure from the government in February 1977, the succession question was equally important.

Gomes favored economic policies focused on the internal market as the engine for growth and advocated going further and faster with liberalization.[31] This led him from being a dissident voice within ARENA, where he was the vice-presidential hopeful linked to Magalhães Pinto, to becoming a member of the MDB—which he would later come to represent in the Senate. But his activity during 1978 served to convince the opposition that potential cleavages within both the army and ARENA, given Magalhães Pinto's extreme frustration, could open the door to let them slip into power. Gomes persuaded his fellow Paulistas that General Bentes Monteiro was the key to this opportunity, for as a nationalist associated in the past with Albuquerque Lima, Bentes Monteiro might receive the support of the influential retired military figures—including Marshal Denys—who initially had sided with Frota. Paulo Brossard of Rio Grande do Sul was chosen for the second spot on the MDB ticket—surviving the electoral debacle to become justice minister in 1986.[32]

Yet Bentes Monteiro had been tied quite closely to Orlando Geisel and had actually been near the top of the regime's list of possible alternatives to Figueiredo. Furthermore, since the latter was quite highly regarded by many who had served with him in the Médici government, no major split in military ranks did occur, and in the end Magalhães Pinto refused to rebel against the ARENA choice.

The acceptability of Figueiredo's candidacy and creation of a favorable environment for his administration were both aided by a series of political reforms put through Congress before the elections. These reforms eliminated the most authoritarian features of the political system by replacing the sweeping arbitrary powers of AI-5 with provisions for a state of siege or a state of emergency that could last 120 days without congressional approval. Other articles of constitutional Amendment No. 11 reinstituted *habeas corpus* for individuals detained on political charges, suspended before-the-fact censorship of radio and television (the press already having been granted this diminution in control), and rescinded a number of the limitations on judicial independence imposed in April.

Against this backdrop on October 15 the electoral college chose Figueiredo over Bentes Monteiro by a vote of 355 to 226 (with eight abstentions, including Magalhães Pinto). The selection of governors also went off smoothly, with the major exception of São Paulo—where upstart Paulo Salim Maluf had managed to defeat Geisel's choice at the ARENA convention. MDB victories were limited to Rio de Janeiro, where the return of Chagas Freitas was perfectly acceptable to the regime as Freitas's control of the MDB there kept it from behaving as an opposition party in any real sense.

With Brazil's electorate up to 46 million in a population of almost 114 million, nearly 38 million of whom actually went to the polls on November 15, the government party elected 231 federal deputies to 189 for the opposition. Yet even more than had been the case in 1974, the gross underrepresentation of populous urban states was crucial to ARENA's comfortable margin of seats, as in terms of popular vote the difference was only 250,000 votes— at a bit over 15 million in favor of ARENA to 14.8 million for the opposition. The government party also won fifteen of the twenty-three Senate seats at stake, a 180-degree turnaround from the 1974 outcome, with twenty-two others having been filled previously by state electoral colleges—ARENA gaining twenty-one of them and the MDB coming away with a single senator. Thus the government's majority in the upper house rose to forty-two against twenty-four, despite the fact that in the popular vote for senators the MDB led by 57 percent to 43 percent.

The opposition's strength in the major urban centers remained impressive, with 8 million of its national total of well over 17 million votes for the Senate coming in São Paulo and Rio de Janeiro alone. In these two states together with Rio Grande do Sul, the MDB elected twice as many federal deputies as did ARENA, but in the other five major states (including number two Minas Gerais, Bahia, Paraná, and Pernambuco) the regime's supporters reversed this result, giving lie to the assertion disseminated in much of the press and accepted uncritically by many U.S. scholars that ARENA victories came only in rural areas and the interior of the country.[33]

Once again the outcome in São Paulo would have the most important long-run influence on national affairs. First, the landslide Senate victory of André Franco Montoro paved the way for him to become governor when direct elections for that post were restored in 1982. Second, the candidacy of Fernando Henrique Cardoso on an MDB subslate made this progressive political sociologist Montoro's senatorial alternate, allowing Cardoso to enter the Senate in 1982 and, after an unsuccessful bid for mayor in 1985, to win reelection to the Senate as the incumbent in 1986.

Nationally the mixed results were in reality most advantageous for the process of political decompression and its transformation into *abertura* (opening). The electoral vitality of the MDB convinced wavering elements associated with the regime of the need for continuing political reforms, while the fact that ARENA remained firmly in control of Congress and state legislatures forestalled any reaction by hardline elements in the armed forces. As generals Frota and Abreu remained the focus of conspiratorial activities on the part of disaffected junior officers, the avoidance of an opposition victory was of utmost importance. Yet this additional "moral victory" for the opposition drew them further into the game of liberalization through elections—the slow and conflict-free road.[34]

Thus, following Geisel's year-end revocation of the banishments of a number of exiles, Figueiredo was inaugurated as constitutional chief executive on March 15, 1979. With AI-5 and its prodigious arbitrary powers now repealed, *distensão* had essentially become *abertura*—in its first stage still part of a process of liberalization, not yet democratization. What Geisel had done at the end of his watershed term was to reduce the regime's reliance upon arbitrary powers by making it far less likely to encounter situations in which the application of such powers might seem necessary. If, at least by the criteria of jurists and political scientists, he did not succeed in legitimizing the regime, he did greatly augment and amplify its viability. Although the opposition still distrusted decompression and was very wary of the government's *abertura* project, they had been drawn completely into the regime-initiated game of how far and how fast development could proceed.

The extreme Left—particularly its violence-oriented and maximalist components—was essentially irrelevant from this point on, and the new government would, much as Geisel had done, contain attempts by the radical Right to derail *abertura*. Geisel's "relative" democracy had been achieved;

his hand-picked successor could move on toward "mitigated representative democracy," while the opposition could endeavor to pull the process further in the direction of actual democracy.[35]

Figueiredo: Political Opening and Economic Difficulties, 1979–1982

With João Figueiredo's inauguration, for the first time since 1926 a Brazilian administration was followed by one committed to continuing the former administration's policies. In fact this would be the course pursued in almost all respects until the last months of 1981, and even then Geisel-like policies would be carried on in many areas through 1983. Paradoxically, a break with what Geisel represented and a loss of control over the situation would occur in 1984—the extra sixth year Geisel had insisted upon tacking onto his successor's term.[36]

As might be expected under these circumstances, there were a considerable number of holdovers in Figueiredo's Cabinet. Not only did Golbery continue as presidential chief of staff, but Simonsen stayed on—shifting over to planning minister, with Karlos Rischbeiter moving from the presidency of the Bank of Brazil to fill the vacancy Simonsen's move created at the Finance Ministry. Petrônio Portella came from the Senate to be justice minister, Mário Andreazza—Médici's transportation minister—was brought back to be interior minister, and former economic czar Delfim Netto took over the Agriculture Ministry with a promise to greatly expand food production on a crash basis.

General Walter Pires de Albuquerque was expected to provide firm leadership for the army while not complicating plans for *abertura* by developing presidential aspirations of his own a la Costa e Silva and Frota. General Octávio Aguiar de Medeiros assumed Figueiredo's old post as head of the SNI, while General Danilo Venturini became chief military aide. Other Cabinet positions were awarded according to the fundamental pattern of providing representation to key states. The result was an administration reflecting all major currents within both the military establishment (Castelistas, Médici followers, and advocates of professionalization) and the technocratic stratum. As a result of this heterogeneity, the government lacked unity and coherence and would require significant personnel changes after the shakedown period.

Not only would Simonsen soon give way to Delfim Netto's powerful drive to return to primacy in the economic realm, but at the beginning of 1980 death would remove the creative Portella from his role as political coordinator. Then near the midpoint of Figueiredo's government, Golbery would leave, permitting a return of Leitão de Abreu as presidential chief of staff. But by this time the sharp deterioration of the president's health had introduced a more profound change into the political equation. Even healthy, Figueiredo was not a strong leader in the Castelo Branco–Geisel tradition; once debilitated by serious cardiovascular problems he would become much more of a Costa e Silva.

Hitting the Ground Running

Attention quickly fixed upon the new government's proposal for a broad, but not all-inclusive amnesty—which left out those who had endangered lives by use of armed force. At the same time as the opposition sought to expand its scope, resorting again to mobilizing public demonstrations, a wave of strikes was unleashed by unions seeking to test the effects, if not the limits, of *abertura*.[37] The Falcão law was revoked in July, but the government refused to do away with the national security law. The opposition continued to overestimate the defections it could expect from ARENA dissidents—as it had in the 1978 presidential election and the subsequent abortive try to defeat the Geisel government's insistence upon a constitutional provision for declaring a state of national emergency and other safeguards to partially replace the arbitrary powers the regime was relinquishing with the repeal of the institutional acts. When push came to shove, many of those who had expressed sympathy for the MDB's efforts to push *abertura* further and faster voted with the government.

Thus amnesty became the law at the beginning of September on the administration's terms. Two months later a reformulation of the party system was approved about as it had been designed by Golbery and Portella, despite a determined attempt on the part of the MDB leaders to defeat provisions abolishing existing parties. Soon there was not only the Social Democracy Party (PDS) as ARENA's replacement and the Party of the Brazilian Democratic Movement (PMDB), but also the Popular Party (PP), the Brazilian Labor Party (PTB), and the Democratic Workers' Party (PDT).

This was exactly what Golbery and Portella had wanted—the government party stayed essentially united while the opposition divided into strong rival parties. Moreover, there was only one really new actor on the party scene: the Workers' Party (PT), headed by the São Paulo metalworkers' leader Luís Inácio Lula da Silva.[38] Some thirty ARENA congressmen did not join the successor PDS—most of them going to the PP—but in return two dozen former MDB national legislators did enter the reformulated government party.[39] The PMDB retained ninety-four deputies and sixteen senators from the old MDB—while failing to hold on to ninety-five from the lower house and nine in the Senate. About half of these entered the new PP, with small numbers opting for the PTB and PDT.

The new year opened with Portella's death from a heart attack—which he had tried to hide in order to preserve his presidential hopes—and Rischbeiter's resignation as finance minister, his replacement being Ernani Galvêas, an old ally of Delfim Netto. Though the economic legacy Figueiredo had received from the Geisel administration was mixed, in many ways it was quite respectable, as GDP growth reached 7.2 percent for 1979, but with inflation nearly doubling to 77 percent. Yet in light of the global energy crisis and its heavy impact upon a country as dependent on imported crude oil as Brazil, Rischbeiter and Simonsen had felt that continued stress on growth would lead to serious problems down the road. Thus they advocated prompt adjustment to the new harsher economic realities, even if this meant a "corrective" recession.

But much as would be repeated by the civilian government in 1985 and 1986, those pushing the politically more appealing course of continued stress on growth would win out, while events would subsequently vindicate the defeated realists. Hence Simonsen had returned to academic life in August 1979 with Delfim Netto taking his place, and in 1980—after Delfim pushed through a 30 percent devaluation of the cruzeiro in response to a seriously deteriorating balance of payments situation—Rischbeiter threw in the towel and went back to the private sector. The Third National Development Plan, covering the 1980–1985 period, approved by Congress in May, embodied the optimistic hypotheses stressed by Delfim Netto and all but ignored the warning signs flashed by his erstwhile colleagues.[40] Indeed, in Delfim's eagerness to duplicate his earlier success in a changed economic environment, he ignored the external crisis of doubling oil prices and rising interest rates until late 1980.

With censorship a dead letter, nearly all political prisoners finally freed, and even the most controversial exiles such as Prestes and Arraes not only returned but also beginning to participate actively in politics, Brazil moved during 1980 to firm up *abertura*. The first test of the regime's ability to implement its version of transition toward—but not all the way to—democracy came in September with passage of a bill postponing municipal elections until November 1982 so that they would coincide with state and national balloting. This measure was made palatable by the reestablishment of direct election of governors in 1982 through constitutional Amendment No. 15 of November 19, 1980. The administration was also able to demonstrate the viability of its new congressional base of support by enacting its own restrictive version of a new immigration law and turning back an alliance of opposition parties with PDS dissidents who were trying to return important prerogatives to Congress.

The military's political profile was lowered substantially during 1979 and 1980 as Figueiredo and Golbery consolidated *abertura*, and Army Minister Pires, a longtime friend of the president, albeit politically well to his Right, restored unity to the army. Still there were elements embedded within the armed forces, particularly in the security and intelligence areas, who had not yet accepted the idea of *abertura*. Though they were not in a position to challenge it nearly as directly as had been the case in 1976–1977 with respect to decompression, they could still create considerable mischief. Thus, 1981 was to provide more serious tests of the military's developing capacity to govern without extraordinary powers than had the early stages of Figueiredo's term.

Riocentro and Dropping the Pilot

Terrorist bombings, which were very largely the work of the extreme Right although they were often blamed on the Left, became more frequent in early 1981 until the Riocentro incident threatened to bring on a major political crisis at the beginning of May. In this episode a noncommissioned officer was killed and his superior was badly injured when a bomb exploded in their car. While a great deal of evidence put forward by the opposition-oriented media supported the popular assumption that this was a "work accident" involving terrorist elements linked to the intelligence arm of the First Army, a military-run investigation declined to reach the same conclusion. For his part, Figueiredo decided to tread very gingerly in a matter in which many military moderates agreed with the hardliners that the armed forces must be spared any undue embarrassment. Thus the official line remained that the sergeant and captain were victims of a terrorist attack, not the would-be perpetrators of an anti-leftist bombing that could have caused substantial loss of life in the crowded convention center. The military institution was unwilling to be subjected to public censure for doing what many believed was their duty in combatting perceived subversion, a fact that temporarily created a near impasse for the regime in pushing ahead with *abertura*.[41]

More than any of his predecessors, however, Figueiredo was able to put his own stamp upon the military high command during the early stages of his presidency. Owing to the rigid "up and out" military retirement system instituted by Castelo Branco to force longtime general officers into retirement earlier than age sixty-six, by August 1981 Figueiredo enjoyed the luxury of working with an army high command made up entirely of those whom he had promoted to four-star rank, most of whom were from Figueiredo's own class at the academy. Moreover, he was able to fill three more posts on this key body that November. Along with consequent shifts in command, this put the president in an excellent position to deal more forcefully with subsequent efforts to disrupt *abertura*—when he had the will to do so.

Golbery's abrupt resignation in August triggered considerable speculation that Figueiredo intended to slow down or cut back on political opening, at least until greater consensus could be achieved within the military establishment. Golbery, who was approaching his seventieth birthday and had been having increasing health problems, had been in the enormously taxing position of presidential chief of staff for nearly seven and a half years with no vacations. But the cause of Golbery's resignation was Figueiredo's failure to act as Geisel or Castelo Branco would have and to accept instead the advice of SNI head Medeiros and others who were already planning on at least one more military-headed administration.[42] Besides, Golbery's closest associate among the president's inner circle of advisors, Private Secretary Heitor Ferreira de Aquino, had earlier been instructed to curb his political pronouncements and lower his political profile. Accustomed to exercising power that was in some ways almost that of a de facto prime minister, Golbery had been encountering increasingly strong opposition to his policies from Medeiros, who recently had been joined on many issues by Delfim Netto. In a very real sense a prisoner of the widely held myth that he was all-powerful within the government, Golbery was being held responsible by the public for some actions that did not have his approval.

Golbery's departure was also deeply rooted in the question of strategy toward the 1982 congressional and gubernatorial elections and the subsequent presidential succession. On this latter point his firmly held view was that the presidency should be returned to civilian hands before the emerging difficult economic conditions further complicated the process. This view clashed head-on with the burgeoning aspirations of Medeiros. Both Médici and Figueiredo had utilized the SNI as a springboard to the presidency, while Golbery—founder of that powerful security institution—felt that it had become a Frankenstein's monster that threatened to catalyze the intelligence community's development into a veto group, if not a state within the state. Golbery had advocated a complete airing of the Riocentro affair and had warned that the matter would be disinterred and exploited by the opposition during the 1982 campaigning. Moreover, given his concern with facilitating political normalization, he was dissatisfied with recent decisions to step up the fight against inflation and maintain solvency of the social security system in ways that might well hurt the PDS at the polls the following year. For, though GDP growth in 1980 had been a high 9.1 percent, inflation had climbed to 110 percent. But the full brunt of recession was being felt in 1981 as GDP actually shrank by 3.1 percent—nearly 5.3 percent in per capita terms—and inflation remained a high 95 percent.

Economic Storm Clouds

The Figueiredo government reaped the whirlwind with respect to the debt situation as interest payments zoomed toward the stratosphere as a result of the sharp upward thrust in interest rates brought about by U.S. policy at the end of the 1970s and in the early 1980s. Interest tied to the New York prime rate rose at a dizzying pace to levels often three times that in effect when the loans had been contracted, with those linked to the LIBOR (London Inter-Bank offered rate) following close behind. From a 7.8 percent average in 1977, the prime shot up to 11.8 percent in 1978 and on to 15.3 percent during 1979 before peaking at an unprecedented 21.5 percent in 1980—a year in which the LIBOR averaged a bloated 17.5 percent. As Brazil's loans were at a significant spread above these benchmarks, interest payments soared. From $2.7 billion in 1978, they grew to $4.2 billion the following year, then on to $7.5 billion in 1980. In conjunction with high amortization payments, this increase in interest led to dramatically higher debt service totals, with 1978's $8 billion jumping to near $10.6 billion the next year before it passed $11.3 billion in 1980.[43]

The interest shock was also felt in the critical current accounts deficit, which leapt from $7 billion in 1978 to over $10.7 billion prior to reaching $12.8 billion for 1980. These huge outflows could only partially be covered by using up foreign exchange reserves, which dropped from the 1978 peak of nearly $12 billion to $9.7 billion at the end of 1979 and were eroded further to $6.9 billion a year later. Moreover, the rapid growth in export revenues was more than eaten up by the once again surging oil prices. Hence, although the former grew substantially, from $12.7 billion in 1978 to over $15.2 billion the next year and on to $20.1 billion for 1980, imports exploded from $13.7 billion to $18.1 billion and then on to $23.0 billion. The resulting trade deficits of nearly $2.9 billion a year helped spur the current accounts deficits to record highs. In this situation principal had to be rolled, leading to a debt of $49.9 billion at the end of 1979 and $53.9 billion by December 31, 1980. The economic recession was still to come, and there was yet another dark cloud on the horizon. Whereas new loans minus debt service had to this point been positive—$1.1 billion in 1970 and almost $2.8 billion in 1975—despite the high total of additional loans, 1980 witnessed a net transfer abroad of over $1.8 billion. Although this outflow would be temporarily reversed the next year, from 1982 on the drain would grow sharply.[44]

Rather than undertake a major adjustment program with its concomitant economic slowdown and consequent political impopularity, Figueiredo chose to push ahead in 1981 along essentially the same lines that had resulted in substantial growth during the first half of his term. With great effort exports were increased to $23.3 billion during 1981, while imports were reduced slightly to $22.1 billion, allowing for a $1.2 billion trade surplus that cut the current accounts deficit to a still unmanageable $11.7 billion. Yet interest payments jumped to $10.3 billion, bringing debt service to $15.4 billion and resulting in a rise in long- and medium-term indebtedness to $61.4 billion. Indeed, to close the balance-of-payments gap, everything possible was done to attract loans, including resorting to shorter term borrowing, with state enterprises even buying unneeded equipment in order to obtain the attached producer credits.[45]

In the political realm, showing greater initiative and resolve than he had heretofore, Figueiredo seized advantage of the opportunity to emerge from the shadow cast over his leadership by the legendary power-behind-the-throne image that had developed over the years to make Golbery seem to be the father and genius of *abertura*. Members of the government's innermost circle were working on a plan for a chain reaction of job shifts that would be beneficial to their interests and ambitions. But the president short-circuited this plan by quickly naming Leitão de Abreu to the job Abreu had previously held under Médici and in which he had been accustomed to working closely with both Figueiredo and Delfim Netto. Although this meant that most of the holdovers from the Geisel administration were gone and that, in terms of personalities, the regime had taken on a profile much like that of the 1969–1974 era, it did not necessarily foreshadow an end to *abertura*. Indeed, rather than a return to the Médici years, it was in large part a co-optation of the Médici faction of the hardline into acceptance of a substantial political opening and a commitment of their support to behind-the-scenes moves to curb the terrorists of the Right. Although preferring the term *decompression* to *abertura*, Leitão de Abreu had not left a particularly conservative stamp in his seven-year stay on the Supreme Court.[46]

Heart Trouble and Loss of Heart

Whereas Golbery's resignation had focused the attention of the political elites on the succession issue, President Figueiredo's heart attack in mid-September raised this question to the public in a dramatic fashion. Although the uncertainties of the first hours after the president's heart attack aroused some fears of a crisis analogous to that that had been triggered by Costa e Silva's stroke in 1969, the outcome was strikingly different. This fact demonstrated the progress that had been made in strengthening the capabilities of the political system during the intervening dozen years. With the army minister issuing a warning that the subject of the vice-president assuming office was not a matter for barracks or officer-club debate, the regime's inner core quickly decided that Aureliano Chaves should occupy the presidency on a temporary basis. In keeping with his background as a successful Minas Gerais politician, Chaves behaved in a most responsible manner during his brief stewardship. Thus, not only did stability prevail, but the net effects of this episode were positive.

By late October it was apparent that Figueiredo's health was not critically undermined and that, as surgery had not been necessary at that time, he could resume his full duties by mid-November. Meanwhile by skillfully avoiding the intrigues in which certain opposition politicians sought to involve him, the civilian acting chief executive had strengthened his public image as a viable future president. On the other hand, those opposed to the idea of an end to the military's hold on the presidency as well as some civilian presidential hopefuls took comfort in the legislative defeat of a government-sponsored electoral bill in late October, as this defeat raised doubt concerning Chaves's ability to exert effective leadership over the government party.

To this point, in spite of opposition efforts to extend the limits of *abertura*, its scope and pace were still clearly under government control. In November the administration pushed through a package of electoral legislation including a requirement for straight-slate voting from top to bottom (*voto vinculado*) accompanied by a ban on coalitions. As a result, the PP under Tancredo Neves decided to merge with the PMDB. Although this was clearly a setback to the regime's divide-and-rule strategy, its impact was not as negative from the government's point of view as many authors have indicated. For, if alliance between the PP and the PMDB had been permitted along with ticket-splitting on the part of the individual voters, the outcome a year later would very likely have been no better for the PDS that the actual results. Furthermore, and far more important in the long run, the merger led to a situation in which the PMDB by 1983 at least was largely led by moderates coming from its PP side. These conciliatory pragmatists were able to neutralize, if not always control, the more intransigent and maximalist elements who otherwise might very well have come to dominate the chief opposition party and carry it leftward and away from compromise.

Indeed, this beneficial result would still be highly operative into 1989, long after the results of the 1982 balloting had been superseded by the subsequent 1986 elections.⁴⁷ Then, too, such changes in the electoral rules were less extensive than those routinely adopted by French governments under the Fourth Republic or even by Charles de Gaulle after he came to power. For that matter, the government of Socialist François Mitterand changed from single-member districts to proportional representation in 1986 to reduce their electoral losses and then switched back again in 1988 to curb the advance of Jean Marie Le Pen's extremist right-wing party. One might well wonder why measures considered pragmatic or even statesmanlike in France are considered opportunistic and immoral for Brazil.

Constitutional Amendment No. 22 in late July 1982 raised the requirement for amending the constitution to its traditional two-thirds level, increased a bit more the heavy overrepresentation of small states, and altered the composition of the electoral college by adding six representatives from each state legislature. These modifications provided security against an eventual opposition majority in Congress. With a number of individuals having shifted around from one party to another to find a good political "space" in their states, the congressional lineup on the eve of new national elections was 224 deputies and thirty-six senators for the PDS against 168 seats in the lower house and twenty-seven in the upper for the PMDB. The PTB with nine deputies and one senator and the PT with five deputies and one senator rounded out the party spectrum at the national level.⁴⁸

Yet a major cost of the protracted period of military rule was becoming apparent: Populist civilian politicians of a centrist to conservative cast— most notably Kubitschek, Lacerda, and Adhemar de Barros—had been gotten rid of, but the ensuing vacuum had not been filled by new civilian leadership. The 1966 crop of governors yielded only the already established and by now rather elderly Luiz Viana Filho and the never-electable Roberto de Abreu Sodré. The permanent residue from the 1970 cohort was really only Antônio Carlos Magalhães, like Viana Filho from Bahia. The only presidential material from 1974 was Chaves, and the grades were not yet in on the 1978 governors. The result was that unless the return to direct election of state chief executives could produce a new cadre of potential national figures, the way could be open for the return to presidential contention of the two individuals who had most directly contributed to the crisis that had brought on military intervention in 1964—Jânio Quadros (the irresponsible quitter) and Leonel Brizola (the equally irresponsible incendiary). Certainly it was possible that these two leaders had learned from the hard lessons of nearly two decades, but there was no assurance that they had really become wiser as well as older.

The 1982 Elections and Their Aftermath

The November 15 voting constituted an important triumph for moderation and a significant step toward sensible political modernization. Essentially, Brazil emerged strengthened rather than divided by elections whose results encouraged all major political actors to pursue their objectives through normal parliamentary and electoral channels. As was crucial for political stability at that juncture, the PDS won in a majority of states—guaranteeing in the process control of the Senate, a near majority in the lower house, and a slim margin in the electoral college that would choose the new president a little over two years later. Yet whereas there had been but a single opposition governor for the preceding four years, the return to direct elections gave the opposition control of ten statehouses to the government's thirteen and created a new situation in which the central government would not only need to negotiate, but also at times to truly compromise. As the executive branch was accustomed to doing little more in this direction than consulting its own party and then informing the opposition of the administration's decisions, this was a major change indeed.

A Near Standoff

Most notable was the fact that, whereas in 1965—the most recent time governors had been directly elected—opposition victories in Rio de Janeiro and Minas Gerais by very moderate figures had led to a hardline coup, this time even Brizola's win in Rio de Janeiro and those of the PMDB in nine other states were accepted by the armed forces with much more resignation than trauma. This acceptance was all the more significant in light of the fact that these states contained roughly 60 percent of the area and population of Brazil and even more of the country's wealth and productive capacity.[49]

Although Rio de Janeiro is only Brazil's third most important state, the election there had the most significant ramifications. With just 1.7 million votes out of nearly 5.5 million cast, Brizola—by far the most feared of all opposition candidates—was elected state chief executive over a promising representative of the new leadership generation of the government party. Yet as disappointing as this victory by the highly personalist but generally leftist Democratic Workers' Party (PDT) was to the president and his close associates, the strong showing of Wellington Moreira Franco and the rest of the PDS slate was in the long run probably worth much more to the regime than winning in three or four of the marginal states.

Four years previously the government party's predecessor, ARENA, had been subjected to a crushing defeat in the former capital, but with the more than 1.5 million votes it received this time around, the PDS not only whipped the favored PMDB, but also almost killed off the PTB in the process. The PMDB's Waldomiro Teixeira garnered fewer than 1.2 million votes—below a tenth of the total—while the PTB's Sandra Cavalcanti, an early frontrunner in the public opinion polls, was all but devastated by the meager half-million-plus votes she received. In addition, the PT's high-flying dreams were dashed by the dismal 150,000 votes it garnered. Moreover, many of the most radical congressional candidates went down to defeat even in the midst of this opposition tide. Thus, most of the more ideological "historical," or "authentic," PMDB candidates for both Congress and the state legislature were defeated as centrist former PP politicians ran more strongly.

In Brazil's true nation within a nation, São Paulo, the PMDB won impressively on the strength of roughly 5.2 million votes to over 2.7 million for the PDS, fewer than 1.5 million for the PTB, and an almost insignificant 1.1 million for the PT—below 10 percent of the vote. Besides sending essentially moderate former Christian Democrat Franco Montoro to the statehouse, the major opposition party elected thirty federal deputies to sixteen for the PDS; yet this outcome compared favorably with ARENA's performance in 1978, with almost all progovernment incumbents who lost reelection bids being MDB turncoats lured over to the government side after those elections by then Governor Maluf. Moreover, Severo Gomes, the most moderate of the three PMDB senatorial nominees, received almost 2.9 million votes compared to fewer than 1.9 million for Almino Afonso (labor minister under Goulart) and only 170,000 for a radical nationalist. In its "home" state the PT, although winning nine congressional seats, saw its strongest vote getter come in no better than ninth overall, while its dominant personality, Lula da Silva, ran only fourth in the governorship race—some 300,000 votes behind third-place Jânio Quadros, who was attempting a comeback on the PTB ticket.

In Minas Gerais the PMDB's Tancredo Neves, formerly national head of the PP and coming off a hard-fought senatorial election in 1978, won the governor's post that had narrowly eluded him in 1960. Yet his vote margin of under 2.7 million to over 2.4 million for the less prominent PDS standard-bearer showed that the opposition was far from dominant in Brazil's second state, a fact brought home by the PMDB's mere 140,000 vote margin over the government party in the congressional races. Though Itamar Franco (who would become Brazil's vice-president in 1990) was reelected to the Senate, he was the only authentic MDB figure to do well, and most of the other victors were from the former PP ranks. Most important, having held almost every office in politics and government that really matters during a career spanning five decades—including justice minister under Vargas and prime minister during the 1961–1962 parliamentary regime—the shrewd and experienced Neves was available for and alert to the possibility of a presidential bid.

The PDS's losses in the three most populous states fully accounted for the nationwide difference in the total gubernatorial vote of nearly 8 million in favor of the four other parties combined over the PDS's 42 percent of the total. In terms of congressional seats the government party came up with fifty-six in the big three states as against sixty-seven for the PMDB, sixteen for the PDT, thirteen for the PTB, and eight for the PT. This substantial deficit was all but wiped out in the rest of the country—where the PDS won 179 Chamber seats compared to 134 for the PMDB and but six for the other three parties combined. Although failing to elect a senator from any of the three major states, the PDS triumphed by a fifteen to seven margin in the rest of the country, thus retaining a majority of exactly two-thirds (forty-six to twenty-three) in the upper house.

The opposition parties' justifiable claim to represent the modern, urbanized sector of Brazil was based upon the PMDB's solid victories in Paraná as well as in São Paulo and Minas Gerais. In Paraná José Richa gained the governorship by 1.7 million to over 1.1 million for the progovernment candidate, with Álvaro Dias victorious in the Senate race. On the other hand, Rio Grande do Sul and Santa Catarina provided the PDS with its major victories outside the northeast and north. In Rio Grande do Sul, Jair Soares defeated the PMDB's Pedro Simon by a mere 22,000 votes only because the PDT's strong bid split the opposition vote. The PDS also ousted Paulo Brossard from the Senate as each of the major parties polled nearly 1.3 million votes while the PDT came in at 750,000. In Santa Catarina the PDS margin was a mere 13,000 as the PDS and the PMDB each drew over 825,000 votes.

Other major triumphs for the government side included Bahia, Pernambuco, and Ceará (fifth, seventh, and eighth in terms of electorate). In Bahia, Antônio Carlos Magalhães, two-time governor, carried off his gamble of putting his political future on the line by delivering a massive victory at over 1.6 million to just above 1 million for a relatively unknown PMDB candidate, while veteran Viana Filho (presidential chief of staff for Castelo Branco and subsequently governor) easily won reelection to the Senate. Although the election in Pernambuco was much closer, it had at least equal impact in light of the state's strong tradition of ideological opposition to the central government and the proven appeal of leftist candidates in Recife. But the PMDB's Senator Marcos Freire lost the governorship to former vice-governor Roberto Magalhães as outgoing governor Marco Maciel gained election to the Senate. In terms of margin, the PDS victory in Ceará was even more impressive, as young economist Gonzaga da Mota garnered nearly 1.2 million votes in burying the PMDB's Mauro Benevides, who failed to reach the half-million mark, and two-time former governor Virgílio Távora ran up the same overwhelming 70 percent margin in his bid to return to the Senate.

Nationally some 48.5 million of 58.6 million registered voters (in a population of slightly over 123 million) turned out, giving the opposition parties—especially the PMDB—victory in ten states that collectively had three-fifths of the country's population and nearly 75 percent of its GDP.[50] Continuing secular trends, the government party won in only twenty-five of the 100 largest cities and, for the first time, failed to get a majority of the valid vote in the balloting for Chamber of Deputies. Yet its 36.7 percent of the total—including null and blank ballots—was only 3.3 percent below ARENA's proportion in 1978, when the artificial two-party system was still in effect. The PDS still enjoyed a very modest 100,000-vote edge over the PMDB on this dimension of national voting, as the PDT got only 2.4 million votes nationally (almost all in Rio de Janeiro and Rio Grande do Sul), with 1.8 million for the PTB and 1.4 million for the PT—more than three-quarters of it in São Paulo.

Significantly, the elections showed a continuation of the drop in invalid votes that had begun in 1974 and carried through 1978. Thus from a high of 30.3 percent in 1970, these "spoiled ballots" in the proportional representation voting had dropped to 21.3 percent in 1974 and 20.7 percent in 1978 before falling to 15.1 percent in 1982—half the level of a dozen years earlier. In the majority races the decline was equally dramatic, down to only 10.2 percent compared with 27.7 percent in 1970 and 18.6 percent in 1978. For the legitimacy of the system, it was far better that these anti-government electors vote for parties other than the PDS rather than cast blank or null ballots. Moreover, the turnout rate was an exceptionally high 82.8 percent.[51]

Although Brizola's election was very difficult for most of the military to swallow, it did not provoke a major crisis. The government calmed the more vocal elements by pointing out that the most important fact was that the PDS emerged from the elections with a solid majority in the electoral college—with 235 federal deputies plus forty-six senators for a nucleus of 281, with control of a dozen state legislatures potentially good for seventy-two additional electors, plus three from Santa Catarina where the legislature was evenly split. This twelve-seat margin over a minimal majority could be increased by the fact that the PTB was at least as much a potential ally of the PDS as it was a possible part of the opposition.[52] The matter of the nonpromotion and hence forced retirement of hardline leader General Coelho Neto was also absorbed within the officer corps without serious consequences.

Economic Woes

With the elections over, the government admitted publicly what it had denied to that point—that the country was on the verge of insolvency. Even before the elections the administration had announced rather stringent fiscal and financial goals for 1983, including a sharp cut in imports in order to generate a $6 billion trade surplus to help cover the unmanageable current accounts deficit—which had swollen to over $16 billion. Now the administration revealed that negotiations had been going on with the IMF for some months because the country's foreign exchange reserves were rapidly approaching zero. Indeed, in the calculations of some specialists this might already have occurred by year's end except for Delfim Netto's insistence upon carrying on the receivables side of the ledger an uncollectable debt from Poland.

To add to the president's woes, not only had 1982 been a bad year economically, but 1983 would prove to be worse in almost every respect. Thus in 1981 interest payments of $9.2 billion were well over three times the figures for Geisel's last year in office.[53] In 1982 GDP growth was a meager 1.1 percent, inflation was up marginally to just under 100 percent, and the current accounts deficit was a whopping $16.3 billion—up $4.6 billion from the preceding year—while net capital inflow had slacked off by $4.9 million. Though imports were reduced significantly to $19.4 billion, exports declined even more sharply to $20.2 billion. With interest payments surging to $12.6 billion, bringing debt service to a staggering $18.3 billion, reserves plummeted to below $4 billion—at the official calculation—but the effective level was approaching zero, as the published figures not only ran some months behind the fast-deteriorating situation but also were padded by such uncollectables as the $1.5 billion owed Brazil by Poland. With around $12.5 billion borrowed "normally" during the year, much of it fairly short-term, the accumulated principal took a quantum jump to at least $69.7 billion. Indeed, more inclusive criteria than those of the Central Bank yielded a total of $79.6 billion for 1982, up from $68.7 billion in 1981.[54]

After mid-year the Mexican moratorium dramatically raised the prospects of default and brought home to the international banking community its dangerous overexposure in Latin America. This not only caused a rapid dropoff in the flow of new loans and credits to Brazil, but also led to a decline of some $4 billion in interbank deposits and of $2 billion to $3 billion in commercial credit lines. The need for IMF funds as well as help from the United States and European governments was clear if even a semblance of continued solvency was to be maintained. Thus, the administration began behind-the-scenes negotiations—while denying vehemently until after the November elections that such negotiations were going on, nor even admitting the existence of a critical balance of payments problem.

Only a hastily thrown together emergency package avoided default on interest payments, with no one really wanting to bring up the question of amortization, which had quietly been suspended in mid-year.[55] Finally the first in a long series of letters of intent—none of which would be fulfilled— was signed with the IMF in January 1983. Although this agreement brought some immediate relief, it provided no medium-range solution to the problem of administering a suffocating debt that the government had expected to continue rolling over as it had in the past without having actually to divert resources from development to payment of the debt. By dint of a 23 percent maxi-devaluation of the cruzeiro, exports were made more competitive, albeit at a high cost in inflation. Brazil embarked full force upon a strategy of attaining greatly increased trade surpluses (involving reduction in oil imports as well as expansion of exports) in order to keep up interest payments as a means of convincing banks to roll over Brazil's debt principal.

In these spheres the country's performance was at least impressive, bordering upon truly dramatic. The nearly $6.5 billion trade surplus of 1983—on exports of $21.9 billion and imports of only $15.4 billion—cut the towering current accounts deficit, which had exceeded $16.3 billion in 1982, to only $6.8 billion. Then 1984's doubling of this trade surplus to $13.1 billion, with foreign sales of just over $27 billion almost twice overseas purchases of $13.9 billion, would keep current accounts nearly balanced. Yet the foreign debt jumped by $11.6 billion in 1983 (to $81.3 billion) and would soar further to $91.1 billion by the end of 1984. Indeed, including short-term debt brought the foreign debt to $102 billion.[56]

Yet the government met with no real success in getting the economy under control and moving forward as the erosion of the previous two years turned into a precipitous drop. GDP shrunk by an alarming 2.8 percent, with the consequent reduction in standards of living causing a sharp rise in social unrest.[57] Despite recessionary austerity measures, inflation more than doubled to a record 211 percent, aggravated by a sharp climb in unemployment. The modest progress made between 1970 and 1980 in reducing income inequalities and alleviating the absolute misery of a very large proportion of the population was washed away. An equally serious problem was the pall of pessimism that hung over the nation as an increasing proportion of the population lost confidence in a speedy economic recovery.[58]

Such a deteriorating economic environment was favorable to the opposition's renewed campaign for a return to direct presidential elections. In mid-year Figueiredo had to take leave from the presidency and go to the United States for bypass surgery. During the month and a half of his absence and through the many months it took before the president could resume even a nearly full work schedule, mass rallies were held in all major cities in support of a constitutional amendment to effect direct presidential elections.[59] Yet the government remained confident that it could deny this proposal the two-thirds majority required and that its margin in the electoral college—which had climbed to thirty-six with postelection shifts by some congressmen—would stand up to any strains induced by conflict over selection of the party's candidate. Even the emergence of PMDB national president Guimarães as a popular symbol—Mr. Direct Elections—did not preoccupy the regime's strategists.

Opening Becomes Transition: 1984—A Crucial Year

As the Figueiredo government limped into its sixth year—a stay in power longer than that of any Brazilian president since Vargas—the transition to a civilian, fully competitive political system was far from assured. Although events during the latter half of 1983 had clearly demonstrated that the regime was losing its control over the process of *abertura*, as late as mid-1984 it still appeared very likely that Figueiredo's successor would come from within his administration or, if not, at least from the conservative wing of the regime's party. The defeat in late April of the opposition's campaign for direct presidential elections reinforced the probability of such an outcome. Yet by the beginning of the final quarter of the year, *abertura* had become democratic transition and the election of a civilian from the opposition's ranks appeared all but certain. Indeed, the crucial turnaround from a controlled opening to a situation in which initiative had completely escaped the government's hands took place in the short span of three months—June through August.

Leadership Falters

Paradoxically, the government's loss of control over the political situation coincided with its success in the economic realm; a year that had begun as a continuation of 1983's disastrous performance would finish with a remarkable second half recovery that led to 5.4 percent growth for the year.

But as most of the expansion came late in the year and was masked by continuing high inflation, it came too late to bolster the badly sagging political prestige of a noticeably tired and divided administration. Yet the crucial factor in *abertura* becoming democratic transition against the government's wishes was a failure of leadership in the political sphere. During Geisel's stewardship, his strong leadership got liberalization on the tracks and moving at a controlled albeit often uneven pace. Although the opening for the purpose of extrication or tactical disengagement had continued through the first part of Figueiredo's term, it began to falter after the triple blows of Portella's death, Golbery's departure, and Figueiredo's cardiovascular problems. It was leadership failure that made it possible for *abertura* to acquire its own dynamism.

If Figueiredo could have brought himself to support his vice-president's logical and popular candidacy, all would probably have gone as planned and the PDS would have continued in power after 1985. Ill-conceived efforts to impose someone closer to the president's inner circle led instead not only to the election of a PMDB leader, but also to the implosion of the PDS and its dizzying descent from majority party to insignificant rump—all by means of abandonment, without even requiring the benefit of elections. Yet through an ironic turn of events, ill health would prevent the PMDB standard-bearer from taking office, opening the way for inauguration of his running mate—who as late as mid-1984 not only had been a bulwark of the PDS, but also its national president. As for Chaves, he would have to settle for becoming a Cabinet member in the Sarney government, when but for Figueiredo's shortsightedness he could have been the one to preside over the transition to democratic civilian rule.

The administration sought, with some success, to weaken congressional support for the Dante de Oliveira amendment for direct presidential elections by introducing its own version, one that retained the electoral college for the 1984 presidential election but provided for a direct election in 1988. Had the opposition accepted this compromise, there would have been direct elections for the national chief executive sooner than was actually the case— 1988 rather than 1989. But the PMDB and its allies again miscalculated, rationalizing that many PDS legislators would bow to popular sentiment as it was expressed in the streets and in the galleries.

When the vote came in the lower house on April 25 it was another moral victory but a concrete defeat. For, although the tally was 298 to 65 in favor, including 55 positive votes from the government party, the amendment was doomed by 113 absences—112 from the PDS—as the requirement was for two-thirds of the total membership, not of those voting, and the final total was 22 votes short. Moreover, even if the measure had passed in the Chamber, it would almost certainly have died in the Senate. The decisive consideration in the lower house's rejection of this long step toward democratization was possible hardline military reaction that could derail *abertura*, and there is no reason to believe that the upper house would have been any less sensitive to this danger—also, many of the senators would not have to face the voters as soon as would the deputies.

Indeed, the lessons of 1965, 1968, and 1969 were still sharply etched on the minds of Brazil's Solons. Misplaced faith that Congress could not resist the manifest will of the people would again crop up in March 1988, when concern over military reaction would lead the constituent assembly to reject both the parliamentary system and reduction of Sarney's term. In 1984 this misplaced faith only gave the regime a chance to recapture the initiative.

As early as August 1983 Figueiredo had decided against Chaves as his successor. Yet by that time it was already apparent that—in light of a number of scandals involving abuses of power by the SNI—General Medeiros was not a viable option, and Leitão de Abreu's prospects existed chiefly in his own mind. Although the president clearly had lost control of the situation and lacked the disposition and ability to lead in a changing environment of increasingly competitive politics, egged on by several of his ministers he flirted with the idea of trying to stay on, at least for an additional two years. He was encouraged in this wildly inappropriate and unrealistic venture by Brizola, for whom direct presidential elections in 1986 appeared the optimum road to the presidency. And with almost all the key figures in the government involved in maneuvers to stay in power—no fewer than six of them harboring personal aspirations to be president—Delfim Netto continued to run economic policy as he saw fit without interference from anyone, least of all Figueiredo.

Thus, this chaotic situation simply became a bit more confused when, in the midst of the disclosure of the miserable economic results for 1983, the president gave up on the task of finding a consensus candidate and threw that problem back into the lap of the PDS. But the government party had itself been seriously weakened in July 1983, when an insurgent slate of backbenchers called Participation gained 35 percent of the seats on the national directorate, very nearly forcing out party President José Sarney and Secretary-General Prisco Viana. As fate would have it, however, within a few years these two, along with Antônio Carlos Magalhães—who at that time was still attempting to engineer an Andreazza-Chaves slate—would be running the country, with Sarney as president and Viana and Magalhães as two of the most influential ministers.

Presidential Succession and Party Realignment

Figueiredo's failure to define his preferred successor, at least in terms of a particular name, led by mid-1984 to increasing disaggregation of the government party that was reflected also in the Cabinet and in higher reaches of the bureaucracy. Indeed, dissension among key advisors was rife by late 1983 and grew thereafter. In this context, Paulo Maluf, who at fifty-two had been actively campaigning to gain the support of PDS delegates and electors since even before the 1982 elections, continued his relentless drive to force the government to accept him as its candidate. Having defeated Figueiredo's favorite at the 1978 São Paulo ARENA convention and then gone on to become governor of that key state, this entrepreneur of Lebanese extraction was certain he could repeat this feat on the national level in 1984. He was encouraged in this belief by Golbery, who saw Maluf as the best chance for getting the detested—by Golbery even more than by the public—"Medeiros crowd" out of power.

Believing that Maluf could be headed off, key presidential staffers continued their work of persuading Figueiredo that Chaves, former president Geisel's clear preference, had been too independent during the times he had exercised the presidency and had made Figueiredo look bad with his vigorous administrative style.[60] With Medeiros at its core, this clique hoped to remain in power behind Interior Minister Andreazza. Convinced that Chaves would have no real choice but to accept the results of the PDS convention, they myopically discounted the possibility of his leading a major schism of the party.[61]

Maluf—determined, hyperactive, and intelligent, but in many ways open to attack as a nonideological demagogue with limitless ambitions who believed that every man had his price and who was often willing to pay that price to get what he wanted—proved capable of winning the PDS nomination. But the fact that this was achieved largely through lavish expenditures and promises of future benefits and offices for delegates coming over to his side sat badly with Maluf's rivals—who could not or would not compete with him in this field. Chaves, a hot-tempered weight lifter capable of bursts of self-righteousness, had already been considering the possibility of not carrying his campaign to a convention seemingly loaded against him—in which case he and his followers would not feel bound by the convention's outcome.

Thus, as the candidate with the lowest national popularity quotient moved ever closer to the government party's nomination, its most popular figure edged gradually toward destabilizing the whole controlled process by reaching an agreement with his fellow Minas Gerais statesman, the diminutive Governor Tancredo Neves. And as the focus of politics returned from the speakers' platform at the *direitas ja* (direct elections now) rallies to the arena of negotiations and alliance building, Neves once again came to overshadow Ulysses Guimarães.[62]

Vice-President Chaves enjoyed very widespread support among business and industry leaders as well as being favored by much of the officer corps. Moreover, Geisel's endorsement still carried very substantial weight with important bellwethers of the military establishment. Clearly, pushing Chaves too far was an unwise move, yet it was a series of additional—some blatantly unnecessary—rebuffs by the now floundering president that convinced Chaves to break openly with Figueiredo and split with the PDS, drove him to get many other regime figures to join him in this risky venture, and led him to transfer his business and military backing to Neves.

Blinded by a propensity to equate loyalty with defense of even the most unsuccessful of his government's policies, the president also failed to see that *abertura* from above required going beyond the hardcore unconditional backers of the 1964 Revolution to find a candidate who could combine a basic commitment to the major goals of the 1964–1984 regimes with an ability to mobilize popular support and channel burgeoning aspirations in directions compatible with those aims. Surrounded by advisors who were playing on his ego for their own purposes, Figueiredo seems either to have lost any capacity for independent judgment or to have hoped that a muddled succession picture might provide him an opportunity to hold on to power.

Although the opposition's campaign for a return to direct election of the president was not successful in attaining its expressed goal, it did help significantly to create an environment in which Figueiredo's continuist project would die aborning and in which the government was prevented from adding insult to injury by foisting an unpopular Maluf upon the frustrated populace. This environment also led many PDS politicians to consider seriously the consequences in terms of their 1986 electoral ambitions of supporting a candidate whom majority public opinion clearly considered not only the antithesis of their desires, but also essentially illegitimate.

Once the excitement and letdown of the campaign for direct elections was over, a few weeks after the crucial vote, the battleground shifted from the public eye to the kind of behind-the-scenes maneuvering that traditionally has proven more effective in changing the course of Brazilian politics. During May and June a significant coalition of PMDB elements and PDS dissidents formed to combat Figueiredo's conciliatory amendment. Their parliamentary skill in finding a loophole for moving up the date for direct presidential elections from 1988 to 1984 led the president to withdraw his proposal on the eve of its scheduled June 27 Chamber vote.

Yet by this time the dominant pragmatic wing of the PMDB had already decided that the more productive course was to do battle within the electoral college in the hope that the respected Tancredo Neves could gain support from a good proportion of the disappointed backers of unsuccessful aspirants for the government party's nomination. This strategy gained substance as Chaves and his followers decided to anticipate their defeat within the PDS and formalize their dissident group as the Liberal Front. In June, following Maluf's predictable rebuff of a proposal that all the PDS contenders step down to allow the president to select a unity candidate, the Chaves contingent had suggested a party primary to choose the candidate who had the broadest backing of the rank and file. Carried to Figueiredo by party President Sarney, this reasonable proposal originally gained the president's halfhearted approval. When faced with Maluf's categorical rejection of the idea, however, Figueiredo abruptly reversed himself. Consequently, Sarney resigned his post on June 16 and was followed in short order by Senator Jorge Bornhausen—Sarney's immediate successor as party head.[63]

As a final conciliatory gesture both Chaves and Senator Marco Maciel again offered to withdraw if Maluf and Andreazza would do likewise. Feeling victory within his grasp, Maluf refused outright, while Andreazza conditioned his agreement to Maluf's assent. While Andreazza almost pitifully pleaded with Figueiredo to throw the government's full support behind him, one of Andreazza's staunch backers—Antônio Carlos Magalhães—announced that he would vote for Neves in the electoral college if the PDS's choice was Maluf. Shortly thereafter Magalhães began to excoriate Maluf as an incorrigible corrupter in a bombshell *Veja* interview. Thus, although Maluf easily prevailed at the mid-August PDS convention—by 493 to 350 over Andreazza—more than 100 individuals entitled to vote stayed away in protest over Maluf's alleged "buying" of the nomination. These Liberal Front elements began immediately to woo deeply disappointed Andreazza backers.

Indeed, on the heels of Maluf's convention victory the marriage of the Liberal Front dissidents and the PMDB was first celebrated, then consummated. Finally faced with the reality that there would be no direct election for the presidency, the progressive wing of the PMDB had no choice but to acquiesce in the nomination of Neves—a particularly bitter pill for Ulysses Guimarães to swallow, as he understandably felt that his long tenure as MDB-PMDB head should have earned him the high honor of being the presidential candidate. Ulysses had long chafed at Neves's seniority, which had been evident as far back as 1961, when Ulysses had become a minister under then Prime Minister Neves. Having been the opposition standard-bearer in 1973, the proud Paulista would never be satisfied with the series of high offices he was yet to attain, but would continue to view the presidency as the prize that his devotion to duty merited. Instead, at the August PMDB convention Ulysses had to watch Neves receive nearly unanimous backing, with Sarney—who until recently had been a ranking figure of the military regime—being named the vice-presidential candidate.

Victory of the Moderates

In a very short time the new Democratic Alliance bandwagon evolved into a steamroller. Almost immediately its Liberal Front component roughly doubled, turning the putative thirty-six-vote PDS margin into at least a 100-vote deficit—at around 300 for the Democratic Alliance to 200 for the PDS, with 160–170 undecided. Moreover, public opinion polls, certain to have a psychological effect upon wavering electoral college members, put Neves ahead by about a three to one margin. Although Maluf remained certain that electors would ultimately prove susceptible to his blandishments— underpinned as they were by promises of ample funding in the 1986 campaigns and patronage in his administration—this was not to be the case. Nor were his hopes to see further manipulation of the rules governing the electoral college to be fulfilled. For the mass rallies held by Neves served as a constant reminder to the 686 electors of the political perils of going against the surging tide of public opinion with a return to competitive democratic politics just around the corner.

Thus the two campaigns followed almost totally different strategies: That of the government candidate was based upon past effectiveness of the instruments of clientelism and the politics of patronage and payoff, and that of Neves was based on the promise of a new era of conciliation and participation and a future worthy of the long-suffering Brazilian people.

Although Figueiredo had already warned Maluf that even if the latter won the PDS nomination he would never manage to be elected, the PDS candidate counted on the president eventually throwing the full weight of the government behind his candidacy.[64] Though Industry and Commerce Minister Camílo Penna—a Mineiro long associated with the rebellious vice-president, Chaves—was forced out, most administration officials merely continued with their regular responsibilities, and some even gave aid and comfort to the new "enemy." This was particularly true in technical agencies and among those second-echelon figures identified with the centrist faction who had left the PDS for the Liberal Front—or who were planning to do so at a strategic moment in the future. As it worked out, a number of these "defectors" would indeed be kept on or even advanced in the new government; others would be rehabilitated in 1987 and 1988 and appointed to important offices.

The replacement in September of the SUDENE and Sugar and Alcohol Institute heads was more of a slap at Maciel for his role in the Liberal Front than it was a move seriously intended to intimidate the northeastern governors. One after another these governors joined the Democratic Alliance, expressing the impossibility of supporting a thoroughly unpopular candidate once their constituents had become excited over Neves. Each in his own way made it clear that being put on starvation rations by an angered federal government for the short period of five months was far preferable to betraying the trust of his electorate—and having to face the consequences at the polls in November 1986. By 1988, two of them, Hugo Napoleão and João Alves, would be in Sarney's Cabinet, and a third would have come very close to attaining that lofty perch.

In October, stung by criticism from his military ministers that he was not doing enough to stave off an opposition victory, Figueiredo resorted to vigorous jawboning and arm twisting of PDS governors. But his efforts were to no avail as the governors' alignment with the Democratic Alliance candidate went forward. As the key to the Maluf candidacy resided in belief in the inevitability of his victory, once such a victory was called seriously into question Maluf's support quickly eroded. Although more vigorous punishment of Liberal Front governors and dissident PDS elements by Figueiredo might have slowed this process, it could not have stopped it.

Maluf's last hope was to gain the lion's share of the 138 state representatives to the electoral college. His energetic efforts during October to win over PDS state legislators who would have a say in the matter were effectively neutralized by the governors, who met his hardball tactics by flexing some of their own muscles. In the end these noncongressional electors would vote 108 to twenty-three in favor of Neves (with seven abstentions). The PMDB came away with fifty-one of these state legislature electors and the Liberal Front with forty, so the handwriting was on the wall—except in the eyes of those observers who either attributed miraculous abilities to the "undefeated" Maluf or had succumbed to his multiple temptations.

Not surprisingly, by mid-October there was an increasingly widespread perception not only that Neves should be elected, but also that he would in fact be the winner. At this juncture Tancredo was favored by almost 70 percent of the voters in the seven largest metropolitan regions, whereas Maluf had the support of fewer than 20 percent. Moreover, 63 percent of those polled expected a win for the Democratic Alliance, while only 30 percent foresaw Maluf as the likely victor. A month later Maluf's approval rate had declined to less than 14 percent with only 21 percent still expecting the government to pull out a win by hook or by crook. More important, private meetings between Neves and the army minister had removed most of Pires's most serious reservations, and the ever-cautious opposition candidate went out of his way to reassure the military that there would be no revanchism under his government and that the armed forces as an institution would be free from political interference.[65]

By a vote of 480 to 180 on January 15, 1985, the electoral college made Neves the country's new chief executive and essentially rendered the incumbent administration totally impotent. Some 271 of the Democratic Alliance's votes came from the PMDB, with the PFL delivering 113 more and PDS dissidents chipping in with fifty-five. (Fourteen PDS electors and three others abstained, and nine electors—five of them from the PT—were absent.)[66] Thus, after nearly twenty-one years of military regimes, Brazil was about to get a civilian government, and a broad-based centrist one to boot.

In the final analysis the successful transition owed a great deal to the reasonableness and moderation demonstrated by almost all significant political actors. Those disappointed by the course of events came to accept their setback and eventually assumed a statesmanlike stance. Thus, Figueiredo himself adapted to the role of the individual who has presided over a peaceful return to civilian government, while even Maluf adopted the pose of a good loser—and immediately began to formulate plans for an eventual comeback. Those of the Center-Left who had pinned their hopes on direct elections consoled themselves with the fact that they would have an active role in the new government and turned their energies to the task of shaping a new constitution. Further over on the Left there were audible sighs of relief that the end of military rule was finally at hand—accompanied by a flurry of activity on the part of the several rival groups to position themselves for the increased opportunities that political legalization would soon bring them. And well they might be content, for Brazil had come a long way indeed in a short time since those days in late 1981 when the bombs at Riocentro had threatened to abort *abertura*.

9

The Sarney Government: From Transition to Consolidation, 1985–1989

As had been the case in 1822, 1889, 1930, and 1946, most observers of the Brazilian scene and many elements of Brazilian society expected that this transition would lead swiftly and almost automatically to a substantially transformed political system. To the extent that they foresaw a sharp break with the past and a regime based on new forms of political organization, these observers and citizens were soon to be disappointed (as in fact earlier generations had been). For this had been a "transition without rupture" in which the adherence to the movement for a change of regime by experienced politicians and powerful interests associated with the prior order would guarantee that the bottle might be new, but the wine would be substantially the same.

Indeed, by 1987 if not earlier, the nation's power configuration would be closer to that prevailing under Figueiredo than to the radically transformed structure envisaged by the would-be architects of a new order.[1] For nothing had really taken place either to change the social and economic bases of Brazilian politics or to place at center stage any new national organizations that could displace the entrenched military and propertied interests. Repeated assertions that the era of ideological politics had finally arrived were based on misreadings of the situation and gross overestimation of the role popular organizations had played in the transition—as this role was distinct from such organizations' high visibility and level of activity. Moreover, there was little consideration of the difficulties of transforming these popular organizations into effective forces in the day-to-day realm of politics that was dominated by bureaucratic decision making and a carry-over Congress.

Forbidding Challenges

Although twenty-one years of military rule had come to an end, transition to a viable system of competitive civilian politics would prove an arduous and divisive chore. Among the tasks confronting the first civilian government in almost a generation were: (1) the need to work out a viable relationship between the executive and legislative branches of government; (2) the urgency of infusing life into the immense and ponderous state machinery that had been built up since 1964; (3) the desirability of restructuring the political party system without returning to the excessive fragmentation that contributed to the protracted crisis of the early 1960s; and (4) the necessity of drafting and putting into effect a new constitutional framework adequate to the needs of a complex society with enormous social inequalities and vast developmental needs.

Moreover, early on there would be elections for mayors of state capitals, and then the government would have to conduct nationwide elections in November 1986 for all governorships, two senatorial seats per state, and the full array of federal and state legislative seats. All this would have to be undertaken quickly and accomplished before the end of 1988 at the latest—a point at which elections in over 4,000 municipalities were to be held. Then the president would have to steer the country through its first direct presidential election in almost three decades.

As if this agenda were not formidable enough, there were also the matters of husbanding a still quite fragile economic recovery and dealing with the forbidding social deficit accumulated through twenty years of concentration on economic growth rather than on societal needs or income distribution. In this regard, continuity in economic policy would be sorely lacking during the early years of civilian government as finance ministers enjoyed precarious tenure and their loudly heralded plans proved bereft of staying power. This policy instability—reminiscent of the early years of the republic nearly a century before—was in sharp contrast with the period of military rule, during which Campos, Delfim Netto, and Simonsen orchestrated economic policy for almost the entire twenty-one years.[2] Yet the consistent historical pattern of letting short-term political considerations take priority over economic rationality and even over any kind of long-range developmental programs—a pattern broken in part by Vargas and Kubitschek—would again prevail.

Zigzags rooted in the contradiction between expectations and the nominal majority party's inability to shape the course of events also marked the political realm. There had been widespread faith that Tancredo Neves, with his vast experience and nearly legendary political sagacity, would find a way to handle the intimidating mass of challenges awaiting the civilian regime. It was also expected that the PMDB would be his partner in this endeavor. But Neves never even had the chance to assume the presidential office, which fell instead to Sarney—who was viewed with reserve, suspicion, distrust, or even distaste by much, perhaps most, of the PMDB, the dominant element of the Democratic Alliance. Moving cautiously, so much so that he earned a reputation for indecisiveness, Sarney would gradually escape from efforts by PMDB leaders to limit his options, and by mid-1988 he had managed to place these efforts in check. But within a few months he became virtually a premature lame duck as the drama of presidential succession surged to the foreground.

Rivalries and Contradictions

The progressive wing of the PMDB and others who had expected that the transition to civilian rule would mean something resembling a return to the structural reform orientation of the Goulart years looked askance at Sarney's reliance upon former ARENA politicians and his cultivation of close relations with the armed forces. In the view of these progressives the changes from the military regime were more formal than profound. For them transition would come only when some authentic opponent of the military governments, not merely a critic of Figueiredo's mishandling of the succession process, came to occupy the presidency. Yet it would be precisely this disdain for Sarney on the part of the historical PMDBers that would push him to rely upon his old allies from the Geisel-Figueiredo years.

Very likely no permanent harmony between the disparate elements of the Democratic Alliance was possible in view of their incompatible concepts of what the socioeconomic content of the "Nova República" should be—much as had been the case after 1930. As it turned out, the insistence of the more progressive elements that Sarney himself constituted a major obstacle to change left the president with no feasible option but to follow what was for him the most natural course—governance in collaboration with the Center and Center-Right.[3]

But this divorce between Sarney and the "authentic" PMDB would occur in stages, as the former early on sought to earn the support of the PMDB's strong Center-Left component. During the initial phase of his presidency, as an "accidental" chief executive, Sarney was forced to govern with a Cabinet that had been selected by Neves for the style of government the wily Mineiro had in mind. Only well after Neves's death would Sarney feel free to make piecemeal changes, and even then he was constrained first by the composition of the Democratic Alliance and subsequently by the functioning of the constituent assembly. Not until well into his fourth year as president did Sarney sense the liberty to rid his Cabinet of PMDB figures closely tied to Guimarães and very clearly not sympathetic to the president's objectives.

For, whereas both Neves and Guimarães had been young men during the 1930s, Sarney's youth came during the 1950s, so his formative experiences were very different—the two PMDB leaders were rooted in the Vargas era, which was for Sarney little more than a childhood memory. Moreover, no matter how cosmopolitan and intellectual he had become, Sarney's roots were in the northeast, whereas Guimarães was almost the archetypal Paulista and Neves was 100 percent Mineiro.

The First Year: Sarney as Tancredo's Stand-in

When Sarney was sworn in on March 15, it was as acting president, with the country purposely misled—a task facilitated by a national penchant for wishful thinking—into expecting that Neves would eventually recover and assume the presidency.[4] The twenty-one civilian ministries had been allotted in a masterful manner combining regional balance and equity among the several components of the Democratic Alliance with the need to maintain equilibrium among the alliance's elements at the state level in view of the upcoming 1986 elections. São Paulo and Minas Gerais came out particularly well, which was justifiable in light of the fact that together they had roughly 46 million inhabitants—more than California and New York combined—as well as the lion's share of the country's productive capacity.

Composition of the Coalition

From São Paulo (1984 population, 30 million) came three members of Governor Franco Montoro's Cabinet plus the premier state's PFL leader. Representatives of Minas Gerais included Foreign Minister Olavo Setúbal (sixty-two), Planning Minister João Sayad (thirty-nine), Industry and Commerce Minister Roberto Gusmão (sixty), and Labor Minister Almir Pazzianotto (forty-eight). Moreover, Paulistas were also given control of the National Economic and Social Development Bank (BNDES), with businessman Dilson Funaro (fifty) as its president and André Franco Montoro Filho as its vice-president. São Paulo would gain even more when Funaro moved up to finance minister in August.

Being Neves's home state, Minas Gerais (with nearly 16 million inhabitants at the time) received proportionately even better treatment, with three members of the state administration he had assembled in 1982 moving into the Cabinet along with the outgoing vice-president and Neves's nephew. The latter, Francisco Dornelles (fifty), held the key Finance Ministry, and Aureliano Chaves (fifty-six)—the PFL's prospective presidential candidate—was minister of mines and energy. Ronaldo Costa Couto (forty-two), formerly Minas Gerais planning secretary, received the politically strategic Interior Ministry (regional affairs and development), and José Hugo Castelo Branco (fifty-nine), former head of the Minas Gerais state banks, became presidential chief of staff. José Aparecido de Oliveira (fifty-six) moved from Minas Gerais secretary of culture to be culture minister, then quickly went on to become governor of the Federal District. The second most populous state still ended up with the Culture Ministry as Aluísio Pimenta (sixty-two) succeeded to that post.

Bahia (population 11 million) and Pernambuco (population 7 million) emerged ahead of more populous Rio de Janeiro and Rio Grande do Sul, gaining third and fourth place, respectively, in the apportionment of top-echelon positions. In Bahia, the PDS dissidents, the former PP wing of the PMDB, and the PMDB's more progressive faction each came away with a ministry. Unquestionably the dominant political figure in the state, two-time former governor Antônio Carlos Magalhães (fifty-seven) gained the Communications Ministry despite the fact that he was still affiliated with the PDS—he did not enter the PFL until January 1986. To balance this patronage advantage, centrist Carlos Sant'Anna (fifty-four) was named health minister and longtime PMDB warhorse Waldir Pires (fifty-nine) became minister of social welfare. Pernambuco received a ministry for the PFL— that of Education, which was headed by Marco Maciel (forty-four)—and one for the PMDB—that of Justice, with Fernando Lyra (forty-six) at its helm. Leadership of the Federal Savings Bank (CEF) was given to Lyra's intramural rival, former senator Marcos Freire (fifty-three). Moreover, Governor Roberto Magalhães was assuaged by the naming of José Maria Aragão (fifty-one) to head the National Housing Bank.

Although it did not receive a civilian Cabinet position, Rio de Janeiro (population 13 million) gained the presidency of the Central Bank through Antônio Carlos Lemgruber (thirty-four) plus the position of Petrobrás chief executive through Hélio Beltrão (sixty-nine), the PFL's leader there. This apparent snubbing of Brazil's third state was really a concession to Governor Brizola, who did not want his opponents strengthened prior to the crucial election for mayor of Brazil's second city. Rio Grande do Sul (population 9 million) came away only with the Agriculture Ministry under Pedro Simon (fifty-five), whereas Paraná did somewhat better with the Transportation Ministry under Senator Affonso Camargo Netto (fifty-five), the Brazilian Coffee Institute headed by former minister Karlos Rischbeiter (fifty-eight), and Itaipu Binacional under former governor Ney Braga (seventy). Western states had to be content with only the new Urban Development Ministry under Goiás's Flávio Peixoto da Silveira (thirty-nine).

The northeast was very well represented in the Neves/Sarney government even beyond the five ministers from Bahia and Pernambuco. Sarney hailed from Maranhão, and in compensation his longtime rival Renato Archer (sixty-two) became minister of science and technology. Ceará won the Debureaucratization Ministry through PFL Deputy Paulo Lustosa (forty) to balance the Bank of the Northeast under former senator Paulo Benevides (fifty-five), the PMDB standard-bearer in Ceará in 1982. Aluísio Alves (sixty-four) of Rio Grande do Norte became minister of administration, Camílo Calazans (fifty-six) of Sergipe's PFL became head of the Bank of Brazil, and Alagoas's José Aprigio Vilela (thirty-six) was tapped to preside over the Sugar and Alcohol Institute. The north's representation came by way of Nélson Ribeiro (fifty-four) of Pará as agrarian reform minister; Amazonas was compensated with control of the Amazon Bank and the Manaus Free Zone as Pará also came away with the regional development agency SUDAM.

Thus no states of real consequence were left out of the upper levels of the administration. Espírito Santo was relatively well taken care of with the presidency of the Rio Doce Valley Company (CVRD), Brazil's multibillion-dollar state mining company, and Santa Catarina could at least point to Senator Jorge Bornhausen as national president of the PFL. Indeed, when second- and third-echelon posts were taken into account, few small states could legitimately feel slighted in terms of present versus past treatment.

On the economic and financial side, the government had a decidedly pragmatic, nearly orthodox cast. Neves was essentially a fiscal conservative convinced of the need to bring inflation under control. Himself once an executive of the Bank of Brazil, he would have been the first Brazilian chief executive since Vargas to have more than a layman's grasp of the workings of the economy and the financial system. Although Sarney originally accepted Neves's position in this realm, he subsequently sided for a time with the structuralist-oriented advocates of growth. As finance minister, Dornelles— a tax expert and Neves's nephew—lacked personal political clout, needing the nearly complete confidence and backing of the president to be effective. Although Sarney gave him this during Neves's illness, Dornelles was forced to throw in the towel in August 1985, subsequently joining the PFL in Rio de Janeiro. With Calazans backed up by Francelino Pereira (sixty-four)— former governor of Minas Gerais—as administrative vice-president, the Bank of Brazil was essentially under PFL control.

There were clearly quite deep political divisions within the governmental orchestra Neves had constructed to respond to his virtuoso direction—a technique he learned as Vargas's justice minister in 1953–1954 and honed as prime minister in 1961–1962. Much weight was still carried by a group of essentially moderate military ministers including Army Minister Leônidas Pires Gonçalves (sixty-four), Navy Minister Henrique Sabóia (fifty-nine), Air Force Minister Octávio Júlio Moreira Lima (fifty-eight), SNI head General Ivan de Souza Mendes (sixty-two), Armed Forces General Staff Chief Admiral José Maria Amaral de Oliveira (fifty-nine), and Military Cabinet Chief Rubens Bayma Denys (fifty-five)—son of the key army figure of the early 1960s.

By and large the military ministers were in basic harmony with the PFL faction of the Cabinet (Chaves, Maciel, Setúbal, Dornelles, and Lustosa) as well as sympathetic to the politically independent Costa Couto. Also aligned with the PFL and the military on most matters was Magalhães, who temporarily stayed in the PDS as a means of attracting part of its congressional delegation to support the government and eventually to enter the PFL during the course of the 1986 campaign. Thus this Center-conservative group made up half the Cabinet from the very beginning.

In the middle, both ideologically and in terms of intramural policy disputes, were those PMDB ministers whose loyalty was much more to Neves personally than to the party that had housed them only since early 1982. This former PP group included Gusmão, Castelo Branco, Sant'Anna, and Pimenta (with Aparecido de Oliveira near at hand). Lyra, with his own political ambitions hemmed in by an excess of strong leaders in Pernambuco, fit quite uncomfortably and restlessly between the PMDB ministers and the group highly responsive to Ulysses Guimarães—Archer, Camargo Netto, Pires, Simon, Ribeiro, and Alves. Sayad and Pazzianotto stood between the Guimarães group and the former PP group because of the close political relationship these two men had with São Paulo Governor Franco Montoro, a friendly rival of Guimarães within the PMDB and São Paulo politics. Peixoto's position responded essentially to that of his mentor, Goiás Governor Iris Resende.

Although members of the "PMDB of Ulysses" faction were highly visible, they controlled essentially the politically least important ministries and their power depended heavily upon the attitudes taken by the PMDB's congressional delegation—which was influenced first and foremost by longtime party President Guimarães, but also by floor leaders Pimenta da Veiga (thirty-seven), Humberto Lucena (fifty-seven), and Fernando H. Cardoso (fifty-three). Though at times responsive to executive pressures, the PMDB's degree of support for government policy in Congress was most heavily conditioned by the presumed preferences of their constituents. This was particularly true of the progressives, who feared that a moderate orientation opened up space for their PDT and PT rivals to exploit sentiment for more dramatic and far-reaching change.

Tentative Beginnings

For the first six weeks of the new administration, the public's attention focused much more upon Neves's brave but hopeless struggle for survival than it did upon the government's actions. Neves's death on April 21, though assuring Sarney's continuance as president also allowed Guimarães to emerge as the PMDB's leading figure. Thus, if Sarney was not to become virtually a figurehead controlled by the PMDB and Guimarães—who took few pains to hide the fact that he felt both better qualified to be president and much more deserving of the honor—he needed to cultivate support elsewhere.

Given the fact that a new Congress would be elected in November 1986, the president's task of devising the best strategy for assuring a parliamentary basis for his government both for 1985–1986 and through the 1987–1989 period was a complex one. Achieving this parliamentary basis not only required victory for the PMDB and PFL in the congressional balloting, but also meant that the moderates within the PMDB representation had to at least counterbalance the progressives. A left-wing preponderance within the PMDB ranks in the constituent assembly would place the president in almost as untenable a position as the one that would result from the lack of a Democratic Alliance majority. Sarney either would have to make such great policy concessions to the leftist elements of the PMDB as to become virtually their prisoner or would risk seeing them cut his presidential term to four years or even less.

Even with substantial success at the polls, patronage criteria for allocation of government resources, which had reemerged in the later stages of the Figueiredo administration, would become dominant as Sarney was required to use patronage to compensate for his lack of natural leadership within the Democratic Alliance in the never-ending battle to obtain acceptable legislative results.

Such efforts to build a congressional base of support, although they began with the PFL, had to involve parties outside the Democratic Alliance. Yet at the same time Sarney was compelled to move cautiously in this direction so as not to alienate the numerically dominant PMDB, for Guimarães and Cardoso had become accustomed to acting as if there was a de facto parliamentary system with Ulysses behaving as prime minister. Indeed, they seemed to feel that, as an accidental occupant of the presidency, Sarney should be willing to accept an essentially ceremonial role and leave running the country to Paulistas like them who were better prepared to lead. Guimarães justified this view with his greater experience and established leadership of the near-majority party, whereas Cardoso—an internationally renowned sociologist and the godfather of dependency theory—had (and has) no doubt that he is intellectually best prepared to preside over the consolidation of democracy in Brazil.[5]

Yet this approach was more in keeping with the formal façade of the party system, not with the reality that the PMDB was an extremely heterogeneous holding company of political groupings that shared little more than a long experience of being in opposition and a consequent difficulty in adapting to being the governing party—or even the party of the government.[6]

Again a Flawed Party System

The party system as it had emerged by 1985 was very mixed, containing both parties and factions that bore a close relationship to those that had existed before 1964 along with others that were products of developments during the long period of military rule. Even the traditionally constituted groups had been heavily affected by the significant societal changes that had taken place during the nearly quarter of a century since the 1962 elections—the last elections held before the drastic 1964 regime change.[7] Moreover, Brazil's electorate had expanded almost four times over during this twenty-three-year period—from 18.5 million to nearly 70 million. Thus, taking deaths into account, little more than a fifth of the New Republic's voters could have had any personal link to the pre-1964 parties.

As shown in Chapter 6, in the early 1960s the Left of the party spectrum was occupied essentially by the PTB—roughly equal in electoral strength to the PSD and stronger than the UDN. But the PTB was divided into a nationalist-leftist wing led by Brizola and a patronage-oriented wing headed by the party's São Paulo leader, Ivette Vargas—Getúlio's niece. Suspended uneasily between the two was President Goulart, who eventually moved closer to the more radical faction. Hit extremely hard by the 1964 wave of cassations, the PTB was largely swallowed up by the MDB in 1966, although some patronage-hungry elements of the PTB opted for ARENA.

With the end of the enforced two-party system, Brizola and Vargas struggled for control of the PTB label, with the latter winning out courtesy of help from Golbery. Following Ivette's death at the beginning of 1984, the PTB came under the control of a quite conservative São Paulo group who would use it in 1985 as the vehicle for electing former president Quadros to the post of São Paulo mayor. Around the country the PTB became a flag of convenience used by diverse elements lacking political space within the larger parties.

Denied the PTB name, with which he had been so prominently identified before 1964, Brizola organized the Democratic Workers' Party (PDT), with which he won election as Rio de Janeiro's governor in 1982. This remained his personalist vehicle, as his *caudilho* personality brooked no real debate, much less competition, within "his" party. Thus, although Brizola's PDT candidate, Senator Saturnino Braga, was elected as Rio's mayor in 1985, Braga soon broke with Brizola—who expected Braga to take orders as if he was a hierarchical subordinate—and with the PDT.[8]

Moreover, the PDT suffered from a lack of any significant base in São Paulo, where the Workers' Party (PT), organized by a coalition of metalworkers and socialist intellectuals at the very end of the 1970s, soon achieved a hold over the very societal elements—the radical wing of the organized working class and the left-wing middle-class intelligentsia—whose support the PDT required. Furthermore, the PMDB's progressive wing also contained elements analogous to the pre-1964 PTB, hemming in the PDT even more tightly.

The dominant party until after 1962, the PSD, was a Vargas-founded holding company of state political machines deeply divided between conservative rural groupings and the Center to Center-Right bulk of the urban bourgeoisie. It differed from the UDN more in terms of state and local rivalries than on major policy positions. Born as a coalition of anti-Vargas forces, the UDN also housed both an essentially conservative rural wing and one composed of Center-Right urban professionals and their middle-class supporters.

The vast majority of the UDN and a very large proportion of the PSD found themselves uncomfortably coexisting within ARENA after the "either-or" choice of affiliation forced upon them in 1966, and they subsequently faced the same situation in the straitjacket of the PDS. A significant minority of the PSD went into the MDB in 1966, with some remaining in the PMDB after 1979 and others joining with Tancredo Neves to form the Popular Party (PP)—until the government perhaps unwisely pushed the PP back into the PMDB prior to the 1982 elections. Though a few of the former PP members opted to join the Popular Front Party (PFL) after its founding in 1984, the PFL was chiefly composed of former UDN figures who abandoned the Maluf-oriented PDS at that point, with Sarney in the van along with Chaves and Maciel.

The lesser legal parties of the pre-1964 era, some ten in all, were swallowed up by the post-1966 two-party system. As they were essentially regional or personalist in nature and not tied to a particular social stratum, they were not an important factor within the 1966–1979 parties, nor did they effectively reemerge subsequently. As their share of the vote in 1962 had totalled only about 20 percent, three-fourths of it won in coalition with one or another of the three major parties, these lesser parties failed to represent significant sectors of society.

Of greatest note was the Social Progressive Party (PSP) of the late São Paulo patronage populist Adhemar de Barros. Most of his followers went into ARENA and hence to the PDS, but his chief heirs subsequently went in opposite directions. Adhemar Filho (Ademarzinho) until 1989 ran the very weak Paulista affiliate of Brizola's PDT, while Reynaldo de Barros—

the *caudilho's* nephew and 1982 PDS candidate for São Paulo governor—joined the PFL. The Republican Party (PR) existed chiefly in Minas Gerais and was largely absorbed by ARENA, whereas the Liberator Party (PL) was a Rio Grande do Sul historical relic that split between ARENA and the MDB. The chiefly São Paulo–based National Workers' Party (PTN) eventually ended up with elements in both the PTB and PDT as well as some in the PMDB. The Christian Democratic Party (PDC) saw its strong base in Paraná divide between followers of Ney Braga, who passed through ARENA and the PDS before ending up in the PFL, and others like Camargo Netto, who found a home in the PMDB by way of the PP before moving on to the PTB. The PDC's main leader in São Paulo, Franco Montoro, became a PMDB stalwart—and in 1982 was elected as São Paulo governor—before participating in the dissidence that, in the form of the Brazilian Social Democratic Party (PSDB), in mid-1988 moved into opposition to both Sarney's government and Guimarães's leadership of the PMDB.

The Brazilian Socialist Party (PSB) was little more than an electoral club of intellectuals with little popular support that reemerged in 1985 as essentially the same highly vocal splinter group. The Popular Representation Party (PRP) was a declining vestige of 1930s fascism, and under the New Republic it languished as an element of the political freak show without even the minimal support needed to move into the sideshow. The Social Workers' Party (PST) and Rural Workers' Party (PRT) were only splinters of a splinter whose demise was essentially unnoticed. The last of the pre-1964 parties, the Renovating Workers' Movement (MRT), was a short-lived personalist offshoot of the PTB, which because of its leader's death was already moribund before the 1964 Revolution.[9]

Although widely heralded as something entirely new on the Brazilian political scene, the PT was not quite as pristine as its advocates and apologists claimed. Certainly Lula da Silva was a refreshingly new type of political leader, having come up through the ranks of the labor movement. Yet encrusted within this "authentically working-class" party from the beginning were a variety of left-wing ideological cliques composed of middle-class intellectuals as well as entire Communist parties either unable to come out into the open because of legal problems or incapable of mobilizing any significant electoral support on their own. Thus, as well as important parts of the PCdoB, the PT housed most of the MR-8 along with such essentially Trotskyite groups as Liberdade e Luta (Libelu), which later became O Trabalho; Convergência Socialista; and the Movement for Proletarian Emancipation (MEP). Also burrowed into the PT were the Revolutionary Brazilian Communist Party (PCBR), the Revolutionary Communist Party (PRC), and the Maoist group Ala Vermelha. Subsequently there would also be the Trotskyite splinters Democracia Socialista and Democratic and Socialist Power, which often worked at cross-purposes to the Lula-led majority faction Articulation (backed by the left wing of the Catholic Church through the ecclesiastical base communities and the Pastoral da Terra).[10]

Whither the Church?

Indeed, though analyses of the PT have focused chiefly upon its links to the labor movement, overoptimistic assumptions concerning its rapid development into a critical if not decisive force were rooted in a belief that its Church support would be a crucial factor in both its organizational spread and its electoral growth. This growth was essential for the regime change to develop into a system change, for only if the PT and other parties of the Left could come to have a real prospect of obtaining power might the New Republic turn into something substantially different from a cross between the pre-1964 situation and the modernizing aspects of the Geisel-Figueiredo period. The ability of these parties to make an actual challenge for power would require the effective support of a much stronger and more nationally organized institution than the labor movement either was or could soon become.[11] Thus, perhaps the most important question with respect to the 1985–1989 period centered on the ability of the Church to maintain the substantial unity it had demonstrated during the period of opening and to support campaigns for social justice as effectively as it had those for an end to repression and a return to democratic politics.

That it could not and would not do so was clear once the position and role of the Vatican were taken into account. Insistence by forces on the Left in viewing the progressive São Paulo Church under Cardinal Arns as the wave of the future was as unrealistic as their belief that the PT would shortly come to exert a heavy, even dominant influence in the nation's political life. The São Paulo segment of the Church would be drastically undercut by concerted efforts of both the Brazilian Church's conservative wing and Rome, whereas the PT would be effectively contained by the renewed—not merely residual—strength of co-optative clientelism and patronage populism.

The progressive wing of the Church certainly fared well during *abertura* and the early stages of transition. Dom Aloísio Lorscheider moved up to the presidency of the National Conference of Brazilian Bishops (CNBB) in the early 1970s, with his progressive cousin, Dom Ivo Lorscheiter, as his secretary-general and eventual successor. Under their leadership the 1977 general assembly of the CNBB concentrated on defining the "Christian Requirements of a Political Order" and that of 1980 stressed "The Church and Land Problems"—both essentially progressive documents. At the same time efforts among workers and landless peasants were picking up steam, and ecclesiastical base communities (CEBs) multiplied, particularly in low-income areas on the periphery of major urban centers.[12]

At the twenty-first CNBB general assembly in April 1983 the progressive wing managed, albeit with some difficulty, to reelect Dom Ivo, bishop of Santa Maria, Rio Grande do Sul, to a second four-year term as president. In what may well have been the toughest electoral battle in the history of the CNBB, Dom Ivo was strongly supported by the hundred-odd left-leaning prelates and vehemently opposed by the forty or so convinced conservatives. Perceived as less radical than Dom Aloísio, cardinal of Fortaleza, Dom Ivo was the recipient of reluctant support by half the hundred-plus moderates—and then only on the third ballot. At the same time Dom Luciano Mendes de Almeida, nearly as much a progressive moderate as a moderate progressive, was overwhelmingly reelected secretary-general and came to play a major role in avoiding excessive polarization of the hierarchy.

Yet deep doctrinal differences continued to be aggravated in the context of transition, as Pope John Paul II worked patiently but persistently to redress the balance in the favor of moderate and conservative clergy. At the end of 1980 the pope cautioned the Brazilian clergy against neglecting primary religious responsibilities due to excessive involvement in social questions. Subsequently the Vatican used its powers of appointment and assignment to weaken the radical progressives and strengthen those elements most in line with papal views, which included a commitment to preserving the essentially hierarchical nature of the Church. Maverick theologian Leonardo Boff, the author of very influential books supporting liberation theology, was censured in 1985 and required to adopt a penitential silence. Conservative Dom Lucas Moreira Neves was returned from Rome to become cardinal of Salvador, a position that made him the country's primate. In this appointment the expressed preferences of the CNBB were pointedly ignored as the Vatican forcefully demonstrated that such decisions remained its exclusive purview. The "conservative reaction" within the Church was well underway.[13]

Clearly the party system of the mid-1980s was not stable, much less did it have deep roots in the electorate. As events would soon clearly prove, the system was not suitable for the task of consolidating the democratic transition. One of the major obstacles to any significant reform or reinforcement of the quite inadequate and undisciplined party system lay in the politicians' unwillingness to do away with the system's most irrational features.[14] For, although the great majority of them were aware of its manifold faults and weaknesses and many even recognized that a drastic overhaul—especially on the electoral side—might significantly improve legislative performance and party responsibility, these considerations were not priorities for the vast majority of politicians. To the Brazilian congressmen the existing procedures had one great, indeed overriding, merit—all of them had managed to get elected through this bizarre system, in most cases repeatedly, and a switch to better defined constituencies and elimination of micro- and mini-parties might weaken their individual chances for reelection.

Early Maneuvering and Mayoral Elections

The first matter on the Sarney government's agenda was the widespread desire for replacement of the authoritarian 1969 constitution. The left half of the political spectrum wanted early elections for an "exclusive" constituent assembly that would draft a democratic and progressive basic charter. Those to the right of Center preferred to leave this task to the regular Congress, which was scheduled to be elected in November 1986.

Knowing that an exclusive assembly would almost certainly cut deeply into his powers and might very well seek to truncate his term as well,

Sarney strongly supported the latter option, getting his way after heated congressional debate that stretched through the whole second half of the year. Meanwhile, without any great hurry or enthusiasm, he implemented Neves's idea of a "Commission of Notables" to prepare a draft that, it was expected, would serve as a basis for the assembly's work on a new constitution during 1987. Although this group attracted considerable media attention, it was marginal to Sarney's plans—particularly after it recommended adoption of a parliamentary form of government.[15]

An end to political censorship and rehabilitation of labor leaders dismissed from their union posts under the military regime served to demonstrate that "authoritarian rubble" was being cleaned away. Legislation in May removed virtually all restrictions on the formation of political parties, extended the right to vote to illiterates, and provided that future presidential elections would be direct. Hence after thirty-eight years the PCB was again a legal party, as was the PCdoB. Moreover, mayoral elections were scheduled for state capitals and other municipalities that had been considered national security areas under the military regime. On the other hand, legislation to reestablish congressional prerogatives, such as voting additional expenditures, and proposals to do away with the national security law encountered significant difficulties and eventually bogged down.

For, although many national legislators had changed from the PDS to the PFL over the matter of presidential succession, the fact remained that a majority of the Congress had been elected in 1982 on the ticket of the government's party and remained deeply suspicious of anything the PMDB's progressive wing strongly favored. For its part, the military held firm against an October bill that would have required reinstating all members of the military purged between 1964 and 1979 with full back pay at the rank they might have achieved had they remained on active duty throughout the period. Military pressure on the Arinos commission to maintain the constitutional provisions legitimizing the armed forces' role in maintaining law and order and acting as guarantor of the country's basic institutions was also heavy and concerted—supported from within by the more conservative members of the commission itself.[16]

Only a few clues as to shifts in voter loyalty emerged from the November 1985 elections of capital city mayors—the first such balloting in over two decades. In São Paulo (with 4.9 million voters) the PTB-PFL alliance behind Quadros received 37.5 percent of the vote, just about the same as the PDS-PTB total within the city in the 1982 gubernatorial elections. The PMDB dropped from 42 percent in 1982 to 34.2 percent—very close to the PT's gain from 14.3 percent to 19.8 percent. Eight lesser parties totalled only 3.8 percent of the 1985 vote, and the PDS and PDT did not field candidates. This lack of significant voter shifts from before the return of civilian government was mirrored in Rio de Janeiro (electorate 3.2 million) where, with nearly 40 percent of the vote, the PDT maintained the dominant position it had established in 1982, with the PFL a respectable second—at over 17 percent—and the PMDB a distant third with less than 9 percent.

None of the fifteen new parties running in Rio de Janeiro gained more than a toehold, while the PTB (at 2 percent) fell well behind its 1982 performance and the PT (with 1 percent) again showed no significant support.

In Belo Horizonte (with 1 million voters), the PMDB held on to the majority position it had accomplished in 1982, with the PFL a distant second. Neither the PDT, PT, nor PTB showed any real strength, and the myriad new parties failed even to get a respectable sliver of the vote. Salvador (with 725,000 voters) witnessed an easy PMDB victory but with well below the proportion of the vote that party had received there in 1982, while the PMDB was soundly defeated at the state level. In Porto Alegre, the PDT winner at a little over 40 percent of the 725,000 voters improved significantly on his own performance in running for governor in 1982, while in Curitiba (electorate 600,000) the PMDB held its own against a strong PDT challenge. Up in Recife (with 600,000 voters), however, the percentages showed considerable change. There both leading candidates came from PMDB ranks, but the PDT came away with 22 percent of the vote—essentially at PMDB expense—while the bulk of the 30 percent PDS vote of 1982 went to the PFL.

The most dramatic shift in party fortunes took place in Fortaleza (with 700,000 voters), where the PT surged from an insignificant 1 percent in 1982 to victory with 33 percent while the PMDB dropped proportionally from 58.4 percent to 30.6 percent. Essentially this resulted from a chain reaction of recent changes in party affiliation by leading figures: The governor elected by the PDS in 1982 left the PFL for the PMDB while the winning PMDB candidate, Maria Luiza Fontanelle, abruptly migrated to the PT— which she would leave in April 1988. On the Center-Right side of the spectrum, the PFL, receiving 25 percent of the vote, was supported by most of those who had given the PDS its 32.1 percent share in 1982. Even in alliance with the PTB, the PDS fell sharply to slightly over 5 percent. In Belém and Manaus the PMDB held on to its dominance, but in Goiânia it was hard pressed by the PT.

Thus, though the PMDB could point to nineteen wins in twenty-five races in state and territory capitals—along with 110 wins out of 201 contests in other localities—it was not really very satisfied with its performance. Senator Fernando Cardoso's loss to "outdated has-been" Quadros was particularly galling, as it could only be written off in part to failure by the distinguished intellectual Cardoso to address the mundane local issues that were on the voters' minds. Indeed, Cardoso's campaign speeches seemed more appropriate to the presidential candidate he hoped to become than to a mayoral aspirant. He projected too much of an image of wanting the job as a springboard to higher office rather than a genuine desire to deal with that overgrown metropolis's manifold and pressing problems.[17] Given Saturnino Braga's win in Rio de Janeiro and Alceu Collares's in Porto Alegre, along with Fontanelle's victory in Fortaleza, the PMDB had ample reason to worry about growth of Brizola's PDT and to look over its shoulder at the PT.

Still Searching for an Identity and a Game Plan

During this time Sarney demonstrated concern with redeeming the "social deficit" built up during the more than two decades of military rule. Thus in August he commissioned noted social scientist Hélio Jaguaribe to organize a team to analyze the country's social problems and prepare a set of proposals for more equitable policies. Throwing himself into this task with all of his considerable talents and energy, Jaguaribe—once a young member of the brain trust in the final Vargas administration—came up with a strategy to lift Brazilian living standards to the present level of Spain by the turn of the century.[18] The president's response was to pledge 12 percent of the federal budget for social programs and to adopt as his administration's slogan "Everything for the Social."

In the political sphere the first year of civilian rule brought no threats of retrogression, limited but significant steps toward consolidation, and a definite improvement in Sarney's position—on balance a quite respectable result taking into account the trauma of Neves's death and consequent public dismay. In the economic realm the balance sheet was even more favorable, although formidable long-term problems remained with regard to foreign debt, inflation, and income distribution. With the exception of inflation, which ran at double-digit rates through the first quarter of the year, the new government inherited a substantially improved and in many ways still improving economic situation. Industrial production was up 6.1 percent in 1984, providing the chief impetus for a 5.7 percent growth in GDP. This not only more than offset the 1981–1983 shrinkage of the economy, but it also held out the prospect that per capita losses could be recovered in 1985. Yet debt had risen to a very troublesome $96 billion.[19]

Initially dependent upon export expansion, this economic recovery had broadened into domestic commerce and agriculture. Unemployment had dropped steadily during 1984, and the record trade surplus of just over $13 billion came largely from a nearly 25 percent increase in exports to over $27 billion—with manufactures leading the way at $15.1 billion, up a full one-third over 1983. Crucial to this was the U.S. market, with sales there up nearly 29 percent to $7.7 billion, along with a significant drop in oil imports for the fourth straight year. Even after massive interest payments, this recovery provided a small current accounts surplus of around $200 million, allowing some room for an increase in essential imports. Moreover, satisfactory debt negotiations made possible an increase in foreign exchange reserves from below zero at the beginning of 1983 to the neighborhood of $7 billion by the change of administrations in March 1985.

During the first year of the civilian government there was substantial progress on most economic fronts despite early contradictions between the policies advocated by the finance minister and those pushed by the Planning Ministry before a kind of synthesis was achieved at the end of August. The trade surplus held near the previous year's record at $12.5 billion—on exports of $25.6 billion and imports of $13.1 billion—and more than 1.7 million persons were added to the rolls of the employed by year's end.

Internal consumption became the engine of economic growth as real salaries rose nearly 13 percent in the industrial sector, and commerce was up in the second semester following a good agricultural harvest—all of which yielded a dramatic 8.4 percent GDP expansion. With industrial production up 9 percent, the 1980 record level was surpassed and the pre-recession high in per capita GDP was within reach. Moreover, the minimum wage rose some 260 percent—more than twenty-five points over the inflation rate.

On the negative side the fight against the dragon of inflation was a casualty of the administration's pursuit of growth. When the cost of living went up a record 14 percent in August, the president replaced Dornelles with the more developmentalist Dilson Funaro. Subsequently inflation continued at a high rate pushed by both the financing needs of the large public sector deficit, which led to a great expansion of internal debt, and continuing price markups in anticipation of continued high inflation. The impact of this cycle on the foreign debt situation was substantial as the new government had inherited a condition of noncompliance with the IMF accord, which was due to expire in early 1986, and was unwilling for political reasons to accept continued close monitoring of the nation's finances by that international body.

Scrapping efforts to reach agreement on an eighth letter of intentions, the government decided to forgo any kind of agreement for 1985, opting instead for direct negotiations with creditor banks—facilitated by a vague IMF acknowledgment of the seriousness and feasibility of Brazil's proposed 1986 economic program.[20] Substantial tax increases, containment of public sector expenditures, and reduction of internal interest rates were enacted in December, a month in which inflation reached 16.2 percent, but the government realized that much more drastic action would soon have to be taken.

The Second Year: The Cruzado Plan, Electoral Triumph, and the Big Letdown

The period from March 1986 to February 1987 would resemble a roller coaster ride through a hall of mirrors that ended up near the house of horrors. The initially prevailing sense of malaise would be quickly dispelled by the apparently painless economic "miracle" of the Cruzado Plan, which brought a marginal decrease in the cost of living in March and a trend in which savings began to be funneled into productive investment rather than the merry-go-round of financial speculations that had run rampant in recent years—a situation quite similar to that during the early stages of the republic more than nine decades in the past. The government staked its future on the success of a program oversold to the public as a great Brazilian discovery— a way to stop inflation dead in its tracks and at the same time enjoy economic growth with high employment and sharply rising purchasing power.

Thus, with the November elections choosing a national legislature that would decide the nature of the governmental system and the tenure of the incumbent administration, neither Sarney nor the PMDB could resist the temptation to continue the program that had produced massive public support for the regime far beyond the point that sound economic thinking dictated. This time it was a case of too much for too long, as what should have been a temporary price and wage freeze accompanied by firm measures to set the government's financial house in order and promptly followed by a gradual reduction of controls was extended several months after it had already begun to distort demand-supply relationships and create serious shortages.

The temporary atmosphere of prosperity shading into a broad-based boom did guarantee an overwhelming electoral victory for the PMDB, with the PFL picking up most of what was left over, and resulted in GDP growth of over 8 percent for 1986; it also set the stage for a massive hangover as much of the public would feel betrayed when the artificial prosperity evaporated soon after the elections and inflation—which the voters had been led to believe had been brought under lasting control—once again threatened to climb back toward new record highs.[21] Thus 1987 would open much as the preceding year—marked by a sense of malaise and skepticism toward government promises.

The First Cabinet Shakeup

In February 1986 Sarney finally moved to put his stamp more fully upon the administration. Taking advantage of some Cabinet members' need to resign so they would be eligible to run for office in November, he carried out a thorough reshuffling and rationalization of the top echelon. When Funaro replaced Dornelles as finance minister the preceding August, the Central Bank had been taken out of the hands of the "Rio banking boys" and entrusted to Fernão Bracher (fifty), who was also of the São Paulo PMDB. Now Maciel became head of the presidential staff, with Castelo Branco shifting over to Industry and Commerce—as Gusmão and his privatizing ideas left the administration. PFL national president Bornhausen took over from Maciel at Education, and Roberto de Abreu Sodré (sixty-seven) replaced fellow PFL Paulista Setúbal in Foreign Relations. Goiás Governor Resende (fifty-three) became agriculture minister in place of Simon, with Rio Grande do Sul having to settle for Paulo Brossard (sixty-one) moving into the Justice Ministry vacated by Lyra. The PMDB of Pernambuco lost a ministry in this shift and was compensated with the top post in the Superintendency for the Economic Development of the Northeast (SUDENE).

The Health Ministry remained in Bahian PMDB hands under Roberto Santos (in place of Sant'Anna), and Maranhão's José Reinaldo Tavares (forty-six) moved up from SUDENE to be transportation minister. In compensation for Camargo Netto's leaving Transportation, Paraná PMDB's Deni Schwartz (forty-eight) became minister of urban development, replacing Peixoto. Internationally renowned economist Celso Furtado (sixty-five), originally of

Paraíba and a PMDB intellectual, took over the Culture Ministry—making one less Cabinet post for overrepresented Minas Gerais—and Rio de Janeiro finally got a Cabinet position as Rafael de Almeida Magalhães (fifty-five) became minister of social welfare in place of Bahia's Pires. The Debureaucratization Ministry was abolished, but Ceará was compensated with a new Irrigation Ministry under former Fortaleza mayor Vicente Fialho (forty-seven), a political independent.

Thus, the government became even more geographically balanced than before, Sarney had some individuals with his personal confidence in key positions, and the political makeup of the administration came to reflect at least partially the parties' support of the government in Congress rather than just their behavior in the January 1985 electoral college. Yet, although the PMDB, which had some 200 federal deputies and one-third of the Senate, survived its April 1986 national convention without serious dissidences, it was still much more of a holding company of diverse political currents than it was a cohesive party. Indeed, failing to win the party's nomination for governor in their home states, several major figures would leave the PMDB to make bids under the banners of lesser parties. Sarney worked to preserve PMDB-PFL alliances in the few states where that was still possible, seeking the victory of one or the other were they were competing at the polls. His greatest concern was to head off significant gains by either the PDT or the PT, both of which hoped to exploit any downturn in the economic situation.

Politics and Economics: The Cruzado Plan and National Elections

As has already been pointed out, the surging inflation of December 1985 and January 1986 had led Sarney to accept a "heterodox shock" based upon the experiences of Argentina and Israel and designed by a group of young economists gathered together by Funaro. With absolute secrecy up until adoption of the new program being a crucial factor, the Cruzado Plan was announced with great fanfare on February 28. It combined as its chief features substituting the new unit of currency from which its name derived for the old cruzeiro at a rate of one to 1,000; abolishing indexation; implementing a one-year freeze on mortgages and rents along with an indefinite price freeze; and promulgating a new wage system. The last feature involved an adjustment of pay to its average value over the past six months accompanied by an 8 percent bonus. From that point on, whenever accumulated inflation reached 20 percent there would be a corresponding upward wage adjustment.[22]

In the short run this "bold and imaginative" program appeared to be a rousing success. Inflation rates stayed below 1 percent a month for March and April and under 2 percent through October. Substantial increases in real income and rising employment led to a consumption boom that often went beyond the bounds of reason as individuals paid premiums well above the regulated price for cars and consumer durables. In this heady, superficially booming but unrealistic situation, repressed inflation began to build up almost volcanic pressures. Thus in mid-year the Cruzadinho, or little cruzeiro, package of measures designed to decrease consumption and increase investment was decreed. The proceeds from the compulsory loans imposed on gasoline, automobile purchases, and foreign travel were to be channeled into a newly created National Development Fund. Moreover, taxes were increased on short-term financial instruments in order to move capital in the direction of longer term productive investments.

Hence it was within a context of euphoric optimism never before experienced by the vast majority of Brazilians that the crucial November elections took place. On November 15, with a very high proportion of the more than 69 million voters actually voting, Brazil elected a Congress that would also function as a constituent assembly to write a new constitution. As it would remain the nation's legislative body through 1990, with senators serving until early 1995, this Congress was slated to play a critical role in the consolidation of the still fledgling democratic regime. Governors and state legislatures were also chosen to hold office for four years.

Taking place in a climate of rapid economic growth, high employment, and improving social well-being, this balloting resulted in a sweeping victory for the governing Democratic Alliance. Composed of the PMDB and PFL, the alliance won all governorships, over three-fourths of the lower house, and at least 80 percent of the Senate. Indeed, in most states the elections were chiefly a contest between the two government parties, with the PMDB coming out on top by a very decisive margin—partly because of its established organization and historic name, but also largely as a result of its identification with the Cruzado Plan and "Saint Dilson" Funaro, the plan's presumed miracle worker. This national balloting constituted an overwhelming popular vote of confidence in the Sarney administration as the government's critics on both the Left and Right went down to crushing defeats that threatened to derail their presidential aspirations. Similarly, some two dozen newly established parties failed to find any voter responsiveness, leaving the party system essentially where it had been before the campaign.[23]

In light of the peculiarities of Brazil's party system, with parties that were allied at the national level not only frequently opposed in many states but also even running locally in coalitions with parties hostile to their national partners, results are most meaningfully analyzed and interpreted at the state level. And as the key states have a predominant weight in the direct election of a president, trends there are of great importance to the future. Indeed, in 1986 the four states of São Paulo, Minas Gerais, Rio de Janeiro, and Rio Grande do Sul contained nearly half the country's voters (33.6 million of a total 69.2 million). With Bahia and Paraná added in, the six largest states had 43 million voters, or roughly 62 percent of the national electorate.

In São Paulo, with an electorate at that time of almost exactly 16 million, Vice-Governor Orestes Quércia (forty-eight), a centrist who had first reached prominence with his 1974 election to the Senate, handily won the governorship over one of the country's leading industrialists, Antônio Ermírio de Moraes (fifty-eight), who was running on the PTB ticket. Equally important was Maluf's third-place finish, a stunning defeat that derailed his comeback attempt. Although the unsuccessful 1985 presidential candidate received nearly 3 million votes, this was far behind the winner's 5.8 million or even the runner-up's 4 million. The Left opposition represented by the PT also fared poorly, with Eduardo M. Suplicy (forty-five) falling short of his third-place performance in the 1985 mayoral race and garnering fewer than 1.4 million votes. Even though PT national president Lula da Silva (forty-two) was sent to the Chamber of Deputies with an impressive individual vote, the party elected only seven others to accompany him to Brasília, while the PMDB won twenty-eight seats and easily elected both senators—Mário Covas and incumbent Cardoso.

Harboring nearly 7.2 million voters, Rio de Janeiro saw Wellington Moreira Franco (forty-one), a Paris-educated sociologist of moderate social democratic leanings, gain the prize that had narrowly eluded him in 1982, leading an alliance of the PMDB, PFL, and ten minor parties to a smashing victory. Stung by its third-place finish in the previous year's mayoral election, the PMDB had decided to shake off the "patronage populism" of Chagas Freitas's legacy (a cross between political boss Frank Hague of Jersey City in the 1940s and Chicago's Mayor Richard Daly in the 1960s). To this end they made the PDS's 1982 standard-bearer their nominee.

Though the immediate victim of this steamroller was Darcy Ribeiro (sixty-four), incumbent vice-governor, anthropologist, and one-time Goulart chief of staff, the real loser was Brizola—who was deprived of any base of operations for his presidential bid. This time Alzira Vargas's son-in-law thrashed Brizola's hand-picked stand-in by a margin of just over 3 million to 2.2 million votes, with popular writer and former urban guerrilla Fernando Gabeira (forty-five) a distant third with 500,000 votes on the PT–Green Party (PV) coalition slate. The PMDB and PFL each elected a senator, putting frosting on the Democratic Alliance's cake.

With an electorate of almost 8 million, Minas Gerais experienced an intramural battle chiefly involving the PMDB. Governor Hélio Garcia (fifty-three)—who had succeeded to the office when Neves resigned to run for president—attempted to further his presidential aspirations by denying the dominant party's nomination to either respected progressive Senator Itamar Franco or conservative patronage populist Newton Cardoso (forty-eight). The latter bulldozed his way to victory at the party convention and, largely on the strength of the small-town vote, pulled out a narrow win by a margin of 3 million to more than 2.7 million for Franco (backed by the PFL, the Liberal Party [PL], and a strong PMDB dissident group engineered by José Aparecido de Oliveira). Although PDS Senator Murilo Badaró limped in with only 500,000 votes, his remaining in the lists contributed materially to Cardoso's victory, one that put a crimp in Mines and Energy Minister Chaves's hopes of attaining the presidential office that had been denied him in 1985. The PMDB elected thirty-five federal deputies and both senators in what was in many ways the most decisive win anywhere in the country.

Rio Grande do Sul (with nearly 5 million voters) was critical to favorite son Brizola's presidential plans. Although his PDT had won the election for Porto Alegre mayor a year earlier, even an opportunistic alliance with the PDS could not save it from a smashing defeat at the hands of Pedro Simon and the PMDB. This centrist with some progressive leanings who was fresh out of the Agriculture Ministry avenged his narrow 1982 defeat with a landslide that included both senators and a majority of the state's congressional delegation—as he rolled up over 2 million votes to the PDT-PSD candidate's 1.2 million and not much more than half that for the PFL standard-bearer.

Rounding out its impressive victories in the south, in Paraná, with some 4.3 million voters, the PMDB consolidated the victories it had scored in 1982 and 1985 as modern centrist Álvaro Dias (forty-two) easily gained the governorship—by 2.3 million votes to but 800,000 for his nearest pursuer—with the outgoing holder of that office, José Richa (fifty-two), winning one Senate seat and incumbent Camargo Netto holding on to the other. Santa Catarina's 2.3 million voters also went lopsidedly for the party of the Cruzado Plan, giving centrist Pedro Ivo Campos (fifty-five) more than 1 million votes compared to roughly 700,000 for the PFL candidate and fewer than a half million for the PDS nominee, while the PMDB also picked up both Senate seats. With some 2.2 million voters, Goiás (which strategically surrounds the Federal District) went decisively to the PMDB as progressive Senator Henrique Santillo (forty-eight) became governor with about 1 million votes to former governor Mauro Borges's 600,000.

Perhaps the most dramatic PMDB triumph came in Bahia (with 4.8 million voters), where the party avenged its 1982 defeat by easily electing Waldir Pires and winning both Senate seats and a majority of the congressional delegation in the process. Thus, the PMDB at least interrupted the long dominance of Communications Minister Magalhães over the state he had twice governed. Pernambuco (with an electorate of 3.1 million) posted a decisive win for the PMDB behind Miguel Arraes (sixty-nine), whose earlier term had been cut off by the 1964 Revolution. Reestablishing himself as a national figure on the strength of his 1.6 million to 1 million victory over the PFL's young candidate, the former nationalist Left warhorse of the 1950s and early 1960s was by now more populist than radical. Ceará, containing an electorate of 2.9 million, experienced not only a massive PMDB victory, but also the devastation of the scheme of co-optative clientelism that had allowed three conservative *coroneis* to control the state for the past generation. Thirty-seven-year-old Tasso Jereissati, a centrist businessman, trounced a conservative former governor backed by two other former governors—both of whom had been Cabinet ministers under the military regime. Maranhão (with 1.8 million voters) saw the PMDB-PFL alliance breeze to victory behind Epitácio Cafeteira (sixty-two) with nearly 80 percent of the vote. Fairly similar results prevailed in the rest of that region and throughout the north.

If it looked just at the figures, the PMDB had a great deal to celebrate. With 261 federal deputies it had a definite majority in the 487-member lower house, and its forty-five senators gave it an even larger mandate in that body. (It had begun the New Republic with 201 and twenty-three seats, respectively.) No fewer than twenty-two of twenty-three governorships came to be held by individuals affiliated with the party—although a number of these posts had been won in coalition with the PFL. At the same time, although certainly disappointed in the electoral outcome, the leaders of the junior partner in the Democratic Alliance were far from ready to throw in the towel. The 119 deputies elected from the PFL were just ten fewer than they had before, and their sixteen senators were more than they had at the beginning of the Sarney administration. (Their initial numbers had been seventy and twelve, although they had quickly gained a significant part of the PDS representations.)

For the PDS it was quite another matter, as thirty-three deputies and five senators was less than half of their congressional representation before the campaign began, which already had been well down from the 165 and thirty-one they had at the beginning of the administration and was a far cry from 1982's total of 235 deputies. The PDT could find little solace in its two dozen deputies and brace of senators—one of them a holdover. As they had begun the Sarney government with twenty-three and one, this represented at best stagnation, not the doubling of seats that was their announced minimum target. Similarly, although they made a great hullabaloo over having "doubled" their congressional representation, fifteen deputies was in reality a very disappointing harvest for the PT, as was its roughly 5 percent of the national vote compared with the 3.3 percent it received in 1982. (Trebling their state legislators meant that they still had only thirty-eight seats throughout the whole country, while the victories of 184 municipal councilmen took on a different perspective when viewed against the background of 4,300 municipalities and over 43,000 local legislators.)

The PTB's seventeen seats left it about where it had been but still well above the twelve Chamber seats it held at the beginning of civilian rule, while the Liberal Party's (PL) six deputies came from Rio de Janeiro and São Paulo, in each case on the coattails of one man—either Álvaro Valle or Guilherme Afif Domingos. Five congressmen was not a promising result for those who hoped to resurrect the PDC, and as for the PCB and PCdoB, three deputies each was a pale shadow of Communist strength in the 1946–1947 Congress and no improvement over what they had possessed when they were still hidden within the PMDB. The PCB polled only 0.7 percent of the vote in São Paulo and even less in Rio de Janeiro, while the PCdoB won one seat in Rio de Janeiro and two in Bahia as part of PMDB-led coalitions that won landslide victories. The PSB came away with one lonely seat, as did the Social Christian Party (PSC) behind Quadros's daughter.

What these results meant in the long run could not really be discerned until after at least the next round of national balloting, for further realignment and cleavages began to take their toll almost as soon as the results were in. Party switching became even more frequent and serious in the context of forging the new constitution and positioning for the 1988 municipal elections. Moreover, the Cruzado Plan, by lifting the Brazilian economy to an artificial high, had contributed to the exaggerated scale of the PMDB victory, a situation not likely to be repeated in the future. Without this exaggerated victory, the 1987–1988 constituent assembly would have had a far less moderate composition, and conflict between it and the executive branch would have been more frequent and more serious.

High Hopes Dashed: The Collapse of the Cruzado Plan

Unfortunately, the Cruzado Plan also led quite directly to the intractable economic problems that characterized 1987. As prices were kept frozen too long, purchasing power climbed well above available supplies—particularly with respect to consumer durables, clothing, and nonessential foodstuffs. Thus, for example, meat consumption, which had been steadily declining in per capita terms, jumped sharply during 1986 as real wages rose substantially and millions of individuals previously living at the subsistence level were brought into the money economy—while millions of others bought goods and services they had long forgone. Desirable in social terms, this trend increased domestic consumption, sharply reduced exports, and created inflationary pressures reflected in actual prices climbing well above the legal limits. The very substantial recovery had taken advantage of unused productive capacity, but the investments were just not there to go beyond this to create the new industrial plants needed to provide the basis for sustained expansion.[24]

Corrective policies decreed just after the elections were designed to reduce consumption and increase savings so as to augment investment in productive capacity and give government additional revenues to decrease the public sector deficit. Coming too late to reverse economic deterioration in the month and a half that remained in 1986, these measures were a poor substitute for directly attacking the deficit by reducing expenditures. Thus, although the GDP growth rate for the year was a robust 8 percent, inflation began to climb again, hitting 7.3 percent for December—a sharp jump over November's 3.3 percent. Moreover, trade surpluses, which had been running at an average of over $1 billion a month, disappeared and actually turned into small deficits. Though premeditated failure to include some imports in the official tabulations masked this fact for some months, the subsequent need to revise the 1986 trade surplus downward from $13.5 billion to $12.5 billion undermined the administration's credibility as did related scandals concerning emergency meat and agricultural imports.

In this context, major investments in expanding industrial capacity in priority sectors were far less than government planners expected, thus requiring reduction of consumption as the major leg of anti-inflation policies. This line was resisted by Funaro and his staff of PMDB economists, who were concerned with preserving the social gains of the Cruzado Plan period and preferred once again to denounce the foreign debt as the real villain. In the face of a drastic fall in foreign exchange reserves stemming from the disappearance of the trade surplus, they convinced Sarney to decree a moratorium on payment of interest on the foreign debt to private banks as of February 22, 1987.

The Third Year:
Economic Downturn and Political Indecision

In the period from March 1987 to February 1988, the constituent assembly, which was doubling as the nation's regular Congress, made excruciatingly slow progress toward producing a new framework for government and public policy. This would take place in the environment of a deteriorating economic situation and a sputtering and sloppy realignment of political forces marked by a lack of decisiveness on the part of most key actors—not the least of whom was the president himself. Such a failure to really rationalize party alignments had its roots not only in uncertainty as to what even the near-term future would bring, but also in a pervasive reticence to assume significant risks. Essentially 1987 was a period during which a scant number of reputations were made, many became frayed, and not a few were flayed. In this context of the politics of hesitancy, the armed forces came to constitute perhaps the strongest bulwark of the Sarney government.

Repeated shifts in government policies and personnel would be closely related to the fluctuating fortunes of the administration and its critics in the constituent assembly. As much of this fluctuation resulted from the ebb and flow of a continuing intramural struggle for dominance between moderates and progressives within the PMDB, relations between the president and Guimarães—who as presiding officer of Congress was Sarney's legal substitute—swung back and forth between collaboration and thinly veiled antagonism. Yet even in the troughs, this situation did not deteriorate into the kind of executive-legislative warfare that had occurred when Pedro I closed down Brazil's first constitution-framing body or when the legislature of the newly born republic turned the tables on Deodoro. Indeed, were it not for the repeated moves within the *constituente* to emasculate Sarney's powers, truncate his term, or do both in one fell swoop, the tension was generally within the limits inherent in a situation in which two independent forces were seeking to maximize their influence.

The Quest for a Basic Charter

The national legislature elected in November 1986 reflected the country's political divisions relatively accurately, tilted slightly toward the Center-Right owing to the underrepresentation of São Paulo. About one in eight of its members could be identified as strongly conservative, being found mostly within the ranks of the PDS and the PFL and constituting a majority of the former party and a strong minority of the latter.[25] Depending upon whether more weight is placed upon actions or rhetoric, some 6 percent to 10 percent of the *constituentes* were well over on the Left, most of them coming from the ranks of the PT, the PDT, and the PMDB—although constituting a quite small fraction of the catchall PMDB. Extremely vocal and active, these leftists would have a very heavy impact at the initial stage of subcommissions and a significant one during the subsequent workings of the commissions, but would not be as effective in the Systematization Commission—where parties were represented proportionately and the representatives were selected by their party leaders. Once action passed onto the floor, the leftists would find themselves waging an often unsuccessful and at times ineffectual battle to preserve a substantial proportion of their earlier gains.[26]

Between one-fifth and one-fourth of the legislators were of a Center-Left persuasion, an orientation most heavily found in the PMDB but also including some individuals in the PFL and the PTB. This grouping was roughly matched in strength by the Center-Right, which dominated the PFL, constituted a major wing of the PMDB, was characteristic of much of the PTB, and marked the small PL as well. The remaining third or a bit more of the *constituentes* were squarely in the Center, from where they had the potential to exercise the balance of power. Yet they were divided between the moderate, often former PP wing of the PMDB and the less conservative half of the PFL. Roughly a quarter of the *constituentes* were rural landowners, with an equal proportion (including some overlapping) having ties to the financial sector. Some thirty-four Protestants, including seven ministers, represented a vast increase over only eleven in the previous Congress.

The constituent assembly had begun its work in February with the election of Guimarães as its presiding officer by a vote of 299 to 155 for former justice minister Lyra—favored by the "progressive" elements.[27] The radical Left early on met with a series of defeats that established the basic parameters within which the body would conduct its work. First their proposal to exclude the senators elected in 1982 was rejected, then lack of support killed their pretension that the assembly be completely sovereign, capable of amending the existing constitution by majority vote, and entitled to disapprove actions of the administration. Finally a 247 to 121 repudiation of their effort to convoke Funaro to explain the government's foreign debt moratorium put an end to their plans to really govern the country while writing the new constitution. Discerning that their real goal was finding a way to cut short his mandate, Sarney managed to stall adoption of that body's rules of procedure until after the new governors took office in mid-March.[28]

From that time through May, the president partially reshaped his Cabinet to reflect the new balance of forces brought about by this changing of the guard at the statehouse level as well as the alignments that were tortuously emerging from the constituent assembly. For, although the PMDB had a majority on paper, with 304 of 559 deputies and senators, it was in reality divided into three relatively distinct currents: a Center to conservative wing consistently supporting Sarney; a left wing with no loyalty to the administration despite a fairly avid appetite for patronage and perquisites; and a moderately Center-Left contingent whose degree of support for the government varied sharply from issue to issue. Thus the PFL with but 134 seats had to carry much of the brunt of the burden of providing a reasonably stable legislative base for the government—indeed, so much so that by late September it would break with the PMDB while seeking enhanced Cabinet representation.

The protracted round of Cabinet changes that would leave the government with a more conservative, northeastern, and "pre-1985" look began in mid-March when Sayad was replaced as planning minister by Aníbal Teixeira (fifty-seven) of Minas Gerais. This change resulted from the incompatibility between Sayad's belief that some more orthodox and politically unpopular austerity measures were necessary and Funaro's conviction that continuation of his policies would soon bring inflation under control without jeopardizing continued high economic growth. The naming of a Mineiro to this post vacated by a Paulista returned São Paulo to the number of ministries it had controlled at the beginning of the administration and helped solidify relations between Sarney and incoming Minas Gerais Governor Cardoso. Then, in a move intended to pave the way for Funaro's defenestration, Maciel abandoned the post of presidential chief of staff in favor of a return to the Senate, the presidency of the PFL, and an enhanced independence from the government. Costa Couto moved over to Maciel's old post from the Interior Ministry, where he was replaced by Maciel ally Joaquim Francisco Cavalcanti (thirty-nine) from Pernambuco.

Only five weeks after Sayad was forced out by presidential rejection of his economic and fiscal proposals, Funaro himself fell from power in the face of soaring inflation, which had reached nearly 17 percent in January, held at just below and then slightly above 14 percent the following two months, and jumped sharply in April to a shocking 21 percent (before going on to over 23 percent and then more than 26 percent in May and June). Funaro's successor as finance minister was cocksure economist/businessman Luíz Carlos Bresser Pereira (fifty-three), also from São Paulo—but he was named only after an imbroglio in which PMDB leaders, with Guimarães in the van, vetoed Sarney's initial choice of Ceará Governor Jereissati for this key post, which the Paulistas had come to consider their privileged domain. This contretemps further strained the uneasy relationship between Sarney and the PMDB national leadership and confirmed the president's belief that he would have to bypass the party as much as possible by working through the state chief executives. Furthermore, it put Bresser in a very difficult position from the beginning, as Sarney felt Bresser had been imposed upon him against his will by the PMDB, while at the same time much of the party lacked any enthusiasm for Bresser's policies—which were based heavily upon his own academic theories and writings.

The Bresser Plan

Confident that he understood the real nature of Brazil's inflation, a topic on which he had published repeatedly and recently, in mid-June Bresser launched an economic plan bearing his name.[29] Centering on a temporary price freeze and a formula for holding pay increases in check, it bore significant similarities to what Sayad had proposed a few months earlier—

which Sarney had discarded at the time in favor of giving Funaro's policies another chance. Although the Bresser Plan brought inflation down temporarily—to 6.36 percent in August and a bit lower in September—it subsequently began to lose momentum as inflation again rose rapidly. The inflation rate reached 9.2 percent for October before hitting 12.8 percent and 14.1 percent for the last two months of the year as GDP growth ceased, causing the total GDP rise for 1987 to fall to only 3.6 percent—by far the lowest since the dark days of the 1981–1983 recession. Such slippage severely undermined already flagging public confidence in the administration's ability to direct the economy—and hence raised doubts as to the government's general competence.

The economy, specifically popular perceptions of economic performance, had clearly become the most important factor conditioning the course of Brazilian politics during the Sarney administration. The president's ability to lead the country toward consolidation of the transition from military rule within a framework of continued presidentialism and centrist policies fluctuated almost directly in proportion to his popularity. His popularity, in turn, was essentially a reflection of the degree of popular satisfaction—or dissatisfaction—with the government's management of the economy. The political price of the government's deep involvement in running the country's economic life—on the upswing since the Médici and Geisel administrations—was having to assume responsibility for shortcomings as well as taking credit for accomplishments. Extremely low on the eve of the launching of the Bresser Plan—after having been intoxicatingly high for much of 1986—public support then demonstrated temporary recuperation on the strength of a sharp drop in inflation combined with apparent avoidance of a recession. Subsequently it sagged badly, never again coming anywhere close to the levels to which Sarney had been accustomed and seriously jeopardizing his ability to lead the country.

A key feature of the Bresser Plan was the temporary nature of the price freeze, which this time was not to exceed ninety days, and thus it was hoped that the grave problems of prices falling sharply behind costs, which had led to the eventual failure of the Cruzado Plan, would be avoided. National labor leaders felt that the more restrictive wage policy that replaced the old "triggers" of 20 percent automatic raises would provide fertile ground for a general strike. Wishing to demonstrate that the labor movement had become a major factor in Brazil's political life and eager to wipe out the bitter memories of an essentially unsuccessful strike staged on December 12, 1986, they also wanted to make an immediate and dramatic impression of strength upon the constituent assembly.

But when it was finally held on August 20, the work stoppage was far from general. Indeed, it was an outright fiasco, with fewer than 10 million participating—compared to participation of at least 20 million eight months earlier. This outcome provided the government with some badly needed breathing space, but more importantly it left the more radical labor leaders demoralized and opened the way for significant realignments in this field—

which would culminate in May 1989 with a changing of the guard. When central union organizations were finally made legal in April 1985, the Single Center of Workers (CUT) was already functioning as a close ally if not an adjunct of the PT. More traditional elements of the labor movement had founded the National Coordination of the Working Class (CONCLAT) and in March 1986 transformed it into the General Labor Center (CGT), which was initially close to the PMDB. This grouping claimed affiliation of some 1,450 unions and the right to speak for 25 million workers nominally represented by those unions (a considerable exaggeration of their effective strength). For its part the more militant CUT claimed the support of over 1,100 unions and some 12.5 million workers—still inflated figures, albeit less so than in the CGT's case. (By 1989 these rival centers would be claiming to represent 29 million and 15 million workers, respectively.) In reality, with few exceptions Brazilian unions remain bureaucratic, unrepresentative, and hence unable to effectively channel, much less control, the aspirations of their rank and file.[30]

Lula and his chief aide, Jair Meneguelli (thirty-nine), had seen their credibility undercut from the lack of significant material gains as a result of the prolonged strike by auto workers and related São Paulo unions in April and May 1985. Now, as CUT president, Meneguelli was the chief loser in the flop of the loudly heralded general strike, being criticized harshly even by his historical ally, PT President Lula, for letting ideological and political considerations blind him to the real interests of the workers. Joaquim dos Santos Andrade (sixty) of the rival CGT, who went along with the strike halfheartedly, lost ground to younger union leaders—particularly Luíz Antônio Medeiros (thirty-nine), who would go on to found the National Confederation of Metalworkers (CNM), and Antônio Rogério Magri of the electricians. These individuals had more accurately gauged the hesitance of their rank and file to embark on such a risky venture at a time when unemployment was rising and employers might be looking for justifications to lay off workers. They would subsequently gain a broadening base of support for their program of "results" unionism (concentrating on material gains rather than political causes).

Ministerial Turnover Continues

Meanwhile, changes in the upper echelon of the government continued apace. In May Agrarian Reform Minister Dante de Oliveira—who had replaced Ribeiro a year earlier when the president had come to consider Ribeiro unacceptably inefficient—quit in frustration to go back to being mayor of Cuiabá. Marcos Freire was forced to leave the presidency of the money-dispensing Federal Savings Bank for this thankless job. Then fellow Pernambucan Cavalcanti quit in a huff in early August, with the PMDB head of SUDENE being dismissed as a consequence. (This would pay off handsomely for Cavalcanti in November 1988, when he easily won election as Recife's mayor.) João Alves, until March governor of Sergipe, took Cavalcanti's place. Then on September 8 Freire was killed in an airplane crash, and former governor Jáder Barbalho (forty-two) of Pará became the fourth individual to head the Agrarian Reform Ministry in the short span of two and a half years. When Sarney attempted to mollify a disgruntled Arraes by offering to name one of the latter's close associates to the patronage-important SUDENE post, PFL Education Minister Bornhausen resigned in late September—a move designed to provoke a crisis between the president and the PMDB as well as accentuate divisions within that party.

The result of the protracted political crisis was far from what Bornhausen and his mentor Maciel had in mind. The president did start out by insisting that members of his Cabinet and the parties they represented fall in line behind his desire to maintain a presidential system of government and support his efforts to guarantee a five-year term. A PMDB national convention in mid-July had ended in a stalemate with a decision to leave this divisive issue up to the constituent assembly. On that occasion Sarney had backed away from a real test of strength—uncertain just what Guimarães might do—and in October he again evaded a showdown, accepting a fairly weak pledge of support from the PMDB national directorate and a slightly stronger affirmation by the party's governors in place of his original insistence on individual commitments from the legislators. Thus instead of a major administrative overhaul and the drastic Cabinet changes that many expected, there was only an anticlimactic reshuffle.[31]

In an attempt to keep the PFL from following through on a threat to leave the government, the intensely partisan Rafael de Almeida Magalhães was dropped as social welfare minister, with fellow PMDB member and Guimarães intimate Archer moving over from the Science and Technology Ministry, where he was replaced by Chamber majority leader Luíz Henrique da Silva (forty-six). This compensated Santa Catarina for Bornhausen's departure, but left Rio de Janeiro without a representative in the Cabinet. Moderate conservative Prisco Viana (fifty-four), a PMDB congressman from Bahia—who once had been ARENA secretary-general—became housing and urban development minister, which necessitated the departure of Deni Schwartz (whose sponsor, Richa, was no longer on the president's good side).

To balance this change, Santos, also from Bahia, was dismissed as health minister, making room there for Paraná Federal Deputy Luíz Carlos Borges da Silveira (forty-six) from the center-right wing of the PMDB. Finally Piauí Senator Hugo Napoleão (forty-four) was named as education minister, leaving the PFL right were they had been before they initiated the crisis. In brief, Sarney had partially rewarded the center-right wing of the PMDB without any sharp rebuff of Guimarães. While Álvaro Dias of Paraná got a pat on the back for his cooperation, Moreira Franco received a slap on the wrist for unreliability. Only the left wing of the PMDB was seriously punished. What had changed, however, was the intraparty power relationships, as Maciel's bid for the PFL to break with the government was soundly defeated by an alliance of Chaves and Antônio Carlos Magalhães—neither of whom had any intention of giving up their strategic ministries. The latter emerged as virtually the innermost of Sarney's inner circle of advisors.

Constitution Writing Drags On

During this time, the work of drafting a new constitution was moving ahead, but it was generating more in the way of political attrition rather than making progress toward a document acceptable to a majority of the *constituentes*. After their initial setbacks, the Left had seen their prospects brighten considerably when São Paulo Senator Covas was elected PMDB floor leader over Luíz Henrique da Silva—a faithful supporter of Guimarães. Although this vote was limited to the PMDB, it put the progressive Covas—who had been purged by the military regime—in a position where he could and did give the more radical elements in the majority party a markedly disproportionate share of control over the twenty-four thematic subcommissions.

Influenced heavily by short-term political considerations, particularly that of holding the PMDB together at any cost—as his presidential aspirations had come to all but determine his decisions—Guimarães acquiesced in this gross overrepresentation of PMDB progressives as first-stage rapporteurs. This resulted in provisions often substantially out of line with the sentiment of the majority of the membership, who were left out of the process as it moved on to nine commissions of less specialized scope at the end of May.

Although the Left was still significantly overrepresented on these bodies, which consolidated the subcommission drafts, some of the highly celebrated—at least by the vocal Left and their media sympathizers—victories of the progressives were trimmed down at this stage. Counting upon the very powerful role given to the ninety-three-member Systematization Commission, Covas—now in full flight as a presidential candidate in the elections he expected to be able to have called for November—felt his allies could push through a constitution closely following the PMDB party program. In his view, and that of the whole historical faction of the PMDB as well as other parties of the Left, the objective was a document meeting their perception of what their constituents wanted. They counted upon the assembly's internal regulations to protect their draft from the more conservative makeup of the body as a whole.

Following the work of these commissions, at the end of June overall rapporteur Bernardo Cabral—who would become Collor de Mello's justice minister in 1990—produced an extremely prolix, overly long, and excessively detailed draft that satisfied virtually no one. Indeed, quickly gaining the nickname of "Frankenstein," the document was inundated in a flood of more than 100 "popular amendments" submitted by societal groups, generally on the Left, and totalling 12 million signatures. Finally by late August Cabral came back with a revised draft, slimmed down from over 500 articles to a "mere" 300. Though most *constituentes* considered it an improvement, few were satisfied with what came to be known as "Rosemary's baby." Chaired by senior statesman Afonso Arinos, a determined advocate of a parliamentary system who was still deeply chagrined that the president had not submitted the work of his earlier body of experts as an official draft, the Systematization Commission worked slowly through September, October, and November. With its membership proportional to each party's strength, it was closer to a cross-section of the larger body but was still biased toward inclusion of articulate Center-Left and Left elements.

After the commission rejected a presidentialist amendment by fifty-seven to thirty-six and on November 15 voted a four-year term for the president by a narrow forty-eight to forty-five margin, Covas, Guimarães, Arinos, and Cabral—who had thus far kept the process under their control—were suddenly faced with what was for them an unexpected backbencher revolt. The fact that they were caught off guard is a reflection of the tendency—quite common in Brazilian politics, particularly on the Left—to confuse winning a battle with having won the war. In Covas's case, he at least had the excuse that he had been laid up by heart surgery from mid-September until shortly before the bubble burst.

In essence, they assumed that the commission's draft would go to the floor under rules that would make far-reaching modifications all but impossible. But the executive had become much more determined by November not to sit by and be emasculated by supposed allies who were in a great hurry to make the Sarney administration a thing of the past. With Antônio Carlos Magalhães emerging as the president's chief political counselor, the government began to woo the large number of federal deputies who had felt affronted by their party's leadership when that leadership had denied them places on the Systematization Commission.

Thus, at the beginning of December the so-called Centrão, or Big Center, pushed through drastic changes in the assembly's rules and procedures. The changes forced upon a very reluctant Guimarães required that all provisions be approved by an absolute majority and provided that substitute articles backed by 280 members would receive precedence in voting even over those from the commission draft.

As the insurgents had won a preliminary vote in late November by 271 to 223 and now triumphed on December 3 by 290 to 116, the balance had tilted sharply and decisively. Most important, almost half of the PMDB's representatives refused to follow Covas's order for a walkout to reduce attendance below the quorum requirement—and 125 of them voted with the Centrão against the party's official position. Now a leader disowned by a large proportion of his party, Covas would begin to pack his bags for departure to a new party composed of fellow progressives.

Hence, as plenary debate and article-by-article voting finally got underway in December, it was clear that the entire membership would have their say in shaping the constitution. If it had not been a good year for Sarney, in most ways it left deeper scars upon his main rivals—with the final showdown still to come in 1988.

The Fourth Year:
Finally, a Framework for the New Republic

After three years, temporizing finally came to an end. The determination of the anti-Sarney elements of the PMDB to cut his term and reduce his powers by approving a parliamentary system and marking presidential elections for November 1988 led the president to throw all his influence into the scales to retain presidentialism and preserve the fifth year of his mandate. Greatly aided by such governors as São Paulo's Quércia and Cardoso of Minas Gerais, Sarney demonstrated the residual strength of patronage clientelism in reversing the tide in favor of shortening his tenure and curtailing his powers. Yet a shadow lingered over his impressive March 22 victories—334 votes for presidentialism and 304 for five years as president (compared to the minimum of 280 required for passage)—because of the perception that outspoken military support for his positions bordering on a none-too-veiled threat of possible armed forces intervention might well have been the decisive factor.

New Year, New Game Plan

Much as elections in 1982 and 1986 prevented the government from adopting needed—but politically unpopular—measures at the proper time, the constituent assembly was cause for delay during 1988. Only after the question of the president's term was finally resolved did the government belatedly take meaningful measures to cut the public sector deficit and curb inflation from escalating into hyperinflation. At least a beginning in this direction came in early January, when Mailson Ferreira da Nóbrega, a career civil servant, was confirmed in the post left vacant by Bresser Pereira's resignation shortly before the end of the old year. As he was a champion of policies close to the essentially orthodox line Dornelles had taken at the beginning of the Neves-Sarney government, Nóbrega's "rice and beans" approach contrasted sharply with the line followed since August 1985. This reorientation back to reality after the fanciful flights of Funaro—who could be accused with substantial justice of having tried to repeal the law of supply and demand—and Bresser Pereira—who suspected that everyone else was wrong about inflation and the debt problem—involved congruent personnel changes down the line. Thus, in late January João Batista de Abreu replaced scandal-tinged fellow Mineiro Teixeira as planning minister and new heads of the Central Bank and Bank of Brazil were soon installed.

To implement semi-austerity policies needed to reach an agreement with the IMF, essential to get the long-stalled debt renegotiations moving again, Sarney required the support of the governors to offset the fundamental hostility of PMDB leadership. Yet he had to attain this without sacrificing his tenure as president. The only feasible way was to push quickly for a victory in the assembly, then implement "realistic and responsible" economic measures so that the government could argue that this was done on its own initiative, not forced upon Brazil by the IMF.

The crux of the problem with this strategy involved keeping the cooperation of key governors in the face of fiscal measures that would increase their already severe headaches. For the substantial success Sarney had enjoyed with the governors during 1987 rested heavily on generous financial support for their priority programs, and only the governors could keep congressional reaction under control. Moreover, given the hiatus in the normal development of new national political leadership resulting from twenty-one years of military regimes, the governors elected in 1986 constituted the most important pool of potential ministerial and chief executive talent.

Key Governors: The Dukes of the New Regime

Certain governors in Brazil are major national actors just because of the vital importance of their states, regardless of their personal strengths and weaknesses. This is most true with respect to São Paulo—which has a population equal to that of Argentina and a GDP rivaling Mexico's. Possessing over 22 percent of the national electorate, this state is critical for presidential contests. Moreover, although grossly underrepresented in Congress, it still has the largest delegation of any one state. Thus, Quércia, experienced spokesman for the interior of the state, came quickly to exercise considerable political clout in Brasília—accentuated by the fact that all other major Paulista PMDB leaders were enemies of the Sarney government to varying degrees (Covas, Cardoso, Guimarães, and Franco Montoro). Quércia's basic aim— with his eye on the presidency in 1989 or 1994—was, at least to November 1988, to maintain fundamentally good relations with the president, but at the same time to maximize Sarney's need for his continued support by not going along with moves that might so consolidate the president's political base that he would no longer require Quércia's periodic efforts to mobilize congressional votes and coordinate joint actions of fellow big-state governors on Sarney's behalf. On the negative side of the ledger, Quércia constituted a constant source of pressure upon the treasury for funds to carry forward the fairly ambitious programs he counted upon to make himself a leading presidential contender. Indeed, when in 1989 São Paulo's revenues rose as a result of the provisions of the new constitution while the central government's ability to supplement those revenues shrank, Quércia would distance himself from Sarney.

Although no other Brazilian governor enjoyed the luxury of being as indispensable to the federal administration as Quércia, three others exercised leverage on the national scene in 1988. Minas Gerais, whose population is only half that of São Paulo, has seen its governors reach the presidency with equal frequency during this century—in part as the other states' perceived best check on the danger of Paulista hegemony. Moreover, its congressional representation is almost equal in size to that of São Paulo, and Minas Gerais possesses the nation's second largest electorate. Thus, although considered quite ordinary—especially compared to such predecessors as Neves, Kubitschek, or even Chaves—Newton Cardoso was a very determined and persistent individual who harbored hopes that Mineiro unity might once again offset a deeply divided São Paulo in the 1989 presidential sweepstakes. Proportionately even more than was the case with his southern neighbor, his stance on national questions was largely determined by his desire for a continued heavy flow of federal funds into his state. Thus, he was essentially opposed to austerity programs and conditioned his support of Sarney upon continuing administration aid to his ambitious public works programs, which centered on paving much of the sprawling state's road network. Unlike Quércia, who had a 1975–1982 stint in the Senate, Cardoso's highest previous office was as mayor of an industrial suburb of the state capital, and his perspective was relatively parochial. (By 1989 his ineffectiveness as governor would reduce him to a minor actor as many presidential candidates took on Mineiros as running mates.)

In sharp contrast, Rio de Janeiro's Moreira Franco was both cosmopolitan and international. With a doctorate in sociology earned in Paris, the youngest of Brazil's major state governors had a much deeper understanding of the complexities of national socioeconomic dynamics and international developments than did any of his fellow governors. Also, well aware that the presidency was not a realistic goal for him this time around, he was playing for the longer run and perceived Brazil as changing more rapidly and profoundly than did Quércia or Cardoso. Hence he tried to articulate a more coherent Center-Left orientation for the PMDB, preferring Miguel Arraes over Guimarães as the party's 1989 standard-bearer.

Though Bahia, Brazil's fourth state, has produced presidential contenders, they have never been able to grasp the brass ring, but Rio Grande do Sul has furnished the country with a disproportionate share of presidents— though not through direct elections. Bahia's Waldir Pires was heavily checked by Antônio Carlos Magalhães, who from his post as minister of communications and presidential confidant was already campaigning actively to regain control of the state in 1990. For his part Rio Grande do Sul's Pedro Simon was up to his ears in the Gaúcho state's near bankruptcy and faced the president's resentment over his unsuccessful efforts to deny Sarney the Democratic Alliance's vice-presidential nomination in 1984. This situation provided an opportunity for Paraná's Álvaro Dias to move to the forefront. Enjoying by far the highest approval rating of any governor and as young as Moreira Franco but having already served a term in the Senate, he demonstrated astuteness in emerging almost immediately from Richa's shadow and keeping the state's finances in good order. And although many observers expected Arraes to provide leadership for his region on the basis of his previous projection on the national scene, he concentrated instead upon Pernambuco's problems. This allowed Fernando Collor de Mello of the small state of Alagoas to become the leading voice of gubernatorial dissatisfaction with the Sarney government—a role he used with devastating effectiveness to project himself onto the national scene.

With the critical decisions within the constituent assembly being made between March and mid-year, the first major political battle resulted in a decisive victory for Sarney, as on March 22 the Systematization Commission's proposal of a parliamentary system was rejected on the floor by a vote of 344 to 212 and a five-year term was approved in place of the leadership's proposal for presidential elections in 1988. The executive demonstrated majority support from all but three states—Bahia, Rio Grande do Sul, and Alagoas. From the rest of the north and northeast the margin was a lopsided

144 to fifty-three, but the largest states also contributed heavily to the outcome with thirty-eight of sixty-three Paulistas, thirty-five of fifty-six Mineiros, and thirty-five of forty-nine from Rio de Janeiro supporting the president along with twenty of thirty-three from Paraná.

On a party basis Sarney's majority was comprised of 144 from the PMDB and 113 PFL votes as well as twenty-two PDS congressmen and sixteen from the PTB. Although generally opposed to the administration, twenty-five representatives of the PDT and fifteen from the PT also voted for presidentialism in keeping with the ambitions of respective party leaders Brizola and Lula to occupy the presidency in the future. Of course, however, they did not support Sarney on the length of his term, making the vote on that measure fall to 304–223 and thirty-one absent.

This victory for the administration required both full use of the government's patronage resources and mobilization of military support. The military ministers had made it very clear that they harbored severe reservations concerning a parliamentary system and viewed the prospect of presidential elections in 1988 with alarm, given the fact that progovernment forces were still involved in forging a new constitution and the PMDB was racked by internal dissension—while Brizola was already in full campaign swing. But Sarney was still faced with the problem of holding on to these votes until the final floor consideration of his term came during debate several months later on the constitution's transitory provisions. This called for a strategy of fulfilling some of the promises made to individual *constituentes* while holding off on others until the final challenge had been turned back.

The PMDB: In and Out of the Government at the Same Time

With a five-year term for Sarney being maintained on June 2 by a comfortable 328 to 222 margin, with three abstentions and an equal number of absences, the constitution moved toward completion. In a reflection of the continuing tension between the chief executive and the leader of the nominal majority party, early August brought the departure of the ministers closest to Guimarães. Luíz Henrique's replacement at Science and Technology was Ralph de Biasi (forty), strongly promoted by São Paulo Governor Quércia; Roberto Cardoso Alves (sixty-one), also from São Paulo and leader of the conservative wing of the PMDB, took over the Industry and Commerce post vacated by Castelo Branco's death (from cancer). To compensate Minas Gerais, Congressman Leopoldo Bessone (forty-six) became agrarian reform minister, as Barbalho moved over to take Renato Archer's place at social welfare. Finally, Aparecido de Oliveira left the Federal District governorship to replace Furtado as culture minister—the same post Oliveira had held at the beginning of the government.

Thus, Sarney was finally free from ministers inevitably "disloyal" to him because of their intimate ties to Guimarães. And as Labor Minister Pazzianotto had accepted an appointment to the superior labor tribunal (with no permanent replacement at the time), this shakeup meant that Chaves and

Magalhães, along with Aparecido—who had gone and returned—were the only civilian ministers remaining from the original 1985 Cabinet. The party picture also underwent an important change as Covas, Fernando Henrique Cardoso, José Richa, and former São Paulo governor Franco Montoro led an exodus of progressives out of the PMDB into a PSDB (Brazilian Social Democratic Party, popularly called the Tucanos after the bird they took as their symbol). Hence the composition and orientation of the Sarney government had come to be very close to what might well have been the case had Figueiredo opted to support Chaves in the 1984 succession and that moderately conservative Mineiro had become president.

The greatest difference was rooted in Sarney's determination to bring the northeast toward center stage and his insistence upon putting into motion major projects designed to foster the development of this vast region. For he believed that it would probably be a long time before another representative of the region came to the presidency, which he felt essentially meant that it was a now-or-never situation with respect to such long-range projects as the north-south railroad and massive irrigation works. (Although Marshal Castelo Branco was originally from Ceará, he had been a career military man for so long that, combined with his overriding priority for putting the national economy in order through austerity, nothing significant was undertaken along these lines.) Not surprisingly, Maranhão in particular held the forefront of Sarney's initiatives.

Finally, a Constitution

On September 22 the protracted and often politically agonizing process of shaping a new constitution came to an end with the final ritual vote, followed by promulgation on October 5.[32] Although the 1987–1988 constituent assembly took a long time to produce an unexceptional charter, the assembly did have several undeniable merits. In the first place, it really wrote a constitution from scratch rather than merely revising and approving a document placed before it. Second, the protracted process of beginning from a tabula rasa did provide for a very thorough airing of almost every significant issue of governance and public policy. Through the subcommissions, commissions, and the Systematization Commission all interests and points of view had an opportunity to be heard during the ten months before plenary debate began. Finally, much more than even in the past a conscious effort was made to decide what institutions and provisions might be most appropriate for Brazil—and this was done on a pragmatic basis rather than being rooted in the naive belief that copying on a wholesale basis features from elsewhere would prove at least a mini-panacea.

The basic structure of government was little altered, although Congress saw its powers amplified and major changes were made at the top of the judicial pyramid. The Security Council was eliminated, being replaced by a Council of the Republic and a National Defense Council. The first was composed of the president, the vice-president, presiding officers from the Chamber of Deputies and the Senate, majority and minority leaders of each house, the justice minister, and six private citizens (two each appointed by the president, the Senate, and the Chamber for three-year terms). The latter council was to be constituted by the president, vice-president, Chamber and Senate presiding officers, and the military ministers plus those of Justice, Foreign Relations, and Planning.

On the one hand workers' rights and benefits were augmented, but on the other no expropriation of productive land was permitted, which amounted to a limitation on agrarian reform more restrictive than that previously in effect. A ban on foreigners owning land near the borders was dropped, but restrictions were placed upon their exploitation of mineral resources. Moreover, a limit on interest rates to 12 percent annually was considered by many observers a demagogic gesture that would be very difficult to enforce without extreme disruption of the financial system. Amendment would be by a three-fifths majority of Congress until 1993, at which time a new constitutional convention would be empowered to change any and all provisions by a simple majority vote.[33]

The northern part of Goiás was immediately transformed into the state of Tocantins, with the federal territories of Amapá and Roraima also to be elevated to that status by 1990. This would further increase the congressional bias in favor of small, underdeveloped states, especially in the Senate. In this context the increase of the limit on federal deputies for São Paulo to seventy was virtually meaningless, not making a significant beginning in correcting that state's gross underrepresentation and still giving Minas Gerais almost the same representation as the twice as populous São Paulo. The franchise was extended to sixteen-year-olds but on a nonobligatory basis.

Article 142 defined the armed forces as "permanent and regular national institutions organized on the basis of hierarchy and discipline, under the express authority of the President of the Republic and intended for the defense of the country, guaranteeing the constitutional powers and, by invitation of any one of these, law and order." Although less of a mandate for the military to function as the moderating power than had been the case in previous constitutions, the new role fell far short of the clear prohibition on this that the Left had advocated. Moreover, the secretariat of the abolished Security Council was reborn as the National Defense Staff Secretariat (SADEN).

Significant changes in the distribution of revenues mandated in the constitution gave directly to states and municipalities fiscal resources that they had been in the habit of bargaining for on a continuing case-by-case basis with the federal executive. This new distribution scheme would give them greater political independence and potentially would weaken the political dominance of the president. In response, in an act viewed by the governors as retaliation, the Sarney administration began an effort to transfer a variety of functions and services to the states and increased pressure upon them to repay part of their foreign debts that had been covered by Brasília. The governors' mobilization of their congressional delegations to block this effort ushered in a new period of executive-legislative conflict.

Grassroots Elections

The 1988 municipal elections mobilized even greater numbers of politicians and political cadres than had the national balloting two years earlier. With over 4,300 mayors, an equal number of vice-mayors, and some 43,600 municipal councilmen (*vereadores*) to be elected, there were roughly 1.2 million candidates involved in a total electorate of just over 75.8 million. When the dust created by the comings and goings of their millions of campaign workers had settled after November 15, very little had occurred to clarify the confused presidential succession picture.[34] As almost every governor failed to elect the mayor of his state capital, none of them improved his prospects and their setbacks cancelled out, leaving them all just about where they had been relative to one another. Furthermore, although the two largest metropolitan centers were won by the PT and the PDT, neither of these parties of the Left demonstrated significant strength on more than a regional basis.

The biggest loser was the PMDB, chiefly in the sense that the artificially high proportion of offices it had gained at the state and national levels in 1986 was not duplicated in the midst of a very different environment of runaway inflation and popular disenchantment with the conduct of the country's affairs by this numerically hegemonic but internally divided behemoth. Yet although it clearly did have serious wounds to lick, the PMDB still remained Brazil's largest party by a substantial margin, electing almost 1,900 mayors and 17,000 councilmen on the strength of roughly 25 percent of the countrywide vote. Despite dramatic defeats in most of the major urban centers, it retained control of five state capitals and in São Paulo possessed a formidable base of 194 mayors and over 1,500 *vereadores*.

Although virtually overlooked in the media hype about the São Paulo and Rio de Janeiro outcomes, on a national basis the PFL consolidated its position as Brazil's second-ranking party. It elected nearly 1,500 mayors and close to 17,000 *vereadores*, while polling over 15 percent of the popular vote. In Recife its candidate, Joaquim Francisco Cavalcanti (who had a very brief stay in Sarney's Cabinet), received almost half the vote (49.5 percent) while swamping not only the PMDB standard-bearer, but also limiting the PDT to less than 14 percent and the PT to only 7.5 percent in a city with a long tradition of favoring the Left. The PFL's total victory of three state capitals tied it for third place in this respect. Even in São Paulo it was second, with 137 mayors and 1,500 city councilmen.

Though continuing gradual progress toward becoming more than just a São Paulo party, the PT was not at all the major victor depicted in much of the U.S. and European media. Certainly the election of Luíza Erundina in São Paulo was a noteworthy accomplishment. Yet she received just 29 percent of the vote in winning by nearly 1.54 million votes to 1.26 million for the PDS's Paulo Maluf. Even this outcome was possible only because many PMDB and PSDB voters—despairing of their own lackluster candidates' minimal chances—threw their support at the last minute to the PT nominee as the only way to stop a Maluf comeback that would have projected him squarely into the middle of the presidential sweepstakes. Although it won in Campinas and several major industrial suburbs, the PT's statewide total of thirteen mayors and 295 local legislators left it vying with the PDT for sixth place.

Furthermore, victories in Porto Alegre and Vitória could not hide the fact that the PT came out disastrously in the two principal places outside São Paulo where it had elected mayors in 1985. In Fortaleza it finished way back in the pack, and in Villa Velha (an important part of greater Vitória) it came in fourth. Even more serious was the fact that, while getting over 18 percent of the Rio de Janeiro city vote for a second-place finish, it elected only one mayor in the whole state, and in Minas Gerais it won but seven of 723 mayoral races (chiefly in steel towns where metalworkers and their families made up a high proportion of the electorate). Nationally it came away with just thirty-six mayors, still a quite limited base for Lula's presidential bid (and within ten months five of these would have defected to other parties).[35]

Although the PDT as a whole proclaimed to all who would listen that the elections demonstrated its own great progress toward becoming a truly national party, the realistic elements within the PDT leadership were in fact highly disappointed with the results. Jaime Lerner's victory in Curitiba was a personal triumph for the twice-former mayor, not a measure of PDT strength. Then, too, Porto Alegre's mayorship was lost to the PT. In São Paulo the PDT came up virtually empty—with only seventeen mayors and 267 *vereadores*—while its just over 30 percent of the vote in electing Rio de Janeiro's mayor continued a downward trend there (as Brizola had gotten 41.4 percent of the vote in 1982; Saturnino Braga, 39.3 percent in 1985; and Darcy Ribeiro, 35.4 percent in 1986). In the party's home state as a whole, its share was only 25 percent of the vote, placing it between the PMDB and the PFL with eighteen of sixty-eight mayors. Its national claims of 200 mayors, 2,200 municipal councilmen, and over 6 million votes seem much less impressive when translated into proportional terms: 4.5 percent of municipal chief executives, under 5 percent of *vereadores*, and 8 percent of the registered electorate. This constituted a precariously narrow organizational base for Brizola's presidential candidacy, a fact that explained his subsequent efforts to form alliances with disaffected elements of other parties.

The PSDB proved to be a party of many chiefs and few Indians, as it ran dismally in São Paulo—home base of most of its top leaders—getting but five mayors and 205 councilmen (compared to eighty-eight and 1,050 for the PTB and seventy-nine and 953 for the PDS). Pimenta da Veiga's election in Belo Horizonte was the only bright spot in an otherwise unrelieved national picture of acute electoral anemia. Indeed, the PSDB was outperformed not only by the PMDB, the PFL, the PDT, and the PT but also by the PTB and the PDS. The PTB came in with almost 400 mayors, while the PDS came back strong in rural areas, electing close to 450 mayors. The PL failed to establish itself as a significant electoral factor, while the PDC demonstrated viability, if not vitality. The other twenty-one parties had very little indeed to show for their often enthusiastic and sometimes exaggerated efforts.

Despite significant shifts in voter support in the larger urban centers, it was clear that parties of the Left had not attained clear electoral superiority in the larger cities taken as a whole, while those of the Center and Right still possessed a marked advantage in the municipalities of under 50,000 inhabitants, where some 40 percent of the electorate was found. Hence the intermediate towns (*municípios* of 50,000–100,000 population) had the potential to be as critical in the 1989 election as frequently are the suburban counties of Westchester, Nassau, and Suffolk in New York State balloting.

Once More to the Well

The new year opened in a climate of malaise and uncertainty similar to that prevailing in early 1986, but with an even greater sense of crisis and urgency. Despite negotiations between representatives of business and industry on the one hand and labor on the other, little real progress had been made toward a "social pact" capable of pulling the country back from the brink of hyperinflation. As the official inflation for 1988 had been 933 percent and accelerating, with other cost of living indices over the 1,000 percent mark, and GDP growth had been marginally negative, the dreaded phenomenon of stagflation had clearly already arrived. (Indeed, 28.8 percent inflation in December had been welcomed as lower than feared.)

The government's response was to launch the Plano Verão on January 15. The "new cruzado" with three zeros lopped off and initially pegged on a par with the U.S. dollar became the unit of currency, with an end to monetary correction being paired with a price freeze and abolition of automatic pay raises as the key elements in an effort to bring inflation under some degree of control. To avoid the problems caused by the original Cruzado Plan, these measures were to be of an indeterminate but clearly temporary duration. Prices went up sharply on the eve of the freeze, and official January inflation was calculated on a statistical basis of over a month and a half, thus reaching an astronomical 70.3 percent (while the other cost of living indices during the calendar month ran about half this figure). The government's patent intention was to clear away the carryover effects of inertial inflation to allow for a dramatically lower mark for February (calculated over a period of less than half a month) and a consequent public impression that prices were being stabilized—the only circumstance in which the absence of major pay raises would be acceptable to the workers.

Credibility for the pledge to eliminate the public sector deficit and limit expenditures to current revenues was to be gained by proposals to dismiss nontenured federal employees and close or combine a number of government agencies. State enterprises were to meet their investment needs not by tapping the treasury or borrowing, their traditional tactics, but rather by issuing more stock, selling off unneeded assets, and "privatizing" subsidiaries that had little or nothing to do with their main productive purpose. All these measures promptly encountered serious opposition in Congress, a situation that would subsequently enable the executive to point the finger at the electorally oriented legislature for the program's very limited results.

At the same time Sarney finally freed himself of those few remaining PMDB ministers whose essential loyalty was to a PMDB electoral victory, if not necessarily to Guimarães's candidacy, and delivered a sign of his displeasure to governors Quércia and Cardoso, who had become critical of the administration's failure to manage the economy without also reducing aid to their states. Moreover, presidential hopeful Chaves also left the Cabinet at this juncture. Fialho, whose Irrigation Ministry was abolished, replaced Chaves at Mines and Energy, and Cardoso Alves acquired most of Science and Technology, merged was with Industry and Commerce. Administration was folded into Planning and Agrarian Reform was merged with Agriculture.[36]

Stepping down from the Supreme Court, tough and wily Mineiro Oscar Dias Corrêa (sixty-eight) assumed the Justice Ministry; Carlos Sant'Anna returned to the Cabinet, this time as education minister; and Paulista Seigo Tsuzuki (fifty-six) took over the Health Ministry. Mineira Dorothéa Werneck (forty), who had held a series of second-echelon posts in Labor and Treasury, was elevated to labor minister on the basis of technical competence and good rapport with important union leaders. With Housing and Social Well-being dismembered, the ministries created since 1985 for essentially political purposes had been eliminated.

Sarney would find the final year of his presidency to be extremely frustrating as presidential succession came to hold center stage. Not only did he face a recalcitrant Congress, whose members were looking ahead to reelection bids in 1990, but all presidential candidates took pains to distance themselves from the administration. Indeed, most would come to attack it, often vying to be the most vehement in this regard. Although the election was still eight months distant, in most important respects Sarney was already a caretaker, if not quite a lame duck—and a largely discredited caretaker at that.

10

Brazil Faces the 1990s

A single event would dominate Brazil during the last year of the Sarney administration—election of a new president and the formation of his government, an administration that would carry Brazil to the middle of the 1990s. All else would take a back seat to directly electing the nation's chief executive for the first time since Quadros had been chosen over Marshal Lott in 1960. The longest previous interruption in popular selection of the nation's helmsman during the century of the republic had been but half as protracted, lasting from 1930 to 1945. And though the choices just after the end of World War I had been quite limited, centering on two senior military figures, this time the array of candidates—all civilians—was virtually as broad as imaginable, running the gamut from the man rejected by the 1985 electoral college to a former guerrilla running on an environmentalist platform. Indeed, there were a highly diversified score of others in between.

The selection, narrowed down to two by the November 15 voting and made final through the December 17 runoff, reflected much more the continuities of Brazil's political life than it marked any dramatic change— although it anticipated possible significant shifts further down the line. For the electorate of over 82 million Brazilians age sixteen and up clearly and decisively expressed their preference for a new face, but one representing the entrepreneurial stratum of the private sector. Fernando Collor de Mello (forty), a handsome and athletic son of an old-line northeastern politician, is an economically conservative populist—in many ways a newer and streamlined version of Quadros, albeit tempered with at least a dash of Kubitschek (and perhaps a pinch of Vargas). His election over Lula da Silva was both a bitter disappointment to those who felt that the Left's day had finally come and a resounding confirmation that large sectors of the Brazilian masses were still little interested in ideological politics.

Indeed, Collor's greatest support came from the broad base of the Brazilian social pyramid, precisely those who according to class-based analyses should have mobilized in support of a Socialist or at least Social Democratic candidate rather than an outspoken advocate of giving free enterprise capitalism a real chance to show what it could do in Brazil.[1] Moreover, the candidate the administration attempted to launch at the last moment in an effort to head off the election of a critic of its alleged corruption and manifest ineffectiveness, television performer, network owner, and megabusinessman Sílvio Santos (fifty-nine), also drew the largest proportion of his potential support from the least privileged strata of Brazilian society.

Although surprising to most foreign observers—and considered shocking by many of them—this outcome was fully in keeping with the historical tendency of Brazilians to seek a personalistic semi-messiah when push comes to shove (as analyzed by Roberto da Matta and discussed in Chapter 1). It also conformed to Przeworski's broadly based comparative finding that, contrary to what the media consistently predict (based upon an erroneous inference that visibility during the campaign for democratization reflects or translates into electoral support), the Left has in no recent case ever won the first post-transition presidential elections.[2] Certainly, the events of 1989, as well as those of 1985 through 1988, also bear out Baloyra's contention that Brazil's was the most complex and confusing of all the Latin American and southern European transitions. For after reviewing all these cases, he concludes that "Brazil witnessed a deterioration that began at the moment of greatest triumph of the most successful bureaucratic authoritarian (BA) regime, the longest process of transition, the largest number of elections between deterioration and breakdown, the most complex, prolonged conflict within the military, and the most convoluted of endgames."[3]

By the return to civilian rule in 1985, Brazil had completed a transition *from* an authoritarian regime; through the 1986 elections and the resulting constitution it had consolidated this and carried out a transition *toward* democracy; by the fully competitive direct election of a president at the end of 1989 it underwent a transition *to* democracy. The crucial challenge of the 1990s is consolidation of a real, viable, and lasting democratic system. Although the array of relevant institutional actors has broadened substantially, as the 1990s opened the armed forces, organized religion, and owners of the property and capital necessary to generate economic growth still remained the key elements of the political equation. Once again the party scene was one of flux bordering on churning confusion as politicians scrambled around seeking a label that might facilitate their election as governor, senator, congressman, or state legislator in October 1990. For the two parties that had dominated the 1985–1988 scene—the PMDB and PFL—had gone down to disastrous defeats of truly epic proportions in the 1989 presidential sweepstakes.

Presidential Succession

The 1988 municipal elections actually marked the beginning of the presidential race. As Brizola and Lula rushed their campaigns to the streets, three facts became apparent. First, the unpopularity of the Sarney government would prevent it from playing a decisive role in shaping the succession; second, despite their top rankings in the early polls, neither Brizola nor Lula managed to ignite the enthusiasm of the bulk of the electorate; and third, only a small, if very vocal, minority of Brazil's voters demonstrated firm ties to the plethora of underinstitutionalized parties. Quite to the contrary, the vast majority still manifested a marked tendency to vote for a candidate rather than for a party, for an image instead of a program. Finding little appeal in ideologies and relatively uninterested in specific policies, they were looking for someone whom they could view as worthy of their trust and capable of pulling Brazil out of its present morass. Anyone associated with the Sarney government or, indeed, having had a prominent position in Brazilian politics in recent years, would encounter serious voter rejection. After a long interruption of popular participation in presidential selection, the electorate naturally lacked experience in choosing a leader for the country. By and large, they had a far clearer idea of what they were against than exactly what they were for.[4]

The Race for the Runoff

Virtual owners of the PDT and PT respectively, Brizola and Lula did not have to concern themselves with winning nomination before beginning their campaigns. As conventions, not primary elections, were still the Brazilian means for determining a party's nominee, other serious candidates had to concentrate first upon consolidating support of their respective party's power brokers before carrying their candidacies to the voters. A number of presidential hopefuls were held back by the even more fundamental task of shopping for a party that would back their bid; when failing at this, some opted to found their own.

Thus, it was quite natural that Brizola and Lula would break out ahead as the early leaders. Neither of them, however, pushed beyond 16 percent in polls—which were marked by extremely high degrees of undecided voters as well as substantial support for nonpoliticians such as television personality Sílvio Santos.[5] Soon they were challenged by a candidate they both mistakenly refused to view as a serious threat. Fernando Collor de Mello, the young governor of the small northeastern state of Alagoas, neatly disposed of the nomination problem by turning the minuscule Youth Party (PJ) into the National Reconstruction Party (PRN), which then formed a coalition with the tiny Social Christian Party (PSC) as well as with the nearly invisible Social Labor Party (PST) and Renovating Workers Party (PTR). Such an alliance allowed him repeated access to the Brazilian public through three different free, one-hour, all-channel television programs. This ideal media candidate made the most of these opportunities to rise rapidly from near obscurity to status as the country's most discussed public figure.

The result was an explosive surge from merely 5 percent of voter preferences in February 1989 to 15 points and a tie for second with Lula in early April before he rocketed to a 20 percent approval rate by the end of the month. At 32–38 percent in late May polls, Collor left Brizola in his dust at 13–15 percent, while the once leading Lula fell to single-digit figures. Meanwhile the country's two strongest parties went from merely wasting time to actually planting and cultivating the seeds of their own demise. The mid-March

PMDB convention showed a deeply divided party. While Ulysses Guimarães formed an alliance with the *históricos* to move the party sharply to the Left and away from the government, a Sarney-backed insurgent slate came away with nearly 38 percent of the delegates. Guimarães prevailed in the heated battle for the party's nomination, with the progressives being placated by the choice of Waldir Pires for the number two spot. But his belief that party organization would prove adequate to overcome his age and ponderous campaign style was to prove completely out of touch with the new electoral realities. Equally mistaken was his conviction that by adopting a strategy of attacking the Sarney government and marginalizing the party's moderates in favor of the Left the PMDB could make the electorate forget that it had held a majority of posts in the national administration from 1985 to 1988.

Indeed, more than any other single development, the PMDB's decision to go with seventy-three-year-old Ulysses rather than a younger candidate not highly involved in the Brasília scene, such as Quércia, paved the way for Collor's eventual triumph. For the electorate could not be convinced of the palpably untrue line that Guimarães and the PMDB had not really been closely associated with the Sarney government. For the same reason, Aureliano Chaves's PFL candidacy developed into an equally sad case of a reasonably distinguished political figure being deserted by most of his own party's leaders as they perceived the infatuation of their electors with the Collor candidacy and the nonviability of the party's own nominee.

While shifts in political affiliations would continue throughout the year and on into 1990, the trends were already clear by May. The PMDB was down to under 200 federal deputies and the PFL slipping toward the 100 mark as the PSDB had reached forty-four in the Chamber and eight in the Senate, chiefly at the expense of the PMDB. The PDS suffered only minor defections, while the PTB edged up to tie the PDT for fifth place in Congressional strength and the PDC came to challenge the PT as the seventh largest legislative grouping. Meanwhile the National Reconstruction Party (PRN) slowly acquired congressional adherents as Collor's candidacy came to offer prospects for their achieving power and undertaking the quest for higher office in 1990.

Meanwhile, the "Summer Plan" slid toward an ignominious end as the rather artificial 3.6 percent inflation rate for February (on the heels of the 70 percent for January) headed into double-digit figures in May on its way to "stabilization" just below the 40 percent monthly level during the Brazilian winter and fall. In mid-March the CUT and CGT proclaimed a two-day general strike against the government's economic program, this time roughly 40 percent effective (compared to 20 percent in 1987 and 30 percent in 1986). The moderate Antônio Rogério Magri subsequently managed to oust Joaquinzão Santos Andrade from the CGT's presidency—later allying with Collor—while a wave of CUT-led strikes, often punctuated with violence, had an adverse impact upon Lula's campaign.

By this time center stage was clearly held by the man who, beginning as a rank outsider, had shrewdly found both the responsive chords in the perplexed electorate and the media and business support necessary to capitalize upon the opportunity afforded by the liabilities of the candidates already in the lists. Touted as a northeasterner on the basis of part of his childhood and short tours of duty as mayor of Maceió (1979–1982) and governor of Alagoas (1987–1989), Collor was in reality very much a product of Brazil's heartland, where he had spent most of his life. Educated through high school chiefly in Rio de Janeiro, where his father was serving in the Senate, he then studied at the University of Brasília before graduating from the Federal University of Alagoas and settling into management of the family's extensive newspaper, radio, and television holdings.

Originally married into a wealthy and socially prominent Rio de Janeiro family—with whom he retained very good relations despite a subsequent divorce, he remarried a local beauty during his stint as mayor. Slightly over 6′ 1″ and weighing in at just about 190 pounds, this boyishly handsome, black-belt karate champion possessed almost all the attributes to appeal to a basically youthful electorate—including an attractive twenty-five-year-old wife who was just finishing college.

The populist Collor, essentially a conservative regarding economics—but socially at least a centrist, demonstrated an unusual aptitude for making resounding criticisms of the existing regime that led voters to see him as a potential reformer of the widely discredited practices of Brazilian politics. Highly photogenic and charismatic (as charisma, like beauty, is essentially in the eye of the beholder), Collor tended to substitute talk about modernization and attacks upon corruption and abusive bureaucratic privileges for any profound criticism of the existing socioeconomic order. As with Quadros in Brazil's last direct presidential election twenty-nine years earlier, "moralization" and scathing denunciation of "politicians" were at the heart of Collor's appeal. Repeated over and over, "we'll put the corrupt maharajahs in jail where they belong" never failed to arouse a near-hysterical response from elements of his audiences, which tended to have a powerful contagious effect upon others.

Collor successfully avoided dealing with economic and social policy issues by asserting that "the moral crisis is the root of all other crises." The public was assured that he represented "the modern against the old, the advanced against the outdated," but with precious few policy specifics. Business audiences were told that he would give modern capitalism a try by reducing state control over the economy. In his official convention program, Collor was most concrete and unambiguous with respect to fostering free enterprise and limiting the economic role of the state while imposing private sector methods of administration and standards of accountability upon government enterprises. He declared a "war against inflation" without providing any details—strongly implying that credibility, determination, and resolute leadership were what was most required.

In gambling on the appeal of the providential man against that of ideologies that may fascinate Brazilian intellectuals but leave the great mass of the electorate cold, Collor seemed to be reading the Brazilian public correctly. It became abundantly clear that much of the Brazilian electorate was looking for leadership, hopefully firm and courageous. The frontrunner was not inclined to turn away any potential supporters by advocating specific policies to which they might take exception. Instead, he asked for their support and collaboration in a crusade to clean up the mess in which a potentially rich and progressing Brazil was unfortunately—and unnecessarily—mired. He involved his listeners through impassioned pleas not to leave him alone in the battle against "them," implying that all his rivals had a common interest in stopping him so that they could go on enriching themselves and abusing the public trust. By assuming a position of intransigent critic of the Sarney government, Collor effectively preempted the efforts of the Left to benefit from the administration's unpopularity and prevalent public dissatisfaction with the economic and social situation.

The fundamental strength of Collor's appeal was reflected in his broad base of support. Down through the first round of balloting in mid-November his position as favorite stood up when viewed from regional, age, education, gender, and class perspectives. Brizola ran ahead of him only in the two states of which he had been governor (Rio de Janeiro and Rio Grande do Sul); Covas edged him out just with the most educated sliver of the population; and Guilherme Afif Domingos (forty-six) challenged him among the upper class. While Lula was strong in capitals and other very large cities, Collor's proportion of voter preferences grew down through medium cities to small towns and the countryside. He was extremely popular among the younger voters whom Brizola and Lula had mistakenly assumed would flock to their leftist banners.

By criticizing the São Paulo Federation of Industries as "backward and reactionary," Collor avoided being tagged as the darling of the Right, a role filled more by Maluf and Afif as well as several minor candidates. His ability to satisfy many centrist constituencies spelled doom to Covas's dream of staking out the middle road in a polarization between Lula and Brizola on the Left and Collor, Maluf, and Afif on the Right. It was also a major factor in the failure of the nominees of the country's two major parties to generate any momentum. Guimarães's pathetic showing gravely mortgaged the PMDB's future, while only a handful of PFL faithful stuck with Chaves in his ill-fated effort to get his campaign off the ground.

Brazil's Voters—Ready and Willing, but How Able?

At just over 82 million the electorate was up sharply even over the preceding November, largely owing to the inclusion of sixteen and seventeen-year olds. Geographically, the dominance of the center and south remained pronounced, as São Paulo led the way with 18.5 million votes, followed by Minas Gerais's more than 9.4 million and Rio de Janeiro's 8.2 million—for a three-state aggregate of over 36.1 million, some 44 percent of the nation's total. Adding in Rio Grande do Sul at 5.7 million and Paraná with more than 5.0 million, plus Santa Catarina's over 2.7 million and the Federal District's nearly 860,000 voters brought the heartland and its southern extension to 49.4 million registered electors—over 60 percent of the country's total. Indeed, outside this more developed area, only Bahia with 5.9 million voters, Pernambuco at nearly 3.8 million, and Ceará at almost 3.4 million constituted significant prizes. Yet to underscore the massive size of Brazil's electoral venture, three other states had more than 2 million enrolled voters each (which was above the size of Uruguay's electorate), while an additional half dozen states possessed at least a million voters.

The electorate was essentially young, nearly half being under thirty, with almost a fifth twenty-one or younger. Fewer than 15 percent were above age fifty. This was to prove a decisive factor, as older candidates—such as Guimarães at seventy-three, Chaves and Covas at sixty, and Brizola nearing sixty-eight—came to fare poorly. Only a sixth of the potential voters had graduated from high school, with one in fourteen having gone to college. At the other extreme, at least a tenth were totally illiterate, with another 30 percent barely able to read and write. Of the rest, an incomplete grade school education was most common, while but 15 percent had finished elementary school, but not graduated from the next level.

But what most distinguished the Brazilian electorate in 1989 was their essential inexperience in voting to fill national offices and their very weak ties to political parties. The overwhelming majority had never voted before the abrupt 1964 regime change. Indeed, only those forty-five or older could have done so in the 1962 congressional elections, while individuals over forty-seven were the only Brazilians who might have voted for a president at some time in their lives. Hence the electorate included some individuals who had never gotten over their pre-1964 loyalties, but several times more who were socialized into the either-or choice of ARENA or the MDB when they were the only parties allowed from 1966 to 1979.

Yet for at least half the potential voters, even these labels meant little or nothing, as their initiation into political participation came after the reemergence of a multiparty system at the beginning of the 1980s. Fully 30 million had turned eighteen since the 1978 elections; at least 4 million of the over 6 million sixteen and seventeen-year olds were registered; and an estimated 10 million older illiterates finally gained the right to vote in late 1985—although not all of these bothered to register. Moreover, a plethora of new parties had emerged during the 1982 state and congressional elections, the partial municipal elections of November 1985, the 1986 gubernatorial and legislative balloting, the nationwide municipal elections of 1988, and the run-up to the 1989 presidential campaign. In light of all these discontinuities, it should not be surprising that by far the greater part of the electorate had no fixed party loyalties and would be voting primarily for the man, or the image of the man.

The Stretch Drive

Collor's support declined from around or even above the 40 percent mark in mid-September to about 30 percent by the beginning of October, where it then stabilized.[6] Largely a result of all his competitors possessing equal or greater free television time after September 15, Collor's slippage gave heart to his rivals. Yet Collor enjoyed the luxury of still having roughly twice the electoral preferences of his leading pursuers, as Brizola—in many ways apparently caught in a kind of mid-1960s time warp—was unable to move up from the 15 percent level at which he had been stuck since the earliest stages of the campaign. Meanwhile, Lula—benefitting greatly from the enthusiastic and determined support of the left-wing of the Catholic Church—steadily reduced the gap that had reached 7 or 8 percentage points in September, pulling even with Brizola by early November. Covas and Maluf also gained during the late stages of the campaign, but only enough to lift their supporters' hopes, not enough to pose a threat to Lula or Brizola, much less Collor.

Collor finally announced his economic and social program in late October. At its heart was a promise to raise some $94 billion in extra revenue over the span of his term, largely through improved tax collection. Historically, evasion in the fields of personal and corporate levies has been estimated at nearly 50 percent, while fraud with regard to foreign trade is also large scale. Hence net tax revenues have run at around 10 percent of GDP, when 15 percent would be more reasonable in light of the existing tax rates. In addition to the $45 billion scheduled to come from rigorous enforcement of the tax laws (which explains the preference of major sectors of the business classes for Maluf or Afif, who made no such threat of clamping down), $31.5 billion was to be garnered from privatization of state enterprises, with $11.4 billion coming from reduced outlays for servicing the foreign debt—where payments would be capped at half the level of the late 1980s—and $6.1 billion through increased administrative efficiency.

All this additional revenue was to be applied to social programs, with health leading the way at $36 billion and $15 billion more for sanitation. Housing was slated to receive $18 billion (for 2.3 million units), education a supplemental $9.6 billion, transportation an additional $9 billion, and science and technology some $6 billion, with $5 billion earmarked for agrarian reform. Over the five-year span of this program, GDP was optimistically projected to rise to over $517 billion, exports to surpass $40 billion a year, and the minimum salary to reach $369 (from under $100). Production of grains was to increase from 70 to 97 million tons annually, while infant mortality was to be cut by a full third.[7] Any similarity to Kubitschek's 1955–1960 Program of Goals was purely and calculatedly intentional.

The campaign got briefly, but dramatically sidetracked in early November, as in a desperate last-minute effort to head off election of a hostile candidate who promised a thorough audit of the administration's stewardship, a clique of Sarney's advisors sought to roil the waters by inserting the candidacy of popular television personality Sílvio Santos (born Senor Abravanel), a half billion dollar per year businessman. Fortunately the Superior Electoral Tribunal (TSE) put a relatively quick end to this diversionary and disruptive ploy by unanimously denying formal registration of Santos's patently illegal candidacy on the dual grounds that the minor party whose candidate had withdrawn in his favor failed to meet minimum standards for continued recognition and that he was ineligible as the holder of a federal concession in the form of television channels.

A few days later the electorate confirmed Collor as its favorite and made Lula his runoff rival, albeit this by the narrowest of margins. Lula's paper-thin lead over Brizola of 425,000 votes—.5 percent of the electorate—could be attributed to his luck in drawing the first line on the ballot, while the PDT standard-bearer was buried in the middle of the long list in the number twelve position. But if it had not been for his broader geographical distribution of support and the effectiveness of progressive Catholic clergy in convincing parishioners to vote for him, the PT candidate would not have been close enough to Brizola for this to have made the difference.[8]

The Final Confrontation: The People Speak

Through November 15 Brazilian voters could choose from among a wide variety of proposals for the near-run future—ranging all across the political spectrum, as well as off it in the case of some personalist populists. For the next month this changed drastically, as a score of candidates were eliminated, leaving only Collor, a centrist to conservative populist professing to be a Social Democrat and championing a "modern" approach, and Lula, advocate of the interests of labor against those of capital and articulator of a consistent ideological position for the Left. The two finalists had youth in common and very little else. The contest was essentially a battle to gain the support of the majority of the electorate orphaned by the defeat of their preferred candidates.

In late November and early December Lula's efforts were concentrated on gaining endorsements by candidates eliminated in the November 15 balloting and formal adherence of their parties to his "Brazil Popular Front." After some initial difficulty, Brizola and his PDT came fully on board, as did the PCB of Roberto Freire. Negotiations with the PSDB dragged out over the incompatibility of economic programs, but eventually the party leadership endorsed Lula, and Covas appeared on the platform with him on a limited number of occasions. The PMDB, still in shock over the magnitude of its first-round fiasco, saw a good proportion of its governors edge over to the Collor camp, with others sitting on the fence to the very end. Only Arraes in Pernambuco provided really effective support to Lula's campaign, with Simon in Rio Grande do Sul making a secondary contribution.[9]

The first of two televised debates on December 3 proved a shot in the arm for Lula, not as much because of his competent, but far from inspiring performance as it was the product of Collor's too restrained posture and his camp's failure to exploit their candidate's better moments on the next day's nationwide electoral program. Working through Sunday night, the Lula team put together a collage of his most telling shots that, unanswered by the Collor campaign, gave the impression that Lula had walked away a hands-down winner. This was quickly reflected in a steady rise for Lula in the polls and a corresponding drop by his opponent.

Stung into action, Collor turned his full energies from crisscrossing the country to revamping his television appearances. Opting to return to his earlier hard-hitting style rather than continuing the statesmanlike stance advocated by the more liberal members of his staff, Collor approved his brother Leopoldo's proposal to exploit a skeleton from Lula's closet. Thus, the country was treated to the spectacle of a highly emotional ex-lover, who denounced Lula for having tried to pay her to have an abortion and for later proposing that they resume their sexual relationship after both were remarried.

Though there may be some doubt as to how directly effective this was in terms of votes, the attack from an unexpected quarter clearly knocked Lula off balance and put him on the defensive, a posture painfully clear in the final climactic television debate on December 14. There, in dramatic contrast to a poised and confident Collor, projecting authority and leadership, Lula put on an almost pitifully inept performance. Obviously nervous and distraught, he fumbled through notes and documents without effectively rebutting Collor's slashing assertions. This time the country's dominant network, TV Globo, presented on its widely watched Friday night news program a series of scenes from the debate that depicted an insecure and at times apparently disoriented Lula being virtually destroyed by a quite presidential Collor.

The net result was to more than merely offset the negative impact for Collor of the earlier debate episode. Momentum was clearly and strongly reversed, a trend only partially caught by the last round of polls. Hence the thinness of the margins favoring Collor led many observers to mistakenly project a very tight race or even a Lula victory. This error was in spite of the fact that no poll ever showed Lula completely even, much less ahead. (Such a commonly shared propensity is attributable to the tendency of observers and journalists to cluster in Rio de Janeiro and Brasília—two centers of pro-Lula sentiment—as well as to wishful thinking inspired by personal preferences and ideological sympathies.)

Despite inclement weather in large parts of the country, the vast majority of Brazil's electorate turned out to put an end to the almost year-long campaign. Some 35.1 million, over 53 percent of the valid vote, opted for Collor, while 31.1 million expressed their preference for Lula.[10] Thus, efforts of the pro-Lula forces to build up from 11.6 million votes for the PT candidate on November 15 to the over 33 million that would be needed for election proved an impossible undertaking. The vast majority of Brizola's 11.2 million supporters heeded their leader's injunction to vote for the "bearded frog" who had until recently been viewed by them as an intense rival who had snatched a well-deserved victory away from them by the narrowest of margins. The mere 790,000 voters who had backed the PCB also generally fell into line with Lula's candidacy despite their deeply rooted rivalry with the PCdoB, a vocal part of Lula's original coalition.

The death blow to his hopes came, however, when a large proportion of those 7.8 million citizens who had voted for Covas failed to accompany PSDB leadership into the Brazil Popular Front—and at least half of the 3.2 million who had voted for the PMDB's Guimarães followed suit. The first of these trends was perhaps not fully predictable, as the PSDB had very few governors or mayors whose stance could be taken as an indication of what their followers might do. Yet the public migration of many PMDB governors over to the Collor side was a strong harbinger of their supporters' eventual choice. As it turned out, the mainly middle-class Brazilians who had opted for Covas or Guimarães as their first choice—when forced to choose between a candidate to the Right of their original preference of one to the Left—drifted in large numbers to the side of Collor. In many cases they were motivated more by fear of his rival's radicalism (which Lula strove to mute during the final stages of the campaign) than by positive attraction to Collor or affinity with his positions. But such negative voting or even going for the lesser of two evils is common in almost all either-or electoral situations throughout the world.

These centrist "orphans," particularly numerous in São Paulo and Minas Gerais but also significant in Paraná, were instrumental in swinging the balance heavily in Collor's favor. Starting with the 20.6 million votes he had put together in the first round and then falling heir to the great majority of Paulo Maluf's nearly 6 million votes, the frontrunner also garnered by far the lion's share of the 1.5 million vote total of the PFL's Aureliano Chaves and PTB nominee Affonso Camargo. To this total he added considerably over half the almost 3.3 million votes received by the PL's Guilhermo Afif Domingos and at least an even split of the minor candidates' votes for something over another 1.5 million. Though the combined total of these votes brought him within striking distance of victory, it was the big slice of the Covas-Guimarães center vote he received that carried him very comfortably past the 33 million plus total needed for victory.

São Paulo proved pivotal as Collor racked up a margin of 2.53 million votes on 58 percent of the valid tally. Minas Gerais supplemented these votes with an additional advantage of 830,000 on better than 56 percent for the winner. Even more important, however, was Paraná, which chipped in with a positive balance of 1.45 million votes, as Collor's share of the vote (some 2.8 million) was more than double that of Lula. Bahia completed the four-state backbone of Collor's triumph by denying Lula victory in the home state of his runningmate. On the strength of votes in the interior mobilized by Governor Nilo Coelho and Communications Minister Magalhães, Collor pulled ahead there at the very last stages of vote counting to win by 138,000.

The bulge from this heartland region was sufficient to offset the landslide victories for Lula in Rio de Janeiro by 3.28 million (on 5.23 million to 1.95 million) and Rio Grande do Sul by a margin of 1.83 million (with 3.37 million to 1.54 million). Lula's win in the Federal District by 452,000 to 269,000 was more than neutralized by Collor's 690,000 to 474,000 drubbing of Lula in Espírito Santo. Combined with a narrow win in Santa Catarina, this gave the victor an edge in the densely populated lower part of the country.

Thus, the less developed northern and western parts of Brazil were not crucial to Collor's election, although they did certainly contribute significantly to its magnitude. In this sixteen-state area, Lula managed only to eke out a paper-thin win in Pernambuco (1.51 million to 1.46 million), while Collor at least doubled his rival's votes in Goiás, Pará, Matto Grosso do Sul, Matto Grosso, Amazonas, Sergipe, Acre, and Tocantins. In his own state of Alagoas he rolled to victory with 76 percent of the valid vote. Collor also carried Sarney's home state of Maranhão by over 330,000 votes and Ceará by a margin of 360,000 while winning handily in Paraíba, Rio Grande do Norte, Piauí, and Rondônia.

Collor's share of the vote was greater the smaller the town or city. Thus, he polled more than two-thirds of the vote in municipalities of under 15,000 and stayed comfortably over the three-fifths mark in those between 15,000 and 30,000 while running at about 55 percent in cities of 30,000 to 80,000 inhabitants. Above that figure he ran into stiff competition from Lula, who dominated over all in state capitals. Yet even there Collor scored a number of dramatic victories, most notably his 700,000 vote margin in São Paulo— South America's largest city—as well as nearly two to one triumphs in Maceió, Campo Grande, and Rio Branco accompanied by a narrower win in Aracajú. He also carried most of the chief cities of populous Paraná and many of those in São Paulo. Most significantly, Collor also won in the great majority of the cities governed by PT mayors, including, besides the São Paulo capital, Santos, Campinas, and Vitória in the million inhabitants bracket.

With respect to social class, the victor retained the strong base in the lowest socioeconomic strata that he had demonstrated in November's first-round balloting while picking up the support Maluf and Afif had enjoyed among the upper stratum. Collor also benefitted from a significantly greater backing from female voters than from males—shades of Charles de Gaulle in France's first direct election of a president back in 1965.

As the Dust Settled

Certainly the PT gained from making it to the runoff and managing to mobilize a very respectable total of just over 31 million votes for Lula. The electoral experience, particularly the national media exposure, was positive for the country's closest approximation to a modern political party. Being number two was vital for the future because, had the PDT rather than the PT gotten into the final round and gained a month in the spotlight, Brizola and his personalist populist party would have at least temporarily eclipsed the PT. As Lula had edged out Brizola by literally the luck of the draw, the PT had avoided by a hair the disaster of coming in third and having to play a supporting role to the PDT while its rival Brizola basked in the sun as the Left's standard-bearer. (In the long run the situation is probably much like that of France in that there is not really room for two mass parties on the Left—the advance of the Socialists in France during the late 1960s and 1970s left the Communists marginalized during the 1980s at under 10 percent of the vote.)

Lula, by virtue of his finalist role, enjoyed an initial advantage as prospective leader of the opposition to Collor's government. Moreover, he was ensconced in Congress, while Brizola continued without political office. On the other hand, the PT's electoral fiasco in São Paulo combined with the obvious fact that Lula would have been ignominiously trounced if it had not been for the strong piggyback ride received from Brizola and the PDT in Rio de Janeiro and Rio Grande do Sul posed a severe obstacle to consolidating PT leadership, much less hegemony, over the Brazilian Left. Lula's strategy was to avoid running for São Paulo governor as this would of necessity both pull him away from the national scene during much of 1990 and expose him to the peril of a defeat at the hands of Maluf, Covas, or whatever candidate Collor might support—especially if this turned out to be the same horse backed by Quércia. Yet sending a lesser contender into the fray would all but guarantee a PT defeat in Brazil's premier state in October 1990.

Looking beyond 1990, Brizola faced a much more favorable prospect as he could almost count upon regaining control of Rio de Janeiro state. Once again governor, he would be in a strong position to contest Lula's primacy as the opposition's leading figure. Beginning from the very solid base he possessed in Rio de Janeiro and Rio Grande do Sul, Brazil's third and fifth states, Brizola could continue at least to block the PT's efforts to become a truly national force (for it has as yet to develop real strength in Minas Gerais, Bahia, or Paraná as well as being decidedly weaker than the PDT in Rio de Janeiro and Rio Grande do Sul). Other than the PT and PDT, the major parties faced doubtful futures in terms of survival, much less positioning toward a bid down the road for power nationally. The once-dominant PMDB emerged from the campaign in shambles, with formerly number two PFL's only hope lying in becoming a pillar of the new government's congressional alliance. And, though Collor would begin to govern with a coalition of factions from a variety of parties, he did not intend to make the present PRN his chief political vehicle.

The Collor Government

As inflation rose to 68 percent in January and 73 percent the following month on its way to 84 percent for March, Sarney left office amidst generally negative assessments of his performance. In sharp contrast, there was considerable optimism concerning Collor's prospective stewardship.

The general outlines of the new administration's program were evident from the campaign and elaborations released during the transition period. Clearly, the program would consist of a substantial reduction of the role of the state in Brazilian society, an attack on excessive government spending—

especially on benefits for the privileged—and prompt attention to halting the inflationary spiral. Longer-term efforts were geared toward settling Brazil's crushing debt burden, attracting new flows of investment and technology, improving commercial relations with the developed world, and generally inserting a rehabilitated and modernized Brazilian economy into the competitive mainstream of international life.

Few Brazilians or foreign observers were prepared, however, for the scope and rigor of the measures that were announced immediately after the March 15 inauguration. The federal bureaucracy was to be substantially reorganized and slimmed down—with many of its traditional privileges slated for abolition. In addition an ambitious program of privatization was outlined to dramatically cut back the country's huge and sprawling network of state companies. Substantial deregulation of the economy was planned, to encourage both imports and foreign private investment. At the same time a large number of costly subsidies to local producers were to be slashed, new revenues found, and income taxes rigorously collected. The result was to be a substantial improvement in the situation at the federal treasury and a truly balanced budget in reasonably short order. Finally, wage and price controls were implanted on a temporary basis and a new currency was issued. But by far the most original and controversial aspect of the Collor Plan was the freezing of the bulk of bank, overnight, and money market accounts—which for a time blocked at least 70 percent of the economy's liquidity in one fell swoop.

The New Team

By cutting the number of ministries in half, Collor both created the possibility of significant changes and returned the federal government to a structure over which the chief executive could at least hope to exercise effective control. The key problem resided in finding individuals capable of heading the two unwieldy superministries that emerged. In this regard, the appointment of University of São Paulo assistant professor Zélia Cardoso de Melo (thirty-six) at the supremely important Economics Ministry was the principal question mark—as this new ministry was composed of the former Finance portfolio plus almost all of what used to be the Planning Ministry and most of Industry and Commerce as well.[11] Although the president clearly had confidence in Zélia (as she is generally known), she came to the job with a quite modest professional background, albeit with a knack for putting together an able team. Consequently, considerable responsibility for the critically important matter of economic policy fell directly on Collor himself, which was apparently the way he wanted it.

The government financial institutions under the economy minister's supervision showed a marked São Paulo dominance combined with professional competence. The presidency of the Central Bank, whose enhanced autonomy was at least a provisional Collor goal, was entrusted to Ibrahim Eris (forty-five), a Turk who had become involved with Brazil while working on a doctorate in economics at Vanderbilt University in the early 1970s. The Bank of Brazil was placed in the keeping of a career executive, Alberto Policaro (former vice-president), and the National Economic and Social Development Bank (BNDES) came to be headed by Eduardo Modiano (thirty-eight), a highly regarded economics professor at Rio de Janeiro's Catholic University who helped design the Cruzado Plan of 1986. The Federal Savings Bank (CEF) went to Lafayette Coutinho Torres (fifty), head of the São Paulo operations of Bahia-based Banco Econômico—and linked to Paulo Maluf by marriage. The Securities and Exchange Commission (CVM) was placed under tax lawyer Ary Oswaldo Mattos Filho (fifty), a São Paulo resident with postgraduate work at Harvard University.

Reform of the most substantial portion of the federal bureaucracy and responsibility for handling most of Brazil's enormous array of state companies fell to retired air force Lieutenant Colonel Ozires Silva (fifty-nine)—also from São Paulo. His new Infrastructure Ministry embraced 50 percent of Brazil's GDP and nearly half of all federal government employees—an inflated workforce of 640,000. Composed of the former ministries of Transportation, Communications, and Mines and Energy, it also contained elements of Industry and Commerce and traces of Interior. This gave Ozires the thorny task of trying to exert effective supervision over most of Brazil's massive state enterprises. His ability to reduce Brazil's huge state sector and instill private sector productivity criteria throughout its residue would be crucial to Collor's plans to bring the $30 billion prospective 1990 public sector deficit under control. Rather paradoxically, this individual whose career had been within state enterprises would shoulder much of the burden of privatization: the selling off or closing down of many governmental economic ventures.

Although no other ministries are so substantively important as those of Zélia and Ozires, Justice Minister Bernardo Cabral (fifty-seven) was entrusted with the delicate and critical role of selling the administration's policies to the Congress. He brought to this task a wide range of political connections across party lines stemming from his function as coordinator of the constitution-writing process during 1987 and 1988. More influential with the president was Secretary-General of the Presidency Marcos Coimbra (sixty-two). This experienced career ambassador, married to Collor's older sister, played a major role during the campaign and remains a trusted and intimate advisor. On the military side Collor chose three competent professionals with reputations for avoiding political involvement: General Carlos Tinoco Ribeiro Gomes (sixty-two), Admiral Mário César Flôres (fifty-eight), and Lieutenant Brigadier Socrates da Costa Monteiro (fifty-nine).

The Foreign Ministry was given to Dr. José Francisco Rezek (forty-six), a native of Minas Gerais, who stepped down from the Supreme Court to supervise both a reorientation of Brazilian international relations in the direction of first-world priorities and a significant reorganization of the nation's foreign policy–making machinery. Antônio Rogério Magri (forty-eight) of São Paulo was, until he took control of the Ministry of Labor and Social Welfare, president of one of the country's two principal labor federations (the CGT, which is a moderate counterweight to the PT-linked CUT). Used as a symbol of administration concern for working-class interests, Magri pushed the double message that lower inflation meant real gains for workers and that workers' views were at last getting to the president's ears. The Cabinet was rounded out by a PFL senator from Rio Grande do Sul, Carlos Chiarelli (forty-nine), as education minister; Paraná Deputy Alceni Guerra (forty-four) at the Health Ministry; Alagoas social services administrator Margarida Procópio (fifty) in the Social Action Ministry; and thirty-year-old Antônio Cabrera Mano Filho of São Paulo in the Ministry of Agriculture and Agrarian Reform. Perhaps the greatest gamble in structuring Collor's executive office was the appointment of a young businessman and personal friend to be special secretary for strategic affairs. Pedro Paulo Leoni Ramos (twenty-nine) inherited the very delicate task of filling the vacuum left by the abolition of the SNI—Brazil's powerful intelligence agency, which had produced two military presidents and made two other of its heads into powers behind the chief executive.

The Game Plan

Collor had promised to explode off the starting blocks with a "credibility shock" to convince the nation that, unlike his predecessor, he was deadly serious about eliminating inflation. Shock was exactly the reaction of Brazilian society as Collor's "war" against inflation was launched with the economic equivalent of nuclear weapons. Overnight the economy's liquidity was reduced from a high 30 percent of GDP to under 10 percent. At one fell swoop roughly $90 billion was temporarily "dried up" by being kept as cruzados in blocked accounts as the cruzeiro became Brazil's new currency. Although the nominal value was one for one, strict limitations on amounts that could be converted made the new monetary unit scarce—and thus valuable.

At least $50 billion of the bloated "overnight" market, which had been a very expensive way of financing the government's domestic debt, was taken out of circulation as a nonmonetary means of payment by limitation of immediate conversion to CZ 25,000 or 20 percent of each holding, whichever was higher. This saved the government several billion dollars in interest payments. Similar restrictions blocked close to $30 billion in savings accounts and $8 billion in certificates of deposit, with additional billions involved in the form of interest-bearing checking accounts, short-term investment funds, debentures, and similar types of financial holdings. Total liquidity dropped initially from perhaps $145 billion to $35 billion before it began to rise gradually under exceptions to Central Bank rules. Moreover, stiff taxes were imposed on many types of financial transactions and conversions of cruzados to cruzeiros. The banning of bearer accounts, bearer checks, and bearer bonds was designed not only to sharply curb tax evasion by recognized firms, but also to bring much of the informal economy into the open. Indeed, it was also hoped that the lack of cruzeiros for essential expenditures such as payrolls would lead many companies to bring back funds held abroad that had been generated by underinvoicing exports and overinvoicing imports.

Other measures sharply raised fuel and public utility prices but rolled private sector prices back to the March 12 level, where they would be held for forty-five days; imposed a future system of prefixing prices and wages that would break the "dog chasing its tail" cycle institutionalized by the comprehensive system of indexing of the economy; and freed the exchange rate from government fixing. Two dozen federal agencies—including the Brazilian Coffee Institute and the Sugar and Alcohol Institute—were abolished; proposals were made for laying off several hundred thousand surplus government employees; and mechanisms for privatization of state enterprises were set up. At the program's heart was a plan to keep inflation down by transforming the massive public sector operating deficit of over $30 billion into a small surplus—a sharp turnaround from a deficit of 8 percent of GDP to a surplus of 2 percent. Compulsory loans for privatization, fiscal reforms, and improved tax collection (evasion traditionally runs close to 50 percent) were to make up the major portion of this transformation. Administrative reform and suspension of subsidies and fiscal incentives rounded out the budget-balancing package.[12]

The vehicle for Collor's sweeping economic and administrative reforms was a collection of twenty-odd "provisional measures" that took effect immediately, but required congressional approval within thirty days—which essentially meant before the Easter weekend. The president maintained that the package was an indivisible whole and that, therefore, only minor details were negotiable. The vital question was whether modifications insisted upon by a Congress inclined to play a truly protagonistic role in the policy-making process would be essentially cosmetic or, instead, sufficiently profound as to affect the integrity of the "New Brazil" Plan.

The greatest opposition was concentrated upon the CZ 50,000 limit on withdrawals from savings accounts. Although over 90 percent of these accounts were below the threshold, the Brazilians who count most politically were strongly affected by this measure. (In fact a very high proportion of parties and politicians had their campaign funds stashed away in savings accounts as well as in the overnight market.) Yet the sweeping and explosive nature of Collor's program had the general effect of focusing adversely affected interests upon a damage-control effort aimed at modifying the program's most rigorous provisions rather than any more comprehensive opposition to the fundamental thrust of the measures. Moreover, Collor opened a strategic series of exceptions for persons who were retired or ill and for companies having extreme difficulty in meeting payrolls.

Justice Minister Cabral and the administration's floor leaders had to convince congressmen under siege by wounded special interests that backing the president would be electorally advantageous. In this effort the administration benefitted from the fact that patronage-important third- and fourth-echelon positions were not filled until Collor's program had been voted on—and those congressmen who were not initially inclined to toe the line were advised that their petitions would fall upon deaf ears if they did not support the president at this crucial juncture. Additionally, they might be singled out in public as enemies of Collor's efforts to save the country from the ravages of runaway inflation. And for many if not most of Brazil's legislators, voting "right" means going the way most likely to pay off both at the polls and in terms of patronage.

On the critical front of public support, important in influencing congressional voting, Collor was off to a strong start, but Brazilian opinion is highly volatile and closely linked to perceptions of how the economy is faring. During his first week in office a poll in the ten major cities showed Collor with 81 percent approval as compared with 58 percent at his inauguration. Some 70 percent expected that his program would cause inflation to decline drastically, with an additional 18 percent expecting a less dramatic turnaround.[13] A different polling institution reported 71 percent rating the new president as excellent or good, plus 18 percent with weaker approval (*regular*). Most remarkably, a full half of those who had voted for Lula gave Collor the clearly favorable ratings, with another 30 percent of them considering him not at all bad.[14]

Congressional voting on the Collor program demonstrated how little parties matter. Despite recent defections (the beginning of April being the deadline for changing affiliation of those intending to run in October), the PMDB still had a few over 130 federal deputies and 23 senators for 28 percent of Congress. At 97 in the lower house and 13 in the upper, the PFL mustered nearly 20 percent of Congressional seats—at least in theory. With 60 deputies and 13 senators, the PSDB claimed 13 percent of congressional strength. Together the PDT, PT, PCB, PCdoB, and PSB (the Left opposition) fell just short of 75 national legislators—also for a 13 percent total. On the Right, the PDS, PRN, PTB, PDC, and PL aggregated 128 seats, or 23 percent. If party discipline could be counted upon to any significant degree, Collor would have the 42 percent held by these parties and the PFL, hence needing less than one-quarter of the PMDB-PSDB legislators to carry his program forward. His negotiating ability, his disposition to wheel and deal, and the extent of his popularity with the public—as reflected in the latest polls—proved to be sufficient in the first important test. During the initial two weeks of April the Collor Plan was approved with surprisingly little modification.[15] The crucial vote came with endorsement on April 13 (249 to 106) of the initial attack on excess liquidity.

In mid-May the government announced plans to cut more than 300,000 employees from the federal payroll in order to eliminate one of the causes of Brazil's chronic public sector deficit. As federal employees have long been the sacred cows of Brazilian national life, this initiative triggered a torrent of criticism and resistance.[16] Despite some adverse court rulings and considerable foot-dragging among the state enterprises, by August the total retired, fired, or put on involuntary furlough reached the 200,000 mark. Although with the latter still receiving base pay the immediate fiscal benefits of this move were limited, it served to hold the line on the $46 billion annual federal payroll, and future savings might be significant.

A new industrial policy announced at mid-year—greatly reducing protectionism and facilitating imports—dealt a stiff blow to those major sectors of the Brazilian economy that were used to virtually guaranteed profits at no real risk. Tariffs were sharply cut while other limitations on imports were eliminated. A sweeping antitrust law was submitted to Congress, and cartels and monopolies found themselves facing the possibility of real competition rather than being allowed to continue with price-fixing practices.

Inflation not only was quickly cut from the surging hyperinflationary rates inherited from the Sarney administration but also was kept under reasonable control, with hopes for future decline. Given the institutionalized system of indexation rooted in the Brazilian economy and the "inflationary" culture that had become part of most Brazilians' everyday life, this was a most difficult task.[17] The consumer price index showed inflation dropping by half in April and falling to 7.9 percent in May. With prices increasingly being freed from government control, this figure rose to 9.5 percent in June and 12.9 percent for July before declining to 12.0 percent in August and climbing to 12.8 percent in September and 14.2 percent in October under the adverse impact of the surge in petroleum prices caused by the Mideast crisis. This unleashed strong pressures for again tying pay raises for lower earning brackets to the cost of living index. The resurgence of inflation to 15.6 percent for November and 18.3 percent in December presented the administration with the dilemma of either adopting more stringent austerity measures or backing off in the battle to curb what it had repeatedly labeled the country's primary problem.

The government's approval rating followed progress on the inflation front quite closely. Thus the poll in the ten largest cities that had given Collor a 63 percent excellent or good rating after a month in office—compared to but 7 percent rating him bad or worse—showed this trend reversing in mid-June to a quite low 25 percent excellent or good rating and 29 percent negative. After worsening slightly in July (23 percent favorable, 31 percent unfavorable, and 43 percent in the middle), positive assessments came to slightly exceed negative ones on August 10—at 28 percent to 26 percent, with 44 percent lukewarm.[18] Similarly, the proportion finding the economic program to be bad fell slightly between July and August (from 43 percent to 26 percent), while those considering it good in whole or in part rose about the same degree. Dissenting from this trend, the PT-led CUT faction of the labor movement unleashed a wave of violent strikes in an attempt to undermine the administration's economic program.

In its efforts to carry through its dismantling of Brazil's *cartorial* state, the Collor government continued to face three major obstacles: (1) the 1988 constitution with its plethora of protective provisions for special interests; (2) a Congress preoccupied with courting votes by favoring the claims of well-organized and well-mobilized interest groups; and (3) a judiciary zealously defending the letter of the still-new constitution without regard for how such actions undermine the administration's reform efforts. Indeed, taking these formidable obstacles into account, Collor's team made surprisingly successful headway on most fronts before the October elections. In fact the administration had already done a number of things unheard of in Brazilian national experience, not just in recent decades. Further progress in the direction of rationalization and modernization would depend on the outcome of the nationwide balloting. Much of Collor's ability to implement his programs during the third quarter of 1990 depended upon lack of a congressional quorum while national legislators were absorbed with electoral survival. This situation would not prevail again until after mid-1994. Hence resort to provisional measures would need to be replaced by a consistent ability to push normal legislation through the two houses of Congress. This would require that a majority of those elected on October 3 be inclined to support the president and his program.

The 1990 Elections

Almost 84 million registered voters went to the polls on October 3 to choose which of nearly 17,000 candidates would fill more than 1,600 posts as governors, vice-governors, senators, alternate senators, federal deputies, and state legislators. Selection of candidates had been overshadowed by the dramatic actions of the Collor government during its first weeks in office; then the slow-developing campaign took a back seat to the soccer World Cup competition in June. It soon became clear that, whereas in the presidential contest the premium had been on new faces, in governors Brazil's voters were looking for experience and proven performance. Thus, 44 percent of the twenty-seven governors chosen have occupied statehouses before—some more than once—with a good proportion of the others coming from the ranks of big-city mayors. On the Senate side, where thirty-one of eighty-one seats were at stake, experience was also in great demand, and the winners were a mix of incumbents, outgoing governors, and former state chief executives. The 503 individuals elected to the lower house of Congress included only 38 percent incumbents, most of the rest being veteran state legislators and mayors seeking to move up to the national scene. Among the victors were only a smattering of newcomers to elective politics who were trying to cash in on their reputations in other fields.[19]

Once again the elections underscored the weakness of Brazil's political parties, and, with local and regional issues playing an important role in state campaigns, a strong Center-Right tilt emerged both in the Congress and in the new lineup of governors. Indeed, the gross underrepresentation of São Paulo combined with the extreme overrepresentation of the smaller, essentially agrarian states made the Left's efforts to significantly increase their weight in Congress an uphill battle. Down by the beginning of the campaign to just 129 federal deputies, the PMDB suffered further erosion, electing only 107 to the lower house, along with but eight senators and a mere seven governors. Its erstwhile junior partner from the 1985–1988 period, the PFL, moved up to near parity on the strength of eighty-seven seats in the Chamber of Deputies and nine of those at stake in the Senate.

On the gubernatorial side the PFL was the big winner, with nine victors coming from among its ranks and four others from coalitions in which it was a major factor. The PSDB fell far short of its goal of catching the PMDB, electing just thirty-seven national congressmen, a lone senator, and but a single governor. Indeed, this dropped the "Tucanos" from third to seventh place, as the PDS elected forty-three deputies, a pair of senators, and a governor, while for the PRN these figures were forty, none, and two. Indeed, with thirty-six seats in the lower house, five in the Senate, and two governors, the PTB also outperformed the PSDB.

The PDT, despite Brizola's easy victory as governor of Rio de Janeiro, made limited national progress, electing forty-seven federal deputies and one senator as well as two other governors (Rio Grande do Sul and Espírito Santo). Still this kept the PDT well ahead of the PT, which elected only one senator and no governors and won only thirty-five seats in the lower house—as Lula opted not to stand for reelection. The PT's frequent allies also fared poorly, as the PCB elected only three federal deputies; the PCdoB, five; and the PSB, eleven—along with one senator. The moderate to conservative "flag of convenience" parties did a little better than hold their own. The PDC came away with twenty-two seats in the lower house, along with two in the upper; and the PL lost ground with but fifteen seats in the Chamber of Deputies.[20]

Most incumbent governors suffered reverses that threatened their political futures, much less their presidential ambitions, as their candidates for statehouse succession went down to defeat. Although Orestes Quércia's candidate won in a runoff in São Paulo; Newton Cardoso's ran fourth in Minas Gerais; and Moreira Franco's was crushed in Rio de Janeiro. Antônio Carlos Magalhães's triumphal return—for a third time—to the Bahia governorship spelled an end for Waldir Pires's aspirations. Pedro Simon saved himself by gaining election to the Senate from Rio Grande do Sul while his party's candidate for governor went down to defeat. Miguel Arraes's record vote for the lower house from Pernambuco was a weaker version of the same tactic, as the winner for governor there, the PFL's Joaquim Francisco, had been strongly opposed by Arraes in 1988, when Arraes was an easy victor in the Recife mayoral contest. Major gainers among governors were Álvaro Dias, who saw his candidate come from behind in the final round in Paraná, and Ceará's Tasso Jereissati—whose hand-picked candidate was easily elected. The most interesting results in lesser states included the triumph of Sarney's allies in Maranhão, Renan Calheiros's corruption-marked failure to capture the Alagoas statehouse, and Gilberto Mestrinho's election as governor of Amazonas for the third time.

Luiz Antônio Fleury Filho's election as São Paulo governor not only placed Paulo Maluf in a most uncomfortable situation—as a presidential hopeful, but also all but knocked Mário Covas (the third-place finisher there) out of the lists. Hélio Garcia (fifty-nine), by becoming governor of Minas Gerais on a minor party label, was placed in a position to take over the PMDB there along with its significant representation in Congress. Hence he might well prove a major obstacle to the hopes of both Dias and Quércia to become the dominant figure of the PMDB. The PFL, PTB, PRN, PDC, and perhaps the PDS and PL as well appeared likely to be swallowed up in the broad new Center party that Collor seemed inclined to build as a more stable political base in the Congress that would take office in February 1991.

Socioeconomic Conditions at the Beginning of the 1990s

Will the 1990s be a period of renewed sustained economic growth, more equitable distribution of income, a substantial diminution in the "social deficit," or some combination of these desirable outcomes? To deliver on such promises and satisfy popular aspirations the Collor government will have to overcome an essentially negative heritage bequeathed it by the Sarney administration. Inflation must not only be brought back from the brink of hyperinflation, but it must also be kept under permanent control. The year's total matched 1989's 1,800 percent, albeit with only 270 points coming under Collor. Also urgently required are significant relief from the crushing burden of foreign debt; control of the soaring internal debt (which depends upon drastic reduction of the public sector deficit); and increased savings and investment over the 1989 level of 18 percent of GDP.

While the picture is bleak, it is far from hopeless. The economy did at least grow by 3.4 percent in 1989 following its marginally positive performance the preceding year (after a modest 3.6 percent growth in 1987). Yet this means that over these three years there had been almost no increase in per capita GDP. Indeed, the just over 7 percent yearly average growth for the 1984–1986 period only made up in per capita terms for the 15 percent decline associated with the deep 1981–1983 recession. Thus, the meager expansion of per capita wealth and output over the decade of the 1980s was a result of its strong beginning in 1980—when the economy expanded by 9.1 percent. By contrast, 1990 saw GDP contract by nearly 4 percent.

But the picture is brightened somewhat by the fact that real economic growth in 1988 and 1989 was significantly higher than the official figures indicate. For the informal sector, often called underground or parallel, did expand substantially. To avoid paying social security and other wage taxes as well as to escape the turnover tax on merchandise and evade income taxes, most small businesses in Brazil operate largely "off the books." Indeed, conservative estimates place that part of the economy not captured through conventional means of calculating GDP on the basis of official figures at an additional $100 billion.[21] This also means, of course, that official numbers on income distribution are unreliable, as many in the informal economy seriously understate their income to researchers, often to the extent of declaring no income at all! even when this is in clear contradiction to their living conditions.

Still the Dragon of Inflation

A major price paid for Brazil's development has been persistent and usually rapid rises in the cost of living. But in the late 1980s this took on a grimmer and more ominous visage. For inflation soared out of control while economic growth slowed nearly to a halt. From pushing 400 percent in 1987, the price index jumped to almost 1000 percent the next year, before reaching 1,765 percent for 1989. As expansion of the economy for these three years barely covered population increase, no longer could inflation be accepted as a price necessarily paid for sustained economic development. Yet in the face of governmental inability to get a handle on the problem, the threshold of toleration kept rising. Thus, the Cruzado Plan had followed February 1986's (then) record 14.4 percent inflation, the Bresser Plan came on the heels of June 1987's new record of over 26 percent, and the Summer Plan wasn't launched until this had been exceeded in December 1988. Yet by the second half of 1989 monthly rates a hair below 40 percent were toasted as victories, because the monster to be feared had escalated to that of hyperinflation—generally defined as over 50 percent a month. Even 41.4 percent in November was written off as "not at all bad for an election month," while a further rise in December to 53.5 percent was rationalized by the observation that a lame duck government certainly couldn't be expected to act energetically and effectively on this front.[22]

A starting point toward bringing the problem under control was the generally reluctant and essentially belated realization on the part of most groups seriously involved in the policy-making process that the public sector deficit, the inertial effects of indexation, and even the large trade surpluses of the mid and late-1980s are indeed among the major roots of Brazil's intractable problem of chronic acute inflation.[23] This led to a slowly spreading awareness that there is no quick fix or painless prescription for reducing the runaway pace of inflation. Although the Sarney administration was able to reduce the public sector deficit to 4 percent of GDP in 1988, entrenched interests—many within the government itself—resisted sharp cuts in subsidies and closing of governmental agencies, while the increasingly independent Congress, looking to reelection bids in 1990, blocked implementation of many of the measures the executive did manage to adopt. Hence public sector deficit financing expanded again in 1989—to 7.2 percent of GDP. Thus the federal government's 1990 treasury surplus was no mean feat.

The explosion of domestic debt further complicated the problem. In recent years the ballooning cost of servicing a snowballing internal debt has helped fuel inflation and has become a major factor in destabilizing government finances. By the end of 1989 outstanding government paper had exploded beyond $65 billion or roughly 17 percent of GDP. From only .5 percent in 1975, the cost of servicing the rolling internal debt had leapt by 1987 to 4 percent of GDP before jumping further as a result of the high interest rates accompanying the subsequently soaring inflation. Whereas in 1970 interest on the internal debt had amounted to only 4.8 percent of the federal government's use of its revenues, this reached 51.3 percent by 1985 before moving steadily higher. Clearly since that time servicing the internal debt has become nearly as serious a burden as the closely related one of foreign debt—hence the importance of its reduction by 17 percent in 1990.

This undisciplined and accelerating expansion of internal debt was rooted in a long series of public sector deficits that ran as high as 7.7 percent of GDP in 1982 before coming down to a 4 percent average in the mid-decade years.[24] This gap between receipts and expenditures rose to an undisciplined 5.5 percent in 1987, with the central government's operating deficit being the chief culprit, followed by those of the states and municipalities and the parastatal companies. Success in reducing the overall deficit to the 4 percent level in 1988 was a transitory victory, as in 1989 it again got out of hand, with prospects for 1990 truly grim unless a much firmer hand were at the helm. Issuing of securities is the chief way of covering these deficits. Most of this paper being short-term, the government has found itself forced to refinance a major proportion of the internal debt at frequent intervals and high interest rates. As a result, the public sector came to absorb an increasingly large proportion of national savings, up from 50 percent in 1980 to 70 percent by 1988.

Although carrying the internal debt by issuance of securities was highly inflationary, alternative methods of financing the public sector deficit were either equally inflationary as in the case of emission of currency, or no longer practicable, which was the situation with respect to borrowing abroad. Moreover, tax increases have been eaten up by additional spending mandated by a Congress preoccupied with reelection. Owing in large part to a wide variety of investment and export incentives, only a few of which faced extinction through the administration's proposed austerity measures, net tax receipts for the federal government declined between 1970 and 1987 from 17 percent of GDP to a low of 9 percent while the gross tax burden dropped only from 26 percent of GDP to 21 percent.[25] With fiscal incentives and tax exemptions keeping net tax receipts running well below current expenditures, the government's capacity to invest underwent a sharp drop. Combined with the abrupt decline in foreign investment, gross fixed capital formation dropped off from the level of about 22 percent of GDP for the 1971–1980 period to an average of just over 18 percent of GDP from 1981 through 1989.

External Factors: Debt, Balance of Payments, Investment, and Trade

Brazil's development, particularly that led since the 1950s by industrialization, has required high rates of investment, a significant share of which has come from abroad. As foreign portfolio investment through the Brazilian stock markets is still quite new and small-scale, this has involved both direct investment and borrowing—with the latter having come to overshadow greatly the former—although in 1988–1989 billions of dollars of conversion of debt into equity began to reverse this two-decade trend. While direct investment sets up a counter flow of financial resources in terms of profits and royalties, this has been of relatively modest dimensions in Brazil, as a substantial proportions of profits have generally been reinvested. But recent trends in this regard are far from reassuring. Indeed, legal remittances of profits and dividends rose from $909 million in 1987 to $1.54 billion the next year before jumping to $2.3 billion in 1989.

For their part, loans require both interest and either amortization of principal or their "rolling over" in the form of additional borrowing to cover payments due on old loans. Such a heavy load of debt service depletes foreign exchange reserves and thus requires massive trade surpluses—earned essentially by expanding foreign sales and reducing imports. This in turn restricts internal consumption and feeds inflationary pressure. Eventually the problem comes around to not only rescheduling payment on the foreign debt, but also renegotiation of its terms and efforts to gain a significant degree of outright relief from creditor banks and governments—something very much on the agenda of Brazil's current administration.

By any meaningful standards of comparison, Brazil with its debt of between $115 and $120 billion is not really one of the region's most indebted countries. True, the sheer bulk of its debt is rivaled only by that of Mexico, but it is at or below the region's norms in terms of relative perspective. Thus, in per capita terms, accumulated foreign debt is about $800 compared with roughly $1,350 for Mexico, $1,700 for Argentina, and over $2,000 for Venezuela. At around 30 percent, the proportion of external debt to GDP is quite low for a region in which for some countries debt equals or exceeds GDP. Also comparatively good within the Latin American experience is the debt to export earnings ratio of just over three to one.[26]

Restoration of civilian democratic government did little to improve the debt problem inherited from the military regime. Continued reduction of imports during 1985 to $13.2 billion compared to $25.6 billion in exports produced a healthy trade surplus of about $12.5 billion, thus avoiding any significant current accounts deficit and leaving the country capable of coping reasonably well with interest payments of $11.4 billion. But with amortization running at $8.9 billion, borrowing to pay old loans pushed the accumulated stock of debt to $103.6 billion—"only" $95.9 billion by the narrower Central Bank calculations. A reduction in net oil imports to $3.9 billion was of major help in holding the line on foreign purchases, and foreign exchange reserves, which had recovered to $12 billion in 1984, kept steady at $11.6 billion.

In 1986, however, the great increase in internal consumption brought on by the temporary prosperity engendered by the Cruzado Plan limited exports to $22.4 billion—which combined with imports of slightly over $14 billion yielded a trade surplus only a bit above $8.3 billion. Fortunately, interest payments had declined to $9.1 billion, but even so total external debt still rose to at least $107.6 billion, while foreign exchange reserves slid to $6.8 billion.

Faced with a patent inability to keep up with scheduled disbursements—as total interest charges for the 1980–1986 period had exceeded $72 billion (a figure that reached $123 billion for the longer 1971–1989 time span)—the government decreed a partial moratorium on interest payments at the end of February 1987. This desperation move, cloaked in nationalist rhetoric but in reality the result of impending insolvency, was intended to stem the rising net outflow of financial resources as well as to strengthen Brazil's position in debt negotiations, which had been dragging on ever since the civilian administration had overoptimistically decided that it could do better than the tentative agreement virtually nailed down by the Figueiredo government in late 1984. Thus, 1987 ended with little real improvement on the debt front. While a trade surplus of almost $11.2 billion was achieved on foreign sales of $26.2 billion and purchases of $15 billion, interest payments still amounted to $8.8 billion. Moreover, interest not paid to the private banks was added to the principal, pushing it over the $115 billion mark (almost $124 billion by the most inclusive of criteria).

More disturbingly, signs of disinvestment and capital flight were increasingly evident, with 1986 having seen a negative figure of $100 million in direct investment along with only $450 million in reinvestment of profits and $300 million in conversion of debt into equity. This meager inflow equalled only a bit over half the outflow of dividends and royalties, culminating a negative trend in this direction begun in 1982. And although the capital flight estimate of $15 billion for the 1983–1987 period was quite low compared to Mexico's massive hemorrhaging or Argentina's disinvestment surge, this was up sharply from the $6 billion total for the longer 1976–1982 span. For 1987 foreign investment was down further, remission of profits and dividends up, and capital flight increasing—reaching over $7 billion in 1988 and nearing $1 billion a month in 1989.

While in 1988 a comprehensive rescheduling of $63.6 billion, the bulk of Brazil's debt to foreign private banks and well over half its total external debt, was achieved, this arrangement quickly began to come apart at the seams, and in 1989 Brazil fell far behind on interest payments, with the banks uninterested in further negotiations with a lame-duck government. With 1988 exports at almost $33.9 billion running higher than predicted, permitting a trade surplus of over $19 billion, Brazil actually managed to show a $4 billion balance of payments surplus after paying off the preceding year's deficit in this regard. This was accomplished despite interest payments of $9.9 billion and amortization of half that much. (Experts believe that the real value of Brazilian exports—frequently underinvoiced—runs between 20 and 25 percent higher than the prices registered with Cacex.) In 1989 some $34.4 billion in recognized foreign sales combined with an increase of imports to $18.3 billion to produce a trade surplus of $16.1 billion. This dropped to $11 billion in 1990, as imports needed for development were increased, some products were diverted from export to domestic consumption, and oil prices shot up as a result of the Mideast crisis. Debt negotiations stalled as Brazil insisted that capacity to pay be the basic criterion.

The Social Deficit

Although social conditions in Brazil still leave a great deal to be desired, they have clearly been changing for the better—quite dramatically so over the past generation.[27] The still massive residual problem is more one of some elements of society being left behind rather than the lot of the great majority showing little or no improvement. Thus, for example, it is very clear that education and income are very closely correlated in Brazil, but the relationship is much more complex than either the interpretation that only those who are relatively better off to begin with have access to education—the approach that income causes or explains educational differences—or the assertion that education leads directly to higher income levels (the "stop complaining and go to school" cop-out).

In reality education is the main vehicle for upward social mobility in Brazil, but the channel is far from unobstructed, and getting higher-paying jobs on the strength of schooling alone is far from automatic. When the economy is at the high tide of rapid sustained growth, the obstacles in the stream of social mobility are relatively submerged, and the opportunity ferry may pass safely over them. But when growth slows down to where the economy is producing fewer new jobs than the number of persons entering the labor market, the sandbar of inadequate employment opportunities and shoals of unemployment imperil passage across class barriers. In these situations the principle that "it's who you know, not what you know" comes massively into play, and the high hopes of many who have struggled and sacrificed for educational attainment founder on the treacherous rocks of color, sex, and even region of origin. As a result, while many millions of Brazilians do manage to improve their status and level of living, millions of others miss the opportunity boat, while millions more become relatively—if not absolutely—worse off.[28]

Material aspects of living have been improving for a very large proportion of Brazilians, particularly those in urban areas. Thus households with running water increased from only 15.6 percent in 1950, to 24.3 percent a decade later, through 33.3 percent in 1970, on to 56 percent in 1980 and 71 percent by 1988. This progress was paralleled with respect to electricity, as the 1950 proportion of 24.6 percent reached 86 percent by 1988. As late as 1970 only 26.1 percent of Brazilian homes had refrigerators, a share that hit 69 percent by 1988—a year in which stoves were found in over 97 percent of all households. Whereas only 24.1 percent of families had a television set in 1970, this had risen to 72 percent by 1988. Automobiles, which were possessed by only 9 percent of Brazilian households in 1970, were found in over a third of all homes by 1988.[29]

In every one of these categories there is a sharp urban-rural disparity, but end of the 1980s figures for the laggard rural areas were in most cases already past the 1960 national proportions and closing in on those for 1970. Hence a continuance of the trends of the past two decades would soon begin to reduce sharply the material gap between the vast urban and diminishing rural sectors of society. This development would be most welcome in the closely related fields of infant mortality and life expectancy—the latter now up to over sixty-five years for Brazil as a whole, but still in the fifties in the most backward states.

Despite considerable progress in recent years, at least on the quantitative side, Brazil's educational system leaves very much to be desired. The quality of teaching is generally poor and often even horrendous, especially at the primary level, where the vast majority attend public schools. Yet in good part this is the price paid for substantially increased access, with space available catching up to demand in some of the more developed urban centers. Secondary schools have not yet fully adjusted to the task of educating millions for functioning in an increasingly complex society rather than just preparing tens of thousands for university entrance—as was the case a short generation ago. Over this same time span Brazil has managed to build Latin America's largest and best system of higher education, albeit one where quality is very uneven between such fine institutions as the University of São Paulo or the State University at Campinas and an array of profit-oriented degree factories.

The most serious of many educational problems is a dual one at the very beginning of the elementary level, which by law begins at age seven. Although there are now at least 26 million children enrolled in the first eight grades, this leaves about 4.3 million seven to fourteen-year olds out of school.[30] Yet unsatisfactory as is the present situation, it marks great progress over the extremely restricted access and highly elitist nature of the educational system in the past. As recently as 1950 there were fewer than 5 million students of all kinds in Brazil. Of this limited number, only 60,000 were in high school, while enrollment in higher education was only 44,000. By 1960 the total number of students had nearly doubled to 8.73 million, with just over 267,000 in high school and 93,000 receiving higher education. A decade later the elementary student population had exploded to 15.9 million, with slightly over an additional million in high schools and 456,000 attending colleges and universities—the latter an amazing fivefold expansion during a single decade.

Great as was this sustained expansion, growth of educational opportunity was to accelerate even more during the 1970s, as by 1980 elementary school enrollment passed 22.5 million and that in secondary schools surpassed 2.8 million. These were respectively almost five, forty-six, and thirty-two times the 1950 figures. And although the rate of growth of education slowed in the early 1980s, largely as a result of the economic recession, by mid-decade Brazil had a total of 31.5 million students—well over six times the 1950 figure—an impressive achievement during a single generation. Still, however, only a little over 20 percent of the fifteen- to nineteen-year-olds in Brazil are among the country's 3.5 million high school students. Moreover, illiteracy is still near 20 percent.

Unfortunately, the striking imbalances in Brazil's social situations tend to be reinforcing, as sharp regional discrepancies—to a high degree coinciding with urban-rural differences—interact with the fact that much of the Afro-

Brazilian population is to be found in the rural areas of the more backward regions. And it is exactly there that Brazil's chief channel of upward social mobility—educational opportunity—is sorely missing.

The Challenge of 1990: Finding the Engine(s) for Growth

As it sought to develop a viable program for maintaining growth while bringing inflation under control, the generally young and imaginative Collor transition team demonstrated a salutary realization that there is no quick fix in the way of a magical, painless, or easy formula. Debt relief, underscored by the 1989 burden of at least $17 billion in debt service due plus profits, dividends, and royalties; continued—if not improved—access to the markets of the industrialized nations; and renewed foreign investment are all badly needed by Brazil. In addition, however, increased investment by the Brazilian private sector and recovery of the state's capacity to invest are essential if near stagflation is to be transformed into a return of the sustained growth required to support a needed attack upon the country's forbidding social problems. The reasonably good start on the inflation and deficit fronts in 1990 still left the rest of these pressing matters to be dealt with in 1991— in an international environment marked by the end of the Cold War combined with an acute crisis in the Middle East that carried potentially devastating economic consequences.

Soldiers, Priests, and Property Owners

The Brazilian armed forces remained at the beginning of the last decade of the twentieth century far more than just a potent veto group, if for the moment at least, something less than the regime's tutor. The country's 1964–1984 ruling institution still retained the capacity to be arbiter of its national life. Recent events, from the 1986 elections through the constituent assembly, and on to presidential succession demonstrated growth, not deterioration, in the power and influence of Brazil's propertied strata. With the military having vacated the center of the political arena, they came increasingly to the forefront. Indeed, never had they directly occupied as high a proportion of seats as in the 1987–1990 Congress—whose role expanded greatly with democratization and the erosion of Sarney's authority. For nearly a third of national legislators were primarily businessmen, with a total of over 45 percent being closely linked to capital.[31] At the same time the Catholic Church remained a key actor on both sides of the political spectrum. The active engagement of its progressive wing was crucial to the Left's pretensions to obtain power and transform the existing social order, while checkmating of this by the conservative wing of the hierarchy was essential to the Right's retention of political control and maintenance of the existing economic system. Hence, for all that Brazil had changed over the past several generations, the armed forces, the Church, and the captains of the national economy still largely controlled the nation's destiny.

In the Wings, the Military

Clearly the Brazilian armed forces, which continued to have a heavy influence within the Sarney government, are highly concerned with the directions the new administration might take. Although it is impossible to predict exactly what may be the evolution of their thought with regard to appropriate attitudes and future actions in the political realm, one key point must be borne in mind. The Brazilian armed forces have not "gone back to the barracks," because they have never been apolitical and fully subject to civilian control as that term implies. They have always at best done a significant degree of coaching from the sidelines and have been ready to step in if the game of politics got out of hand—they being the judge of whether this has occurred. In their preponderant self-image—although this is far from universal and subject to significant variations in degree and intensity—the Brazilian military has saved the nation, constitutional order, the republic, or the country's "Christian, Western, and democratic" values on at least twenty-seven occasions.[32]

As they see the historical record and the obligations imposed upon them by the patriotic tradition established by the actions of their predecessors, the chain began almost 170 years ago with expelling the Portuguese, battling the Argentines, and thwarting a whole series of efforts to split off pieces of the country—all during the very first generation of national life. This was followed, with the great Caxias as the bridge between generations, by repulsing Paraguayan aggression and then unleashing the forces of modernization by refusing to enforce slavery in the 1870s. Then came establishment of the republic and guiding it through the first perilous years— with Deodoro and Floriano firmly enshrined in the pantheon of military heroes, safe in military minds from derogatory efforts to tarnish their memories by pointing out political and administrative shortcomings.

Ensconced as trustees of the moderating power, the next generation defeated the southern secessionists in the mid-1890s, redeemed the republic's honor at Canudos, and defended the country's borders in Acre before following Hermes's leadership in battling the retrograde oligarchies who had perverted the republic. Shortly thereafter they put down the subversive threat of peasant insurgency in the Contestado, stood ready to defend the territorial integrity of the nation during World War I, and then—by way of *tenentismo* and the 1930 Revolution—brought a new and more modern republic into being.

Again in the officer corps' predominant perception, these thirteen patriotic ventures were only the beginning, as over the next decade the *tenente* generation had to defeat the São Paulo revolt, put down a Communist revolution, and turn back the Integralist coup—all before they and their younger brothers risked and sacrificed their lives in large numbers helping to save Western Christian Democracy from Axis powers on the battlefields of Italy during World War II. The present generation's personal experience begins at about this point, as today's generals were at least entering the military schools if not active service.

After restoring the domestic democratic order by ousting Vargas in 1945, the armed forces had to do the job again in 1954 and contain the threat of civil war the following year—before providing stability in the Kubitschek years behind Lott and Denys (whose son is still an active duty general). Thus the military had played the savior role twenty-one times when the present generation of colonels finished going through the academy and got their careers under way. These were participants in what they see as a combination of firmness and moderation on the part of military leaders averting a potentially bloody crisis in 1961. Led by the great figure of Castelo Branco in 1964 and joined by most of today's lieutenant colonels, they acted decisively to save the country from Communism, corruption, and chaos.

Coming into the lives and experiences of the present junior and field grade officers, in the late 1960s and early 1970s the Brazilian armed forces— in the version of events being inculcated among cadets and recruits at the end of the 1980s—were compelled to perform the thankless task of stamping out subversion at the same time as under Médici's inspiration they set the country firmly on the road to modernization, development, and being taken seriously in the world. Subsequently, through the still present and presti- gious—almost revered—figure of Geisel, they conducted the country back toward resumption of fully competitive political life.

Most recently they have provided stability to a beleaguered civilian government as selfish and self-seeking political interests have sought to undo much of the "progress" achieved under military auspices between 1964 and 1985. As they see it, if this proud tradition is not to be betrayed, they must now see that the country does not return to the excessive polarization that marked the early 1960s. Never mind that this view of their role and accomplishments is refuted, rejected, and belittled by politicians and "self-proclaimed intellectuals whose bloated egos are matched by their lack of patriotism." This only confirms the military's pervasive reservations about the fundamental untrustworthiness of such elements and the threat to national security their coming to power would pose.

Apart from this perception of the situation and their weighty inheritance as guardians of the nation's fundamental values and basic institutions, the Brazilian armed forces have increased their internal unity and enhanced their professional capabilities since relinquishing control of the government. In particular, ground forces are being augmented and modernized in keeping with the lessons of the 1982 British-Argentine conflict and realization of the need to establish an effective military presence on the vast reaches of the country's northern frontier. The latter consideration is particularly salient in light of the present inability to control either drug smugglers or the estimated half million gold prospectors spread across the inaccessible border regions running from Surinam in the east all the way past Venezuela and Colombia to Peru and Bolivia in the west. Then, too, there is the new preoccupation with possible developments in Paraguay brought on by the fall in 1989 of the generation-long Stroessner government.[33] Moreover, they view with substantial concern the deteriorating political situation in Colombia and Peru as well as the precarious alliance of traditionally opposed elements upon which Bolivia's government rests.[34]

Clearly as 1990 came to a close, the Brazilian armed forces manifested little disposition to again become directly responsible for the conduct of government—balanced by no perceptible inclination to lose the capacity to do so should conditions sharply deteriorate. Campello de Souza's closely reasoned and carefully pondered analysis comes close to the mark. Despite the military's late 1980s "lack of interest" in again assuming power, she concludes that they might be brought to intervene as a result of a "crisis of government" resulting from party disarray, disorder of the state apparatus, and "above all" the reinforcement of populism.[35] For this realistic observer, the "most probable outcome" would be that "the Brazilian democratization effort will be slowly debilitated by the suffocating weight of the military's presence." Short of this, there can be little doubt that Brazil's armed forces remain much more than just a potent veto group, if currently less than an active tutor or intrusive arbiter.

A Church Divided but Still a Critical Factor

The Catholic Church remains the short leg of the tripod of national institutions. Divisions previously pointed out as existing in the early 1980s have since deepened and become more open. The progressive clergy's close identification with the PT and accelerating attacks upon the capitalist order were met with escalation of the Vatican-conservative hierarchy's counter offensive. Maverick theologian Leonardo Boff, one of the continent's leading popularizers of Liberation Theology, was censured in 1985 and required to adopt a penitential silence.[36]

Although some observers had hoped that the election of Dom Luciano Mendes de Almeida in 1987 to preside over the CNBB would help ameliorate the deepening divisions within the Brazilian church, he acted essentially as an ally of the progressives. Tension between that wing of the Brazilian Catholic clergy and the Vatican escalated during 1988 as the latter stepped up its counter attack on several fronts. First the most highly placed advocates of this extremely vocal wing received cautionary letters ranging up to the level of warnings to desist from certain activities or face punishment, while Dom Luciano was removed from his position at the right hand of Cardinal Arns in São Paulo and sent to an out-of-the-way bishopric in Minas Gerais. Second, the massive São Paulo Archdiocese, containing nearly 15 million persons, was dismembered in order to reduce the power of Cardinal Arns. More than 7 million persons were taken out from under this extremely liberal prelate's jurisdiction as four new dioceses were created. These were headed by three moderates and a conservative, while Dom Paulo's team of progressive auxiliary bishops was broken up in the process and the vast majority of the CEB's came under the sway of the new bishops.

One politically important result of this dismemberment was a reduction in the scope and range in São Paulo of the very close cooperation between lower clergy and PT militants so essential to Lula's presidential bid—a partnership that had led to many CEBs functioning almost as PT campaign organizations (as they continued to do in several parts of the country). The third line of attack saw moderates and conservatives named to other key posts around the country as the Papal Nuncio worked closely with Dom Lucas Moreira Neves and other pillars of tradition and Vatican supremacy.[37] Nationally it has been estimated that Brazil's bishops are divided as about 31 percent progressives, 53 percent moderates, and but 16 percent conservatives, with the ratio among priests roughly 30, 50, and 20 percent.[38] A key difference is that most of the progressives are heavily involved in politics, while some conservatives and many of the moderates believe that the Church should stay out of partisan political activities.

One of the major problems of the Catholic Church continues to be its serious undermanning. Nearly 7,000 parishes may appear adequate on paper, but with fewer than 14,000 priests—many of them engaged in education and administration—staffing is often skeletal. This religious army has enough generals, with bishops totalling 378, but there is a critical and worsening lack of vocations—aggravated by the fact that in recent decades at least 4,000 priests have left to get married. Over the years a large number of priests have been imported from European countries and the United States— now making up 45 percent of the total—and several of them have emerged as leaders of the clergy's left wing. Most prominent of these are Pedro Casaldáglia, Bishop of São Felix do Araguaia (a Spaniard); his close ally. Frenchman Tomás Balduino (Bishop of Goiás Velho); and Germany's Erwin Krautler, Bishop of Xingu.[39]

Sadly, the need for so many foreign priests stems largely from the fact that very few Afro-Brazilians have been able to enter the priesthood. At around 200, they amount to an essentially disgraceful 1.5 percent of the country's priests. In addition, although women are much more intensely Catholic than men in Brazil, their requests to play a less frustratingly secondary role have been consistently rebuffed. Under these conditions, it is quite natural that in much of the country a kind of folk Catholicism, relatively unfettered and undisciplined by the clergy, not only flourishes, but often prevails over the "pure" variety. Most apparent in the smaller towns of the interior, it has also become important in more populated areas.

The Challenge of Other Religions

Protestant sects have been growing very rapidly in Brazil, especially during the past quarter century. Catalogued at a million in 1940 and estimated at only five percent of the population just two decades ago, Protestants were enumerated at just under 8 million in the 1980 census, but this appears to reflect a serious undercount. Current estimates run as high as 28 million persons—nearing 20 percent of the population. Indeed, the Assembly of God alone claims 8 million followers (a count that ignores the losses resulting from a number of important spinoffs). But it is the more evangelical pentecostal sects that are making the greatest headway as a significant number of Afro-

Brazilians and erstwhile spiritualists turn to them, along with neglected and disenchanted Catholics. A clear demonstration of their growth was the fact that they elected thirty-four representatives to Congress in 1986 compared to only twelve in 1982. Much of their expansion stems from the recent success of religious television ministries, with ownership of a channel in Rio de Janeiro and late 1989 purchase of one in São Paulo as well as programs in almost all other major cities.[40]

Whereas earlier progress by mainstream Protestant denominations was chiefly among middle-class groups, the pentecostal/evangelical sects have made dramatic headway lower in the socioeconomic pyramid. Yet gains by both types of non-Catholic Christian churches have often been largely by default, seizing upon the manifold opportunities afforded by the failure of the Catholic Church to have an active presence in many large neighborhoods or new centers of population. Protestants in general, but the pentecostals in particular, played an active and effective role in the Collor campaign, helping to offset the progressive Catholics' support for Lula.

Property Owners: Still in the Saddle

Civilian democratic politics has not put a crimp in the political dominance of the propertied elements of Brazilian society. Indeed, the withdrawal of the military from direct exercise of power and the at least temporary neutralization of the progressive wing of the Catholic Church has increased their scope of political activity and range of influence since 1985. On top of this, the outcome of the 1989 presidential elections was highly advantageous to their continued leading role in national political life. Not only did a representative of their ranks win the presidency, but spokesmen for the São Paulo core of the entrepreneurial strata—Maluf and Afif Domingos—ran strongly as well. Thus, propertied elements' fears that the balance of power would shift drastically to the Left through competitive electoral politics proved unfounded, or at least distinctly premature.

As 1990 progressed they looked ahead with renewed confidence to consolidating the presidential victory by capturing control of those state administrations that had slipped into the hands of Center-Left PMDB elements through the 1986 balloting. Furthermore, they may even have increased the pro–private sector interest contingent of the Congress to take office in 1991. Then, too, they can expect to be influential in a national administration coming to power through having defeated the Left at the ballot box and facing strong and uncompromising opposition from the coalition of parties that participated in Lula's powerful, if ultimately unsuccessful, campaign of "labor versus capital."

Diniz and Boschi, concentrating on the industrial sector, but touching on other propertied groups, point out a significant to dramatic strengthening of their organizational capabilities, clearly evident in the 1987–1988 constituent assembly. This extends to both seeking other elective offices and occupying positions in the economic side of the federal government.[41] Tavares, focusing on the landowners and their Ruralist Democratic Union (UDR), concludes that they were very effective in defending their interests within the constituent assembly. In his view:

> One doesn't know for certain how many congressmen this entity managed to elect in the November 15, 1986 elections, but it was certainly a sufficient number to articulate the guarantee of a majority for its principal proposals: the prohibition of any type of agrarian reform in "productive" lands and amnesty of interest from the Cruzado [Plan]. In the constituent process, the UDR acted as a pressure group and was able to "domesticate" a significant faction, even frustrating political agreements among parliamentary blocs seeking conciliatory solutions for the agrarian reform question.[42]

The entrepreneurial strata have also come to realize the space available to them from the fact that "side by side with its extreme force in the sense of concentration of powers," the Brazilian state also demonstrates "its extreme weakness due to ineffectiveness and inefficiency in policy implementation."[43]

The negative impact of the expanded role of the entrepreneurial elites in terms of political development is aptly summed up by Camargo and Diniz when they point out: "the strengthening of their capacity for organization was done without breaking the historical pattern of representation of business interests in the state apparatus. The direct access of groups, associations and individual companies to segments of the state bureaucratic apparatus persisted as the dominant trait in articulation between the public and private sectors."[44] Dreifuss goes further in attributing both great political power and retrograde influence on policy to the propertied strata—as well as stressing their close ties to the military establishment. For him, and other radical leftist critics of the existing order, urban and rural elites act in an "oligarchic, caudilhesque, patrimonial, and clientelistic" manner.[45] The entrepreneurial sector, possessing a clear sense of its interests and capacity to act in the policy-making arena, constitutes a "true power structure."[46] In addition to such sectoral organizations as the National Confederation of Industries (CNI) and its functional components and state affiliates—especially the São Paulo branch (FIESP)—urban propertied groups operate through a wide variety of associations and institutions. These include the Chamber for Economic and Social Studies and Debates, the Liberal Institute, the Brazilian Union of Entrepreneurs, the National Confederation of Financial Institutions, The Brazilian Association for Defense of Democracy, The Free Enterprise Front, the Informal Forum, and the National Thought of Entrepreneurial Bases.[47]

The effectiveness of such groups is facilitated by the fact that state clientelism is still very much alive and operative; in conjunction with still vigorous populism, it allows for the propertied groups to co-opt support for their colonization—even quasi-capture—of those parts of the state apparatus most critical to their interests.[48]

Prospects for the 1990s

As demonstrated in Chapters 8 and 9, the broad-based movement of the first half of the 1980s for a return to civilian government and competitive politics did not reflect a consensus on the appropriate institutional framework for the new regime, much less agreement on policies in the social and economic realms. Thus, the post-1984 transition opened the door for intense competition over these fundamental questions. Their resolution through the 1987–1988 constituent assembly was both incomplete and tentative—especially in light of the non-self-implementing nature of almost all the social advances and progressive features of the somewhat schizophrenic basic charter that finally emerged.

The late 1989 presidential elections were another important, but far from determining, much less final, round in the ongoing battle over what kind of democratic order would emerge in Brazil. Indeed, while in many important ways the options were made public and perhaps even clarified, this was as much in an atmosphere of polarization as one of consensus building. The 1990 state and congressional elections will prove to be at least equally important in defining the nature of the future order, as the ability of Collor to implement his vision of a Brazil ready to face the challenges of the new century will be heavily conditioned by the need for a stable base of parliamentary support. Cooperation in this and other respects from the governors of the major states will also be important as both the new Congress and new governors will serve to the end of Collor's term.

Collor's Complex Challenges

Clearly the stewardship of Collor will be critical, particularly because the party system with which he began governing was no more rational nor coherent than it has been in the past. In the short run at least, the party panorama will remain somewhere between fragmented and chaotic as the rapid disaggregation of the PMDB has left the country in a situation close to that of the French Third and Fourth Republics, with a dozen parties represented in Congress and none of them approaching a majority. Essentially the combination of an almost absurdly permissive law with regard to minimum requirements for recognition as a national party and failure to institute a less irrational electoral system encourage the continuation of parties that, rather than aggregating demands, aggravate the divisions within the body politic.

To say that a drastic restructuring of the party system is badly needed is not to imply that it is possible, much less likely. Indeed, better opportunities for doing so may well have already passed by. A major obstacle resides in the peculiar electoral system—one that not only minimizes both any degree of responsibility of representatives to constituencies or meaningful party discipline, but also encourages alliances of transitory electoral convenience at the state and local levels. These are often contrary to the parties' positions on the national scene. This critically dysfunctional feature remains highly resistant to reform for the very powerful reason that those with the ability to change it—the sitting Congress—are exactly the chief beneficiaries of the existing highly flawed system. Time and again national legislators have backed away from significant change for fear that their individual prospects for reelection would be lessened by rationalization of the electoral system.

As representation in the national legislature continues to be far different from the national distribution of popular votes, Collor quickly needed to forge some type of viable coalition within the carryover Congress as well as establish workable relationships with the incumbent governors—most of whom preferred someone else as chief executive. In gaining election, he made promises not compatible with the restraints and limitations imposed by a very difficult economic situation, entered into commitments to groups and interests that sometimes conflicted with his public promises, and raised aspirations and expectations to highly unrealistic levels—much of the latter in the final round of bidding against Lula for electoral support. The forces who backed his opponent in the hotly contested runoff race continue seeking to exploit and aggravate the resulting problems and place roadblocks in the way of his legislative program.[49]

Moreover, it will be extremely difficult for him to get the country's administrative house in order, for he assumed office in the midst of yet another nationwide election year—this time for most of the Senate and all the Chamber of Deputies as well as for the country's governors and state legislators. Hence the nation's political forces would act with one or both eyes on their voters, much of the time quite impervious to the president's cries for responsible behavior and generally unimpressed with his claim to have a mandate from the electorate—especially as he was the first choice of only a decided minority.

Once the dust and debris clear from the electoral carnival, Collor will have to begin his second year in office trying to shape a new parliamentary base in keeping with the results of the October 1990 balloting. Only then will Brazil settle down from the dizzying round of campaigns and elections kicked off with the electoral college's voting in January 1985 and including mayors of major cities in November 1985, governor and national and state legislators the following year, municipal elections in 1988, presidential balloting in 1989, and a repeat of the 1986 array of elections in 1990. As by 1994 the country will once more be in the process of choosing a new president—this time combined with the full set of gubernatorial, congressional, and legislative elections—the 1991–1993 period may afford the only opportunity for rational measures and programs at least relatively insulated from the distorting influence of immediate electoral considerations.

Yet as municipal balloting is scheduled for 1992 and a national referendum on adoption of the parliamentary form of government is likely the following year, this respite will be far from complete. Indeed, the 1989 losers may well try to roil the political waters even earlier with pressures for such a change. To further complicate matters, there is little doubt that sentiment and mobilization for much larger-scale agrarian reform will build up during the early 1990s, and the Brazilian political system has yet to demonstrate any capacity to deal effectively with this major and divisive issue of public policy.[50]

A State and System Resistant to Reform

Obstacles to modernizing and democratizing the political system are not, however, limited to the party/electoral/legislative sphere. The bureaucratic apparatus inherited by the new government manifests strong continuities with the undemocratic past. As seen by the leading Brazilian students of the subject of private sector–government interaction, "certain distinguishing characteristics of the structure and functioning of the state apparatus in Brazil present a high degree of continuity in relation to authoritarian style, despite political opening, attempts at rationalizing through reforms of an administrative nature, and the immense degree of diversification and complexity reached by the State machine in the last two decades."[51] Among the persisting features they single out are closed style, low transparency, very limited accountability, strong clientelistic ties, and most importantly, a low capacity for implementation and enforcement.[52]

What Camargo and Diniz have termed "the overload of expectations about the State's performance" still persists as Brazil enters the 1990s, for nothing has happened to change the situation of a state "strong in terms of the prerogatives accumulated, but weak in its capacity for implementation."[53] Camargo has perceived the space for and even functionality of populism as rooted in the "irrational configuration of a political market constituted by the persistent and dramatic hiatus between the increasing demands for goods and services and the public power's deficient supply of them."[54] O'Donnell emphasizes the "predominance of personal relations, clientelism, strong regionalism, scarce or nonexistent party discipline, and highly diffuse ideologies" as obstacles to consolidating Brazil's democratic transition.[55] Collor must not only take all of these factors into account and deal effectively with them, but will also have to come to terms with the Left's perception of a urgent need to reduce the "historical distance that almost always exists between political institutions and social processes—between the mechanisms and *loci* of public decision making and popular experiences and expectations."[56]

For Brazil's modernization is incompatible with the elites' use of traditional political culture to justify delay in erecting new political institutions; as Moisés argues, the latter must be done so that political culture can itself undergo the "transforming effect of new basic structures."[57] After six years of transition, Brazil must get past the situation in which extraordinary uncertainty prevails. The Sarney period was deeply marked by the undetermined processes of change O'Donnell and Schmitter find characteristic of the recent wave of Latin American and southern European transitions with their "elements of accident and unpredictability, of crucial decisions taken in a hurry with very inadequate information, of actors facing unresolvable ethical dilemmas and ideological confusions, of dramatic turning points reached and passed without an understanding of their future significance."[58]

Jaguaribe's analysis of the country's predicament is not only highly perceptive and relevant, but also essentially congruent with views articulated by Collor and some of his more intellectual advisors. The dean of Brazil's political scientists sees *cartorial* corporatism as prevailing at the level of all social classes, as "*Cartorial* groups de facto and frequently *de jure* acquire parcels of public power that confer on them control of strategic sectors and are superimposed upon the regulatory action of the state in detriment to collective interests. Niches of immunities and privileges are created, favoring minorities at the expense of the general interests of society."[59] Incompatibility between a comparatively modern state and a primitive party system leads to a situation in which, if the latter is not soon modernized, the former is likely to cease to be democratic.[60]

The situation is further complicated by the fact that the constitution gives Congress broad powers without responsibility for governing, while leaving the president with powers insufficient for his nearly complete responsibility for conducting the nation's governance.[61] Hence both party reform and adoption of a parliamentary system are seen as urgently needed. Meanwhile the country faces multiple crises, and

> the government that follows that of President Sarney will right away come up against a frontal contradiction between what is suitable to do to get the solution of the structural problematic underway and what it needs to do to defeat inflation. The solution of problems of a structural nature requires, in addition to other measures, important investments. . . . Anti-inflationary policies to be put into effect immediately by the future government, on the other hand, require a drastic reduction of public expenditures and a series of measures with inevitable short-run recessive effects.[62]

A drastic anti-inflation program must be implemented at the very beginning of the new administration, as Collor has certainly done, so that a program of development and reforms of a social democratic nature may be undertaken in 1991. Yet the battle against inflation may well not be won so quickly, and as seen dramatically in Vargas's last term, societal pressures and electoral exigencies might still force Collor's hand on the developmental task before inflation is fully brought under control.

A Look Down the Long Road

Despite the formidable agenda facing the Collor administration, prospects for its reasonable performance, while quite uncertain, are far from totally bleak, much less downright dismal. Balancing economic, political, and military, the situation he inherited was no more unfavorable than that found by Kubitschek in 1956 or by Prudente de Morais in 1894. The key question is whether Brazil's new helmsman will prove to be of Juscelino's stature or even that of the republic's earliest civilian chief executive. On the plus side, the human and institutional resources for consolidating democracy are present should the will and skill to mobilize them for this purpose be found. The experience needed to avoid past mistakes and other countries' errors is also available—if political leaders, not just the president, will take a long and deep look at Brazil's real historical experience and show better judgment than in the past as to what comparative lessons are truly appropriate to their country.

If Collor is not fully up to the stiff challenge, Brazil will still somehow limp along to 1994, when there will have been more time for new leadership to emerge and mature following the long 1964–1984 hiatus of military rule. And there will also have been further opportunities for the electorate to have become more discriminating in exercising their power of choice. Beyond these reasons for cautious and restrained hope, there is some consolation to be taken from the fact that Brazil has come this far with very few outstanding chief executives and many who were at best only marginally adequate. Opportunities have undoubtedly been lost as a result, yet much ground has been made up on those rare occasions when exceptional individuals have come to captain the ship of state.

Even if the 1989 elections prove in the long run not to have produced such a man, they at least almost certainly spelled an end to the presidential bids of an array of political figures in their sixties and seventies whose ambitions to be president far outran their abilities to be an effective head of government. This will open space for new national leadership—including the 1990 crop of governors—to occupy center stage and gain the requisite experience to provide a more substantial menu of options for the 1994 presidential succession. If by then, as may well be the case, Brazil has switched over to a parliamentary system, they will take a back seat as the recruitment pool for prime ministers will essentially be those of the Congress elected in 1990 who manage to achieve reelection in 1994—if not Collor himself should he deliver on his promises. The leadership stratum in Congress will at least potentially be deeper in quality and more seasoned in the give and take of truly competitive democratic politics than are the present national legislators. Then, too, there remains the possibility that a less artificial and irrational party system might by then have developed to lessen the burden on executive leadership—if Collor can accomplish in this realm what Vargas did with respect to the machinery of government.

The bottom line is that during the first half of the 1990s Brazil will likely experience a variety of "crises," some of which will severely strain the system's capabilities. But a crisis of regime, either in the form of a popular revolution or military intervention, is not on the horizon—although these spectres may be raised in political rhetoric and invoked by the dissatisfied extremes.

Notes

Chapter 1

1. The author has made this argument concerning Brazil's increasing international importance in a variety of publications since 1973, in greatest detail in his *Brazil: Foreign Policy of a Future World Power* (Boulder, CO: Westview Press, 1976).

2. This theme was developed by the author in "Política Internacional e a Estratégia das Grandes Potências," *Política e Estratégia* 1, 1 (October–December 1983), pp. 54–62.

3. Distinguished economist Angus Maddison, in a paper delivered in São Paulo and quoted in Brazilian newspapers and magazines in early 1989, stated that in terms of 1965 U.S. dollars Brazil's GDP went from $1.063 billion in 1870 to $166.372 billion in 1987. Over this long time span Brazil showed the greatest proportional growth at 4.4 percent a year, followed by Japan at 3.9 percent and the United States with 3.4 percent annual growth. As Brazil's population rose 14.4 times over during these 117 years, per capita GDP growth averaged 2.1 percent. Among Maddison's many relevant publications are *Phases of Capitalist Development* (Oxford: Oxford University Press, 1982) and *Two Crises: Latin America and Asia 1929–38 and 1973–83* (Paris: Development Centre, Organisation for Economic Co-operation and Development [OECD], 1985).

4. Economic analysts in and on Brazil have a pronounced tendency to assume that their preferred policies and personal panaceas, if adopted and followed, would have led to better results than those that actually occurred. Yet the record regarding those few occasions when an erstwhile critic's suggestions were put into effect—such as the 1986 Cruzado Plan and the subsequent Bresser Plan—raises considerable doubt as to whether this assuredness is justified. Recent examples of such second-guessing include Luiz Carlos Bresser Pereira, *A Dívida e a Inflação: A Economia dos Anos Figueiredo, 1978–1985* (São Paulo: Gazeta Mercantil, 1985); João Manoel Cardoso de Melo, *O Capitalismo Tardário: Contribuição à Revisão Crítica de Formação e do Desenvolvimento da Economia Brasileira* (São Paulo: Editora Brasiliense, 1982); Ignácio Rangel, *Economia: Milagre e Anti-Milagre* (Rio de Janeiro: Jorge Zahar Editor, 1985); Maria da Conceição Tavares and J. Carlos de Assis, *O Grande Salto para o Caos: A Economia Política e Política Econômica do Regime Autoritário* (Rio de Janeiro: Jorge Zahar Editor, 1985); and Paul Singer, *O dia de largarta: Democratização e conflito distributivo no Brasil do Cruzado* (Rio de Janeiro: Jorge Zahar Editor, 1985).

5. The phrase is taken from Edmar L. Bacha and Herbert S. Klein, eds., *A Transição Incompléta: Brasil desde 1945*, 2 volumes (Rio de Janeiro: Editora Paz e Terra, 1986).

6. The official Brazilian classification for an urban center is the seat of any *município,* or district. But because the Brazilian *município* is often more comparable to a county in the United States than to a town, this includes some rather sparsely populated places. For this reason I have chosen a much higher cutoff point (in terms of population) to ensure that only distinctively urban environments fall into this category.

7. Positivism is an outlook rooted in the philosophy of Auguste Compte and his original French disciples.

8. Useful for comparative perspective, although of no direct value on Brazil, is Eric A. Nordlinger, *Soldiers in Politics: Military Coups and Governments* (Englewood Cliffs, NJ: Prentice-Hall, 1977). Other key books on the military in politics in broad comparative perspective, albeit also extremely weak on Brazil, are Amos Perlmutter, *The Military and Society in Modern Times: Professionals, Praetorians, and Revolutionary Soldiers* (New Haven, CT: Yale University Press, 1977) and Samuel E. Finer, *The Man on Horseback: The Role of the Military in Politics,* 2nd rev. ed. (Boulder, CO: Westview Press, 1988).

9. Alexandre de Souza Costa Barros, "The Brazilian Military: Professional Socialization, Political Performance and State Building" (unpublished Ph.D. dissertation, Department of Political Science, University of Chicago, 1978) is very useful, and two works of José Murilo de Carvalho are essential. See the latter's "As Forças Armadas na Primeira República: O Poder Desestabilisador," *Cadernos de Ciência Política da Universidade Federal de Minas Gerais* 1 (March 1974), pp. 111–188; and *Armed Forces and Politics in Brazil 1930–1945,* Working Paper No. 95 of the Latin American Program of the Woodrow Wilson Center for International Scholars (Washington, DC: Smithsonian Institution, 1980), published also in *Hispanic American Historical Review* 62, 2 (May 1982), pp. 193–223. The most valuable source by a "Brazilianist" (as opposed to a Brazilian) is Frank D. McCann, "The Military," in Michael L. Conniff and Frank D. McCann, eds., *Modern Brazil: Elites and Masses in Historical Perspective* (Lincoln: University of Nebraska Press, 1989), pp. 47–80. Of interest regarding recent times is John Markoff and Silvio R. Duncan Baretta, "Professional Ideology and Military Activism in Brazil: Critique of a Thesis of Alfred Stepan," *Comparative Politics* 17, 2 (January 1985), pp. 175–191; John Markoff and Silvio R. Duncan Baretta, "Brazil's *Abertura:* Transition from What to What?" in James M. Malloy and Mitchell A. Seligman, eds., *Authoritarians and Democrats: Regime Transitions in Latin America* (Pittsburgh, PA: University of Pittsburgh Press, 1987), pp. 43–65; and John Markoff and Silvio R. Duncan Baretta, "Economic Crises and Regime Change in Brazil: The 1960s and the 1980s," *Comparative Politics* 22, 4 (July 1990), pp. 421–444.

10. Barros, "The Brazilian Military," p. 57.

11. Ibid., p. 151, drawing on research by José Murilo de Carvalho.

12. The "dominant actual or potential power" of the Brazilian military in national political life was dated by Anthony Leeds to the time of the Paraguayan War. See his *Brazil as a System* (Amherst: University of Massachusetts International Studies Program, June 1977), pp. 6–7. See also Robert A. Hayes, *The Armed Nation: The Brazilian Corporate Mystique* (Tempe, AZ: Arizona State University, 1989).

13. Campos Coelho, *Em Busca de Identidade: O Exército e a Política na Sociedade Brasileira* (Rio de Janeiro: Editora Forense-Universitária, 1976).

14. Carvalho, "As Forças Armadas," *Cadernos de Ciência Política,* p. 141.

15. Eurico Dutra, *O Exército em dez anos de govêrno do Presidente Vargas* (Rio de Janeiro: Imprensa Militar, 1941), p. 27.

16. José Murilo de Carvalho, "As Forças Armadas na Primeira República: O Poder Desestabilisador," in *História Geral da Civilização Brasileira,* Tomo 3, Vol. 2, *Sociedade*

e Instituições (1889–1930) (São Paulo: Difusão Editorial, 1977), especially pp. 221–224.

17. Carvalho, "As Forças Armadas," *Cadernos de Ciência Política*, p. 161.
18. Barros, "The Brazilian Military," p. 139.
19. Ibid., pp. 53–54.
20. Ibid., p. 48.
21. Simon Schwartzman, "Representação e Cooptação Política no Brasil," *Dados* 6 (1969), pp. 24–56. See also Simon Schwartzman, *São Paulo e o Estado Nacional* (São Paulo: Difusão Editorial do Livro, 1975).
22. June E. Hahner, *Poverty and Politics: The Urban Poor in Brazil, 1870–1920* (Albuquerque: University of New Mexico Press, 1986), p. 37.
23. Eleven Brazilian economists make these points clear in Marcelo de Paiva Abreu, ed., *A Ordem do Progresso: Cem Anos de Política Econômica Republicana, 1889–1989* (Rio de Janeiro: Editora Campus, 1989). See especially pp. 7–9. The editor of the work, Marcelo de Paiva Abreu, became a high-ranking Economics Ministry official in March 1990.
24. A graphic analysis of the factors leading to the near disappearance of the Brazilian Indians is found in John Hemming, *Amazon Frontier: The Defeat of the Brazilian Indians* (Cambridge, MA: Harvard University Press, 1988), which carries to 1910 the story begun in John Hemming, *Red Gold: The Conquest of the Brazilian Indians* (Cambridge, MA: Harvard University Press, 1978).
25. See Roberto da Matta, "The Quest for Citizenship in a Relational Universe," in John D. Wirth, Edson de Oliveira Nunes, and Thomas E. Bogenschild, eds., *State and Society in Brazil: Continuity and Change* (Boulder, CO: Westview Press, 1987), pp. 307–335, especially p. 315. For background consult Manuel Diegues, *Regiões Culturais do Brasil* (Rio de Janeiro: Centro Brasileira de Pesquisas Educacionais/Ministério da Educação e Cultura, 1960).
26. Charles Wagley, *An Introduction to Brazil*, rev. ed. (New York: Columbia University Press, 1971), pp. 167–185.
27. See Linda Lewin, *Politics & Parentela in Paraíba: A Case Study of Family-based Oligarchy in Brazil* (Princeton, NJ: Princeton University Press, 1987).
28. Roberto DaMatta, *O que faz o brasil, Brasil?* (Rio de Janeiro: Editora Rocco, 1984), especially pp. 23–33. These ideas are expanded upon in Roberto DaMatta, *A Casa e a Rua: Espaço, cidadania, mulher e morte no Brasil* (São Paulo: Editora Brasiliense, 1985).
29. Roberto DaMatta, "The Ethic of *Umbanda* and the Spirit of Messianism: Reflections on the Brazilian Model," in Thomas C. Bruneau and Philippe Faucher, eds., *Authoritarian Capitalism: Brazil's Contemporary Economic and Political Development* (Boulder, CO: Westview Press, 1981), pp. 239–264.
30. Ibid., p. 251. Also of use is Roberto DaMatta, *Carnavais, malandros e heróis: Para uma sociologia de dilema Brasileira* (Rio de Janeiro: Zahar Editores, 1979).
31. This subject is well treated in Anthony Leeds, "Brazilian Careers and Social Structure," *American Anthropologist* 66, 6 (December 1964), pp. 1321–1347.
32. Consult DaMatta, *O que faz o brasil, Brasil?* pp. 97–101. It may be argued that DaMatta is primarily concerned with literate and urban Brazilians. For an approach stressing popular culture, consult Renato Ortiz, *Cultura Brasileira e Identidade Nacional* (São Paulo: Editora Brasiliense, 1985).
33. Aspásia Camargo and Walder de Góes, *Meio Século de Combate, Diálogo com Cordeiro de Farias* (Rio de Janeiro: Editora Nova Fronteira, 1981).

Chapter 2

1. Emília Viotti da Costa, *The Brazilian Empire* (Chicago: University of Chicago Press, 1985), p. xxiv. Her more detailed views are contained in *Da senzala à colônia* (São Paulo: Difusão Européia do Livro, 1966).

2. A scheme for integrating economic, social, and political factors is included in Ronald M. Schneider, "Brazil's Political Future," in Wayne A. Selcher, ed., *Political Liberalization in Brazil: Dynamics, Dilemmas, and Future Prospects* (Boulder, CO: Westview Press, 1986), pp. 217–260.

3. Nathaniel H. Leff, *Underdevelopment and Development in Brazil*, Vol. 2, *Reassessing the Obstacles to Economic Development* (London: Allen & Unwin, 1982), p. 103.

4. Viotti da Costa, *The Brazilian Empire*, p. xvii.

5. Caio Prado Júnior, *The Colonial Background of Modern Brazil* (Berkeley and Los Angeles: University of California Press, 1969), pp. 4–5. Here and in Caio Prado Júnior, *Evolução Política do Brasil e Outros Estudos*, 4th ed. (São Paulo: Editora Brasiliense, 1963), he provides a coherent Marxist interpretation of Brazil's history, something also found in Nelson Werneck Sodré, *Formação Histórico do Brasil*, 3rd ed. (São Paulo: Editora Brasiliense, 1964).

6. See Immanuel Wallerstein, *The Modern World-System 1: Capitalist Agriculture and the Origins of the European World-Economy in the Sixteenth Century* (New York: Academic Press, 1974), pp. 38–52. Of great value for putting Brazil in perspective regarding the global interests of Portugal are the writings of Charles R. Boxer, particularly *The Portuguese Seaborne Empire, 1415–1825* (New York: Alfred A. Knopf, 1969) and *Salvador de Sá and the Struggle for Brazil and Angola, 1602–1686* (London: University of London Press, 1952). A comprehensive treatment of Portugal's exploration and settlement of Brazil can be found in Sérgio Buarque de Holanda, ed., *História Geral da Civilização Brasileira*, Tomo 1, Vol. 1, *A Época Colonial: Do Descobrimento à Expansão Territorial* (São Paulo: Difusão Editorial do Livro, 1960) and Alexander Marchant, *From Barter to Slavery: The Economic Relations of Portuguese and Indians in the Settlement of Brazil, 1500–1580*, 2nd ed. (Gloucester, MA: P. Smith, 1966).

7. The detailed workings of the Portuguese system and its application to Brazil are explored by Raymundo Faoro in *Os Donos do Poder: Formação do Patronato Político Brasileiro*, 2nd ed. (Porto Alegre, Brazil: Editora Globo, 1975), particularly Vol. 1, pp. 97–137. Fernando Uricoechea in *The Patrimonial Foundations of the Brazilian Bureaucratic State* (Berkeley and Los Angeles: University of California Press, 1980), pp. 11–12, maintains that neither Faoro's emphasis upon the king and the several organs of royal administration nor those interpretations that attribute the leading role in colonization to private groups is correct. In his view there was a "complex pattern of active participation by both protagonists." See also Vicente Costa Santos Tapajós, *A Política Administrativa de D. João III* (Brasília: Editora Universidade de Brasília, 1983) and Vicente Costa Santos Tapajós, *Organização Política e Administrativa do Império* (Brasília: Fundação Centro de Formação do Servidor Público, 1984).

8. Useful on colonial administration are the essays in Dauril Alden, ed., *Colonial Roots of Modern Brazil* (Berkeley and Los Angeles: University of California Press, 1973). E. Bradford Burns, *A History of Brazil*, 2nd ed. (New York: Columbia University Press, 1980) and Rollie E. Poppino, *Brazil: The Land and People* (New York: Oxford University Press, 1968) are more than serviceable surveys of Brazilian history.

9. See Instituto Brasileiro de Geografia e Estatística (IBGE), *Estatísticas Históricas do Brasil* (Rio de Janeiro: IBGE, 1987), p. 28. Less up-to-date is Armin K. Ludwig, *Brazil: A Handbook of Historical Statistics* (Boston: G. K. Hall, 1985). Still useful on the colonization and life of the several regions are the works of João Fernando de

Almeida Prado, including, among many others, *Primeiros Povoadores do Brasil, 1500–1530* (São Paulo: Companhia Editora Nacional [CEN], 1935); *O Brasil e o Colonialismo Europeu* (São Paulo: CEN, 1956); *São Vicente e as Capitanias do Sul do Brasil* (São Paulo: CEN, 1961); *Pernambuco e as Capitanias do Norte do Brasil* (São Paulo: CEN, 1939); *A Bahia e as Capitanias do Centro do Brasil*, 3 volumes (São Paulo: CEN, 1945–1950); and *A Conquista da Paraíba* (São Paulo: CEN, 1964).

10. John Hemming, in *Red Gold: The Conquest of the Brazilian Indians* (Cambridge, MA: Harvard University Press, 1978), pp. 487–492, carefully constructs this figure for the Indian population. Earlier works had placed this number as high as over 4 million or as low as 1 million. IBGE, *Estatísticas Históricas do Brasil*, p. 20, note 2, attributes to Maria Luiza Marcílio a figure of 2,432,000.

11. João Alfredo Libânio Guedes and Joaquim Ribeiro, *A União Ibérica—Administração do Brasil Holandes* (Brasília: Editora Universidade de Brasília, 1983).

12. IBGE, *Estatísticas Históricas do Brasil*, p. 58.

13. Charles R. Boxer, *The Dutch in Brazil, 1624–1654* (Oxford: Clarendon Press, 1957).

14. The character and role of the Brazilian frontiersmen are vividly treated in Poppino, *Brazil: The Land and People*, pp. 72–94, as well as in Richard M. Morse, ed., *The Bandeirantes: The Historical Role of the Brazilian Pathfinders* (New York: Borzoi Books, 1965) and in Clodomir Vianna Moog, *Bandeirantes and Pioneers* (New York: Alfred A. Knopf, 1964). On urban life, see Vivaldo Coaracy, *O Rio de Janeiro no Século Dezessete*, 2nd ed. (Rio de Janeiro: Livraria José Olympio Editora, 1965).

15. Eduardo Canabrava Barreiros, *Episódios da Guerra dos Emboabas e sua Geografia* (Belo Horizonte, Brazil: Editora Itatiaia, 1984).

16. Charles R. Boxer, *The Golden Age of Brazil, 1695–1750: Growing Pains of a Colonial Society* (Berkeley and Los Angeles: University of California Press, 1962), pp. 61–125, provides a masterful account of these events.

17. The African community had been in existence for almost a century. See Clóvis Moura, *Rebeliões da Senzala: Quilombos, insurreições guerillhas* (São Paulo: Edições Zumbi, 1959); Décio Freitas, *Palmares, A Guerra dos Escravos* (Rio de Janeiro: Edições Graal, 1976); Edison Carneiro, *O Quilombo dos Palmares*, 2nd ed. (São Paulo: Companhia Editora Nacional, 1958); and João Alves Filho, *Memorial dos Palmares* (Rio de Janeiro: Xenon Editora e Produtora Cultural, 1988). The community's leader, Zumbi, evaded capture and death until November 1695. For a broader treatment of the issue, see A.J.R. Russell-Wood, *The Black Man in Slavery and Freedom in Colonial Brazil* (New York: St. Martin's Press, 1982).

18. Detail on the second half of the eighteenth century is found in Dauril Alden's *Royal Government in Brazil with Special Reference to the Administration of the Marquis of Lavradio, 1769–1779* (Berkeley and Los Angeles: University of California Press, 1968). On the southern Brazilian colonies (which have frontiers with Spanish colonies), see Moysés Vellinho, *Capitania d'El-Rei: Aspectos Polêmicos da Formação Rio-Grandense* (Porto Alegre, Brazil: Editora Globo, 1964). There is also interesting material in Rudolph W. Bauss, "Rio de Janeiro: The Rise of Late Colonial Brazil's Dominant Emporium" (unpublished Ph.D. dissertation, Department of History, Tulane University, ca. 1977).

19. Consult Nelson Werneck Sodré, *As Razões da Independência* (Rio de Janeiro: Editora Civilização Brasileira, 1965), pp. 15–53.

20. Essential for this period is Tomo 1, Vol. 2 of the *História Geral da Civilização Brasileira*—henceforth *HGCB*—entitled *A Época Colonial: Administração, Economia, Sociedade* (São Paulo: Difusão Européia do Livro, 1960). Also consult Hélio de Alcântara Avellar, *Administração Pombalina* (Brasília: Editora Universidade de Brasília,

1983). Useful material on all the period is in Mitchell Gurfield, *Estrutura das Classes e Poder Político no Brasil Colonial* (João Pessoa, Brazil: Edições da Universidade Federal de Paraíba, 1983).

21. IBGE, *Estatísticas Históricas do Brasil*, p. 29.

22. Invaluable on this subject is Kenneth Maxwell, *Conflicts and Conspiracies: Brazil and Portugal, 1750-1808* (New York: Columbia University Press, 1973). Also essential is A.J.R. Russell-Wood, ed., *From Colony to Nation: Essays on the Independence of Brazil* (Baltimore, MD: Johns Hopkins University Press, 1975). Viotti da Costa, *The Brazilian Empire*, pp. 2–4, suggests the context of independence as a double crisis of the colonial system and absolute monarchy. Also of value is Vicente Barretto, *A Ideologia Liberal no Processo da Independência do Brasil, 1789-1824* (Brasília: Câmara dos Deputados, 1973).

23. Very useful for this whole period is Roderick J. Barman, *Brazil: The Forging of a Nation, 1798-1852* (Stanford, CA: Stanford University Press, 1988), with the decade before the arrival of the Portuguese court probed in pp. 9–41. See also Alexandre José de Mello Moraes, *História do Brasil-reino e do Brasil-império*, 2 vols. (Belo Horizonte, Brazil: Editora Itatiaia, 1982).

24. Rich detail on the late eighteenth century and early 1800s is found in Barman, *Brazil: Forging of a Nation*, pp. 9–64, and in Faoro, *Os Donos do Poder*, pp. 203–275. On the British dominance resulting from the 1810 treaties see Werneck Sodré, *As Razões da Independência*, pp. 125–173, as well as Alan K. Manchester, *British Preeminence in Brazil: Its Rise and Decline* (Chapel Hill: University of North Carolina Press, 1933).

25. IBGE, *Estatísticas Históricas do Brasil*, p. 28. José Honório Rodrigues, in *Independência: Revolução e ContraRevolução*, Vol. 2, *Economia e Sociedade* (Rio de Janeiro: Livraria Francisco Alves, 1975), p. 87, provides the number 3.96 million for 1823, while Nathaniel H. Leff, in *Underdevelopment and Development in Brazil*, Vol. 1, *Economic Structure and Change, 1822-1947* (London: Allen & Unwin, 1982), p. 15, puts the 1822 population at 4.7 million. On the events leading up to independence see Barman, *Brazil: Forging of a Nation*, pp. 42–96, and Emília Viotti da Costa, "Introdução ao Estudo da Emancipação Política do Brasil," in Carlos Guilherme Mota, ed., *Brasil em Perspectiva*, 3rd ed. (São Paulo: Difusão Européia do Livro, 1971), pp. 64–125.

26. On José Bonifácio see Viotti da Costa, *The Brazilian Empire*, pp. 24–52, and on other key figures of this drama consult Vol. 4, *A Liderança Nacional*, of Rodrigues, *Independência*.

27. For a description of the intricate maneuvering during this preliminary stage of independence, see Vol. 4, *A Evolução Política*, of Rodrigues, *Independência*; Pedro Octávio Carneiro da Cunha, "A fundação de um Império liberal," in *HGCB*, Tomo 2, *O Brasil Monárquico*, Vol. 1, *O Processo de Emancipação*, 2nd ed. (São Paulo: DIFEL, 1965), pp. 135–178; and the masterful reconstruction in Barman, *Brazil: Forging of a Nation*, pp. 97–129. Also useful is Carlos Guilherme Mota, ed., *Mil Oitocentos e Vinte e Dois: Dimensões* (São Paulo: Editora Perspectiva, 1972). The benchmark biography of Pedro is Sérgio Corrêa da Costa, *Every Inch a King* (New York: Alfred A. Knopf, 1950), but Neil Macaulay's *Dom Pedro: The Struggle for Liberty in Brazil and Portugal, 1798-1834* (Durham, NC: Duke University Press, 1986) is clearly the most important work on this controversial figure. Barman, *Brazil: Forging of a Nation*, pp. 97–129, treats the early years of Pedro's reign.

28. See Wanderley Pinho, "A Bahia, 1808-1856," in *HGCB*, Tomo 2, *O Brasil Monárquico*, Vol. 2, *Dispersão e Unidade* (São Paulo: Difusão Européia do Livro, 1964), pp. 242–311.

29. Consult Arthur Cézar Ferreira Reis, "O Grão-Pará e o Maranhão," in ibid., pp. 71–172, especially pp. 140–149, and Rodrigues, *Independência*, Vol. 3, *As Forças Armadas*, pp. 218ff.

30. In spite of its short life, this legislative body of roughly 100 members would furnish the empire with thirty-three senators, twenty-eight ministers, eighteen provincial presidents, seven counselors of state, and four regents. See Pedro Octávio Carneiro da Cunha, "A fundação de um Império liberal: Discusão de princípios," in *HGCB*, Tomo 2, Vol. 1, pp. 238–262.

31. Amaro Quintas, "A agitação republicana no Nordeste," in *HGCB*, Tomo 2, Vol. 1, pp. 207–237, provides a detailed treatment of developments in Pernambuco and neighboring provinces. Also useful is Manuel Correia de Andrade, *Movimentos Nativistas em Pernambuco: Setembrizada e Novembrada* (Recife, Brazil: Universidade Federal de Pernambuco, 1977).

32. See David Carneiro, *História da Guerra Cisplatina* (Brasília: Editora Universidade de Brasília, 1983). J. S. Soares de Souza, "O Brasil e o Prata até 1828," in *HGCB*, Tomo 2, Vol. 1, pp. 300–328, discusses independent Brazil's first war and its political ramifications. See also Euripedes Simões de Paula, "A organização do exército brasileiro," pp. 265–277 of the same volume. A broader context is furnished by Ron Seckinger, *The Brazilian Monarchy and the South American Republics, 1822–1831: Diplomacy and Statebuilding* (Baton Rouge: Louisiana State University Press, 1984).

33. The complex story of this impasse and its resolution is told in Pedro Octávio Carneiro da Cunha, "A fundação de um Império liberal: Primeiro reinado, reação, e revolução," in *HGCB*, Tomo 2, Vol. 1, pp. 379–404, as well as in Paulo Pereira Castro, "A 'Experiência Republicana,' 1831–1840," in *HGCB*, Tomo 2, Vol. 2, pp. 9–67. Barman, *Brazil: Forging of a Nation*, pp. 130–159, analyzes the 1825–1831 period, as does Afonso Arinos de Mello Franco in his and Jânio Quadros's *História do Povo Brasileiro*, Vol. 4, *O Império, O Escravismo, e o Unitarismo Político* (São Paulo: J. Quadros Editores Culturais, 1967), pp. 128–160.

34. Pedro's decision may well have been far less painful than most scholars have imagined. He had for several years been deeply concerned with the succession question in his native Portugal, and with his brother Miguel's seizure of the Portuguese throne in March 1828 in detriment to the rights of Miguel's child wife—Pedro's nine-year-old daughter—the emperor, still in his early thirties, could view his subsequent abdication as exchanging a new and somewhat uncomfortable crown for a time-honored throne. He did in fact become king of Portugal before his untimely death in 1834. Neil Macaulay, on the other hand, in his book *Dom Pedro*, portrays Pedro as less absolutist and depicts his enemies as far from truly liberal. Barman, in *Brazil: Forging of a Nation*, stresses the continuing desire of Brazilians to cut Portuguese-born down to size.

35. A law of May 4, 1831, had reduced the manpower ceiling to 14,342; that of August 30 cut the ceiling to 10,000. A law establishing the national guard was promulgated the following day. The most comprehensive treatment of the guard during the empire is Jeanne Berrance de Castro, "A Guarda Nacional," in *HGCB*, Tomo 2, Vol. 4, *Declínio e Queda do Império* (São Paulo: Difusão Européia do Livro, 1971), pp. 274–298, and this is expanded upon in Jeanne Berrance de Castro, *A milícia cidadã: A Guarda Nacional de 1831 à 1850* (São Paulo: Companhia Editorial Nacional, 1977). Consult also Uricoechea, *Patrimonial Foundations of the Brazilian Bureaucratic State*, pp. 61–154, and Werneck Sodré, *As Razões da Independência*, pp. 177–261. The best concise treatment of the first part of the 1830s is Barman, *Brazil: Forging of a Nation*, pp. 160–188.

36. Luíz Viana Filho, *A Sabinada: A República Baiana de 1837* (Rio de Janeiro: Editora José Olympio, 1938) and Paulo César Souza, *A Sabinada: A Revolta Separatista da Bahia, 1837* (São Paulo: Editora Brasiliense, 1987).

37. Júlio José Chiavenato, *Cabanagem: O Povo no Poder* (São Paulo: Editora Brasiliense, 1983) and João José Reis, *Rebelião Escrava no Brasil: A História do Levante dos Malês, 1839* (São Paulo: Editora Brasiliense, 1986).

38. See Maria de Lourdes Mônaco Janotti, *A Balaiada* (São Paulo: Editora Brasiliense, 1987) and Maria Januária Vilela Santos, *A Balaiada e a insurreição de escravos no Maranhão* (São Paulo: Editora Ática, 1983).

39. The late stages of the Regency and beginning of the era of Pedro II are thoughtfully analyzed in Barman, *Brazil: Forging of a Nation*, pp. 189–216.

40. Sandra Jatahy Pesavento, *A Revolução Faroupilha* (São Paulo: Editora Brasiliense, 1987); Morivalde Calvet Fagundes, *História da Revolução Faroupilha* (Caxias do Sul, Brazil: Editora da Universidade de Caxias do Sul, 1984); Spencer Leitman, *Raízes Sócio-Econômicas da Guerra dos Farrapos* (Rio de Janeiro: Edições Graal, 1979); and Fernando Henrique Cardoso, "Rio Grande do Sul e Santa Catarina," in *HGCB*, Tomo 2, Vol. 2, pp. 473–505, are all useful.

41. See Isabel Andrade Marson, *O Império do Progresso: A Revolução Praieira em Pernambuco, 1842-1855* (São Paulo: Editora Brasiliense, 1987) and Amaro Quintas, *O Sentido Social da Revolução Praieira* (Rio de Janeiro: Editora Civilização Brasileira, 1967).

42. Olavo Brasil de Lima, Jr., and Lúcia Maria Gomes Klein, "Atôres Políticos do Império," *Dados* 7 (1970), p. 74.

43. *Civic* and *praetorian* are basic concepts of Samuel Huntington, developed in his *Political Order in Changing Societies* (New Haven, CT: Yale University Press, 1968). Huntington's framework has been applied to Brazil in my *The Political System of Brazil: Emergence of a 'Modernizing' Authoritarian Regime, 1964-1970* (New York: Columbia University Press, 1971).

44. Useful sources on the political system of pre-independence Brazil include Antônio Octávio Cintra, "A Função Política no Brasil Colonial," *Revista Brasileira de Estudos Políticos* 18 (January 1965), pp. 81–104, and Fernando José Leite Costa, "Processo de Diferenciação na Sociedade Colonial," *Dados* 7 (1970), pp. 42–61. The 1840s and opening of the next decade are aptly assessed in Barman, *Brazil: Forging of a Nation*, pp. 206–232.

45. See Alan K. Manchester, "The Growth of Bureaucracy in Brazil," *Journal of Latin American Studies* 4, 1 (May 1971), pp. 77–83.

46. Uricoechea, *Patrimonial Foundations of the Brazilian Bureaucratic State*, pp. 64ff.

47. Berrance de Castro, "A Guarda Nacional," pp. 274–291.

48. In English on Pedro II there is Mary Wilhelmina Williams, *Dom Pedro the Magnanimous, Second Emperor of Brazil* (Chapel Hill: University of North Carolina Press, 1937). Much more fully researched is Pedro Calmon, *História de D. Pedro II*, 5 vols. (Rio de Janeiro: Livraria José Olympio Editora, 1975). The first volumes are titled *Infância e Mocidade, 1825-1853* and *Cultura e Política, Paz e Guerra, 1853-1870*.

49. IBGE, *Estatísticas Históricas do Brasil*, p. 58, provides the figures at five-year intervals; Leff, *Underdevelopment and Development in Brazil*, Vol. 1, pp. 20, 49, 53, Vol. 2, p. 6, gives other relevant data. Useful analysis is found in Emília Viotti da Costa, "O Escravo na Grande Lavora," in *HGCB*, Tomo 2, Vol. 3, *Reações e Transações* (São Paulo: Difusão Européia do Livro, 1967), pp. 135–188; Carlos Oberacker, Jr., "A Colonização Baseada no Regime da Pequena Propriedade Agricola," in ibid., pp. 220–244; and Paula Beiguelman, "O Encaminhamento Político do Problema da Escravidão no Império," in ibid., pp. 188–219. It seems that the slave population in

the mid-1860s, although declining, was still over 1.7 million. The number that had arrived from Africa between 1781 and 1852 was just over 2.1 million.

50. Leff, *Underdevelopment and Development in Brazil*, Vol. 1, pp. 15, 36–37, Vol. 2, p. 73, and Burns, *History of Brazil*, p. 183.

51. Nícia Vilela Luz, *A Luta Pela Industrialização do Brasil* (São Paulo: Editora Alfa-Omega, 1975), pp. 23–24. See also Stanley J. Stein, *The Brazilian Cotton Manufacture: Textile Enterprise in an Under Developed Area, 1850–1950* (Cambridge, MA: Harvard University Press, 1957).

52. Consult Stanley J. Stein, *Vassouras: A Brazilian Coffee County, 1850–1900* (Cambridge, MA: Harvard University Press, 1957).

53. See Faoro, *Os Donos do Poder*, pp. 390–399; Cléa Sarmento, "Estabilidade Governmental e Rotatividade de Elite Política no Brasil Imperial," *Dados* 29, 2 (1986), pp. 139–174; and Hélgio Trinidade, "A Construção do Estado Nacional na Argentina e no Brasil (1810–1900): Esboço de um Análise Comparada," *Dados* 28, 1 (1985), pp. 61–87. Also useful for the political issues and debates of the period is Nelson Werneck Sodré, *A História da Imprensa no Brasil* (Rio de Janeiro: Editora Civilização Brasileira, 1966), pp. 50–200.

54. José Murilo de Carvalho, *A Construção da Ordem: A Elite Política Imperial* (Rio de Janeiro: Editora Campus, 1980), p. 39. Consult also José Murilo de Carvalho, "A Bureaucracia Imperial: A Dialética de Ambigüidade," *Dados* 21 (1979), pp. 7–31, and José Murilo de Carvalho, *Teatro de Sombras: A Política Imperial* (São Paulo: Edições Vértice, 1988).

55. A *cartorio* is a very powerful kind of notary public whose stamp is required for any document to have validity. Because he usually has a monopoly in his area, he can charge high fees. *Cartorial* has come to describe a system in which private interests almost appropriate areas of government activity and enjoy near impunity.

56. Hélio Jaguaribe, *Brazilian Nationalism and the Dynamics of Its Political Development*, Studies in Comparative International Development 2, 4 (1966), p. 59. See also his *Condições Institucionais de Desenvolvimento* (Rio de Janeiro: Instituto Superior de Estudos Brasileiros, 1958).

57. Uricoechea, *Patrimonial Foundations of the Brazilian Bureaucratic State*, pp. 25ff.

58. Ibid., pp. 56–57, and Barman, *Brazil: Forging of a Nation*, p. 226.

59. The most systematic treatment of the political system as relatively democratic is João Camilo de Oliveira Torres, *A Democracia Coroada: Teoria Política do Império do Brasil*, 2nd ed. (Petrópolis, Brazil: Editora Vozes, 1964). More specialized and empirical works include Phillip N. Evanson, "The Liberal Party and Reform in Brazil, 1860–1889" (unpublished Ph.D. dissertation, Department of History, University of Virginia, 1969), and Eul-Soo Pang and Ron L. Seckinger, "The Mandarins of Imperial Brazil," *Comparative Studies in History and Society* 9, 2 (April 1971), pp. 215–244. Also useful is Vamireh Chacon, *História dos Partidos Brasileiros* (Brasília: Editora Universidade de Brasília, 1980). The quite different view from below comes through in Thomas Flory, *Judge and Jury in Imperial Brazil, 1808–1871: Social Control and Political Stability in the New State* (Austin: University of Texas Press, 1981).

60. See Murilo de Carvalho, *Teatro de Sombras*, pp. 140–141.

61. Ibid., pp. 107–138.

62. On the parties see Murilo de Carvalho, *A Construção da Ordem*, chap. 8, and Barman, *Brazil: Forging of a Nation*, pp. 224–229.

63. See Murilo de Carvalho, *Teatro de Sombras*, pp. 50–83.

64. The politics of this period are covered by Francisco Iglésias, "Vida política 1848/1868," in *HGCB*, Tomo 2, Vol. 3, pp. 9–112, and Faoro, *Os Donos do Poder*, pp. 329–394.

65. John Schulz, "O Exército e o Império," in *HGCB*, Tomo 2, Vol. 4, *Declínio e Queda do Império* (São Paulo: Difusão Européia do Livro, 1971), pp. 235–238, is most reliable on these matters. More detail is provided in his "The Brazilian Army and Politics, 1850–1894" (unpublished Ph.D. dissertation, Department of History, Princeton University, 1973). Also of very substantial value for the period after 1865 is William S. Dudley, "Reform and Radicalism in the Brazilian Army, 1870–1889" (unpublished Ph.D. dissertation, Department of History, Columbia University, 1972). Consult also Dudley's articles "Institutional Sources of Officer Discontent in the Brazilian Army, 1870–1889," *Hispanic American Historical Review* 55 (February 1974), pp. 44–65, and "Professionalism and Politicization as Motivational Factors in the Brazilian Army Coup of 15 November 1889," *Journal of Latin American Studies* 8, 1 (May 1976), pp. 101–124.

66. Schulz, "O Exército e o Império," p. 240.

67. Brasil de Lima, Jr., and Gomes Klein, "Atôres Políticas no Império," p. 79, furnish the breakdown of the several chambers by members' occupations for the period 1826–1858.

68. Berrance de Castro, "A Guarda Nacional," p. 29, provides figures for 1839 to 1870. Those from 1865 on, however, apparently cover only troops stationed in Brazil, excluding the far greater numbers participating in the war with Paraguay. A table of force levels from 1830 to 1888 is furnished in Dudley, "Reform and Radicalism," pp. 244–247.

69. Dudley, "Reform and Radicalism," pp. 232–238, is the best source on military expenditures and troop levels for the latter half of the empire, with figures up to mid-century in Brasil de Lima, Jr., and Gomes Klein, "Atôres Políticas no Império," pp. 66–71. Consult also Luis Aureleano Gama de Andrade, "Dez Anos de Orçamento Imperial (1867/1877)," *Revista Brasileira de Estudos Políticos* 31 (May 1971), pp. 181–206, and Murilo de Carvalho, *Teatro de Sombras*, pp. 23–49.

70. See Umberto Peregrino, *História e Projeção das Instituições Culturais do Exército* (Rio de Janeiro: Biblioteca do Exército, 1967).

71. The most useful treatments of the Paraguayan War are Augusto Tasso Fragoso, *História da Guerra entre a Triplice Aliança e o Paraguay*, 5 vols. in 3 (Rio de Janeiro: Imprensa do Estado Maior de Exército, 1934) and Antônio de Souza, Jr., "Guerra do Paraguai," *HGCB*, Tomo 2, Vol. 4, pp. 299–314. A revisionist view, particularly in its sympathy to the plight of the Paraguayan masses, is found in Anatólio Alves de Assis, *Genocídio na Guerra do Paraguay* (Belo Horizonte, Brazil: Imprensa Oficial de Minas Gerais, 1986).

72. Iglésias, "Vida política 1848/1868," pp. 102–112, treats the political reflections of the war, and Faoro, *Os Donos do Poder*, pp. 444–447, views it as a watershed in the evolution of the army as a political force. See also Frederick M. Nunn, "Military Professionalism and Professional Militarism in Brazil, 1870–1970: Historical Perspectives and Political Implications," *Journal of Latin American Studies* 4, 1 (May 1972), pp. 29–54.

73. De Souza, Jr., "Guerra do Paraguai," p. 314. Dudley, "Reform and Radicalism," p. 48, calculates the Brazilian military mobilization at 111,650 men (excluding civilians), and some estimates of casualties reach 50,000—although this figure probably includes those who contracted disabling illnesses.

74. Consult Nícia Vilela Luz, "As Tentativas de Indústria no Brasil," in *HGCB*, Tomo 2, Vol. 3, pp. 28–41.

75. Burns, *History of Brazil*, p. 156.

76. On this period see Calmon, *História de D. Pedro II*, Vol. 3, *No País e no Estrangeiro, 1870–1887; HGCB*, Tomo 2, Vol. 4, especially Roque Spencer M. de Barros,

"A Questão Religiosa," pp. 338–365; and *HGCB*, Tomo 2, Vol. 5, *Do Império a República* (São Paulo: Difusão Européia do Livro, 1971), passim.

77. See June E. Hahner, *Poverty and Politics: The Urban Poor in Brazil, 1870–1920* (Albuquerque: University of New Mexico Press, 1986), p. 40. Somewhat lower figures are found in Leff, *Underdevelopment and Development in Brazil*, Vol. 1, pp. 49–53, and Vol. 2, pp. 7, 60.

78. Ibid., Vol. 2, pp. 84–89, 107.

79. The best estimates for growth in these years are found in Raymond W. Goldsmith, *Brasil 1850–1984: Desenvolvimento Financeiro sob um Século de Inflação* (São Paulo: Harper & Row do Brasil, 1986), pp. 20–27.

80. Vilela Luz, *A Luta Pela Industrialização do Brasil*, pp. 49–66. Consult Anyda Marchant, *Viscount Mauá and the Empire of Brazil: A Biography of Irineu Evangelista de Souza, 1813–1889* (Berkeley and Los Angeles: University of California Press, 1965), and Roderick Barman, "Business and Government in Imperial Brazil: The Experience of Viscount Mauá," *Journal of Latin American Studies* 13, 2 (November 1981), pp. 239–264.

81. See Murilo de Carvalho, *Teatro de Sombras*, pp. 84–106.

82. Leff, *Underdevelopment and Development in Brazil*, Vol. 2, p. 85.

83. Dudley, "Reform and Radicalism," p. 6.

84. Berrance de Castro, "A Guarda Nacional," p. 298.

85. See Frank D. McCann, *A Nação Armada: Ensaios sobre a História de Exército Brasileiro* (Recife, Brazil: Editora Guararapes, 1982), p. 16. On the broader question of the decline of the monarchical system consult Francisco José de Oliveira Vianna, *O Occaso do Império* (São Paulo: Companhia Melhoramentos de São Paulo, 1925), and Heitor Lyra, *História da queda do império* (São Paulo: Companhia Editora Nacional, 1964).

86. Joseph L. Love, "Political Participation in Brazil, 1881–1969," *Luso-Brazilian Review* 7, 2 (December 1970), pp. 3–24. Compared to these 142,000 electors, under the old system there had been an estimated 1 million *votantes*, albeit eligible to vote only at the local-level first stage, while the parliamentary electors had been far fewer. The best figures on elections and the electorate are in Walter Costa Porto, *O Voto no Brasil: Da Colônia à Quinta República* (Brasília: Gráfica do Senado Federal, 1989).

87. For a detailed treatment of this period see Calmon, *História de D. Pedro II*, Vol. 4, *A Abolição e a República, 1887–1889*, as well as George C. A. Boehrer, *Da monarquia à república: História do Partido Republicano do Brasil, 1870–1889* (Rio de Janeiro: Ministério de Educação e Cultura, 1954), and Reinaldo Carneiro Pessoa, *A Idéia Republicana no Brasil, Através dos Documentos* (São Paulo: Editora Alfa-Omega, 1973).

88. Schulz, "O Exército e o Império," p. 241, concludes that the salaried source of income and educational level of Brazilian officers during the second half of the nineteenth century are more important in explaining their political behavior than their social or geographic origins.

89. Dudley, "Reform and Radicalism," pp. 199, 200, 202, provides in tabular form the military experience of a sample of these three generational groups of officers broken down by branch of service. For a Brazilian military perspective see Tristão de Alencar Araripe, *Tasso Fragoso: Um pouco de história do nosso Exército* (Rio de Janeiro: Biblioteca de Exército, 1960).

90. Gama de Andrade, "Dez Anos de Orçamento Imperial," p. 205. Irene Maria Magalhães, "Antecedentes da República: Intervencionismo Militar e Legitimidade," *Dados* 7 (1970), pp. 172–178, samples the press during the 1884–1889 period, finding

that, though the monarchy was viewed as lacking in legitimacy, only a small proportion of the public considered military intervention a legitimate alternative.

91. Dudley, "Reform and Radicalism," p. 427.

92. Viotti da Costa, *The Brazilian Empire*, pp. 202ff., makes a persuasive case that the religious question was not an important cause of the monarchy's demise. For greater detail consult her *Da Monarquia à República—Momentos Decisivos* (São Paulo: Editorial Grijalbo, 1977). Also useful on the church-state conflict of the 1870s is Nilo Pereira, *Conflito Entre a Igreja e o Estado no Brasil* (Recife, Brazil: Universidade Federal de Pernambuco, 1970).

93. June E. Hahner, *Civilian-Military Relations in Brazil, 1889–1898* (Columbia: University of South Carolina Press, 1969), p. 10n, points out that thirty-six of sixty-three war ministers during the reign of Pedro II were civilians. Before 1865, however, the proportions were eighteen military to seven civilians, and during the 1875–1882 period army heroes in this post came to be the rule.

94. See Raimundo Magalhães Júnior, *Deodoro: A Espada contra o Império* (São Paulo: Companhia Editora Nacional, 1957), especially Vol. 1, *O Aprendiz de Feiticeiro (da Revolta Praieira ao Gabinete Ouro Preto)*.

95. The most comprehensive study of the Military Club is in Robert Hayes, "The Formation of the Brazilian Military Class and Its Political Behavior, 1807–1930" (unpublished Ph.D. dissertation, Department of History, University of New Mexico, 1969).

96. Standard sources on the abolitionist movement include Robert Conrad, *The Destruction of Brazilian Slavery, 1850–1888* (Berkeley and Los Angeles: University of California Press, 1972) and Robert Brent Toplin, *The Abolition of Slavery in Brazil* (New York: Atheneum, 1971). See also Conrad's *Brazilian Slavery: An Annotated Bibliography* (Boston: G. K. Hall, 1977); Leslie Bethell, *The Abolition of the Brazilian Slave Trade: Britain, Brazil, and the Slave Trade Question, 1807–1869* (Cambridge: Cambridge University Press, 1970); and Seymour Drescher, "Brazilian Abolition in Comparative Perspective," *Hispanic American Historical Review* 68, 3 (August 1988), pp. 429–460. José Maria dos Santos, *Os Republicanos Paulistas e Abolição*, 2nd ed. (São Paulo: Livraria Martins, 1965) and Célia Maria Marinho de Azevedo, *Onda Negra, Medo Branco: O Negro no Imaginário das Elites do Século XIX* (Rio de Janeiro: Editora Paz e Terra, 1988) are also useful, as are two studies by Evaristo de Moraes, *A Escravidão Africana no Brasil* (Brasília: Editora Universidade de Brasília, 1986) and *A Campanha Abolicionista (1879–1888)* (Brasília: Editora Universidade de Brasília, 1986), both reprints of pre-1930 works.

97. For a detailed discussion of Republican attitudes toward the military see Hahner, *Civilian-Military Relations in Brazil*, pp. 19–28. Dudley, "Reform and Radicalism," pp. 458–479, treats military attitudes toward republicanism.

98. Magalhães Júnior, *Deodoro*, Vol. 1, pp. 289–299.

99. Consult Américo Albuquerque, *Floriano Peixoto. O consolidador da república* (Rio de Janeiro: Typografia Moreira Maximino, 1894); Arthur Vieira Peixoto, *Biografia do Marechal Floriano Peixoto* (Rio de Janeiro: Ministério da Educação, 1939); and Francolino Camêu and Artur Vieira Peixoto, *Floriano Peixoto—Vida e Governo* (Brasília: Editora Universidade de Brasília, 1983).

100. On orders and honors more broadly in the imperial regime see Eul-Soo Pang, *In Pursuit of Honor and Power: Noblemen of the Southern Cross in Nineteenth-Century Brazil* (Tuscaloosa: University of Alabama Press, 1988).

101. Hélio Silva, *1889: A República não Esperou o Amanhecer* (Rio de Janeiro: Editora Civilização Brasileira, 1972), pp. 117–119.

102. Magalhães Júnior, *Deodoro*, Vol. 2, *O Galo na Torre (do desterro em Mato Grosso a fundação da República)*, pp. 56–82, and Dudley, "Reform and Radicalism," pp. 538–

551. If anything more was needed to push Deodoro into the arms of the conspirators it was the very ill-advised naming of a longtime personal enemy, Senator Gaspar da Silveira Martins, to be the next prime minister.

103. Goldsmith, *Brasil 1850–1984*, p. 27. See also Frank Colson, "On Expectations— Perspectives on the Crisis of 1889 in Brazil," *Journal of Latin American Studies* 13, 2 (November 1981), pp. 265–292.

104. Viotti da Costa, *The Brazilian Empire*, pp. 230–232. São Paulo would insist upon federalism in the new regime's constitution and would continue to champion federalism, especially at those times when a Paulista did not occupy the presidency.

105. Huntington, *Political Order in Changing Societies*, p. 199.

106. Ibid., pp. 204–205.

107. These totals are based primarily upon Vilela Luz, *A Luta Pela Industrialização do Brasil*, p. 63.

Chapter 3

1. Thomas E. Skidmore, *Black into White: Race and Nationality in Brazilian Thought* (New York: Oxford University Press, 1974), p. viii.

2. José Murilo de Carvalho, *Os bestializados: O Rio de Janeiro e a República que não foi* (São Paulo: Companhia das Letras, 1987), p. 42. Useful on these years are José Enio Casalecchi, *O Partido Republicano Paulista: Política e Poder, 1889–1926* (São Paulo: Editora Brasiliense, 1987); Maria de Lourdes Mônaco Janotti, *Os Subversivos da República* (São Paulo: Editora Brasiliense, 1986); Suely Robles Reis de Queiroz, *Os Radicais da República: Jacobinismo—Ideologia e Ação, 1893–1897* (São Paulo: Editora Brasiliense, 1986); and Décio Saes, *A Formação do Estado Burgues no Brasil, 1888–1891* (Rio de Janeiro: Editora Paz e Terra, 1985). A broader treatment can be found in Saes's earlier work *Classe Média e Política na Primeira República Brasileira, 1889–1930* (Petrópolis, Brazil: Editora Vozes, 1975).

3. Insightful on the decline of the northeast are Peter L. Eisenberg, *The Sugar Industry in Pernambuco: Modernization Without Change* (Berkeley and Los Angeles: University of California Press, 1974), and Richard Graham, "Government Expenditures and Political Change in Brazil, 1880–1899, Who Got What," *Journal of Interamerican Studies and World Affairs* 19 (August 1977), pp. 339–368.

4. Figures are from June Hahner, *Poverty and Politics: The Urban Poor in Brazil, 1870–1920* (Albuquerque: University of New Mexico Press, 1986), p. 7; Nathaniel H. Leff, *Underdevelopment and Development in Brazil*, Vol. 2, *Reassessing the Obstacles to Economic Development* (London: Allen & Unwin, 1982), p. 10; and Fernando H. Cardoso, "Dos Governos Militares à Prudente-Campos Sales," in *História Geral da Civilização Brasileira* (HGCB), Tomo 3, Vol. 1, *Estrutura de Poder e Economia, 1889–1930* (São Paulo: Difusão Européia do Livro, 1975), p. 14. Also see Edgard Carone, *A República Velha I (Instituições e Classes Sociais)*, 2nd ed. (São Paulo: Difusão Européia do Livro, 1972), pp. 147–246. Extremely valuable is Angela Porto, Lilian de A. Fritsch, and Sylvia F. Padilha, *Processo de Modernização do Brasil, 1850–1930* (Rio de Janeiro: Fundação Casa de Rui Barbosa, 1985), an annotated bibliography that includes over 2,050 items.

5. Consult Aspásia de Alcântara Camargo, "A Questão Agrária. Crise do Poder e Reformas de Base (1930–1964)," in *HGCB*, Tomo 3, Vol. 3, *Sociedade e Política, 1930–1964*, 3rd ed. (São Paulo: Difusão Editorial, 1986), p. 130.

6. Roderick J. Barman, *Brazil: The Forging of a Nation, 1798–1852* (Stanford, CA: Stanford University Press, 1988), p. 242.

7. The best sources on the economy and economic policy in the period of the mid-1880s to mid-1890s include Anníbal Villanova Villela and Wilson Suzigan, *Política do Governo e Crescimento da Economia Brasileira, 1889–1945* (Rio de Janeiro: Instituto de Planejamento Econômico e Social, 1973); Wilson Suzigan, *Indústria Brasileira: Origem e Desenvolvimento* (São Paulo: Editora Brasiliense, 1986); Leff, *Underdevelopment and Development in Brazil;* Nícia Vilela Luz, *A Luta Pela Industrialização do Brasil* (São Paulo: Editora Alfa-Omega, 1975); and Carone, *A República Velha I*, pp. 72–129. See also Paula Beiguelman, *A Formação de Povo no Complexo Cafeeiro: Aspectos Políticos* (São Paulo: Livraria Pioneira Editora, 1968); Eugene W. Ridings, "Interest Groups and Development: The Case of Brazil in the Nineteenth Century," *Journal of Latin American Studies* 9, 2 (November 1977), pp. 225–250; Eugene W. Ridings, "Class Sector Unity in an Export Economy: The Case of Nineteenth-Century Brazil," *Hispanic American Historical Review* 58, 3 (August 1978), pp. 432–444; Eugene W. Ridings, "Business, Nationality and Dependency in Late Nineteenth-Century Brazil," *Journal of Latin American Studies* 14, 1 (May 1982), pp. 55–96; and Steven Topik, "The Evolution of the Economic Role of the Brazilian State, 1889–1930," *Journal of Latin American Studies* 11, 2 (November 1979), pp. 325–342. Topik argues that although the state came to intervene extensively in the economy, such intervention was not at all opposed to private capitalist interests, but rather often was on behalf of those interests.

8. Leff, *Underdevelopment and Development in Brazil*, Vol. 2, p. 144.

9. See Richard Graham, *Britain and the Onset of Modernization in Brazil, 1850–1914* (Cambridge: Cambridge University Press, 1968), pp. 51–72.

10. On the 1888–1898 period, consult Gustavo H. B. Franco, "A Primeira Década Republicana," in Marcelo de Paiva Abreu, ed., *A Ordem do Progresso: Cem Anos de Política Econômica Republicana, 1889–1989* (Rio de Janeiro: Editora Campus, 1989), pp. 11–30; Vilela Luz, *A Luta Pela Industrialização do Brasil*, pp. 168–174; and Raymond W. Goldsmith, *Brasil 1850–1984: Desenvolvimento Financeiro sob um Século de Inflação* (São Paulo: Harper & Row do Brasil, 1986), p. 110. Goldsmith puts money-supply expansion at a very big level, with M1 expansion at 98.9 and 50.6 percent for 1890 and 1891 while M2 lagged just behind at 94.5 and 42.5 percent. (M1 includes currency, checking accounts, and other demand deposits; M2 adds to these savings accounts, time deposits, money market funds, and similar means of payment of high liquidity.)

11. Villanova Villela and Suzigan, *Política do Governo e Crescimento da Economia Brasileira*, pp. 31–32.

12. Richard Graham, "Landowners and the Overthrow of the Empire," *Luso-Brazilian Review* 7, 2 (December 1970), pp. 44–56.

13. See John D. Wirth, *Minas Gerais in the Brazilian Federation, 1889–1937* (Palo Alto, CA: Stanford University Press, 1977), pp. 12ff.

14. Cardoso, "Dos Governos Militares à Prudente-Campos Sales," p. 38.

15. Leoncio Basbaum, *História Sincera da República*, Vol. 2, *De 1889 à 1930* (São Paulo: Editôra Fulgor, 1958), p. 27. Maria Antonieta de A. G. Parahyba, "Abertura Social e Participação Política no Brasil," *Dados* 7 (1970), pp. 89–102, compares social participation (in terms of literacy, urbanization, and economically active population) with political participation (measured by eligibility to vote) for the period 1872–1920. She finds no opening of the political sphere under the Old Republic, except in the center-south, particularly in São Paulo and Rio Grande do Sul. Yet even in that more dynamic part of the country, political participation lagged far behind that in the social sphere. The same data is related to more strictly economic changes in Nancy Alessio, "Urbanização, Industrialização e Estrutura Ocupacional (1872–1920)," *Dados* 7 (1970), pp. 103–117.

16. Raimundo Magalhães Júnior, *Deodoro: A Espada contra o Império*, Vol. 2 (São Paulo: Companhia Editora Nacional, 1957), pp. 83–141, gives detail on the organization of the new regime, as does Edgard Carone, *A Primeira República (1889–1930) Texto e Contexto* (São Paulo: Difusão Européia do Livro, 1969), pp. 13–16, and Edgard Carone, *A República Velha II (Evolução Política)* (São Paulo: Difusão Européia do Livro, 1971), pp. 7–28.

17. See June E. Hahner, *Civilian-Military Relations in Brazil, 1889–1898* (Columbia: University of South Carolina Press, 1969), pp. 34–42, and Afonso Arinos and Jânio Quadros, *História do Povo Brasileiro*, Vol. V, *A República, as Oligarquias Estaduais* (São Paulo: J. Quadros Editores Culturais, 1967), pp. 13–25. José Maria Bello, *A History of Modern Brazil* (Palo Alto, CA: Stanford University Press, 1966), pp. 59–62, sketches government figures.

18. Magalhães Júnior, *Deodoro*, Vol. 2, pp. 127–137, 283–309, deals with the work of the assembly and its election of Deodoro. See also Hahner, *Civilian-Military Relations*, pp. 40–46, and Bello, *History of Modern Brazil*, pp. 77–84. In Rio de Janeiro only 28,585 voted out of a potential 109,421 literate males over twenty-one not serving as soldiers or priests. See Murilo de Carvalho, *Os bestializados*, p. 85.

19. Magalhães Júnior, *Deodoro*, Vol. 2, pp. 238–264.

20. The center of the dispute between Deodoro and the Congress was a law of October 2 that specified "crimes of responsibility" by a president. Deodoro objected to Congress saying that various acts by a president would be illegal and hence would be just cause for the president's removal. Deodoro's veto was overridden through a questionable maneuver of Congress's presiding officer, Prudente de Morais. Deodoro's short tenure as constitutional chief executive is treated in ibid., pp. 327–358; Carone, *A República Velha II*, pp. 34–51; and Hélio Silva, *1889: A República não Esperou o Amanhecer* (Rio de Janeiro: Editora Civilização Brasileira, 1972), pp. 161–184.

21. Basbaum, *História Sincera da República*, Vol. 2, p. 15. Carone, *A Primeira República*, pp. 17–24, contains key statements by Deodoro and Floriano.

22. Bello, *History of Modern Brazil*, pp. 89–106, has an excellent brief sketch of Floriano and his administration. Hahner, *Civilian-Military Relations*, pp. 51–72, provides relevant detail, as do Carone, *A República Velha II*, pp. 51–132, and Silva, *1889: A República não Esperou o Amanhecer*, pp. 187–233. See also Francolino Camêu, *Floriano Peixoto* (Brasília: Editora Universidade de Brasília, 1983), a reprint of a work originally published in 1925.

23. The best brief treatment of this episode is in Glauco Carneiro, *História das Revoluções Brasileiras*, Vol. 1, *Da Revolução da República à Coluna Prestes, 1889/1927* (Rio de Janeiro: Edições "O Cruzeiro," 1965), pp. 50–62. More detailed is Felisberto Freire, *História da Revolta da 6 de Setembro de 1893* (Brasília: Editora Universidade de Brasília, 1982).

24. Hahner, *Civilian-Military Relations*, pp. 56–69, provides a useful analysis of the motivations and goals of the several contending forces, as does Joseph L. Love, *Rio Grande do Sul and Brazilian Regionalism: 1882–1930* (Palo Alto, CA: Stanford University Press, 1971), pp. 47–75. For greater detail, consult Wenceslau Escobar, *Apontamentos para a História da Revolução Rio-grandense de 1893* (Brasília: Editora Universidade de Brasília, 1983). See also Eduardo Klugelmas, "A Primeira República no Periodo de 1894 à 1909," in Paula Beiguelman, *Pequenos Estudos de Ciência Política* 2 (São Paulo: Livraria Pioneira Editora, 1968), pp. 145–170, and Maria do Carmo Campello de Souza, "O Processo Político Partidário na Primeira República," in Carlos Guilherme Mota, ed., *Brasil em Perspectiva*, 3rd ed. (São Paulo: Difusão Européia do Livro, 1971), pp. 162–226.

25. See Raúl Oliveira Rodrigues, *Um Militar contra o militarismo: A vida de Saldanha da Gama* (Rio de Janeiro: Edições "O Cruzeiro," 1959).

26. For a discussion of the legalist versus reformist doctrines within the army during the first half of the twentieth century, consult Estevão Leitão de Carvalho, *Dever Militar e Política Partidária* (São Paulo: Companhia Editora Nacional, 1959). Hahner, *Civilian-Military Relations*, pp. 73–97, provides a sound introduction to the situation in the 1890s. Key for understanding the military's role is José Murilo de Carvalho, "As Forças Armadas na Primeira República: O Poder Desestabilisador," in *HGCB*, Tomo 3, Vol. 2, *Sociedade e Instituições (1889–1930)* (São Paulo: Difusão Editorial, 1977), pp. 181–234.

27. *Jornal do Comércio*, June 16, 1893, as quoted in Hahner, *Civilian-Military Relations*, p. 94.

28. Consult Fernando de Azevedo, *Canaviais e Engenhos na Vida Política de Brasil: Ensaio sociológico sobre o elemento político na civilização do açucar*, 2nd ed. (São Paulo: Edições Melhoramentos, 1959), pp. 75–83, 93–103, as well as his *A Cultura Brasileira*, 4th ed. (São Paulo: Edições Melhoramentos, 1964), pp. 178–200.

29. Hélio Jaguaribe, *Condições Institucionais de Desenvolvimento* (Rio de Janeiro: Instituto Superior de Estudos Brasileiros, 1958), pp. 14–22. A useful sketch of the bureaucracy in the nineteenth century is Robert T. Daland, *Exploring Brazilian Bureaucracy: Performance and Pathology* (Washington, DC: University Press of America, 1981), pp. 45–52.

30. Vilela Luz, *A Luta Pela Industrialização do Brasil*, pp. 104–117; Raymundo Faoro, *Os Donos do Poder: Formação do Patronato Político Brasileiro*, Vol. 2, 2nd ed. (Porto Alegre, Brazil: Editora Globo, 1975), pp. 506–518; and Goldsmith, *Brasil 1850–1984*, pp. 106–109. More detail is in Luiz Antônio Tannuri, *O Encilhamento* (São Paulo: Editora Hucitec, 1981). Franco, "A Primeira Década Republicana," p. 23, refers to "hesitations and omissions" on the part of Ruy's two short-lived successors. One of those successors, Francisco de Paula Rodrigues Alves, finding little political support for his "responsible" conservative policies, quit after just nine months.

31. Hahner, *Civilian-Military Relations*, pp. 25–48, presents an analysis of São Paulo's exploitation of the civil war and naval revolt to end the Republican dictatorship and put into effect a civilian administration.

32. Consult Heloisa Rodrigues Fernandes's comprehensive *Política e Segurança* (São Paulo: Editora Alfa-Omega, 1974), and her essay "A Força Pública do Estado do São Paulo," in *HGCB*, Tomo 3, Vol. 2, pp. 235–256.

33. See Hahner, *Civilian-Military Relations*, pp. 110–124, and Carone, *A República Velha II*, pp. 128–132.

34. Bello, *History of Modern Brazil*, p. 137, maintains that "Even on the day power was transferred to his successor, he could have tried, and probably could have carried off, the dreaded coup, had he not been more inclined to stubborn resistance than to bold ventures."

35. Government–armed forces relationships during this period are well treated in Hahner, *Civilian-Military Relations*, pp. 149–182. Carone, *A República Velha II*, pp. 135–173, and Silva, *1889: A República não Esperou o Amanhecer*, pp. 237–294, provide rich detail on policy and politics.

36. A good summary of this incident is in Carneiro, *História das Revoluções Brasileiras*, Vol. 1, pp. 96–117. The flavor of this tragedy is immortalized in Euclydes da Cunha's classic *Rebellion in the Backlands* (Chicago: University of Chicago Press, 1944). See also Maria Isaura Pereira de Queiroz, *O Messianismo no Brasil e no Mundo* (São Paulo: Dominus Editora/Edusp, 1965), pp. 324ff.; Edmundo Moniz, *A Guerra Social de Canudos* (Rio de Janeiro: Editora Civilização Brasileira, 1978); Edmundo Moniz, *Canudos* (Rio de Janeiro: Elô Editora, 1987); J. C. Ataliba Nogueira, *Antônio Conselheiro e Canudos* (São Paulo: Companhia Editora Nacional, 1974); Robert M.

Levine, " 'Mud-Hut' Jerusalem: Canudos Revisited," *Hispanic American Historical Review* 68, 3 (August 1988), pp. 525–572; and Tristão de Alencar Araripe, *Expedições Militares contra Canudos: Aspecto Marcial* (Rio de Janeiro: Biblioteca do Exército, 1960).

37. On the political ramifications of the Canudos affair, consult Francisco de Assis Barbosa's treatment in Arinos and Quadros, *História do Povo Brasileiro*, Vol. 5, pp. 79–88.

38. Joseph L. Love, "Political Participation in Brazil, 1881–1969," *Luso-Brazilian Review* 7, 2 (December 1970), pp. 7–9, calculates electoral participation at 2.7 percent of the total population, as contrasted with 117,700 voters, or .89 percent, of total population for the 1886 parliamentary elections. Consult also Emmanuel Sodré, *Lauro Sodré na História da República* (Rio de Janeiro: Edição do Autor, 1970).

39. Assis Barbosa, in Arinos and Quadros, *História do Povo Brasileiro*, Vol. 5, p. 121. Campos Salles had but one finance minister, Joaquim Murtinho, who was an advocate of extreme austerity.

40. Love, "Political Participation," is the most systematic expansion of this thesis. Renato Lessa, *A Invenção Republicana: Campos Sales, as Bases e a Decadência da Primeira República Brasileira* (São Paulo: Edições Vértice, 1987), is a thoughtful analysis. Carone, *A Primeira República*, pp. 99–114, contains insightful selections from Campos Salles's writings on this system and style of politics. Carone's *A República Velha II*, pp. 174–196, is also useful.

41. Celso Peçanha, *Nilo Peçanha e a Revolução Brasileira* (Rio de Janeiro: Editora Civilização Brasileira, 1969), p. 60. See also Carone, *A República Velha II*, pp. 196–226, and Afonso Arinos de Mello Franco, *Rodrigues Alves: Apogeu e Declínio do Presidencialismo*, Vol. 2 (Rio de Janeiro: Livraria José Olympio Editora, 1973).

42. See Murilo de Carvalho, *Os bestializados*, pp. 91–139, and Jeffrey D. Needell, "The *Revolta Contra Vacina* of 1904: The Revolt Against 'Modernization' in Belle-Époque Rio de Janeiro," *Hispanic American Historical Review* 67, 2 (May 1987), pp. 233–268, as well as Needell's broader *A Tropical Belle Époque: Elite Culture & Society in Turn-of-the-Century Rio de Janeiro* (New York: Cambridge University Press, 1988). Carneiro, *História das Revoluções Brasileiras*, Vol. 1, pp. 136–150, also analyzes the 1904 revolt. Manuel Ferraz de Campos Salles, *Da Propaganda à Presidência* (São Paulo: Typografia "A Editora," 1908), is valuable for an understanding of the period. See also Alcindo Guarabara, *A Presidência Campos Sales* (Brasília: Editora Universidade de Brasília, 1983), and Antônio Joaquim Ribas, *Perfil Biográfico do Dr. Manoel Ferraz de Campos Sales* (Brasília: Editora Universidade de Brasília, 1983). These are reprints of works originally published early in the century.

43. See João Neves da Fontoura, *Memórias*, Vol. 1, *Borges de Medeiros e seu Tempo* (Porto Alegre, Brazil: Editora Globo, 1958), pp. 79–80. All 211 officers and 394 cadets expelled received amnesty in September 1905. See Frank D. McCann, "The Military," in Michael L. Conniff and Frank D. McCann, eds., *Modern Brazil: Elites and Masses in Historical Perspective* (Lincoln: University of Nebraska Press, 1989), pp. 50–51, and João Batista Mascarenhas de Moraes, *Memórias*, Vol. 1 (Rio de Janeiro: Livraria José Olympio Editora, 1969), pp. 102–103.

44. Paulo Sérgio Pinheiro, "O Proletariado Industrial na Primeira República," in *HGCB*, Tomo 3, Vol. 2, p. 139.

45. See Leff, *Underdevelopment and Development in Brazil*, Vol. 1, pp. 123, 166; Maria Tereza Schorer Petrone, "Imigração," in *HGCB*, Tomo 3, Vol. 2, pp. 93–133; and Boris Fausto, "Expansão de Café e Política Cafeeira," in *HGCB*, Tomo 3, Vol. 1, pp. 195–248. Also relevant are Maria Lígia Coelho Prado and Maria Helena Rolim Capelato, "A Borracha na Economia Brasileira da Primeira República," in *HGCB*, Tomo 2, Vol. 1, pp. 287–307, and Carone, *A República Velha I*, pp. 27–68.

46. On economic and fiscal policy of this era, consult Villanova Villela and Suzigan, *Política do Governo e Crescimento da Economia Brasileira*, pp. 35–38, 99–133; Vilela Luz, *A Luta Pela Industrialização do Brasil*, pp. 180–190; and Steven Topik, *The Political Economy of the Brazilian State, 1889–1930* (Austin: University of Texas Press, 1987).

47. Joaquim Duarte Murtinho, finance minister for almost all of Campos Salles's term, stressed a fairly consistent policy of reducing the quantity of paper money in circulation. In many respects Murtinho was a precursor of today's advocates of combatting inflation through a drastic reduction of liquidity—as was done by the Collor government in March 1990.

48. Afonso Arinos, *Rodrigues Alves*, Vol. 2, pp. 448–465, and Thomas H. Holloway, *Vida e Morte do Convênio de Taubaté: A Primeira Valorização do Café* (Rio de Janeiro: Editora Paz e Terra, 1978).

49. A useful reassessment of the economic policy of the governments from Rodrigues Alves through the end of the Old Republic is Winston Fritsch, "Apogeu e Crise na Primeira República: 1900–1930," in Paiva Abreu, ed., *A Ordem do Progresso*, pp. 31–72.

50. Biographies of Pinheiro Machado include José da Costa Porto, *Pinheiro Machado e seu Tempo* (Porto Alegre, Brazil: L & PM Editores, 1985), and Ciro Silva, *Pinheiro Machado* (Brasília: Editora Universidade de Brasília, 1982).

51. Love, *Rio Grande do Sul and Brazilian Regionalism*, pp. 138–141, details the maneuvering for the presidential nomination. On Pena's brief administration, see Bello, *History of Modern Brazil*, pp. 196–207, and Carone, *A República Velha II*, pp. 226–244.

52. Cardoso, "Dos Governos Militares à Prudente-Campos Sales," pp. 46–49.

53. See Frank D. McCann, *A Nação Armada: Ensaios sobre a História de Exército Brasileiro*, (Recife, Brazil: Editora Guararapes, 1982), pp. 33–36.

54. The intricate story of the precampaign maneuvering by all parties and factions is well told in Arinos and Quadros, *História do Povo Brasileira*, Vol. 5, pp. 161–177.

55. Bello, *History of Modern Brazil*, pp. 208–215, usefully sketches this interim regime and the campaign. See also Peçanha, *Nilo Peçanha e a Revolução Brasileira*, passim, and Luíz Viana Filho, *A Vida de Ruy Barbosa*, 7th ed. (São Paulo: Livraria Martins Editora, 1965), pp. 330–339.

56. The fullest account of this incident is in Edmar Morel, *A Revolta da Chibata: Subsídios para a História da Revolta na Esquadra pelo Marinheiro João Cândido em 1910* (Rio de Janeiro: Irmões Pongetti Editores, 1959), which should be supplemented by the more recent Marcos A. Silva, *Contra a Chibata: Marinheiros Brasileiros em 1910* (São Paulo: Editora Brasiliense, 1982).

57. Bello, *History of Modern Brazil*, p. 169.

58. Gláúcio Ary Dillion Soares, *Sociedade e Política no Brasil (Desenvolvimento, Classe e Política durante a Segunda República)* (São Paulo: Difusão Européia do Livro, 1973), pp. 17–31.

59. Alcântara Camargo, "A Questão Agrária," pp. 131–132.

60. Among the best sources on the political system of the Old Republic are Vitor Nunes Leal, *Coronelismo, Enxada e Voto: O Município e o Regime Representativo no Brasil* (Rio de Janeiro: Revista Forense, 1948); José Maria dos Santos, *A Política Geral do Brasil* (São Paulo: J. Magalhães, 1930); Maria Isaura Pereira de Queiroz, *O mandonismo local na vida política brasileira e outros ensaios* (São Paulo: Editora Alfa-Omega, 1976); Maria Isaura Pereira de Queiroz, "O Coronelismo: Numa Interpretação Sociológica," in *HGCB*, Tomo 3, Vol. 1, pp. 155–190; Carone, *A República Velha I*, pp. 249–342;

and Marcos Vinícius Vilaça and Roberto de Albuquerque, *Colonel, Coroneis* (Rio de Janeiro: Edições Tempo Brasileiro, 1965).
    61. On Hermes's presidential term see Carone, *A República Velha II*, pp. 255–296.
    62. See José de Costa Porto, *Os Tempos de Rosa e Silva* (Recife, Brazil: Concórdia, 1970), pp. 161–192.
    63. Consult Raymundo Giro, *Pequeno História de Ceará*, 2nd ed. (Fortaleza, Brazil: Instituto de Ceará, 1962), and Abelardo Montenegro, *História dos partidos políticos Cearenses* (Fortaleza, Brazil: A Batista Fontenele, 1965).
    64. The most comprehensive and systematic study of Padre Cícero and his movement is Ralph della Cava, *Miracle at Joazeiro* (New York: Columbia University Press, 1970). Consult also Rui Facó, *Cangaceiros e Fanáticos* (Rio de Janeiro: Editora Civilização Brasileira, 1963); Otacílio Anselmo, *Padre Cícero: Mito e Realidade* (Rio de Janeiro: Editora Civilização Brasileira, 1968); Amalia Xavier de Oliveira, *O Padre Cícero que Eu Conheci (Verdadeira História de Juazeiro do Norte)* (Rio de Janeiro: Gráfica Olmpica Editora, 1969); and Edmar Morel, *Padre Cícero: O Santo do Juazeiro* (Rio de Janeiro: Editora Civilização Brasileira, 1966).
    65. Neves da Fontoura, *Memórias*, Vol. 1, pp. 188–189, and Love, *Rio Grande do Sul and Brazilian Regionalism*, pp. 156–163.
    66. This Canudos-type problem is most throughly treated in Maurício Vinhas de Queiroz, *Messianismo e Conflito Social: A guerra sertaneja do Contestado, 1912–1916* (Rio de Janeiro: Editora Civilização Brasileira, 1966); Oswaldo R. Cabral, *A Campanha do Contestado* (Florianópolis, Brazil: Editora Lunardelli, 1979); Marli Auras, *Guerra do Contestado* (Florianópolis, Brazil: Editora da Universidade Federal de Santa Catarina, 1984); Duglas Teixeira Monteiro, *Os Errantes do Novo Século* (São Paulo: Livraria Duas Cidades, 1974); and Duglas Teixeira Monteiro, "Um Confronto entre Juazeiro, Canudos, e Contestado," in *HGCB*, Tomo 3, Vol. 2, pp. 39–92.
    67. Neves da Fontoura, *Memórias*, Vol. 1, p. 201. Good on the years from 1910 to 1918 are Love, *Rio Grande do Sul and Brazilian Regionalism*, pp. 165–171; Arinos and Quadros, *História do Povo Brasileiro*, Vol. 5, pp. 207–216; and Faoro, *Os Donos do Poder*, Vol. 2, pp. 579–654.
    68. See Frank D. McCann, "The Formative Period of Twentieth-Century Brazilian Army Thought 1900–1922," *Hispanic American Historical Review* 64, 4 (November 1984), pp. 737–765; Leitão de Carvalho, *Dever Militar e Política Partidária*, pp. 42–44; and Carone, *A República Velha I*, pp. 345–372.
    69. McCann, *A Nação Armada*, pp. 31–42, and Nelson Werneck Sodré, *História Militar do Brasil* (Rio de Janeiro: Editora Civilização Brasileira, 1965), pp. 198–200.
    70. Neves da Fontoura, *Memórias*, Vol. 1, pp. 202–203, and Love, *Rio Grande do Sul and Brazilian Regionalism*, pp. 168–174. Carone, *A República Velha II*, pp. 296–315, treats the Bráz administration.
    71. See Afonso Arinos, *Rodrigues Alves*, Vol. 2, pp. 828–833.
    72. Consult Linda Lewin, *Politics and Parentela in Paraíba: A Case Study in Family-based Oligarchy in Brazil* (Princeton, NJ: Princeton University Press, 1987), especially Chapter 7, "Pessoa in Power," pp. 308ff. See also Carone, *A República Velha II*, pp. 319–360. Also of use are Assis Barbosa, in Arinos and Quadros, *História do Povo Brasileiro*, Vol. 5, pp. 239–268; Epitácio Pessôa, *Pela Verdade* (Rio de Janeiro: Nacional, 1926); and Laurita Pessoa Raja Gabaglia, *Epitácio Pessôa (1865–1942)*, 2 vols. (Rio de Janeiro: Livraria José Olympio Editora, 1951).
    73. Fritsch, "Apogeu e Crise na Primeira República," pp. 37–41, treats the "Gold Era" of 1900–1913, with analysis of the wartime period (World War I) on pp. 41–45. He concludes that these latter years did not give a boost to industry overall owing to the difficulty of acquiring necessary components and inputs from abroad.

74. Goldsmith, *Brasil 1850–1984*, pp. 84, 144, 155, and Leff, *Underdevelopment and Development in Brazil*, Vol. 1, p. 166, Vol. 2, p. 9.

75. Hahner, *Poverty and Politics*, p. 88. Hahner's total for immigration from 1884–1923 comes to 2.76 million, somewhat lower than Leff, *Underdevelopment and Development in Brazil*, Vol. 1, p. 67, which gives a figure of 2.8 million for 1885 through 1909. See also Michael M. Hall, "The Origins of Mass Immigration in Brazil, 1871–1914" (unpublished Ph.D. dissertation, Department of History, Columbia University, 1969).

76. See Suzigan, *Indústria Brasileira*, pp. 43–44, 48–58, as well as Goldsmith, *Brasil 1850–1984*, p. 147.

77. Suzigan, *Indústria Brasileira*, pp. 72, 347; Vilela Luz, *A Luta Pela Industrialização do Brasil*, pp. 150–157, 193–200; and Villanova Villela and Suzigan, *Política de Governo e Crescimento da Economia Brasileira*, pp. 42–44, 135–150.

78. Edgard Carone, *Revoluções do Brasil contemporâneo 1922/1938* (São Paulo: Desa Editôra, 1965), pp. 23–24, and Eul-Soo Pang, *Bahia in the First Republic: Coronelism and Oligarchies, 1889–1934* (Gainesville: University of Florida Press, 1979).

79. Neves da Fontoura, *Memórias*, Vol. 1, pp. 235–250, develops the thesis that 1921 was the true root of the 1930 Revolution.

80. Carone, *Revoluções do Brasil contemporâneo*, pp. 26–35, furnishes a good summary of the 1921–1922 replay of the Military Question as army and civilian government authorities again came to loggerheads. See also his *A Primeira República*, pp. 57–58, 119–121, as well as Peçanha, *Nilo Peçanha e a Revolução Brasileira*, pp. 113–146.

81. The literature on the letters affair and the subsequent revolt has reached enormous proportions. Hélio Silva, *1922: Sangue na Areia da Copacabana* (Rio de Janeiro: Editora Civilização Brasileira, 1964), contains almost overwhelming detail and copious documentation. Glauco Carneiro, *O Revolucionário Siqueira Campos*, 2 vols. (Rio de Janeiro: Gráfica Record Editora, 1966), pp. 67–171, deals with events leading up to the revolt, with the events of the July 5 revolt detailed on pp. 173–265. See also Nair de Teffe Hermes da Fonseca, *A Verdade Sôbre a Revolução de 22* (Rio de Janeiro: Gráfica Portinho Cavalcanti, 1974). On the marshal's life and personality, see Hermes da Fonseca Filho, *Marechal Hermes: Dados para uma biografia* (Rio de Janeiro: Instituto Brasileiro de Geografia e Estatística, 1961).

82. Silva, *1922: Sangue na Areia da Copacabana*, pp. 71–72. Carone, *A República Velha II*, pp. 361–392, covers the Bernardes administration. In many ways the best book on the topic of *tenentismo* is José Augusto Drummond, *O Movimento Tenentista: Intervenção Militar e Conflito Hierárquico (1922–1935)* (Rio de Janeiro: Edições Graal, 1986).

83. Neves da Fontoura, *Memórias*, Vol. 1, pp. 251–261, provides some interesting sidelights on these developments. Significantly the turnout in this hotly contested election was 50 percent above the previous high.

84. Silva, *1922: Sangue na Areia da Copacabana*, p. 49.

85. The violence of the polemic can be seen from the excerpts of the Military Club session of June 25 included in Werneck Sodré, *História Militar do Brasil*, pp. 202–208. A balanced assessment is in Lawrence H. Hall, "João Pandiá Calogeras, Minister of War, 1919–1922: The Role of a Civilian in the Development of the Brazilian Army" (unpublished Ph.D. dissertation, Department of History, New York University, 1983).

86. See Everardo Dias, *História das Lutas Sociais no Brasil* (São Paulo: Editora Edaglit, 1962), pp. 87–130; Silva, *1922: Sangue na Areia da Copacabana*, passim; Edgard Carone, *O Tenentismo: Acontecimentos, Personagens, Programas* (São Paulo: Difusão

Editorial, 1975), pp. 21–43; and Henry Hunt Keith, "Soldiers as Saviors: The Brazilian Military Revolts of 1922 and 1924 in Historical Perspective" (unpublished Ph.D. dissertation, Department of History, University of California, Berkeley, 1969).

87. Silva, *1922: Sangue na Areia da Copacabana*, pp. 188–208, provides many details on the Military Academy and Vila Militar uprisings.

88. See Drummond, *O Movimento Tenentista*, p. 99.

89. On the 1922–1923 Rio Grande do Sul crisis, consult ibid., pp. 283–359; Neves da Fontoura, *Memórias*, Vol. 1, pp. 261–301; and Love, *Rio Grande do Sul and Brazilian Regionalism*, pp. 199–215. Edgard Costa, *Os Grandes Julgamentos do Supremo Tribunal Federal, Primeiro Volume (1892–1925)* (Rio de Janeiro: Editora Civilização Brasileira, 1964), pp. 326–335, 376–393, 442–450, covers the court proceedings concerning those arrested with respect to the 1922 uprising, with a similar treatment of 1924 on pp. 494–516.

90. See Fernando Setembrino de Carvalho, *Memórias—Dados para a História do Brasil* (Rio de Janeiro: n.p., 1950).

91. Carone, *O Tenentismo*, pp. 47–83, 271–279, 301–308. Dias, *História das Lutas Sociais no Brasil*, pp. 130–138, recounts early contacts between dissatisfied military and radical labor leaders. João Alberto Lins de Barros, *Memórias de um Revolucionário* (Rio de Janeiro: Editora Civilização Brasileira, 1954), pp. 19–22, points out how five months in prison following the 1922 uprising brought him together with scores of young officers and facilitated their indoctrination by Joaquim Távora and other revolutionary leaders.

92. The standard monograph is Ana Maria Martínez Correa, *A rebelião de 1924 em São Paulo* (São Paulo: Editora Hucitec, 1976). Silva, *1922: Sangue na Areia da Copacabana*, pp. 363–412, and Carneiro, *História das Revoluções Brasileiras*, Vol. 1, pp. 263–284, provide detail on the revolt itself. See also John F. W. Dulles, *Anarchists and Communists in Brazil, 1900–1935* (Austin: University of Texas Press, 1973), pp. 233–266, and Drummond, *O Movimento Tenentista*, pp. 100–118.

93. See Juarez Távora's *A Guisa de Depoimento sôbre a Revolução Brasileira de 1924*, Vol. 1 (São Paulo: Editora "O Combate," 1927) and Vol. 3 (Rio de Janeiro: Mendonça e Machado, 1928), as well as his *Uma Vida e Muitas Lutas*, Vol. 1, *Da Planície a Borda do Altiplano* (Rio de Janeiro: Livraria José Olympio Editora, 1973), pp. 111–219.

94. See José Ibere Costa Dantas, *O Tenentismo em Sergipe* (Petrópolis, Brazil: Editora Vozes, 1974).

95. Silva, *1922: Sangue na Areia da Copacabana*, pp. 415–424.

96. Carneiro, *O Revolucionário Siqueira Campos*, Vol. 1, pp. 311–342; Hélio Silva, *1926: A Grande Marcha* (Rio de Janeiro: Editora Civilização Brasileira, 1965), pp. 43–72; and Carone, *O Tenentismo*, pp. 85–119, 294–300, cover events in Rio Grande do Sul.

97. See Neil Macaulay, *The Prestes Column: Revolution in Brazil* (New York: Franklin Watts, 1974), passim; Nelson Werneck Sodré, *A Coluna Prestes: Análise e depoimentos* (Rio de Janeiro: Editora Civilização Brasileira, 1980), passim; Carone, *O Tenentismo*, pp. 123–147, 301–316; and Lins de Barros, *Memórias de um Revolucionário*, pp. 61–189. An excellent synthesis is in Drummond, *O Movimento Tenentista*, pp. 119–166. Drummond points out that many did not believe in the prospects for a "war of movement," preferring to go into exile instead.

98. Drummond, *O Movimento Tenentista*, pp. 153–155, says that Bertholdo Klinger (then a major about to be promoted), in August 1925 on his own initiative, ceased to pursue the rebels in the field, calling for a political solution. Drummond concludes that both groups of professional soldiers were not eager for a battlefield confrontation

of the type and scale that would leave permanent scars and prevent future cooperation in the military realm.

Chapter 4

1. June E. Hahner, *Poverty and Politics: The Urban Poor in Brazil, 1870–1920* (Albuquerque: University of New Mexico Press, 1986), pp. 290–291.

2. Ibid., p. 291.

3. Hélio Jaguaribe, *Political Strategies of National Development in Brazil*, Studies in *Comparative International Development* 3, 2 (1967–1968), pp. 29–30.

4. Hélio Jaguaribe, *Brazilian Nationalism and the Dynamics of Its Political Development*, Studies in *Comparative International Development* 2, 4 (1966), p. 59.

5. Hahner, *Poverty and Politics*, p. 292.

6. José Augusto Drummond, *O Movimento Tenentista: Intervenção Militar e Conflito Hierárquico (1922–1935)* (Rio de Janeiro: Edições Graal, 1986), p. 78.

7. Maria do Carmo Campello de Souza, "O Processo Político-Partidário na Primeira República," in Carlos Guilherme Mota, ed., *Brasil em Perspectiva*, 3rd ed. (São Paulo: Difusão Européia do Livro, 1971), p. 221. Other formulations of the position and role of the middle class in the 1930s and 1940s include Boris Fausto, *A Revolução de 1930. Historiografia e História* (São Paulo: Editora Brasiliense, 1970); Boris Fausto, *Pequenos Ensaios de História da República (1889–1945)* (São Paulo: Centro Brasileiro de Análise e Planejamento, 1972); Celina do Amaral Peixoto Moreira Franco, Lucia Lippi de Oliveira, and Maria Aparecida Alves Himes, "O Contexto Político da Revolução de Trinta," *Dados* 7 (1970), pp. 118–136; Décio A. M. Saes, *Classe Média e Política na Primeira República Brasileira, 1889–1930* (Petrópolis, Brazil: Editora Vozes, 1975); Décio A. M. Saes, *Classe média e sistema política no Brasil* (São Paulo: T. A. Queiroz Editor); Décio A. M. Saes, "Classe Média e Política no Brasil, 1930–1964," in *História Geral da Civilização Brasileira (HGCB)*, Tomo 3, Vol. 3, pp. 447–506; and Paulo Sérgio Pinheiro, "Classes Médias Urbanas: Formação, Natureza, Intervenção na Vida Política," in *HGCB*, Tomo 3, Vol. 2, pp. 8–37.

8. Campello de Souza, "O Processo Político-Partidário," p. 225.

9. See Gláúcio Ary Dillon Soares, *Sociedade e Política no Brasil (Desenvolvimento, Classe e Política durante a Segunda República)* (São Paulo: Difusão Européia do Livro, 1973), pp. 38–39.

10. A good analysis of Luís's administration is in Edgard Carone, *A República Velha II (Evolução Política)* (São Paulo: Difusão Européia do Livro, 1971), pp. 392–430.

11. On the Communist Party during this period, see Astrojildo Pereira, *Formação do PCB, 1922–1928* (Rio de Janeiro: Editorial Vitória, 1962); Edgard Carone, *O PCB*, Vol. 1, *1922–1943* (São Paulo: Difusão Editorial, 1982); Eliezer Pacheco, *O Partido Comunista Brasileira, 1922–1964* (São Paulo: Editora Alfa-Omega, 1984); and Edgard Carone, *O Marxismo no Brasil: Das Origens à 1964* (São Paulo: DIFEL, 1986). Ronald H. Chilcote, *The Brazilian Communist Party: Conflict and Integration, 1922–1972* (Oxford: Oxford University Press, 1974), pp. 16–33, and John F. W. Dulles, *Anarchists and Communists in Brazil, 1900–1935* (Austin: University of Texas Press, 1973), pp. 233–306, are useful English-language treatments.

12. Paulo Nogueira Filho, *O Partido Democrático e a Revolução de 1930*, 2nd ed. (Rio de Janeiro: Livraria José Olympio Editora, 1965), pp. 152–272, deals with the establishment of the Democratic Party. Very useful is Maria Ligia Prado, *A Democracia Ilustrada: O Partido Democrático em São Paulo—1926–1934* (São Paulo: Editora Ática, 1986). See also Boris Fausto, "Expansão de Café e Política Cafeeira," in *HGCB*, Tomo

3, Vol. 2, pp. 415–417. Mauricio Font makes a strong case that dissatisfied large coffee planters played a key, if not dominant, role in the Democratic Party (PD), particularly between 1926 and 1930. See his "Coffee Planters, Politics, and Development in Brazil," *Latin American Research Review* 22, 3 (1977), pp. 69–90. Also highly relevant are Sérgio Silva, *Expansão Cafeeira e Origens da Indústria no Brasil* (São Paulo: Editora Alfa-Omega, 1981), and Thomas Holloway, *Immigrants on the Land: Coffee and Society in São Paulo* (Chapel Hill: University of North Carolina Press, 1980). Afonso Arinos de Mello Franco, *A Alma do Tempo* (Rio de Janeiro: Livraria José Olympio Editora, 1961), pp. 191–192, recounts how Antônio Carlos made a major effort to bring into his government representatives of the new generation from each of the state's traditionally important political families. The most perceptive contemporary study covering the decline of the Old Republic is Sertório de Castro, *A República que a Revolução Destruiu* (Rio de Janeiro: Freitas Bastos, 1932).

13. Drummond, *O Movimento Tenentista*, p. 171.

14. Dalcidio Jurandir as quoted in Glauco Carneiro, *O Revolucionário Siqueira Campos*, Vol. 2 (Rio de Janeiro: Gráfica Record Editora, 1966), p. 59.

15. A classic contemporary interpretation of *tenentismo* up to the São Paulo revolt is Virgínio Santa Rosa, *O Sentido do Tenentismo* (Rio de Janeiro: Schmidt, 1933). Other essential sources include Maria Cecília Spina Forjaz, *Tenentismo e Política: Tenentes e Camadas Médias Urbanas na Crise de Primeira República* (Rio de Janeiro: Editora Paz e Terra, 1982); Maria Cecília Spina Forjaz, *Tenentismo e Forças Armadas na Revolução de 30* (Rio de Janeiro: Editora Forense-Universitária, 1989); Edgard Carone, *O Tenentismo: Acontecimentos, Personagens, Programas* (São Paulo: Difusão Editorial, 1975); Eurico de Lima Figueiredo, ed., *Os Militares e a Revolução de 30* (Rio de Janeiro: Editora Paz e Terra, 1979); Octávio Malta, *Os Tenentes na Revolução Brasileira* (Rio de Janeiro: Editora Civilização Brasileira, 1969); and Paulo Sérgio Pinheiro, *Política e Trabalho no Brasil dos Anos Vinte ao 1930* (Rio de Janeiro: Editora Paz e Terra, 1975), pp. 53–68.

16. Estevão Leitão de Carvalho, *Dever Militar e Política Partidária* (São Paulo: Companhia Editora Nacional, 1959), p. 72. A useful interpretation of civil-military relations during the Old Republic is Edmundo Campos Coelho, *Em Busca de Identidade: O Exército e a Política no Sociedade Brasileira* (Rio de Janeiro: Editora Forense-Universitária, 1976), pp. 65–96. Essential on this for the Vargas era is José Murilo de Carvalho, "Armed Forces and Politics in Brazil 1930–1945," *Hispanic American Historical Review* 62, 2 (May 1982), pp. 193–223. Besides reconstructing the competition of the professionals versus the reformist-interventionist elements within the context of the political process of the times, Murilo de Carvalho provides figures for the size of the army and its budget over these years (pp. 211–212). See also Vanda Maria Ribeiro Cosa, "Com Rancor e com Afeto: Rebeliões Militares na Década de 30," *Estratégia e Política* 4, 2 (April–June 1986), pp. 174–200.

17. Carneiro, *O Revolucionário Siquiera Campos*, pp. 104–105. Also useful is Juarez Távora, *Uma Vida e Muitas Lutas*, Vol. 1 (Rio de Janeiro: Livraria José Olympio Editora, 1973), pp. 241–286. Though he stresses their concern for the military's interests over any social class ties or political program, Drummond agrees that the *tenentes* definitely saw the military as a special arbiter of the nation's political life. See Drummond, *O Movimento Tenentista*, p. 31.

18. Drummond, *O Movimento Tenentista*, pp. 63, 86.

19. See Raymond W. Goldsmith, *Brasil 1850–1984: Desenvolvimento Financeiro sob um Século de Inflação* (São Paulo: Harper & Row do Brasil, 1986), pp. 147, 155, as well as Anníbal Villanova Villela and Wilson Suzigan, *Política do Governo e Crescimento da Economia Brasileira, 1889–1945* (Rio de Janeiro: Instituto de Planejamento Economico

e Social, 1973), pp. 44–45, 151–178. Also useful is Joan L. Bak, "Cartels, Cooperatives, and Corporatism: Getúlio Vargas in Rio Grande do Sul on the Eve of Brazil's 1930 Revolution," *Hispanic American Historical Review* 63, 2 (May 1983), pp. 255–275. Winston Fritsch, "Apogeu e Crise na Primeira República: 1900–1930," in Marcelo de Paiva Abreu, ed., *A Ordem do Progresso: Cem Anos de Política Econômica Republicana, 1889–1989* (Rio de Janeiro: Editora Campus, 1989), pp. 46–71, analyzes the 1919–1930 period. See also Michael L. Conniff, *Rio de Janeiro in the Depression Era, 1920–1937* (Stanford, CA: Stanford University Press, 1975).

20. João Neves da Fontoura, *Memórias*, Vol. 2, *A Aliança Liberal e a Revolução de 1930* (Porto Alegre, Brazil: Editora Globo, 1963), p. 25.

21. Although a massive literature exists concerning Vargas and his more than two decades of national prominence, no fully adequate biography has yet been written. John F. W. Dulles, *Vargas of Brazil* (Austin: University of Texas Press, 1967), is more a chronicle of the era than an analytical study of the man. Similarly, Hélio Silva's multivolume "Vargas cycle" provides a vast amount of detail and documentation on the course of events but generally lacks systematic interpretation and focused study of the chief actor in the political drama. The third volume of the cycle, *1930: A Revolução Traida* (Rio de Janeiro: Editora Civilização Brasileira, 1966), treats developments through October of that fateful year. Affonso Henriques, *Ascensão e Queda de Getúlio Vargas* (Rio de Janeiro: Distribuidora Record, 1966), a three-volume work spanning 1930 to 1954, is consistently more harshly critical of Vargas than either Dulles or Silva is favorable to the *caudilho*. Official "court" biographies abounded in the 1930s and early 1940s, with the most useful work by an intimate admirer being Alzira Vargas do Amaral Peixoto, *Getúlio Vargas, meu Pai* (Porto Alegre, Brazil: Editora Globo, 1960). Also favorable is Luiz Vergara, *Fui Secretário de Getúlio Vargas: Memórias dos Anos de 1926–1954* (Porto Alegre, Brazil: Editora Globo, 1960), while Cláudio de Araújo Lima, *Mito e Realidade de Vargas*, 2nd ed. (Rio de Janeiro: Editora Civilização Brasileira, 1955), is a less than sympathetic psychological study. See also Rubens Vidal Araújo, *Os Vargas* (Porto Alegre, Brazil: Editora Globo, 1985); Vavy P. Borges, *Getúlio Vargas e a Oliguarquia Paulista* (São Paulo: Editora Brasiliense, 1985); Valentina de Rocha Lima, ed., *Getúlio: Uma história oral* (Rio de Janeiro: Editora Record, 1986); Paulo Brandi, *Vargas, da Vida para a História* (Rio de Janeiro: Zahar Editores, 1983); and Pedro Cezar Dutra Fonseca, *Vargas: O Capitalismo em Construção* (São Paulo: Editora Brasiliense, 1989). Fernando Jorge, *Getúlio Vargas e seu tempo: Um Retrato com Luz e Sombra*, Vol. 1, *1883–1900* (São Paulo: T. A. Queiroz Editor, 1987), is the beginning of a new multivolume study.

22. For a treatment of the second half of 1928 from the perspective of the São Paulo opposition, see Nogueira Filho, *O Partido Democrático*, pp. 273–334. The *tenentes* in exile are discussed in Carone, *O Tenentismo*, pp. 151–168, 317–365.

23. A wealth of detail on preliminary political maneuvering, including most of the relevant correspondence, is contained in Hélio Silva, *1926: A Grande Marcha* (Rio de Janeiro: Editora Civilização Brasileira, 1965), pp. 127–240. The broader context is provided in Raymundo Faoro, *Os Donos do Poder: Formação do Patronato Político Brasileiro*, 2nd ed. (Porto Alegre, Brazil: Editora Globo, 1975), pp. 663–685, 708–714, as well as Maria Cecília Spina Forjaz, *Tenentismo e Aliança Liberal* (São Paulo: Livraria Editora Polis, 1978). Neves da Fontoura, *Memórias*, Vol. 2, pp. 3–67, relates the Rio Grande do Sul vice-governor's role, and Nogueira Filho, *O Partido Democrático*, pp. 367–384, provides the São Paulo perspective on these developments. In English, see Dulles, *Anarchists and Communists*, pp. 307–399.

24. Silva, *1926: A Grande Marcha*, pp. 240–322, relates in detail the discussions and communications from the signing of the pact to the formal launching of Vargas's

candidacy in September. Neves da Fontoura, *Memórias*, Vol. 2, pp. 68–129, covers the same period from a more immediate perspective.

25. Silva, *1926: A Grande Marcha*, pp. 323–407, and Silva, *1930: A Revolução Traida*, pp. 36–105, provide an account of the exciting campaign with all its intrigues. Neves da Fontoura, *Memórias*, Vol. 2, pp. 130–307, recounts the campaign from the viewpoint of one of the Liberal Alliance's most active and militant architects. Nogueira Filho, *O Partido Democrático*, pp. 385–440, presents the strikingly different view from São Paulo. In English, see Dulles, *Anarchists and Communists*, pp. 401–444, and Jordan M. Young, *The Brazilian Revolution of 1930 and the Aftermath* (New Brunswick, NJ: Rutgers University Press, 1967), pp. 30–54.

26. For documents summarizing the AL program, see Nogueira Filho, *O Partido Democrático*, pp. 687–698, 702–706, 718–720. The full program can be found in Getúlio Vargas, *A Nova Política do Brasil*, Vol. 1 (Rio de Janeiro: Livraria José Olympio Editora, 1938), pp. 19–54. These two should be read in conjunction with Drummond, *O Movimento Tenentista*, pp. 167–203.

27. Neves da Fontoura, *Memórias*, Vol. 2, pp. 307–329, details the period.

28. See Silva, *1930: A Revolução Traida*, pp. 154–182; Adhemar Vidal, *João Pessoa e a Revolução de 30* (Rio de Janeiro: Edições Graal, 1978); Luiz Nunes, *A Morte de João Pessoa e a Revolução de 30* (João Pessoa, Brazil: Edições Aquarius, 1978); Henriques, *Ascensão e Queda de Getúlio Vargas*, pp. 104–116; and Neves da Fontoura, *Memórias*, Vol. 2, pp. 330–364.

29. For details, consult Silva, *1930: A Revolução Traida*, pp. 25–35, 106–120, as well as Lourival Coutinho, *O General Góes Depõe*, 2nd ed. (Rio de Janeiro: Livraria Editora Coelho Branco, 1956), pp. 59–87; Nogueira Filho, *O Partido Democrático*, pp. 441–492; Alexandre José Barbosa Lima Sobrinho, *A Verdade sôbre a Revolução de Outubro* (São Paulo: Gráfica-Editora Unidas, 1933); Virgílio A. de Mello Franco, *Outubro, 1930*, 2nd ed. (Rio de Janeiro: Editora Schmidt, 1931); and Maurício de Lacerda, *Segunda República* (Rio de Janeiro: Freitas Bastos, 1931).

30. Pereira, *Formação do PCB*, pp. 105–109. Consult also Abguar Bastos, *Prestes e a Revolução Social* (Rio de Janeiro: Editorial Calvino, 1946). Prestes moved to Buenos Aires, where he engaged in lengthy discussions with leaders of that country's Communist movement and rapidly evolved toward doctrinaire radical positions that set him apart from the mainstream of *tenentismo*. He continued to be active on the political scene until his death in early 1990.

31. João Alberto Lins de Barros, *Memórias de um Revolucionário* (Rio de Janeiro: Editora Civilização Brasileira, 1954), pp. 217–226, relates the conversations between Prestes and *tenente* leaders, and Silva expands upon them in *1930: A Revolução Traida*, pp. 121–147.

32. See Carneiro, *O Revolucionário Siquiera Campos*, Vol. 2, pp. 494–519, 527–567, and Juarez Távora, *Uma Vida e Muitas Lutas*, Vol. 1, pp. 288–334.

33. The texts of Prestes's statements are in Silva, *1930: A Revolução Traida*, pp. 417–426; Carneiro, *O Revolucionário Siquiera Campos*, Vol. 2, pp. 702–716; and Nogueira Filho, *O Partido Democrático*, pp. 710–718.

34. Coutinho, *O General Góes Depõe*, pp. 3–58, covers Góes Monteiro's pre-1930 activities.

35. Tristão de Alencar Araripe, *Tasso Fragoso: Um pouco de história do nosso Exército* (Rio de Janeiro: Biblioteca de Exército, 1960), pp. 525–611, treats Tasso Fragoso's role in the revolution.

36. Silva, *1930: A Revolução Traida*, pp. 185–364, provides ample details on the fighting. Also useful are Coutinho, *O General Góes Depõe*, pp. 78–148; Leitão de Carvalho, *Dever Militar e Política Partidária*, pp. 180–199; Agildo Barata, *Vida de um*

Revolucionário (Rio de Janeiro: Editora Melso, ca. 1963), pp. 89–146; and Nogueira Filho, *O Partido Democrático*, pp. 493–542.

37. Klinger's ideas, which led to his becoming the military chief of the 1932 São Paulo constitutionalist revolt, are summarized in Leitão de Carvalho, *Dever Militar e Política Partidária*, pp. 200–210, with Klinger's October 1930 role analyzed in pages 210–229. Klinger subsequently published a number of volumes on his views and experiences, the most relevant of which is *Parada e Desfile duma Vida de Voluntário do Brasil na primeira metade do século* (Rio de Janeiro: Empresa Gráfica "O Cruzeiro," 1958).

38. On the period of junta government, see Silva, *1930: A Revolução Traida*, pp. 364–416.

39. Coutinho, *O General Góes Depõe*, pp. 134–137; Klinger, *Parada e Desfile*, pp. 336–350; Pedro Aurélio de Góes Monteiro, *A Revolução de 30 e a Finalidade Político do Exército* (Rio de Janeiro: Aderson, 1934); and Alencar Araripe, *Tasso Fragoso*, pp. 571–608.

40. Silva, *1930: A Revolução Traida*, pp. 411–416, contains the speeches made at this time.

41. Hélio Silva, *1931: Os Tenentes no Poder* (Rio de Janeiro: Editora Civilização Brasileira, 1966), pp. 54–55, contains a summary of Vargas's "Program of National Reconstruction." See also Dulles, *Vargas of Brazil*, pp. 77–89, and Dulles, *Anarchists and Communists*, pp. 445–509. Fundamental sources on the Vargas era include Fundação Getúlio Vargas, *A Revolução de 30: Seminário Internacional* (Brasília: Editora Universidade de Brasília, 1980); Fundação Getúlio Vargas, *A Revolução de 30: Textos e Documentos*, 2 vols. (Brasília: Editora Universidade de Brasília, 1982); Ricardo Antônio Silva Seitenfus, *O Brasil de Getúlio Vargas e a Formação dos Blocos, 1930–1942* (São Paulo: Companhia Editora Nacional, 1985); Dulce Chaves Pandolfi, *Da Revolução de 30 ao Golpe de 37* (Rio de Janeiro: Fundação Getúlio Vargas, 1987); and Ana Ligia Medeiros and Monica Hirst, eds., *Bibliografia Histórica: 1930–45* (Brasília: Editora Universidade de Brasília, 1982).

42. Góes Monteiro, *A Revolução de 30*, pp. 98–99.

43. Nelson Werneck Sodré, *Memórias de um Soldado* (Rio de Janeiro: Editora Civilização Brasileira, 1967), p. 53. A more detached and analytical view than that of this Marxist army officer (Werneck Sodré) is in Drummond, *O Movimento Tenentista*, Chapter 9, "Do exílio ao poder: Tensões entre a retomada da carreira militar e a militância política," pp. 205–247.

44. See John Wirth, "Tenentismo in the Brazilian Revolution of 1930," *Hispanic American Historical Review* 44, 2 (May 1964), pp. 162–179, and Robert J. Alexander, "Brazilian Tenentismo," in ibid., pp. 229–242.

45. See Ernani do Amaral Peixoto with Aspásia Camargo, Lucia Hippolito, Maria Celina Soares D'Araújo, and Dora Flaksman, *Artes da Política: Diálogo com Amaral Peixoto* (Rio de Janeiro: Editora Nova Fronteira, 1986), pp. 69–82, 97–139.

46. For analysis of the struggle between the *tenentes* and oligarchies in the period to mid-1932, see Edgard Carone, *A República Nova* (São Paulo: Difusão Editorial, 1974), pp. 283–315, and Carone, *O Tenentismo*, pp. 171–191. A participant's view is Juarez Távora, *Uma Vida e Muitas Lutas*, Vol. 2, *A Caminhada no Altiplano* (Rio de Janeiro: Livraria José Olympio Editora, 1975), pp. 5–171. Ideological trends in the revolution are traced in Antônio José Azevedo do Amaral, *O Estado Autoritário e a Realidade Nacional* (Rio de Janeiro: Livraria José Olympio, 1938), pp. 80–105, augmented by Hélgio Trinidade, "Bases da democracia Brasileira: Lógica liberal e práxis autoritária (1822/1945)," in Alain Rouquié, Bolívar Lamounier, and Jorge Schvarzer, eds., *Como Renascem as Democracias* (São Paulo: Editora Brasiliense, 1985), pp. 47–72. On Rio

Grande do Sul, see Carlos E. Cortes, *Gaúcho Politics in Brazil: The Politics of Rio Grande do Sul, 1930–1964* (Albuquerque: University of New Mexico Press, 1974), pp. 24–67, and Joan L. Bak, "Political Centralization and the Building of the Interventionist State in Brazil: Corporatism, Regionalism, and Interest Group Politics in Rio Grande do Sul, 1930–1937," *Luso-Brazilian Review* 22, 1 (Summer 1985), pp. 9–25.

47. Neves da Fontoura, *Memórias*, Vol. 2, pp. 431–437, treats Neves da Fontoura's alienation from Vargas, while two more works by Neves da Fontoura, *Por S. Paulo e pelo Brasil!* (São Paulo: n.p., 1932) and *Acuso!* (Rio de Janeiro: n.p., 1933), contain strong denunciations of Vargas.

48. Carone, *O Tenentismo*, pp. 197–220, 431–460, provides detail on the intramural rivalries and infighting in São Paulo. Also useful are Silva, *1931: Os Tenentes no Poder*, pp. 85–146; Peter Flynn, "The Revolutionary Legion and the Brazilian Revolution of 1930," in Raymond Carr, ed., *Latin American Affairs* (London: St. Anthony's Papers, 1970), pp. 65–103; and Edgard Carone, *A Segunda República* (São Paulo: Difusão Européia do Livro, 1973), pp. 252–279.

49. The complex story of political developments during 1931 is told in Silva, *1931: Os Tenentes no Poder*, pp. 147–240, with even more detail in Paulo Nogueira Filho, *A Guerra Cívica 1932*, Vol. 1, *Ocupação Militar* (Rio de Janeiro: Livraria José Olympio Editora, 1965), pp. 3–321. Also see Michael L. Conniff, "The Tenentes in Power: A New Perspective on the Brazilian Revolution of 1930," *Journal of Latin American Studies* 10, 1 (May 1978), pp. 61–82.

50. The text of the manifesto is in Nogueira Filho, *A Guerra Cívica*, Vol. 1, pp. 408–415, with the events of January narrated in pages 322–378.

51. Paulo Nogueira Filho, *A Guerra Cívica 1932*, Vol. 2, *Insurreição Civil* (Rio de Janeiro: Livraria José Olympio Editora, 1966), pp. 3–92, provides an exhaustive treatment of developments relevant to the civil war from February through mid-March.

52. Ibid., pp. 93–219, and Silva, *1931: Os Tenentes no Poder*, pp. 308–361, describe the period from mid-March to late May.

53. On the May–June 1932 period, see Hélio Silva, *1932: A Guerra Paulista* (Rio de Janeiro: Editora Civilização Brasileira, 1967), pp. 31–81; Nogueira Filho, *A Guerra Cívica*, Vol. 2, pp. 20–378; and Coutinho, *O General Góes Depõe*, pp. 171–191. Drummond, *O Movimento Tenentista*, pp. 242–244, treats the switch of ministers, which was closely tied to the reintegration of *tenentes* who had been expelled before 1930.

54. Flynn argues this point persuasively in "The Revolutionary Legion."

55. Paulo Nogueira Filho, *A Guerra Cívica 1932*, Vol. 3, *Povo em Armas* (Rio de Janeiro: Livraria José Olympio Editora, 1967), deals with events of July; Vol. 4, *Resistência Indômita*, Tomo 1, *Epopéia Militar* (Rio de Janeiro: Livraria José Olympio Editora, 1971), deals with August; and Tomo 2, *Mobilização Épica* (São Paulo: Usina Açucareira Ester, SA, 1981), pulls together loose ends. A participant as well as observer, the author blends a day-by-day account of the political happenings and press coverage with a similarly detailed reportage of military operations. (Owing to Nogueira Filho's death in 1969, the announced volume on September—*Prodigiosa Retaguarda*—was never completed.) Silva, *1932: A Guerra Paulista*, pp. 82–193, covers the fighting, and Stanley Hilton, *1932 A Guerra Civil Brasileira (História da Revolução Constitucional de 1932)* (Rio de Janeiro: Editora Nova Fronteira, 1982), provides a useful synthesis.

56. Hilton, *1932 A Guerra Civil Brasileira*, p. 121.

57. Coutinho, *O General Góes Depõe*, pp. 193–229, contains Góes's account of military operations, while Silva, *1932: A Guerra Paulista*, pp. 194–248, wraps up the final stage of the struggle.

58. Consult Drummond, *O Movimento Tenentista*, pp. 249–261, and Campos Coelho, *Em Busca de Indentidade*, pp. 97–126, for interpretations of the military during the Vargas era.

59. Silva, *1932: A Guerra Paulista*, pp. 353–358, reprints the text of this decree, Decree No. 22,194 of December 8, 1932.

60. Hélio Silva, *1933: A Crise do Tenentismo* (Rio de Janeiro: Editora Civilização Brasileira, 1968), furnishes ample detail on the period from November 1932 to November 1933.

61. Consult Carone, *O Tenentismo*, pp. 223–246, 366–430, 449–501.

62. Drummond, *O Movimento Tenentista*, p. 226.

63. Boris Fausto, "A Revolução de 1930," in Mota, ed., *Brasil em Perspectiva*, pp. 227–255. Silva, *1933: A Crise do Tenentismo*, pp. 99–109, 137–217, treats the Paulista infighting and the election.

64. On this succession episode, see Benedicto Valladares, *Tempos Idos e Vividos* (Rio de Janeiro: Editora Civilização Brasileira, 1966), pp. 36–70, and Silva, *1933: A Crise do Tenentismo*, pp. 218–239. Also vital are Afonso Arinos de Mello Franco, *Um Estadista da República*, 3 vols. (Rio de Janeiro: Livraria José Olympio Editora, 1955), especially Vol. 3, *Fase Internacional*, pp. 1485–1508; and Coutinho, *O General Góes Depõe*, pp. 244–253.

65. A useful "insider" view of the military institution in the mid-1930s is Juracy M. Magalhães, *Minhas Memórias Provisorias* (Rio de Janeiro: Editora Civilização Brasileira, 1982), pp. 51–88.

66. Afonso Arinos de Mello Franco, *Um Estadista da República*, Vol. 3, pp. 1407–1420, covers the work of the Itamaraty Commission (named for the palace that housed the Foreign Ministry). Hamilton Leal, *História das Instituições Políticas do Brasil* (Rio de Janeiro: Editora Nacional, 1962), pp. 369–420, analyzes the functioning of the first constituent assembly, with treatment of the 1933–1934 body in pages 469–505. See also Angela Maria de Castro Gomes, "Confronto e Compromiso no Processo da Constitucionalização (1930–1935)," in *HGCB*, Tomo 3, Vol. 3, pp. 1–75, and Angela Maria de Castro Gomes, Dulce Chaves Pandolfi, and Maria Tereza Lopes Teixeira, eds., *Regionalismo e Centralização Política: Partido e Constituente nos anos 30* (Rio de Janeiro: Editora Nova Fronteira, 1980).

67. Aspásia Camargo, Dulce Chaves Pandolfi, Eduardo Rodrigues Gomes, Maria Celina Soares D'Araújo, and Mario Grynszpan, *O Golpe Silencioso: As Origens da República Corporativa* (Rio de Janeiro: Rio Fundo Editora, 1989), p. 30. Karl Lowenstein, *Brazil Under Vargas* (New York: Macmillan, 1942), pp. 212–226, provides an incisive analysis of this constitution from a contemporary perspective.

68. The best analysis of this period is Robert Levine's *The Vargas Regime: The Critical Years, 1934–1938* (New York: Columbia University Press, 1970). Carone, *A República Nova*, pp. 316–341, provides an able synthesis of developments from late 1932 through 1935, while Hélio Silva, *1934: A Constituente* (Rio de Janeiro: Editora Civilização Brasileira, 1969), and Hélio Silva, *1935: A Revolta Vermelha* (Rio de Janeiro: Editora Civilização Brasileira, 1969), give much greater detail. Camargo et al., *O Golpe Silencioso*, pp. 75–84, discusses Vargas's maneuvering to neutralize Flôres's efforts to project himself onto the national political scene.

69. Camargo et al., *O Golpe Silencioso*, pp. 31–33, 88–92, treats Vargas's dealings with the military through 1936.

70. The key source for this discussion is Hélgio H. Trinidade, *Integralismo: O Fascismo Brasileiro na Década de 30* (São Paulo: Difusão Editorial, 1974), a briefer version of which is "Integralismo: Teoria e Práxis Política nos anos 30," in *HGCB*, Tomo 3, Vol. 3, pp. 297–335. In English, there is Elmer Broxson, "Plínio Salgado

and Brazilian Integralism, 1932–1938" (unpublished Ph.D. dissertation, Department of History, Catholic University of America, 1972). The doctrine of Brazilian Integralist Action (AIB) is contained in the many writings of Plínio Salgado, particularly *O Integralismo perante a Nação*, 3rd ed. (Rio de Janeiro: Livraria Classica Brasileira, 1955). Olbiano de Melo, *A Marcha da Revolução Social no Brasil* (Rio de Janeiro: Edições "O Cruzeiro," 1957), is a useful contribution by one of the movement's leading figures, who later became disenchanted. See also Jarbas Medeiros, *Ideologia Autoritário no Brasil, 1930–1945* (Rio de Janeiro: Fundação Getúlio Vargas, 1978), pp. 379–599. The best treatment in English is Levine, *The Vargas Regime*, pp. 81–99.

71. The most objective treatment of the ANL is Levine, *The Vargas Regime*, pp. 58–80, with Dulles, *Anarchists and Communists*, pp. 511–530, also useful. Great detail is contained in Lélia M. G. Hernandez, *Aliança Nacional Libertadora: Ideologia e Ação* (Porto Alegre, Brazil: Mercado Aberto, 1985), and Silva, *1935: A Revolta Vermelha*, pp. 115–192, with brief sketches in Carone, *A República Nova*, pp. 136–141, and Leoncio Basbaum, *História Sincera da República*, Vol. 3, *De 1930 à 1960*, 3rd ed. (São Paulo: Editôra Fulgor, 1968), pp. 66–101. Among works by the participants, consult Luís Carlos Prestes, *Problemas Atuais da Democracia* (Rio de Janeiro: Editoral Victória, 1947), pp. 167–182; Abguar Bastos, *Prestes e a Revolução Social*, pp. 297–336; and Barata, *Vida de um Revolucionário*, pp. 225–250. Also useful is Drummond, *O Movimento Tenentista*, pp. 263–269. On the level of ideas more than actions, see Ludwig Lauerhauss, Jr., *Getúlio Vargas e o Triunfo do Nacionalismo Brasileiro: Estudo do Advento da Geração Nacionalista de 1930* (Belo Horizonte, Brazil: Editora Itatiaia, 1986), especially pp. 110–131.

72. Levine, *The Vargas Regime*, pp. 100–124; Nelson Werneck Sodré, *A Intentona Comunista de 1935* (Porto Alegre, Brazil: Mercado Aberto, 1986); and Stanley Hilton, *A Rebelião Vermelha* (Rio de Janeiro: Editora Record, 1986). Barata, *Vida de um Revolucionário*, pp. 253–300, provides the account of a leading participant in the events in Rio de Janeiro.

73. See Camargo et al., *O Golpe Silencioso*, p. 35.

74. Levine, *The Vargas Regime*, p. 43, discusses this episode.

75. Leal, *História das Instituições Políticas*, pp. 515–516, treats these amendments, while Nelson Werneck Sodré, *História Militar do Brasil* (Rio de Janeiro: Editora Civilização Brasileira, 1965), pp. 263–270, and Levine, *The Vargas Regime*, pp. 125–137, contain useful observations.

76. The text of Góes Monteiro's December 3, 1935, memorandum to the war minister is in Coutinho, *O General Góes Depõe*, pp. 307–313. There is a detailed treatment in Camargo et al., *O Golpe Silencioso*, pp. 114–118.

77. Camargo et al., *O Golpe Silencioso*, p. 250.

78. Coutinho, *O General Góes Depõe*, pp. 281–298, presents Góes Monteiro's account.

79. Hélio Silva, *1937: Todos os Golpes Se Parecem* (Rio de Janeiro: Editora Civilização Brasileira, 1970) is the most detailed work on this topic. Also of value for the events of 1937 are Juracy M. Magalhães, *Minha Vida Pública na Bahia* (Rio de Janeiro: Livraria José Olympio Editora, 1957) and John F. W. Dulles, *Brazilian Communism, 1935–1945: Repression During World Upheaval* (Austin: University of Texas Press, 1983), pp. 1–133.

80. Carone, *A República Nova*, pp. 342–378; Regina Portella Schneider, *Flôres da Cunha: O último gaúcho legendário* (Porto Alegre, Brazil: Martins Livraria, 1981); and Cortes, *Gaúcho Politics in Brazil*, pp. 68–111.

81. For their campaign speeches see Armando de Salles Oliveira, *Jornada Democrática: Discursos Políticos* (Rio de Janeiro: Livraria José Olympio Editora, 1937) and José

Américo de Almeida, *A Palavra e o Tempo: 1937–1945* (Rio de Janeiro: Livraria José Olympio Editora, 1965). Levine, *The Vargas Regime,* pp. 138–148, and Dulles, *Brazilian Communism, 1935–1945,* pp. 88–107, synthesize the environment within which the campaign progressed.
    82. Camargo et al., *O Golpe Silencioso,* pp. 10, 125–135, 157–179.
    83. A great deal has been written about the Cohen Plan by both critics and defenders of the Vargas regime, with "new" evidence periodically reawakening interest in the episode. See, for example, Silva, *1937: Todos os Golpes Se Parecem,* pp. 375–387, and Peter Flynn, *Brazil: A Political Analysis* (Boulder, CO: Westview Press, 1978), pp. 87–88. Amaral Peixoto, *Artes da Política,* p. 136, states that a meeting of key generals on September 27 decided on a coup with, without, or even against Vargas.
    84. Levine, *The Vargas Regime,* p. 95.
    85. Silva, *1937: Todos os Golpes Se Parecem,* pp. 448–450.
    86. In Virgílio A. de Mello Franco, *A Campanha da UDN (1944–1945)* (Rio de Janeiro: Livraria Editora Zélio Valverde, 1946), pp. 95–100.
    87. Camargo et al., *O Golpe Silencioso,* pp. 12–13, 251, with pages 193–208 providing details on the military role in 1937 events.
    88. Ibid., p. 252.
    89. The characterization is from ibid., p. 243.
    90. On the first days of the Estado Novo, see Silva, *1937: Todos os Golpes Se Parecem,* pp. 477–542, and Levine, *The Vargas Regime,* pp. 149–158. Very useful are Edgard Carone, *A Terceira República* (São Paulo: Difusão Editorial, 1976); Edgard Carone, *O Estado Novo (1937–1945)* (São Paulo: Difusão Editorial, 1976); Lourdes Sola, "O Golpe de 37 e O Estado Novo," in Mota, ed., *Brasil em Perspectiva,* pp. 256–282; Lucia Lippi Oliveira, Mônica Pimenta Velloso, and Angela Maria Castro Gomes, eds., *Estado Novo: Ideologia e Poder* (Rio de Janeiro: Zahar Editores, 1982); Simon Schwartzman, ed., *Estado Novo: Auto-retrato* (Brasília: Editora Universidade de Brasília, 1983); Reynaldo Pompeu de Campos, *Repressō judicial no Estado Novo: Esquerda e direita no banco dos réus* (Rio de Janeiro: Editora Achioné, 1982); and Nelson Jahr Garcia, *O Estado Novo, ideologia e propaganda política: A legitimação do estado autoritário perante as classes subalternas* (São Paulo: Edições Loyola, 1982). Camargo et al., *O Golpe Silencioso,* pp. 11–12, stresses that the coup was without real resistance because the principal conflicts had been neutralized before they materialized and, because everyone could see it coming, the coup seemed like the logical outcome of events when it finally happened.
    91. Vargas, *A Nova Política do Brasil,* Vol. V, pp. 17–32.
    92. This tendency was not, of course, unique to Brazil. In Argentina, Chile, and other Latin American countries that had significant experience with representative regimes, authoritarian political movements came to exert significant influence after 1930. Indeed, at the time of the November 1937 Brazilian coup only five governments in all Latin America could by any stretch be termed democratic, while nine were clearly dictatorial. Six others fell somewhere in between, with ostensibly constitutional systems vitiated by rigged elections or resort to force as the ultimate arbiter. Useful on Brazil during this time period are Amaral Peixoto, *Artes da Política,* pp. 145–230; Juracy M. Magalhães, *Minhas Memórias Provisorias,* pp. 91–115; and Lauerhauss, *Getúlio Vargas,* pp. 132–153.
    93. Camargo et al., *O Golpe Silencioso,* p. 253.
    94. See Carone, *A Terceira República,* pp. 142–155, and Carone, *O Estado Novo,* pp. 156–161. Lowenstein, *Brazil Under Vargas,* provides a detailed analysis of the institutional arrangements from the highly legalistic perspective of political science in those days.

95. On the political views and ideology of "Chico Ciência" Campos, see Jarbas Medeiros, *Ideologia Autoritário no Brasil*, pp. 9–51. Among Campos's own writings are *O Estado Nacional: Sua estrutura, Seu contuedo ideológico*, 2nd ed. (Rio de Janeiro: Livraria José Olympio Editora, 1940) and *Antecipações a Reforma Política* (Rio de Janeiro: Livraria José Olympio Editora, 1940). The formative influences upon this generation that resulted in a view of the state as tutor of society are explored by Bolívar Lamounier, "Formação de um Pensamento Político Autoritário na Primeira República: Uma Interpretação," in *HGCB*, Tomo 3, Vol. 2, pp. 343–374; Wanderley Guilherme dos Santos, "A Imaginação Político-Social Brasileira," *Dados* 2–3 (1967), pp. 182–193; and Wanderley Guilherme dos Santos, "Raizes da Imaginação Política Brasileira," *Dados* 7 (1970), pp. 136–156. Co-optation of intellectuals is discussed in Sérgio Miceli, *Intelectuais e Classe Dirigente no Brasil (1920–1946)* (São Paulo: Difusão Editorial, 1979).

96. Faoro, *Os Donos do Poder*, p. 704.

97. On this period detail is in Hélio Silva, *1938: Terrorismo em Campo Verde* (Rio de Janeiro: Editora Civilização Brasileira, 1971).

98. Glauco Carneiro, *História das Revoluções Brasileiras*, Vol. 2 (Rio de Janeiro: Edições "O Cruzeiro," 1965), pp. 437–457, sketches the attempted coup, with greater detail in Silva, *1938: Terrorismo em Campo Verde*, pp. 161–273. David Nasser, *A Revolução dos Covardes* (Rio de Janeiro: Empresa Gráfica "O Cruzeiro," 1947) is based on the diary of rebel Lieutenant Severo Fournier, and Amaral Peixoto, *Getúlio Vargas, meu Pai*, pp. 175–199, gives an account from the presidential palace perspective.

99. See Dulles, *Vargas of Brazil*, pp. 169–230, for the 1938–1942 period. More detail is in Hélio Silva, *1939: Vespera de Guerra* (Rio de Janeiro: Editora Civilização Brasileira, 1972), and Hélio Silva, *1942: Guerra no Continente* (Rio de Janeiro: Editora Civilização Brasileira, 1972), as well as Carone, *A Terceira República*, pp. 38–54.

100. On the origins of the complex machinery of the modern Brazilian state, consult Mário Wagner Vieira da Cunha, *O Sistema Administrativo Brasileiro, 1930–1950* (Rio de Janeiro: Ministério de Educação e Cultura, 1963); Lawrence S. Graham, *Civil Service Reform in Brazil: Principles Versus Practice* (Austin: University of Texas Press, 1968); Octávio Ianni, *Estado e Planejamento Econômico no Brasil (1930–1970)* (Rio de Janeiro: Editora Civilização Brasileira, 1971), pp. 13–71; and Barbara Geddes, "Building 'State' Authority in Brazil, 1930–1964," *Comparative Politics* 22, 2 (January 1990), pp. 217–235. Economic policy making is probed by John D. Wirth in *The Politics of Brazilian Development, 1930–1954* (Palo Alto, CA: Stanford University Press, 1970). More generally on the policies of the Estado Novo, see Flynn, *Brazil: A Political Analysis*, pp. 94–116; Thomas E. Skidmore, *Politics in Brazil, 1930–1964: An Experiment in Democracy* (Oxford: Oxford University Press, 1967), pp. 33–47; and Faoro, *Os Donos do Poder*, pp. 685–708, 714–725.

101. Luíz Werneck Vianna, *Liberalismo e Sindicato no Brasil* (Rio de Janeiro: Editora Paz e Terra, 1970), and Kenneth P. Erickson, *The Brazilian Corporative State and Working Class Politics* (Berkeley and Los Angeles: University of California Press, 1977) are the most systematic studies of this development, with José de Segadas Viana, *Organização Sindical Brasileira* (Rio de Janeiro: Empresa Gráfica "O Cruzeiro," 1943) reflecting the thinking of the Vargas regime. On the urban working class and trade unions, see also Timothy F. Harding, "The Political History of Organized Labor in Brazil" (unpublished Ph.D. dissertation, Department of History, Stanford University, 1973); Moisés Vinhas, *Estudos Sobre o Proletariado Brasileiro* (Rio de Janeiro: Editora Civilização Brasileira, 1970); José Albertino Rodrigues, *Sindicato e Desenvolvimento no Brasil* (São Paulo: Difusão Européia do Livro, 1968); Boris Fausto, *Trabalho Urbano e Conflito Social, 1880–1920* (São Paulo: Difusão Editorial do Livro, 1977); Juarez R.

Brandão Lopes, *Sociedade Industrial no Brasil* (São Paulo: Difusão Européia do Livro, 1964); Juarez R. Brandão Lopes, *Crise do Brasil Arcaico* (São Paulo: Difusão Européia do Livro, 1967); Azis Simão, *Sindicato e Estado: Suas relações na formação do proletariado de São Paulo* (São Paulo: Dominus Editôra, 1966); Neuma Aguiar Walker, "The Mobilization and Bureaucratization of the Brazilian Working Class" (unpublished Ph.D. dissertation, Department of Sociology, Washington University, 1969); and the key works of Leôncio Martins Rodrigues, *Conflito industrial e sindicalismo no Brasil* (São Paulo: Difusão Européia do Livro, 1966), and "Sindicalismo e Classe Operária (1930–1964)," in *HGCB*, Tomo 3, Vol. 3, pp. 507–555.

102. Instituto Brasileiro de Geografia e Estatística, *Estatísticas Históricas do Brasil* (Rio de Janeiro: Instituto Brasileiro de Geografia e Estatística, 1987), pp. 34, 94, 348–349.

103. Villanova Villela and Suzigan, *Política do Governo e Crescimento da Economia Brasileira*, pp. 216, 219, and Goldsmith, *Brasil 1850–1984*, pp. 8, 114. Nathaniel H. Leff, *Underdevelopment and Development in Brazil*, Vol. 1 (London: Allen & Unwin, 1982), p. 166, gives an even higher figure of 58 percent a year from 1930 through 1939. Very useful on this period is Marcelo de Paiva Abreu, "Crise, Crescimento e Modernização Autoritária: 1930–1945," in Paiva Abreu, ed., *A Ordem do Progresso*, pp. 73–104, with pages 74–82 covering 1930–1934 and pages 82–90 covering the 1934–1937 period.

104. Wilson Suzigan, *Indústria Brasileira: Origem e Desenvolvimento* (São Paulo: Editora Brasiliense, 1986), pp. 344–346.

105. Ibid., pp. 36, 58–60. Paiva Abreu, "Crise, Crescimento e Modernização Autoritário," pp. 90–103, covers the second half of Vargas's stay in power.

106. Many Brazilians have analyzed this development. In addition to Caio Prado Júnior, Boris Fausto, and Nelson Werneck Sodré—whose works have already been cited—consult Luiz C. Bresser Pereira, *Desenvolvimento e Crise no Brasil, Entre 1930 e 1967* (Rio de Janeiro: Zahar, 1968); Juarez Rubens Brandão Lopes, *Desenvolvimento e Mudança Social: Formação da sociedade urbano-industrial no Brasil* (São Paulo: Companhia Editora Nacional, 1968); Paul Singer, *Desenvolvimento e Crise* (São Paulo: Difusão Européia do Livro, 1968); Octávio Ianni, *Industrialização e Desenvolvimento Social no Brasil* (Rio de Janeiro: Editora Civilização Brasileiro, 1963); Octávio Ianni, *Estado e Capitalismo* (Rio de Janeiro: Editora Civilização Brasileira, 1965); and the many relevant works of Florestan Fernandes, especially *A Sociologia numa Era de Revolução Social* (São Paulo: Companhia Editora Nacional, 1963); *Sociedade de Classes e Subdesenvolvimento* (Rio de Janeiro: Zahar, 1968); and *Mudanças Sociais no Brasil: Aspectos do desenvolvimento da sociedade brasileira*, rev. ed. (São Paulo: Difusão Européia do Livro, 1974).

107. Villanova Villela and Suzigan, *Política do Governo e Crescimento da Economia Brasileira*, pp. 193–200.

108. Ibid., pp. 189, 226–228, and Silva, *1942: Guerra no Continente*, p. 137.

109. Consult especially the works of Eli Diniz, including "O Estado Novo: Estrutura de Poder. Relações de Classes," in *HGCB*, Tomo 3, Vol. 3, pp. 77–120; *Empresário, Estado e Capitalismo no Brasil: 1930–1945* (Rio de Janeiro: Editora Paz e Terra, 1978); and, with Renato Raul Boschi, *Empresariado Nacional e Estado no Brasil* (Rio de Janeiro: Editora Forense-Universitária, 1978). Also useful are Maria do Carmo Campello de Souza, *Estado e Partidos Políticos no Brasil, 1930 à 1964* (São Paulo: Editora Alfa-Omega, 1976), pp. 96–101, and Philippe C. Schmitter, *Interest Conflict and Political Change in Brazil* (Palo Alto, CA: Stanford University Press, 1971), pp. 110–126, 137–150.

110. Diniz, "O Estado Novo," p. 114.

111. Graham, *Civil Service Reform in Brazil*, pp. 27–30.

112. Campello de Souza, *Estado e Partidos Políticos*, pp. 87–95, provides a sound discussion of the role of interventors. The writings of Eli Diniz cited in note 109 above are the only systematic work on the real politico-bureaucratic mechanisms of the Estado Novo.

113. Aspásia de Alcântara Camargo, "A Questão Agrária. Crise do Poder e Reformas de Base (1930–1964)," in *HGCB*, Tomo 3, Vol. 3, *Sociedade e Política, 1930–1964*, 3rd ed. (São Paulo: Difusão Editorial, 1986), p. 141.

114. Diniz, "O Estado Novo," pp. 80–81.

115. Ibid., p. 84.

116. Ibid., p. 92. For much greater evidence see Edgard Carone, *O Pensamento Industrial no Brasil, 1880–1945* (São Paulo: Difusão Editorial, 1977), and Italo Tronca, "O exército e a industrialização: Entre as Armas e Volta Redonda (1930–1942)," in *HGCB*, Tomo 3, Vol. 3, pp. 337–360.

117. Diniz, "O Estado Novo," p. 97.

118. Ibid., p. 105.

119. Wirth, *The Politics of Brazilian Development*, p. 8.

120. See Frank D. McCann, *The Brazilian-American Alliance, 1937–1945* (Princeton, NJ: Princeton University Press, 1973); Stanley E. Hilton, *Brazil and the Great Powers, 1930–1939: The Politics of Trade Rivalry* (Austin: University of Texas Press, 1975); Stanley E. Hilton, *O Brasil e a Crise Internacional: 1930–1945* (Rio de Janeiro: Editora Civilização Brasileira, 1977); and Hélio Silva, *1944: O Brasil na Guerra* (Rio de Janeiro: Editora Civilização Brasileira, 1974).

121. Brazil's participation in the war effort is meticulously analyzed in McCann, *The Brazilian-American Alliance*, and is chronicled in Manoel Thomaz Castello Branco, *O Brasil na II Grande Guerra* (Rio de Janeiro: Biblioteca do Exército, 1960); João Batista Mascarenhas de Moraes, *Memórias* (Rio de Janeiro: Livraria José Olympio Editora, 1969); Floriano Lima Brayner, *A Verdade Sobre a FEB: Memórias de um Chefe de Estado Maior na Campanha da Itália, 1943–1945* (Rio de Janeiro: Editora Civilização Brasileira, 1968); and Floriano Lima Brayner, *Recordando os Bravos* (Rio de Janeiro: Editora Civilização Brasileira, 1977).

122. Coutinho, *O General Góes Depõe*, pp. 380–386. McCann, *The Brazilian-American Alliance*, p. 352, places the formal request in April 1943.

123. Coutinho, *O General Góes Depõe*, pp. 386–392. Also useful is Estevão Leitão de Carvalho, *A Serviço do Brasil na Segunda Guerra Mundial* (Rio de Janeiro: Editora "A Noite," 1952).

124. See Arthur José Poerner, *O Poder Jovem: História da Participação Política dos Estudantes Brasileiros* (Rio de Janeiro: Editora Civilização Brasileira, 1968), pp. 131–163.

125. Key sources on this period include Hélio Silva, *1945: Porque Depuseram Vargas* (Rio de Janeiro: Editora Civilização Brasileira, 1976); Antônio Mendes de Almeida Júnior, "Do Declínio do Estado Novo ao Suicídio de Getúlio Vargas," in *HGCB*, Tomo 3, Vol. 3, pp. 225–255; Carone, *O Estado Novo*, pp. 285–349; John F. W. Dulles, *A Faculdade do Direito de São Paulo e a Resistência Contra Vargas, 1938–1945* (Rio de Janeiro: Editora Nova Fronteira, 1984); and Stanley Hilton, *O Ditador e o Embaixador: Getúlio Vargas e Adolf Berle Jr. e a Queda do Estado Novo* (Rio de Janeiro: Editora Record, 1987). See also Dulles, *Vargas of Brazil*, pp. 249–274, and Skidmore, *Politics in Brazil*, pp. 48–63.

126. Silva, *1945: Porque Depuseram Vargas*, pp. 62–77; Carone, *O Estado Novo*, pp. 299–302; and Virgílio A. de Mello Franco, *A Campanha da UDN*, pp. 103–111.

127. Werneck Sodré, *História Militar do Brasil*, pp. 285–287. A strongly pro-Dutra interpretation is contained in José Caó, *Dutra: O Presidente e a Restauração Democrática* (São Paulo: Instituto Progresso Editorial, 1949).

128. See Silva, *1945: Porque Depuseram Vargas*, pp. 39–47, 78–104. The interview is reprinted in Virgílio A. de Mello Franco, *A Campanha da UDN*, pp. 136–146.

129. Additional Act No. 9 of February 28 is analyzed in depth in Campello de Souza, *Estado e Partidos Políticos*, pp. 111–142. Also consult Silva, *1945: Porque Depuseram Vargas*, pp. 107–113, and Carone, *A Terceira República*, pp. 11–117.

130. Juarez Távora, *Uma Vida e Muitas Lutas*, Vol. 2, pp. 177–203, and Silva, *1945: Porque Depuseram Vargas*, pp. 114–144.

131. The text of Prestes's addresses are in Prestes, *Problemas Atuais da Democracia*, pp. 77–163. On the PCB at this juncture, see Carone, *O PCB*, Vol. 2, *1943–1964*, and Dulles, *Brazilian Communism, 1935–1945*, pp. 179–220.

132. Consult Maria Victoria de Mesquita Benevides, *A UDN e o Udenismo: Ambigüidades de Liberalismo Brasileiro, 1945–1965* (Rio de Janeiro: Editora Paz e Terra, 1981), pp. 23–61. A firsthand account is Juracy M. Magalhães, *Minhas Memórias Provisorias*, pp. 115–126.

133. Gomes's campaign pronouncements are contained in his *Campanha da Libertação* (São Paulo: Livraria Martins Editora, 1946). The UDN platform is in Carone, *A Terceira República*, pp. 426–432.

134. Carone, *A Terceira República*, pp. 421–426, contains the PDS program.

135. See Carone, *O Estado Novo*, pp. 329–332.

136. The PTB program of 1946 is in Edgard Carone, *A Quarta República* (São Paulo: Difusão Editorial, 1980), pp. 433–436.

137. This is the interpretation of Afonso Arinos, *A Alma do Tempo*, pp. 418–419. See also Silva, *1945: Porque Depuseram Vargas*, pp. 213–266.

138. Silva, *1945: Porque Depuseram Vargas*, pp. 273–274.

Chapter 5

1. Key sources on the 1946–1960 period include Hélio Silva, *1945: Porque Depuseram Vargas* (Rio de Janeiro: Editora Civilização Brasileira, 1976), pp. 273–488; Hélio Silva, *1954: Um Tiro no Coração* (Rio de Janeiro: Editora Civilização Brasileira, 1978); Edgard Carone, *A Quarta República (1945–1964)* (São Paulo: Difusão Editorial, 1980); Edgard Carone, *A República Liberal I (Instituições e Classes Sociais, 1945–1964)* (São Paulo: Difusão Editorial, 1985); Edgard Carone, *A República Liberal II (Evolução Política, 1945–1964)* (São Paulo: Difusão Editorial, 1985); Sérgio Miceli, "Carne e Osso da Elite Política Brasileira Pós-1930," in *História Geral da Civilização Brasileira (HGCB)*, Tomo 3, Vol. 3, *Sociedade e Política, 1930–1964*, pp. 557–596; and Maria Victoria de Mesquita Benevides, *A UDN e o Udenismo: Ambigüidades de Liberalismo Brasileiro, 1945–1965* (Rio de Janeiro: Editora Paz e Terra, 1981), pp. 62–76. In English see Thomas E. Skidmore, *Politics in Brazil, 1930–1964: An Experiment in Democracy* (Oxford: Oxford University Press, 1967), pp. 65–80; Peter Flynn, *Brazil: A Political Analysis* (Boulder, CO: Westview Press, 1978), pp. 132–149; and John F. W. Dulles, *Vargas of Brazil* (Austin: University of Texas Press, 1967), pp. 275–299.

2. Hélio Jaguaribe, *Brazilian Nationalism and the Dynamics of Its Political Development*, Studies in Comparative International Development 2, 4 (1966), p. 61, and Hélio Jaguaribe, *Political Strategies of National Development in Brazil*, Studies in Comparative International Development 3, 2 (1967–1968), p. 32.

3. Francisco Weffort, *State and Mass in Brazil*, Studies in Comparative International Development 2, 12 (1966), p. 190.

4. Francisco Weffort, "Política de Masses," in Octávio Ianni, ed., *Política e Revolução Social no Brasil* (Rio de Janeiro: Editora Civilização Brasileira, 1965), pp. 163–75. In the absence of a good study of Arraes, see Miguel Arraes, *O Jogo do Poder no Brasil* (São Paulo: Editora Alfa-Omega, 1981).

5. The phenomenon of Brazilian populism has been too often approached from an ideological rather than empirical point of departure. Reflective of this is Francisco Weffort's *O Populismo na Política Brasileira* (Rio de Janeiro: Editora Paz e Terra, 1978), which should be contrasted with Vamireh Chacon, *Estado e Povo no Brasil: As Experiências do Estado Novo e da Democracia Populista, 1937–1964* (Rio de Janeiro: Livraria José Olympio Editora, 1977), and Gláucio Ary Dillon Soares, *Sociedade e Política no Brasil (Desenvolvimento, Classe e Política durante a Segunda República)* (São Paulo: Difusão Européia do Livro, 1973). For background consult Michael L. Conniff, *Urban Politics in Brazil: The Rise of Populism* (Pittsburgh: University of Pittsburgh Press, 1981).

6. See Aspásia de Alcântara Camargo, "A Questão Agrária. Crise do Poder e Reformas de Base (1930–1964)," in *HGCB*, Tomo 3, Vol. 3, 3rd ed. (São Paulo: Difusão Editorial, 1986), p. 123, and Simon Schwartzman, *São Paulo e o Estado Nacional* (São Paulo: Difusão Editorial do Livro, 1975), passim.

7. Consult Edmundo Campos Coelho's analysis of the post-1945 period in *Em Busca da Identidade: O Exército e a Política na Sociedade Brasileira* (Rio de Janeiro: Editora Forense-Universitária, 1976), pp. 127–152.

8. Maria do Carmo Campello de Souza, *Estado e Partidos Políticos no Brasil, 1930 à 1964* (São Paulo: Editora Alfa-Omega, 1976), p. 123. Fourth in the congressional voting was the remains of the old Republican Party with but 220,000 votes, followed by the PDC with under 102,000 and the PRP with fewer than 95,000. Maria do Carmo Campello de Souza also expresses some interesting ideas in "A democracia populista (1945/1964): Bases e limites," in Alain Rouquié, Bolívar Lamounier, and Jorge Schvarzer, eds., *Como Renascem as Democracias* (São Paulo: Editora Brasiliense, 1985), pp. 73–103. Carlos Lacerda's view of the 1945 campaign is in his *Depoimento* (Rio de Janeiro: Editora Nova Fronteira, 1977), pp. 62–71. Useful on the longer period is Lacerda's *Discursos Parlamentares* (Rio de Janeiro: Editora Nova Fronteira, 1982).

9. See the discussion of the *constituente* in Silva, *1945: Porque Depuseram Vargas*, pp. 323–350; Hamilton Leal, *História das Instituições Políticas do Brasil* (Rio de Janeiro: Editora Nacional, 1962), pp. 575–599; and João Almino, *Os democratas autoritários: Liberdades individuais, de associação política e sindical na Constituente de 1946* (São Paulo: Editora Brasiliense, 1980). Gastão Pereira da Silva, *Constituentes de 46: Dados Biográficos* (Rio de Janeiro: Editora Tupy, 1947) is useful for information about the composition of this body, while Osny Duarte Pereira, *Que é A Constituição?* (Rio de Janeiro: Editora Civilização Brasileira, 1964) is highly critical of the assembly as conservative and U.S. influenced. See also Evaristo Giovannetti Netto, *A Bancada do PCB na Assembléia Constituente de 1946* (São Paulo: Editora Novos Rumos, 1986).

10. See Silva, *1945: Porque Depuseram Vargas*, pp. 155–210.

11. On the background and characteristics of the PSD and UDN congressional representatives, consult Miceli, "Carne e Osso da Elite Política," and Campello de Souza, *Estado e Partidos Políticos*, pp. 124–136.

12. Useful on an important aspect of politics that has strong reflections even today is Sérgio Adorno, *Os Aprendizes do Poder—O bacharelismo liberal na política Brasileira* (Rio de Janeiro: Editora Paz e Terra, 1988).

13. See Ronald H. Chilcote, *The Brazilian Communist Party: Conflict and Integration, 1922–1972* (Oxford: Oxford University Press, 1974), pp. 49–57, and Edgard Carone, *O PCB*, Vol. 2, *1943–1964* (São Paulo: Difusão Editorial, 1982).

14. Benevides, *A UDN e o Udenismo*, p. 71, stresses the high degree of UDN adherence to the government. See also Otávio Soares Dulci, *A UDN e o anti-populismo no Brasil* (Belo Horizonte, Brazil: Editora Universidade Federal de Minas Gerais, 1986).

15. Prestes's clarification of the PCB's position can be found in Luís Carlos Prestes, *Problemas Atuais da Democracia* (Rio de Janeiro: Ed:toral Vitória, 1947), pp. 263–328, and, less directly, pp. 331–360. On Dutra's views see Mauro R. Leite and Novelli Júnior, *Marechal Eurico Dutra, o dever da verdade* (Rio de Janeiro: Editora Nova Fronteira, 1983). Dutra's presidential addresses are collected in abridged form in José Teixeira de Oliveira, ed., *O Governo Dutra* (Rio de Janeiro: Editora Civilização Brasileira, 1956). Afonso Arinos, *A Escalada* (Rio de Janeiro: Livraria José Olympio Editora, 1965), pp. 88–92, 106–107, 114–119, treats congressional debate on the cassation of Communist mandates and the role of military pressures in this episode. See also Silva, *1945: Porque Depuseram Vargas*, pp. 383–488. Getúlio Vargas, *A Política Trabalhista no Brasil* (Rio de Janeiro: Livraria José Olympio Editora, 1950), pp. 58–183, reveals the former president's strategy.

16. For the situation of labor under Dutra consult Ricardo Maranhão, *Sindicatos e Democratização* (São Paulo: Editora Brasiliense, 1979), and John D. French, "Workers and the Rise of Adhemarista Populism in São Paulo Brasil, 1945–47," *Hispanic American Historical Review* 68, 1 (February 1988), pp. 1–43.

17. Alcântara Camargo, "A Questão Agrária," pp. 144–146.

18. Most useful is Sérgio Bresserman Vianna, "Política Econômica Externa e Industrialização: 1946–1951," in Marcelo de Paiva Abreu, ed., *A Ordem do Progresso: Cem Anos de Política Econômica Republicana, 1889–1989* (Rio de Janeiro: Editora Campus, 1989), pp. 105–122. For a good, brief discussion for the layperson, see Skidmore, *Politics in Brazil*, pp. 69–73. Werner Baer, *Industrialization and Economic Development in Brazil* (Homewood, IL: Richard D. Irwin, 1965) is the most useful single source on the Brazilian economy following World War II. See also Octávio Ianni, *Estado e Planejamento Econômico no Brasil (1930–1970)* (Rio de Janeiro: Editora Civilização Brasileira, 1971), pp. 75–105.

19. Nelson Werneck Sodré, *Memórias de um Soldado* (Rio de Janeiro: Editora Civilização Brasileira, 1967), pp. 65, 80. About the only biography of Lott is Joffre Gomes da Costa, *Marechal Henrique Lott* (Rio de Janeiro: n.p., 1960).

20. Werneck Sodré, *Memórias de um Soldado*, pp. 273–277, describes the beneficial impact of Castelo upon the quality of education at the EEM. See also John F. W. Dulles, *Castello Branco: The Making of a Brazilian President* (College Station: Texas A & M University Press, 1978), pp. 31–61.

21. Nelson Werneck Sodré, *História Militar do Brasil* (Rio de Janeiro: Editora Civilização Brasileira, 1965), pp. 292–304, and Werneck Sodré, *Memórias de um Soldado*, pp. 258–260.

22. On the 1950 campaign see Getúlio Vargas, *A Campanha Presidencial* (Rio de Janeiro: Livraria José Olympio Editora, 1951); Silva, *1954: Um Tiro no Coração*, pp. 35–100; Maria Celína Soares D'Araújo, *O Segundo Governo Vargas, 1951–1954: Democracia, Partidos e Crise Política* (Rio de Janeiro: Zahar Editores, 1982), pp. 37–102; and Ana Lígia Silva Medeiros and Maria Celína Soares D'Araújo, *Vargas e os Anos Cinquenta* (Rio de Janeiro: Fundação Getúlio Vargas, 1982). Vargas's enemies' perspective is articulated in Lacerda, *Depoimento*, pp. 97–102, and the Rio Grande do Sul ramifications are illuminated in Carlos Cortes, *Gaúcho Politics in Brazil: The Politics of Rio Grande do Sul, 1930–1964* (Albuquerque: University of New Mexico Press, 1974), pp. 115–134, with the rest of the Vargas period on pp. 135–151. Also useful is Ernani do Amaral Peixoto with Aspásia Camargo, Lucia Hippolito, Maria Celína Soares D'Araújo, and Dora Rocha Flaksman, *Artes da Política: Diálogo com*

Amaral Peixoto (Rio de Janeiro: Editora Nova Fronteira, 1986), pp. 240–259, 389–434.

23. The UDN's role in this period is analyzed in Benevides, *A UDN e o Udenismo*, pp. 77–86.

24. Café Filho, *Do Sindicato ao Catete: Memórias Políticas e Confissões Humanas*, 2 vols. (Rio de Janeiro: Livraria José Olympio Editora, 1966), pp. 184–187. Café was strongly opposed by the Catholic Church and its Electoral League (LEC), and Vargas was seeking a favorable attitude from the politically potent Church.

25. João Cândido Maio Neto, *Coluna por Um* (Rio de Janeiro: Edições Gernasa, 1963), p. 43. This is more fully analyzed in Maria Victoria Benevides, *O PTB e o Trabalhismo: Partido e Sindicato em São Paulo: 1945–1964* (São Paulo: Editora Brasiliense, 1989), pp. 44–49.

26. Flynn, *Brazil: A Political Analysis*, pp. 141–149; Skidmore, *Politics in Brazil*, pp. 75–80; and Dulles, *Vargas of Brazil*, pp. 290–299, treat the 1950 election. For comparison of this with the 1945, 1955, and 1960 presidential balloting, see Ronald M. Schneider, *Brazil Election Factbook* (Washington, DC: Institute for the Comparative Study of Political Systems, 1965), pp. 53–61.

27. Werneck Sodré, *História Militar do Brasil*, pp. 304–306; Werneck Sodré, *Memórias de um Soldado*, pp. 294–299; Plínio de Abreu Ramos, *Brasil, 11 de Novembro* (São Paulo: Editôra Fulgor, 1960), pp. 62–63; and Joaquim Justino Alves Bastos, *Encontro com o Tempo* (Porto Alegre, Brazil: Editora Globo, 1966), pp. 156–161.

28. Skidmore, *Politics in Brazil*, pp. 82–100, provides a detailed discussion of the policy issues and debates of the 1951–1953 period, as does Flynn, *Brazil: A Political Analysis*, pp. 148–166. See also Adelina Maria Alves Novaes e Cruz et al., eds., *Impasse na Democracia Brasileira, 1951–1954: Coletânia de documentos* (Rio de Janeiro: Editora da Fundação Getúlio Vargas, 1983), and Ianni, *Estado e Planejamento Econômico*, pp. 109–138. The social and economic infrastructure of Brazil at this time is aptly analyzed in Hélio Jaguaribe, "A Crise Brasileira," *Cadernos do Nosso Tempo* 1 (October–December 1953), pp. 120–160.

29. Hélio Jaguaribe, *Desenvolvimento Econômico e Desenvolvimento Político* (Rio de Janeiro: Editora Fundo da Cultura, 1962), pp. 184–213, presents a discussion of the different approaches under the major division between cosmopolitanism and nationalism. By 1952 the young intellectuals associated with the developmental nationalism approach had expanded from their association with Vargas's "Assessoria Econômica" to establish a research institution and journal. Radical nationalist views can be found in the *Revista Brasiliense* from its inception in September 1955 on through the Goulart regime.

30. On economic policy consult Sérgio Bresserman Vianna, "Duas Tentativas de Estabilização: 1951–1954," in Paiva Abreu, ed., *A Ordem do Progresso*, pp. 123–150.

31. Soares D'Araújo, *O Segundo Governo Vargas*, p. 165.

32. Ibid., pp. 102–164, makes a case for viewing Vargas's aim as that of building as broadly inclusive a coalition of forces as possible with little attention to parties as such. See also Dulles, *Vargas of Brazil*, pp. 303–314.

33. Consult Carone, *A República Liberal I*, pp. 133–171, and Luciano Martins, *Industrialização, Burgesia Nacional e Desenvolvimento* (Rio de Janeiro: Editora Saga, 1968), p. 78.

34. Vargas's policies during the first year of his administration are spelled out in the statements and documents collected in his *O Governo Trabalhista do Brasil*, Vol. 1 (Rio de Janeiro: Livraria José Olympio Editora, 1952). Robert T. Daland, *Brazilian Planning: Development Politics and Administration* (Chapel Hill: University of North Carolina Press, 1967), pp. 30–35, 97–99, provides a useful analysis of economic

planning efforts and disputes during this period. Novaes e Cruz et al., *Impasse na Democracia Brasileira*, pp. 67–199, contains many relevant documents.

35. The policy conflict between the finance minister and the head of the Bank of Brazil foreshadowed the tensions between the finance and planning ministries in the 1970s and 1980s.

36. On the PCB during this period, see Chilcote, *The Brazilian Communist Party*, pp. 57–62, as well as Carone, *A República Liberal I*, pp. 348–354.

37. Werneck Sodré, *História Militar do Brasil*, pp. 306–329, and Werneck Sodré, *Memórias de um Soldado*, pp. 295–363, provide a detailed account from the viewpoint of a member of the nationalist-Communist faction.

38. See Abreu Ramos, *Brasil, 11 de Novembro*, pp. 84–90, 93–100, and Almir Mattos, *Em Agôsto Getúlio Ficou Só* (Rio de Janeiro: Problemas Contemporâneos, 1963), pp. 11–14. The text of the treaty is in Carone, *A Quarta República*, pp. 35–41, with the controversy reconstructed in Werneck Sodré, *Memórias de um Soldado*, pp. 402–409, and Luis Alberto Moniz Bandeira, *Presença dos Estados Unidos no Brasil (Dois séculos de história)* (Rio de Janeiro: Editora Civilização Brasileira, 1973), pp. 332–337. Important documents on Vargas's relations with the military are reprinted in Novaes e Cruz et al., *Impasse na Democracia Brasileira*, pp. 31–66.

39. Hélio Jaguaribe, "A Crise Ministerial e a Nova Política do Getúlio Vargas," *Cadernos do Nosso Tempo* 1 (October–December 1953), pp. 90–98; Hélio Jaguaribe, "Situação Política Brasileira" and "O Moralismo e a Alienação das Classes Médias," *Cadernos do Nosso Tempo* 2 (January–June 1954), pp. 103–120 and 150–159. In English consult Skidmore, *Politics in Brazil*, pp. 107–122.

40. The most detailed account of Vargas-Perón dealings is Affonso Henriques, *Ascensão e Queda de Getúlio Vargas*, Vol. 3, *Declínio e Morte* (Rio de Janeiro: Distribuidora Record, 1966), pp. 119–173.

41. In the wake of Perón's fall in September 1955, revelations concerning suspiciously large payments to Goulart in a pinewood deal with the Argentine regime played a major role in the November military-political crisis. Even with Perón out of power for nearly a decade, as late as 1964 Lacerda could continue to exploit this issue along with the fact that Goulart was Vargas's protégé to arouse suspicion concerning the Goulart's supposed intentions to establish a "syndicalist republic" of the Peronist type in Brazil. Hence in 1964 as in 1954, awareness by the military of the Vargas-Goulart ties to Perón would distort their perception not only of government favors to the labor movement but also of government emphasis upon basic reforms and the government's anti-U.S. strain of nationalism.

42. Soares D'Araújo, *O Segundo Governo Vargas*, stresses a continuation of such conciliating efforts meeting with declining success rather than a major shift in policy or tactics by Vargas.

43. For a defense of *Ultima Hora* see Werneck Sodré, *Memórias de um Soldado*, pp. 428–430, with the case against Vargas presented in Henriques, *Declínio e Morte*, pp. 250–266, and Lacerda, *Depoimento*, pp. 120–131. See also Silva, *1954: Um Tiro no Coração*, pp. 183–215, and Armando Falcão, *Tudo à Declarar* (Rio de Janeiro: Editora Nova Fronteira, 1989), pp. 59–79. Wainer finally told all shortly before his death in *Minha Razão de Vivir* (Rio de Janeiro: Editora Record, 1987).

44. See Alcântara Camargo, "A Questão Agrária," pp. 148–149.

45. For Vargas's position on this question see his *A política nacionalista do petróleo no Brasil* (Rio de Janeiro: Edições Tempo Brasileiro, 1964). For a sharply divergent position with considerable backing among the military, consult Juarez Távora, *Petróleo Para o Brasil* (Rio de Janeiro: Livraria José Olympio Editora, 1955). Peter S. Smith, *Oil and Politics in Modern Brazil* (Toronto: Macmillan of Canada, 1976) is the best

historical study of the oil question. See also Gabriel Cohn, *Petróleo e Nacionalismo* (São Paulo: Difusão Européia do Livro, 1968). Strongly favorable to Vargas and the Left is Maria Augusta Tibirça Miranda, *O Petróleo é Nosso: A luta contra o "entreguismo" pelo monopólio estatal* (Petrópolis, Brazil: Editora Vozes, 1983). For a participant view of Vargas's policies, see Medeiros Lima and Jesus Soares Pereira, *Petróleo, Energia Elétrica, Siderúgica: A Luta Pela Emancipação, um depoimento de Jesus Soares Pereira sobre a política de Vargas* (Rio de Janeiro: Editora Paz e Terra, 1975). Among more recent works, see Getúlio Carvalho, *Petrobrás: De Monopólio aos Contratos de Risco* (Rio de Janeiro: Editora Forense-Universitária, 1977), especially pp. 45–76, and Bernardo Kucinski, ed., *Petróleo: Contratos de Risco e Dependência* (São Paulo: Editora Brasiliense, 1977), particularly pp. 133–183.

46. Jover Telles, *O Movimento Sindical no Brasil* (Rio de Janeiro: Editorial Vitória, 1962), pp. 55–77, is useful on labor during this period.

47. Carone, *A República Liberal II*, pp. 68–77, treats this development. Relevant documents on Vargas's dealings with labor are brought together in Novaes e Cruz et al., *Impasse na Democracia Brasileira*, pp. 200–217.

48. See Carone, *A República Liberal II*, pp. 79–84, and Silva, *1954: Um Tiro no Coração*, pp. 216–263, on deterioration of the political situation. In English see Dulles, *Vargas of Brazil*, pp. 315–335, and Skidmore, *Politics in Brazil*, pp. 122–142.

49. Juarez Távora, *Uma Vida e Muitas Lutas*, Vol. 2, *A Caminhada no Altiplano* (Rio de Janeiro: Livraria José Olympio Editora, 1975), pp. 226–254. See also Afonso Arinos, *A Escalada* (Rio de Janeiro: Livraria José Olympio Editora, 1965), pp. 245–278, and Benevides, *O PTB e o Trabalhismo*, pp. 49–56.

50. See Werneck Sodré, *Memórias de um Soldado*, pp. 430–435, and Alves Bastos, *Encontro com o Tempo*, pp. 219–222. The manifesto is in Carone, *A Quarta República*, pp. 556–564, and Oliveiros S. Ferreira, *As Forças Armadas e o Desafio da Revolução* (Rio de Janeiro: Edições GRD, 1964), pp. 122–129.

51. João Neves da Fontoura, *Depoimentos de um ex-Ministro* (Rio de Janeiro: Editora Simões, 1957) contains the bombshell interview, and Hélio Jaguaribe, "A denuncia João Neves," *Cadernos do Nosso Tempo* 2 (January–June 1954), pp. 83–100, provides insight into the political ramifications of this episode. See also Limeira Tejo, *Jango: Debate Sôbre A Crise dos Nossos Tempos* (Rio de Janeiro: Editora Andes, 1957).

52. Armando Boito, Jr., *O Golpe de 1954: A Burguesia contra o Populismo* (São Paulo: Editora Brasiliense, 1982); Araken Távora, *O Dia em que Vargas Morreu* (Rio de Janeiro: Editora do Reporter, 1966); and Silva, *1954: Um Tiro no Coração*, pp. 267–296. The most profound analysis of the anti-Vargas movement's political roots and ties to the middle class's reliance upon the military is Hélio Jaguaribe, "O Golpe de Agôsto," *Cadernos do Nosso Tempo* 3 (January–March 1955), pp. 1–20. Carlos Lacerda's perspective is in his *Depoimento*, pp. 132–141. Among the vast journalistic literature on this dramatic event, see Hugo Baldessarini, *Crônica de uma Época: Getúlio Vargas e o Crime de Toneleros* (São Paulo: Companhia Editora Nacional, 1957); Lourival Fontes and Glauco Carneiro, *A face final de Vargas* (Rio de Janeiro: Edições "O Cruzeiro," 1966); and F. Zenha Machado, *Os Ultimos Dias de Govêrno de Vargas* (Rio de Janeiro: Editora Lux, 1955). Vargas's opponents have their say in Café Filho, *Do Sindicato ao Catete*, pp. 298–355; Arinos, *A Escalada*, pp. 318–347; and Henriques, *Declínio e Morte*, pp. 324–381.

53. Gileno Dé Carli, *Anatomia da Renúncia* (Rio de Janeiro: Edições "O Cruzeiro," 1962), pp. 25–26. Key documents concerning the crisis are found in Novaes et al., *Impasse na Democracia Brasileira*, pp. 229–323.

54. The full text is in Dulles, *Vargas of Brazil*, pp. 334–335, as well as Carone, *A Quarta República*, pp. 88–89, and Silva, *1954: Um Tiro no Coração*, p. 375.

55. Sensitivity and insight are shown in "O Legado Político de Vargas," *Cadernos do Nosso Tempo* 3 (January–March 1955), pp. 49–56. Understandably, Lacerda was not so sympathetic as shown in his *Depoimento*, pp. 142–150.

56. The reaction is dramatically described in Arinos, *A Escalada*, pp. 345–351, and Café Filho, *Do Sindicato ao Catete*, pp. 349–361.

57. The most useful and perceptive treatment of Café Filho's administration in English is Rollie E. Poppino, "Brazil Since 1954," published with José Maria Bello, *A History of Modern Brazil* (Palo Alto, CA: Stanford University Press, 1966), pp. 323–354, especially pp. 326–333. See also Skidmore, *Politics in Brazil*, pp. 143–162; Flynn, *Brazil: A Political Analysis*, pp. 172–181; and John F. W. Dulles, *Unrest in Brazil: Political Military Crises, 1955–1964* (Austin: University of Texas Press, 1970), pp. 7–28. Carone, *A República Liberal II*, pp. 84–112, provides an adequate narrative. Café Filho, *Do Sindicato ao Catete*, pp. 363–483, is of use for the president's perception, supplemented by Juarez Távora, *Uma Vida e Muitas Lutas*, Vol. 3, *Voltando a Planície* (Rio de Janeiro: Livraria José Olympio Editora, 1976), pp. 9–44, and Lacerda, *Depoimento*, pp. 151–162.

58. See Benevides, *A UDN e o Udenismo*, pp. 91–99. By far the most useful study of economic policy at this juncture is Demosthenes Madureira de Pinho Neto, "O Interregno Café Filho: 1954–1955," in Paiva Abreu, ed., *A Ordem do Progresso*, pp. 151–169.

59. The best contemporary treatment of these elections is "As Eleições de Outubro," *Cadernos do Nosso Tempo* 3 (January–March 1955), pp. 31–48.

60. See Bento Munhoz da Rocha, *Radiografia de Novembro*, 2nd ed. (Rio de Janeiro: Editora Civilização Brasileira, 1961), pp. 123–129, and Café Filho, *Do Sindicato ao Catete*, pp. 484–494. The most detailed and systematic study of the campaign is Edward Anthony Riedinger, *Como Se Faz um Presidente: A Campanha de JK* (Rio de Janeiro: Editora Nova Fronteira, 1988).

61. Arinos, *A Escalada*, pp. 351–357. Also relevant on this period is Juracy M. Magalhães, *Minhas Memórias Provisorias* (Rio de Janeiro: Editora Civilização Brasileira, 1982), pp. 129–147, especially pp. 140ff. See also Amaral Peixoto, *Artes da Política*, pp. 263ff. Key documents on the campaign are gathered in Novaes e Cruz et al., *Impasse na Democracia Brasileira*, pp. 333–389.

62. Távora, *Uma Vida e Muitas Lutas*, Vol. 3, pp. 44–95; Café Filho, *Do Sindicato ao Catete*, pp. 494–532; and Arinos, *A Escalada*, pp. 358–374, are among the best sources on the inter- and intraparty politics of the electoral period. Hélio Jaguaribe, "A Sucessão Presidencial," *Cadernos do Nosso Tempo* 4 (April–August 1955), pp. 1–23, is of value as are Etelvino Lins, *Um Depoimento Político: episódios e observações* (Rio de Janeiro: Livraria José Olympio Editora, 1977), pp. 62–68; Gomes da Costa, *Marechal Henrique Lott*, pp. 233–259; Viriato de Castro, *O Fenômeno Jânio Quadros* (São Paulo: Palacio do Livro, 1959), pp. 120–129; and Carlos Castilho Cabral, *Tempos do Jânio e Outros Tempos* (Rio de Janeiro: Editora Civilização Brasileira, 1962), pp. 65–72. See also Benevides, *O PTB e o Trabalhismo*, pp. 57–62.

63. See Pinho Neto, "O Interregno Café Filho," pp. 157–162.

64. For the leftist military faction's interpretation of the Café period, see Werneck Sodré, *História Militar do Brasil*, pp. 358–367, and Werneck Sodré, *Memórias de um Soldado*, pp. 444–485, as well as José Loureiro Júnior, *O Golpe de Novembro e Outros Discursos* (Rio de Janeiro: Livraria Classica Brasileira, 1957).

65. See Schneider, *Brazil Election Factbook*, p. 56. Useful on the aftermath is Viriato de Castro, *Espada X Vassoura: Marechal Lott* (São Paulo: Palacio do Livro, 1959). On Adhemar see Hélio Jaguaribe, "Que é o Adhemarismo?" *Cadernos de Nosso Tempo* 2 (January–June 1954), pp. 139–149; Regina Sampaio, *Adhemar de Barros e o PSP* (São

Paulo: Global Editora, 1982); F. Rodrigues Alves Filho, *Um Homen Ameaça o Brasil: A história secreta e espantosa da 'caixinha' de Adhemar de Barros* (São Paulo: n.p., 1954); and Lopes Rodrigues, *Adhemar de Barros perante a Nação* (São Paulo: Editora Piratininga, 1954).

66. The speech is in Carone, *A Quarta República*, pp. 76–79, while the best account is Dulles, *Unrest in Brazil*, pp. 31–61. See also Juscelino Kubitschek de Oliveira, *Meu Caminho para Brasília*, Vol. 2, *A Escalada Política* (Rio de Janeiro: Bloch Editores, 1976), pp. 421–453, and Hélio Silva, *O Poder Militar* (Porto Alegre, Brazil: L & PM Editores, 1985), pp. 103–166. Important documents on the military conspiracy and crisis are reprinted in Novaes e Cruz et al., *Impasse na Democracia Brasileira*, pp. 390–430.

67. Café Filho, *Do Sindicato ao Catete*, pp. 543–559. Also consult Távora, *Uma Vida e Muitas Lutas*, Vol. 3, pp. 96–103, and Falcão, *Tudo à Declarar*, pp. 101–112.

68. For Luz's perspective, see his *Em Defesa da Constituição: Discurso* (Rio de Janeiro: Editora Simões, 1956). Lacerda's views are in his *Depoimento*, pp. 163–173.

69. Loureiro Júnior, *O Golpe de Novembro*, pp. 301–317.

70. Juscelino Kubitschek de Oliveira, Vol. 1, *A Experiência de Humilidade*, of his *Meu Caminho para Brasília* (Rio de Janeiro: Bloch Editores, 1974), covers up to 1940, with Vol. 2, *A Escalada Política*, carrying on to his election. Vol. 3, *50 Anos em 5* (Rio de Janeiro: Bloch Editores, 1978), deals with his term as president. Kubitschek's *Por Que Construi Brasília* (Rio de Janeiro: Bloch Editores, 1975) and his earlier *A Marcha de Amanhecer* (São Paulo: Bestseller, 1962) are also pertinent. Riedinger, *Como Se Faz um Presidente*, contains useful insights.

71. For a perceptive sketch of the problems Kubitschek encountered upon taking office, see "Sentido e Perspectivas do Govêrno Kubitschek," *Cadernos do Nosso Tempo* 5 (January–March 1956), pp. 1–17. Kubitschek's ancestry and early life is covered in Francisco de Assis Barbosa, *Juscelino Kubitschek: Uma Revisão na Política Brasileira*, Vol. 1, *Da Chegada de João Alemão à Revolução de 1932* (Rio de Janeiro: Livraria José Olympio Editora, 1960). Kubitschek's presidency is analyzed in Maria Victoria Benevides, *O Governo Kubitschek: Desenvolvimento Econômico e Estabilidade Política, 1956–1961* (Rio de Janeiro: Editora Paz e Terra, 1976); Ricardo Maranhão, *O Governo Juscelino Kubitschek* (São Paulo: Editora Brasiliense, 1981); and Carone, *A República Liberal II*, pp. 112–139. In English consult Skidmore, *Politics in Brazil*, pp. 163–186; Flynn, *Brazil: A Political Analysis*, pp. 190–207; and Dulles, *Unrest in Brazil*, pp. 65–100.

72. Useful are Celso Lafer, *The Planning Process and the Political System in Brazil: A Study of Kubitschek's Target Plan, 1956–1961* (Ithaca, NY: Cornell University Dissertation Series, 1970); Celso Lafer, "Premissas operacionais do Plano de Metas," *Dados* 9 (1972), pp. 72–83; Conselho do Desenvolvimento, *Programa de Metas*, 3 vols. (Rio de Janeiro: Presidência da República, 1958); Daland, *Brazilian Planning*, pp. 38–39, 51–55; Ianni, *Estado e Planejamento Econômico*, pp. 142–187; and Hélio Jaguaribe, *Economic and Political Development: A Theoretical Approach and a Brazilian Case Study* (Cambridge, MA: Harvard University Press, 1968), pp. 151–162. A perceptive synthesis of economic policy is in Luiz Orenstein and Antônio Claudio Sochaczewski, "Democracia com Desenvolvimento: 1956–1961," in Paiva Abreu, ed., *A Ordem do Progresso*, pp. 171–195.

73. Alcântara Camargo, "A Questão Agrária," pp. 152–155.

74. See Amélia Cohn, *Crise Regional e Planejamento. O Processo de Criação da SUDENE* (São Paulo: Editora Perspectiva, 1976), and Francisco Oliveira, *Elegia para uma re(li)gião: Sudene, Nordeste, Planejamento e conflitos de classes*, 2nd ed. (Rio de Janeiro: Editora Paz e Terra, 1978). Also of interest is José Almeida, *A Implantação da Indústria Automobilística no Brasil 1910/1976* (São Paulo: Editora Brasiliense, 1976).

75. Glauco Carneiro, *História das Revoluções Brasileiras*, Vol. 2 (Rio de Janeiro: Edições "O Cruzeiro," 1965), pp. 504–517, and Dulles, *Unrest in Brazil*, pp. 65–73, offer the most complete accounts of this episode.

76. Benevides, *O Governo Kubitschek*, pp. 147–193, emphasizes good relations between Kubitschek and Lott, while the former's memoirs show that he didn't perceive any alternative to making the best of the situation.

77. De Castro, *Espada X Vassoura*, though it seeks to appear impartial, is really quite a vicious hatchet job by a pro-Quadros propagandist, while da Costa, *Marechal Henrique Lott*, is a routine campaign biography.

78. Details on the "Golden Sword" homage by leftist elements and the subsequent provocative stance by Juarez Távora are found in Kubitschek, *50 Anos em 5*, pp. 95–125; Távora, *Uma Vida e Muitas Lutas*, Vol. 3, pp. 119–121; and Silva, *O Poder Militar*, pp. 173–186. Odylio Denys revealed only part of his thoughts and activities in his *Ciclo Revolucionário Brasileira: Memórias, 5 do Julho de 1922 à 31 de Março de 1964* (Rio de Janeiro: Editora Nova Fronteira, 1980).

79. Benevides, *O Governo Kubitschek*, pp. 59–103, examines the PSD-PTB alliance as a cornerstone of Kubitschek's stable interlude and analyzes his military support on pages 147–193. See also Miriam Limoeiro Cardoso, *Ideologia do Desenvolvimento Brasileiro. Juscelino Kubitschek e Jânio Quadros* (Rio de Janeiro: Editora Paz e Terra, 1977). Falcão, *Tudo à Declarar*, pp. 117–205, treats the Kubitschek government from the perspective of a close political collaborator.

80. For a partial listing see Benevides, *O Governo Kubitschek*, pp. 187–188, and John J. Johnson, *Military and Society in Latin America* (Palo Alto, CA: Stanford University Press, 1964), pp. 211–212.

81. Alves Bastos, *Encontro com o Tempo*, pp. 306–307. Of course in the long run the "Democratic Crusade" would come out on top, with Castelo becoming Brazil's president in 1964.

82. On the developing divergence of interests between the PSD and PTB, consult Benevides, *O Governo Kubitschek*, pp. 109–141. Cortes, *Gaúcho Politics in Brazil*, pp. 152–177, covers the course of events in that state during the latter half of the 1950s and 1960.

83. The literature on and by the Brazilian nationalist movement during this period is voluminous, with the publications of the Institute of Advanced Brazilian Studies (ISEB) generally representing the most systematic attempt to develop a coherent approach to the analysis of Brazilian "reality." Among the most important studies during ISEB's more representative stage—before moderates left in 1958—were a collection of essays, *Introdução aos Problemas do Brasil* (1956); Alberto Guerreiro Ramos, *A Redução Sociológica* (1958); Alberto Guerreiro Ramos, *Ideologias e Segurança Nacional* (1958); Hélio Jaguaribe, *O Nacionalismo na Actualidade Brasileira* (1958); and Cândido Antônio Mendes de Almeida, *Perspectiva Atual da América Latina* (1959). Editôra Fulgor published a great number of works by such radical nationalists as Dagoberto Salles, Osny Duarte Pereira, Gabriel de Resende Passos, and Sérgio Magalhães. *Revista Brasiliense*, an independent Marxist journal whose pages were open to authors of diverse ideological orientations, and *Estudos Sociais*, the PCB's theoretical review, are useful for following the development of positions of the Left.

84. See Schneider, *Brazil Election Factbook*, pp. 43–46, 58–61, for a discussion of the congressional elections. Further detail is furnished in *Revista Brasileira de Estudos Políticos* 8 (April 1960), passim.

85. Luís Carlos Prestes, *A Situação Política e a Luta por um Governo Nacionalista e Democrático* (Rio de Janeiro: Editorial Vitória, 1959). See also Chilcote, *The Brazilian Communist Party*, pp. 64–74.

86. Brazil, Ministério da Fazenda, *Programa de Estabilização Monetária para o Período de Setembro de 1958 à Dezembro de 1959* (Rio de Janeiro: Imprensa Nacional, 1958).
87. See Kubitschek, *50 Anos em 5*, pp. 207–213, 217–222, 227–229, 239–242, 249–256, 279–281.
88. The views of Roberto Campos, although they were temporarily eclipsed by Kubitschek's policy shift, were to be of continuing importance to the present. These views are expressed in several of Campos's many works, such as *Ensaios de História Economia e Sociologia* (Rio de Janeiro: APEC Editora, 1963); *A Moeda, o Govêrno, e o Tempo* (Rio de Janeiro: APEC Editora, 1964); and *Economia, Planejamento e Nacionalismo* (Rio de Janeiro: APEC Editora, 1963). Ignácio Rangel, *A Inflação Brasileira*, 2nd ed. (Rio de Janeiro: Edições Tempo Brasileiro, 1963) presents a view more compatible with the analyses of the radical developmentalists.
89. In 1950 agriculture accounted for 26.7 percent of GDP and industry but 23.5 percent, according to Raymond Goldsmith, *Brasil 1850–1984: Desenvolvimento Financeiro sob um Século de Inflação* (São Paulo: Harper & Row do Brasil, 1986), p. 225.
90. See Kubitschek, *50 Anos em 5*, pp. 447–450, and Pedro Sampaio Malan, "Relações Econômicas Internacionais do Brasil, 1945–1964," in *HGCB*, Tomo 3, Vol. 4, *Economia e Cultura (1930–1964)* (São Paulo: Difusão Editorial, 1984), pp. 77–93.

Chapter 6

1. Gláucio Ary Dillon Soares, *Sociedade e Política no Brasil (Desenvolvimento, Classe e Política durante a Segunda República)* (São Paulo: Difusão Européia do Livro, 1973), p. 14, with a wealth of examples on pp. 99–114. The best studies of politics at the local level include Fanny Tabak, "Estudos de Política Local—A Experiência do Brasil," *Revista de Ciência Política* 5, 4 (June 1971), pp. 61–90; José Murilo de Carvalho, "Estudos do Poder Local no Brasil," *Revista Brasileira de Estudos Políticos* 25/26 (July 1968), pp. 231–248; Bolívar Lamounier, "Política Local e Tensões Estruturais no Brasil: Teste Preliminar de uma Hipótesis," *Dados* 4 (1968), pp. 186–198; Antônio Octávio Cintra, "A Integração do processo Político no Brasil: Algumas Hipoteses Inspiradas na Literatura," *Revista de Administração Pública* 5, 2 (July–December 1971), pp. 7–29; and Lúcia Maria Gaspar Gomes and Fernando José Leite Costa, "Contribuição ao estudo da sociedade tradicional: Bibiografia comentada (1)," *Dados* 5 (1968), pp. 167–180.
2. Simon Schwartzman, *São Paulo e o Estado Nacional* (São Paulo: Difusão Editorial do Livro, 1975), pp. 22–23, and Simon Schwartzman, "Um Enfoque Teórico do Regionalismo Político," in Jorge Balán, ed., *Centro e Periferia no Desenvolvimento Brasileiro* (São Paulo: Difusão Européia do Livro, 1974), pp. 79–107.
3. Hélio Jaguaribe, *Political Strategies of National Development in Brazil, Studies in Comparative International Development* 3, 2 (1967–1968), pp. 39–40.
4. This interpretation is fundamentally congruent with the analyses of Alcântara Camargo, Schwartzman, and Soares, although it disagrees with them in emphases and a number of specifics. The most systematic effort to conceptualize the events leading to the 1964 system change is Wanderley Guilherme dos Santos, *Sessenta e Quatro: Anatomia da Crise* (São Paulo: Edições Vértice, 1986). See also Olavo Brasil de Lima Júnior, Fabiano Guilherme M. Santos, and Octávio Amorim Neto, "Fragmentação Eleitoral e Radicalização no Rio de Janeiro: Impacto Estadual na Política Nacional (1945–1964)," *Dados* 30, 2 (1987), pp. 169–187.
5. On the Quadros period the best English sources are Thomas E. Skidmore, *Politics in Brazil, 1930–1964: An Experiment in Democracy* (Oxford: Oxford University

Press, 1967), pp. 187–204; John F. W. Dulles, *Unrest in Brazil: Political Military Crises, 1955–1964* (Austin: University of Texas Press, 1967), pp. 103–140; and Peter Flynn, *Brazil: A Political Analysis* (Boulder, CO: Westview Press, 1978), pp. 207–220. Edgard Carone, *A República Liberal II (Evolução Política, 1945–1964)* (São Paulo: Difusão Editorial, 1985), pp. 139–171, is useful, as is Maria Victoria de Mesquita Benevides, *O Governo Jânio Quadros* (São Paulo: Editora Brasiliense, 1981). Mário Victor, *Cinco Anos que Abalaram o Brasil: De Jânio Quadros ao Marechal Castelo Branco* (Rio de Janeiro: Editora Civilização Brasileira, 1965), pp. 1–286, provides an uneven journalistic coverage of the Quadros campaign and presidency. See also Maria Victoria Benevides, *O PTB e o Trabalhismo: Partido e Sindicato em São Paulo: 1945–1964* (São Paulo: Editora Brasiliense, 1989), pp. 66–71, and Ernani do Amaral Peixoto with Aspásia Camargo, Lucia Hippolito, Maria Celína Soares D'Araújo, and Dora Rocha Flaksman, *Artes da Política: Diálogo com Amaral Peixoto* (Rio de Janeiro: Editora Nova Fronteira, 1986), pp. 437–444.

6. In addition to Carlos Castilho Cabral, *Tempos de Jânio e Outros Tempos* (Rio de Janeiro: Editora Civilização Brasileira, 1962), and Viriato de Castro, *O Fenômeno Jânio Quadros* (São Paulo: Palacio do Livro, 1959), sources on Quadros's political style and techniques include Vidal dos Santos and Luiz Monteiro, *Diário de uma Campanha* (São Paulo: Exposição do Livro, n.d.); Oliveiros S. Ferreira, "Comportamento Eleitoral em São Paulo," *Revista Brasileira de Estudos Políticos* 8 (April 1960), pp. 162–228; Francisco Weffort, "Raízes Sociais do Populismo em São Paulo," *Revista Civilização Brasileira* 1, 2 (May 1965), pp. 137–158; Asiz Simão, "O Voto Operário em São Paulo," *Revista Brasileira de Estudos Políticos* 1 (December 1956), pp. 130–141; "Porque Venceu Jânio Quadros," *Cadernos do Nosso Tempo* 1 (October–December 1953), pp. 99–102; Hélio Damante, "O Movimento de 22 de Março de 1953 em São Paulo," *Revista Brasileira de Estudos Políticos* 18 (January 1965), pp. 105–112; and João Mello Neto, *Jânio Quadros* (São Paulo: Editora Renovação, 1982).

7. Viriato de Castro, *O Fenômeno Jânio Quadros*, pp. 99–108, covers the 1954 campaign.

8. Kubitschek's views of this succession race are in his *50 Anos em 5* (Rio de Janeiro: Bloch Editores, 1976), pp. 283–291, 301–302, 317–320, 387–390, 402–410. Carlos Lacerda's views are in *Depoimento* (Rio de Janeiro: Editora Nova Fronteira, 1977), pp. 202–224.

9. Araken Távora, *Vôo Rebelde* (Rio de Janeiro: Gráfica Vida Doméstica, 1964); Glauco Carneiro, *História das Revoluções Brasileiras*, Vol. 2 (Rio de Janeiro: Edições "O Cruzeiro," 1965), pp. 519–531; and Dulles, *Unrest in Brazil*, pp. 91–100, treat this vest-pocket revolt.

10. Dos Santos and Monteiro, *Diário de uma Campanha*, pp. 85–281. Lucia Hippólito, *De Raposas e Reformistas: O PSD e A Experiência Democrática Brasileira, 1945–64* (Rio de Janeiro: Editora Paz e Terra, 1985), p. 205, treats Lott's selection. For Lott's campaign see Milton Senna, *Como Não Se Faz um Presidente* (Rio de Janeiro: Edições Gernasa, 1968).

11. On the voters' choice, see Glaúcio Ary Dillon Soares, "Classes Sociais, Strata Sociais e as Eleições Presidenciais de 1960," *Sociologia* 23, 3 (September 1961), pp. 217–238, and Glaúcio Ary Dillon Soares, "Interesse Político, Conflito de Pressões e Indecisão Eleitoral," *Sintese Política, Econômica, e Social* 9 (January–March 1961), pp. 5–34.

12. See Odylio Denys, *Ciclo Revolucionário Brasileiro: Memórias, 5 do Julho de 1922 à 31 de Março de 1964* (Rio de Janeiro: Editora Nova Fronteira, 1980). Also useful is Juarez Távora, *Uma Vida e Muitas Lutas*, Vol. 3, *Voltando a Planície* (Rio de Janeiro: Livraria José Olympio Editora, 1976), pp. 136–173.

13. Hélio Silva, *O Poder Militar* (Porto Alegre, Brazil: L & PM Editores, 1985), pp. 192–240, is useful on events of 1961.

14. On Quadros's centralizing tendencies, see Benevides, *O Governo Jânio Quadros,* p. 32. For the Congress with which Quadros had to deal, see Maurício Vaitsman, *Sangue novo no Congresso: Deputados de 1959–1962, esboço biográfico* (Rio de Janeiro: J. Ozon Editora, 1960).

15. Alberto Guerreiro Ramos, *A Crise do Poder no Brasil* (Rio de Janeiro: Zahar, 1961), pp. 21–104, is of considerable value for understanding the changes occurring at this time. Perspective on economic policy can be found in Marcelo de Paiva Abreu, "Inflação, Estagnação e Ruptura: 1961–1964," in Marcelo de Paiva Abreu. ed., *A Ordem do Progresso: Cem Anos de Política Econômica Republicano, 1889–1989* (Rio de Janeiro: Editora Campus, 1989), pp. 197–212.

16. Consult Aspásia Alcântara Camargo, "A Questão Agrária. Crise do Poder e Reformas de Base (1930–1964)," in *HGCB,* Tomo 3, Vol. 3, 3rd ed. (São Paulo: Difusão Editorial, 1986), pp. 168–188, for the details.

17. The administration's foreign policy is explained in Jânio Quadros, "Brazil's New Foreign Policy," *Foreign Affairs* 40, 1 (October 1961), pp. 19–27, and Afonso Arinos de Mello Franco, *Evolução da Crise Brasileira* (São Paulo: Companhia Editora Nacional, 1965), pp. 244–258.

18. Victor, *Cinco Anos que Abalaram o Brasil,* pp. 259–260, and Gileno Dé Carli, *Anatomia da Renúncia* (Rio de Janeiro: Edições "O Cruzeiro," 1962), pp. 184–185. See also the following works by Gileno Dé Carli: *JQ—Brasília e a Grande Crise* (Rio de Janeiro: Irmões Pongetti, 1961); *Os Tempos de Jânio Quadros* (Recife, Brazil: Companhia Editora de Pernambuco, 1982); and *Visão da Crise* (Brasília: Editora Universidade de Brasília, 1980), which carries the story down to March 1964.

19. Lacerda's views can be gathered from his speeches, collected in *O Poder das Ideas* (Rio de Janeiro: Distribuidora Record, 1963), as well as from his *Depoimento,* pp. 202–266.

20. See Silva, *O Poder Militar,* pp. 241–310; Hélio Silva, *1964: Golpe ou Contragolpe* (Rio de Janeiro: Editora Civilização Brasileira, 1975), pp. 37–148; Amir Labaki, *1961: A Crise da Renúncia e a Solução Parlamentarista* (São Paulo: Editora Brasiliense, 1986); and Luiz Alberto Moniz Bandeira, *A Renúncia de Jânio Quadros e a Crise Pre-1964* (São Paulo: Editora Brasiliense, 1979). This brings together Moniz Bandeira's two earlier works: *O 24 de Agôsto de Jânio Quadros* (Rio de Janeiro: Editora Melso, 1961) and *O Caminho da Revolução Brasileira* (Rio de Janeiro: Editora Melso, 1962). In English consult Skidmore, *Politics in Brazil,* pp. 200–215, and Dulles, *Unrest in Brazil,* pp. 124–150.

21. Lacerda, *O Poder das Ideas,* pp. 329–343, and Lacerda, *Depoimento,* pp. 239–246.

22. A perceptive interpretation is Hélio Jaguaribe, "A Renúncia de Jânio Quadros e a Crise Política Brasileira," *Revista Brasileira de Ciências Sociais* 1, 1 (November 1961), pp. 272–311. Lacerda's view is in his *Depoimento,* pp. 246–266. Armando Falcão, *Tudo à Declarar* (Rio de Janeiro: Editora Nova Fronteira, 1989), pp. 211–222, is also relevant.

23. In Jânio Quadros and Afonso Arinos de Melo Franco, "O Porque da Renúncia," *Realidade* 20 (November 1967), pp. 31–35. See also Quadros's long interview in *Pasquim* June 24–30, 1977. Even discounting Quadros's obvious desire to portray his actions as patriotic and self-sacrificing, the purposeful, if not fully rational, aspects of his "plan" merit greater attention than the largely psychological explanations in vogue at the time.

24. Brizola's proclamation is in Labaki, *1961: A Crise da Renúncia*, pp. 151–152. See also Luiz Alberto Moniz Bandeira, *Brizola e Trabalhismo* (Rio de Janeiro: Editora Civilização Brasileira, 1979), pp. 75–85.

25. See José Machado Lopes, *O III Exercito na Crise da Renúncia de Jânio Quadros: Um depoimento* (Rio de Janeiro: Editorial Alhambra, 1980).

26. Victor, *Cinco Anos que Abalaram o Brasil*, pp. 357–358.

27. For a conceptualization of this process, see Juan Linz and Alfred Stepan, eds., *Breakdown of Democratic Regimes* (Baltimore, MD: Johns Hopkins University Press, 1978), particularly the latter's "Political Leadership and Regime Breakdown: Brazil," in Vol. 3, *Latin America*, pp. 110–137.

28. Olavo Brasil de Lima Júnior, *Os Partidos Políticos Brasileiros: A Experiência Federal e Regional, 1945–1964* (Rio de Janeiro: Edições Graal, 1983), argues strongly for viewing the party system—although not all the individual parties—in a less negative light, holding that trends prior to 1964 were moving the system in a more rational direction that involved the natural growth of the PTB to become the country's leading party.

29. Dos Santos, *Sessenta e Quatro*, p. 10.

30. The rationale for the position assumed by Tancredo Neves can be found in his *O Regime Parlamentar e a Realidade Brasileira* (Belo Horizonte, Brazil: Revista Brasileira de Estudos Políticos, 1962), and Francisco Brochado da Rocha's strong preference for a presidential system is clear in *Falando ao Brasil* (Porto Alegre, Brazil: Editora Globo, 1964). Goulart's government is treated at length in Luiz Alberto Moniz Bandeira, *O Governo João Goulart: As lutas sociais no Brasil, 1961–1964* (Rio de Janeiro: Editora Civilização Brasileira, 1978); briefly in Caio Navarro de Toledo, *O Governo Goulart e o Golpe de 64* (São Paulo: Editora Brasiliense, 1982); descriptively in Carone, *A República Liberal II*, pp. 172–221; extensively in Skidmore, *Politics in Brazil*, pp. 211–302; more sympathetically in Flynn, *Brazil: A Political Analysis*, pp. 226–307; and in detail in Dulles, *Unrest in Brazil*, pp. 150–300. Lacerda's perspective is in his *Depoimento*, pp. 267–281.

31. See Victor, *Cinco Anos que Abalaram o Brasil*, pp. 419–429.

32. Ibid., pp. 432–443, and San Thiago Dantas, *Política Externa Independente* (Rio de Janeiro: Editora Civilização Brasileira, 1962). An interesting volume by a Dantas disciple who by the late 1980s would be Brazil's ambassador in Washington is Marcílio Marques Moreira, *Indicações para o Projeto Brasileiro* (Rio de Janeiro: Edições Tempo Brasileiro, 1971).

33. See Osny Duarte Pereira, *Quem Faz as Leis no Brasil* (Rio de Janeiro: Editora Civilização Brasileira, 1962), pp. 60–79.

34. The most comprehensive study of IPES is René Armand Dreifuss, *1964: A Conquista do Estado, Ação Política, Poder e Golpe de Classe* (Petrópolis, Brazil: Editora Vozes, 1981).

35. Almost all available sources on IBAD are by its leftist critics, with the most useful being Eloy Dutra, *IBAD, Sigla da Corupção* (Rio de Janeiro: Editora Civilização Brasiliera, 1963). The 1963–1964 vice-governor of Guanabara demonstrates that IBAD spent very sizeable sums—far above the financial capabilities of its domestic supporters—on the 1962 elections.

36. See Olympio Mourão Filho, *Memórias: A Verdade de um Revolucionário* (Porto Alegre, Brazil: L & PM Editores, 1978), as well as José Stacchini, *Março 1964: Mobilização da Audacia* (São Paulo: Companhia Editora Nacional, 1965).

37. Dulles, *Unrest in Brazil*, pp. 168–173, provides some interesting observations on this cabinet crisis.

38. Brochado da Rocha, *Falando ao Brasil*, pp. 45–87.

·

39. Levi Carneiro, *Uma Experiência de Parlamentarismo* (São Paulo: Livraria Martins Editora, 1965), pp. 182–185, 204–205, 309.

40. The most comprehensive sources on the 1962 elections on a state-by-state basis are a special issue of *Revista Brasileira de Estudos Políticos* 16 (January 1964), edited by Orlando M. Carvalho; and Themistocles B. Cavalcante and Vladimir Reisky Dubnic, eds., *Comportamento Eleitoral no Brasil* (Rio de Janeiro: Fundação Getúlio Vargas, 1964). Hélio Jaguaribe, "As Eleições de 62," *Tempo Brasileiro* 2 (December 1962), pp. 7–38, puts a fairly heavy stress upon ideological factors. Useful, if limited, perspectives are in Benevides, *O PTB e o Trabalhismo*, pp. 72–75, and Juracy M. Magalhães, *Minhas Memórias Provisorias* (Rio de Janeiro: Editora Civilizaçãon Brasileira, 1982), pp. 161ff. See also Daniel Krieger, *Desde as Missões Saudades, Lutas, Esperanças* (Rio de Janeiro: Livraria José Olympio Editora, 1976), pp. 147–171, covering the 1961–1963 period.

41. The 1945 and 1958 figures are from Soares, *Sociedade e Política no Brasil*, p. 59, with that for 1962 my own from fieldwork at the time.

42. Francisco Weffort, *State and Mass in Brazil, Studies in Comparative International Development* 2, 12 (1966), p. 192.

43. The Chamber had been enlarged from 326 to 409. The turnout at 14.7 million was nearly two-and-a-half times that of 1945 and up some 62 percent from 1955. The 1910 total had been only 700,000 and that of 1933 a little over 1.2 million. São Paulo's electorate nearly doubled between 1945 and 1958, as did that of Rio Grande do Sul, while that of Minas Gerais rose by well over 70 percent. See the discussion in Soares, *Sociedade e Política no Brasil*, pp. 51–57.

44. Osny Duarte Pereira, *Que é a Constituição?* (Rio de Janeiro: Editora Civilização Brasileira, 1964), pp. 280–286.

45. The peasant league movement had begun in Pernambuco in the early Kubitschek years, and in November 1961 a national Peasants' Congress was held in Belo Horizonte. Two volumes by Antônio Callado, *Os Industriais de Sêca e Os 'Galileus' de Pernambuco* (Rio de Janeiro: Editora Civilização Brasileira, 1960) and *Tempo de Arraes: Padres e Communistas na Revolução sem Violência* (Rio de Janeiro: José Álvaro Editorial, 1965), provide a perceptive interpretation of the region's problems in very human terms. More accurate is Joseph A. Page, *The Revolution that Never Was: Northeast Brazil, 1955–1964* (New York: Grossman, 1972). Manoel Correia de Andrade's *A Terra e o Homen no Nordeste* (São Paulo: Editora Brasiliense, 1963), and Josué de Castro's *Death in the Northeast* (New York: Random House, 1966), are also useful sources on rural discontent and its roots. Marta Cehelsky, *Land Reform in Brazil: The Management of Social Change* (Boulder, CO: Westview Press, 1979), painstakingly reconstructs the debate and government impasse on the agrarian issue from Kubitschek on, as does Alcântara Camargo, "A Questão Agrária." Important works on the rural sector of Brazilian society include Alberto Passos Guimarães, *A Crise Agrária* (Rio de Janeiro: Editora Paz e Terra, 1979); Otávio G. Velho, *Capitalismo Autoritário e Campesinato* (São Paulo: Difusão Editorial, 1976); and José Gomes de Silva, *A Reforma Agrária no Brasil* (Rio de Janeiro: Zahar Editores, 1971).

46. For an analysis of this period, consult Robert T. Daland, *Brazilian Planning: Development Politics and Administration* (Chapel Hill: University of North Carolina Press, 1967), pp. 146–179; Skidmore, *Politics in Brazil*, pp. 229–260; Dulles, *Unrest in Brazil*, pp. 193–211; Flynn, *Brazil: A Political Analysis*, pp. 242–280; Carone, *A República Liberal II*, pp. 190–201; and Octávio Ianni, *Estado e Planejamento Econômico no Brasil (1930–1970)* (Rio de Janeiro: Editora Civilização Brasileira, 1971), pp. 204–222. The atmosphere of the times is well preserved in Carlos Castello Branco, *Introdução à Revolução de 1964*, Vol. 1, *Agonia do Poder Civil* (Rio de Janeiro: Editora Artenova, 1975).

47. A significant role in the radicalization of public opinion was played by Editora Civilização Brasileira's "Notebooks of the Brazilian People," commissioned in 1962 and 1963, written by leftist intellectuals, and designed to reach a mass readership. At the same time Editôra Fulgor of São Paulo launched a similar "Peoples' University" series.

48. Kenneth P. Erickson, *The Brazilian Corporative State and Working Class Politics* (Berkeley: University of California Press, 1977), pp. 106–107, and Lucília de Almeida Neves Delgado, *O Comando Geral dos Trabalhadores no Brasil, 1961–1964*, 2nd ed. (Belo Horizonte, Brazil: Editora VEGA, 1986).

49. Erickson, *The Brazilian Corporative State*, pp. 107–150. Also consult Dulles, *Unrest in Brazil*, pp. 296–300.

50. Daland, *Brazilian Planning*, pp. 55–67, 146–181, for a knowledgeable analysis of the plan and its political function. Celso Furtado's interpretations of Brazil's economic problems and political realities are more fully developed in several of his works, including *The Economic Growth of Brazil* (Berkeley and Los Angeles: University of California Press, 1964); *Diagnosis of the Brazilian Crisis* (Berkeley and Los Angeles: University of California Press, 1965); *Development and Underdevelopment* (Berkeley and Los Angeles: University of California Press, 1967); *A Pre-Revolução Brasileira* (Rio de Janeiro: Editora Fundo de Cultura, 1962); and *Dialéctica do Desenvolvimento* (Rio de Janeiro: Editora Fundo de Cultura, 1964).

51. This document is in Sérgio Magalhães, *Prática da Emancipação Nacional* (Rio de Janeiro: Editora Civilização Brasileira, 1964), pp. 158–212.

52. Treatment of the Hanna case from a Brazilian nationalist viewpoint is found in Osny Duarte Pereira, *Ferro e Independência* (Rio de Janeiro: Editora Civilização Brasileira, 1967), pp. 79–182, with the profits remittance problem discussed in Sérgio Magalhães et al., *A Questão da Remessa de Lucros* (Rio de Janeiro: Editora Universitária, 1962). The other side of the parliamentary battle can be found in Daniel Faraco and Mem de Sá, *A Remessa de Lucros: Um problema nacional* (Porto Alegre, Brazil: Editora Globo, 1963). See also Silva, *1964: Golpe ou Contragolpe*, pp. 182–195, and Silva, *O Poder Militar*, pp. 310–344.

53. See José de Souza Martins, "O Plano Trienial e a Marcha da Revolução Burguesa," *Revista Brasiliense* 49 (September–October 1963), pp. 41–52.

54. J. J. Faust, *A Revolução Devora Seus Presidentes* (Rio de Janeiro: Editora Saga, 1965), p. 54.

55. Hélio Jaguaribe, *Brazilian Nationalism and the Dynamics of Its Political Development*, Studies in Comparative International Development 2, 4 (1966), p. 65.

56. Moniz Bandeira, *Brizola e o Trabalhismo*, pp. 51–87.

57. Cehelsky, *Land Reform in Brazil*, pp. 86–97, 132–153, treats the agrarian reform question at this juncture. Carlos Castello Branco, *Introdução à Revolução de 1964*, Vol. 2, *A Queda de João Goulart* (Rio de Janeiro: Editora Artenova, 1975) provides a day-by-day account of politics from mid-1963 to the end of the Goulart government.

58. Leoncio Basbaum, *História Sincera da República*, Vol. 4, *De Jânio Quadros à Costa e Silva (1961–1967)*, 3rd ed. (São Paulo: Editôra Fulgor, 1968), pp. 83–99, has an insightful critique of parties and political leaders.

59. Castello Branco, *Introdução à Revolução de 1964*, Vol. 1, p. 187.

60. PSD Federal Deputy Abelardo Jurema became justice minister with the task of trying to hold the government coalition together, serving as a voice for moderation within the regime. See his *Sexta-Feira 13: Os últimos dias de governo Goulart* (Rio de Janeiro: Edições "O Cruzeiro," 1964), pp. 17–105.

61. Bilac Pinto, *Guerra Revolucionária* (Rio de Janeiro: Editora Forense, 1964), pp. 11–44.

62. The Sergeants' Revolt is analyzed in Oliveiros S. Ferreira, *As Forças Armadas e o Desafio da Revolução* (Rio de Janeiro: Edições GRD, 1964), pp. 79–91; Carneiro, *História das Revoluções Brasileiras*, Vol. 2, pp. 533–550; and Jurema, *Sexta-Feira 13*, pp. 107–121. Dulles, *Unrest in Brazil*, pp. 223–226, argues that the revolt was triggered prematurely by an anti-Communist infiltrator.

63. Quoted in Dulles, *Castello Branco: The Making of a Brazilian President* (College Station: Texas A & M University Press, 1978), p. 296.

64. *Jornal do Brasil*, September 19, 1963.

65. Dulles, *Unrest in Brazil*, pp. 230–238; Pinto, *Guerra Revolucionária*, pp. 49–50; Fernando Pedreira, *Março 31: Civis e Militares no Processo de Crise Brasileiro* (Rio de Janeiro: José Álvaro Editor, 1964), pp. 13–14; and Araken Távora, *Brasil: 1 de Abril* (Rio de Janeiro: Bruno Buccini, 1964), pp. 46–51.

66. Dulles, *Castello Branco: The Making of a Brazilian President*, pp. 297–299.

67. The interview is originally from *Manchete*, November 30, 1963, and is reprinted in Castello Branco, *Introdução à Revolução Brasileira*, Vol. 2, pp. 234–245.

68. Castello Branco, *Introdução à Revolução Brasileira*, Vol. 2, p. 150.

69. Dantas had first used this term in reply to Brizolista attacks in April and defined it more precisely in "A Evolução da Política Brasileira," *O Digesto Econômico* 174 (November–December 1963), pp. 77–85.

70. On the Church at this juncture, consult Emanuel de Kadt, *Catholic Radicals in Brazil* (London: Oxford University Press, 1970), pp. 51–189; Thomas C. Bruneau, *The Church in Brazil: The Politics of Religion* (Austin: University of Texas Press, 1982), pp. 48–53; Thomas C. Bruneau, *The Political Transformation of the Brazilian Catholic Church* (London: Cambridge University Press, 1974), pp. 71–100; and Scott Mainwaring, *The Catholic Church and Politics in Brazil, 1916–1985* (Stanford, CA: Stanford University Press, 1986), pp. 43–75.

71. Jaguaribe, *Political Strategies*, p. 45.

72. Jaguaribe, *Brazilian Nationalism*, p. 65.

73. On the peasantry see Moisés Vinhas, *Problemas Agrário-Camponeses do Brasil* (Rio de Janeiro: Editora Civilização Brasileira, 1972); José de Souza Martins, *Os Camponeses e a Política no Brasil: As lutas sociais no campo e seu lugar no processo político* (Petrópolis, Brazil: Editora Vozes, 1981); Fernando Antônio F. Azevedo, *As Ligas Camponeses: Campesinato e Política, 1955/1964* (Recife, Brazil: Universidade Federal de Pernambuco, 1982); Maria Isaura Pereira de Queiroz, *O Campesinato Brasileiro: Ensaios sôbre civilização e grupos rústicos no Brasil* (Petrópolis, Brazil: Editora Vozes, 1973); Alberto Passos Guimarães, *Quatro Séculos de Latifúndio* (São Paulo: Editôra Fulgor, 1963); and Francisco Julião, *Cambão—The Yoke: The Hidden Face of Brazil* (Harmsworth, Engl.: Penguin Books, 1972).

74. In addition to Edgard Carone, *O PCB*, Vol. 2, *1943–1964* (São Paulo: Difusão Editorial, 1982), and Ronald H. Chilcote, *The Brazilian Communist Party: Conflict and Integration, 1922–1964* (Oxford: Oxford University Press, 1974), pp. 64–81, see Leôncio Martins Rodriguez, "O PCB: Os Dirigentes e Organização," in *HGCB*, Tomo 3, Vol. 3, pp. 363–443, especially pp. 422–431.

75. For the factionalism of the 1955–1957 period, consult Osvaldo Peralva, *O Retrato* (Belo Horizonte, Brazil: Editora Itatiaia, 1960), pp. 253–358.

76. Criticisms of the PCB for its conservatism were frequent in 1963–1964. Alberto Guerreiro Ramos, *Mito e Verdade da Revolução Brasileira* (Rio de Janeiro: Zahar, 1963), pp. 14–15, 180–191, called for the Brazilian Left to create a revolutionary road in both theory and practice that would be in keeping with national reality, not shaped by the dogmas and myths that were a straitjacket for the PCB, while Marcos Peri, *Perspectiva da Revolução Brasileira* (Rio de Janeiro: Edições Autores Reunidos, 1964),

denounced the PCB line as reformist and opportunist and suggested that the party had betrayed the proletariat. Also useful is Octávio Ianni, *Crisis in Brazil* (New York: Columbia University Press, 1971).

77. See Dênis de Moraes and Francisco Vianna, *Prestes: Lutas e autocriticas* (Petrópolis, Brazil: Editora Vozes, 1982). Also useful is Leandro Konder, *A democracia e os communistas no Brasil* (Rio de Janeiro: Edições Graal, 1980). Perceptive and with the perspective gained from an additional two decades plus is Dênis de Moraes, *A Esquerda e o Golpe de 64: Vinte e cinco anos depois, as forças populares repensam seus mitos, sonhos. e ilusões* (Rio de Janeiro: Editora Espaço e Tempo, 1989). Various groupings on the extreme Left are discussed on pages 64–82.

78. Dênis de Moraes, *A Esquerda e o Golpe de 64*, pp. 83–93.

79. For criticism of the PCB's failure to appreciate the changing rural situation, see Caio Prado Júnior, "Marcha da Questão Agrária no Brasil," *Revista Brasiliense* 51 (January–February 1964), pp. 1–9.

80. One of the most penetrating analyses of the radicalization of Catholic youth is contained in Cândido Antônio Mendes de Almeida, *Memento dos Vivos: A Esquerda Católica no Brasil* (Rio de Janeiro: Edições Tempo Brasileiro, 1966), particularly pp. 173–215. See also Haroldo Lima and Aldo Arantes, *História da Ação Popular de JUC ao PC do B* (São Paulo: Editora Alfa-Omega, 1984), pp. 13–58; Luiz Alberto Gomes de Souza, *A JUC: Os estudantes católicos e a política* (Petrópolis, Brazil: Editora Vozes, 1984); and Luiz Gonzaga de Souza Lima, *Evolução política dos Católicos e da Igreja no Brasil* (Petrópolis, Brazil: Editora Vozes, 1979).

81. The most comprehensive analysis of the role of the UNE is Robert Myhr, "The Political Role of the Brazilian Student Movement" (unpublished Ph.D. dissertation, Department of Government, Columbia University, 1968). Also useful are João Roberto Martins Filho, *Movimento Estudantil e Ditadura Militar, 1964–1968* (Campinas, Brazil: Papirus Livraria Editora, 1987), pp. 52–70, and José Luis Sanfelice, *Movimento Estudantil: A UNE na resistência ao golpe de 64* (São Paulo: Cortez Editora, 1986), pp. 17–67. On the university context of the time, see Luiz Antônio Constant Rodrigues da Cunha, *A Universidade crítica no ensino superior na República Populista* (Rio de Janeiro: Francisco Alves Editora, 1983).

82. A public opinion poll taken only a few days before Goulart's ouster gave Kubitschek 28 percent, Lacerda 22 percent, and Carvalho Pinto 12 percent. Arraes and Adhemar de Barros followed with 8 percent each, trailed by Magalhães Pinto with but 2 percent. See *O Globo*, October 6, 1989, p. 5.

83. On Arraes, see Callado, *Tempo de Arraes*; Adison de Barros, *Ascenção e Queda de Miguel Arraes* (Rio de Janeiro: Editora Equador, 1965); and Miguel Arraes et al., *Palavras de Arraes* (Rio de Janeiro: Editora Civilização Brasileira, 1965).   .

84. The major sources on this episode are Dreifuss, *1964: A Conquista do Estado*, pp. 329–337, and Dutra, *IBAD, Sigla da Corupção*. Also useful are Silva, *1964: Golpe ou Contragolpe*, pp. 253–256, and Silva, *O Poder Militar*, pp. 355–365.

85. Dreifuss, *1964: A Conquista do Estado*, pp. 162–337.

86. See Stacchini, *Março 64*, pp. 20–22, and Ferreira, *As Forças Armadas*, pp. 65–69, 138–141.

87. Alberto Dines et al., *Os Idos de Março e a Queda em Abril* (Rio de Janeiro: José Álvaro Editora, 1964), pp. 288–290; Stacchini, *Março 64*, pp. 67–68; and Dulles, *Castello Branco: The Making of a Brazilian President*, pp. 293–318.

88. Discussed in Stacchini, *Março 64*, pp. 70–84, with the text in Silva, *1964: Golpe ou Contragolpe*, pp. 466–471.

89. For Brizola's actions during the regime's final crisis, see Moniz Bandeira, *Brizola e o Trabalhismo*, pp. 94–99. Also useful for this juncture as well as for sidelights on

earlier events is Moniz Bandeira, *Juscelino & Jango—PSD & PTB* (Rio de Janeiro: Editora Artenova, 1979). The PCB was aligned with Jango, while the PCdoB favored Brizola's side. Basbaum speculates that Goulart even preferred to be overthrown rather than see power slip into the hands of Brizola and the CGT. See Basbaum, *História Sincera da República*, Vol. 4, pp. 90–91, 127. Almost all those Goulart government figures interviewed in Moraes, *A Esquerda*, agree that Brizola was driven by a thirst for power and that his actions seriously weakened the administration. For something from a very different position on the political spectrum, see Falcão, *Tudo à Declarar*, pp. 239–250.

90. Pinto, *Guerra Revolucionária*, pp. 45–131.

91. Dines, *Os Idos de Março*, pp. 15–33, and Dulles, *Unrest in Brazil*, pp. 254–257.

92. The events of the month immediately preceding the armed uprising are covered in Silva, *O Poder Militar*, pp. 366–407, and Silva, *1964: Golpe ou Contragolpe*, pp. 315–340, as well as in Skidmore, *Politics in Brazil*, pp. 273–298; Flynn, *Brazil: A Political Analysis*, pp. 280–295; Dulles, *Castello Branco: The Making of a Brazilian President*, pp. 330–361; and Carlos Chagas, *A Guerra das Estrelas (1964–1984): Os Bastidores das Sucessões Presidenciais* (Porto Alegre, Brazil: L & PM Editores, 1985), pp. 11–53. See also Cibilis da Rocha Viana, *Estratégia do desenvolvimento Brasileiro: Uma política nacionalista para vencer a atual crise econômica* (Rio de Janeiro: Editora Civilização Brasileira, 1967), and Cibilis da Rocha Viana, *Reformas de base e a política nacionalista de desenvolvimento de Getúlio à Jango* (Rio de Janeiro: Editora Civilização Brasileira, 1980).

93. The text is in Silva, *1964: Golpe ou Contragolpe*, pp. 457–466. See also Dulles, *Unrest in Brazil*, pp. 267–274, and Dines, *Os Idos de Março*, pp. 34–41, 195–199, 249–257, 309–312.

94. The important role of the press in creating public opinion favorable to the coup is analyzed in Jonathan P. Lane, "Functions of the Mass Media in Brazil's 1964 Crisis," *Journalism Quarterly* 44, 2 (Summer 1967), pp. 297–306. Marcos Sá Corrêa, *1964: Visto e comentado pela Casa Branca* (Porto Alegre, Brazil: L & PM Editores, 1977), stresses the U.S. role, as does Phyllis R. Parker, *Brazil and the Quiet Revolution* (Austin: University of Texas Press, 1979). Economic factors are emphasized in Michael Wallerstein, "The Collapse of Democracy in Brazil: Its Economic Determinants," *Latin American Research Review* 15, 3 (1980), pp. 3–40.

95. The text is in Castello Branco, *Introdução à Revolução Brasileira*, Vol. 2, pp. 268–271.

96. The end of Alberto Dines's assessment of Dutra's pronouncement bears repeating: "It was the professional soldier speaking for the immense majority of the professional soldiers." Dines, *Os Idos de Março*, p. 318.

97. The march is discussed in Dulles, *Unrest in Brazil*, pp. 274–278; Solange de Deus Simões, *Deus, patria, e família: As mulheres no golpe de 1964* (Petrópolis, Brazil: Editora Vozes, 1985); and José Louzeiro et al., *Assim Marcha a Família* (Rio de Janeiro: Editora Civilzação Brasileira, 1965).

98. Goulart's views are treated in Moniz Bandeira, *O Governo João Goulart*, pp. 75–125.

99. The text is in Dines, *Os Idos de Março*, pp. 392–393, and Pinto, *Guerra Revolucionária*, pp. 199–202.

100. Moniz Bandeira, *O Governo João Goulart*, pp. 64–74, 126–162, reconstructs events in a way more sympathetic to Brizola than to Goulart.

101. The naval crisis is covered by Dulles, *Unrest in Brazil*, pp. 278–289, as well as Dines, *Os Idos de Março*, pp. 51–58, 225–233, 263–265, 296–298, 325–330.

102. See Marco A. Borba, *Cabo Anselmo* (São Paulo: Global Editora, 1981).

103. Edmar Morel, *O Golpe Comeou em Washington* (Rio de Janeiro: Editora Civilização Brasileira, 1965), pp. 91–94, provides detail, as does Assis Brasil's testimony reported in *O Estado de S. Paulo*, July 2 and 4, 1964. Admission that this was a fatal mistake in Goulart's judgment and allocation of the blame to Brizola, Assis Brasil, and others is found in Moraes, *A Esquerda*, pp. 99–107, 192ff., 312–316.

104. See Silva, *1964: Golpe ou Contragolpe*, pp. 353–381; Mourão Filho, *Memórias*, pp. 216–366; and Heloisa Maria Murgel Starling, *Os senhores das Gerais: Os novos inconfidentes e o golpe de 1964* (Petrópolis, Brazil: Editora Vozes, 1986).

105. See Costa e Silva's text in Pinto, *Guerra Revolucionária*, pp. 202–204. Dines, *Os Idos de Março*, pp. 59–62, 233–237, 266–273, 330–338, covers this brief period.

106. The total number of noncoms in the area was estimated at 25,000 to 30,000. On this speech see Dulles, *Unrest in Brazil*, pp. 290–294.

107. For a basically pro-Goulart interpretation of the final days, see Moniz Bandeira, *O Governo João Goulart*, pp. 163–186. See also Carone, *A República Liberal II*, pp. 201–221.

108. Sound treatments of these crucial days are in Dulles, *Castello Branco: The Making of a Brazilian President*, pp. 365–381, and Dulles, *Unrest in Brazil*, pp. 303–337. Also useful is Luis Carlos Guedes, *Tinha que ser Minas* (Rio de Janeiro: Editora Nova Fronteira, 1979). Lacerda's account is in his *Depoimento*, pp. 282–291.

109. Stacchini, *Março 64*, pp. 67, 96–99, and Hernani d'Aguiar, *A Revolução por Dentro* (Rio de Janeiro: Editora Artenova, 1976), pp. 102–104. The latter credits Costa e Silva's recruitment to Jayme Portella.

110. D'Aguiar, *A Revolução por Dentro*, pp. 176–180, and Silva, *1964: Golpe ou Contragolpe*, pp. 418–429.

111. On São Paulo's role, see Silva, *1964: Golpe ou Contragolpe*, pp. 247–252, 260–267, 382–393, as well as d'Aguiar, *A Revolução por Dentro*, pp. 142–169.

112. See Mário Poppe de Figueiredo, *A Revolução de 1964: Um depoimento para a história pátria* (Rio de Janeiro: APEC Editora, 1970), pp. 27–72, and Silva, *1964: Golpe ou Contragolpe*, pp. 307–312, 430–446. The broader Rio Grande do Sul environment of these events is provided in Carlos Cortes, *Gaúcho Politics in Brazil: The Politics of Rio Grande do Sul, 1930–1964* (Albuquerque: University of New Mexico Press, 1974), pp. 178–195.

113. Silva, *1964: Golpe ou Contragolpe*, pp. 275–295, 408–412. On the exception, see Seixas Doria, *Eu, Reu sem Crime* (Rio de Janeiro: Editora Equador, 1964).

114. The best case in point, aside from the false note of bellicosity in the rhetoric of the student and labor organizations, was Brizola's "Groups of 11." Defended recently by him as a "desperate" effort to develop an organized base for resisting the impending coup, they came nowhere close to the 24,000 cells of which he had boasted. See Moraes, *A Esquerda*, p. 353. Although Brizola now says they were civic clubs of "democratic resistance" and were never intended as the nucleus of a paramilitary capability, this is both contradicted by his 1964 words and not at all as the surviving members recall the experience. As it turned out, the clubs' chief impact was in adding to public concern that the Left was about to resort to force to impose its goals.

Chapter 7

1. Greater detail on the immediate post-coup situation can be found in Ronald M. Schneider, *The Political System of Brazil: Emergence of a "Modernizing" Authoritarian Regime, 1964–1970* (New York: Columbia University Press, 1971), pp. 108–145, as

well as in John F. W. Dulles, *Castello Branco: The Making of a Brazilian President* (College Station: Texas A & M University Press, 1978), pp. 389–433; John F. W. Dulles, *President Castello Branco: Brazilian Reformer* (College Station: Texas A & M University Press, 1980), pp. 1–63; Carlos Castello Branco, *Os Militares no Poder*, Vol. 1, *Castelo Branco* (Rio de Janeiro: Editora Nova Fronteira, 1976), pp. 5–85; and Luíz Viana Filho, *O Governo Castelo Branco* (Rio de Janeiro: Livraria José Olympio Editora, 1975), pp. 46–84. Very useful for understanding the underlying developments is Wanderley Guilherme dos Santos, *Crise e Castigo: Partidos e Generais na Política Brasileira* (São Paulo: Edições Vértice, 1987). Another stimulating formulation is Simon Schwartzman, *Bases do Autoritarismo Brasileiro*, 2nd ed. (Rio de Janeiro: Editora Campus, 1982), with the views of several scholars contained in Bernardo Sorj and Maria Hermínia Tavares de Almeida, eds., *Sociedade e Política no Brasil pós-64* (São Paulo: Editora Brasiliense, 1983). Interesting sidelights are contained in Ernani do Amaral Peixoto with Aspásia Camargo, Lucia Hippolito, Maria Celína Soares D'Araújo, and Dora Rocha Flaksman, *Artes da Política: Diálogo com Amaral Peixoto* (Rio de Janeiro: Editora Nova Fronteira, 1986), pp. 468–486. See also Wanderley Guilherme dos Santos et al., *Trilogia do terror: A implantação 1964* (São Paulo: Edições Vértice, 1989).

2. Useful interpretations of the confused political scene of 1964–1966, in addition to those cited in note 1, above, include Thomas E. Skidmore, *Politics in Brazil: An Experiment in Democracy, 1930–1964* (Oxford: Oxford University Press, 1967), pp. 303–321; Thomas E. Skidmore, *The Politics of Military Rule in Brazil, 1964–85* (New York: Oxford University Press, 1988), pp. 18–45; Alfred Stepan, *The Military in Politics: Changing Patterns in Brazil* (Princeton, NJ: Princeton University Press, 1971), pp. 213–236; Georges-André Fiechter, *Brazil Since 1964: Modernization Under a Military Regime* (London: Macmillan, 1975), pp. 37–112; and Peter Flynn, *Brazil: A Political Analysis* (Boulder, CO: Westview Press, 1978), pp. 308–352.

3. Valuable for those seeking insight into how this period appeared at the time are three works by distinguished political scientist Cândido Antônio Mendes de Almeida: "Sistema político e modelos de poder no Brasil," *Dados* 1 (1966), pp. 7–41; "O govêrno Castelo Branco: Paradigma e prognose," *Dados* 2/3 (1967), pp. 63–111; and *Beyond Populism* (Albany: State University of New York Press, 1977). Also useful are Amaury de Souza, "Março o Abril? Uma bibliografia comentada sôbre o movimento político de 1964 no Brasil," *Dados* 1 (1966), pp. 160–175, and Lucia Maria Gaspar Gomes, "Cronologia do govêrno Castelo Branco," *Dados* 2/3 (1967), pp. 112–132.

4. Carlos Chagas, *A Guerra das Estrelas (1964/1984): Os Bastidores das Sucessões Presidenciais* (Porto Alegre, Brazil: L & PM Editores, 1985), pp. 50–77; Carlos Lacerda, *Depoimento* (Rio de Janeiro: Editora Nova Fronteira, 1977), pp. 292–302; and Mauro Borges Teixeira, *O Golpe em Goiás: História de um Grande Traição* (Rio de Janeiro: Editora Civilização Brasileira, 1965), pp. 109–119, cover Castelo Branco's selection, as do Juracy M. Magalhães, *Minhas Memórias Provisorias* (Rio de Janeiro: Editora Civilização Brasileira, 1982), pp. 171–174, and Armando Falcão, *Tudo à Declarar* (Rio de Janeiro: Editora Nova Fronteira, 1989). A bitterly disillusioned perspective on this period is found in Olympio Mourão Filho, *Memórias: A Verdade de um Revolucionário* (Porto Alegre, Brazil: L & PM Editores, 1978), pp. 322–328, 371–438. See also Hélio Silva, *1964: Golpe ou Contragolpe* (Rio de Janeiro: Editora Civilização Brasileira, 1975), pp. 408–419.

5. The totals for the three services were about 1,200 during 1964, with twenty-eight more in 1967–1968. See Maria Helena Moreira Alves, *State and Opposition in Military Brazil* (Austin: University of Texas Press, 1985), p. 42. Of interest is Hélio

Silva, *A Vez e a Voz dos Vencidos: Militares x Militares* (Petrópolis, Brazil: Editora Vozes, 1988).

6. The literature on the 1964 repression is substantial, with Márcio Moreira Alves's *Torturas e Torturados* (Rio de Janeiro: Idade Nova, 1966) bringing together most of the essentials.

7. Detail on the second half of 1964 is contained in Dulles, *President Castello Branco*, pp. 63–109; Viana Filho, *O Governo Castelo Branco*, pp. 85–203; and Castello Branco, *Os Militares no Poder*, Vol. 1, pp. 87–180. Lacerda's reconstruction is in his *Depoimento*, pp. 303–326, with a less personally involved perspective in Daniel Krieger, *Desde as Missões Saudades, Lutas, Esperanças* (Rio de Janeiro: Livraria José Olympio Editora, 1976), pp. 179–189.

8. Mitra Arquidiocesana de São Paulo, *Perfil dos Atingidos* (Petrópolis, Brazil: Editora Vozes, 1988), and Dulles, *President Castello Branco*, p. 76. Slightly different figures are given by Marcus F. Figueiredo, "A Política da Coação no Brasil Pós 64," in Lucia Klein and Marcus F. Figueiredo, *Legitimidade e coerção no Brasil pós 64* (Rio de Janeiro: Editora Forense-Universitária, 1978), pp. 109–202.

9. For other interpretations of the doctrinal and career differences between these groups, see Stepan, *The Military in Politics*, pp. 172–187, 236–259; Fernando Pedreira, *Março 31: Civis e Militares no Processo de Crise Brasileiro* (Rio de Janeiro: José Álvaro Editor, 1964), pp. 26–67; Eurico de Lima Figueiredo, *Os Militares e a Democracia: Analise Estrutural da Ideologia do Presidente Castelo Branco* (Rio de Janeiro: Edições Graal, 1980), passim; and Wilfred A. Bacchus, "Long-Term Military Rulership in Brazil: Ideologic Consensus and Dissensus, 1963–1983," *Journal of Political and Military Sociology*, 13, 2 (Spring 1985), pp. 99–123. See also *Revista Brasileira de Estudos Políticos* 21 (July 1966) and *Cadernos Brasileiros* 38 (November–December 1966), passim, as well as C. Neale Ronning and Henry Hunt Keith, "Shrinking Political Arena: Military Governments Since 1964," in Henry Hunt Keith and Robert A. Hayes, eds., *Perspectives on Armed Politics in Brazil* (Tempe: Arizona State University Press, 1976), pp. 25–252.

10. On the economic policy disputes of the Castelo Branco period and their aftermath, consult André Lara Resende, "Estabilização e Reforma: 1964–1967," in Marcelo de Paiva Abreu, ed., *A Ordem do Progresso: Cem Anos de Política Econômica Republicana, 1889–1989* (Rio de Janeiro: Editora Campus, 1989), pp. 213–231; Octávio Ianni, *Estado e Planejamento Econômico no Brasil (1930–1970)* (Rio de Janeiro: Editora Civilização Brasileira, 1971), pp. 225–238; Skidmore, *The Politics of Military Rule*, pp. 29–39, 55–56, 58–63; Antônio Dias Leite, *Caminhos do Desenvolvimento* (Rio de Janeiro: Zahar, 1966); Paul Singer, *Desenvolvimento e Crise* (São Paulo: Difusão Européia do Livro, 1968); Fernando Gasparian, *Em Defesa da Economia Nacional* (Rio de Janeiro: Editora Saga, 1966); Fernando Gasparian, *Capital Estrangeiro e Desenvolvimento da América Latina* (Rio de Janeiro: Editora Civilização Brasileira, 1973); Roberto Campos, *Política Econômica e Mitos Políticos* (Rio de Janeiro: APEC Editora, 1965); Roberto Campos, *A Técnica e o Riso* (Rio de Janeiro: APEC Editora, 1966); Roberto Campos, *Do Outro Lado da Cérca* (Rio de Janeiro: APEC Editora, 1968); Roberto Campos, *Ensaios Contra a Maré* (Rio de Janeiro: APEC Editora, 1969); and Roberto Campos, *Temas e Sistemas* (Rio de Janeiro: APEC Editora, 1969). Also of importance for understanding the ramifications of this increasingly polemical debate are Octávio Gouveia de Bulhões, *Dois Conceitos de Lucro* (Rio de Janeiro: APEC Editora, 1969); Carlos Lacerda, *Reforma e Revolução* (Rio de Janeiro: Distribuidora Record, 1964); Carlos Lacerda, *Palavras e Ação* (Rio de Janeiro: Distribuidora Record, 1965); and Carlos Lacerda, *Brasil entre a Verdade e a Mentira* (Rio de Janeiro: Bloch Editores, 1965. Perspective on the longer period, particularly after 1964, is provided in João

Paulo dos Reis Velloso, *Último Trem para Paris: De Getúlio ao Sarney, "Milagres," choques, e crises do Brasil Moderno*, 2nd ed. (Rio de Janeiro: Editora Nova Fronteira, 1986).

11. See Marta Cehelsky, *Land Reform in Brazil: The Management of Social Change* (Boulder, CO: Westview Press, 1979), pp. 197–212. The positive face of the Castelo Branco government is portrayed in José Wamberto, *Castelo Branco, Revolução e Democracia* (Rio de Janeiro: n.p., 1970), and Luíz Viana Filho, ed., *Castello Branco, Testemunhos de uma Época* (Brasília: Editora Universidade de Brasília, 1986).

12. Campaign issues, strategies, and results are analyzed in Schneider, *The Political System of Brazil*, pp. 163–169.

13. Consult Skidmore, *The Politics of Military Rule*, pp. 42–48; Dulles, *President Castello Branco*, pp. 163–201; Moreira Alves, *State and Opposition in Brazil*, pp. 62–65; Flynn, *Brazil: A Political Analysis*, pp. 338–340; and Viana Filho, *O Governo Castelo Branco*, pp. 332–355. Lacerda's break with Castelo is discussed in Lacerda, *Depoimento*, pp. 327–343.

14. For the last stages of Castelo's government, see Lacerda, *Depoimento*, pp. 356–554; Dulles, *President Castello Branco*, pp. 202–495; and Castello Branco, *Os Militares no Poder*, Vol. 1, pp. 356–680.

15. The MDB is thoroughly analyzed in Maria D'Avila G. Kinzo, *Legal Opposition Politics Under Authoritarian Rule in Brazil: The Case of the MDB, 1966–79* (New York: St. Martin's Press, 1988). See also Amaral Peixoto, *Artes da Política*, pp. 495–521. The new party rules were laid down in Complementary Act No. 4 of November 19, 1965. A majority of the state's delegation of congressmen entered the MDB only from Guanabara, Rio de Janeiro, Rio Grande do Sul, Goiás (seven to six), and Amazonas (four to three). In all other cases the majority faction joined the government party. Even for São Paulo the split was thirty-four to twenty-five in favor of ARENA. Consult also Paulo Roberto Motta, *Movimentos Partidários no Brasil: A Estratégia da Elite e dos Militares* (Rio de Janeiro: Fundação Getúlio Vargas, 1971), pp. 61–72.

16. Costa e Silva's campaign is covered in Chagas, *A Guerra das Estrelas*, pp. 90–114, and Hernani D'Aguiar, *A Revolução por Dentro* (Rio de Janeiro: Editora Artenova, 1976), pp. 263–286. Also useful are Krieger, *Desde as Missões*, pp. 221–237, and Falcão, *Tudo à Declarar*, pp. 299–302.

17. Lacerda's several key articles and addresses are collected in Carlos Lacerda, *Crítica e Autocrítica* (Rio de Janeiro: Editora Nova Fronteira, 1966).

18. See Krieger, *Desde as Missões*, pp. 211–221, and Magalhães, *Minhas Memórias Provisorias*, pp. 189–214.

19. On these elections, see Schneider, *The Political System of Brazil*, pp. 178–195, and Ronald M. Schneider, *Brazil Election Factbook 2* (Washington, DC: Institute for the Comparative Study of Political Systems, 1966), passim, as well as *Revista Brasileira de Estudos Políticos* 23/24 (July 1967–January 1968).

20. Essential for understanding the 1967 constitution in the context of Brazilian experience and the exceptional acts and decrees of the Castelo administration are two volumes by Osny Duarte Pereira: *A Constituição do Brasil 1967* (Rio de Janeiro: Editora Civilização Brasileira, 1967) and *A Constituição Federal e Suas Modificações Incorporados ao Texto* (Rio de Janeiro: Editora Civilização Brasileira, 1966). Pereira's highly critical view is balanced out by the much more favorable Themistocles B. Cavalcanti et al., *Estudos Sôbre a Constituição de 1967 e Sua Emenda No. 1*, 2nd ed. (Rio de Janeiro: Fundação Getúlio Vargas, 1977). Innovations with respect to political rights and the party system are discussed in Paulo Bonavides, *A Crise Política Brasileira* (Rio de Janeiro: Editora Forense, 1969), and the incisive Oscar Dias Corrêa, *A Constituição de 1967* (Rio de Janeiro: Editora Forense, 1968). Dias Corrêa left the Supreme Court to become justice minister in January 1989.

21. Costa e Silva has not yet been the subject of an even partially satisfactory biography. Nelson Dimas Filho, *Costa e Silva: O Homen e o Líder* (Rio de Janeiro: Edições "O Cruzeiro," 1966) is the weakest kind of campaign biography, while Jayme Portella de Melo, *A Revolução e o Governo Costa e Silva* (Rio de Janeiro: Guavira Editores, 1979) is a collection of materials and papers assembled by Costa's chief military aide and largely devoted to putting Costa in the best possible light. Thus Carlos Castello Branco, *Os Militares no Poder*, Vol. 2, *O Ato 5* (Rio de Janeiro: Editora Nova Fronteira, 1978) and Vol. 3, *A Baile das Solteironas* (Rio de Janeiro: Editora Nova Fronteira, 1979) become of even greater importance for reconstructing this period than is their companion volume covering the Castelo years. These volumes should be supplemented by Fernando Pedreira, *Brasil Política, 1964–1975* (São Paulo: Difusão Européia do Livro, 1975), pp. 27–145. Selected aspects of the Costa administration are covered in Kinzo, *Legal Opposition Politics*, pp. 96–120, and Moreira Alves, *State and Opposition in Brazil*, pp. 80–105, with the most comprehensive analyses being Skidmore, *The Politics of Military Rule*, pp. 66–104; Flynn, *Brazil: A Political Analysis*, pp. 366–438; Fiechter, *Brazil Since 1964*, pp. 123–170; and Schneider, *The Political System of Brazil*, pp. 203–240. Sidelights on some episodes are provided by Krieger, *Desde as Missões*, pp. 269ff.

22. Still useful is the perceptive interpretation of the transition provided by James W. Rowe in "Brazil Stops the Clock, Part I: 'Democratic Formalism' Before 1964 and in the Elections of 1966," and "Brazil Stops the Clock, Part 2: The New Constitution and the New Model," *American Universities Field Staff Reports*, East Coast Latin American Series, Vol. 13, Nos. 1 and 2 (March 1967).

23. On Delfim Netto's policy views see his *Planejamento para o Desenvolvimento Econômico* (São Paulo: Livraria Editora Pioneira, 1966).

24. Useful for following the course of events is Lucia Maria Gaspar Gomes, "Cronologia do primeiro ano do Govêrno Costa e Silva," *Dados* 4 (1968), pp. 199–220.

25. Lacerda's account is in his *Depoimento* (Rio de Janeiro: Editora Nova Fronteira, 1977), pp. 356–364.

26. Consult Arthur José Poerner, *O Poder Jovem: História da Participação Política dos Estudantes Brasileiras* (Rio de Janeiro: Editora Civilização Brasileira, 1968), pp. 267–310; João Roberto Martins Filho, *Movimento Estudantil e Ditadura Militar, 1964–1968* (Campinas, Brazil: Papirus Livraria Editor, 1987), pp. 75–109; José Luis Sanfelice, *Movimento Estudantil: A UNE na resistência ao golpe de 64* (São Paulo: Cortez Editora, 1986), pp. 68–111; and Fay Haussman and Jerry Haar, *Education in Brazil* (Hamden, CT: Archon Books, 1978), pp. 80–88.

27. For background, see José Oscar Beozzo, "A Igreja Entre a Revolução de 1930, O Estado Novo e a Redemocratização," in *História Geral da Civilização Brasileira* (HGCB), Tomo 3, Vol. 4, *Economia e Cultura (1930–1964)* (São Paulo: Difusão Editorial, 1984), pp. 271–341, and Antônio Flávio de Oliveira Pierucci, Beatriz Muniz de Souza, and Cândido Procópio Ferreira de Camargo, "Igreja Católica: 1945–1970," in ibid., pp. 343–380. Also see Cândido Procópio Ferreira de Camargo, *Igreja e Desenvolvimento* (São Paulo: Centro Brasileiro de Análise e Planejamento [CEBRAP], 1971); Sérgio Miceli, *A elite eclesiástica brasileira (1890–1930)* (São Paulo: Editora Bertrand Brasil, 1988); and João Camilo de Oliveira Torres, *História das Idéias Religiosas no Brasil* (São Paulo: Editorial Grijalbo, 1968).

28. Useful are Luiz Gonzaga de Souza Lima, *Evolução Político dos Católicos e da Igreja no Brasil* (Petrópolis, Brazil: Editora Vozes, 1979), and Fred Gillette Sturm, "Religion," in Michael L. Conniff and Frank D. McCann, eds., *Modern Brazil: Elites and Masses in Historical Perspective* (Lincoln: University of Nebraska Press, 1989),

pp. 246–264. The key role of the Centro Dom Vital and of outstanding Catholic intellectuals Jackson de Figueiredo and Alceu Amoroso Lima is covered in almost all works on the Church, as is the importance in the elections of the 1940s and 1950s of the Catholic Electoral League (LEC) as the Church's political arm.

29. Thomas C. Bruneau, *The Political Transformation of the Brazilian Catholic Church* (London: Cambridge University Press, 1974), pp. 107–236; Thomas C. Bruneau, *The Church in Brazil: The Politics of Religion* (Austin: University of Texas Press, 1982), pp. 11–92; Scott Mainwaring, *The Catholic Church and Politics in Brazil, 1916–1985* (Stanford, CA: Stanford University Press, 1986), pp. 79–141; and Emanuel de Kadt, *Catholic Radicals in Brazil* (London: Oxford University Press, 1970), pp. 190–229, are all useful, with Margaret Todaro, "Pastors, Prophets and Politicians: A Study of the Political Development of the Brazilian Church, 1921–1945" (unpublished Ph.D. dissertation, Department of History, Columbia University, 1969) key for its historical role in politics. For perspective of the times, see Márcio Moreira Alves, *O Cristo do Povo* (Rio de Janeiro: Editora Sabiá, 1968).

30. See Haroldo Lima and Aldo Arantes, *História da Ação Popular: Da JUC ao PC do B* (São Paulo: Editora Alfa-Omega, 1984), pp. 59–109, and Álvaro Caldas, *Tirando o Capuz* (Rio de Janeiro: Editora Codecri, 1981). Caldas spent almost all the early 1970s as a political prisoner.

31. Consult Jacob Gorender, *Combate nas Trevas: A Esquerda Brasileira das Ilusões Perdidas a Luta Armada* (São Paulo: Editora Ática, 1987), pp. 85–92. Useful are Moisés Vinhas, *O Partidão: A luta por um partido de massas, 1922–1974* (São Paulo: Editora Hucitec, 1982); Dênis de Moraes and Francisco Viana, *Prestes: Lutas e Autocríticas* (Petrópolis, Brazil: Editora Vozes, 1982); and Edgard Carone, *O PCB*, Vol. 3, *1964–1982* (São Paulo: Difusão Editorial, 1982).

32. Marighella's most influential writings include *Porque resistí a prisão* (Recife, Brazil: Edições Contemporâneas, 1965) and *For the Liberation of Brazil* (Middlesex, Engl.: Penguin Books, 1971). A series of participant accounts are brought together in Antônio Caso et al., *A esquerda armada no Brasil, 1967–1971* (Lisbon: Editora Moraes, 1976). For the emergence of these and other groups, see Gorender, *Combate nas Trevas*, pp. 94–160.

33. José Emiliano and Oldeck Miranda, *Lamarca, o capitão da guerrilha* (São Paulo: Editora Global, 1980).

34. Useful on the armed struggle are Gilson Rebello, *A Guerrilha de Caparaó* (São Paulo: Editora Alfa-Omega, 1980), which is based on a series of *O Estado de S. Paulo* articles in February 1980, and Alfred Syrkis, *Os Carbonários: Memórias da guerrilha perdida* (São Paulo: Editora Global, 1980).

35. Though the choice of terminology and historical parallelism is my own, stimulus for considering the late 1960s generational differences within the army in terms of *as teses sorbonianas* comes from Fernando Pedreira's essay "O nosso Exército antes e depois," in *Correio da Manhã*, February 11, 1968. Also useful are Oliveiros S. Ferreira, *O Fim do Poder Civil* (São Paulo: Editora Convívio, 1966); Edmund Campos Coelho, *Em Busca de Identidade: O Exército e a Política na Sociedade Brasileira* (Rio de Janeiro: Editora Forense-Universitária, 1976), pp. 153–172; and Alexandre de Souza Barros, "The Brazilian Military: Professional Socialization, Political Performance and State Building" (unpublished Ph.D. dissertation, Department of Political Science, University of Chicago, 1978).

36. This theme is explored in Schneider, *The Political System of Brazil*, pp. 242–261, as well as in Eliezer Rizzo de Oliveira, *As Forças Armadas: Política e ideologia no Brasil, 1964–1969* (Petrópolis, Brazil: Editora Vozes, 1976).

37. Wanderley Guilherme dos Santos, "Uma Revisão da Crise Brasileira," *Cadernos Brasileiros* 38 (November–December 1966), p. 56.

38. *Jornal do Brasil*, August 24, 1968, reports on this debate.

39. For a denunciation of repression and right-wing terror, see Flávio Deckes, *Radiografia do Terrorismo no Brasil, 1966/1980* (São Paulo: Icone Editora, 1985), pp. 49–67; João Quartim, *Dictatorship and Armed Struggle in Brazil* (New York: Monthly Review Press, 1971), pp. 146–147; Daniel Aarão Reis Filho and Jair Ferreira de Sá, eds., *Imagens da Revolução: Documentos políticos das organizações clandestinos de esquerda dos anos 1961-1971* (Rio de Janeiro: Editora Marco Zero, 1985); Gorender, *Combate nas Trevas*, pp. 141–152; and Daniel Aarão Reis Filho and Pedro de Moraes, *1968 a paixão de uma utopia* (Rio de Janeiro: Editora Espaço e Tempo, 1988).

40. "A corrente inconformada do Governo," *Visão*, October 11, 1968, pp. 21–23. In English, see Margaret Sarles Jenks, "Political Parties in Authoritarian Brazil" (unpublished Ph.D. dissertation, Department of Political Science, Duke University, 1979).

41. See Luiz Henrique Romagnoli and Tânia Gonçalves, *A volta de UNE: De Ibiúna à Salvador* (São Paulo: Editora Alfa-Omega, 1979), pp. 11–13. The press first reported 1,240 arrests, although official figures on those actually booked totalled only 712. See *O Estado de S. Paulo* and *Jornal do Brasil* of October 13 through October 17, 1968. Useful on the student movement in 1968 are Martins Filho, *Movimento Estudantil e Ditadura Militar*, pp. 117–166, and Sanfelice, *Movimento Estudantil*, pp. 145–175.

42. Moreira Alves's views are recounted in *A Grain of Mustard Seed: The Awakening of the Brazilian Revolution* (New York: Doubleday, 1973), pp. 1–25. Compare with Krieger, *Desde as Missões*, pp. 327–341.

43. A detailed discussion of this crisis is in Schneider, *The Political System of Brazil*, pp. 271–278; Moreira Alves, *State and Opposition in Military Brazil*, pp. 93–104; Skidmore, *The Politics of Military Rule*, pp. 79–83; and Flynn, *Brazil: A Political Analysis*, pp. 418–427. Officers opposed to AI-5 met with congressional leaders who included Covas and Humberto Lucena, who would be Senate president in 1988.

44. The text is in *Visão*, December 20, 1968, pp. 21–23, as well as in the daily papers of December 14. Lacerda's perspective is in his *Depoimento*, pp. 364–378.

45. See Figueiredo, "A Política de Coação," pp. 150–155, for a breakdown by year, category, and degree of punishment. The first two months of 1969 are treated in Castello Branco, *Os Militares no Poder*, Vol. 3, pp. 13–82.

46. On economic policy, see Luiz Aranha Corrêa do Lago, "A Retomada do Crescimento e as Distorções do 'Milagre': 1967-1973," in Paiva Abreu, ed., *A Ordem do Progresso*, pp. 233–294.

47. I analyze the March–August period in Schneider, *The Political System of Brazil*, pp. 279–294. For greater detail, see Castello Branco, *Os Militares no Poder*, Vol. 3, pp. 103–309.

48. Carlos Chagas, *113 Dias de Angustia: Impedimento e Morte de um Presidente*, 2nd ed. (Porto Alegre, Brazil: L & PM Editores, 1977), is valuable on the rest of the year, although it puts Costa e Silva in the best possible light—which is quite natural as the author was the presidential press secretary.

49. See ibid., pp. 139–148, for the exchange of letters.

50. Skidmore, *The Politics of Military Rule*, pp. 99–104, and Schneider, *The Political System of Brazil*, pp. 295–304. The kidnapping is in Gorender, *Combate nas Trevas*, pp. 166–170, and is told by a participant in Fernando Gabeira, *Carta sobre a anistia* (Rio de Janeiro: Editora Codecri, 1979), pp. 41–57, and Fernando Gabeira, *O que é isso, Companheiro?* (Rio de Janeiro: Editora Codecri, 1980), pp. 107–130.

51. *Constituição da República Federativa do Brasil, Emenda No. 1* (Brasília: Imprensa Nacional, 1969). See also the texts of Institutional Acts 12 through 17 (August 31 through October 14) in Chagas, *113 Dias da Angustia*, pp. 231–238. Albuquerque

Lima's strength was centered in the navy, where he was the favorite, and in the First, Third, and Fourth Armies—where in each case he ran second to Médici. Within the army Alto Commando on September 29 Albuquerque was edged out for third place by Antônio Carlos Muricy by a margin of six to five, so his name was not on the list of three forwarded by the army to the armed forces high command (see Chagas, *113 Dias da Angustia*, pp. 170–189). Castello Branco, *Os Militares no Poder*, Vol. 3, pp. 310–358, covers September and October.

52. On the unfolding of the Médici government, see Skidmore, *The Politics of Military Rule*, pp. 105–159; Flynn, *Brazil: A Political Analysis*, pp. 441–455; Schneider, *The Political System of Brazil*, pp. 297–329; Pedreira, *Brasil Política*, pp. 149–205; and Castello Branco, *Os Militares no Poder*, Vol. 3, pp. 359–757. Also useful is Fernando José Leite Costa and Lucia Gomes Klein, "Um Ano de Govêrno Médici," *Dados* 9 (1972), pp. 156–221.

53. Marighella's demise is covered in Gorender, *Combate nas Trevas*, pp. 171–178. See also Frei Betto, *Batismo de Sangue: Os dominicanos e a morte de Marighella* (Rio de Janeiro: Editora Civilização Brasileira, 1982).

54. On the influence of soccer, consult Peter Flynn, "Sambas, Soccer, and Nationalism," *New Society* 463 (August 12, 1971), pp. 327–330, and Robert M. Levine, "The Burden of Success: *Futebol* and Brazilian Society Through the 1970s," *Journal of Popular Culture* 14, 3 (Winter 1980), pp. 453–464. Brazil's loss in the championship game in 1950 certainly didn't strengthen the regime against Vargas's comeback, but the 1958 victory probably helped Kubitschek's position in the state and congressional balloting of that year. Repeating as world champions in 1962 on balance helped the Goulart government stabilize itself in the analogous voting of that year. A dismal 1966 performance had limited impact because of the very restricted competition of that year's elections.

55. See Schneider, *The Political System of Brazil*, pp. 319–324.

56. On his political machine, see Eli Diniz, *Voto e Máquina Política—Patronagem e Clientelismo no Rio de Janeiro* (Rio de Janeiro: Editora Paz e Terra, 1982). A defense of his government by one of its ranking members is Francisco Manoel de Melo Franco, *O Governo Chagas Freitas: Uma Perspectiva Nacional Através de uma Experiência Local* (Rio de Janeiro: Livraria José Olympio Editora, 1977).

57. See Gorender, *Combate nas Trevas*, pp. 179–213; Jaime Sautchuk et al., *A Guerrilha do Araguaia* (São Paulo: Editora Alfa-Omega, 1978); Fernando Portela, *Guerra de Guerrilhas no Brasil* (São Paulo: Global Editora, 1979), which is based upon his series of articles in *Jornal da Tarde* in mid-January 1979; Wladimir Pomar, *Araguaia, o Partido e a Guerrilha* (São Paulo: Editora Brasil Debates, 1980), which gives the PCdoB's line chiefly through party texts and participants' perspectives; Moreira Alves, *State and Opposition in Military Brazil*, pp. 103–137; and Clóvis Moura, ed., *Diário da Guerrilha do Araguaia* (São Paulo: Editora Alfa-Omega, 1979), which reproduces the version written in 1975 by the leaders of the ill-fated 1972–1974 attempt.

58. The fundamental sources on repression include Dom Paulo Evaristo Arns et al., *Brasil: Nunca Mais* (Petrópolis, Brazil: Editora Vozes, 1985); Mitra Arquidiocesana de São Paulo, *Perfil dos Atingidos*; and Antônio Carlos Fon, *Tortura: A história da repressão política no Brasil* (São Paulo: Global Editora, 1979). Joan R. Dassin, "Press Censorship and the Military State in Brazil," in Jane L. Curry and Joan R. Dassin, eds., *Press Control Around the World* (New York: Praeger Publishers, 1982), pp. 149–186, and Paolo Marconi, *A Censura política na imprensa Brasileira: 1968–1978* (São Paulo: Global Editora, 1980), are key on this important topic. Skidmore, *The Politics of Military Rule*, pp. 125–135, provides an abundantly documented account of repression

under Médici. Presidential pronouncements are contained in the following works by Emílio Garrastazú Médici: *O Jôgo da Verdade* (Brasília: Imprensa Nacional [IN], 1970), *Nova Conciência do Brasil* (Brasília: IN, 1970), *A Verdadeira Paz* (Brasília: IN, 1971), *Tarefa de Todos Nós* (Brasília: IN, 1971), *O Povo não Está Só* (Brasília: IN, 1972), and *O Sinal da Amanhã* (Brasília: IN, 1972). Médici's post-presidential reflections are in Antônio Carlos Scartezini, *Segredos de Médici* (São Paulo: Editora Marco Zero, 1985). Lacerda's account of the regime's destruction of the Frente Ampla is in Lacerda, *Depoimento*, pp. 379–397, while Castello Branco, *Os Militares no Poder*, Vol. 3, pp. 540–679, treats May through September 1970.

59. See Joseph Comblin, *A Ideologia da Segurança Nacional: O Poder Militar na América Latina* (Rio de Janeiro: Editora Civilização Brasileira, 1978), which puts this into broader comparative perspective.

60. In addition to works already cited in notes 27, 28, and 29, three studies by Ralph della Cava are essential for understanding the Church's role in society and politics. See Ralph della Cava, ed., *A Igreja em Flagrante: Catolicismo e Sociedade na Imprensa Brasileira, 1964–1980* (Rio de Janeiro: Editora Marco Zero, 1985); Ralph della Cava, "Catholicism and Society in Twentieth-Century Brazil," *Latin American Research Review* 11, 2 (1976), pp. 7–50; and Ralph della Cava, "The 'People's Church,' the Vatican, and *Abertura*," in Alfred Stepan, ed., *Democratizing Brazil: Problems of Transition & Consolidation* (New York: Oxford University Press, 1989), pp. 143–167, especially pp. 144–147.

61. Murilo Filho's fact-filled books are *O Desafio Brasileiro* (Rio de Janeiro: Bloch Editores, 1970), *O Milagre Brasileiro* (Rio de Janeiro: Bloch Editores, 1972), *O Modelo Brasileiro* (Rio de Janeiro: Bloch Editores, 1974), and *O Progresso Brasileiro* (Rio de Janeiro: Bloch Editores, 1974). Murilo Filho was a ranking staffer of the Manchete publishing firm. In a similar vein were texts for the required courses of "Moral and Civic Education" and "Brazilian Problems," with Arnaldo Niskier's *Nosso Brasil* (Rio de Janeiro: Bloch Editores, 1973) being one of the best and José Alfredo Amaral Gurgel's *Segurança e Democracia* (Rio de Janeiro: Livraria José Olympio Editora, 1975) reflecting the content at the university level. On the other side were a barrage of works by leftist intellectuals, with the van composed of Paul Singer, *O "Milagre Brasileiro" Causas e Consequências* (São Paulo: Centro Brasileiro de Análise e Planejamento [CEBRAP], 1972), pp. 57–77; Celso Furtado, *Análise do "Modelo" Brasileiro* (Rio de Janeiro: Editora Civilização Brasileira, 1972); Celso Furtado, *O Mito do Desenvolvimento Econômico* (Rio de Janeiro: Editora Paz e Terra, 1974); Celso Furtado, *Um Projeto para o Brasil* (Rio de Janeiro: Editora Saga, 1969); and Celso Furtado, *A Hegemonia dos Estados Unidos e o Subdesenvolvimento da América Latina* (Rio de Janeiro: Editora Civilização Brasileira, 1973). Also relevant are Maria da Conceição Tavares, *Da substituição de importações ao capitalismo financeiro: Ensaios sôbre economia Brasileira* (Rio de Janeiro: Zahar Editores, 1973); Francisco de Oliveira, *A Economia da Dependência Imperfeita* (Rio de Janeiro: Edições Graal, 1977); Dionísio Dias Carneiro, ed., *Brasil: Dilemas da Política Econômica* (Rio de Janeiro: Editora Campus, 1977); Fernando H. Cardoso, *O Modelo Político Brasileiro e Outros Ensaios* (São Paulo: Difusão Européia do Livro, 1972); Evaldo Amaro Vieira, *Estado e Miséria Social no Brasil: De Getúlio à Geisel, 1951 à 1978* (São Paulo: Cortez Editora, 1983); and Ricardo Tolipan and Arthur Carlos Tinelli, eds., *A Controvérsia Sôbre Distribuição da Renda e Desenvolvimento* (Rio de Janeiro: Zahar, 1975). See also Luiz Alberto Moniz Bandeira, *Cartéis e Desnacionalização (a experiência brasileira: 1964–1974)* (Rio de Janeiro: Editora Civilização Brasileira, 1975), and Osny Duarte Pereira, *Multinacionais no Brasil: Aspectos Sociais e Políticos* (Rio de Janeiro: Editora Civilização Brasileira, 1974).

62. Roberto Campos and Mário Henrique Simonsen consistently refuted such allegations—both those made within Brazil and those by foreign scholars. See the

former's *Temas e sistemas* and *O Mundo que Vejo e no Desejo* (Rio de Janeiro: APEC Editora, 1976). Jointly Campos and Simonsen produced *A Nova Economia Brasileira* (Rio de Janeiro: Livraria José Olympio Editora, 1974) and *Formas Criativas no Desenvolvimento Brasileiro* (Rio de Janeiro: APEC Editora, 1975). See also Simonsen's *Inflação, Gradualismo x Tratamento de Choque* (Rio de Janeiro: APEC Editora, 1970), *Brasil 2001* (Rio de Janeiro: APEC Editora, 1969), and *Brasil 2002* (Rio de Janeiro: APEC Editora and Bloch Editores, 1972). Also of value are Carlos Geraldo Langoni, *Distribuição da Renda e Desenvolvimento Econômico do Brasil* (Rio de Janeiro: Editora Expresso e Cultura, 1973), and Carlos Geraldo Langoni, *A Economia da Transformação* (Rio de Janeiro: Livraria José Olympio Editora, 1975). In English, consult Samuel A. Morley, *Labor Markets and Inequitable Growth* (Cambridge: Cambridge University Press, 1982); Lance Taylor, Edmar L. Bacha, Eliana A. Cardoso, and Frank J. Lysy, *Models of Growth and Distribution for Brazil* (New York: Oxford University Press, 1980); and Stefan H. Robock, *Brazil: A Study in Development Progress* (Lexington, MA: Lexington Books, 1975).

63. Chagas, *A Guerra das Estrelas*, pp. 199–222.

Chapter 8

1. The Geisel period is treated in considerable detail in Thomas E. Skidmore, *The Politics of Military Rule in Brazil, 1964–1985* (New York: Oxford University Press, 1988), pp. 160–209; Peter Flynn, *Brazil: A Political Analysis* (Boulder, CO: Westview Press, 1978), pp. 472–512; and Roberto Attila Amaral Vieira, *Crônica dos Anos Geisel* (Rio de Janeiro: Editora Forense-Universitária, 1987). Walder de Góes, *O Brasil de General Geisel* (Rio de Janeiro: Editora Nova Fronteira, 1978), is quite useful. Adirson de Barros, *Março: Geisel e a Revolução Brasileira* (Rio de Janeiro: Editora Artenova, 1976), is worth consulting, along with Armando Falcão, *Tudo à Declarar* (Rio de Janeiro: Editora Nova Fronteira, 1989), pp. 323–396.

2. André Gustavo Stumpf and Merival Pereira Filho, *A Segunda Guerra: Sucessão de Geisel* (São Paulo: Editora Brasiliense, 1979), pp. 16–17, 19, 22, is categorical on the point that Figueiredo's candidacy was in Geisel's mind from the very beginning. Carlos Chagas, *A Guerra das Estrelas (1964/1984): Os Bastidores das Sucessões Presidenciais* (Porto Alegre, Brazil: L & PM Editores, 1985), pp. 223–225, is less certain of this. See also Getúlio Bittencourt, *A Quinta Estrela: Como se tenta fazer um presidente no Brasil* (São Paulo: Livraria Editora Ciências Humanas, 1978).

3. As cited in Bernard Kucinski, *Abertura: A história de uma crise* (São Paulo: Editora Brasil Debates, 1982), p. 20.

4. Examples of the views of PMDB leaders at this juncture include Ulysses Guimarães, *Rompendo o Cerco* (Rio de Janeiro: Editora Paz e Terra, 1978); André Franco Montoro, *Da "Democracia" que Temos para a Democracia que Queremos* (Rio de Janeiro: Editora Paz e Terra, 1974); Alencar Furtado, *Salgando a Terra* (Rio de Janeiro: Editora Paz e Terra, 1977); Freitas Nobré, *Debate Sôbre Problemas Brasileiras* (Brasília: Coordenada Editora, 1974); Freitas Nobré, *Constituente* (Rio de Janeiro: Editora Paz e Terra, 1978); Marcos Freire, *Oposição no Brasil, hoje* (Rio de Janeiro: Editora Paz e Terra, 1974); and Marcos Freire, *Nação Oprimida* (Rio de Janeiro: Editora Paz e Terra, 1977). Contrast these with the views of Geisel's justice minister, in the following works by Armando Falcão: *A Revolução Permanente* (Brasília: Imprensa Nacional, 1975), *A Democracia Moderna* (Brasília: Imprensa Nacional, 1976), and *Tudo à Declarar*.

5. The best analysis of the views of Geisel and Golbery is Alfred Stepan, *Os Militares: Da Abertura à Nova República* (Rio de Janeiro: Editora Paz e Terra, 1986),

pp. 44–55, also found in Alfred Stepan, *Rethinking Military Politics: Brazil and the Southern Cone* (Princeton, NJ: Princeton University Press, 1988), pp. 33–44. Stepan's position on Golbery's views is quite close to the picture I gathered from six discussions with Golbery between 1966 and 1983. Golbery's most complete published formulation of his political views is in the 1980 speech to the Escola Superior da Guerra, published in Golbery do Couto e Silva, *Conjuntura Política Nacional: O Poder Executivo e Geopolítica do Brasil* (Rio de Janeiro: Livraria José Olympio Editora, 1981), pp. 3–37. Elio Gaspari's forthcoming *Geisel e Golbery: O Sacerdote e o Feiticeiro* explores these two complex and very nonpublic, public figures. Indications of its thrust can be found in Gaspari's "O bruxo fez seu ultímo arte," *Veja*, September 23, 1987, pp. 20–31, and in *Veja*, August 12, 1981, pp. 20–33.

6. Golbery was an insatiable student of relevant comparative experience. In addition to facilitating the fieldwork of such scholars as Alfred Stepan, he had proven willing to read through long manuscripts, in the process of which he was intrigued by my application of Huntington's concepts to Brazilian experience from the monarchy through the 1960s. Golbery met Huntington for the first time in late 1969, being "enormously impressed" (letter from Golbery to Ronald Schneider, November 12, 1969). Moreover, Golbery was familiar with the more focused views of Huntington on the Brazilian situation presented to Leitão de Abreu during an October 1972 visit and in a subsequent paper. In February and August 1974 Huntington consulted with Golbery and other Geisel advisors. On Huntington's advice to them, see Skidmore, *The Politics of Military Rule*, pp. 165–167.

7. Wanderley Guilherme dos Santos's September 1973 paper, "Estratégias de descompressão política," is in Wanderley Guilherme dos Santos, *Poder e Política: Crônica do Autoritarismo Brasileiro* (Rio de Janeiro: Editora Forense-Universitária, 1978), pp. 145–211, and is accompanied by insightful articles published by him during the second half of 1974. For a somewhat less pragmatic approach to the question, see dos Santos's essay, "Para um Novo Pacto Social," in Hélio Jaguaribe, *Brasil: Crise e Alternativas* (Rio de Janeiro: Zahar Editores, 1974), pp. 91–120.

8. Wanderley Guilherme dos Santos, "As eleições e a dinâmica do processo político brasileira," *Dados* 14 (1977), pp. 211–239, reprinted in dos Santos, *Poder e Política*, pp. 93–142, is very insightful on this period.

9. The ensuing sections of this chapter expand upon some passages from Ronald M. Schneider, *Brazil: Foreign Policy of a Future World Power* (Boulder, CO: Westview Press, 1976), and Ronald M. Schneider, "The Brazilian Military in Politics," in Robert Wesson, ed., *New Military Politics in Latin America* (New York: Praeger Publishers, 1982), pp. 51–77.

10. Superior Electoral Tribunal, *Dados Estatísticos*, Vol. 11 (Brasília: Imprensa Nacional, 1977). Among the most useful sources on these elections are *Revista Brasileira de Estudos Políticos* 43 (July 1976); Margaret Sarles Jenks, "Political Parties in Authoritarian Brazil" (unpublished Ph.D. dissertation, Department of Political Science, Duke University, 1979), pp. 253–262; Margaret J. Sarles, "Maintaining Control Through Political Parties: The Brazilian Strategy," *Comparative Politics* 15, 1 (1982), pp. 41–72; and Sebastião Nery, *Os 16 Derrotas que Abalaram o Brasil* (Rio de Janeiro: Francisco Alves Editora, 1975).

11. Vargas had only presided over the 1933–1934 balloting, his demise in 1954 coming before that year's elections. Dutra, like Geisel, had both 1946–1947 and 1950, but Kubitschek had only 1958, Goulart just 1962, Castello 1966, and Médici but 1970. Quadros and Costa e Silva failed to last even to one election. Figueiredo, despite a six-year term, would preside over congressional and gubernatorial elections only in 1982, while Sarney would do so just in 1986. Fernando Collor de Mello is

scheduled to parallel Geisel's experience, with elections in 1990 and 1994—the latter including presidential balloting.

12. Bolívar Lamounier, "Comportamento Eleitoral em São Paulo: Passado e Presente," in Bolívar Lamounier and Fernando Henrique Cardoso, eds., *Os Partidos e as Eleições no Brasil* (Rio de Janeiro: Editora Paz e Terra, 1975), pp. 15–44. This important work contains four other studies on São Paulo plus useful ones on Minas Gerais and Rio Grande do Sul. On the resulting Congress, see Câmara dos Deputados, *Deputados Brasileiros: Repertório biográfico dos membros da Câmara dos Deputados, oitava legislatura (1975-1979)* (Brasília: Câmara dos Deputados, 1975). This can usefully be compared with Câmara dos Deputados, *Deputados Brasileiros: Repertório biográfico dos membros da Câmara dos Deputados, Sétima Legislatura (1971-1975)* (Brasília: Biblioteca da Câmara dos Deputados, 1971).

13. Jenks, "Political Parties in Authoritarian Brazil," pp. 235, 251. Useful on the 1972–1977 period is Paulo J. Krishke, ed., *Do "Milagre" à "Abertura"* (São Paulo: Cortez Editora, 1982).

14. Consult Ernesto Geisel, *Mensagem ao Congresso Nacional 1975* (Brasília: Imprensa Nacional, 1975). Fernando Pedreira, "Decompression in Brazil?" *Foreign Affairs* 53, 3 (April 1975), pp. 498–512, is useful.

15. On the Herzog case, see Hamilton Almeida Filho, *A sangue-quente: A morte do jornalista Vladimir Herzog* (São Paulo: Editora Alfa-Omega, 1978); Fernando Jordão, *Dossiê Herzog: Prisão, Tortura, e Morte no Brasil* (São Paulo: Global Editora, 1979); and Paulo Markun, ed., *Vlado, Retrato de um homen e de uma época* (São Paulo: Editora Brasiliense, 1985).

16. See Carlos Alberto Luppi, *Manoel Fiel Filho: Quem vai pagar por este crime?* (São Paulo: Editora Escrita, 1980).

17. Useful on this confused period are Eliezer Rizzo de Oliviera, "Conflits militaires et décisions sous la présidence du General Geisel (1974–1979)," in Alain Roquié, ed., *Les Partis Militaires au Brésil* (Paris: Presses de la Fondation Nationale des Sciences Politiques, 1980), pp. 105–140, and Marcus Faria Figueiredo and José Antônio Borges Cheibub, "A Abertura Política de 1973 à 1981: Quem disse o que, quando— Inventário de um debate," *Boletim Informativo e Bibliográfico de Ciências Sociais* 14 (second semester 1982), pp. 29–61.

18. This is based on a careful reading of the press and very extensive interviews that I carried out in 1975 and 1976 in all major centers.

19. Kucinski, *Abertura*, p. 52. The most thorough analyses of these elections are Fábio Wanderley Reis, ed., *Os Partidos e o Regime: A lógica do processo eleitoral Brasileiro* (São Paulo: Editora Símbolo, 1978), and Jenks, "Political Parties in Authoritarian Brasil," pp. 289–303.

20. The Lei Falcão is analyzed in Celina Rabello Duarte, "A Lei Falcão: Antecedentes e impacto," in Bolívar Lamounier, ed., *Voto de Desconfiança: Eleições e Mudança Política no Brasil, 1970-1979* (Petrópolis, Brazil: Editora Vozes, 1980), pp. 173–216.

21. Regime thinking in the economic sphere is reflected in João Paulo dos Reis Velloso, *Brasil: A Solução Positiva* (São Paulo: ABRIL-TEC Editora, 1978). Evaluation of the Geisel administration's policies is contained in Antônio Barros de Castro and Francisco Eduardo Pires de Souza, *A Economia Brasileira em Marcha Forçada* (Rio de Janeiro: Editora Paz e Terra, 1985), pp. 27–47. Much more critical is Carlos Lessa, "A Estratégia de Desenvolvimento de 1974–1976. Sonho e Fracasso" (thesis for the Faculdade de Economia e Administração da Universidade Federal do Rio de Janeiro, 1978). See also Dionísio Dias Carneiro, "Crise e Esperança: 1974–1980," in Marcelo de Paiva Abreu, ed., *A Ordem do Progresso: Cem Anos de Política Econômica Republicana, 1889-1989* (Rio de Janeiro: Editora Campus, 1989), pp. 295–322.

22. Cogent critiques of the Geisel government's economic policies are contained in Edmar L. Bacha, *Os Mitos de uma Década: Ensaios de Economia Brasileira* (Rio de Janeiro: Editora Paz e Terra, 1976), and Edmar L. Bacha, *Política Econômica e Distribuição de Renda* (Rio de Janeiro: Editora Paz e Terra, 1978). See also Albert Fishlow, "A Tale of Two Presidents: The Political Economy of Crisis Management," in Alfred Stepan, ed., *Democratizing Brazil: Problems of Transition & Consolidation* (New York: Oxford University Press, 1989), pp. 83–119. On the social policy side, consult Pedro Demo, *Política Social nas Décadas de 60 e 70* (Fortaleza, Brazil: Universidade Federal de Ceará, 1981), and, more broadly, Florestan Fernandes, *A Revolução Burguesa no Brasil* (Rio de Janeiro: Zahar Editores, 1975).

23. Fundamental sources on Brazil's foreign debt up to the early 1980s include Sérgio Goldenstein, *A Dívida Externa Brasileira 1964–1982, Evolução e Crise* (Rio de Janeiro: Editora Guanabara, 1986), pp. 91–121; Paulo Davidoff Cruz, *Dívida Externa e Política Econômica—A Experiência Brasileira nos anos 70* (São Paulo: Editora Brasiliense, 1984); and Jeffry Frieden, "The Brazilian Borrowing Experience from Miracle to Debacle and Back," *Latin American Research Review* 22, 1 (1987), pp. 95–131.

24. Useful from here on into the next administration is Enrique A. Baloyra, "From Moment to Moment: The Political Transition in Brazil, 1977–1981," in Wayne A. Selcher, ed., *Political Liberalization in Brazil: Dynamics, Dilemmas, and Future Prospects* (Boulder, CO: Westview Press, 1986), pp. 9–53. See also Sérgio Henrique Abranches, "Crise e Transição: Uma Interpretação do Momento Político Nacional," *Dados* 25, 3 (1982), pp. 317–323, and Hélgio Trinidade, ed., *Brasil em Perspectiva: Dilemas da Abertura Política* (Porto Alegre, Brazil: Editora Sulina, 1982).

25. See Paulino Jacques, *As Emendas Constitucionais Nos. 7, 8 e 9 Explicadas* (Rio de Janeiro: Editora Forense, 1977); Kucinski, *Abertura*, pp. 59–65; and Maria Alva G. Kinzo, *Legal Opposition Politics Under Authoritarian Rule: The Case of the MDB, 1966–79* (New York: St. Martin's Press, 1988), pp. 178–182. Deeper on the societal setting of politics are Peter McDonough, *Power and Ideology in Brazil* (Princeton, NJ: Princeton University Press, 1981), pp. 55–106, and Riordan Roett, *Brazil: Politics in a Patrimonial Society*, 3rd ed. (New York: Praeger Publishers, 1984).

26. Vital for understanding this issue and episode are Stumpf and Pereira Filho, *A Segunda Guerra*, pp. 125–138; Góes, *O Brasil do General Geisel*, pp. 75–102; and Chagas, *A Guerra das Estrelas*, pp. 249–270.

27. See Hugo Abreu, *O Outro Lado do Poder* (Rio de Janeiro: Editora Nova Fronteira, 1979), pp. 91–102, 125–151.

28. In mid-1977 Frota had wanted all the MDB leaders who had appeared on a TV program that the military considered "insulting" to be purged. This would have included both moderates Ulysses Guimarães and Franco Montoro as well as radical Alencar Furtado—Furtado being the only one Geisel did agree to punish. The other two would go on to play very important roles in the subsequent political opening and 1984–1989 transition.

29. Abreu has told his version in *O Outro Lado do Poder* and has detailed his participation in the quest to find a viable opposition candidate in *Tempo de Crise* (Rio de Janeiro: Editora Nova Fronteira, 1980).

30. Realization that they had fallen into the government's trap was slow and incomplete on the part both of opposition leaders and of the wide array of analysts highly sympathetic to them and unduly dependent upon their view of events. Influenced by the interpretations of such analysts and too hostile to Geisel to be at all objective in this matter, several outside scholars who have tried carefully to reconstruct this series of events have missed the main point. See, for example, William C. Smith, "The Political Transition in Brazil: From Authoritarian Liberalization and Elite

Conciliation to Democratization," in Enrique A. Baloyra, ed., *Comparing New Democracies: Transition and Consolidation in Mediterranean Europe and the Southern Cone* (Boulder, CO: Westview Press, 1987), pp. 179–240, especially pp. 200–201. Worse, of course, is ignoring the matter completely, as has been done by Luciano Martins, "The 'Liberalization' of Authoritarian Rule in Brazil," in Guillermo O'Donnell, Philippe C. Schmitter, and Laurence Whitehead, eds., *Transitions from Authoritarian Rule: Latin America* (Baltimore, MD: Johns Hopkins University Press, 1986), pp. 72–94. Even Skidmore fails to grasp the real significance of the Bentes Monteiro candidacy and—largely following Cardoso—greatly overemphasizes the role of the business community in the events of 1978. See Skidmore, *The Politics of Military Rule*, pp. 200–202. My interpretation is firmly rooted in an extensive program of interviews and close observation of the campaign in several parts of Brazil from June to September 1978 (backed up by the experience of studying firsthand all Brazilian elections since 1958).

31. See Severo Gomes, *Tempo de Mudar* (Porto Alegre, Brazil: Editora Globo, 1977).

32. Brossard's views at about that time can be found in his *É Hora de Mudar* (Porto Alegre, Brazil: L & PM Editores, 1977).

33. The most useful sources on these elections include Lamounier, *Voto de Desconfiança*, and Fundação Milton Campos, *As Eleições Nacionais de 1978* (Brasília: Edições da Fundação Milton Campos, 1979), of which Vol. 1 provides countrywide essays and Vol. 2 brings together nineteen state analyses plus a national overview. Another useful source is *Revista Brasileira de Estudos Políticos* 51 (July 1980).

34. An important sign of the changing times was the "Encontro Nacional Pela Democracia" held in early December with the participation of over 1,500 intellectuals and activists. The seminar was sponsored by the Centro Brasil Democrático to discuss what could be done to turn liberalization into full democratization, and its proceedings provide a broad cross-section of the views of the left half of the political spectrum. See Centro Brasil Democrático, *Painéis da Crise Brasileira*, 4 vols. (Rio de Janeiro: Editoras Civilização Brasileira, Avenir, and Paz e Terra, 1979).

35. The term was coined by Bolívar Lamounier in Bolívar Lamounier and José Eduardo Faria, eds., *O Futuro da Abertura: Um Debate* (São Paulo: Cortez Editora, 1981), p. 35. This insightful little volume contains the proceedings of a small seminar held in mid-1981 to weigh how far political opening had come and where it might go in the aftermath of the Riocentro affair. Consult also Bolívar Lamounier et al., *Direito, Cidadania, e Representação* (São Paulo: T. A. Queiroz Editor, 1981), for the proceedings of a mid-1979 conference.

36. Though there is by now a massive literature on *abertura*, this section rests heavily upon the integrated program of interviews and observations I conducted during twelve trips to Brazil for field research spanning the Figueiredo years. Important balanced treatments of this period include Skidmore, *The Politics of Military Rule*, pp. 210–255; Baloyra, "From Moment to Moment," pp. 36–48 (through 1981); and Wayne A. Selcher, "Contradictions, Dilemmas, and Actors in Brazil's *Abertura*, 1979—1985," in Selcher, ed., *Political Liberalization in Brazil*, pp. 55–95. A quite different ideological point of view is in José Álvaro Moisés, *Alternativas Populares da Democracia: Brasil anos 80* (Petrópolis, Brazil: Editora Vozes, 1982), and José Álvaro Moisés, *Cenas de Política Explícito: Descaminhos de uma longe transição política* (São Paulo: Editora Marco Zero, 1986). Also interesting are Michel Debrun, *A "Conciliação" e Outros Estratégias* (São Paulo: Editora Brasiliense, 1983), and Nelson Paes Leme, *1982, a Conquista da Democracia* (Rio de Janeiro: Edições Graal, 1982), the latter a collection of articles published from November 1981 through July 1982.

37. A Brazilian Amnesty Committee had been established as early as February 1978. An early work in this field was Roberto Ribeiro Martins, *Liberdade para os*

Brasileiros: Anistia ontem e hoje (Rio de Janeiro: Editora Civilização Brasileiro, 1978). See also Kucinski, *Abertura*, pp. 108–112, 134–137. On labor at this junction, consult José Álvaro Moisés, *Lições de Liberdade e Opressão: Os trabalhadores e luta pela democracia* (Rio de Janeiro: Editora Paz e Terra, 1982).

38. On this party, see Rachel Meneguello, *PT: A Formação de um Partido, 1979–1982* (Rio de Janeiro: Editora Paz e Terra, 1989); Mário Pedrosa, *Sobre o PT* (São Paulo: CHED Editora, 1980); Francisco Weffort, *Por que democracia?* (São Paulo: Editora Brasiliense, 1984); Emir Sader, ed., *E agora, PT?: Caracter e identidade* (São Paulo: Editora Brasiliense, 1986); and Raul Pont, *Da Crítica ao Populismo na Construção do PT* (Porto Alegre, Brazil: Editora Serima, 1985).

39. David V. Fleischer, "The Brazilian Congress: From *Abertura* to New Republic," in Selcher, ed., *Political Liberalization in Brazil*, p. 100. For the perspective of the party's elder statesman, see Ernani do Amaral Peixoto with Aspásia Camargo, Lucia Hippolito, Maria Celína Soares D'Araújo, and Dora Rocha Flaksman, *Artes da Política: Diálogo com Amaral Peixoto* (Rio de Janeiro: Editora Nova Fronteira, 1986), pp. 525–541.

40. *III Plano Nacional de Desenvolvimento: 1980–1985* (Brasília: Imprensa Nacional, 1987). As the Figueiredo government found itself caught in a $72 billion "scissors" between deteriorating terms of trade and higher interest rates, Rischbeiter's mid-1979 predictions of real trouble ahead were borne out. Simonsen probably could have returned to be finance minister in 1988 or 1990 had he so wished.

41. On this episode, consult Belisa Ribeiro, *Bomba no Riocentro* (Rio de Janeiro: Editora Codecri, 1981).

42. See Elio Gaspari, "O bruxo fez seu ultímo arte," *Veja*, September 23, 1987, pp. 20–31, as well as *Veja*, August 12, 1981, pp. 20–33.

43. The 1979–1982 period is treated in detail in Goldenstein, *A Dívida Externa Brasileira*, pp. 123–148. Some sources include short-term amounts not registered with the Central Bank, thus reaching totals of $54 billion for 1979 and $60 billion for 1980. Such an approach gives a total of $70.6 billion for 1980, $80.4 billion for 1981, almost $92 billion in 1982, $97.5 billion for 1983, and $104.9 billion by the end of 1984.

44. See Luiz Carlos Bresser Pereira, "Da crise fiscal à redução da dívida," in Luiz Carlos Bresser Pereira, ed., *Dívida Externa: Crise e Soluções* (São Paulo: Editora Brasiliense, 1989), pp. 16–19, and Luiz Carlos Bresser Pereira, *A Dívida e a Inflação: A Economia dos Anos Figueiredo, 1978–1985* (São Paulo: Gazeta Mercantil, 1985).

45. Varied perspectives on the economic situation at this juncture include Celso Furtado, *A nova dependência: Dívida externa e monetarismo* (Rio de Janeiro: Editora Paz e Terra, 1982); Maria de Conceição Tavares and J. Carlos de Assis, *O Grande Salto para o Caos: A Economia Política e Política Econômica do Regime Autoritário* (Rio de Janeiro: Jorge Zahar Editor, 1985); and João Manoel Cardoso de Melo, *O Capitalismo Tardário: Contribução à Revisão Crítica de Formação e do Desenvolvimento da Economia Brasileira* (São Paulo: Editora Brasiliense, 1982). See also the essays by Riordan Roett, Sérgio Corrêa da Costa, Edmar Bacha, and Julian M. Chacel in Julian M. Chacel, Pamela Falk, and David V. Fleischer, eds., *Brazil's Economic and Political Future* (Boulder, CO: Westview Press, 1988).

46. This interpretation is based largely upon my contemporary fieldwork and observations.

47. See, for example, David V. Fleischer, "Constitutional and Electoral Engineering in Brazil: A Double-Edged Sword, 1964–1982," *Inter-American Economic Affairs* 37, 4 (Spring 1984), pp. 3–36. See also Gláucio A. D. Soares, *Colégio Eleitoral, Convenções Partidários e Eleições Diretas* (Petrópolis, Brazil: Editora Vozes, 1984).

48. Fleischer, "The Brazilian Congress," p. 122. Useful material is in Câmara dos Deputados, *Deputados Brasileiros: Repertório biográfico dos membros da Câmara dos Deputados Nona Legislatura (1979–1983)* (Brasília: Biblioteca da Câmara dos Deputados, 1979), and Câmara dos Deputados, *Deputados Brasileiros: Repertório biográfico dos membros da Câmara dos Deputados da 47ª Legislatura (1983–1987)*, 2nd ed. (Brasília: Câmara dos Deputados, 1984).

49. This section draws heavily on my fieldwork and personal observations of the campaign and election as detailed in a series of a dozen reports disseminated through the Center for Strategic and International Studies during the second half of 1982. See also *Revista Brasileira de Estudos Políticos* 57 (July 1983), and, on the PT, Meneguello, *PT: Formação*, pp. 123–194.

50. Other useful sources on the elections include David V. Fleischer, ed., *Da Distensão à Abertura: As Eleições de 1982* (Brasília: Editora Universidade de Brasília, 1988); David V. Fleischer, "Brazil at the Crossroads: The Elections of 1982 and 1985," in Paul W. Drake and Eduardo Silva, eds., *Elections and Democratization in Latin America, 1980–1985* (San Diego: University of California at San Diego, Center for Iberian and Latin American Studies, 1986), pp. 299–327; Raimundo Pereira, Alvaro Caropreso, and José Carlos Ruy, *Eleições no Brasil pós 64* (São Paulo: Global Editora, 1984); and Joaquim de Arruda Falcão Neto, ed., *Nordeste: Eleições* (Recife, Brazil: Fundação Joaquim Nabuco and Editora Massangana, 1985).

51. See figures in Fleischer, "The Brazilian Congress," p. 118. The myriad laws, decrees, and regulations impinging on parties and elections in 1982 are compiled in Walter Costa Porto, ed., *Eleições e Partidos*, Vol. 6 of *Coleção Textos Legais* (Brasília: Fundação Petrônio Portella, 1982).

52. Nothing justifies the tendency of many authors to assume that the PTB was an opposition party. Indeed, its availability to be co-opted by the government bordered on unseemly eagerness. Moreover, Golbery had been instrumental in facilitating its founding. Relevant material on this is in Maria Victoria Benevides, *PTB e o Trabalhismo—Partido e Sindicato em São Paulo: 1945–1964* (São Paulo: Editora Brasiliense, 1989), pp. 157–159.

53. On the debt question, see Goldenstein, *A Dívida Exterior Brasileira;* Persio Arida, ed., *Dívida Externa, Recessão, e Ajuste Estrutural: O Brasil diante da crise* (Rio de Janeiro: Editora Paz e Terra, 1983); Paulo Nogueira Batista, Jr., *Mito e Realidade na Dívida Exterior Brasileira* (Rio de Janeiro: Editora Paz e Terra, 1983); and Marcílio Marques Moreira, *The Brazilian Quandary* (New York: Priority Press, 1986), which was written shortly before Marques Moreira became ambassador to the United States. Useful on economic policy of the period is Dionísio Dias Carneiro and Eduardo Modiano, "Ajuste Externa e Desequilíbrio Interno: 1980–1984," in Paiva Abreu, ed., *A Ordem do Progresso*, pp. 323–346.

54. Goldenstein, *A Dívida Externa Brasileira*, p. 147, places the real end of 1982 debt at $83.3 billion, a figure with which Bresser Pereira, "Da crise fiscal," p. 17, agrees (up from $75.5 including short-term loans in 1981). See also Paulo Roberto Souza, *Quem Paga a Conta: Dívida, Déficit e Inflação nos Anos 80* (São Paulo: Editora Brasiliense, 1989), pp. 115–160.

55. See Regis Bonelli and Pedro S. Malan, "Industrialization, Economic Growth, and Balance of Payments: Brazil, 1970–1984," in John D. Wirth, Edson de Oliveira Nunes, and Thomas E. Bogenschild, eds., *State and Society in Brazil: Continuity and Change* (Boulder, CO: Westview Press, 1987), pp. 13–47, and Edmar L. Bacha and Pedro S. Malan, "Brazil's Debt: From the Miracle to the Fund," in Stepan, ed., *Democratizing Brazil*, pp. 120–140.

56. A sound work by a once ranking technocrat is Antônio Dias Leite, *A Transição para a Nova República* (Rio de Janeiro: Editora Nova Fronteira, 1985). See also Ernani

Galvêas, *Brasil, Economia Aberta ou Fechada* (Rio de Janeiro: APEC Editora, 1977), and Ernani Galvêas, *A Crise do Petróleo* (Rio de Janeiro: APEC Editora, 1985).

57. Skidmore exaggerates negative growth—as did many opposition academics in Brazil at the time—putting it at 5 percent and per capita at a minus 7.3 percent, making things out to be somewhat worse than they actually were. See Skidmore, *The Politics of Military Rule,* p. 238. It should be borne in mind that official figures tend to overstate the extent of negative growth, as in many cases activity previously reported and included in statistics now goes "off the books" or "underground"; it does not really cease to exist.

58. An analysis useful for putting these developments in perspective is Bolívar Lamounier and Alkimar R. Moura, "Economic Policy and Political Opening in Brazil," in Jonathan Hartlyn and Samuel A. Morley, eds., *Latin American Political Economy* (Boulder, CO: Westview Press, 1986), pp. 165–196. A popular attack on government policies was Celso Furtado, *Não à Recessão e Desemprego* (Rio de Janeiro: Editora Paz e Terra, 1983).

59. See Ricardo Kotscho, *Explode um Novo Brasil: Diário da Campanha das Direitas* (São Paulo: Editora Brasiliense, 1984). Useful as background are Teotônio Vilela, *A Pregação da Liberdade: Andanças de um liberal* (Porto Alegre, Brazil: L & PM Editores, 1977), and Márcio Moreira Alves, *Teotônio, Guerreiro da Paz* (Petrópolis, Brazil: Editora Vozes, 1983). Severo Gomes, *Entre o Passado e o Futuro* (São Paulo: Livraria Duas Cidades, 1982), is also of some interest. A searing criticism of the existing order by an outstanding social scientist poised to enter electoral politics can be found in Florestan Fernandes, *A Ditadura em Questão* (São Paulo: T. A. Queiroz Editor, 1982), and Florestan Fernandes, *Nova República?* (Rio de Janeiro: Jorge Zahar, 1985). Also essential for understanding the process is Luíz Werneck Viana, *Travessia da Abertura à Constituente* (Rio de Janeiro: Livraria Taurus Editora, 1986), while Olavo Brasil de Lima, Jr., and Sérgio Henrique Abrantes, eds., *As Origens da Crise: Estado Autoritário e Planificação no Brasil* (São Paulo: Edições Vértice, 1987), casts light on the place of central government agencies in the post-1964 system. The second of these authors has functioned as one of Governor Moreira Franco's inner circle of advisors and administrative coordinators.

60. See Gilberto Dimenstein et al., *O Complô que Elegeu Tancredo* (Rio de Janeiro: Editora JB, 1985), p. 20.

61. The rest of this chapter draws heavily upon a monthly series, *Brazil Political Report,* by Ronald M. Schneider and William Perry, published by the Center for Strategic and International Studies from July 1984 through January 1985.

62. The array of aspirants to the presidency are sketched in Villas-Boas Corrêa et al., *Os Presidenciaveis: Quem é Quem no Maratona do Planalto* (Rio de Janeiro: RETOUR, 1983), with cover stories on Maluf, Chaves, and Andreazza in *Veja* of January 25, February 8, and February 22, 1984, respectively. On Neves, see Vera Alice Cardoso Silva, *Tancredo Neves* (Petrópolis, Brazil: Editora Vozes, 1985).

63. See Dimenstein et al., *O Complô que Elegeu Tancredo,* pp. 44–47, 98–101. Also see Walder de Góes and Aspásia Camargo, *O Drama da Sucessão e A Crise do Regime* (Rio de Janeiro: Editora Nova Fronteira, 1984), and the several pieces making up the cover article "A História Secreta da Sucessão," *Veja,* January 16, 1985, pp. 20–55.

64. Maluf's briefing papers in Dimenstein et al., *O Complô que Elegeu Tancredo,* pp. 193–222, are revealing in this respect. For his platform, see Paulo Maluf, *O Caminho da Esperança* (Rio de Janeiro: Scorpio Editora, 1984). The atmosphere of scandals and disenchantment that prevailed is reflected in Dickson Melges Grael, *Aventura, Corrupção e Terrorismo* (Petrópolis, Brazil: Editora Vozes, 1965), and José Carlos Assis, *Os Mandarins da República: Anatomia dos escândalos na Administração*

Pública, 1968–1984 (Rio de Janeiro: Editora Paz e Terra, 1984). See also Nelson Werneck Sodré, *Vida e Morte da Dictadura: Vinte Anos de Autoritarismo no Brasil* (Petrópolis, Brazil: Editora Vozes, 1984).
    65. Dimenstein et al., *O Complô que Elegeu Tancredo*, p. 61, cites a December 31, 1982, meeting, shortly after Tancredo's election as governor, while "A História Secreta da Sucessão" speaks of another meeting at the beginning of September 1984.
    66. Interesting perspective is provided by Glaúcio Ary Dillon Soares, "Elections and the Redemocratization of Brazil," in Drake and Silva, *Elections and Democratization,* pp. 273–298. The PMDB contribution included 196 federal deputies, 24 senators, and 51 state assembly delegates, while that of the PFL was 63, 10, and 40, respectively. The PDS contingent was 39, 5, and 11.

Chapter 9

    1. The first part of this chapter draws upon several of my writings, especially "Brazil's Political Future," in Wayne A. Selcher, ed., *Political Liberalization in Brazil: Dynamics, Dilemmas, and Future Prospects* (Boulder, CO: Westview Press, 1986), pp. 217–260, and "Transition Without Rupture: Parties, Politicians, and the Sarney Government," in Julian Chacel, Pamela Falk, and David V. Fleischer, eds., *Brazil's Economic and Political Future* (Boulder, CO: Westview Press, 1988), pp. 188–198. In a scheme for comparative classification of recent transitions from authoritarian rule, Alfred Stepan considers the Brazilian case a "redemocratization initiated by the military as government." See Alfred Stepan, "Paths for Redemocratization: Theoretical and Comparative Considerations," in Guillermo O'Donnell, Philippe C. Schmitter, and Laurence Whitehead, eds., *Transitions from Authoritarian Rule: Comparative Perspectives* (Baltimore, MD: Johns Hopkins University Press, 1986), pp. 75–76. A sound effort to assess the 1985–1988 period is Maria do Carmo Campello de Souza, "The Brazilian 'New Republic': Under the Sword of Damocles," in Alfred Stepan, ed., *Democratizing Brazil: Problems of Transition and Consolidation* (New York: Oxford University Press, 1989), pp. 351–394. Contrary to the volume's subtitle, the other essays in this comprehensive symposium essentially treat the pre-1985 stages of transition, with very little to say about 1985–1988, much less about "consolidation." Works by authors who struggle to understand why the transition did not lead to a new order substantially free of the clientelism, populism, and military influence that had marked Brazilian politics to 1985 include Aspásia Camargo and Eli Diniz, eds., *Continuidade e Mudança no Brasil da Nova República* (São Paulo: Edições Vértice, 1989); Eli Diniz, Renato Boschi, and Renato Lessa, *Modernização e Consolidação Democrática no Brasil: Dilemas da Nova República* (São Paulo: Edições Vértice, 1989); José Álvaro Moisés and J. A. Guilhon Albuquerque, eds., *Dilemas da Consolidação da Democracia* (Rio de Janeiro: Editora Paz e Terra, 1989); Lourdes Sola, ed., *O Estado da Transição: Política e Economia na Nova República* (São Paulo: Edições Vértice, 1988); Guilhermo O'Donnell and Fábio Wanderley Reis, eds., *A Democracia no Brasil: Dilemas e Perspectivas* (São Paulo: Edições Vértice, 1988); and Guilhermo O'Donnell, *Contrapontos: Autoritarismo e Democratização* (São Paulo: Edições Vértice, 1986).
    2. The basic similarity of Campos's and Simonsen's views is apparent from several collaborative works, including their *A Nova Economia Brasileira* (Rio de Janeiro: Livraria José Olympio Editora, 1974). Delfim's articles and speeches from 1973 to early 1986 are brought together in Antônio Delfim Netto, *Só o Político Pode Salvar o Economista* (Rio de Janeiro: Edição do Autor, 1986), which can usefully be compared with Antônio Delfim Netto, ed., *Alguns aspectos da inflação Brasileira* (São Paulo: Editora Piratininga, 1965).

3. My interpretation of the Sarney administration differs significantly from that offered in Thomas E. Skidmore, *The Politics of Military Rule in Brazil, 1964–1985* (New York: Oxford University Press, 1988), pp. 256–310. This prominent historian's painstaking treatment of events goes only through July 1986, with a brief postscript covering the ensuing eleven months.

4. A detailed account of the president-elect's illness and death is Antônio Britto, *Assim Morreu Tancredo* (Porto Alegre, Brazil: L & PM Editores, 1986).

5. The scholarly quality of Cardoso's writings appears to have dropped off as his political career came to have top priority. Thus, *Autoritarismo e Democratização* (Rio de Janeiro: Editora Paz e Terra, 1975), is in a number of ways superior to his essay "Associated Dependent Development and Democratic Theory," in Stepan, ed., *Democratizing Brazil*, pp. 299–326, and his "Entrepreneurs and the Transition Process: The Brazilian Case," in O'Donnell, Schmitter, and Whitehead, eds., *Transitions from Authoritarian Rule*, pp. 137–153.

6. I made two extended trips per year to Brazil from 1985 through 1989 to accompany the effort to establish and consolidate a democratic regime.

7. Useful sources on the contemporary party system and its links to the past include Bolívar Lamounier and Rachel Meneguello, *Partidos Políticos e Consolidação Democrática: O Caso Brasileiro* (São Paulo: Editora Brasiliense, 1986); David V. Fleischer, "Brazilian Elections in the 1980s: Transition or Transformation," in Chacel, Falk, and Fleischer, eds., *Brazil's Economic and Political Future*, pp. 153–167; David V. Fleischer, "The Brazilian Congress: From 'Abertura' to New Republic," in Selcher, ed., *Political Liberalization in Brazil*, pp. 97–133; Bolívar Lamounier, "Authoritarian Brazil Revisited: The Impact of Elections on the *Abertura*," in Stepan, ed., *Democratizing Brazil*, pp. 43–79; and Associação Nacional de Pós-graduação e Pesquisas em Ciências Sociais (ANPOCS), *Estado, Participação Política e Democracia* (São Paulo: Conselho Nacional de Pesquisas, 1985). The underlying economic and social changes are analyzed in John D. Wirth, Edson de Oliveira Nunes, and Thomas E. Bogenschild, eds., *State and Society in Brazil: Continuity and Change* (Boulder, CO: Westview Press, 1987).

8. On Brizola, see Gláucio Ary Dillon Soares and Nelson do Valle e Silva, "O Charme Discreto de Socialismo Moreno," *Dados* 28, 2 (1985), pp. 253ff.

9. Consult Fernando Ferrari, *Mensagem Renovadora* (Porto Alegre, Brazil: Editora Globo, 1960), and Fernando Ferrari, *Minha Campanha* (Porto Alegre, Brazil: Editora Globo, 1961).

10. See the many writings of such PT intellectuals as Florestan Fernandes, Francisco Weffort, and Paul Singer, particularly Florestan Fernandes, *Que Tipo de República?* (São Paulo: Editora Brasiliense, 1986), and Florestan Fernandes, *Nova República?* (Rio de Janeiro: Jorge Zahar Editor, 1985).

11. Many observers and several recent works on the "new unionism" generally confuse decreased dependence upon the state with a greatly enhanced capacity to influence national affairs. A useful analysis of recent developments in the labor field is Margaret E. Keck, "The New Unionism in the Brazilian Transition," in Stepan, ed., *Democratizing Brazil*, pp. 252–296. See also Leôncio Martins Rodrigues, *CUT: Os Militantes e a Ideologia* (Rio de Janeiro: Editora Paz e Terra, 1990).

12. See especially Ralph Della Cava, "The 'People's Church,' The Vatican, and *Abertura*," in Stepan, ed., *Democratizing Brazil*, pp. 143–167; Marcos de Castro, *A Igreja e o Autoritarismo* (Rio de Janeiro: Jorge Zahar Editor, 1985); Paulo Krischke and Scott Mainwaring, eds., *A igreja nas bases em tempo de transição* (Porto Alegre, Brazil: L & PM Editores, 1986); and Thomas C. Bruneau and W. E. Hewitt, "Patterns of Church Influence in Brazil's Political Transition," *Comparative Politics* 22, 1 (October 1989), pp. 39–61.

13. The term is from della Cava, "The 'People's Church,' " p. 153.
14. The peculiar Brazilian nonlist, ultralarge constituency, extreme preferential vote form of proportional representation electoral system is analyzed in Ronald M. Schneider, *Brazil Election Factbook Number 2* (Washington, DC: Institute for the Comparative Study of Political Systems, 1965), and Ronald M. Schneider, *Brazil Election Factbook Number 2, Supplement* (Washington, DC: Institute for the Comparative Study of Political Systems, 1966).
15. The final version of the Comissão de Estudos Constitucionais proposal was published in *Constituente (Anteprojeto da Comissão Afonso Arinos comentado por Osny Duarte Pereira)* (Brasília: Editora Universidade de Brasília, 1987). Also useful, by a member of the group, is Cândido Mendes de Almeida, *A inconfidência brasileira: A nova cidadania interpela a Constituente* (Rio de Janeiro: Editora Forense-Universitária, 1986). Useful background is provided in João Gabriel Teixeira, ed., *Cidadão, Estado e Políticas no Brasil Contemporâneo* (Brasília: Editora Universidade de Brasília, 1986).
16. On the early stages of the "New Republic," see Flávio Koutzii, ed., *Nova República: Um Balanço* (Porto Alegre, Brazil: L & PM Editores, 1986); Lourenço Dantas Mota, ed., *A Nova República: O Nome e o Coisa* (São Paulo: Editora Brasiliense, 1985); Emir Sader, ed., *Movimentos Sociais na Transição Democrática* (São Paulo: Cortez Editora, 1987); and Olavo Brasil de Lima, Jr., and Sérgio Henrique Abranches, *As Origens da Crise: Estado Autoritário e Planifcação no Brasil* (São Paulo: Edições Vértice, 1987).
17. For rather different interpretations of the results, see Instituto Universitário de Pesquisas do Rio de Janeiro, *Cadernos de Conjuntura 3* (December 1985), and David V. Fleischer, "Brazil at the Crossroads: The Elections of 1982 and 1985," in Paul W. Drake and Eduardo Silva, eds., *Elections and Democratization in Latin America, 1980–1985* (San Diego: University of California at San Diego, Center for Iberian and Latin American Studies, 1986), pp. 299–327. On São Paulo specifically, consult Bolívar Lamounier, ed., *1985: O Voto em São Paulo* (São Paulo: Instituto de Estudos Econômicos, Sociais e Políticos de São Paulo, 1986).
18. See Hélio Jaguaribe et al., *Brasil, 2.000: Para um novo Pacto Social* (Rio de Janeiro: Editora Paz e Terra, 1986), and Hélio Jaguaribe et al., *Brasil: Reforma ou Caos* (Rio de Janeiro: Editora Paz e Terra, 1989). In some ways these works built upon Hélio Jaguaribe et al., *Brasil: Sociedade Democrática* (Rio de Janeiro: Livraria José Olympio Editora, 1985). Other relevant works by this prolific scholar include *O Novo Cenário Internacional* (Rio de Janeiro: Editora Guanabara, 1986), *Brasil: Crise e Alternativas* (Rio de Janeiro: Zahar Editores, 1974), and *Problemas do Desenvolvimento Latino Americano: Estudos de Política* (Rio de Janeiro: Editora Civilização Brasileira, 1966). In English there is Jaguaribe's monumental tour de force, *Political Development: A General Theory and a Latin American Case Study* (New York: Harper & Row, 1973).
19. See Luiz Carlos Bresser Pereira, "Da crise fiscal à redução da dívida," in Luiz Carlos Bresser Pereira, ed., *Dívida Externa: Crise e Soluções* (São Paulo: Editora Brasiliense, 1989), p. 17. The most restrictive figure for 1984 is $91.1 billion, with the medium number being $95.9 billion (inclusion of short-term debt brings the total to $102 billion). A useful synthesis of the economy under Sarney is Eduardo Modiano, "A Ópera dos Três Cruzados: 1985–1989," in Marcelo de Paiva Abreu, ed., *A Ordem do Progresso: Cem Anos de Política Econômica Republicana, 1889–1989* (Rio de Janeiro: Editora Campus, 1989), pp. 347–386. Modiano became the Collor administration's head of the National Economic and Social Development Bank (BNDES).
20. See Eduardo Modiano, *Da Inflação ao Cruzado: A Política Econômica no Primeiro Ano da Nova República* (Rio de Janeiro: Editora Campus, 1986), and Monica Baer, "A dívida externa brasileira: Estratégias de negociações e impactos internas (1983–1987)," in Bresser Pereira, ed., *Dívida Externa*, pp. 184–218.

21. There is a voluminous and often polemical literature on the Cruzado Plan. The best place to begin is Werner Baer and Paul Beckerman, "The Decline and Fall of Brazil's Cruzado," *Latin American Research Review* 34, 1 (1989), pp. 35–64. They conclude that the plan was fatally flawed by the substantial pay increase it included as well as by the public sector deficit, the low exchange rate of the cruzado, and loose monetary policy. Another reasonably balanced treatment is Hayden Coutinho Pimenta, ed., *Plano Cruzado: Ataque e Defesa* (Rio de Janeiro: Editora Forense-Universitária, 1987). Also useful are Francisco Lopes, *O Choque Heterodoxo: Combate à Inflação e Reforma Monetária* (Rio de Janeiro: Editora Campus, 1986); Persio Arida, ed., *Inflação Zero: Brasil, Argentina e Israel* (Rio de Janeiro: Editora Paz e Terra, 1986); Persio Arida and André Lara-Resende, "Inflationary Inertia and Monetary Reform: Brazil," in Chacel, Falk, and Fleischer, eds., *Brazil's Economic and Political Future*, pp. 27–41; Hugo Presgrave de A. Faria, "Macroeconomic Policymaking in a Crisis Environment: Brazil's Cruzado Plan and Beyond," in ibid., pp. 42–59; Lourdes Sola, "Choque Heterodoxo e Transição Democrática sem Ruptura: Uma Abordagem Trans-disciplina," in Sola, ed., *O Estado da Transição*; and Gilberto Dupas, *Crise Econômica e Transição Democrática 83/86: A Delicada Trajetória Brasileira* (São Paulo: Editora Klaxon, 1987). A critical view by an accomplished PT economist is Paul Singer, *O dia de largata: Democratização e conflito distributivo no Brasil do Cruzado* (São Paulo: Editora Brasiliense, 1987).

22. The situation with respect to social conditions is analyzed by Sérgio Henrique Hudson de Abranches, *Os Despossídos: Crescimento e Pobreza no País do Milagre* (Rio de Janeiro: Jorge Zahar Editor, 1985).

23. The following section draws heavily upon my more detailed study, *Brazil's 1986 Elections*, disseminated in December 1986 by the Center for Strategic and International Studies.

24. Strong attacks on the Cruzado Plan are found in Carlos Alberto Sardenberg, *Aventura e Agonia: Nos Bastidores de Cruzado* (São Paulo: Companhia das Letras, 1987), and Alex Solnik, *Por Que Não Deu Certo?* (São Paulo: L & PM Editores, 1987). Also useful is Paulo Renato Souza, "O Plano Cruzado: Sonho e Fracasso," in Paulo Renato Souza, *Quem Paga a Conta?: Dívida, Déficit e Inflação nos Anos 80* (São Paulo: Editora Brasiliense, 1989), pp. 161–183. The broader background of the problem is treated in Ernesto Lozardo, ed., *Déficit Público Brasileiro: Política Econômica e Adjuste Estrutural* (Rio de Janeiro: Editora Paz e Terra, 1987).

25. Useful sources for determining the political orientation of *constituentes*, but which only supplement the essential work of analyzing their voting behavior issue by issue, include Leôncio Martins Rodrigues, *Quem é Quem na Constituinte: Uma Análise Socio-Político dos Partidos e Deputados* (São Paulo: O Estado de S. Paulo/ Maltese, 1987), and República Federativa do Brasil, *Assembléia Nacional Constituinte—1987* (Brasília: Câmara dos Deputados, 1987). The latter contains official biographical sketches of the *constituentes*, while the former is based upon a questionnaire plus research by *Jornal da Tarde* staffers, but excludes the senators.

26. For David Fleischer as well as for the *Folha de S. Paulo*, the proportions are 12, 14, 32, 23, and 9 percent, respectively, for the Far Right, Center Right, Center, Center Left, and Far Left (as cited in Martins Rodrigues, *Quem é Quem*, p. 98). The heart of the real Left was composed of the PT, PCdoB, PCB, and PSB as well as a part of the PDT and some thirty-five or so of the PMDB—most of whom later joined the PSDB. Roughly 100 from the PMDB and the majority of the PDT could accurately be labeled progressives or Center Left, while another fifty or so of the PMDB along with thirty or so of the PFL and half the PTB could best be considered dead Center. Another 100 or so of the PMDB, half that number from the PFL, most of the rest

of the PTB, nearly half the PDS, and the PL and PDC were "moderates" or Center Right. The really conservative fringe consisted of some fifty from the PFL, a score or so from the PMDB, and about half the PDS. The landowners formed a very effective lobbying organization called the Ruralist Democratic Union (UDR), with at least 230,000 members, that subsequently launched its founder, young rancher-doctor Ronaldo Caiado, as a presidential candidate. This event is analyzed in Ricardo Tavares, "Reforma e Contra-Reforma Agrária na Transição Política—Brasil (1979–1988)," *Série Estudos de IUPERJ* (Rio de Janeiro: Instituto Universtário de Pesquisas de Rio de Janeiro [IUPERJ], May 1989), pp. 13–32. The ineffectiveness of traditional business and industry organizations led to the emergence of such groups as the National Front for Free Enterprise (FNLI), the Brazilian Union of Entrepreneurs (UBE), the National Thought of Entrepreneurial Bases (PNBE), Liberal Institute, and Convergência Democrática. Basically since the time of the empire, conservatives have dominated Brazilian politics by keeping the effective competition for office within their own ranks. In the future, to continue in power they will have to line up with a much higher degree of unity versus a really significant progressive counterelite. The long-prevalent system of weak, dependent, essentially controlled from the top-down system of political participation, "political patrimonialism" in Simon Schwartzman's terminology, would face a serious challenge. Yet the interests this system has served so well may not soon be displaced from power, as the forces of the political Left would go into the 1989 elections deeply divided and facing the unexpected and victorious threat of a charismatic modernizing populist from within elite ranks.

27. Of a spate of books that deal with the role of the constitutent assembly, the standouts include João Gilberto Lucas Coelho and Antônio Carlos Nantes de Oliveira, *A Nova Constituição: Avaliação do Texto e Perfil dos Constituentes* (Rio de Janeiro: Editora Revan, 1989); David V. Fleischer and João Gilberto Lucas Coelho, *O Processo Constituente 1987–1988* (Brasília: Centro de Estudos e Acompanhamento da Constituente da Universidade de Brasília, 1988); and Francisco Iglésias, *Constituentes e Constituições Brasileiras* (São Paulo: Editora Brasiliense, 1986). See also *Revista Brasileira de Estudos Políticos* 60/61 (January/July 1985) as well as V. Bastos and T. da Costa, eds., *Constituente: Temas em Análise* (Brasília: Editora Universidade de Brasília, 1987), and V. Bastos and T. da Costa, eds., *Constituente: Questões Polêmicas* (Brasília: Editora Universidade de Brasília, 1988).

28. On the new crop of governors, see the special issue of *Senhor*, March 21, 1987, titled "As Promessas e o Poder dos Novos Governadores."

29. Two works by Bresser Pereira available in English reflect his basic worldview, analysis of Brazilian reality, and policy orientation. They are *Development and Crisis in Brazil, 1930–1983* (Boulder, CO: Westview Press, 1984), and, with Yoshiashi Nakano, *The Theory of Inertial Inflation: The Foundation of Economic Reform in Brazil and Argentina* (Boulder, CO: Lynne Rienner Publishers, 1987). See also Luiz Carlos Bresser Pereira, *O Colapso de uma Aliança de Classes: A Burguesia e a Crise do Autoritarismo Technoburocrática* (São Paulo: Editora Brasiliense, 1978) and essays by Bresser Pereira in *Dívida Externa* as well as Carlos Alberto Sardenberg, ed., *Jogo Aberto: Entrevistas com Bresser Pereira* (São Paulo: Editora Brasiliense, 1989).

30. Labor in Brazil has finally emerged as a major political factor, albeit not at all yet comparable to the situation in Argentina or most industrialized countries. For the Brazilian trade union movement has yet to demonstrate ability either to deliver a large vote to one party or candidate—rather than some support to several candidates (by definition offsetting and often countervailing)—or to conduct a successful general strike. The CUT has over 1,150 affiliated unions, with the real strength of the CGT something over 1,000. The main current of the latter has been linked to the PSDB

through "Joaquinzão" Santos Andrade, who was Covas's senatorial alternate, but the coalition lost control in April–May 1989 to the followers of Antônio Rogério Magri (who would later become the Collor government's minister of labor and social welfare). Santos Andrade then formed a splinter CGT. A new Corrente Sindical Classista (CSC) is linked to the PCdoB but is largely limited to Rio Grande do Sul and Bahia. The total number of unions, many of which exist only on paper to qualify for Labor Ministry funding, is just over 9,500, with 100,000–150,000 union functionaries on their payrolls. Useful are Roque Aparecido da Silva, ed., *Os Sindicatos e a Transição Democrático: O que Pensam os Interessados?* (São Paulo: Instituto Brasileiro das Relações de Trabalho [IBRART], 1986); Maria Hermínia Tavares de Almeida, "*Novo Sindicalismo* and Politics in Brazil," in Wirth, Nunes, and Bogenschild, eds., *State and Society in Brazil*, pp. 147–178; Maria Hermínia Tavares de Almeida, "Difícil caminho: Sindicatos e política na construção da democracia," in O'Donnell and Reis, *A Democracia no Brasil*, pp. 327–367; Heloisa Helena Teixeira de Souza Martins, *O estado e a burocratização do sindicatos no Brasil* (São Paulo: Editora Hucitec, 1979); Keck, "The New Unionism," pp. 252–296; and Kenneth S. Mericle, "Corporatist Control of the Working Class: Authoritarian Brazil Since 1964," in James M. Malloy. ed., *Authoritarianism and Corporatism in Latin America* (Pittsburgh: University of Pittsburgh Press, 1977), pp. 308–338.

31. The episode would initiate the decline of Maciel as PFL leader and aggravate already deep divisions within the PMDB. A very useful compilation of a vast amount of data relevant to understanding Brazil around this period is Wanderley Guilherme dos Santos, Violeta Maria Monteiro, and Ana Maria Lustoso, *Que Brasil é Este? Manual de Indicadores Políticos e Sociais* (Rio de Janeiro: Instituto Universitário de Pesquisas de Rio de Janeiro, 1988). Sarney could never consistently pursue a strategy of splitting the PMDB or breaking with Guimarães for fear of finding himself with no parliamentary base. Efforts in this direction included: (1) reducing his dependence on the PMDB by bringing smaller parties into the government coalition; (2) accentuating cleavages within the PMDB to weaken Guimarães's control; (3) reinforcing the role of the northeast and, to a lesser extent, the PFL in general; and (4) strengthening ties with moderate PMDB governors. Both before and after the 1987 appointment of crafty former deputy Thales Ramalho as a special advisor, Sarney flirted with the idea of forming a clearly pro-administration parliamentary bloc and then transforming it into a centrist party, but he used this more as a bargaining club with Guimarães than as an option to be pursued vigorously.

32. The text of the constitution was carried in the major newspapers on October 5 and October 6 and published in a variety of editions, one of which contained a rather pretentious preface by Guimarães intended to launch his presidential candidacy as "father" of the new basic charter. The constitution's provisions are analyzed in Lucas Coelho and Nantes de Oliveira, *A Nova Constitução.*

33. One of the transitory provisions paves the way for a possible referendum on return to a monarchical form of government, but adoption of a parliamentary system is the most likely major change.

34. Material on these elections is spotty, as definitive results from the rural areas trickled in slowly to the Superior Electoral Tribunal, which soon turned its interest to preparations for the 1989 presidential elections.

35. Claims accepted uncritically by much of the press and many academicians that the elections projected the PT into a role of favorite for the presidential sweepstakes rested on superficial and incomplete consideration of national results. The fact that the PT was favored by a very large proportion of journalists heavily influenced this distortion.

36. Before Vargas created four new ones, there were only seven ministries. Quadros added two more, as did Goulart. Castelo Branco created the SNI, and Costa e Silva established three others before Geisel set up another. Two more were brought into existence by Figueiredo. Under Sarney another seven came into being, with the Ministry of Culture narrowly surviving the reversal of ministerial proliferation in 1989. In March 1990, Collor would reduce the number of ministries to twelve as part of sweeping administrative reform.

Chapter 10

1. See my series of reports, most done with the collaboration of William Perry, *The 1989 Brazilian Elections*, published by the Center for Strategic and International Studies, especially Report No. 5, "The Final Tally" (Washington, DC: Center for Strategic and International Studies, January 1990).

2. Adam Przeworski, "Como e onde se bloqueiam as transições para a democracia?" in José Álvaro Moisés and J. A. Guilhon Albuquerque, eds., *Dilemas da Consolidação da Democracia* (Rio de Janeiro: Editora Paz e Terra, 1989), p. 34 n. 21.

3. Enrique A. Baloyra, "Democratic Transition in Comparative Perspective," in Enrique A. Baloyra, ed., *Comparing New Democracies: Transition and Consolidation in Mediterranean Europe and the Southern Cone* (Boulder, CO: Westview Press, 1987), p. 16.

4. Ronald M. Schneider with William Perry, *The 1989 Brazilian Elections*, Report No. 2, "The Campaign at Midstream" (Washington, DC: Center for Strategic and International Studies, September 1989).

5. Ibid. For further information on the electorate, see Ronald M. Schneider with William Perry, *The 1989 Brazilian Elections*, Report No. 1, "Background" (Washington, DC: Center for Strategic and International Studies, September 1989).

6. Ronald M. Schneider with William Perry, *The 1989 Brazilian Elections*, Report No. 3, "The Stretch Drive" (Washington, DC: Center for Strategic and International Studies, November 1989).

7. Ibid., pp. 7–8.

8. Detailed analysis of the November 15 balloting is in William Perry with Ronald M. Schneider, *The 1989 Brazilian Elections*, Report No. 4, "The First Round and the Campaign for the Second," (Washington, DC: Center for Strategic and International Studies, December 1989).

9. Schneider with Perry, "The Final Tally."

10. In addition to the 66.1 million valid votes, blank ballots totalled 986,446, with nullified ones hitting 3.1 million (including many cases in which the voter insisted on writing in the name of his preferred candidate from the first round). At just under 11.9 million (14.4 percent of the electorate), abstentions were up slightly over the November 15 total—albeit the increase was very small, taking into account the inclement weather and the elimination of the first choices of more than half of those voting. In light of the fact that three decades had passed without direct presidential voting, the near exemplary nature of the elections themselves was something in which Brazilians could justifiably take pride. The presiding officer of the Superior Electoral Tribunal earned accolades for efficiently engineering the massive tasks of administering the elections and vote-counting, being named to head the Foreign Ministry in March 1990.

11. The following two sections draw heavily upon Ronald M. Schneider and William Perry, *The 1989 Brazilian Elections*, Report No. 6, "The Collor Government: A New Team Charts a New Course" (Washington, DC: Center for Strategic and

International Studies, May 1990). See also William Perry, *The 1990 Brazilian Elections*, Special Report, "The Collor Government's First Six Months: Forging a New Brazil" (Washington, DC: Center for Strategic and International Studies, September 1990).

12. "Zélia vai à luta," *Veja*, March 7, 1990, pp. 32–34; "O presidente disparou sua bomba," *Veja*, March 21, 1990, pp. 58–76; and "Tiro de Canhão," *Isto É Senhor*, March 21, 1990, pp. 23–31.

13. *Folha de S. Paulo*, March 18, 1990, pp. B1, B16, and March 23, 1990, p. B1; and *O Globo*, March 24, 1990, p. 8.

14. *Folha de S. Paulo*, April 15, 1990, pp. A4, A6, B1, B4.

15. "Vitória estrondosa," *Veja*, April 18, 1990, pp. 22–27.

16. "O país dos barnabés," *Veja*, June 20, 1990, pp. 28–35.

17. "A cultura da inflação," *Veja*, July 11, 1990, pp. 46–53.

18. *Folha de S. Paulo*, August 15, 1990, pp. A5, B1.

19. Greater detail is in Ronald M. Schneider with William Perry, *The 1990 Brazilian Elections*, Report No. 1, "Pre-Election Analysis: The Setting" (Washington, DC: Center for Strategic and International Studies, September 1990), and Report No. 2, "Pre-Election Analysis: Into the Homestretch" (Washington, DC: Center for Strategic and International Studies, September 1990).

20. Further analysis and detailed results are in William Perry with Ronald M. Schneider, *The 1990 Brazilian Elections*, Report No. 3, "Post-Election Analysis" (Washington, DC: Center for Strategic and International Studies, December 1990), and William Perry with Ronald M. Schneider, *The 1990 Brazilian Elections*, Report No. 4, "New Congress + New Governors = New Game Plan?" (Washington, DC: Center for Strategic and International Studies, February 1991).

21. Avoidance of government regulations is another incentive to staying in the "submerged" economy. A major debate is going on in Brazil over how much of the informal economy may be inferred through the government's methodology for calculating GDP and how much is still slipping through. Even if $46 billion is "imputed" and added by the government to the observed and registered economic activity, the "invisible" component is still almost certainly well in excess of another $50 billion.

22. Important studies of Brazilian inflation include Mário Henrique Simonsen, ed., *Alguns aspectos da inflação Brasileira* (São Paulo: Editora Piratininga, 1965); Luiz Carlos Bresser Pereira and Yoshiashi Nakano, *The Theory of Inertial Inflation: The Foundation of Economic Reform in Brazil and Argentina* (Boulder, CO: Lynne Rienner Publishers, 1987); Francisco Lopes, *O Choque Heterodoxo: Combate à Inflação e Reforma Monetária* (Rio de Janeiro: Editora Campus, 1986); José Marcio Rego, ed., *Inflação Inercial e Teorias sôbre Inflação* (Rio de Janeiro: Editora Paz e Terra, 1986); and Pamela S. Falk, ed., *Inflation: Are We Next? Hyperinflation and Solutions in Argentina, Brazil, and Israel* (Boulder, CO: Lynne Rienner Publishers, 1989).

23. Useful are Ernesto Lozardo, ed., *Déficit Público Brasileiro: Política Econômica e Ajusto Estrutural* (Rio de Janeiro: Editora Paz e Terra, 1988), and Paulo Renato Souza, *Quem Paga a Conta? Dívida, Déficit e Inflação nos Anos 80* (São Paulo: Editora Brasiliense, 1989).

24. Federal internal debt, loosely called "national debt," by late 1989 was over $110 billion, over half of it in the hands of the public and the rest retained by the Central Bank. If well administered, which has not not the case in recent years, this debt could potentially even be a way of capturing resources for public sector investments. This could be accomplished through a drastic reduction of the need to "buy" the trade surplus–generated hard currencies from exporters and a near elimination of the primary deficit of the public sector. Real interest rates of 25–34

percent on internal debt in 1989 need to be reduced by the new government to something approximating the 8 percent average of the early and mid-1980s. Collor's initial moves in this direction would prove to be quite dramatic.

25. Former Planning Minister João Sayad gives taxes for 1970–1974 at 25.9 percent of GDP and those for 1980–1984 at 23.6 percent. See his "Brazil's Economic Stabilization Program: An Analysis," in Julian Chacel, Pamela Falk, and David V. Fleischer, eds., *Brazil's Economic and Political Future* (Boulder, CO: Westview Press, 1988), p. 14. Net tax revenues of 17 percent of GDP were down to 8.8 percent by 1988 as a result of the wildfire growth of fiscal incentives—many of which were massively abused.

26. For Argentina the foreign debt is 83 percent of GDP and 5.2 times export earnings, and Mexico's is 6.2 times exports and 54 percent of GDP. A good beginning on the vast literature regarding Brazil's debt problem can be made through Luiz Carlos Bresser Pereira, ed., *Dívida Externa: Crise e Soluções* (São Paulo: Editora Brasiliense, 1989), and Paulo Nogueira Batista, Jr., *Da Crise Internacional à Moratória Brasileira* (Rio de Janeiro: Editora Paz e Terra, 1988).

27. Essential is Edmar Bacha and Herbert S. Klein, eds., *A Transição Incompléta: Brasil desde 1945,* 2 vols. (Rio de Janeiro: Editora Paz e Terra, 1986). See also Hélio Jaguaribe, *Alternativas do Brasil* (Rio de Janeiro: Livraria José Olympio Editora, 1989).

28. A good portrait of the situation up to the mid-1980s is Hélio Jaguaribe, Wanderley Guilherme dos Santos, Marcel de Paiva Abreu, Winston Fritsch, and Fernando Bastos de Avila, *Brasil, 2000: Para um novo Pacto Social* (Rio de Janeiro: Editora Paz e Terra, 1986). This should be supplemented by Hélio Jaguaribe, Nelson do Valle e Silva, Marcelo de Paiva Abreu, Fernando Bastos de Avila, and Winston Fritsch, *Brasil: Reforma ou Caos* (Rio de Janeiro: Editora Paz e Terra, 1989).

29. Figures are calculated from data in Instituto Brasileiro de Geografia e Estatística (IBGE), *Anuario Estatístico do Brasil, 1986* (Rio de Janeiro: IBGE, 1987), pp. 207–209, with the most recent estimates from IBGE, *Pesquisa Nacional Por Amostra de Domicílios 1988* (Rio de Janeiro: IBGE, 1989).

30. See Claudio de Moura Castro, "O Que Está Acontecendo com a Educação no Brasil," in Bacha and Klein, eds., *A Transição Incompléta,* pp. 103–161, as well as IBGE, *Anuario Estatística do Brasil 1987–1988* (Rio de Janeiro: IBGE, 1988), pp. 199–242.

31. The best source for these proportions is Leôncio Martins Rodrigues, *Quem é Quem na Constituinte: Uma Análise Socio-Político dos Partidos e Deputados* (São Paulo: O Estado de S. Paulo/Maltese, 1987). See also René Dreifuss, *O Jogo da Direita na Nova República* (Petrópolis, Brazil: Editora Vozes, 1989), pp. 99–107.

32. Brazilian scholarship on the country's military has progressed substantially in recent years. See Edmund Campos Coelho, "A Instituição Militar no Brasil: Ensaio Bibliográfico," *Boletim Informativo e Bibliográfico de Ciências Sociais—BIB* No. 19 (1985), pp. 5–19. Important is José Murilo de Carvalho, "Militares e Civis: Um Debate além da Constituinte," in Aspásia Camargo and Eli Diniz, eds., *Continuidade e Mudança no Brasil da Nova República* (São Paulo: Edições Vértice, 1989), pp. 137–152. On the current situation, see Eliezer Rizzo de Oliveira, Geraldo L. Cavagnari Filho, João Quartim de Moraes, and René Armand Dreifuss, *As Forças Armadas no Brasil* (Rio de Janeiro: Editora Espaço e Tempo, 1987); Eliezer Rizzo de Oliveira, Wilma Peres Costa, and João Quartim de Moraes, *A tutela militar* (São Paulo: Edições Vértice, 1987); Eliezer Rizzo de Oliveira, ed., *Militares: Pensamento e ação política* (Campinas, Brazil: Papirus Livraria Editora, 1987); Clóvis Brigagão, *A Militarização da Sociedade* (Rio de Janeiro: Jorge Zahar Editor, 1985); and Oliveiras S. Ferreira, *Forças Armadas, para que?* (Rio de Janeiro: Edições GRD, 1989). See also *Política e Estratégia* 3, 3 (July–September 1985); Alfred Stepan, *Rethinking Military Politics: Brazil and the*

Southern Cone (Princeton, NJ: Princeton University Press, 1988); and Stanley E. Hilton, "The Brazilian Military: Changing Strategic Perceptions and the Problem of Mission," *Armed Forces and Society* 13, 3 (Spring 1987), pp. 329–351. In assessing trends within the armed forces it should be kept in mind that while lieutenants and captains are only a few years out of the academy, majors have averaged fourteen years since commissioning or eighteen since becoming cadets, with the figure rising to twenty-one years for lieutenant colonels—of whom the army has 822, compared to 1,800 majors—and twenty-eight for colonels. For the ninety-four brigadier generals, thirty-five years of service is the average, going up to thirty-nine for the slightly more than two score divisional generals. The dozen and a half top-ranking generals average forty-three years since graduation—having been born around 1924—and attended the academy during World War II. Hence, direct memories of Vargas will persist in the upper reaches of the military until the turn of the century, with pre-1964 experience only fading out during the first decade of the twenty-first century. For a distillation and analysis of some of the issues and debates that greatly concerned these officers at earlier stages of their careers, see Frank D. McCann, "The Brazilian Army and the Problem of Mission, 1930–1964," *Journal of Latin American Studies* 12, 1 (May 1980), pp. 107–126.

33. The array of geopolitical treatises and related studies on strategy by Brazilian scholars, mostly military figures, is quite substantial. Much of the debate can be followed in *Política e Estratégia* as well as the frequent books of General Carlos de Meira Mattos, especially *Estratégias Militares Dominantes* (Rio de Janeiro: Biblioteca de Exército, 1986). In English, see Philip Kelly and Jack Child, eds., *Geopolitics of the Southern Cone and Antarctica* (Boulder, CO: Lynne Rienner Publishers, 1988), as well as Kelly's paper "Geopolitical Tension Areas in South America: The Question of Brazilian Territorial Expansion," in Robert E. Biles, ed., *Inter-American Relations: The Latin American Perspective* (Boulder, CO: Lynne Rienner Publishers, 1988). Riordan Roett and Richard Sacks treat relations with Brazil in their forthcoming volume *Paraguay: The Personalist Legacy* (Boulder, CO: Westview Press, 1990).

34. Consult Waltraud Queiser Morales's forthcoming book *Bolivia: Land of Struggle* (Boulder, CO: Westview Press, 1990).

35. Maria do Carmo Campello de Souza, "The Brazilian 'New Republic': Under the Sword of Damocles," in Alfred Stepan, *Democratizing Brazil: Problems of Transition and Consolidation* (New York: Oxford University Press, 1989), p. 382.

36. Boff's many books began with *Jesus Cristo Libertador* (Petrópolis, Brazil: Editora Vozes, 1972). *E a Igreja se fez povo* (Petrópolis, Brazil: Editora Vozes, 1985), is an example of his more recent works.

37. The division of São Paulo left Cardinal Arns with 241 parishes in an area embracing a still extremely large population of 7.6 million. The largest of the new dioceses was São Miguel, with fifty-two parishes serving 2.5 million inhabitants of a region in which CEB's were most active. Santo Amaro has thirty-three parishes and a potential flock of 1.6 million, and the figures for Campo Limpo are twenty-eight parishes serving a population of 1.3 million.

38. *Veja*, December 6, 1989, p. 57.

39. Vatican letters of warning were sent not only to Cardinal Lorscheider and Bishop Casaldáglia, but also to Archbishop José Maria Pires of João Pessoa (Dom Pelé, the ranking dark-skinned member of the hierarchy) and seven other bishops including Balduino, Adriano Hypolito of Nova Iguaçu, Waldir Calheiros of Volta Redonda, and José Rodrigues of Juazeiro, Bahia. Bulwarks of conservatism include, in addition to the cardinal of Salvador, Dom José Falcão of Brasília, Dom José Rodrigues Cardoso Sobrinho of Recife, and (on most matters) Dom Claudio Colling of Porto Alegre, as well as Cardinal Eugênio Salles of Rio de Janeiro.

40. On popular Catholicism, consult Alba Zaluar, *Os Homens de Deus: Um estudo dos Santos e das festas no Catolicismo popular* (Rio de Janeiro: Zahar Editores, 1983); Luís da Câmara Cascudo, *Religião no Povo* (João Pessoa, Brazil: Imprensa de Universidade da Paraíba, 1978); and Carlos Rodrigues Brandão, *Os deuses do Povo: Um estudo sobre a religião popular* (São Paulo: Editora Brasiliense, 1980).

41. Eli Diniz and Renato R. Boschi, "Empresarios e Constituente: Continuidades e Rupturas no Modelo de Desenvolvimento Capitalista no Brasil," in Camargo and Diniz, eds., *Continuidade e Mudança no Brasil da Nova República*, pp. 133–134.

42. Ricardo Tavares, "Reforma e Contra-Reforma Agrária na Transição Política— Brasil (1979–1988)," *Série Estudos*, No. 70 (Rio de Janeiro: Instituto Universitário de Pesquisas do Rio de Janeiro, May 1970), p. 24. The UDR is also discussed in Dreifuss, *O Jogo da Direita*, pp. 69–85, 135–149, 276–284.

43. Eli Diniz and Renato R. Boschi, "A Consolidação Democrática no Brasil: Atores Políticos, Processos Sociais e Intermediação de Interesses," in Eli Diniz, Renato Boschi, and Renato Lessa, *Modernização e Consolidação Democrática no Brasil: Dilemas da Nova República* (São Paulo: Edições Vértice, 1989), p. 59.

44. Aspásia Camargo and Eli Diniz, "Introdução: Dilemas da Consolidação Democrática no Brasil," in Camargo and Diniz, eds., *Continuidade e Mudança no Brasil da Nova República*, p. 16. Also useful is Frances Hagopian, "Democracy by Undemocratic Means?' Elites, Political Pacts, and Regime Transition in Brazil," *Comparative Political Studies* 23, 2 (July 1990), pp. 147–170.

45. Dreifuss, *O Jogo da Direita*, p. 11.

46. Ibid., pp. 26, 40–45.

47. Ibid., pp. 50–65, 85–99, 120–134.

48. José Álvaro Moisés, "Dilemas da consolidação democrática no Brasil," in Moisés and Guilhoŋ Albuquerque, eds., *Dilemas da Consolidação da Democracia*, p. 174.

49. Schneider and Perry, "The Collor Government: A New Team Charts a New Course," pp. 16–21.

50. Recent works on agrarian reform include Tavares, "Reforma e Contra-Reforma Agrária"; Lygia Sigaud, "A Presença Política dos Camponeses: Uma Questão de Reconhecimento," in Camargo and Diniz, eds., *Continuidade e Mudança no Brasil da Nova República*, pp. 163–178; José da Souza Martins, *A Reforma Agrária e os Limites da Democracia na 'Nova República'* (São Paulo: Editora Hucitec, 1986); and Cândido Grzybowski, *Caminhos e Descaminhos dos Movimentos Sociais do Campo* (Petrópolis, Brazil: Editora Vozes, 1987).

51. Diniz and Boschi, "A Consolidação Democrática no Brasil: Atores Políticos, Processos Sociais e Intermediação de Interesses," p. 58.

52. Ibid., pp. 58–59.

53. Camargo and Diniz, "Introdução: Dilemas da Consolidação Democrática no Brasil," p. 12.

54. Aspásia Camargo, "As Dimensões da Crise," in Camargo and Diniz, eds., *Continuidade e Mudança no Brasil da Nova República*, p. 24.

55. Guillermo O'Donnell, "Hiatos, Instituições e Perspectivas Democráticas," in Fábio Wanderley Reis and Guillermo O'Donnell, eds., *A Democracia no Brasil: Dilemas e Perspectivas* (São Paulo: Edições Vértice, 1988), p. 81. See also O'Donnell's essay "Transições, continuidade, e alguns paradoxos," in ibid., pp. 41–71, and the essay by Reis, "Partidos, Ideologia e Consolidação Democrática," in ibid., pp. 296–326.

56. Moisés, "Dilemas da consolidação democrática no Brasil," p. 122.

57. Ibid., p. 123. See also the views expressed by a number of public figures in José Yunes, ed., *E Agora Brasil?* (São Paulo: Departamento Editorial da Ordem dos Advogados do Brasil, 1988).

58. Guillermo O'Donnell and Philippe C. Schmitter, *Transitions from Authoritarian Rule: Tentative Conclusions About Uncertain Democracies* (Baltimore, MD: Johns Hopkins University Press, 1986), pp. 3–4.

59. Jaguaribe, *Alternativas do Brasil,* p. 123.

60. Ibid., p. 67.

61. Ibid., p. 57.

62. Ibid., p. 18.

Chief Executives
of Republican Brazil

The Old Republic	From	To
Marechal Manoel Deodoro da Fonseca	11/15/1889	11/23/1891
Marechal Floriano Peixoto	11/23/1891	11/15/1894
Prudente José de Morais Barros	11/15/1894	11/15/1898
Manuel Ferraz de Campos Salles	11/15/1898	11/15/1902
Francisco de Paula Rodrigues Alves	11/15/1902	11/15/1906
Afonso Augusto Moreira Pena	11/15/1906	6/14/1909
Nilo Peçanha	6/14/1909	11/15/1910
Marechal Hermes Rodrigues da Fonseca	11/15/1910	11/15/1914
Wenceslau Bráz Pereira Gomes	11/15/1914	11/15/1918
Delfim Moreira de Costa Ribeiro	11/15/1918	7/28/1919
Epitácio Lindolfo da Silva Pessôa	7/28/1919	11/15/1922
Artur da Silva Bernardes	11/15/1922	11/15/1926
Washington Luís Pereira de Sousa	11/15/1926	10/24/1930

The Vargas Era and Its Aftermath	From	To
Getúlio Dornelles Vargas	11/03/1930	10/29/1945
José Linhares	10/29/1945	1/31/1946
Marechal Eurico Gaspar Dutra	1/31/1946	1/31/1951
Getúlio Dornelles Vargas	1/31/1951	8/24/1954
João Café Filho	8/24/1954	11/08/1955
Carlos Luz	11/08/1955	11/11/1955
Nereu Ramos	11/11/1955	1/31/1956
Juscelino Kubitschek de Oliveira	1/31/1956	1/31/1961
Jânio da Silva Quadros	1/31/1961	8/25/1961
Ranieri Mazilli and military junta	8/25/1961	9/07/1961
João Belchior Marques Goulart	9/07/1961	3/31/1964
military junta	4/01/1964	4/15/1964

Note: Indentation signifies vice presidents or others who succeeded to office.

The Military Regime

	From	To
Marechal Humberto de Alencar Castelo Branco	4/15/1964	3/15/1967
Gen. Arthur da Costa e Silva	3/15/1967	8/30/1969
military junta	8/30/1969	10/07/1969
Gen. Emílio Garrastazú Médici	10/07/1969	3/15/1974
Gen. Ernesto Geisel	3/15/1974	3/15/1979
Gen. João Baptista de Oliveira Figueiredo	3/15/1979	3/15/1985

Redemocratization

	From	To
José Sarney	3/15/1985	3/15/1990
Fernando Collor de Mello	3/15/1990	

About the
Book and Author

Brazil's often turbulent political life has revolved in part around the difficult task of reconciling the two goals of its national motto—order and progress. In this definitive political history, one of the leading authorities on Brazil examines the causes and consequences of the tension between these two desirable but seldom compatible goals.

Drawing on an extensive body of scholarly literature, Dr. Schneider focuses on the roles of the three actors that have continuously been at the center of national life, shaping the course of events through the difficult transition from colony to nation, through the changing fortunes of the nineteenth-century monarchy, and through the alternating democratic and authoritarian phases of the following century of republican government. First is the military establishment, zealous for order and historically viewing progress in the narrow perspective of economic development and institutional modernization. Second is the Catholic Church, almost invariably allied with the state in the interests of preserving the status quo. Third is Brazil's propertied classes—colonial landowners, nineteenth-century coffee planters, and modern-day industrialists and bankers—who have wielded considerable influence in state affairs.

Careful consideration is also given to the forces advocating change, such as the urban professionals of the colonial era, the nineteenth-century intelligentsia, the middle class of the republican period, and present-day working-class militants. Dr. Schneider argues that these champions of progress have often found that dramatic regime shifts did not bring about hoped-for social and economic changes and that support for progressive reforms in the urban centers often did not extend to the country's vast interior. Contained and co-opted, reform movements have repeatedly given way to the forces favoring order over progress.

Throughout, Dr. Schneider skillfully weaves in discussion of the social life and economic life of the country and how they have influenced political development. Taken as a whole, the book offers a penetrating look at the sequence of increasingly sophisticated political experiments that began with independence from Portugal in 1822 and culminated in the recent return to democracy.

Ronald M. Schneider is professor of political science at Queens College and the City University of New York Graduate School.

Index